S. Vijay

 *Oracle Press*™

Oracle E-Business Suite Manufacturing & Supply Chain Management

Bastin Gerald
Nigel King
Dan Natchek

Tata McGraw-Hill Publishing Company Limited
NEW DELHI

McGraw-Hill Offices

New Delhi New York St Louis San Francisco Auckland Bogotá Caracas
Kuala Lumpur Lisbon London Madrid Mexico City Milan Montreal
San Juan Santiago Singapore Sydney Tokyo Toronto

About the Authors

Bastin Gerald is a software architect at Oracle Corporation. He is currently leading the designs for the various modules of Oracle Product Development Exchange. He played a significant role in designing the Oracle Warehouse Management System. He worked in the Consulting Organization before joining Development, and has lead Oracle Applications implementation for various clients. Bastin has acquired the CPIM and CIRM certifications from APICS. He is also a Sun Certified Java Programmer.

Nigel King is senior director of design and architecture. His professional career spans finance, manufacturing, and distribution in three countries. He has worked as in both pre- and post-sales consulting before joining development at Oracle six years ago. Nigel's career within development has seen many if not most of the major initiatives within the manufacturing and supply chain applications. He chairs the Architecture Review Group for Oracle Applications, a design oversight group that coordinates the design across the more than 100 applications that make up the E-Business Suite. Nigel is a certified Manufacturing engineer, a certified instructor for the American Production and Inventory Control Society, and a chartered management accountant.

Dan Natchek has documented and taught manufacturing and distribution systems, as well as implemented and sold them, for more than 20 years. He is an APICS-certified Fellow in production and inventory management. For the past eight years he has been employed by Oracle Corporation in the areas of customer education, consulting, and pre-sales support. He participates on several Field Advisory boards, including Flow Manufacturing, Warehouse Management, and Manufacturing Scheduling.

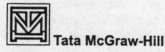 **Tata McGraw-Hill**

Tata McGraw-Hill Edition 2002

Third reprint 2003
RLXYCRYDDDDCX

Reprinted in India by arrangement with The McGraw-Hill Companies, Inc.,
New York

Sales territories: India, Nepal, Bangladesh, Sri Lanka and Bhutan

ISBN 0-07-049531-9

Published by Tata McGraw-Hill Publishing Company Limited,
7 West Patel Nagar, New Delhi 110 008, and printed at
Ram Book Binding House, Okhla, New Delhi 110 020

The **McGraw·Hill** *Companies*

To my beloved parents Sebastian and Rosary.
—*Bastin Gerald*

To my parents whom I miss so much and see so rarely.
—*Nigel King*

To my parents, Larry and Adele, to whom I owe so much.
—*Dan Natchek*

Table of Contents

PART I
Introduction

PART II
Design and Manufacturing Engineering

PART III
Supply Chain Planning

PART IV

Supply Chain Execution

PART V
Support Functions

PART VI
Business Intelligence

Acknowledgments

It was a great pleasure working with the Oracle Press team at Osborne. Jeremy Judson, Athena Honore and Ross Doll helped us in keeping up with the project schedule. Special thanks to Pamela Woolf and her team for all their contributions. We thank Ron Wohl, EVP, E-Business Suite for writing the foreword and providing his encouragement. Finally we thank Larry Ellison, CEO, Oracle Corporation for giving us an opportunity to be a part of such an outstanding company.

—Bastin Gerald, Nigel King, Dan Natchek

Prior to joining Oracle, I spent four years in Sundaram Clayton Ltd .and I thank my friends and former colleagues there, where I gained a lot of insights into the modern manufacturing technologies. I'd like to thank Venkat Subramaniam for the confidence he had in me, and for encouraging me to participate in various cross-functional projects that helped me acquire this knowledge. Truly, this knowledge provided the launch pad for my career in software.

During my tenure in Oracle Consulting, I had the opportunity to study and understand diverse business practices at various client locations. The implementations helped to hone my Oracle Applications knowledge. I thank all my fellow consultants and project managers for this.

After joining Applications Development, my primary role has been to design applications. I had the opportunity to work with some of the greatest software designers. Thanks to all of them for sharing their knowledge with me. Thanks to Nigel King, my co-author for guiding me through the various designs. I thank Jeff Barton and Kurt Robson for allowing me to author this book.

Milan Bhatia helped a lot with timely reviews and encouraging e-mails during the authoring process. I thank him for that. I thank Richard Rodgers, Amin Sikander, and Vishy Parthasarathy for spending their valuable time in reviewing the material.

I thank all my friends, especially Sathish, Manoj and Naveen, for their encouragement. I am very grateful to my wife Jacintha, daughter Nikita, and our family members for their support and encouragement. It would have been lot harder to achieve this feat without the support and encouragement of my family and friends.

—Bastin Gerald; Fremont, California; November, 2001

I really hope that this book makes the random walk of my career look like a series of planned moves. I have many people to thank for their knowing or unknowing contribution to the knowledge I have gained along the way. Many of the companies now exist in different forms and some of my greatest mentors are sadly no longer with us. Most notable to thank are the happy folks at Philips Industrial Electronics for letting me loose on the New Commercial System project, Mary Campbell and Mike Evens of Business Technology Consultants for starting my career in applications, and Jimmy Moyer of Jeyes Group plc for giving me my first international assignment. My instructors; Master Johnson, Master Kahn, and Mr. Kitagawa have been a constant statement of human possibility to me. Their guidance is with me always. I need to thank Kurt Robson Vice President of Design and Architecture for his momentary lack of judgement in recruiting me into development, showering me with intractable problems ever since and granting his permission to write the book.

My thanks to my colleagues in this venture, messes Gerald and Natchek. Their knowledge and application humble me. I must thank Alison Schofield and Leena Subramanian for the reviews beyond the call of duty by. My thanks goes out to Danial Soosai for his guidance on Demand Planning. It really is impossible to work at Oracle and not have the brilliance of the people around you reflect, however, dully from your surface.

The patience of my beautiful wife Anita is without measure. Her support for the moody man locked away in his office deserves accolade that is beyond this world to give. I hope my son forgives me for the hours spent away from play.

Nigel King; San Mateo, California; November, 2001

Writing a book like this taught me more than I ever imagined—it taught me how much I still can learn about the Oracle product suite. My thanks to the development teams that provided us such rich subject matter; I hope we have done it justice.

Oracle has such a wealth of talent in its employees and its customers that acknowledging everyone who has helped me in my career and with this project would fill another book. I thank all the educators, consultants, and customers with whom I have worked; they provided a cumulative perspective that would take many lifetimes to acquire on my own. At the risk of offending through omission, I give special mention to the following people: Michael Alfano, who prided himself on hiring good people—I hope I've lived up to your expectations; Nadeem Syed, Roger Goossens, Scott Malcolm, and the APS team—thank you for your patience and support; John Paramore, Nancy Beck, Rod Sernett, and countless other email junkies at Oracle—many thanks for your dedication and willingness to share your knowledge with Oracle and its customers; Terry Most and the management team—thanks for helping shepherd this book through the Oracle approval process.

My sincere gratitude to Arthur Fink, who took a chance on an aspiring writer many years ago; thank you for your open-mindedness and for giving me my big break.

And very special thanks to my loving wife, Sally, without whose infinite patience, encouragement, and critical copy editing this work would not have been possible.

Dan Natchek; Brookfield, Wisconsin; November, 2001

Introduction

racle's E-Business Suite is the only end-to-end business application that runs entirely on the Internet, supporting e-business across manufacturing, supply chain management, customer relationship management, business-to-business, financials, projects, human resources, and business intelligence functions. The Internet environment drives short cycle times and high customization. An e-business responds by leveraging the strengths of its manufacturing processes to gain a compelling strategic advantage. These companies require high-velocity hybrid manufacturing solutions to meet customer demand.

The Oracle E-Business Suite consists of more than 100 modules built on a single data model—any piece of data is stored only once. This alone provides a level of data integrity and consistency that is difficult if not impossible to attain using multiple data models, often the result when attempting to integrate disparate "best of breed" software. And consistent, accurate data is the cornerstone of good decision-making and good business.

Oracle Manufacturing provides a comprehensive selection of manufacturing solutions combined on one ERP backbone, along with the flexibility to employ these solutions concurrently for maximum efficiency. Oracle is a leader in manufacturing solutions and has developed significant innovations in Flow Manufacturing and mass customization techniques. These manufacturing products are fully integrated with Oracle's E-Business Suite and offer a high-performance manufacturing solution that will enable you to compete and win in today's volatile marketplace.

Distribution support is another key component of the ERP backbone. Oracle provides a full suite of Inventory and Warehouse Management functions fully integrated with Order Management and Procurement capability. This is what enables an e-business to collaboratively execute its supply and distribution plans across its entire supply chain—not just within its four walls.

Support functions, including Costing, Quality, and Pricing are also critical elements of the Oracle E-Business Suite. They provide accurate measurement of profit margin and product quality. These results, in turn, enable true business intelligence, which facilitates continuous improvement.

Who Should Read this Book

Anyone who wants to improve his or her perspective of Oracle Manufacturing and Supply Chain Management products from a business process point of view will find this book an interesting companion. It should appeal to both functional and technical implementation team members. Major functional challenges are thoroughly illustrated, and the possible ways to face these challenges are discussed in detail.

Reviewing the areas of greatest interest to you will improve your overall understanding of the software, because the book is organized by manufacturing and supply chain functions rather than individual modules. You will have a greater appreciation of the integration between the application modules, and increased ability to address business issues using the full power of the Oracle E-Business Suite.

Organization of the Book

The book is divided into six parts:

- Introduction
- Design and Manufacturing Engineering
- Supply Chain Planning
- Supply Chain Execution
- Support Functions
- Business Intelligence

Chapters within these parts focus on Manufacturing and Supply Chain functions rather than individual Oracle modules. This approach will help you to understand how the various modules in Oracle Applications integrate with each other to support a functional or business process. Each chapter might cover features from more than one module. For example, Chapter 7 covers features from Oracle Bills of Material, Oracle Work in Process, and Oracle Flow Manufacturing. A module might appear in more than one chapter, but the features that are covered in each of those chapters will be different. For example, the features of Oracle Work in Process are covered in both Chapters 7 and 16. Logical data models are included in various places to further the understanding on various subjects. Reading logical data models is not difficult and there are various published materials on this subject all over the Internet.

Where appropriate, there are sections that explain the usage of business object interfaces (APIs or Application Programming Interfaces) and open interfaces that should be used by technical implementers while interfacing with third-party or legacy systems. Chapter 22 is a case study that discusses a hypothetical company and its business operations. Each section includes a list of suggested activities that are intended to trigger your thought process. Use these activities to think about the hypothetical business and design your solutions for the various problems posed by the business.

PART
I

Introduction

CHAPTER
1

Introduction to
Oracle Manufacturing and
Supply Chain Products

n the 1970s and 1980s, corporations achieved tremendous productivity gains by improving their production and material handling processes. Most of the improvement efforts were centered on the premise "elimination of waste in every possible way." These corporations had many different ways to identify and eliminate waste. Material waiting to be consumed was considered a waste, and as a result the Just-In-Time (JIT) philosophy was born. In that era, however, the software systems that were used to manage the information needs were highly compartmentalized and companies had to invest millions in integrating and maintaining those software products. With the advent of Enterprise Resource Planning (ERP) software, these corporations are presented with an opportunity to realize tremendous benefits using software that manages the entire business.

Enterprise Business Flows

Optimizing your resources by individual companies or locations is less likely to result in a breakthrough than optimizing the business processes of your enterprise as a whole. A shift in thinking is required to move up to a higher level of the enterprise view from the traditional company view. From an operational standpoint, most of the effort in a typical enterprise is spent in the management of the important flows that are shown in Figure 1-1.

Identification/Creation of Demand

When a company develops a product or a concept, it tries to establish a customer base for that product. At a high level, this involves generating quality leads and converting these leads to sales. At an operational level, this information flow also includes advertising, marketing promotions, market research, gathering competitive intelligence, etc.

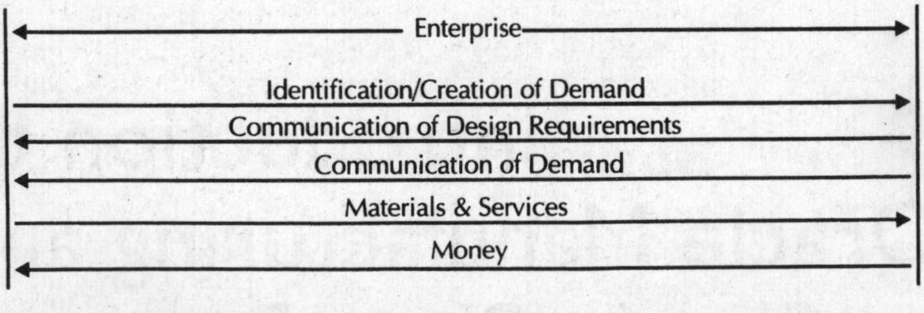

Enterprise

Identification/Creation of Demand

Communication of Design Requirements

Communication of Demand

Materials & Services

Money

FIGURE 1-1. *A high level view of the Enterprise business flows*

Communication of Design Requirements

Customers communicate their needs and product specifications during the product development process. This information is used to design a suitable product and is also shared with a set of chosen suppliers to build a robust supply chain for the product. When a product is designed, the product is tested extensively before being released for manufacturing. Identifying potential problems earlier in the cycle is very important.

Communication of Demand

Customers communicate their demand in the form of firm orders or forecasts. This information is used to plan the material and resource needs to satisfy the demand and is also shared with the appropriate suppliers so that they can plan their material and resource needs. The planning process derives the demand for components from the parent assemblies.

Materials and Services

In order to satisfy the customer demand, materials and services are procured from various suppliers and, after the appropriate value-add, are delivered to the customer. There is also a small amount of reverse material flow, especially in cases where

- Raw materials are provided by the customer.
- Defective products must be reworked.

But for the most part, material flow is from suppliers to customers.

Money

Upon receipt of the products and services, customers begin paying for them in regular cycles. Thus money flows backward from the customers of the final product through the enterprise until it reaches the suppliers who supplied the raw materials for the product. A set of business processes is established to manage this money flow in an enterprise, while satisfying all the legal requirements.

Oracle E-Business Suite

Oracle Applications provides global visibility and facilitates instantaneous information exchange across the supply chain by leveraging the Internet. Businesses can focus on fulfilling customer demand profitably by delivering high-quality products in the shortest time and at the lowest cost.

Oracle Applications is a fully integrated, end-to-end Internet-based supply chain management solution designed to help you operate successfully as an e-business. Oracle's e-business supply chain solutions can help you to transform your business processes—from demand capture to delivery and customer service. Oracle Applications comprises more than 100 modules that are grouped into various product families.

Oracle Customer Relationship Management (CRM)

This family of products manages the information needs of the arrow called Identification/Creation of Demand in Figure 1-1. The Customer Relationship Management (CRM) family of products enables sales and marketing professionals to maximize their effectiveness by providing a comprehensive set of automation and analysis tools with multi-channel execution capabilities, while providing seamless integration with operations and financials. CRM also has the "Service" suite, which deals with contracts and field service.

Oracle Manufacturing and Supply Chain Management

This family of products manages the information needs of the arrows called Communication of Design Requirements, Communication of Demand, and Materials and Services in Figure 1-1. Oracle Manufacturing and Supply Chain Management Applications provide support in establishing an efficient and responsive supply chain linking all customers, suppliers, manufacturing facilities, warehouses, distributors, carriers, and other trading partners through the Internet.

Oracle Financials

This family of products manages the information needs of the arrow called Money in Figure 1-1. Oracle Financials is a comprehensive financial management solution and provides support for accounting, project management, cash and treasury management, and property management. It also has modules that help in strategic planning.

These three families share a common data model, as shown in Figure 1-2. Because the data model is common between these application families, duplication of data is avoided. For example, if you define an item in Oracle Inventory, that item is available to be used by the CRM and Financials modules, or if you define accounts in Oracle Financials, they are available for you to use in Oracle Manufacturing and Oracle CRM modules. Besides this direct sharing of data, Oracle also provides several table-based and program-based interfaces for integration with third-party and legacy applications.

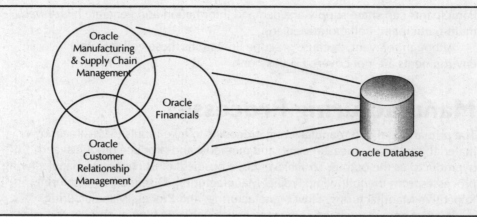

FIGURE 1-2. *Oracle Applications modules share a common data model*

Inter-Enterprise Collaboration

Although Oracle Applications supports multi-company operations using the Multi-org feature, it is a single-enterprise solution. To support the multi-enterprise collaboration needs, Oracle has built the Exchange suite of products.

Oracle Exchange Marketplace

Oracle Exchange Marketplace is a global online marketplace. Trading partners can collaborate in real time to buy and sell any type of goods and services. The variety of transactions range from complex auctions for configured production goods to high-velocity, repetitive purchases of frequently used items.

Oracle Product Development Exchange

Oracle Product Development Exchange offers an Internet-based and secure collaborative product-development environment and leverages the power of the Internet to synchronize all of product, project, people, and document information required to usher a product from concept to obsolescence on a single hub. Designers, buyers, manufacturers, suppliers, service representatives, and customers can collaborate to solve problems, come up with fresh ideas, and find ways to save time and money.

Oracle Supply Chain Exchange

Oracle Supply Chain Exchange is a multi-enterprise supply chain solution that provides all trading partners with a common platform to communicate, collaborate, and plan, optimizing supply and demand across all tiers of the supply chain.

Participants can share supply and demand information and generate high-level, multi-participant, collaborative plans.

Although relevant, because of scope limitations these collaborative environments are not covered in this book.

Manufacturing Processes

The primary goal of a manufacturing process is to take inputs (5Ms—manpower, material, machines, measurement, and methods) and produce products (and byproducts) as the output. To achieve this, a business must choose its manufacturing processes from the following: Project Manufacturing, Discrete Manufacturing, Repetitive Manufacturing, Flow Manufacturing, and Process Manufacturing.

It is not necessary that a company choose only one type of process and stick with it. Companies typically have a mixture of one or more of these processes, depending on the products they produce and the markets they serve.

Oracle has products specifically designed and built to operate in these environments. Oracle Project Manufacturing along with Oracle Project Accounting is widely used to manage an environment such as Aircraft Manufacturing or Ship Building. At the other extreme, Oracle Process Manufacturing is available to manage a process-manufacturing environment such as the manufacturing of chemicals and beverages. Although many of the manufacturing and business processes are similar, these modules are beyond the scope of this book. This book covers the modules in Oracle Manufacturing Applications, which support the following environments:

Discrete Manufacturing

You use discrete manufacturing for assemblies that you make in discrete batches. You can also use discrete manufacturing to track activities such as rework, field service repair, upgrade, disassembly, maintenance, prototype development, etc. Typically, you use a process layout where you move your products in batches between operations to the various shops/departments to carry out the work. You track and associate all costs with the job.

Repetitive Manufacturing

You use repetitive manufacturing when you produce assemblies on a continuous or semi-continuous basis over a predefined interval. You have production lines that can be used to produce either one assembly (dedicated line) or many assemblies (mixed model line). In repetitive manufacturing, you charge the cost of production directly to the assembly and line.

Flow Manufacturing

You use flow manufacturing when you want to establish a highly responsive manufacturing system. In this approach, production is aligned with customer demand. You design flow production lines so that you can produce a family of assemblies at the appropriate rate and mix.

Oracle Manufacturing supports mixed-mode manufacturing; hence, discrete jobs, repetitive schedules, and flow schedules can coexist. Oracle Manufacturing supports Configure-to-Order and enables you to be responsive to your customers' needs. Your customers can choose the product configuration that best suits them. Once you receive your customers' preferred configuration through a sales order, you will be able to create final assembly schedules based on the sales order and deliver the product when it is completed.

Supply Chain Stocking Strategies

Oracle Manufacturing and Supply Chain Applications enable customers to operate using various supply-chain stocking strategies. The term *stocking strategy* denotes a process that identifies and maintains the optimum level of your bills of material at which you should maintain your inventory, so that your inventory investment is a minimum. For example, in the ship building industry, you would not keep any inventory, whereas you would have to keep inventory in your retail outlets if you were selling shoes.

The amount of time a customer is willing to wait to buy a product (delivery lead-time) is a very important determinant of the supply-chain stocking strategy. As the delivery lead-time decreases, the finished goods inventory moves closer to the consumption point. To a certain extent, product complexity can also be an important determinant of a supply-chain stocking strategy. Figure 1-3 shows the typical position of each of these strategies in a lead-time–product complexity graph.

The following strategies are widely used across various industries.

Engineer-To-Order (ETO)

The product is engineered when the customer places the order, and the order typically carries the engineering specifications with it. Each product has unique characteristics; all the resources (design and production) are involved in the delivery process. Each customer order is associated with a project, which is broken further into tasks and subtasks. An example of this would be a new building.

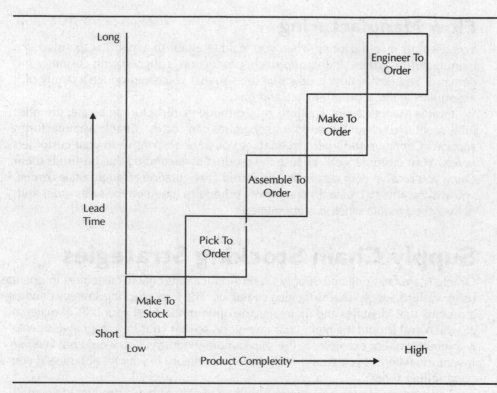

FIGURE 1-3. *Supply chain stocking strategies*

Make-To-Order (MTO)

Standard products are designed and published in catalogs. The actual product is built on receipt of the customer order. Customers might be able to choose certain characteristics optionally. An example of this would be machine building. Each customer order may have an associated project to manage the production and delivery schedule.

Assemble-To-Order (ATO)

These are also standard products and are often configured by customers. You don't wait until the order is received to build an ATO product. Subassemblies are manufactured prior to receiving the order and when the order is received, the subassemblies are assembled to make the finished product. Automobiles and computers are examples of this type of production.

Pick-To-Order (PTO)

Under this strategy, a variety of shippable components are stocked. Customers order "kits" or collections of these parts under a single item number; kits can be either predefined or configured by the customer during the order entry process. The components of the kit are picked and shipped from stock; there is no additional value added after the customer order, other than perhaps packing the components for shipment. A computer system (including the central processing unit, monitor, and printer) is an example of this.

Make-To-Stock (MTS)

In an MTS environment, you produce your products and stock them in anticipation of customer orders. A good forecasting system is very important to this environment because most of the material and capacity planning is done using forecasts rather than actual demand. Examples include stereo systems and television sets.

Choosing a Strategy

As businesses move from ETO to MTS, the lead-time available for the manufacturer decreases dramatically. So, the manufacturer's reliance on a good forecasting/demand planning solution increases as the manufacturer moves down from ETO to MTS.

Though it might seem that these stocking strategies have a direct correlation with the manufacturing processes described earlier, it need not be the case. The optimum stocking level for a model or a product family (in the model/family's bills of material structure) is the level where the number of components and subassemblies is the minimum. This is a general guideline followed across industries and is not a rule. Oracle Manufacturing and Supply Chain Applications allow you to use one or more of the stocking strategies that were described earlier.

With this as a framework, let's briefly examine the Oracle products that address these needs.

Overview of Oracle Manufacturing Products

Oracle provides a set of applications to enable you to model the landscape and products of a manufacturing company. These applications let you define the organization of your business, the products you manufacture, the parts you use, your manufacturing process, and changes to your products over time. Using them, you can track purchases, on-hand inventory balances, and production, and record and analyze quality statistics about your purchase receipts and production process. And Oracle's manufacturing products maintain cost data and cost history for the parts you use or manufacture, and pass that data to Oracle Financial applications.

As a supplier of manufacturing applications, one of Oracle's strengths is the integration of its products. As such, it is relatively unimportant where a given piece of functionality resides; like the old spaghetti sauce ads boasted, "it's in there." The built-in application security makes it easy for you to assign functions to the users of your choosing, regardless of Oracle's assignment of functions to a specific module. However, it's helpful to know Oracle's function/product matrix, if for no other reason than to know where to look in the documentation for details on a particular topic.

The following sections describe each of the products commonly considered baseline manufacturing products. The forecasting and planning products are described later, in the section "Overview of Supply Chain Products."

Oracle Inventory

Oracle Inventory is the foundation of the Oracle Manufacturing suite. It is here that you model the structure of your enterprise; define the items (parts) you use in manufacturing; and maintain perpetual inventory balances through transactions that reflect daily activities, such as receipts, issues, and material movement.

The enterprise structure model lets you define multiple legal entities, containing one or more operating units, which in turn contain one or more inventory organizations. The *legal entity* establishes the relationship to Oracle Financial applications. Each legal entity identifies the set of books within which it operates; this in turn determines the set of books of the operating units and inventory organizations within its hierarchy. You establish many purchasing and order management controls at the operating unit level, while you set most manufacturing controls at the inventory organization level. Though it is subject to discussion and creativity during an implementation, an inventory organization most often corresponds to a manufacturing plant or distribution center. To transfer material between organizations, you define a shipping network that controls which organizations can send and receive material.

Inventory organizations are further subdivided into subinventories, a unique word in the Oracle vocabulary. A *subinventory* is a subdivision of an organization's inventory; frequently it represents a physical location, e.g., a stockroom within a plant, although it also controls the fiscal accounting for inventory. A subinventory also specifies certain characteristics of the inventory quantities stored there—whether such quantities are nettable, reservable, or included in the Available to Promise (ATP) balance. The final level in the enterprise structure is the *locator*; it represents a physical location within a subinventory (e.g., a specific bin). The locator is one of several key flexfields (configurable fields) in the Oracle Suite and can be configured to model your location scheme—row, rack, and bin is a typical example.

Oracle Inventory is the owner of the Item Master, where you define the items or parts that you use in your operation. Each raw material, purchased part, manufactured subassembly, phantom subassembly, and finished good must be identified by an item number, another key flexfield in the Oracle suite. Item definition involves defining each item master, and then assigning that item to each inventory organization where you need to use it. The item master has well over a hundred attributes, individual fields that store discrete pieces of data—for example, description, unit of measure, and minimum or maximum order quantities. You can specify whether most of these attributes will be maintained globally, or maintained individually for the item in each inventory organization. Seeded and user-defined templates simplify the process of item definition. Within Oracle Inventory, you can categorize items as many ways as you want; these categories are used in Inventory and other applications to group items for reporting or processing.

Oracle Inventory provides the transactions needed to maintain on-hand quantities. These transactions record most inventory movement (receipts, issues, and location changes); Work in Process and Order Management provide the inventory transactions related to manufacturing activities and shipping, respectively. Inventory transactions let you receive material from purchase orders, customer returns, or inter-organization shipments. They let you move material from place to place and record miscellaneous adjustments on either an ad-hoc basis or driven by a cycle count or physical inventory process.

Finally, Oracle Inventory provides basic inventory planning—Min–Max planning, and Reorder Point planning—and basic forecasting capabilities, though it is not nearly as robust as the functionality provided in Oracle Demand Planning.

Oracle Bills of Material

Oracle Bills of Material lets you define multi-level bills of material and associated routings that model your manufacturing process. The application builds on the organization and item definitions of Oracle Inventory and provides information to Cost Management, Work in Process, and the planning products.

Within Oracle Bills of Material, you define additional characteristics of your manufacturing operation, including the workday calendar used by each inventory organization, and the manufacturing departments and resources (typically, labor and machinery) used to make your products. The capacity of each resource that you define here is used in Capacity Planning and is the basis of resource constraints used in a constrained or optimized plan in Oracle Advanced Supply Chain Planning.

A bill of material is a structured list of the parts needed to make a product. You define a separate bill of material for each subassembly and finished product; the application lets you view the result as a multi-level bill of material in the traditional indented display. A bill of material identifies the component or child parts and the required quantity per unit of the assembly or parent. Effectivity dates let you model pending changes in your product structure, and allow the planning applications to time-phase those changes. The bill of material also specifies a yield factor for each component. It includes an optional link to the routing operation where the component is consumed, and the WIP Supply Type for each component, indicating how the material is supplied to WIP—for example, whether the material is explicitly issued or back-flushed at point of use. These characteristics affect the processing of jobs or repetitive schedules in Work in Process and also affect the planning process.

Oracle Bills of Material supports the definition of several types of special-purpose bills of material. Model and Option bills define a set of optional components or groups of components, used by Oracle Configurator to support configure-to-order manufacturing, and by Order Management to support the pick-to-order process. Model and Option bills include attributes that affect the shipping of pick-to-order components and the revenue recognition for such pick-to-order products. Planning bills and Product Family bills represent groupings of finished products and are used to simplify the forecasting and planning process—if you forecast the planning bill or family, the process will spread the aggregate forecast across the components of the Planning bill according to percentage factors you define within the bill. While both Planning bills and Product Families support aggregate planning, only Product Families support true two-level master scheduling, where the forecast is consumed at both the Family and the component levels.

Oracle Bills of Material maintains the routings for your products. A routing lists the sequence of steps required to manufacture a product from its components; it specifies the department where each step occurs and typically lists the resources needed at each department. This resource information is used by Work in Process and Manufacturing Scheduling to schedule jobs and is used to calculate planning lead times from your routings, if you choose. It is the basis of the resource requirements used in Capacity Planning and the resource and overhead cost calculations in Cost Management.

Oracle Engineering

Oracle Engineering provides a separate environment for defining items, bills of material, and routings prior to their release to production and supports controlled changes to bills through the use of *Engineering Change Orders* (ECOs).

If you choose, you can define your items, bills, or routings as engineering items, bills, or routings before you release them to manufacturing. While this process uses the same database tables as used for the corresponding released (or manufacturing) objects, it sets an attribute that allows you more selective control over access to those items, bills, and routings than you have for their manufacturing counterparts. This would let you control, for example, who can modify a manufacturing bill or release a discrete job to make an item if it is still under engineering control. Releasing an item, bill, or routing to manufacturing simply switches the controlling attribute and makes the object accessible to all users who have access to manufacturing data.

Engineering Change Orders, sometimes called *Engineering Change Notices* (ECNs), let you make changes to bills of material in a more formal and controlled environment than that provided by Oracle Bills of Material. You can specify changes to one or more bills of material on an ECO, in order to group related product changes. The ECO makes it easy to reschedule or cancel the set of changes as a unit and to control the visibility of those changes to the planning process; it also lets you specify whether the ECO should update WIP jobs and repetitive schedules when it is implemented. Oracle Workflow provides a robust approval process for ECOs.

Oracle Work in Process (WIP)

Oracle Work in Process (WIP) records actual production activity. It lets you report production against discrete jobs or repetitive schedules, or by using a work order-less completion transaction (also part of Oracle Flow Manufacturing).

Discrete jobs in WIP (also called work orders, production orders, or shop orders) represent the production of a specific quantity of a specific item, completed on a specific date. They can be generated by the planning products, created automatically in response to Sales Orders for assemble-to-order products, or created manually. Discrete jobs define a discrete item to be built and have a fixed quantity, start date, and due date. Activity against a discrete job is reported by a unique job number.

Repetitive schedules model high-volume production of an item on an ongoing basis. They represent a rate of production over a period of time. Repetitive schedules have four key dates—the start and completion date and time for the first unit produced on the schedule, and the start and completion date of the last unit. Repetitive schedules model a daily production rate, and the planning process reacts accordingly—while planning assumes that the entire quantity of a discrete job will magically appear on the due date, it recognizes the daily production quantities that a repetitive schedule represents.

Though discrete jobs and repetitive schedules are fundamentally different, they do share some common characteristics, and use the same transactions to report and track activity. Both discrete jobs and repetitive schedules provide pick lists, pull lists, and shortage reporting. You can modify material requirements in advance, or on the fly, based on how you configure the system. You report material issues, returns, and substitutions using the same transaction for discrete and repetitive production. You use the same transactions for discrete and repetitive production, to report movement from operation to operation and to charge resources (e.g., to manually report labor).

Discrete and repetitive also support outside processing through their integration with Oracle Purchasing. A move into an outside processing operation creates a purchase requisition to buy the outside processing service from a supplier.

Receiving transactions (in Oracle Inventory or Oracle Purchasing) update the WIP information and typically advance the job or schedule to its next operation.

Work in Process also lets you report production through a work order-less completion transaction. While this was added to the application as part of Oracle's Flow Manufacturing initiative, it is available in WIP to customers who have not licensed Oracle's Flow Manufacturing product.

Oracle Manufacturing Scheduling

Though Oracle Work in Process provides some simple methods to reschedule discrete jobs on the shop floor, Oracle Manufacturing Scheduling lets you graphically reschedule jobs while respecting the same material and capacity constraints you model in an Advanced Supply Chain plan. You can view your shop floor schedule in a Gantt chart format, drill down to the detail on operations or resources, and reschedule production by simply dragging the entire job or individual operations to the desired point on the time line.

Oracle Flow Manufacturing

Flow Manufacturing is based on the premise that production should be driven only by actual customer demand and then should be rapid enough to satisfy that demand without large investments in inventory or safety stock. Oracle Flow Manufacturing supports high-velocity manufacturing activities by simplifying the planning, scheduling, and reporting of manufacturing activities, and by reducing or eliminating non-value-added activities. Flow Manufacturing provides a method for evaluating the suitability of manufacturing lines for flow production, initiating material replenishment using visual signals, reporting production without use of work orders, and sequencing daily production to maintain a smoothly flowing rate of production.

To be able to produce exactly to customer demand in a lot size of one, you need a production line that is designed and balanced to facilitate production of the mix and volume of items you anticipate. Flow Manufacturing provides a Mixed Model Map to simulate and evaluate line design. Using flow routings (variations on the standard routings defined in Oracle Bill of Material) and some statement of anticipated demand from the planning products or Order Management, the Mixed Model Map identifies potential bottlenecks in the manufacturing process that would impede a smooth flow of production.

Material handling and paperwork are examples of non-value-added activities than can be reduced or eliminated by kanban replenishment. *Kanban*, a Japanese word suggesting "sign" or "signal," implies that the actual execution of material replenishment should be initiated by simple, visual signals, based on some event on the shop floor; for example, emptying a container or rack of parts might be the signal to refill that container or rack from the stockroom, from manufacturing, or directly from the supplier. For kanban replenishment to be effective, the kanbans must be sized appropriately, based on the mix and volume of production you anticipate and the time it takes to replenish. Oracle Flow Manufacturing provides tools to evaluate kanban sizing on an ongoing basis and to execute replenishments from Inventory, Purchasing, or WIP based on kanban signals. Kanban execution is also provided in Oracle Inventory, but the planning capability resides in Oracle Flow Manufacturing.

Proper production sequencing facilitates the smooth flow of product on a mixed-model assembly line. Oracle Flow Manufacturing provides a Line Scheduling Workbench, to allow you to schedule production on your flow lines in the appropriate sequence. You want to satisfy demand, of course, but you also might want to mix the production flow—for example, alternating products with optional steps in order to avoid bottlenecks in the line.

Finally, as mentioned previously, Oracle Flow Manufacturing provides the same work order–less completion transaction as Oracle Work in Process. This eliminates all shop floor reporting except one transaction, which reports completion, back-flushes component material, and automatically charges labor. The process is designed to be extremely simple, yet it also allows for many types of exception activities as needed, e.g., material substitution, use of alternate bills or routings, or production of non-current revisions.

Oracle Cost Management

Oracle Cost Management is the primary point of integration between Oracle Manufacturing and Financial applications. It enables you to maintain the standard or average cost of your items and collects cost information from Inventory, Purchasing, and Work in Process to transfer to Oracle General Ledger.

Oracle Cost Management provides five system-defined cost elements: Material, Resource (e.g., Labor), Overhead, Material Overhead, and Outside Processing. These elements model the typical constituents of a part's cost. You can define as many subelements of these elements as you need; for example, you might have different types of labor or machinery as subelements of the Resource element or different overheads, representing different types of expenses to absorb. You can define an unlimited number of cost types, or sets of costs, for historical or simulation purposes. For example, in a standard cost environment you will have a Frozen cost for valuation, but you might have historical costs, a pending cost to develop next year's standard, and simulated cost types for what-if analysis.

In Release 11i, Oracle Cost Management supports standard, average, FIFO (first in, first out), or LIFO (last in, first out) valuation of your items. You set the choice of costing methods for each of your inventory organizations. Most transactions involving inventory movement, including purchase order receipts, WIP issues, physical or cycle count adjustments, etc., have accounting implications. Oracle Cost Management evaluates these transactions, assigns the appropriate cost, and transfers the costed transactions periodically to Oracle General Ledger. Similarly, most WIP movement transactions also have financial implications; they typically involve the application of resources and absorption of overhead. Cost Management also values these transactions and transfers the results to the general ledger.

Oracle Quality Management

You can track and analyze the quality of your products and your suppliers' products using Oracle Quality Management. It lets you define and maintain the elements for which you need to track quality information, group those elements into collection plans, enforce the collection of that data in Purchasing and Work in Process, and analyze the results.

Collection elements represent the data you need to collect in order to measure and analyze quality. A collection element might record the inner or outer diameter of a piece of tubing, the electrical current between two pins on a circuit board, a taster's subjective evaluation of a flavor, or the corresponding item, discrete job, or purchase order for which the measurement was taken. Numeric elements can have a range of specification values you can use in your collection plans.

A collection plan identifies the elements you need to track and the circumstances that trigger its execution; for example, a receipt of a certain item or group of items from a certain supplier might invoke one collection plan, whereas receiving different items might invoke another plan. A collection plan also defines the acceptable values for its collection elements and the actions you want to take based on the values reported. You can trigger multiple actions, for example, displaying a message to the operator, putting a WIP job on hold, or rejecting the transaction. Currently, Oracle Quality Management is integrated with Work in Process and Purchasing; you can invoke collection plans based on Purchase receipts or WIP transactions. And you can maintain and populate collection plans manually for other sorts of activities; for example, you could define a collection plan to record customer response to a new product offering.

Overview of Supply Chain Products

Oracle's Supply Chain Planning and Execution products are a broad and robust set of tools. They allow you to model your facilities and lanes connecting your facilities. They allow you to record estimations of demand and see how that demand would play through the whole distribution network including customer facilities and supplier facilities. It might be useful to think of the suite as having three layers as shown in Figure 1-4.

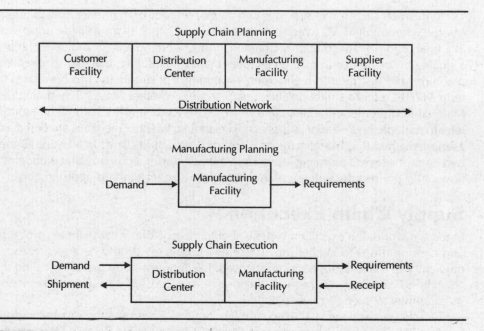

FIGURE 1-4. *Supply chain management processes*

Manufacturing and Supply Chain Planning

To compete effectively and operate efficiently, a company must plan the acquisition of the material and resources that it needs to produce and distribute its products. The process involves the recognition of independent (or external) demand and netting of on-hand quantities. In a manufacturing environment the process must explode bills of material to calculate component requirements. The logic of this process is clear and consistent—"inescapable," in the words of Ollie Wight, one of the pioneers of manufacturing planning. And the general process is well documented in numerous external sources. Therefore, the basic logic is not the subject of this book.

As it has evolved over the years, manufacturing planning process has gone by many different names: *Material Requirements Planning* (MRP, sometimes called *little MRP*), implying planning of material only; Manufacturing Resource Planning (MRP-II or *big MRP*), implying planning of material and capacity; and Enterprise Resource Planning (ERP), implying fuller integration with the financial and customer-facing applications of a typical manufacturing enterprise.

In Release 11i, Oracle provides two major methods of manufacturing planning: Master Scheduling/MRP, which plans material and capacity for a single organization at a time; and Advanced Supply Chain Planning, which plans for multiple plants in a single run. In turn, each method includes master scheduling, material requirements planning, and distribution requirements planning. For simplicity, this book uses the term *MRP* to refer to single organization planning, whether Master Scheduling or Material Requirement planning, and *ASCP* (Advanced Supply Chain Planning) to refer to multiple organization, supply chain planning, whether the plans are designated as master schedules, manufacturing plans, or distribution plans. In addition to these two enterprise-wide planning methods, a manufacturing company that embraces a flow or JIT philosophy will use planning tools to size its kanbans appropriately.

Supply Chain Execution

In today's world, the execution systems should closely follow the planning processes and cannot afford to lag behind. These two processes should be coordinated efficiently so that the business can succeed. Execution systems are often called the "backbone" of a business because the long-term success of a business depends on its capability to execute on its plans.

Oracle supports the vital execution functions of a business through the various features in Oracle Order Management, Oracle Pricing, Oracle Release Management, Oracle Shipping, Oracle Inventory, Oracle Warehouse Management, Oracle Purchasing, and Oracle Supplier Scheduling. These modules offer a bundle of rich functionality that satisfies the needs of the "Demand to Delivery" process of a business. With this background, let's take a look at the modules that offer the supply chain planning and execution features.

Oracle Demand Planning

This is the module of Oracle Applications where you create predictions of future demand. You can create these predictions yourself, or you can use the history created through the shipping system to create your time series data. Oracle offers the normal cast of characters for forecasting models—e.g., single, double, and triple exponential smoothing, Holt-Winters, and an expert method which will automatically determine the model that best fits your needs. Demand Planning comes with tracking signals that will alert you when your forecasting model no longer fits your data. You can combine calculated forecast data and adjust for knowledge outside of the historical data, such as promotions, price increases, cannibalization from new product lines, etc.

Oracle Master Scheduling/MRP

In the Oracle lexicon, the Master Scheduling/MRP Application provides single-organization planning. While you can use a series of MRP plans to plan multiple plants and distribution centers in a supply chain, the process is cumbersome and requires the synchronization of multiple plans. In fact, if the supply chain is complex, with the several plants both sending and receiving material at multiple levels of a bill of material, you might never truly synchronize the plans—by the time you've planned the last link in the supply chain, it's likely to be incorrect due to changes in earlier links in the chain.

Master Scheduling/MRP plans for capacity on an infinite basis only; given the demand you want to satisfy, the plan will tell you how much capacity you need to achieve that plan. It supports detailed Capacity Requirements Planning in conjunction with a true MRP plan and Rough Cut Capacity Planning to evaluate a plan designated as a Master Schedule.

Oracle Advanced Supply Chain Planning

Advanced Supply Chain Planning lets you plan across your entire supply chain in a single planning run. You can include all your manufacturing and distribution sites, even those on earlier releases (as early as 10.7) of Oracle Applications or sites running other ERP software. A single plan can encompass requirements from your customers and show the demand to your suppliers in the form of Purchase Orders or Supplier Schedules. And in the plan, you can include all of the manufacturing methods you utilize—project manufacturing, discrete, repetitive, flow, or process.

While ASCP can plan capacity on an infinite supply model, just like MRP, it provides the option of constraint-based and optimized planning.

You can plan the entire time horizon within one plan and choose the appropriate level of granularity at each point in the horizon. Your plan might plan the immediate future down to the minute, the next few weeks in daily buckets planning for each item and detailed routing resource, the period after that in weekly buckets, and the long-term portion of the horizon in monthly periods, perhaps planning only at the product family and using aggregate bills of resource for capacity planning. You can choose to respect or ignore capacity and material constraints in each section of the horizon.

To describe this comprehensive planning model, Oracle has coined the term *holistic planning*. While it's a rather trendy, California-sounding word, it carries an important message—you can plan your entire supply chain, material and capacity, all manufacturing methods, and all time periods in one integrated plan. This can greatly reduce the time you spend synchronizing plans and increase your manufacturing flexibility, velocity, and competitiveness.

Order Management

Oracle Order Management offers a full range of commercial management and sales administration capabilities. Orders can originate from customers or can be replenishment orders to restock a warehouse or internal orders from a requisition. Oracle Order Management allows fulfillment from your own facilities, from facilities of other companies within your enterprise, or from a third party. The demand for these "Drop Shipped" orders is passed to purchasing through the creation of Purchase orders.

You can enter orders for configured products with the same ease as you would for "sell from stock" products. While entering orders, you will be able to check the Available to Promise and Available to Reserve quantities for that particular item. Integration with ATP allows you to source materials from multiple facilities and review delivery lead-time and estimated arrival dates. You can schedule your shipments to depart at the same time using a "ship set" and even to arrive at the same time if departing from different facilities.

Order workflows can be configured to represent RFQs, Quotes, or Orders and include holds and processing constraints capability. Holds are a facility that prevents processing an order at a given process step. Holds can be applied manually or automatically. Releasing a hold is a secured function. Processing Constraints disallow processing after a given step. An example of this might be preventing the update of price and promised delivery date after the acknowledgment been sent.

Change Management capability is workflow driven and is closely related to the processing constraints capability mentioned earlier. If a person who is not authorized to make the change violates a constraint, a notification is sent to the authorized party requesting the change to be effected. Sales Credits are stored and can be passed directly to sales compensation for sales people who are compensated on order bookings or can be passed to receivables for those compensated on invoiced sales.

You will be able to mass update many sales orders to bring a change into effect. You can use the order copy capability to create a return from an outbound order, an order from a quote, etc. It marks the source order type and order number on the resultant order allowing audit trail through the view orders form.

Oracle Pricing

Oracle Pricing is a very comprehensive tool that rests on a few key components. There are Price Lists and Discount Lists that you can qualify for. Price List lines can be for all items in a category, a particular item, or attributes of an item. Once you have a price list line for your request you might also qualify for discounts (or any modifier including a surcharge). It comes with a complete set of pricing tools, including

- Tiered Pricing based on Item Hierarchies
- Volume discounts with Point and Range breaks
- Formula Based Pricing
- Usage Based Pricing
- Accrued or Retrospective Discount

Oracle Pricing also includes the following sales incentive tools:

- Coupons
- Gift Certificates
- Free Upgrade
- Buy One/Get One Free

Oracle Release Management

This is the module of Oracle Applications where you can take some of the uncertainty out of your planning, by letting your customers tell you their requirements in both the short and long term. They can tell you a series of shipments that they expect from you, and they can tell you the sequence that the vehicle must be loaded in when they unload it. This is very important where variants in a product family are all manufactured on the same production line. The sequence of the assemblies running down the line must match the loading of the vehicle.

Customers can inform you of requirements in flexible time buckets, and you get to agree on how far out in the future you will regard the demand as fixed and from when it should be considered as guidance only. Your demand stream from your customer might also specify a commitment to pay for the raw materials needed to manufacture and to pay for the manufacture without actually requiring shipment. The colloquial terms for these are High Fab and High Raw. You can agree with your customer the days of the week that they will accept deliveries. You can define the shipping pattern from your own warehouses to the customer site. The release management application allows you to operate on cumulative quantities rather than discrete shipments. As each demand stream received will overlay its predecessor you agree with your customer how to identify the same piece of demand. Release management is very focused on customer item definition. Many of the shipping and delivery terms are agreed on an item or item and customer location basis. The release management workbench allows you to review the full picture of demand from a customer including the planning, shipping, and sequenced schedules. It allows you to review whether you are ahead or behind the cumulative quantities requested by your customer.

Oracle Shipping

Oracle Shipping is where the inventory is prepared for shipment to the customer. The shipping system dovetails with the order and release management application to allow assemblies of loads in the correct sequence for the trip. This is very important where variants in a product family are all manufactured on the same production line. The sequence of the assemblies running down the line must match the loading of the vehicle. The vehicle needs to be loaded in the correct sequence to be unloaded when it makes deliveries. The packing entails the management over containers that are tracked through the carrier's system. Shipping is the event in the order lifecycle that triggers the invoice to be created and passed to receivables.

Oracle Warehouse Management

Oracle Warehouse Management supports the business needs of managing a complex and highly automated distribution center. You can model the physical layout of a warehouse using the three physical elements in Oracle WMS: Warehouse, Zones, and Locators. You will be able to model the optimized pick path that is most suitable to your layout using the locator sequences, which will be used during the dispatching of picking tasks.

You can group your warehouses according to the skill levels, so that the resources are utilized in an optimal manner. A resource can execute many different types of tasks. Many times, a task can require multiple resources. For example, picking a large pallet might require a pallet picker and a forklift. This combination of resources could be captured as the resource requirements for that warehouse task.

Oracle WMS allows you to perform your warehouse duties using an RF-based mobile computer. All the warehouse transactions and tasks are supported in a mobile user interface. Some of the important query capabilities such as "on hand query" are also available as a mobile user interface.

You will be able to combine sales orders to be released for picking in more than a dozen ways. Pick waves are released from Oracle Shipping. Oracle WMS sources material in the warehouse using a set of predefined picking rules, breaks these pick released lines into warehouse tasks based on equipment capacity, and dispatches these pick tasks to the warehouse resources with the appropriate role—pallet picks to pallet pickers and case picks to case pickers, for example.

When you receive material from your supplier, Oracle WMS creates putaway tasks for you, allows you to containerize your incoming material, and helps you to track them using a License Plate Number (LPN) from then on. Putaway tasks aren't dispatched, but rather, the put away operators are allowed to choose the material that they want to putaway. They do this by scanning the LPN. Oracle WMS directs the operator to the most appropriate place to put away the material, using the predefined putaway rules. Integration with Oracle Quality module allows you to inspect the incoming material if such inspection is needed.

Oracle Purchasing

Oracle Purchasing addresses the needs of the purchasing professional, planning professional, and the users who request material to be purchased. The module covers direct and indirect procurement with a full requisitioning system that can present both internally hosted and supplier hosted catalogs. A highlight of the suite is the Internet procurement capability. This allows a self-service requisitioning system to be brought up very quickly alongside any purchasing or manufacturing system. It also addresses the needs of corporate spending control with approval routing through an authorization chain. The workflow-based approval processes cover requisitions and ordering. It has built-in encumbrance accounting to hold Requisitions and Purchase Orders without funding.

Requisitions can be sourced internally through internal orders or externally through purchase orders. Oracle Purchasing is a complete supply base management solution for the purchasing professional that includes

- RFQ, Quoting
- Approved Supplier Lists
- Sourcing Rules
- Blanket Purchase Agreements and Releases

Purchasing professionals can use the Autocreate function to review the requisition pool and create a purchase order or release against an agreement.

Oracle Supplier Scheduling

Supplier Scheduling enables you to communicate short- and long-range requirements to suppliers. It takes inputs from the planning and purchasing systems and applies sourcing rules and approved supplier lists to create planning schedules and shipping schedules. You can also create material authorizations for procurement of raw materials and processing to satisfy the requirements in your planning schedules, requisitions, and releases. Sources of requirements from the planning system include unreleased MPS/MRP/DRP orders. Sources of requirements from the purchasing system include approved requisitions and supplier agreement releases. These requirements will be included in the schedule if they are within the schedule horizon.

You can build and communicate the schedule in date buckets of days, weeks, months, and quarters. You can record your supplier's capacity for any given item and if the requirements would exhaust this capacity, the schedule will be split between approved suppliers in order of priority. Supplier scheduling is cumulative focused. Rather than communicating in discrete quantities, requirements are communicated as a cumulative quantity since some datum point agreed by both parties. You can let the system create these schedules, or you can create them manually as real schedules or simulation schedules. These will not be sent to suppliers. Supplier scheduling integrates with the Oracle E-Commerce Gateway for transmitting the planning, shipping, and sequenced schedules to suppliers.

PART
II

Design and
Manufacturing
Engineering

CHAPTER
2

Enterprise Structure

odeling your enterprise structure is the first step in implementing Oracle Applications, or in fact any *enterprise resource planning* (ERP) system. The implementation decisions you make while establishing your enterprise structure have a long-lasting impact on your day-to-day operations. When you are in production, changing these decisions can be very costly, if not impossible, depending on the level at which you are initiating the change. For example, changing the way a manufacturing area is structured can be less costly than attempting to change the structure at the business unit level. This chapter first takes a holistic view of the enterprise structure as modeled in Oracle Applications and then discusses each component.

Enterprise Structure Components

At a high level, an enterprise is structured in terms of its global headquarters, country headquarters, legal companies in different countries, and their operating units. If you drill down deeper, you might have various distribution facilities and manufacturing plants. Before discussing the entities that constitute the enterprise structure in detail, let's take a look at the way a global enterprise might be structured and the modeling of this enterprise structure in Oracle Applications.

Global Enterprise

The database instance is at the top of the hierarchy. The second level is a set of enterprises (having many enterprises in a single instance might not be very common, but it's possible). Each enterprise consists of many divisions. For example, Neptune is a large enterprise, and Computers is one of its divisions. Each division has a country headquarters, which could be a consolidation of various companies that operate in that country. Figure 2-1 depicts one possible structure of a global enterprise.

Each company can have many business units, which in turn might control many manufacturing plants and distribution centers. Customer orders are handled at the business unit level and routed to the appropriate manufacturing plant/distribution center for fulfillment. Purchasing is handled at the business unit level as well. But the manufacturing plants and distribution centers receive their own goods.

Enterprise Structure Modeling in Oracle Applications

Software should model the real world as closely as possible, and Oracle doesn't offer any surprises from that viewpoint. Figure 2-2 shows the hierarchy of entities that help you model your enterprise structure in Oracle Applications; this structure closely resembles the structure illustrated in Figure 2-1.

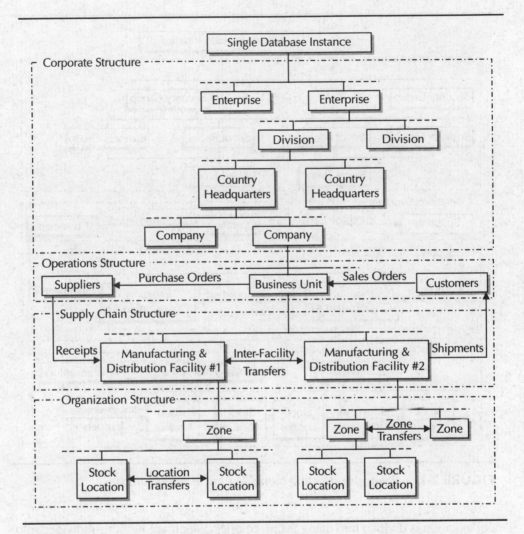

FIGURE 2-1. *Structure of a global enterprise*

Security groups serve the purpose of slicing a single database and using it for multiple enterprises. Business Group and Set of Books together provide you the capability to model both corporate divisions and country headquarters. Legal Entity models a company that reports to a country headquarters.

Operating Unit models a business unit within a legal entity. An Inventory Organization is used to model manufacturing plants and distribution centers. An operating unit can contain many inventory organizations. An inventory

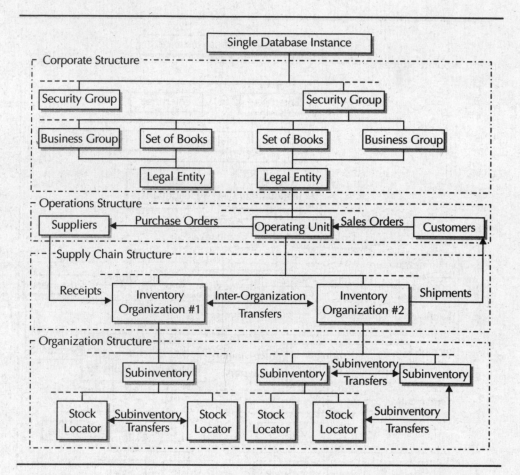

FIGURE 2-2. *Enterprise structure model in Oracle Applications*

organization is divided into many Subinventories, which are further subdivided into many Stock Locators.

As already highlighted, Enterprise Structure decisions can have a long-lasting impact. So, it is very important that you make the right decisions in the beginning of your implementation cycle. Table 2-1 suggests the experts that you should involve for each of the structures that were discussed.

Participation of Experts

Structure Type	Oracle HRMS	Oracle Fin.	Oracle Dist.	Oracle Mfg.	Oracle CRM
Corporate	Required	Required	Required	Not Required	Required
Operations	Required	Required	Required	Required	Required
Supply Chain	Not Required	Not Required	Required	Required	Required
Organization	Not Required	Not Required	Required	Required	Required

TABLE 2-1.   *Expert Participation while Establishing Enterprise Structure*

The logical data model that is presented in Figure 2-3 will help you to get a better understanding of the information presented thus far. As you can see, the Organization entity is used to store information about business groups, operating units, legal entities, and inventory organizations. An inventory organization can have many subinventories, which in turn can contain many locators. Staging lanes and dock doors are subtypes of locators.

NOTE
Security Group ID will be stored in all tables to provide data security across enterprises. Security group entity will have a foreign key to all the tables in Oracle Applications and hence is not included in Figure 2-3.

The rest of this chapter discusses these structural components in detail. Almost all the components of corporate structure do not directly impact the manufacturing and distribution modules and hence will not be covered as extensively, as we cover the components in the remaining three structures.

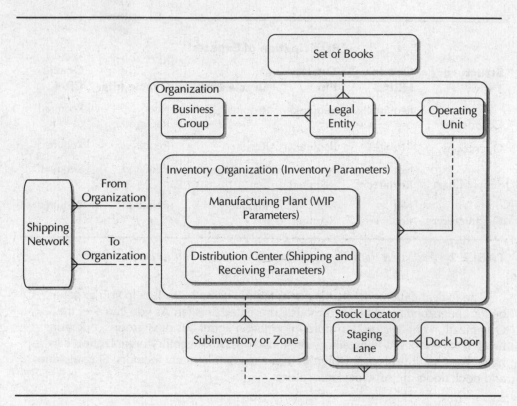

FIGURE 2-3. *Enterprise structure logical data model*

Multi-Org

The *Multi-Org* (MO) feature provides an optimized and simple solution for partitioning the data—taking advantage of the enhanced database views. Multi-Org enables companies to have varied organization models. Companies can have data secured to individual operating centers even if they are situated in another country or if they transact in a different currency and legal structure.

Multi-Org allows consolidated reporting across the enterprise, enabling you to look at your information with a global perspective. A consolidated instance provides better and consistent data and also saves time in collecting information for decision-making.

Because all the data are associated with an organization, it is easy to isolate the data of an operating unit. This would facilitate quick and easy management in case of a spin-off or inactivation of the operating unit and also fast retrieval of the data for a particular operating unit for integration with other systems.

You can use the various features in Multi-Org to model independent operating divisions within a company and independent companies within an enterprise. Multi-Org allows you to report across sets of books, legal entities, and operating units. This allows you to get a consolidated view of your finances irrespective of the number of operating units and legal entities.

NOTE
Multi-Org is the name of a feature that allows you to have multiple sets of books for multiple organizations. (Organizations are covered in the following section.) You can just have one set of books and still operate with multiple organizations.

Organization

Organizations in Oracle Applications are used to represent business groups, legal entities, operating units, and inventory organizations. You define an organization in the Organizations form that is shown in Figure 2-4.

NOTE
All the organization definitions are stored in the HR_ALL_ORGANIZATION_UNITS and HR_ORGANIZATION_INFORMATION tables.

You can identify the location of this organization using the Location field. You can associate only one location with an organization in this form. If you want to associate more than one organization with a location, you can do that from the Locations form.

The different types of organizations are identified using the Organization Classifications. This enables you to place an organization into many classifications. For example, an organization can be a legal entity, as well as an operating unit and inventory organization at the same time.

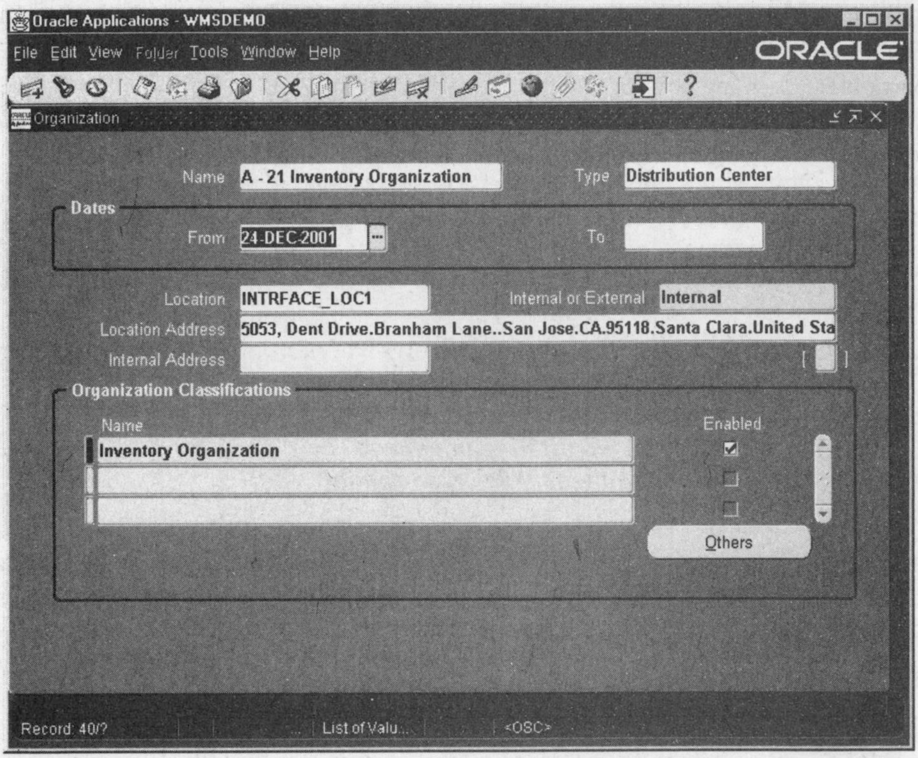

FIGURE 2-4. *The Organization form allows you to define the various types of organizations in Oracle Applications*

Corporate Structure

The corporate structure forms the top of the enterprise. Human resource management and financial accounting policies are established at the country level. A holding company can hold more than one company within a country. This section discusses the four entities in Oracle Applications that provide you with the capability to establish your corporate structure—Security Group, Business Group, Set of Books, and Legal Entity.

Security Group

Security Group is a new feature that is available starting in Release 11i in limited areas. This functionality was not completely available when this book went to press.

Security Group slices your database into many groups using a Group Identifier, allowing you to run multiple enterprises in the same instance. This will be especially useful if you are running as an application service provider, where you want to serve multiple customers and want to provide data security between those customers.

Business Group (BG)

All the country-specific HR policies are identified at the *Business Group* (BG) level. HR allows you to set up different skills, profiles, and job classifications by BG. If you are a conglomerate or if you acquire different companies, you might have more than one business group within a country. The profile HR:Business Group identifies the business group that is tied to the responsibility.

Business Group is defined as an organization in the Organizations form, by including Business Group as one of the organization classifications.

Set of Books

Set of Books is a financial reporting entity that is identified by three important attributes popularly called the 3 Cs—Chart of Accounts, Currency, and (Accounting) Calendar. You can define sets of books in Oracle General Ledger (GL); GL keeps track of accounting information by sets of books. Each responsibility is identified with a set of books using the profile option GL: Set of Books Name; a responsibility can only see the accounting information for that set of books in Oracle GL.

NOTE
Business Group and Set of Books together provide you the capability to model your country headquarters. You can model corporate divisions using consolidated Set of Books.

Legal Entity

A legal entity represents a legal company for which you prepare fiscal or tax reports. A *legal entity* is defined as an organization in the Organizations form, by including Legal Entity as one of the organization classifications. When you define a legal entity, it is automatically attached to the Business Group that is associated with your responsibility. You assign tax identifiers and other legal entity information to this type of organization.

In a global enterprise you can ship products from a warehouse that belongs to a legal entity that is different from the legal entity that sold it. The intercompany invoicing feature in Oracle Applications will automatically record an intercompany sale between these two organizations, by generating intercompany invoices.

Cross Organization Reporting

Cross organization reporting allows you to generate financial reports at the level of legal entity and set of books in addition to the operating unit level. The profile option MO:Top Reporting Level allows you to restrict the reporting level for each responsibility. The possible values are Set of Books, Legal Entity, and Operating Unit.

TIP
Specify the value of MO:Top Reporting Level as Operating Unit, at the site level. This will ensure that users have access to data only from their operating unit.

When you run your reports, you have to select a reporting level. The allowed list for you might vary depending on your responsibility's top reporting level. After selecting the level, you have to select the Reporting Context that you want to report on. For example, if your reporting level is Legal Entity, your reporting context could be Neptune Networks Inc.

A number of reports have been enabled for cross-organization reporting in the areas of payables, receivables, and tax. Other than these functional reports, various country-specific reports have also been enabled for cross-organization reporting.

Operations Structure

The operations structure identifies your customers, suppliers, and the operating units that handle the business processes that interact with your customers and suppliers. This section discusses the three entities that are part of this structure—operating units, customers, and suppliers.

Operating Unit

Operating Unit (OU) is defined as an organization in the Organizations form, by including Operating Unit as one of the organization classifications. Operating Units are a part of a legal entity. You have to associate every OU with a set of books and a legal entity within that set of books.

The profile MO:Operating Unit identifies the OU that is associated with a responsibility. A responsibility can only access information from the OU that is associated with the responsibility. Chapters 12 and 13 cover some of the features that are available at the OU level.

Customer

Customers are defined in the Customers form. You can enter multiple addresses for a customer and assign a business purpose for each address. You can also define contact people, bank accounts, payment methods, telephone numbers, and relationships for each customer. You can change the status of a customer from Active to Inactive, if you want to temporarily disable a customer. The only information that is required for a new customer is a customer name, number, and address.

If you are using Multi-Org, you cannot enter a salesperson or a tax code at the customer level; you can only assign this information to a customer site (for example, Bill To, Ship To, or Dunning site). If you are not using Multi-Org, you can assign a salesperson and tax code at both the customer and site levels. Customers are covered in detail in Chapter 12.

Supplier

Suppliers are defined in the Suppliers form, which enables you to record information about each of the members of your supply base. When you enter a supplier that does business from multiple locations, you store supplier information only once and enter Supplier Sites for each location. You can designate supplier sites as pay sites, purchasing sites, RFQ only sites, or procurement card sites. Suppliers and Supply Base Management are covered in detail in Chapter 13.

Supply Chain Structure

The supply chain management modules in Oracle Applications provide you with the capability to accurately model your supply chain. A supply chain consists of manufacturing plants and distribution centers, with generic and item-specific sourcing relationships. An inventory organization is used to represent a manufacturing plant or a distribution center in Oracle Applications. Once you define an inventory organization, you can enable further functionality (both manufacturing and distribution) by defining additional parameters. This section discusses inventory organizations and then talks about distribution centers and manufacturing plants. The section concludes with shipping networks. Chapter 11 discusses the details of defining your supply chain.

Inventory Organization

You define an inventory organization in the Organizations form by including the Inventory Organization classification. This classification requires you to define various parameters that affect the various functions in an organization—accounting, costing, materials management, engineering, and manufacturing.

Accounting Information

You choose the Set of Books, the Legal Entity within that set of books, and the Operating Unit within that legal entity to which the current organization belongs.

Organization Parameters

The Organization Parameters window allows you to define various parameters that control the inventory, costing, and accounting functions within an organization. This section discusses these parameters in detail.

Inventory Parameters   The Organization Code uniquely identifies the organization within the installation. The Item Master Organization is an organization that contains all the item definitions. Whenever you define an item in an organization, the item will first be defined in the Item Master organization that you identify here. This field will default to the current organization. Item Master Organization is covered in detail in Chapter 3. Figure 2-5 shows the Inventory Parameters tab of the Organization Parameters window.

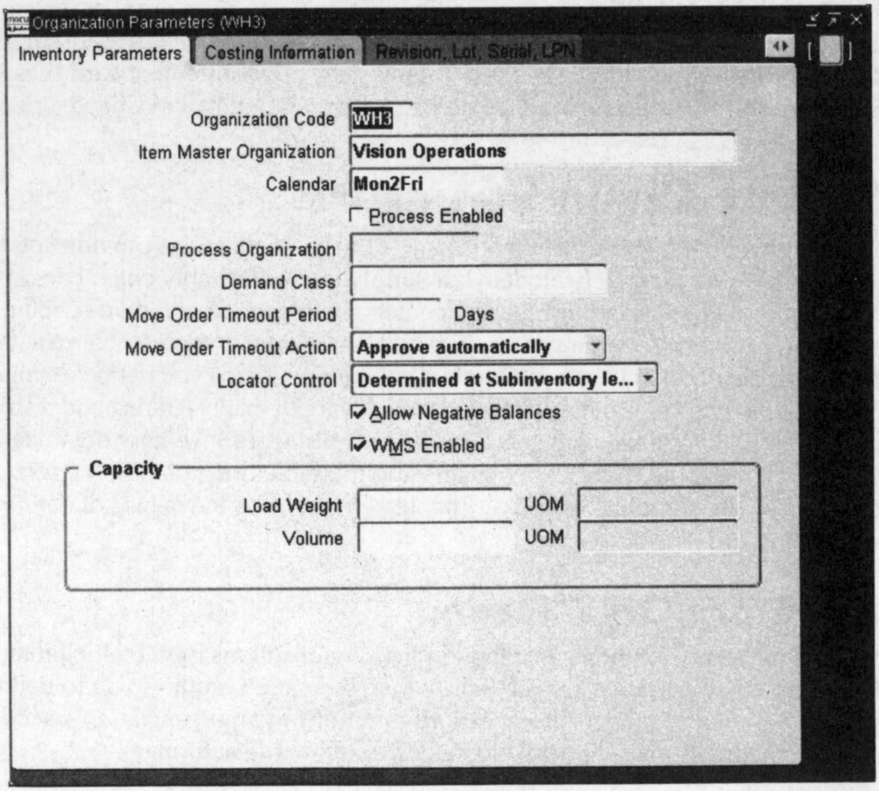

FIGURE 2-5.   *Inventory parameters allow you to determine the behavior of inventory functions at the organization level*

NOTE
If you want to use a single item master organization across business groups, set the profile option HR:Cross Business Groups to Yes at the site level. If the profile is No, you cannot see organizations that are outside your business group, and hence cannot select an organization outside your business group as your item master. You can override this profile value at the responsibility level and specify No for the HR Responsibilities so that you won't see cross-business group information.

The Workday Calendar identifies the amount of time available for planning applications and is covered in detail in Chapter 4. Process Enabled and Process Organization are applicable in a Process Manufacturing context, if you have Oracle Process Manufacturing installed. Demand Classes are used to segregate demand and production into groups, so that you can track and consume those groups independently. Demand Classes are covered in detail in Chapter 8.

The Move Order Timeout Period field identifies the number of days that move order requisition can wait for approval. The item planner is notified when a move order requisition requires approval. After timeout period days, if the planner has not approved or rejected the order, a reminder notice is sent. After another timeout period days, the order is automatically approved or rejected, depending on whether you select Approve Automatically or Reject Automatically in the Move Order Timeout Action field. For example, if your time period is three days and the action is to approve automatically, a planner who has not approved or rejected a move order after three days receives a notification. After another three days (six days from the requisition date), the order is automatically approved if it is still not approved.

TIP
If you don't intend to use approval for move orders in an organization, specify the Move Order Timeout Period as 0 days and the Move Order Timeout Action as Approve automatically.

Locator Control determines the extent to which you want to use locators in an inventory organization. You can choose None if you don't intend to use locators in an organization. Prespecified Only mandates inventory transactions within this organization to require a valid, predefined locator for each item. If the setting is Dynamic Entry Allowed, locators are required in inventory transactions within this organization, but the locator can be either predefined or dynamically entered during the transaction. You can delegate this decision to the individual subinventories within the organization by choosing Determined At Subinventory Level.

NOTE
Unlike default settings at various points in the applications (where the most specific setting prevails), the Locator control setting is a true control—if locator control is set to anything other than Determined at subinventory level, it establishes control for the entire organization; lower-level settings have no effect.

Allow Negative Balances determines whether the on-hand balances in the organization can be driven negative by manual inventory transactions. Regardless of the setting, shipping transactions cannot drive inventory negative. Backflush transactions are controlled by the profile INV:Override Neg for Backflush.

To use Oracle WMS, you should check WMS Enabled. Warehouse Parameters are covered under the Distribution Center section.

Costing Parameters   The Ccsting Organization enables you to decide whether you want to use centralized costing or decentralized costing. The choices are the current organization or the Item Master organization. You can choose a Costing Method if the current organization is the costing organization. A complete coverage of the costing methods can be found in Chapter 18. If you are using Oracle Work in Process, you must choose decentralized costing (i.e. the costing organization must be the current organization) because resources and overheads are considered to be organization-specific objects.

You can choose to transfer only the summaries of the transactions by selecting Summary in Transfer to GL. The posting time for transferring detail transaction distributions to the General Ledger will be longer than the time for summaries, due to the number of records created.

If you intend to use the encumbrance accounting feature in Oracle Purchasing, indicate whether to reverse encumbrance entry upon receipt in inventory. Select a material subelement that this organization uses as a default when you define item costs.

NOTE
Since a material subelement is organization-specific you must define the organization first, then the subelement, then select that subelement as the default in organization parameters.

Valuation Accounts   You choose a set of valuation accounts in the organization parameters. In standard costing organizations, a cost group that contains these accounts is defaulted when you define subinventories and can be overridden.

During inventory transactions, entries will be posted into the accounts of the default cost group at the subinventory level for standard costing organizations.

In average costing organizations, these accounts (except for Expense) are used for subinventory transactions and cannot be updated. You can choose an account each for Material, Material Overhead, Resource Overhead, Outside Processing, and Expense. Inventory transactions are covered in detail in Chapter 15.

Item Controls   The Starting Revision will be used as the default for each new item. Lot Number Uniqueness allows you to specify if you want your lot numbers to be unique across all items. You can choose to generate lot numbers automatically using lot number information at the item or organization level or choose to define lot numbers manually by setting Lot Number Generation appropriately. If the setting is User-defined, lot numbers have to be entered when you receive items that are lot-controlled. If the setting is At Organization Level, the Prefix, Zero Pad Suffix, and Total Length of the organization are used to generate lot numbers automatically when you receive items. If the setting is At Item Level, the item attributes Starting Lot Prefix and Starting Lot Number are used to generate lot numbers automatically when you receive items.

Serial Number Uniqueness allows you to specify the uniqueness controls for serial-controlled items within an organization. If the setting is Within Organization, serial numbers within the organization are always unique. Within Inventory Items enforces unique serial numbers within an inventory item in the organization. Across Organizations enforces unique serial numbers across all organizations.

You can choose the serial number generation to be either at the Item Level or Organization Level. The Prefix and the Starting Serial Number at either of these will be used to generate serial numbers depending on the choice of Generation.

Available to Promise (ATP) and Picking Defaults   You can select an ATP Rule and a Picking Rule as defaults for the organization. The ATP process (covered in Chapter 12) will use the default ATP Rule at the organization level if the item does not have an associated ATP Rule.

Oracle WMS comes with a flexible rules engine that you can use to define your picking rules. If you are not using Oracle WMS, you can use the standard picking rules that are seeded with Oracle Inventory. You can select one of the standard picking rules as the default picking rule for an organization.

You can specify the Subinventory Order (default subinventory picking order) and the Locator Order (default locator picking order) that will be used as a default for all the subinventories and locators in the organization. Picking order is covered in detail in later sections.

Check Pick Confirmation Required if you want your pickers to manually confirm each pick. If you do not check the box, pick confirmation will occur automatically. Manual Pick Confirm allows you to track your inventory more closely than automatic pick confirm. Pick Confirmation is explained in detail in Chapter 15.

Item Sourcing Defaults   You can specify the source type as Supplier, Inventory, or None. If you want to replenish items from a supplier, specify Supplier as the source type. If you want to replenish from another organization (with which you have a shipping network defined) or the same organization, choose Inventory as the source type and also choose an inventory organization. If you are sourcing from the same organization, choose a subinventory within the current organization. Choose None, if you don't want to provide a default source. Sourcing Rules is covered in detail in Chapter 11.

Inter-Organization Transfers   You can choose your Inter-Organization Transfer Charge option from four possible choices—None, Predefined Percent, Requested Value, and Requested Percent. If you chose Predefined Percent, you should specify a percentage value to add to a material transfer. You can choose a set of default inter-organization transfer accounts. These accounts are defaulted when you set up shipping information in the Inter-Organization Shipping Networks window (covered later in the section "Shipping Networks").

Receiving Accounts   In a standard costing organization, the purchase price variance and invoice price variance are recorded during the receipt and invoicing of goods. You choose an account each for posting Purchase Price Variance and Invoice Price Variance for the current organization.

When goods are received, Oracle Receiving records accrual of payables for this organization. You choose an account to accumulate Inventory AP Accrual for this organization. If you use encumbrances in Oracle Purchasing, choose a default account to accumulate Encumbrance for this organization. This will be defaulted when you define your subinventories.

Profit and Loss Accounts   The revenue account and cost of goods sold account are captured at the item level. You can choose the Sales and Cost of Goods Sold accounts at the organization level, which will be defaulted for the items in the organization.

NOTE
The accounts recorded here are used as a starting point by the account generation engines (e.g., Flexbuilder). They are only a starting point, however; the actual account that is generated might be different.

Average Cost Variance   If you are using average costing and allow negative inventory balances, choose an account to represent the inventory valuation error caused by issuing your inventory before processing your receipts.

Organization Access

You can restrict the organizations that can be accessed by a responsibility using the Organization Access form. You have to specify the access list for all responsibilities if you are planning to use this feature. Also, organization access only restricts the list of organizations during logon and while changing organizations—if you use a feature that spans multiple organizations such as ATP, you can specify any valid organization.

Distribution Center

A distribution center is concerned with receiving, storing, and shipping materials. The detailed functionality is discussed in Chapters 14, 15, and 17. In this section, we briefly discuss the various parameters that need to be set up at the organization level.

Receiving Parameters

Use the Receiving Options window to define options that govern receipts in your system. The receiving options allow you to establish the policy at the organization level. For example, you can specify the number of days a receipt can be either early or late. Receiving parameters are covered in detail in Chapter 14. Most of these options can be overridden for specific suppliers, items, and purchase orders.

Warehouse Parameters

If you enable Oracle WMS in an organization, you can define a set of warehouse parameters that will be used by the various WMS features. Figure 2-6 shows the Warehouse tab of the Organization Parameters window.

You can choose to generate put-away tasks as soon as you receive goods from your suppliers by checking Pregenerate after Receipt. Pregeneration will invoke the rules engine to determine the best location to put away the received goods. The Regeneration Interval specifies the time in minutes after which the putaway suggestion is considered to be outdated and will be regenerated.

Time Zone is not being used currently. In the future WMS will support warehouses operating in multiple time zones.

Default Cycle Count Header is used for automatic cycle count generation. For example, if a warehouse user finds that the inventory in a locator doesn't match with that of the system, he or she can cause a new cycle count task to be automatically generated. These tasks will be defined under the default cycle count header for the warehouse.

You can enable crossdocking operations in the warehouse by checking Enable Crossdock.

You select the default rule that will be used for Picking and Put Away if the rules engine is unable to find a rule in a given situation. The default Pick Task Type and Replenish Task Type are used for scheduling picking and replenishment tasks if the rules engine is unable to find a task type for a given situation.

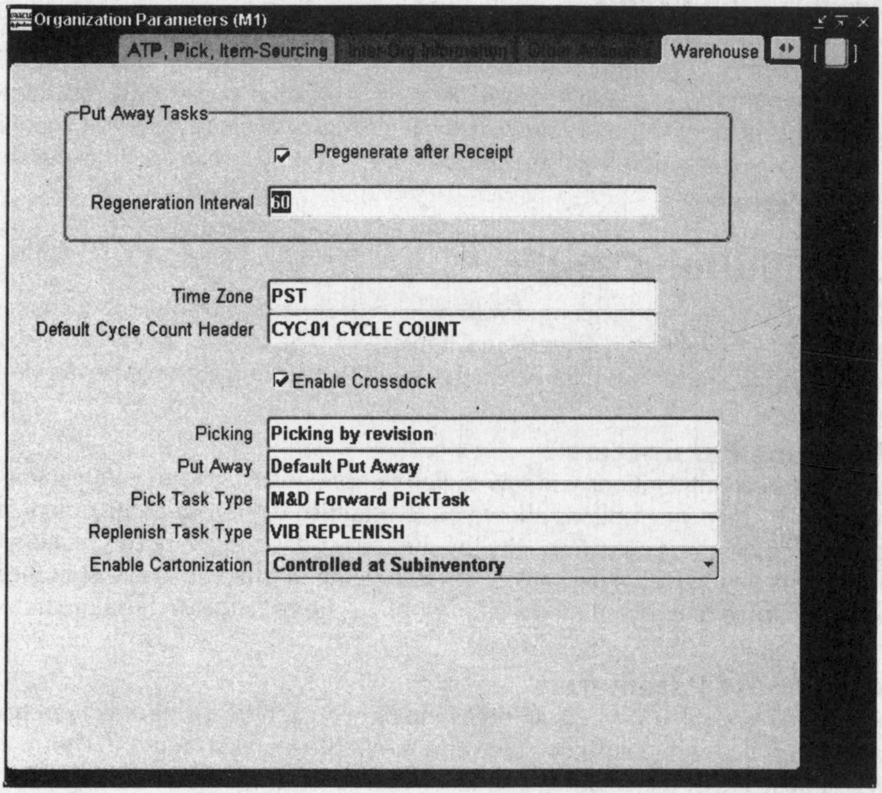

FIGURE 2-6. *Warehouse Parameters*

You can enable cartonization for the warehouse by choosing Yes for Enable Cartonization. If you are not sure, you can delegate the decision to the subinventory level by choosing Controlled at Subinventory.

Shipping Parameters
In the Shipping Parameters window, you can define the default values for basic shipping information such as units of measurement, pick release rules, weight and volume calculations, and delivery grouping rules. These parameters are covered in detail in Chapters 15 and 17.

Manufacturing Plant
You can enable the manufacturing features in an organization by setting up the parameters of the appropriate modules. For example, you set up WIP Parameters to

use Oracle Work In Process, BOM Parameters to use Oracle Bills of Material, and Planning Parameters to use the planning products. These parameters will be covered in the appropriate chapters.

Shipping Networks

The Inter-Organization Shipping Network form allows you to define accounting information and relevant shipping information between inventory organizations. The relationship can be two way or just one way. These relationships are not item specific.

If the transfer lead-time is significant, or if you require explicit acknowledgment at the receiving organization, you can use Intransit as the transfer type. Otherwise, you can use Direct as the transfer type. If the transfer is direct, inventory is immediately visible in the destination organization. You have to identify the FOB point if you use intransit transfers. Inter-Organization Transfers are covered in detail in Chapter 15.

NOTE
Sourcing Rules and Bills of Distribution allow you to create item-specific sourcing networks. These are covered in detail in Chapter 11.

You must choose the accounts that should be used during the transfer. There are five accounts that are affected during a transfer—Transfer Credit, Purchase Price Variance, Payable, Receivable, and Intransit Inventory.

Organization Structure

A manufacturing plant produces the products that are sold in the market using various distribution centers. Manufacturing plants and distribution centers will have to be further divided into zones and stocking locations for easy material handling. This will facilitate you in identifying stocking areas by material type. For example, you might choose to stock all the chemicals in the northeast part of your manufacturing plant. Planning your zones and locators properly can provide you with significant savings in handling and obsolescence costs. In this section, we discuss the internal structure of an inventory organization.

NOTE
The structure of a manufacturing plant has to be established considering two aspects—material handling and the layout of production lines. The material handling aspects are covered in this chapter, and the line layout aspects are covered in Chapter 7.

Subinventory

Subinventory represents a subdivision of an inventory organization. Currently, a
Subinventory is used to represent either a physical zone or to identify the ownership
of inventory. You can also use subinventory to track the materials in a production
line/manufacturing cell. Figure 2-7 shows the Subinventory form. You can define
some item attributes at the subinventory level—this is covered in detail in Chapter 15.

NOTE
*Throughout this book, Subinventory and Zone have
the same meaning and are used interchangeably.*

In a WMS Enabled organization, a subinventory represents a physical area
(a zone or a manufacturing cell). To identify the ownership of inventory, you use
Cost Groups.

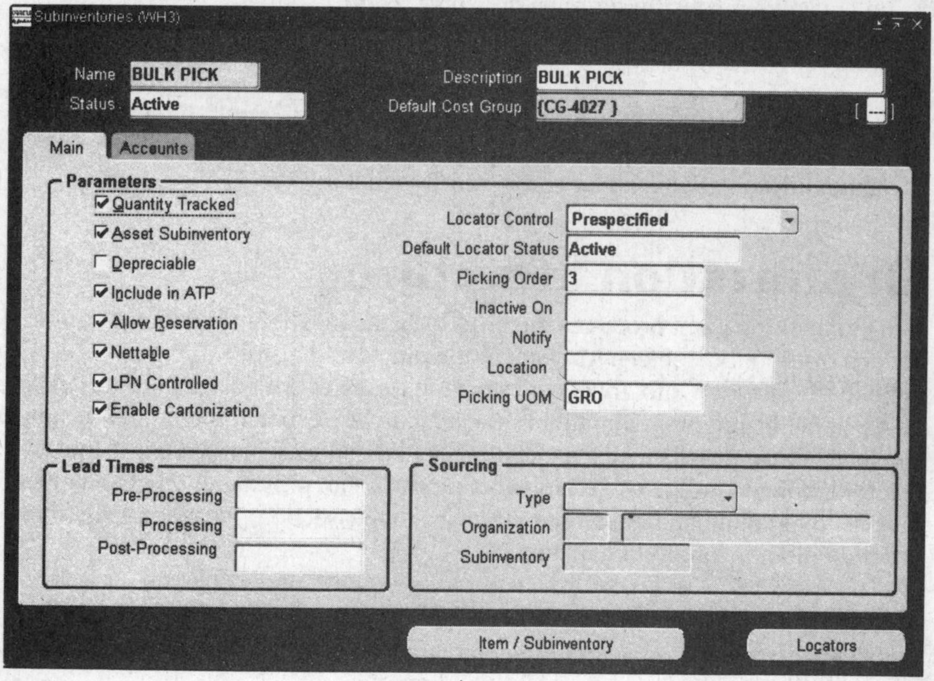

FIGURE 2-7.   *The Subinventory form allows you to define and maintain
subinventories*

NOTE
*In project manufacturing, Cost Group serves as
both a costing entity and an accounting entity.
In WMS organizations, Cost Group is just an
accounting entity—the costing entity is still the
inventory organization.*

This separation of ownership from physical location allows you to manage
consigned inventory. The cost group rules engine will suggest the default cost
group of a subinventory for costing transactions if there are no specialized rules.
Complete coverage of this new feature can be found in Chapter 15.

NOTE
*The table MTL_SECONDARY_INVENTORIES is
used to store subinventories.*

Subinventory Parameters

On-hand balances are maintained for a Quantity Tracked subinventory. If you want
to include the value of the materials in a subinventory on the balance sheet, you
can check the Asset Inventory flag. You cannot update this flag if a subinventory has
on-hand quantity.

The assets in Oracle Fixed Assets can be related to inventory items. This feature
is available with Oracle Network Logistics. Depreciable is used to indicate if the
items in a subinventory that are related to a fixed asset are depreciable.

To include the items in a subinventory in Available to Promise, Available to
Reserve, and Planning Calculations, check the flags Include in ATP, Allow Reservation,
and Nettable, respectively. A non-quantity-tracked subinventory cannot hold asset
inventory, cannot be enabled for ATP, cannot be allowed for reservation, and
cannot be nettable.

If you chose to decide the type of locator control at the subinventory level, you
can choose a type in Locator Control. The options are the same as in the organization
level. Additionally, you can choose to decide locator control for each item by
choosing the Determined at Item Level option. Specify the default status of the
locators in a subinventory using the Default Locator Status field. Locator status is
used to temporarily disable a locator.

You can disable a subinventory by specifying a date in the Inactive On field.
You can select an ECO Approval List (covered in Chapter 5) as the list of people to
be used for move order approvals using the Notify field. If the move order doesn't
specify an approval list, the default list at the subinventory level will be used. You
can optionally associate a Location with a subinventory.

WMS Specific Parameters

Some of the parameters at the subinventory level are only used for WMS Enabled organizations. These parameters allow you to manage the inventory in each zone with much more flexibility and control. This section discusses these parameters.

LPN Controlled   If a zone is LPN controlled (LPN—License Plate Number), the subinventory can contain both loose items and items in an LPN. If a zone is not LPN controlled, the zone can contain only loose items. Containers are covered in detail in Chapter 15.

NOTE
If you use a subinventory/locator as default supply sources for manufacturing, you should ensure that you store loose items in them, because the backflush transactions (covered in Chapter 16) cannot perform an automatic unpack transaction. All inventory transactions will perform an unpack transaction automatically, if necessary.

Enable Cartonization   If you enable cartonization on a zone, all the items that are picked from that zone will be cartonized. Cartonization is a process that splits a picking line based on the packaging constraints and the availability of cartons, before dispatching it to the pickers. Cartonization is covered in detail in Chapter 15.

Picking Order   Picking Order allows you to establish zone sequences. The pick release and pick detailing process (described in Chapter 15) will use this while identifying the material to be picked for a sales order. For example, if you want to always consider the FP (for forward picking) zone before the BK (for Bulk) zone for picking, you can establish the picking order of FP and BK to be 1 and 2, respectively. The pick detailing process will first look at zone FP to source material and then look at zone BK if it doesn't find enough material in zone FP.

Picking UOM   To optimize the productivity of your warehouse, you might want to split your order lines into multiple picking lines to minimize the number of picks. The pick detailing process splits order lines into different picking lines, based on the subinventory's Picking UOM and the material availability in that subinventory. This is illustrated by Figure 2-8.

As you can see from Figure 2-8, a single order line is split into three picking lines based on the UOM Conversion (covered in Chapter 15) and the Picking UOM of subinventories. These picking lines will be routed to the same staging for consolidation.

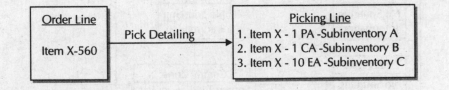

FIGURE 2-8. *Order line splitting based on Picking UOM*

Lead Times

You can specify the Pre-Processing, Processing, and Post-Processing lead times if you want your Min–Max planning to consider the lead time while planning for a subinventory. You can find a detailed explanation of these lead times in Chapter 8. Min–Max planning is covered in Chapter 15.

Sourcing

You can specify the source type as Supplier, Inventory, or Subinventory. Supplier and Inventory behave exactly in the same way as at the organization level. If you want to replenish from a subinventory within the same organization, choose Subinventory as the source type and choose a subinventory within the current organization.

As illustrated by Figure 2-9, you can use the source types at the organization level and at the subinventory level to manage centralized materials management within an organization. Designate a central zone as the source for all the material requirements in your organization. The central subinventory can source material from an external source—either a supplier or another inventory organization. The inventory replenishment programs will create move orders (covered in Chapter 15) from the central zone to replenish zones 1–5 and purchase requisitions/internal requisitions to replenish the central zone.

You can achieve decentralized materials management within an organization by having each zone manage its sourcing on its own, either internally or externally.

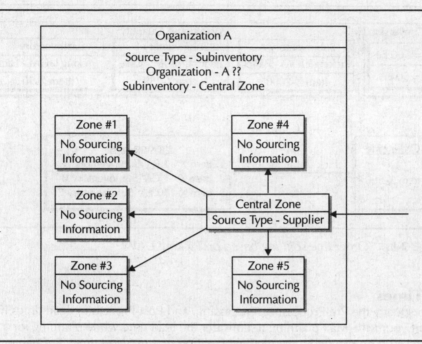

FIGURE 2-9. *Multiple zones sourcing from a central zone*

Stock Locator

Stock Locator represents the smallest physical location in Oracle Applications that allows you to stock and track your materials. Stock Locator is a single structure key flexfield; design your locator structure after taking inputs from all the stakeholders because it has to satisfy the requirements of everyone. You define stock locators in the Stock Locators window that is shown in Figure 2-10. You can access this window by pressing the Locators button in the subinventory form.

NOTE
The table MTL_ITEM_LOCATIONS is used to store stock locators.

As in subinventories, some of the parameters at the locator level are only used for WMS-enabled organizations.

Locator Status

The Status field identifies the current status of a locator. A locator can be temporarily put on Hold; if a locator is on hold, the locator will not be allowed in any inventory transactions.

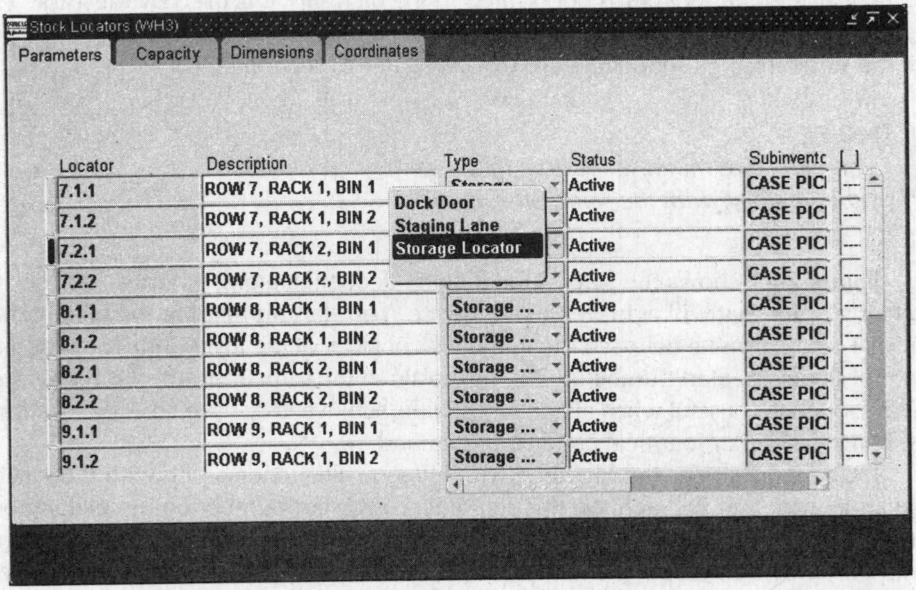

FIGURE 2-10. *The Stock Locators form allows you to define and maintain inventory stocking locations*

NOTE
You can also put lots and serialized items on hold.

Locator Types

The Locator Type further qualifies locator into stocking locator, staging lane, or dock door. A stocking locator is used to store material. Staging lanes are used for staging and consolidating inventory that has been picked for shipment.

During the load process, all the materials are transferred from the staging lane to the dock door or the truck. You can associate staging lanes to dock doors; this is covered in a later section. The usage of staging lanes and dock doors is covered in detail in Chapter 15.

Picking Order

Optimizing your pick path in the warehouse is very important because it is wasteful to have your pickers walking around without getting the real work accomplished. Suboptimal paths can also introduce unnecessary traffic in the warehouse, bringing down the overall productivity. The picking order at the subinventory level allows you to sequence your zones before you sequence your locators. You can use the Picking Order in stock locators to model the pick sequence that is the most appropriate for the subinventories in your warehouse.

Locator Picking Order is not printed in the pick slip. It is used by the Task Dispatching Engine of Oracle WMS for sequencing the picker's task batch. A couple of the standard pick sequences are discussed in this section.

NOTE
You can have multiple locators in the same subinventory, with the same picking order.

Figure 2-11 shows the Serpentine Picking Sequence along with the locator picking order that will achieve this sequence. You start numbering the picking order from 1 and alternate between the left and right sides of the aisle until you reach the end of the aisle. Start numbering the next aisle in the same fashion, but backward. This sequence is useful when all the items in the subinventory have an equal likelihood of being picked or identical patterns of demand.

Figure 2-12 shows the Mainline with Sidetrips Sequence along with the locator picking order that will achieve this sequence. You start numbering the picking order from 1 along the mainline. You stop at some appropriate point along the mainline and continue numbering the first aisle. While numbering the locators in the aisle,

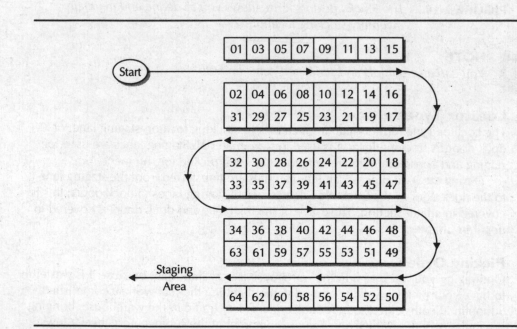

FIGURE 2-11.   *Serpentine picking*

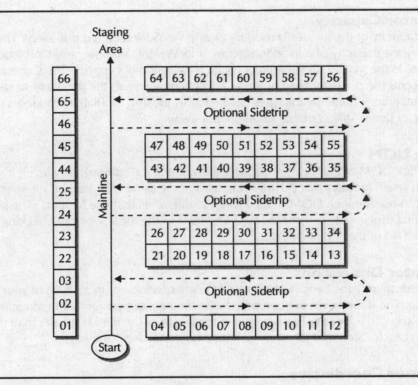

FIGURE 2-12.   *Mainline with sidetrips*

you don't alternate because you go forward and come back on the same aisle. Instead, you number one side of the aisle in forward sequence and number the other side from backward. You continue this pattern for the rest of the subinventory.

You can unify the two pick sequence patterns in Figures 2-11 and 2-12 easily. You can also model various standard pick sequence patterns and any complex patterns in your organization using Locator Picking Order once you identify the pattern.

TIP
To lend additional flexibility during normal operations, you can number your locators with gaps. For example, instead of numbering your locators as 1, 2, 3, 4, ..., you could've numbered your locators as 10, 20, 30, ... and so on. If you later on want to insert a new locator with a different number, you can use an unused number.

Locator Capacity

The capacity of the locator is used by Oracle WMS for directed put-away. You can specify the capacity of a locator in terms of its Weight, Volume, and Unit (countable pieces) in the Maximum field under each classification of capacity. The Current field represents the currently filled quantity. Suggested represents the put-away suggestions that have been made by the rules engine to this locator. Available represents the capacity that is still available for future put-away.

Pick UOM

The Pick UOM at the locator overrides the value at the subinventory level. If you have certain locators that do not store items in the same UOM as the subinventory, you can use the Pick UOM of the locator to differentiate those locators. The pick detailing process always checks the Pick UOM of the locator before checking the Pick UOM of the subinventory.

Locator Dimensions

You can specify the Length, Width, and Height of a locator in a UOM of your choice. The dimensions are compared with the item dimension before directing a put-away to a locator. For example, if the length of the item is greater than the length of a locator, that locator will not be suggested for put-away.

Locator Coordinates

As an alternative to Picking Order, you can use the X, Y, and Z coordinates of a locator from a fixed point in your warehouse or zone to minimize the distance traveled by your pickers. You can use any criteria to come up with your coordinate system. Figure 2-13 illustrates a coordinate system in a zone.

The reference point (or the origin) is imaginary and is purely an implementation consideration. You can mark one end of your warehouse or zone as the reference point and start defining the coordinates of your locators.

If the picking order is not specified, locator coordinates are taken into consideration while dispatching pick tasks to pickers. The distance is calculated using the formula:

$$\text{Distance between Locators} = \sqrt{(X_1 - X_2)^2 + (Y_1 - Y_2)^2 + (Z_1 - Z_2)^2}$$

The locator that has the least distance from the current locator will be the next locator from where the picker will pick.

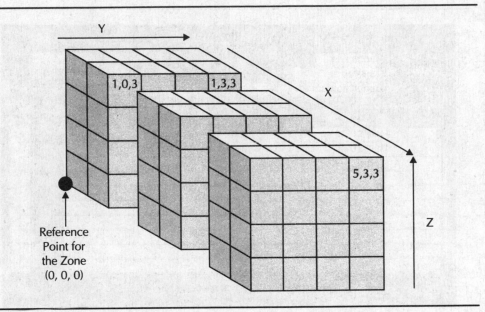

FIGURE 2-13. *Locator coordinates*

Assigning Staging Lanes to Dock Doors

You can assign staging lanes to dock doors so that you can stage all the deliveries that belong to a trip appropriately. Later on you can associate a trip to a dock door and the individual deliveries within the trip to the staging lanes that are associated with that dock door. Figure 2-14 shows the Associate Staging Lanes to Dock Doors window.

NOTE
Dock Door – Staging Lane assignment is stored in the table WMS_STAGINGLANES_ASSIGNMENTS.

Staging and Dock Scheduling is covered in detail in Chapter 15.

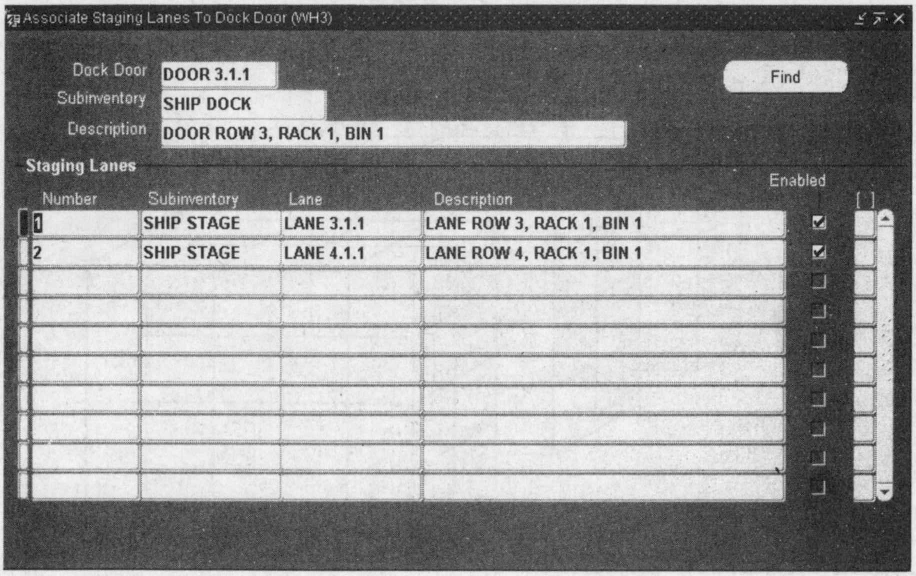

FIGURE 2-14. *Assign staging lanes to dock doors in the Staging Lane Assignment form*

Summary

This chapter described a global enterprise and discussed the various entities in Oracle Applications that could be used to model this global enterprise. Security groups could be used if you are planning to host multiple enterprises in a single database instance. Business Group and Set of Books together provide you the capability to model both corporate divisions and country headquarters. Legal Entity models a company that reports to a country headquarters (combination of Business Group and Set of Books).

An operating unit accepts sales orders from customers and passes them on to the various warehouses/manufacturing plants. The purchasing activities for all the distribution centers and manufacturing plants are consolidated at the operating unit level. Although purchasing is centralized through operating units, items are received in the manufacturing plants and distribution centers.

An inventory organization can be further divided into zones and locators. Planning your zones and locators properly can result in significant savings in handling costs and obsolescence costs. In organizations where WMS is enabled, a number of advanced material handling capabilities are available. For example, locator sequences can be used to minimize the distance traveled by your pickers.

Various examples and illustrations were provided to help you understand the implications of your choices in the most fundamental step in any implementation process—modeling the enterprise structure.

CHAPTER
3

Managing Items

n Oracle Manufacturing, items are used to represent products, services, components of an assembly, and indirect materials. Oracle Manufacturing provides you with many features that will help you in managing your item information. There are many tools that can help you to maintain your item information during the lifecycle of a product.

Product Lifecycle Management

The various modules within Oracle Manufacturing provide a means of modeling and recording activity during all phases of a product's life, starting with the design stage. Figure 3-1 shows a typical product's lifecycle phases, including the design phase with revenue on the y-axis and time on the x-axis. In the design and development phase, however, revenue is negative.

Although it might seem that the investment that is made during the design phase is very little when compared to the revenue that is generated in the other phases, not all concepts are successfully developed and launched. So, it's very important that you only pursue the most promising concepts from a financial and operational standpoint. The product lifecycle (PLC) shown in Figure 3-1 has the following phases:

- **Concept & Design**   The conception phase is where the product idea is conceived and proposed to the product approval committee. This concept is evaluated with respect to a set of criteria, before the committee endorses the concept and allocates budget. At this point, a product development project is started. The team gathers requirements, identifies the features, and designs and develops the prototypes, before field-testing them. Test results are compiled, and this iterative cycle goes on until the product is proved and is ready to be produced on a mass scale.

- **Launch**   In the launch phase, you have to make sure that you have built capacity to satisfy the forecasted demand. You have to lay out your production lines and plan your distribution chain so that you can deliver your products in the least possible time. You may have to carry some inventory, as a safety stock against unforeseen fluctuations in demand and production problems. You also have to plan the marketing structure of your product to enable your customers to easily choose the various options that are available in your product.

- **Growth**   This phase is very important from the point of view of supply chain management. You need to expand your capacity to meet the growing demand without losing your customers to your competitors, yet without building up excessive inventory. Features to manage this phase, such as line design, are covered Chapter 7.

■ **Maturity** In this phase, typically you concentrate on improving margins on the product by cutting costs. You can use the various intelligence reports that are available with the manufacturing products to help you in your cost-cutting efforts in this phase.

■ **Maintain/Decline** During this phase, based on the course of action that you take, you may have to cut costs and allow the product to die slowly or you may invest heavily in promotion, anticipating the decline phase and trying to prolong the maturity phase as much as possible. Most of the software tools to manage a product in this phase such as marketing and promotional activities are available in the CRM Suite of Oracle Applications.

The item attribute Item Status allows you to control the availability of an item to the various business functions during the different phases of a product's lifecycle with the help of eight other item attributes. In this chapter and the following few chapters, we discuss the features that are available in Oracle Manufacturing to manage an item during the different phases of its lifecycle.

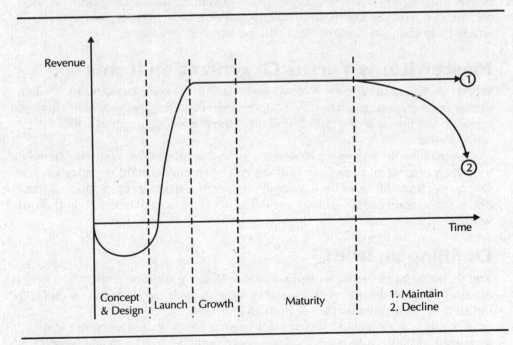

FIGURE 3-1. *The phases in a product lifecycle*

Items

The items in Oracle Applications represent products or services that you sell and their components. If necessary, items can be used to represent other aspects of a product such as product requirements and product features. The difference between a product and a product requirement is that a product is sold in the market, whereas a requirement is just for internal tracking purposes.

Item Master Organization

Item master organization is an inventory organization that holds the definition of the items that are used in your system. The item master organization is defined and maintained just like any other inventory organization.

All the organizations that use the items defined in a master organization are referred to as the child organizations. You define this relationship by choosing the master organization in the organization parameters of the child organization. Unless you have strong reasons to do otherwise, you should use a single item master for your installation. It's a good idea to treat the item master organization as a repository of item definitions and not use that organization to conduct regular business. This way, an item in the master organization will be available as a reference, whereas you would have changed the attributes in all the other organizations.

Master Items Versus Organization Items

When you define an item, the item will be created in the context organization's item master organization. You have to enable the item in all the organizations where you intend to use the item. The item definition in the master organization is like a reference item.

Some of the item attributes (covered later in this chapter) are controllable only at the master organization level, while others can be controlled at the organization level. The master level attributes have a single value across all child organizations. The organization level attributes may have different values in each of the organizations where the item is enabled.

Defining an Item

You define items in the Master Items window. When you define an item, the item is always defined in the master organization. When you define an item, you can copy the attributes from another item or from an item template.

You can apply multiple templates to an item, and you should recognize that template application is additive. So, if you apply a template to an item and subsequently apply another template, the item will have retained the values of all the attributes that were not enabled in the second template and the values of non-updateable attributes from the first template, which may not be your intention. Figure 3-2 shows the Master Item window.

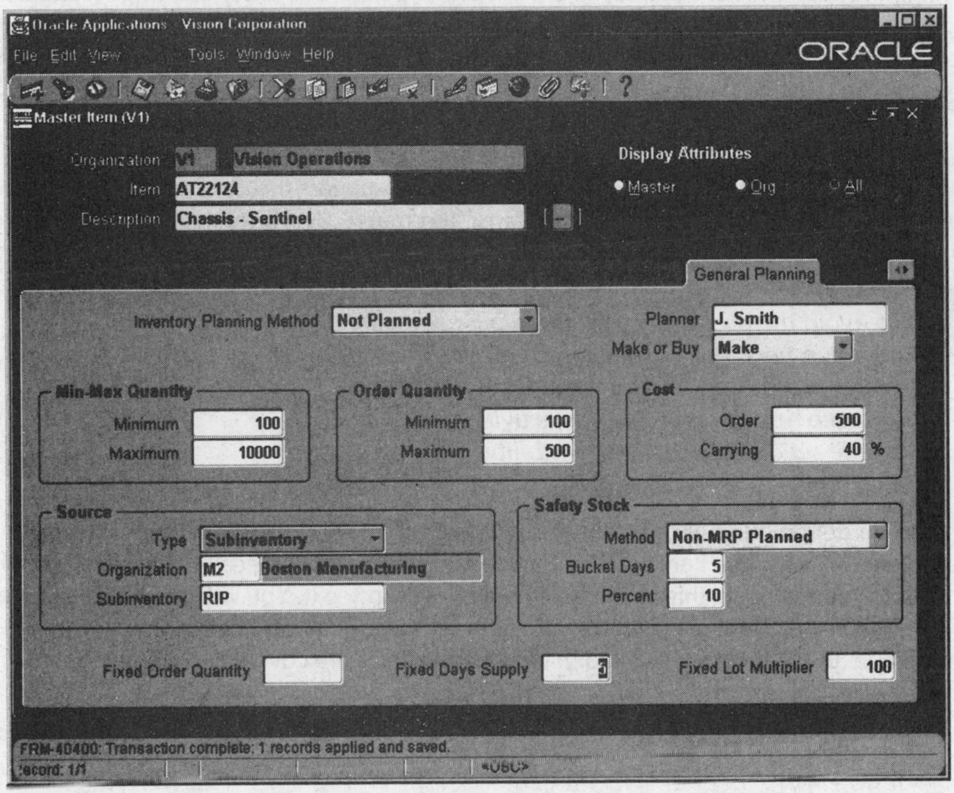

FIGURE 3-2. *Define new items using the Master Item window*

After defining an item, you use the Organization Assignment window from the Tools menu to enable the item in all the organizations where the item will be used. When you enable the item in multiple organizations, all the item attributes are copied in the enabled organization. After that, if you modify an organization level attribute in the Organization Items window, the change will be visible only in the organization where it is modified. This also applies to the item master organization. All the master level attributes can be edited only in the master organization, but they will be visible in all the organizations where the item is enabled.

If necessary, you can change item numbers after you have defined them. This capability is often useful in a pilot environment, where you want to keep an item number consistent with a test script, for example, but may need to change some item attributes that are now difficult to change without a lot of data cleanup (e.g., Primary Unit of Measure or BOM Item Type). In this case, you might rename the existing item and then re-create the item with the correct attributes. The profile option INV: Updateable Item Name controls this process. If it is set to Yes, you can query the existing item on the Master Items form, change the item number, and save. Note that this does not create a new item with the same attributes; it actually changes the item number just as if you changed the item's description, planning method, or cost. And the new item number now appears throughout the system—bills of material, forecasts, plans, and transaction history.

CAUTION
To avoid the possibility of accidentally changing item numbers, you should carefully control access to this profile option. You may want to create a separate responsibility for this activity, with the profile set only for that responsibility.

You define engineering items in the Master Engineering Items window. For an engineering item, the item attribute Engineering Item is automatically checked. You will not be able to update this attribute, although you can see it. You will not be able to view an engineering item using the Master Items or Organization Items window that is available through Oracle Inventory. Engineering items are covered in Chapter 5.

Item Templates

Templates allow you to define an item easily. A template contains a list of item attributes with predefined values. You should consider defining templates for each of the item types in your scenario. Oracle Applications comes with 16 predefined templates; you can define additional templates if you need more in the Item Templates window. Enter a name and description and choose an organization if you want to make the template local to an organization. Navigate to the attributes region. Choose the attributes that you want to be part of the template by enabling them and define the attribute values for those attributes.

CAUTION
Organization level templates cannot be applied to an item in the Master Items window, unless the organization is the master organization itself.

If you only have a few different types of items, you can define a template for each type of item. On the other hand, if you have numerous combinations, it may be easier for you to define templates for a subset of attributes and apply a series of templates to an item. For example, imagine that you have raw material, subassemblies, and finished goods, any of which can be under lot control, serial control, or both. Rather than defining nine templates to cover all the permutations, you can have three base templates (raw material, subassembly, and finished goods) and then two more templates that add lot and serial controls.

NOTE
Templates are simply tools to help you define an item; there is no link maintained between an item and the templates you used to create it. So, if you modify a template, the items that were defined with that template will not recognize the change. If you make any changes to a template, and if you want this to be reflected in all items that used the same template, you have to reapply the template again.

Item Attributes

Item attributes are additional information about an item. Some of the item attributes identify critical item information such as the planning method for an item. Some other attributes such as the Default Shipping Organization provide defaulting information. In this section we discuss item attribute setup and a few attribute groups.

Item Attribute Controls

You specify the control level for your attributes in the Item Attribute Controls window. If the control level of an attribute is Master Level, the attribute is maintained at the item master organization level and can only be edited in that organization. The value of an attribute at the item master organization defaults to the child organizations when the item is enabled and can be changed at the organization level, if the control level is Org Level.

CAUTION
If the control level is organization, and if you change an attribute in the item master organization, it won't reflect in the child organizations. You are only changing the value of that attribute in the master organization.

You can safely switch the control level of an attribute from master to organization. But if you attempt to change the control level of an attribute from organization to master, you will get a warning that your change may cause data inconsistencies. This is because the attribute you are trying to change might already have different values in the individual organizations than it has in the master.

Changing the control level will affect the creation of all items in the future, but it will not change values in any items that are already in the database. If you need to make this kind of change after you have begun defining items, you should take care to ensure that the affected attribute first does have the same value in all the functional organizations as it has in the master, to avoid potential errors or confusion.

Status Attributes

The following eight attributes, known as the *Status Attributes*, have additional controls other than the organization control level discussed earlier in this chapter:

- BOM Allowed
- Build in WIP
- Customer Orders Enabled
- Internal Orders Enabled
- Invoice Enabled
- Transactable
- Purchasable
- Stockable

These status attributes can be controlled by the value of the attribute called Item Status. If you specify a Status Setting as Sets Value, you won't be able to modify that attribute individually; the attribute is controlled by the item's status. If the status setting is Defaults Value, the item status defaults to the value for the attribute, but the attribute can be changed individually. If the status setting is None, the attribute has to be maintained individually and not by changing the item's status.

Item-Defining Attributes

An item-defining attribute describes the nature of an item and identifies the functional areas that are associated with the item. There are seven functional areas in Oracle Applications, for which you have item-defining attributes as listed in Table 3-1.

All the item-defining attributes with the exception of MRP Planning Method are check boxes. You enable an item to the Planning functional area by having any value other than None for MRP Planning Method. The user cannot explicitly set the attribute

Functional Area	Item-Defining Attribute(s)
Inventory	Inventory Item
Procurement	Purchased Item or Internally Ordered Item
Planning	MRP Planning Method
Costing	Costing Enabled
Engineering	Engineering Item
Order Management	Customer Ordered Item
Service	Support Service or Serviceable Product

TABLE 3-1. *Item-Defining Attributes*

Engineering Item; this attribute is set automatically if the item is defined using the Master Engineering Items window.

Attribute Groups

There are over 180 item attributes, and these attributes are arranged into meaningful groups, for better control and usability. Each attribute group relates to a business function in most cases. Sometimes, a group is just a broad classification. We will take a look at these attribute groups in this section.

TIP
Each attribute group is controlled by a security function of the form "Items: group name," where group name represents the name of the attribute groups. You can restrict access to an attribute group by excluding the associated security function from a responsibility. For example, if you want the purchasing manager to update the item, but only the purchasing and inventory groups, you can exclude all the attribute groups except purchasing and inventory. When you do so, you should make sure that you also take away the function "Items: Copy From." Otherwise, the purchasing manager can always update everything by applying templates or copying from other items.

Main Attribute Group

The *Primary Unit of Measure* (UOM) is the UOM in which on-hand balances are held. The primary UOM is defaulted from the profile option INV: Default Primary Unit of Measure. You also select what type of conversions you want to use for an item during transactions using the Conversions radio group. When you transact an item, you can specify any UOM that has an item specific or a standard conversion with the item's primary UOM, based on your selection in the Conversions radio group. Oracle Inventory will always convert the transactions into the primary UOM, before posting the transactions to on-hand balances. You cannot update the primary UOM for an item, once it is saved the first time.

TIP

You should probably not set the primary UOM in the profile INV: Default Primary Unit of Measure or in your templates, because you cannot change the primary UOM once defined. This will force you to think about the item's UOM and prevent you from inadvertently saving an item with the wrong unit of measure.

User Item Type is a code to identify the type of item from your business's perspective. A number of reports have this attribute as a parameter, allowing you to compile reports for specific groupings of items based on the user item type. You can define your item types in the Lookup Codes window.

As discussed before, Item Status potentially controls the eight status attributes, based on your attribute controls. The Item Status window allows you to define new status codes and specify the setting of each status attribute for your status codes.

Item Status allows you to manage your item's transactional behavior during its life-cycle. You can set an item's status in one of two ways. You can make an immediate status change by entering a new status code on the Master Items or Organization Items window, or you can specify a pending status (to become effective at a future date) using Tools | Pending Status when you are on the Item window. The concurrent program Update item statuses with pending statuses makes these pending statuses effective; if you are using this functionality, you should run this program at the beginning of every day.

The Pending Status function also lets you view a history of an item's status changes, whether these changes were made immediately or as pending changes.

Invoicing Attribute Group

You turn on an item for the receivables function by checking the Invoiceable Item attribute. You should make an item as an Invoice Enabled, if you want to include this item in an invoice. You can make an item Invoice Enabled only if it is an invoiceable item. Invoice Enabled could optionally be set by the Item Status.

Accounting Rule determines the number of periods and percentage of total revenue to record in each accounting period. This attribute enables you to identify revenue recognition rules for the item. Invoicing Rule lets you determine the period in which to send an invoice for invoices that span more than one accounting period.

The Tax Code attribute identifies the tax code to use for the item when calculating tax based on location and tax codes. Sales Account provides the general ledger account code combination to record the revenue when a customer is invoiced. Payment Terms identifies payment terms for an item and is for reference information only.

Service Attribute Group

To distinguish between a product and a service, you use the Support Service attribute. If this option is checked, the item represents a service. On the other hand, if you want to indicate that support service is available for an item, you do that using the Serviceable Product attribute. These attributes are mutually exclusive. In other words, a service cannot be a serviceable product.

You can choose a Coverage Template for your service, such as round-the-clock, six-to-six, etc. from a list of predefined coverage schedules in Oracle Service. You can specify the estimated duration of your service using the attributes in Service Duration.

When you have warranty on your product, you indicate that using the Warranty attribute. Enabling this attribute automatically adds an entry in the item's bill of material to include a warranty component. Only serial number controlled items can have warranty enabled, since it will not be possible to trace a claim to a sold item otherwise.

NOTE
The attributes from the other groups are covered in the respective functional chapters.

Item Relationships and Cross-References

You can define item relationships in the Item Relationships window. The relationship types supported are Related and Substitute. Related items include generic relationships and are for information and reporting purposes only. Substitute items can be received from suppliers, if the item attribute Allow Substitute Receipts is checked for an item.

You can define manufacturer part numbers for items, which can be used in catalog search and for reporting purposes. You define manufacturer part numbers in the Manufacturer Part Numbers window that you can access directly from the navigator or through Tools | Manufacturer Part Numbers. You can associate an item with multiple manufacturer part numbers.

Item cross-references can be used to create custom cross-reference types and use those to relate items. For example, you can track succession of assemblies using a cross-reference type called Superceded By. You define cross-reference types in the Cross-Reference Types window. You assign cross-references to an item using Tools | Cross References.

Customer items can be defined in the Customer Items Summary | Detail windows. Your customer item can be related to your item at the customer level, the address category level, or the address level. You can also associate a commodity code with a customer item. Once you have defined customer items, you can select customer items while entering a sales order.

Item Revisions

When you make slight modifications to your item, without changing the form, fit, or function of the item, you may want to define a new revision for that item for tracking purposes. You can define any number of revisions for an item. A new revision should be greater than the previous revision according to the ASCII format. To avoid confusion, alphabetic characters are always in uppercase and the revision itself can be alphanumeric.

You define your revisions in the Item Revisions window. The starting revision for an item is defined at the organization level. You can have multiple revisions effective at the same time, and in that case, you will be able to choose a revision from the available set during inventory/manufacturing transactions.

Figure 3-3 presents you with the logical data model of an item and the related entities. This will help you to understand the bigger picture of the item management features provided in Oracle Inventory.

Categorizing Items

Category sets and item categories in Oracle Inventory let you look at your items from different points of view. Category sets represent the point of view, and the individual item categories inside the category set represent the classification scheme within a point of view. For example, the accounting department might look at items by product line, whereas an inventory analyst might look at items as raw materials, subassemblies, and finished goods.

Category Codes and Category Sets

Category Code or Item Category is a multiple structure *key flexfield* (KFF). You define your category codes in the Categories window and your category sets in the Category Set window. Starting with Release 11i, you can assign an item to multiple

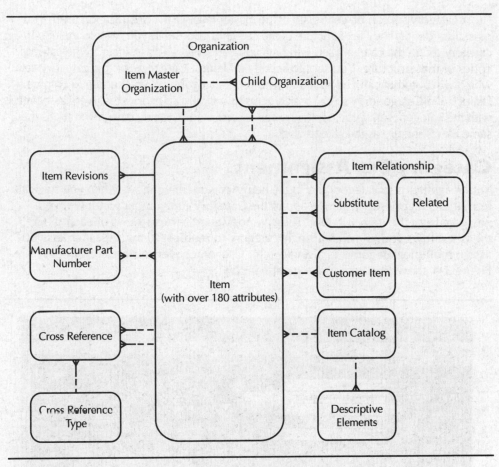

FIGURE 3-3. *Item management logical data model*

category sets within a category set by checking Allow Multiple Item Category
Assignments.

NOTE
*When you allow multiple category assignments
within a category set, you should realize that this
could lead to double counting. For example, if you
run an inventory value report by a category set that
allows multiple category assignment, the same item
can be reported many times.*

A category set can be controlled at the master level or the organization level. You must also identify the Flex Structure of the category codes that you want to include in a category set. In the category sets window, you can select and associate all the category codes of that structure. You should specify a Default Category for this category set, which will automatically be added to your list of categories. If you choose to Enforce List of Valid Categories, you can assign items to only the categories that were associated with the category set. If you don't, you can assign an item to any category that has the same Flex Structure as the category set.

Category Set Assignment

You assign items to category sets in the Item Assignment window, when you navigate from the category sets window, and in the Category Assignment window if you navigate from the item window. These windows are reverse views of each other; the first allows you to assign a single category to multiple items, the latter lets you assign multiple categories to a single item. Use whichever is more convenient. Figure 3-4 shows the Item Assignment window.

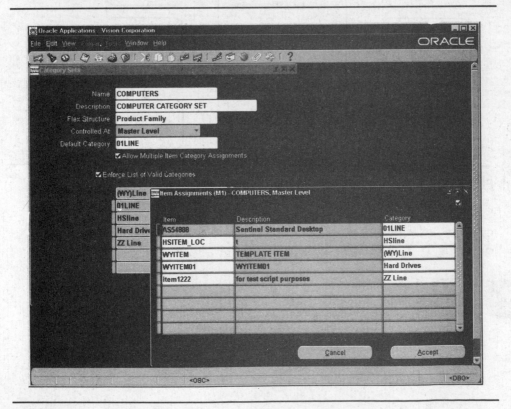

FIGURE 3-4.   *Assign items to categories using the Item Assignment window*

Default Category Sets

There are eight default category sets in Oracle Inventory that map to eight functional areas. With the exception of Product Line Accounting, all the functional areas are associated with a corresponding item-defining attribute.

NOTE
The item-defining attributes and the default category sets should have the same organization control level.

When you define an item, you can enable it for a functional area by enabling the item defining attribute that is associated with the functional area. If you do so, the item will be assigned to the default category within the default category set for the functional area. The defaulting chain is illustrated by Figure 3-5.

TIP
Create a category code called "Unassigned" or "To be determined" and use this as the default category for each of the default category sets, so that you can distinguish between user assignments and default assignments.

When you enable an item to another organization after assigning categories in the master organization, the master level category sets and the default category sets (irrespective of organization control level) will be copied over. After enabling an item in an organization, if you disable an item for a functional area, the defaulted category assignment will not be removed automatically. You should delete the assignment explicitly, if that is what you want.

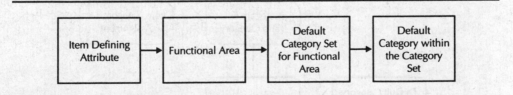

FIGURE 3-5.   *Default Category Assignment*

NOTE
When you create an item by copying from an item, the category assignments are not copied. Even in the case of default category sets, the default category code will be assigned instead of the category code value from the copied item.

Figure 3-6 identifies the important entities in the item category feature and the relationships between them.

Item Catalogs

Item catalogs let you assign an unlimited number of descriptive elements to your items, and use those descriptive elements to search for items throughout the applications. You can use the catalog to help locate items, to avoid duplicating parts that already exist. And the item catalog also lets you generate a more meaningful item description for configured items; this will be described in Chapter 6. Figure 3-7 shows the item search window using item catalog descriptive elements.

You define item catalog groups in the Item Catalog Groups window. You can specify a name for the catalog and a description. You can disable a catalog by putting an end date to the catalog. You can add descriptive elements to a catalog group by pressing the Details button and navigating to the Item Catalog Group Details window. In the Descriptive Elements region, you will be able to add the descriptive elements.

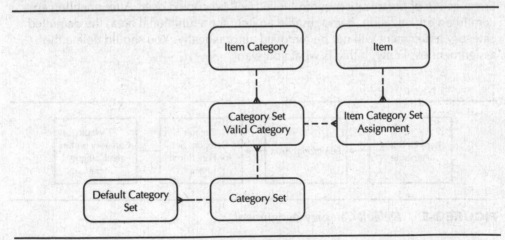

FIGURE 3-6. *Item Category Logical Data Model*

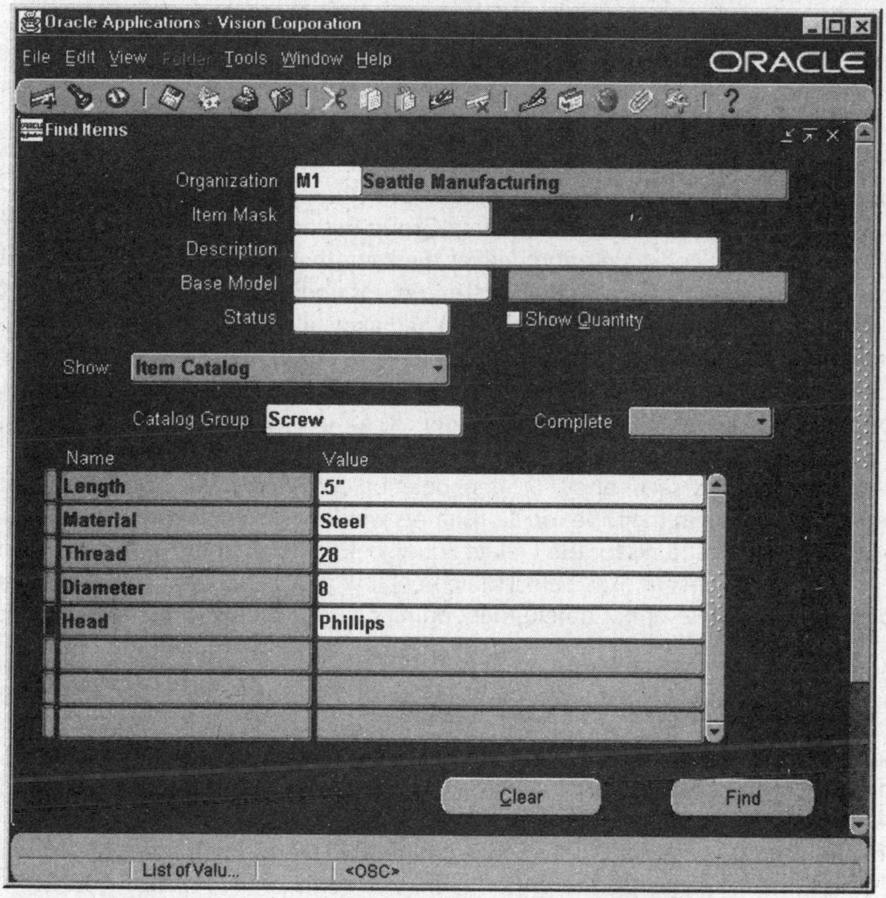

FIGURE 3-7. *Search Items using Catalog Descriptive Elements*

TIP
*You can use item catalogs to implement a variety
reduction program at your company. For example,
you can have a group called Screws, which has the
thread pitch, thread length, etc. as attributes. When
an engineer wants to use a screw in his design, he
can search the Screws catalog and if possible, could
use a screw that already exists rather than creating
another item for the exact same specification.*

You can add aliases in the Aliases region and specify categories in the Categories region for reporting purposes.

Item Deletion

You can delete an item by including an item in a deletion group in the Deletion Groups window. Once you include an item in a group, you can delete the items in the deletion group by pressing the Delete Group button. The delete group process checks for deletion constraints and deletes the items that were included in the group. If there are any violations, the delete group process updates the Status to Error on the Results tab. You can press the Errors button and view all errors and the associated deletion constraints.

If you just want to check if you can delete, you can do so by pressing the Check Group button. The check group process checks for deletion constraints and updates the Status to Error on the Results tab.

Oracle Inventory seeds about 50 item deletion constraints. You can define custom deletion constraints in the Deletion Constraints window. The deletion process checks all the Enabled constraints for the Delete Entity, before deleting the entity. During the check process, it runs the SQL Select Statement that you associate with the constraint and decides to delete or not delete, depending on your setting of the Delete If field.

Items Open Interface

Open interfaces are tables provided for you to put in your information while interfacing with home-grown or third-party applications. A standard process will pick up the rows in the open interface table, validate them and then import the validated rows into Oracle Applications tables. This section will provide you with the tables that are to be used to import items and some of the related objects.

Item

You import item definitions using the Import Items concurrent program. Before running the concurrent program, you should populate the interface table MTL_SYSTEM_ITEMS_INTERFACE (MSII) with the appropriate values for your new item(s). You can define the item, all the item attributes, and the cost details in this table. You can import cost information by specifying the appropriate cost values in MSII. You can also import the revisions of an item along with the item itself, by populating corresponding records in the table MTL_ITEM_REVISIONS_INTERFACE for each row in MSII.

Item open interface supports multi-threaded import. So, you can divide the items that are to be imported using a Set ID and launch multiple item import processes, each with a different set ID.

Starting from 11i.3, you will be able to import category assignments along with items. You cannot create category sets or category codes through this interface. Populate the interface table MTL_ITEM_CATEGORY_INTERFACE with your category assignments and make sure that the process set ID for your category assignments and items are the same. You must make sure that the category sets and category codes have already been defined.

NOTE
APIs for creating and updating items and related
information will be available in a future release.

Customer Item

Import customer item definitions using the interface table MTL_CI_INTERFACE. You must make sure that customers, address category and the customer address information are already defined. To define cross-references between customer items and existing inventory items, use the interface MTL_CI_XREFS_INTERFACE.

Summary

This chapter covered the aspects of creating and maintaining items. Items can be used to represent your products, service, components, and indirect materials. Items are always defined in the item master organization and later on enabled in the using organizations. Item templates help you in defining and maintaining your items.

Item relationships allow you to capture the relationship between items such as substitute items. Item cross-references allow you to define cross-references between your items and items from your trading partners.

Categorize your items using category sets and item categories. Category sets represent the viewpoint and item categories represent the classification scheme. Item catalogs allow you to capture descriptive information about your items, which can be used for searching later on.

Items open interface and the customer item open interface provide you with the capability to import item definitions and customer item definitions into Oracle Applications.

CHAPTER
4

Managing Bills
and Routings

anagement in a manufacturing plant or a distribution center is all about utilizing resources effectively. You have a product to deliver in a certain amount of time that consumes some materials, manpower, and machine time and can be produced using one or more methods.

Materials represent both the direct raw materials and indirect materials such as lubricants and coolants that are used during the production process. The manpower and machine resources perform the work in producing your products. The method resource is a collection of operations that in turn contain the manpower and machine resources; it allows you to model different ways of producing a product.

Before deploying these resources, you should define these resources. Oracle Applications allow you to accurately model these resources and the corresponding constraints. Figure 4-1 shows the different types of resources that exist in such environments.

This chapter focuses on these five resources and explains how to define and maintain these resources in Oracle Applications.

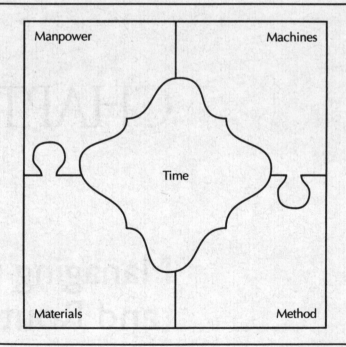

FIGURE 4-1.   *Resources in a Manufacturing/Distribution environment*

Materials

When you manufacture a product, you use raw materials or purchased components. These raw materials are just one type of a resource that is consumed by the finished product. You can produce a product from a variety of different combinations of raw materials. Oracle provides you with the capability to define all the material requirements using primary and alternate bills of material for a finished product. The components of an item have a set of attributes. For example, you can define the default source location for a component. This section explains the bill of materials feature.

Bill of Material Setup

Before you define a bill of materials for items, you should define the parent items and components as items. Item management was covered in Chapter 3. This section discusses the setup of Alternates and the item attributes that control the behavior of an item in the bill of material (BOM).

Alternates

Oracle enables you to create alternate versions of your bills of material and routings to represent the different ways to build a product. For example, if you want to keep a copy of the design bill, you might create an alternate called *As Designed* and use it to define a separate copy of the bill before it is changed for manufacturing purposes. Or, you might want to represent alternate methods of manufacturing an item or a set of alternate components; you can define these alternatives as alternate bills and routings, and Oracle Advanced Supply Chain Planning can use its optimization logic to pick the appropriate bill and routing.

NOTE
ASCP will only choose alternate bills and routings in pairs—i.e., for ASCP to recommend using an alternate routing, there must be an alternate bill with the same designator (even if it is identical to the primary bill).

You create the names you will use for alternates in the Alternates window. You can later on reference an alternate in both bills and routings. Bills and routings (covered later in this chapter) can share alternate labels.

Item Attributes—Bills of Material Attribute Group

The Bills of Material Attribute Group enables you to define the behavior of an item in Oracle Bills of Material and Oracle Engineering. BOM Allowed identifies whether the item can be part of a bill of material; this attribute is a status attribute.

NOTE
BOM Allowed should be yes for an item to have a bill of material as well as to be part of a bill of material.

The BOM Item Type identifies the item's type of bill of material. An item's BOM Item Type can be one of the following:

- **Standard** A standard item represents a product, service, or component. (Phantom items are also classified as standard items.)

- **Option Class** An option class represents an option group and has a collection of options as its components. Options can be either standard items or other option classes.

- **Model** A model is used to represent a configurable ATO or PTO product.

- **Planning** A planning item is a conceptual grouping of items and is used to distribute demand when you know the overall demand for a group of items and when you're reasonably sure about the share of each of these products in the overall demand. For example, if you know that the demand for your personal computers would be $2 billion in 2003, you can distribute the demand to the individual products by using a planning bill.

- **Product Family** A product family is a grouping of items that are planned and produced together. When you design a line, you define it for a family and not for individual products.

The Base Model identifies the model item based on which a configuration item has been defined. This attribute is applicable for Assemble to Order/Pick to Order items only. Effectivity Control enables you to identify the type of effectivity control that is applicable in your environment—date or model/unit effectivity. Model/unit effectivity is available only if you have Oracle Project Manufacturing.

Bill of Material Types

From a manufacturing standpoint, every unique assembly has its own material requirements. When an item is configurable, you have to define a model item to represent the configurable end item and option classes to represent the option groups. If you have a family of items, you have to define a product family item to represent this family during manufacturing planning and for the purposes of designing production lines. The item attribute *BOM Item Type* is used to identify the *BOM Type* of an item.

Access Control by BOM Type

You can control access to bills of material by item type using the profile options—BOM: Standard Item Access, BOM: Planning Item Access, and BOM: Model Item Access. These profiles indicate if you can create and update bills for the associated item type, but they don't control queries. A user can query all types of bills, even without access to maintain those bill types.

Phantom Subassemblies

A phantom assembly is a non-stocked assembly. You can use phantoms to represent the intermediate subassemblies that are created during the production process. Items are designated as phantoms by the value of their WIP Supply Type, but you can override this value for a component in a bill of material. A component can represent a phantom subassembly for one parent item and a stocked subassembly for another parent item.

In general, phantom assemblies behave like normal assemblies when they represent a top-level assembly, such as when you master schedule them or manufacture them using a discrete job. As a subassembly, however, they lose their identity as distinct assemblies and are a collection of their components. The components of the phantom subassembly are included on the job and on the pick list of the job—not the phantom itself.

You can define routings (covered in the section "Method") for phantom assemblies. Oracle WIP automatically explodes through phantom assemblies and ignores their routings when you define discrete jobs or repetitive schedules. In the BOM Parameters window, if you set the Replace with Sequence to No, the individual operation sequence numbers for phantom subassemblies will be retained. If Replace with Sequence is Yes, the phantom components will inherit the operation sequence from the parent assembly. If you set the Use Phantom Routings BOM parameter as Yes, all the phantom assembly resources and overhead costs will be charged to the parent or higher-level assembly.

Defining a Bill of Material

A Bill of Material (BOM) contains the first-level component information of an item. Other than the components, a BOM can have attachments and descriptive elements. Each standard component on a bill can have multiple reference designators and substitute components. You can create a bill from scratch, copy an existing bill, or reference a common bill. When you create a BOM, the BOM is specific to the current organization. To use a bill in another organization, you must either copy it or reference it as a common.

You create a BOM using the Bills of Material window. You must select a parent item for which you are creating the BOM; you can choose an alternate if you are defining an alternate bill. Bills and routings share alternate labels. If you create an alternate bill with the same label as an alternate routing for the same parent item, components are assigned to operations on the alternate routing instead of the primary routing. If there is no routing with the same alternate label, components are assigned to operations on the primary routing.

NOTE
You must define the primary bill or routing before you can define an alternate.

If you are updating or viewing a bill, you can view all the components, only the current components, or both the future and current components effective as of the revision date you specify by choosing an appropriate value in the Display field. If you only want to see the implemented components, check the Implemented Only field. That will exclude pending ECO changes.

BOM Components
A bill contains many components, which are items as well. Table 4-1 identifies the components that can be assigned to a parent, based on their BOM item types.

A component can be included many times in the bill, provided that each entry has a different operation sequence or has a different non-overlapping effectivity.

Component Attributes   The component item sequence will default based on the BOM: Component Item Sequence Increment profile option. You can override the default value with a sequence that is unique within the bill.

You can identify the quantity that is required to make one unit of this assembly at the associated operation. This can include negative or decimal values, with a few exceptions. Pick-to-Order bills cannot have fractions if Oracle Order Management is installed. Pick-to-Order option class components cannot have negative values.

	Component BOM Type			
Parent BOM Type	**Planning**	**Model**	**Option Class**	**Standard**
Planning	✓	✓	✓	✓
Model	X	✓	✓	✓
Option Class	X	✓	✓	✓
Standard	X	X	X	✓

TABLE 4-1.   *Parent BOM Types versus Component BOM Types*

Components with Check ATP turned on cannot have negative or zero quantities. If the component has Quantity Related reference designators, then the component quantity cannot be fractional or negative.

NOTE
*Negative component quantity usually indicates
a byproduct.*

Revision displays the current revision of the component as of the revision date of the parent item. You can specify the effective date range for this component in the Effectivity tab. The Implemented check box indicates whether the component is implemented through an ECO or if it is pending on an ECO.

The planning process uses Planning Percent for Planning Bills, Product Families, Models, and Option classes to calculate the component requirements of an item. Yield is used to represent the expected loss of a component during the production of an item. You can include the component in cost rollups. If included, the material cost of this component is included in the cost of the parent item.

You can enter the Supply Type, Supply Subinventory, and the Locator in the Material Control tab. These values default from the item attributes based on the profile option BOM: Default WIP Supply Values for Components. If set to Yes, the item attribute values are physically copied into the bill of material. You can change them if necessary, but the BOM values will take precedence over the item attributes—if you subsequently change the item attribute settings, the BOM values will not change. If the profile is set to No, you can leave the attributes blank in the BOM, and WIP will read these values from the item attributes.

For model, option class, and kit bills, you can specify the minimum and maximum sales order quantities in the Order Entry tab. You can disable ATP Check of a component in this bill if it is already enabled by the components item attribute. Indicate whether the component is optional and mutually exclusive.

NOTE
*The flag Mutually Exclusive is applicable only
to Option classes. The flag is set at the option
class level, and it indicates if the options within
the Option class are mutually exclusive during the
configuration process.*

In the Shipping tab you can indicate if the component should be listed on shipping documents, required to ship, or required for revenue.

Substitute Components

You assign substitutes in the Substitute Components window that you can access by clicking the Substitutes button from the Bills of Material form. You can select a substitute item and enter the quantity of the substitute item that is needed to replace the full component quantity. This quantity can differ from the quantity of the bill component.

Oracle Work in Process does not consider substitute items in its pick lists. Oracle ASCP will plan for substitutes if your constraints are set up appropriately. Advanced Planning is covered in Chapter 11.

Global Substitutes versus Local Substitutes   If an item is a substitute of another item irrespective of the using assembly, this substitute item is called a global substitute. On the other hand, if the substitute relationship is applicable on certain assemblies, the substitute item is called a local substitute. You should define global substitutes using generic item relationships that was covered in Chapter 3. You should define local substitutes using the bill component substitutes.

NOTE
Oracle ASCP recognizes only local substitutes, and Oracle Purchasing recognizes only global substitutes.

Reference Designators

Reference designators are comments/instructions that are attached to a component. Sometimes called *find numbers* or *bubble numbers,* they often correspond to a notation on a drawing. Planning bills and model, option class, and planning components cannot have reference designators. Reference designators are sorted in alphanumeric order on inquiries and reports. You create reference designators in the Reference Designators window by clicking the Designators button from the Bills of Material window. If you check Quantity Related, the system will ensure that the number of reference designators equals the quantity of the associated component; if unchecked, you can have an unlimited number of reference designators.

You can enter the reference designator names manually or generate them automatically by choosing the Add Range or Delete Range button to open the Range window. You can enter a prefix, a suffix, and starting and ending values for the range of reference designators to add or delete. For example, if you enter NN (for Neptune Networks) as the prefix, 1 and 4 as the starting and ending values, and SW (for Switch) as the suffix, NN1SW, NN2SW, NN3SW, and NN4SW are the reference designators.

Descriptive Elements

If the parent item is a model or an option class, you can specify a list of item catalog descriptive elements in the Descriptive Elements window that you can access by clicking the Elements button from the Bills of Material form. Values are assigned to catalog descriptive elements when new configuration items are created. The descriptive element value of the chosen option is assigned for each descriptive element.

If the parent item is a model, you can only specify a descriptive element name within the catalog group that is associated with the model item. If the parent item is an option class, you can specify a descriptive element name from any catalog group. These descriptive elements are especially helpful to generate a meaningful description for system-generated configured items, as well as to catalog those items.

Defining Bill Documents

You can attach documents to bills of material using the Bill Documents window that you can access using the Attachments icon. You can attach text and files, such as spreadsheets, graphics, and OLE objects.

NOTE
Bills of Material information is stored using the tables BOM_BILL_OF_MATERIALS, BOM_INVENTORY_COMPONENTS, BOM_REFERENCE_DESIGNATORS, BOM_DEPENDENT_DESC_ELEMENTS, and BOM_SUBSTITUTE_COMPONENTS.

Copying Bills

You can save time defining new, similar bills by copying their information rather than creating them manually. You can copy a bill or routing from your current organization or from another organization that shares the item master organization. You can then modify your new bill as necessary. You can copy any revision of a primary or alternate bill or routing.

You can only copy bills between items having the same BOM Item Type attribute. The copy function only copies the single level bill. When you copy a bill across organizations, the components and substitute components on the bill you are copying from must exist in the target organization. The supply subinventories and locators are not copied in the case of cross organization bill copies.

When you copy bills from your current organization, everything is copied to the new bill including the supply type and the supply subinventories and locators. You can copy bills using in the Copy Bill/Rtg From window that you can access by choosing Tools | Copy Bill/Rtg From when you are in the Bill of Materials form.

Sharing Bills

If two or more organizations manufacture the same item using the same bill of material, you can define the bill in one organization and reference it from the other organizations. Using common bills of material, you can share bills of material that exist in your manufacturing organizations with your item master organization.

You cannot create a chain of common references. You can only reference another bill or routing as a common if it has the same alternate name assigned to it. If the current bill you are creating is a manufacturing bill, the common bill must also be a manufacturing bill. If you are referencing an assembly from a different organization, all components and substitute components must exist in the new bill's organization.

When you define a bill for a new assembly, you can reference another assembly and organization as a common bill of material. You cannot reference another bill as a common if components already exist for this bill. You share bills using the Common Bill window that you can access by choosing Tools I Assign Common Bill.

Checking for Bill Loops

Bill loops occur when a bill is assigned as a component to itself somewhere in the multilevel structure of the bill. This is illustrated by Figure 4-2 where A is defined as a component of itself, three levels down. This will cause the planning programs (specifically the explosion process) to abort. The loop check program searches for such loops.

The Check for Loops concurrent program can be submitted from the Tools menu of the Bills of Material window, after a new bill has been saved. You can also run the loop check from the menu for all or a subset of your bills of material.

Mass Changing Bills of Material

You can implement a component change across many assemblies using the mass change bills feature in Oracle Bills of Material. You can define a mass change to add, delete, or replace a component or to change other component information. You can mass change a component information in all the using assemblies or choose a subset of assemblies by item range, item category, or item type. You can mass change primary and alternate bills of material for each using assembly. You can report effective changes for all using assemblies or components. Mass changes using ECOs is covered in Chapter 5.

All the mass change actions that you enter are used to determine if the change is applicable. Let's say you are adding component A and deleting component B in a single mass change order. This change is made only if component A does not exist and component B does exist on the selected bills. The change is applied only if both conditions are met. It's an all or nothing transaction.

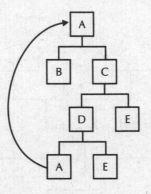

FIGURE 4-2. *Bill loop scenario*

TIP
If you inadvertently performed a mass change that shouldn't have been performed, you can reverse the effects of that mass change using another mass change.

The Entire Structure

You might want to see the extent to which a component is used across all your assemblies, especially if you want to perform a mass change or if you are embarking on a variety reduction program. If you want to understand the complexity of a product, you might want to explode the bills up to the leaf level components. These two scenarios are illustrated by Figure 4-3. Oracle provides you with two tools—Indented Bills and Item Whereused—that will help you achieve this.

Indented (Multilevel) Bill of Material

An indented (multilevel, exploded) manufacturing or engineering bill of material displays the structure of a manufacturing or engineering item. You can view the multilevel BOM using the Indented Bill of Material window that is shown in Figure 4-4. If you entered an alternate, the explosion process will search for all components with the same alternate label. In case an alternate with the same label is not found at some level, the primary is used. The explosion process then continues searching for the original alternate label. You can indicate the default number of explosion levels using the profile option BOM: Default Bill of Material Levels, though, you can override this default for an explosion, if necessary.

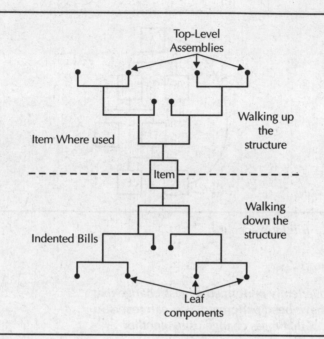

FIGURE 4-3. *Walking up and down the structure*

To view more than the basic information, you can specify the level of detail you want to see (e.g., Material Control attributes, costing information, etc.).

Item Whereused
You can view an imploded list of all the using assemblies of an item in the Item Whereused window. The level of the bill of material where the inventory item appears in the parent assembly is displayed. You can view the parent assembly details in the Item Details tab and component details of the queried item in each of the using assembly in the Component Details tab.

Bill Compare
You can compare any two bills to identify the similarities and differences between them using the Bill Components Comparison form or the Bill of Material Comparison report. Two columns of check boxes, one for assembly 1 and one for assembly 2, indicate if the component appears in the assembly. The Main tabbed region displays the item and operation sequences, the planning percent, the quantity, and whether the item is optional. You can also view other component information using the other tabs.

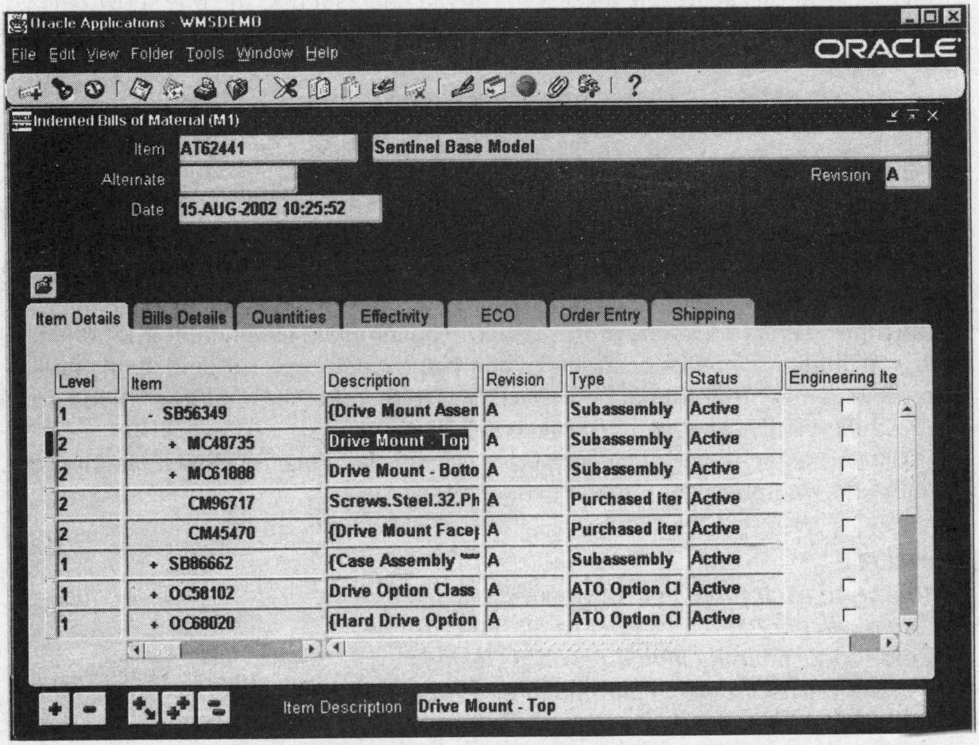

FIGURE 4-4. *Indented BOM enables you to walk down the bill structure of an item*

Deleting Bills

You can delete bills using the Delete Group functionality that was discussed in Chapter 3. Several deletion constraints are installed with Bills of Material. However, you can define custom deletion constraints. Files or objects that are attached to bills are not deleted. Instead, the association between the bill or routing and the attached file is severed. When you delete an entire bill, you delete all the components for the assembly along with their reference designators and substitute items. You can archive bill (and routing) information, but *not* item information.

Product Families

A product family is a grouping of products that have similar production processes. When you have your product families, you can perform material planning and design lines at this aggregate level. Typically, a chart such as the one shown in Figure 4-5 will be used for grouping your products into product families. An item can belong to only one product family. You will be able to plan based on the planning percentages and effectivity of the product family members.

Creating a Product Family

Product families are items themselves, and you can define them in the Master Items window. You can also define a product family using the Define Product Family menu. In this case, the Product Family template is automatically applied. You can designate the default template for product family items using the INV: Product Family Item Template Name profile option. The template assigned in this profile option will be automatically applied when you create a new product family item. A product family item should be an Inventory Item, and the BOM Item Type must be Product Family. The item must also be BOM allowed.

A new category is added for each product family item that is defined. The category has the same name as the product family item.

NOTE
Because each product family corresponds to an item category in the Product Family category set, the Product Family Item Categories Flexfield structure should match the structure of your System Items Flexfield.

	Cutting	Planing	Milling	Grinding
X3454523	X	X	X	X
X3454356	X	X		X
X3454545	X		X	
X34543423	X	X	X	X
X34548778	X	X	X	X

FIGURE 4-5. *Create product families using a Process/Product map*

Each product family member item and the product family item itself are assigned to the corresponding category within the Product Family category set. The assignment is removed when an item is no longer a member of a product family.

Assigning Product Family Members

The Product Family form enables you to assign product family members. You can select a product family item and choose the items that are the members of the product family. The description, type, forecast control, and planning method for the member items are displayed for the items selected.

Planning Percentages for Product Family Members   You can assign planning percentages for a member item, by clicking the Allocation button in the Product Family form. The default planning percent is 100, and the default effectivity date is the system date.

Co-Products

The co-products feature enables you to generate several end items using one primary component. Co-products are available if you have Oracle Shop Floor Management, and you use the Co-Products window to define co-products.

When you enter information in to the Co-Products window, the bills of material of the end items are automatically created. Check the Primary box to identify the primary co-product. There should be only one primary co-product for a component. Non-primary co-products are set up as common bills of material pointing to the primary co-product's bill. The primary co-product's bill can be an alternate or a primary bill.

You can define component details, component substitutes, and co-product substitutes using the Details, Substitutes, and Co-Product Substitutes buttons.

Oracle ASCP calculates supply for multiple assemblies based on the demand for any one of the possible co-product assemblies. The planner can generate and release planned orders for the item for which demand was realized and then view the co-product supplies being generated for the rest of the items in the co-product relationship.

BOM Business Object

You can use the BOM business object API to integrate with other software systems. The BOM business object API can be used to create or update a BOM in Oracle Applications by calling a PL/SQL procedure directly instead of using the open interface.

You need to initialize certain system information before you call the BOM API because each applications table has some system information such as the Who columns. The initialization API sets up some session variables, which is available for the BOM API. Substitute the appropriate values in the following code listing to initialize the system variables:

```
FND_GLOBAL.apps_initialize
(user_id IN NUMBER
-- user_id in FND_USER
, resp_id IN NUMBER
-- responsibility_id in FND_RESPONSIBILITY
, appl_id IN NUMBER
-- application_id in FND_RESPONSIBILITY
)
```

NOTE
The method requires a security_group_id, but you can ignore this parameter; in this case the default of 0 will be used. Security group is used to identify the reports and concurrent programs that are available to a user.

The steps for importing bills of material using the BOM business object API are as follows:

1. Construct a PL/SQL Record for the Engineering Change Order (ECO) header information, say p_eco_header of type `Eng_Eco_Pub.eco_rec_type`, if you want to reference an ECO header. ECO is covered in detail in Chapter 5.

2. Use Table 4-2 to construct the following PL/SQL tables for all the information that is associated with the BOM:

Variable Name	Type	Meaning
p_assembly_items	Bom_bo_ pub.assembly_item_ tbl_type	Bill header information. The record type for this table is bom_bo_ pub.assembly_item_ rec_type

TABLE 4-2. *PL/SQL Tables for the BOM Business Object*

Variable Name	Type	Meaning
`p_rev_components`	`Bom_bo_pub.rev_component_tbl_type`	List of the components for each bill. The record type for this table is `bom_bo_pub.rev_component_rec_type`
`p_ref_designators`	`Bom_bo_pub.ref_designator_tbl_type`	List of reference designators for each component. The record type for this table is `bom_bo_pub.ref_designator_rec_type`
`p_sub_components`	`Bom_bo_pub.sub_component_tbl_type`	List of substitute components for each component. The record type for this table is `bom_bo_pub.sub_component_rec_type`

TABLE 4-2. *PL/SQL Tables for the BOM Business Object* (continued)

3. Call the procedure **process_bom** with the parameters that you constructed in step 2. You don't have to supply all the parameters in every case. If you browse through the signature of this procedure in the manual, you would note that most of the parameters have a default value. So, if you were inserting a whole new BOM, you would provide all the information. On the other hand, if you are modifying a component attribute, you just provide the header and the component information:

```
process_bom
(p_api_version_number
-- IN API version for compatibility checking
,p_init_msg_list
-- IN Should the message list be initialized?
,x_return_status
-- OUT Return status, indicates success or failure
,x_msg_count
```

```
        -- OUT Number of messages during the process
        , x_msg_data
        -- OUT Content of messages during the process
        , p_ECO_rec
        --IN ECO Reference
        , p_assembly_items
        --IN List of top level assemblies
        , p_rev_components
        --IN List of bill components
        , p_ref_designators
        --IN List of reference designators for each component
        , p_sub_components
        --IN List of substitute components for each component
        , x_assembly_items
        --OUT List of top level assemblies
        , x_rev_components
        --OUT List of bill components
        , x_ref_designators
        --OUT List of reference designators for each component
        , x_sub_components
        --OUT List of substitute components for each component
        )
```

Time

Time is money. Execution (both manufacturing and supply chain) happens in real time, but the planning activities, both long-term and short-term, are based on an estimate of available work time. Oracle Applications provide you with the ability to create these time estimates using Workday Calendars. The planning and scheduling systems use workday calendars for lead-time calculations and to calculate the total resource availability. In this section, we will discuss this feature and its components.

Workday Calendar

A workday calendar identifies the valid working days for a manufacturing organization and consists of a repeating pattern of days on and days off and the exceptions to that pattern. You can define any number of workday calendars and assign them to any number of organizations. The form Workday Calendar enables you to define workday calendars.

Calendar Attributes

The quarterly calendar type identifies how the manufacturing calendar is laid out in terms of weeks and months. The 4/4/5 Week Pattern specifies that a quarter of a year consists of two four-week periods followed by one five-week period. 5/4/4 Week Pattern specifies that a quarter contains one five-week period followed by two four-week periods. Calendar Months implies that the year has twelve periods based on calendar months. 13 Periods implies that the year contains thirteen four-week periods.

ASCP enables you to report in both weekly and period buckets if you choose 4/4/5 Weekly Pattern or the 5/4/4 Weekly Pattern as the quarterly calendar type. You can only generate reports in monthly buckets if you choose 13 Periods or Calendar Months as the quarterly calendar type.

CAUTION
You must use a 4/4/5 or 5/4/4 weekly pattern to forecast in period buckets in the planning applications; you cannot forecast in monthly buckets.

The date range identifies the start date and end date of the calendar. The default end date is four years from the start date. Days on and off are calculated based on the start date and the day of the week. So, you would typically specify a Monday as your calendar start date.

Workday Pattern

You can define a series of repeating workday on/off sequences for a given calendar. For example, if you have a work sequence where you work four days the first week (three days off) and three days the second week (four days off), you can define these in sequence. When you build the calendar, the valid workdays are automatically determined for you, based on your workday pattern. You define workday patterns in the Workday Patterns window that you can access by clicking the Workday Pattern button on the Workday Calendar form.

Workday Exceptions

You define exception templates in the Exception Templates form. An exception template enables you to create groups of exception dates and apply them to different calendars. Multiple exception templates can be applied to the same calendar. As each template is applied, new exception dates are added to the exception list for that calendar. This enables you to define different holidays or scheduled down times, for example, for organizations in different countries.

Shifts

For a given workday calendar, you can specify any number of shifts. Shifts inherit workday exceptions and workday patterns from the base calendar. Shift exceptions can either add to or override those of the base calendar. If you create a shift without first creating a workday pattern, a default workday pattern of five days on and two days off is created. You can then update that workday pattern.

If an exception on the base calendar changes, those shifts that do not have an overriding exception on that date will automatically reflect the change. Those shifts that do have an overriding exception on that date will not reflect the change and must be changed manually if they are to reflect the change in the base calendar.

You create shifts in the Shifts window that you can access by clicking the Shifts button from the Workday Calendar form. You must specify a shift number and enter the description for the shift. You can enter multiple start and stop times in the Shift Times window, but the start and stop times for a shift cannot overlap.

NOTE
Multiple start times and end times enable you to model intervals (e.g., break periods) in shifts, though it is not always necessary to maintain this level of detail.

Reviewing the Workday Calendar/Shift
Review your calendar in the Calendar Dates window (or Shift Calendar Dates window) that is shown in Figure 4-6. You can access this window by clicking the Dates button from either the Workday Calendar form or Shifts window.

Apply exceptions to the calendar or shift by clicking the Exception List button in this window. Exceptions can be applied to the workday calendar by selecting individual exception days, by loading them from an exception template, another calendar, and another calendar shift, or by copying a set of exceptions from another calendar.

Building the Workday Calendar
When you have created a workday pattern, assigned shifts, assigned workday and shift exceptions, and reviewed your work, you must build the calendar and assign it to one or more organizations. You can build a calendar using Tools | Build when you are in the Workday Calendar form.

CAUTION
Rebuilding an existing workday calendar affects all organizations that reference the same calendar and exception template.

Copying Calendar and Shift Information
You can copy the entire calendar, including workday patterns, exceptions, and all the shifts. Or, you can just copy a specific shift, including the workday patterns, exceptions, and shift times. If you invoke Tools | Copy from the Workday Calendar, Calendar Dates, and Workday Patterns windows, all workday patterns, all exceptions,

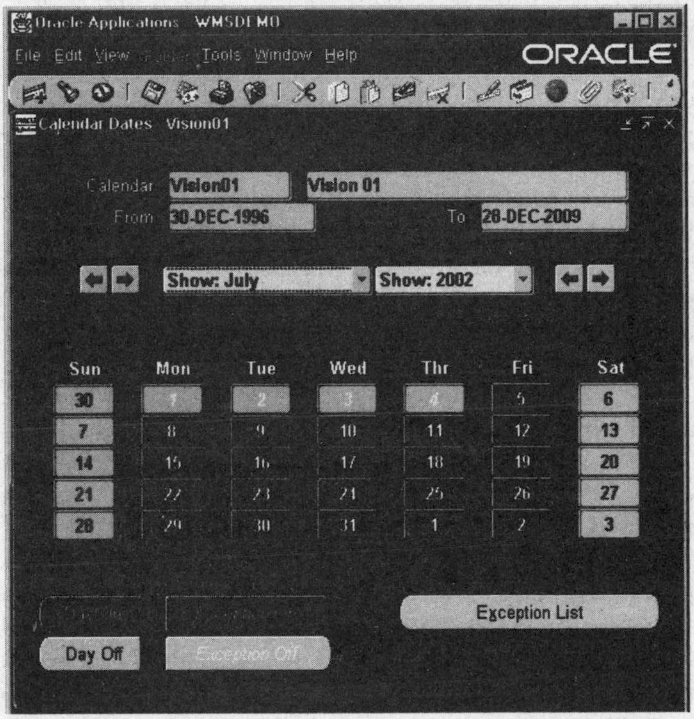

FIGURE 4-6. *Reviewing calendar dates*

and shift information are copied. If you invoke Tools | Copy from the Shifts, Shift Times, Shift Dates, or Shift Workday Patterns window, the shift workday patterns, shift exceptions, and all shift times for the specified shift are copied.

CAUTION
If you copy calendar information to an existing calendar, all new information is appended to the existing calendar information.

Manpower and Machines

A product is manufactured using labor and machines. These are the resources that convert the raw materials into a finished product. Oracle provides you with the capability to define these resources at three levels—Resource Groups, Resources, and Resource Instances. Resources are then grouped into Departments, which represent the various workgroups in the organization. In this section, we will explain the resources, resource instances, and departments.

Resources

Resources represent anything (other than material) that you require to perform, schedule, or cost your manufacturing activities, including persons, machines, outside processing services, and physical space. Starting from Release 11i.4, Oracle enables you to define resource instances for person resources and machine resources.

When you define your departments, you assign the resources available in each department and the shifts that each resource is available for. For each operation you define, you specify a department and list of resources and usages. An operation can use any resource that is available in the department.

Resource Group

Resource Groups provide you the ability to segregate your resources into major groupings. *Rough Cut Capacity Planning* (RCCP) allows you to report by using resource groups. RCCP is covered in detail in Chapter 10.

Defining a Resource

You define resources in the Resources form. The resource name must be unique within the organization. For example, you could assign W12 to represent workman grade 12 or PP for pallet pickers. The resource type identifies if the resource is of type person, machine, etc.

Specify a *unit of measure* (UOM) that describes how you measure the resource. The site-level profile BOM: Hour UOM indicates the unit of measure that represents an hour. You cannot schedule resources whose units of measure are not in the same class as the hour unit of measure (UOM is covered in Chapter 15).

NOTE
You cannot update the resource UOM if the BOM: Update Resource UOM profile option is set to No. Use caution if you do change the resource UOM after you have used the resource—changing the resource UOM does not change any effected cost or routing information.

When an operation is completed, the resource units are applied to the job or repetitive schedule either manually or automatically, based on the charge type. The basis type enables you to specify if you want to charge and schedule the resource for each assembly or for the total job/schedule quantity. Jobs and Schedules are covered in detail in Chapter 16.

If you are performing some of the processing at a supplier site, you can model that part of the process as an *outside processing* (OSP) resource by checking the outside processing flag. The service itself is modeled as a combination of the resource and the associated item; you should enter an item number that represents the outside processing service for this resource. Outside processing is covered in detail in Chapter 16.

Check the Costed flag to collect and assign costs to this resource. If you are using Activity Based Costing, enter an Activity for the resource. You can use activities to group resource charges for cost-reporting purposes.

NOTE
The security functions Privilege To View Cost Information and Privilege To Maintain Cost Information control the ability to view and maintain cost information.

If the resource is costed, indicate whether to charge jobs and repetitive schedules based on a standard rate you define. If you don't charge at the standard rate, you can maintain individual pay rates by employee and charge these rates to the job. In the case of outside processing, if you do not charge the standard resource cost, you will charge the actual PO price to the job. Variances will be posted to the appropriate *rate variance* accounts in this case. For costed resources, you must enter an absorption account that is used to offset resource charges earned in work in process and a rate variance account to collect the variance from charging actual rates to the job.

NOTE
The table BOM_RESOURCES stores information about resources.

For outside processing resources, the default absorption account is the receiving valuation account as defined in the receiving options; the default rate variance account is the organization's Purchase Price Variance account. If you change the default account, your receiving valuation account will have an incorrect balance because of the two accounting transactions that are shown in Figure 4-7.

You can define the direct costs associated with a resource in the Resource Costs window that you can access by clicking the Rates button from the Resources window. You can associate overheads with a resource in the Resource Overhead Associations window that you can access by clicking the Overheads button from the Resources window.

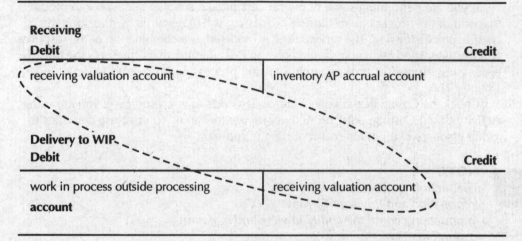

Receiving

Debit	Credit
receiving valuation account	inventory AP accrual account

Delivery to WIP

Debit	Credit
work in process outside processing account	receiving valuation account

FIGURE 4-7. *Accounting transactions for OSP receipt*

If a resource is a setup resource, you can identify the setup type using the Setup Types window that you can access by clicking the Setups button. This can be used for Changeover Time Reduction studies (covered in more detail in Chapter 7).

Resource Instances

Resources identify the skills that are required to perform one or more activities. This aggregate representation is very useful in planning work. When it comes to scheduling/dispatching work, you need to know the actual instance that does the work, as highlighted in Figure 4-8. This is especially true in the case of person and machine resources.

Instances of Manpower Resources   You can identify the employees who are instances of a person resource, by clicking the Employees button that will be enabled for person resources in the Resources form that is shown in Figure 4-9.

In the case of person resources, you can think of a resource as a role that many persons can play. For example, Assembly Operator can be a role, and both Jim and John can play this role. Also note that an employee can be multi-skilled. That is, Jim can be an assembly operator as well as a machine operator.

Instances of Machine Resources   You can identify the machines that are instances of a machine resource by clicking the Equipment button that will be enabled for machine resources in the Resources form that is shown in Figure 4-9.

The instances of a machine are serialized inventory items. You can select any items that have the Equipment flag enabled in the Physical Attributes group.

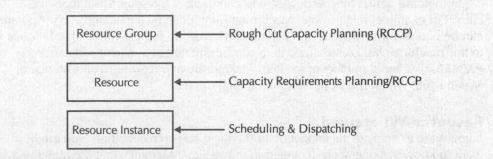

FIGURE 4-8. *Work is scheduled/dispatched to resource instances*

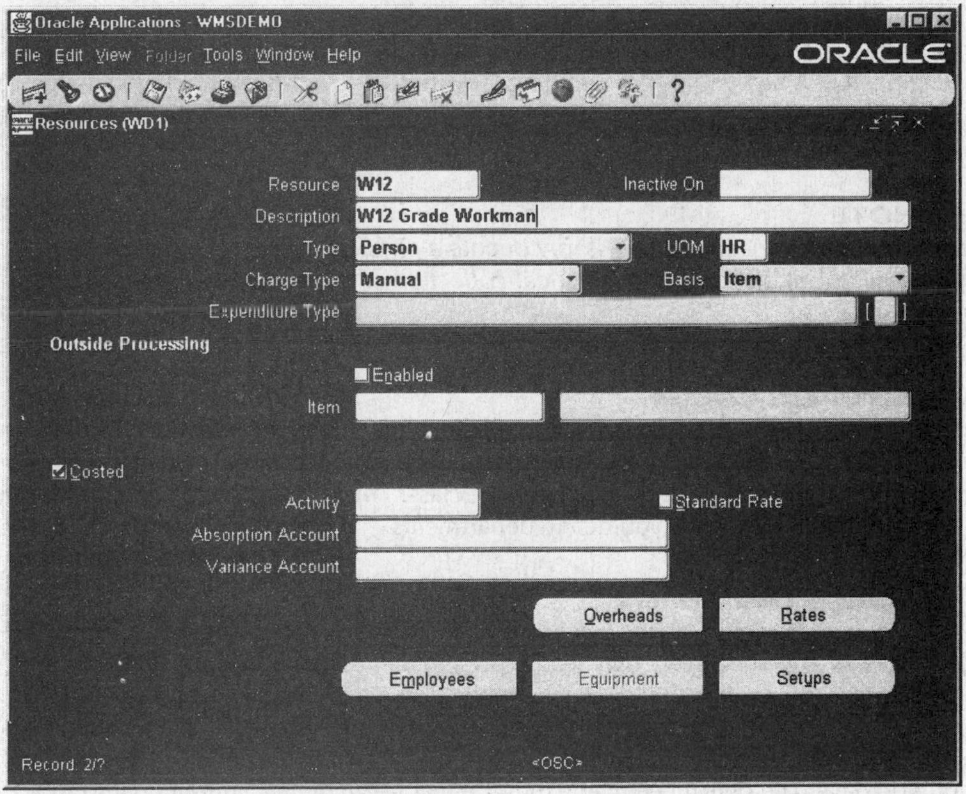

FIGURE 4-9. *Resources*

In the case of machine resources, you can think of a resource as a machine class. For example, a Horizontal Machining Center can be a machine class. An item can be equated to a model of a machine class. Makino-J66 is a model that belongs in this machine class. A serialized item can be equated to a machine instance. AX34535 is a serial number of the item Makino-J66 and represents an instance of Makino-J66, which is a Horizontal Machining Center.

Resource Whereused

If you want to analyze the impact of modifying a resource definition, you might want to know the operations (covered in the section "Method") that are utilizing a resource. You can perform this query using the Resource Whereused form.

Departments

A department is a collection of resources. It can be used to represent a work group, a manufacturing cell, etc. A department consists of one or more people, machines, or suppliers and enables you to collect costs, apply overhead, and compare load to capacity. When you define a routing (covered later in this chapter), you assign a department to each operation in a routing and choose the resources that are available in that department.

NOTE
Department need not necessarily denote a physical area. It can also represent a logical collection of resources.

Department Classes

Department classes group departments and are used for reporting purposes. Department classes are created in the Department Classes form. The Departments button enables you to assign departments to a department class. You can also assign departments to department classes when you define departments.

Defining a Department

You define departments in the Departments form. When you define a department, you specify any department overhead costs and the resources that are available. A department can contain an unlimited number of resources. For each resource, you can specify the shifts that the resource is available. For each resource shift, you can also specify capacity modifications that change the available hours per day, units per day, or workdays. The department name must be unique within the current organization. You must assign a location to a department if it will likely be referenced in a routing, following an outside processing operation. Specify a project expenditure organization if you are using Project Manufacturing. You can make a department inactive by specifying an inactive date, after which you can no longer assign this department to routing operations.

> **NOTE**
> *The tables BOM_DEPARTMENTS, BOM_ DEPARTMENT_RESOURCES, and BOM_ RESOURCE_CHANGES are used to store department and department resource information.*

Overhead Rates

You can enter the department overhead rates in the Overhead Rates window that you can access by clicking the Rates button. For each cost type, specify the various over-head cost components and the corresponding rates.

Assign Resources

You assign resources to a department in the Resources window (shown in Figure 4-10) that you can access by clicking the Resources button from the Departments form. The window shows owned and borrowed resources in two sections. Each resource can be assigned to any number of departments; multiple resources can be assigned to each department.

Owned Resources

Indicate whether the resource is available 24 hours a day and whether this department can share the resource and capacity with other departments. The Check CTP check box enables you to specify whether this resource needs to be included in a Capable to Promise (CTP) check. Specify a resource group for the resource in this department that will be used in Rough Cut Capacity Planning. Indicate if you want scheduling to be done at the resource instance level by checking Schedule by Instance. If this box is not checked, scheduling will occur at the resource level. Assign an exception set that will be used to identify capacity problems. Assign an expenditure type for the resource.

Department Resource Instances   If you schedule at the instance level, you can choose the resource instances that are available for this department. You cannot define new instances; the list is restricted to instances that were defined for the resource.

Tolerance Fences   Tolerance fences let you specify the rate at which you can ramp up capacity. For example, you might have no flexibility for a week or two (a tolerance of zero), but after three weeks, you might be able to increase capacity

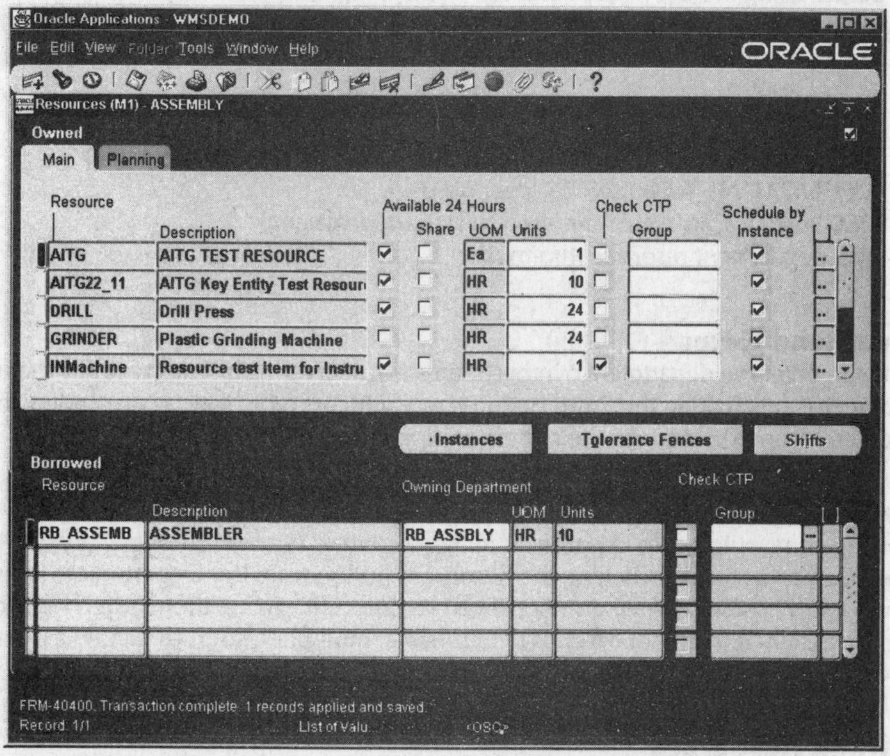

FIGURE 4-10. *Owned and borrowed resources of a department*

by working overtime. If you define these tolerances, ASCP can use them as part of its optimization logic; see Chapter 11.

Shifts For owned resources that are not available 24 hours, you can assign shift information in the Shifts window that you can access by choosing the Shifts button. Choose a shift number that is available in the workday calendar that is assigned to the organization.

You can define temporary capacity changes of a resource by choosing the Capacity Changes button. Capacity modifications can add or delete a day, or add or reduce capacity for a shift. A simulation set must be associated with each capacity change. You can use this to simulate different scenarios during capacity requirements planning (CRP). CRP is covered in Chapters 10 and 11.

If you want to add or remove a workday from a shift, choose the action as Add or Delete. On the other hand, if you intend to add or reduce capacity for a resource in a shift, choose Add or Reduce Capacity. Enter positive numbers to add capacity and negative numbers to reduce capacity.

You can increase or decrease the number of resource units available in a shift by entering positive or negative numbers to increase or decrease the number of resource units, respectively.

The effective date identifies the start date of the capacity change. When you add or remove workdays, the effective start date represents the day that is being added or removed. If you are adding or reducing capacity, the start date represents the first day of the capacity change; in this case, you must also enter a date and time on which the change is no longer in effect.

Borrowed Resources

Identify the owning department for borrowed resources, and specify the number of capacity units (resource units) available for this department. Enable CTP Check and include a resource group for the resource in this department, optionally. Figure 4-11 illustrates how Borrowed Resources would be set up.

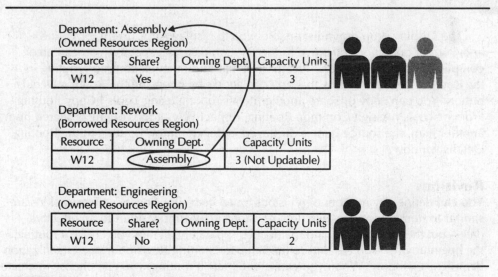

FIGURE 4-11. *How to define Borrowed Resources*

Method

You can utilize different combinations of manpower and machines to produce a product. For example, you can achieve an operation with a lathe or using a drilling/milling machine combination. Oracle provides you with three flavors of routings—Routing, Flow Routing, and Network Routings. Routing is part of the standard product, Flow Routings are part of Oracle Flow Manufacturing, and Network Routing is part of Oracle Shop Floor Management. Each of these three flavors is built on the same premise—a product is produced in a sequence of steps. There are some additional capabilities in Flow Routings and Network Routings. This section explains these features.

Routing

You create a routing in the Routings window. Choose an item and specify an alternate if this is an alternate routing. If you would like this routing to be used in capable to promise calculations, enable the Capable to Promise (CTP) check box.

NOTE
Only one routing for an item can be CTP enabled.

The Display drop-down list enables you to display All, Current, or Future and Current operations effective as the revision date you specify. You can enter completion subinventory and locator information or view a common routing in the Routing Details window that you can access by choosing the Routing Details button. You can copy or share another item's routing using Tools | Copy Routing From or Tools | Assign Common Routing, respectively. If the routing is shared from another item, the source item is displayed under Common Routing in the Routing Details window.

Revisions

You can define any number of revisions for an item's routing. Routing revisions are similar to item revisions—like item revisions, they simply point to an effective date—but they are created and maintained separately. When you create a routing, the beginning revision defaults to the value for Starting Revision in the Organization Parameters window. When you create or update a routing, you can choose to create a new revision or modify an existing revision.

Standard Operations

If your products have operations that are similar, you can define those operations as Standard Operations and use them in your routings. You can either copy or reference a standard operation when you create routings. If you copy, you can modify the operation details. If you reference, you cannot modify any of the operation details. The fields of a standard operation are exactly the same as an operation in a routing and are covered in the section "Operations."

Standard Warehouse Tasks   Oracle WMS uses standard operations as standard warehouse tasks. If you are defining a standard warehouse task, you should identify the Task Type. The Task Type can be Pick, Putaway, Cycle Count, etc. The task assignment engine in Oracle WMS assigns each warehouse task with a standard warehouse task to identify the resource requirements of the task.

Operations

Specify the operation sequence, and optionally select an Operation Code to copy or reference a standard operation.

TIP
If you want to create a standard operation on the fly, you can do so by using Tools | Standard Operations menu.

If you are not using a standard operation, enter the department in which the operation is performed and an effective date range. You can indicate if the operation is option-dependent in the case of model/option class routings (Option dependent-operations are covered in Chapter 6).

Lead Time % indicates the percent of the item's total lead time that is required to complete all previous operations on the routing. This value is used by planning to schedule material to arrive on the operation start date (instead of the order start date). It is calculated by the Calculate Manufacturing Lead Times concurrent program, but can be overridden.

Countpoint operations are gateways in a product's routing and indicate whether you typically report an operation; only countpoint operations default on the WIP move transaction. The Count Point check box enables you to identify these gateway operations.

Autocharge indicates whether you always perform an operation. If you designate an operation as an autocharge operation, it is automatically completed if you skip over it, and any resource charges and material backflushing is performed as if you had explicitly completed it. You would designate an operation as a non-autocharge operation if it were a rework type of operation that you do not want to charge unless you explicitly transact it. Although they are two separate check boxes, the Count Point and Autocharge check boxes work together, and you cannot set Autocharge off if Count Point is on.

Backflush indicates whether a move transaction will attempt to backflush any operation pull material as the operation is completed. If backflushing is disabled for an operation, material will not be backflushed at that operation, even if components are linked to that operation in the bill of material. It will be backflushed when the next backflush operation is completed. (For this reason, you should make sure that the last operation in a routing has backflushing enabled.)

Theoretically, the backflush flag in the routing should correspond to assignment of material in the BOM—if you have assigned Operation pull components to a routing operation in your bills, that operation should normally be identified as a backflush operation in the routing. In practice, all operations default to backflush operations, and the default is appropriate in most cases—if an operation is designated as a backflush operation, but has no material assigned, no backflushing occurs.

You might want to designate an operation as a non-backflush operation, even if material is associated with that operation, if you want to defer backflushing to a more efficient point. If, for example, your material is actually consumed in an operation where you typically report one unit at a time, you might gain a slight performance advantage by deferring the backflushing to a later operation where you report larger quantities—you end up generating one large backflush transaction, rather than a lot of smaller backflush transactions. You should strike a balance between this performance improvement and the potential inaccuracies in inventory by not backflushing at the point of use.

The Minimum Transfer Quantity is used to specify the minimum quantity of the assembly that can be moved from this operation. You will get a warning if you attempt to move a number that is less than this value. The default minimum transfer quantity is 0.

Specify the Operation Yield for each operation. The valid values range between zero and one. This represents the percent of the assembly that is output from this operation. For example, if the operation yield is 0.9, only 90 percent of the assemblies that enter this operation are expected to make it to the next operation.

Operation Resources

Define the resources that will be used in each routing operation. Designate each resource as lot-based or unit-based using the Basis field. A lot-based resource is used only once per order, whereas the usage of an item-based resource is multiplied by the job quantity. Specify the Usage of the resource in the resource UOM. The inverse field automatically reflects the amount of resource requirement per unit of the resource UOM. For example, if the usage is 0.1 and the resource UOM is HR, the inverse will be 6. You can alternatively enter the inverse, and the usage will be automatically calculated for you.

Indicate if this resource is available for 24 hours using the Available 24 Hours flag. If you want your resources to be scheduled in a different sequence than the order in which they are defined, specify that sequence using Schedule Seq. Resources with the same schedule sequence are considered as simultaneous resources, and you can select one of the resources as a primary resource using the Principal flag.

You can associate alternate (substitute) resources to operation resource groups that have the same schedule sequence. The alternate resources have a Replacement Group number. When considering alternates, all the resources with the same replacement group will be considered as a potential replacement. For example, if you have a lathe operation that can in turn be achieved using a milling machine and a drilling machine, you can combine the milling and drilling machines as one replacement group for the lathe, in the alternate Operation Alternate Resources window. Within the alternate resources, identify the primary resource using the Principal flag.

NOTE
As in the case of items, there are global and local (within a routing operation) substitutes for resources as well. At the time of writing this book, the global substitute feature was still being designed.

Indicate the number of resource units that are required for this operation using Assigned Units.

Include or Exclude a resource when scheduling an operation and when calculating manufacturing lead-time for the assembly by setting the Schedule field to Yes or No, respectively. If you want to indicate that a resource can operate in tandem with the prior or next resource, you can achieve that by setting the Schedule field to Prior or Next, respectively. Figure 4-12 illustrates these different scheduling options.

The Resource Offset % indicates the percent of time in the item's manufacturing lead-time when this resource completes. In concept, this is similar to the lead-time percent of the operation. It is used by MRP for capacity planning to estimate the timing of resource load. Like the operation's lead time percent, it is calculated by the lead-time calculation process or can be manually entered.

If you are using activity-based costing, identify the activity type of this resource using the Activity field. Specify if you want to collect resource charges at the standard resource rate using the Standard Rate flag. Determine how each resource is charged using Charge Type. If the charge type is Manual, you must manually charge the job or repetitive schedule. If the charge type is WIP Move, Oracle WIP will automatically charge this type of resource to a job or repetitive schedule when you complete an operation.

Use PO Receipt and PO Move as the charge types for outside processing operations if you want to charge the job when the outside processing PO is received. In both these cases, the job is charged at the receipt of the PO. The difference between PO Move

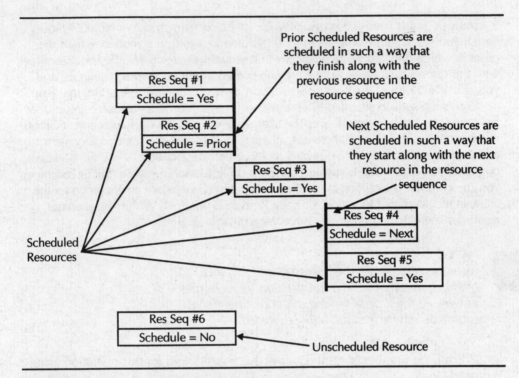

FIGURE 4-12. *Operation Resource Scheduling options*

and PO Receipt is that a PO Move resource charges the job and performs a move at the same time (via the open interface); a PO Receipt resource just charges the job and waits for a separate move transaction. You might use both PO Move and PO Receipt resources in a single operation (e.g. there might be a separate setup charge and a separate run charge); no more than one resource at an operation can be a PO Move resource.

NOTE
The tables BOM_OPERATIONAL_ROUTINGS, BOM_OPERATION_SEQUENCES, and BOM_OPERATION_RESOURCES are used to store information about routings.

Switching Between Primary and Alternate Routings
If you want to switch between primary and alternate routings, query the alternate routing that you want to switch to primary and choose Tools I Switch to Primary.

This will make the current routing the primary routing; rename the previous primary routing with the alternate designator of the current routing, though you can specify a different alternate if you choose. This does not affect any jobs, plans, or costs that were based on the former primary routing.

Cost Rollup

You can perform a single-level cost rollup for the current routing using Tools | Rollup Cost. Specify the cost type. The effective date and time are used to determine the structure of the bill of material to use in the cost rollup. This enables you to roll up historical and future bill structures using current resource rates and component costs. You can optionally include unimplemented engineering change orders (ECO) in the rollup. (ECO is covered in detail in Chapter 5.) After the rollup is completed, the cost rollup process can optionally produce the Indented Bill of Material Cost Report, which lists the detailed cost structure by level.

Flow Routing

Flow routing is simply a sequence of events that can be organized and grouped into two views—the As Designed view (Processes) and the As Manufactured view (Line Operations). This is illustrated by Figure 4-13.

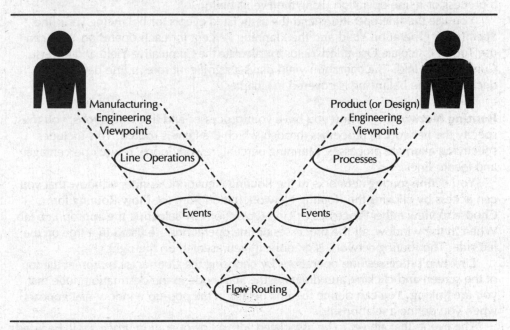

FIGURE 4-13. *Flow routings provide you As Designed and As Manufactured views*

Events represent the smallest unit of work in a flow line. These events identify the resource requirements and are grouped under processes or line operations. To be included in the Mixed Model Map calculations, event resources should be scheduled (any value other than No). Mixed Model Map is covered in detail in Chapter 7.

Standard Events, Standard Processes, and Standard Line Operations

Define standard events, standard processes, and standard line operations using the Standard Events, Standard Processes, and Line Operations forms, respectively. All the attributes are essentially the same, and most of them are available in the standard routing feature that was covered earlier. A significant difference is that a production line is associated with all of these. Flow routings are always defined for a combination of a product and a production line. Production lines will be covered in Chapter 7.

Flow Routing

You define flow routings in the Flow Routings form shown in Figure 4-14. Include standard processes, line operations, and their associated events. You can view the processes, line operations, and all the events in the flow routing itself by choosing the appropriate view option. However, you edit the events that are associated with a process or a line operation using the Events button.

You use the line operations and the associated events for balancing your line. Specify the Operation Yield and the Planning Percent for each operation. You can use Tools | Calculate Operation Yields to calculate the Cumulative Yield and Reverse Cumulative Yield. The operation yield plays a significant role in line balancing decisions. Line balancing is covered in Chapter 7.

Routing Network　When you have your processes and line operations, you must specify the network of processes through which the item is routed. This includes specifying alternate processes, planning percent, rework loops, rework percentage, and feeder lines.

You define routing networks in the Routing Network Designer window that you can access by clicking the Routing Network button from the Flow Routing form. Choose to view either Processes or Line-Operations by selecting the appropriate tab. When in the window, all the processes or line operations are listed in a tree on the left side. The routing network is graphically represented on the right.

Link two processes/line operations by choosing the Connector button at the top of the screen and clicking and dragging the Start node to the destination node that you are linking. You can define the link details in the pop-up window that appears when you define a relationship.

The events that are yet to be associated with a line operation/process will be listed on the bottom left of the screen. You can associate an event with a process/line

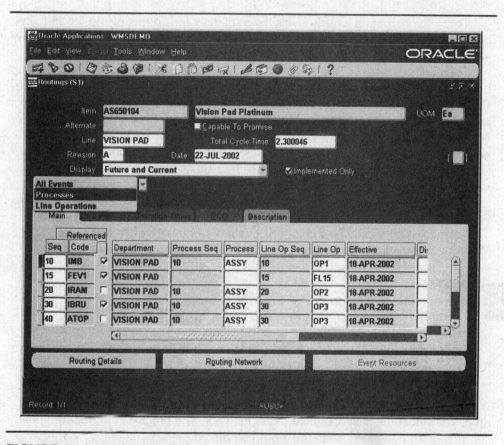

FIGURE 4-14. *Associate processes and line operations to an assembly/line combination in the Flow Routings form*

operation by dragging the event to a process or line operation. You can drill down into a process or line operation to view the events that make up the process/line operation, and you can move events from one another by dragging and dropping.

Network Routings

Network routings comprise a collection of routing operations that include primary paths and alternate paths and allow flexible routing for lot-based jobs. This type of routing is used in scenarios where the paths that jobs take are not always known at the time the job is created.

Network routings use only standard operations; therefore, you must define all the possible operations as standard operations. Define the network routing for an item in the Routings form. This routing should contain all the possible operation paths.

The network routing is really an extension of the standard routing. All the attributes of the standard routing are available in the network routing as well. There are a few additional attributes such as the cumulative and reverse cumulative yield.

The major extension, however, is the routing network. The network relationships between the different operations and the sequence of operations are defined in the Routing Network window that you can access by clicking the Routing Network button in the Routing form. This button will be enabled only in Shop Floor Management enabled organizations. In this window the primary and alternate paths are outlined along with the percentage; each is likely to be used. Although the number of paths from start to end could be numerous, there must be a unique starting operation and a unique ending operation in the entire network.

Define your routing network by entering the operation sequence and the values From and To in the Code fields. Identify the primary path with the Link Type field. The primary path should be a complete chain of operations from start to finish. The Planning % indicates the percentage of material flow through each operation.

NOTE
The operation relationship in the routing network is defined using operation codes. This is the reason network routings mandate you to use standard operations.

When a complete network routing is defined, a WIP Job for a Lot begins with a routing comprising only the first and the last steps. As the job completes the first step, you select the next operation in the network. The process continues until the job reaches the last step when the job is completed.

Logical Data Model of Manpower, Machines, and Methods

Figure 4-15 will help you to reinforce your understanding of the various entities that constitute the method definition in Oracle Applications and the relationships between them.

Although the figure implies operations, events, and standard operations have relationships to both departments and resources separately, the relationships need to be looked at collectively. We always select a department before selecting a resource in the operation (or event) resources form. Also this is a many-to-many relationship and is resolved by the table BOM_OPERATION_RESOURCES in the physical data model.

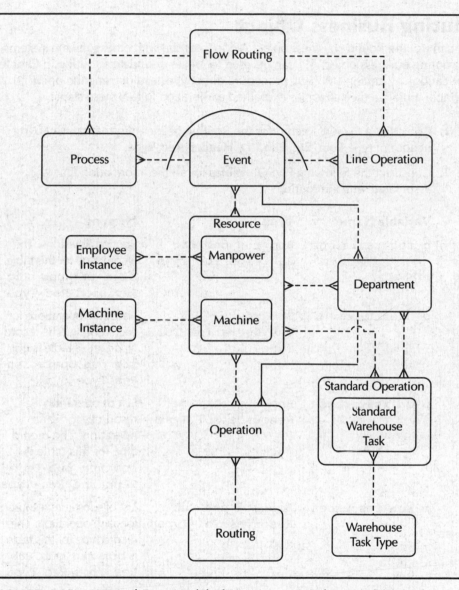

FIGURE 4-15. *Logical Data Model of Manpower, Machine, and Method Definitions*

Routing Business Object

You can use the Routing business object API to integrate with other software systems. The routing business object API can be used to create or update a routing in Oracle Applications by calling a PL/SQL procedure directly instead of using the open interface. Initialize the system (as explained earlier) and follow these steps:

1. Construct a PL/SQL Record for the Routing header information, say p_rtg_ header of type **Bom_Rtg_Pub.Rtg_Header_Rec_Type**.

2. Construct the following PL/SQL Tables for all the information that is associated with the routing:

Variable Name	Type	Meaning
p_rtg_revisions	Bom_rtg_pub.Rtg_ Revision_Tbl_Type	Routing Revisions. The record type for this table is bom_rtg_pub. Rtg_ Revision_Rec_Type
p_operations	Bom_rtg_ pub.Operation_Tbl_ Type	List of the operations for each routing. The record type for this table is bom_ rtg_pub.Operation_ Rec_Type .
p_op_resources	Bom_rtg_pub.Op_ Resource_Tbl_Type	List of operation resources for each operation. The record type for this table is bom_rtg_pub.Op_ Resource_Rec_Type
p_sub_resources	Bom_rtg_pub.Sub_ Resource_Tbl_Type	List of substitute resources for each operation. The record type for this table is bom_rtg_pub.Sub_ Resource_Rec_Type
p_op_networks	Bom_rtg_pub.Op_ Network_Tbl_Type	List of operation relationships identifying the routing network The record type for this table is bom_rtg_pub.Op_ Network_Rec_Type

3. Call the procedure **process_rtg**, with the parameters that you constructed in step 2.

```
Bom_Rtg_Pub.process_rtg
(p_bo_identifier
-- IN Type of business object
,p_api_version_number
-- IN API version for compatibility checking
,p_init_msg_list
-- IN Should the message list be initialized?
, p_rtg_header
--IN Routing Reference
, p_rtg_revisions
--IN List of routing revisions
, p_operations
--IN List of operations
, p_op_resources
--IN List of operation resources
, p_sub_resources
--IN List of substitute resources
, p_op_networks
--IN Operation network relationships
, x_rtg_header
--OUT Routing Reference
, x_rtg_revisions
--OUT List of routing revisions
, x_operations
--OUT List of operations
, x_op_resources
--OUT List of operation resources
, x_sub_resources
--OUT List of substitute resources
, x_op_networks
--OUT Operation network relationships
,x_return_status
-- OUT Return status, indicates success or failure
,x_msg_count
-- OUT Number of messages during the process
)
```

Summary

This chapter identified the types of resources (materials, manpower, machines, methods, and time) in a manufacturing environment. Bills of material and co-products represent the material resource. You can define alternate bills to represent the different groupings of raw materials for a particular item. A number of the attributes at the item level are also available at the bill component level.

Workday calendars and shifts allow you to model the Time resource. You can model complex workday patterns using the workday calendar. For example, you can create a pattern that has four days on and three days off in the first week and three days on and four days off in the following week.

The manpower and machine resources allow you to model high-level groupings of manpower and machines. For example, you can define a W12 grade worker as a manpower resource. Similarly, you can define a CNC machining center as a machine resource. Employees are instances of manpower resources. Equipment type of inventory items are instances of machines.

Routings, Flow Routings, and Network Routings allow you to model the method resource. Routings are a collection of manufacturing operations or steps that identify the required manpower and machine resources at each step. Standard operations can be defined and reused across many routings. Standard WMS tasks identify the WMS task type, in addition to the resource requirements.

CHAPTER
5

Design Engineering

racle Engineering allows you to provide your design engineers with controlled access to item information, bills of material, and routings for items that are being designed. During the product lifecycle phases, Oracle Engineering allows you to record, track, and implement engineering changes to items, bills of material, and routings.

Developing Prototypes

While developing a product, most enterprises try to track the development in one engineering organization and then manufacture it in many plants. This concept of one engineering organization is not in the context of physical location. You may have designers/engineers who are located all over the world, but all of them belong to this virtual engineering community of a company.

You can define a single inventory organization in Oracle Applications to model your virtual engineering community and enable all the engineering items in this organization; when you're ready to manufacture an item, you can transfer/copy that item to manufacturing and enable it in the appropriate manufacturing/distribution organizations.

Engineering Items

The difference between an engineering item and a manufacturing item is that they are controlled through different security functions. Typically, the ability to access (view and update) engineering items is given to a smaller group of users. Other than the ability to view and update the item information, engineering items behave exactly the same way as manufacturing items. For example, whether you can purchase an item or not is determined by the item attribute Purchaseable irrespective of that item being an engineering or a manufacturing item.

You define engineering items in the Define Engineering Item form. In the real world, an item has many characteristics that could be identified by the item itself, or sometimes by the location in which it is stored. You can model these characteristics of an item using one of the two features—item attributes and item-subinventory attributes. Both of these are covered in detail in various parts of this book. For an engineering item, the item attribute Engineering Item is automatically checked. You will not be able to update this attribute, although you can see it. You will not be able to view an engineering item using the Define Item form that is available through Oracle Inventory. You will be able to purchase, build, and sell an engineering item, based on the setting of its other item attributes.

The Engineering Items: Revisions security function secures the ability to create revisions for an engineering item, whereas Engineering Items: Delete secures the ability to delete engineering items.

Engineering Bills and Routings

You can define the structure of your item as an engineering bill in the Engineering Bills of Material form. Because this is an "as designed" structure, it might not be used for manufacturing the product. So, you can define an Alternate called As Designed and use that to represent all your engineering structures.

You can define the operations to produce your item as an engineering routing in the Engineering Routing form. Similar to the component structure, you can use the As Designed label to distinguish your prototype routings.

NOTE
Unlike some ERP systems, Oracle Applications allow a particular item, bill of material, or routing to exist only in one environment (engineering or manufacturing) at a time; once you transfer the object from engineering to manufacturing, it no longer exists in engineering. To keep a separate copy of a bill or routing, you can create an alternate as described here. Alternatively, you can copy the engineering objects to manufacturing under a new item number; this alternative is discussed later in this chapter.

Accessing Engineering Information

The ability to access engineering items is controlled using function security. Any user who has the function Master Engineering Items in their menu has the ability to define/update engineering items. There is a corresponding function at the organization level called Organization Engineering Items, which controls the ability to edit engineering items in the enabled organizations.

Similarly, you can access engineering bills and routings if you have the functions Engineering Bills of Material and Engineering Routings in your responsibility.

Transferring to Manufacturing

Once you have completed the development of a new product and the product is proven through various tests, you release this product for manufacturing. You accomplish this by transferring or copying the item and its related information to manufacturing.

Typically, you do a transfer if the item is handed over to manufacturing and from then on that item's information will be maintained by manufacturing. During the development cycle, if an item has reached a stage so that it can be built and sold in the market, you may want to start manufacturing that item and at the same time continue its development. In such cases, you copy an engineering item to manufacturing by giving a new name for the item. Manufacturing will maintain this item's information from now on, whereas engineering will own the original item and carry out the development on that item. When you transfer an item, the transfer is done only in the organization where you're performing the transfer. Later on, you can enable this item in the appropriate manufacturing organizations.

NOTE
Transferring an item from engineering to manufacturing in a child organization does not automatically result in a transfer to the master organization also. Conversely, transferring the item in the master organization does not result in a transfer in its child organizations. Transfers must be done separately in each organization; this allows you to be very specific in your engineering controls.

As illustrated by Figure 5-1, transferring engineering information is a one-way process. You can transfer information from engineering to manufacturing, but you cannot transfer information back from manufacturing into engineering.

To transfer an engineering item to manufacturing, navigate to the Transfer to Manufacturing form. Once there, select the item that you want to transfer in the Revisions tab and choose the information that you want to transfer by checking one or more of Item, Bill, and Routing. The current revision of the item and the routing

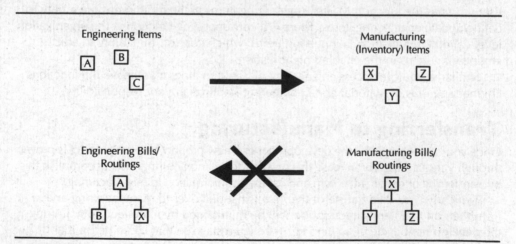

FIGURE 5-1. *Transfer of items, bills, and routings is a one-way process*

will be shown, and you can optionally specify new revisions for the item and routing that will be effective after the transfer. In the alphanumeric sequence, the new revisions should be higher than the current revisions.

Because a manufacturing bill might not include engineering items, transferring an engineering bill of material will automatically transfer any first-level engineering components of that bill. This is a single-level transfer. It transfers the items only; it does not transfer the bills of material of any engineering components; you must transfer these separately.

NOTE
*There is no separate revision for bills. The item
revision is used as the bill revision.*

If you don't specify a specific alternate in the Alternates tab, all the alternates defined for the item including the primary will be transferred. You can choose the information that you want to transfer by selecting one of the three possible values in the Selection field. If you want to transfer a specific alternate, choose Specific to Transfer, and then specify an alternate to transfer. You should choose Primary to Transfer if you want to transfer just the primary. Choosing All to Transfer will have the same effect as not specifying anything in this tab.

If you want to relate this transfer with an Engineering Change Order (ECO; explained in more detail in the following section), you can choose an ECO in the ECO, Description tab; this might be useful for you in inquiries, though there is no additional functionality provided by ECO.

If you want to create a copy of an engineering item in manufacturing, you should use the Copy to Manufacturing form that is shown in Figure 5-2. In addition to the information in the transfer form, this form has a Manufacturing tab, which has the new item name and description.

CAUTION
*When you copy an engineering item to
manufacturing, you must provide a new name for
the item. Also, if you want to copy bills and routing
from engineering to manufacturing, you must copy
them at the same time that you copy the item. This
is because the copy function doesn't allow you to
reference an item after you have copied it to
manufacturing. So, if you want to copy, copy
everything in one step.*

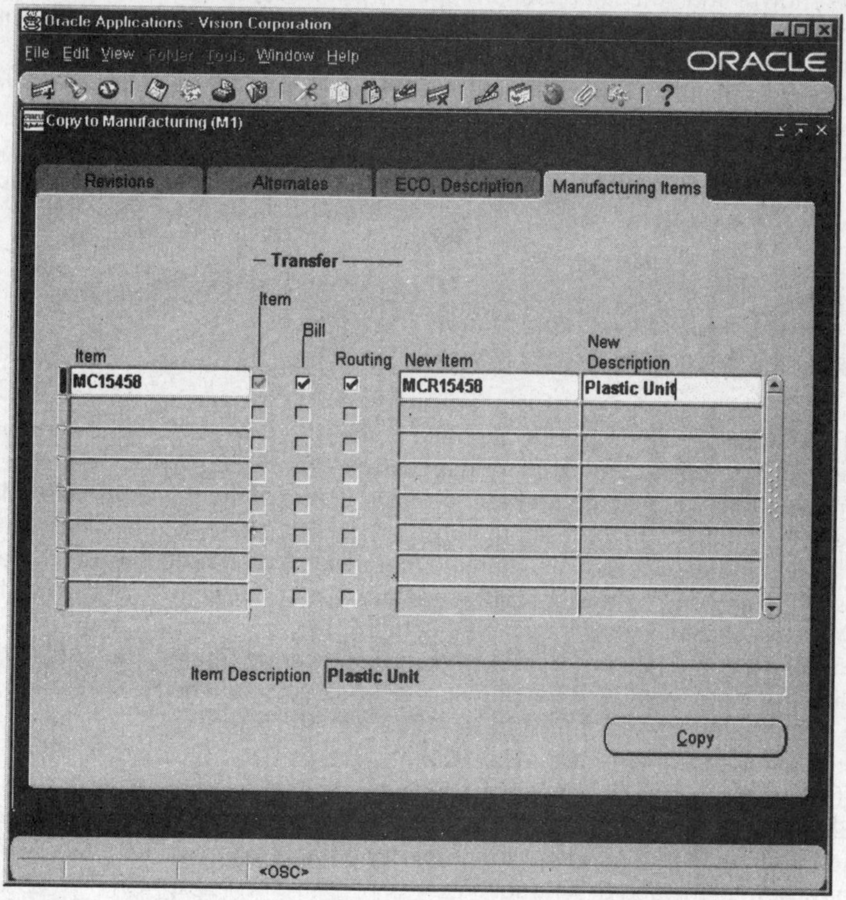

FIGURE 5-2. *The Copy to Manufacturing form duplicates an item from engineering in manufacturing*

The security function Engineering Items: Transfer secures the ability to transfer engineering items to manufacturing.

Engineering Change Orders

In a manufacturing organization, a standard document is used as the vehicle for communicating new product releases and changes in existing products. There are several names for this document, such as Engineering Change Note, Engineering Change Notification, etc. Oracle Engineering supports this business process with the Engineering Change Order (ECO) feature. You will be able to define an ECO that can consist of multiple items, bills, and routings, allowing you to group your changes logically as illustrated by Figure 5-3. Once the ECO is defined, you can submit this ECO for approval from various people. Later on, you will implement this ECO. The approval process is carried out using workflows defined using Oracle Workflow. You can either use the seeded workflow or define custom workflows and use them.

ECO Setup

ECOs allow you to manage engineering changes to your items, bills, and routings. You can update your existing items or release new items using an ECO. Although most of the setup steps are optional, defining and using the following would help in simplifying the process of defining and using ECOs.

ECO Autonumbering

You can configure the way ECOs are automatically numbered and control this numbering pattern on a user-by-user basis. If this level of control is not necessary in your environment, the next level is to have a numbering pattern for each organization. Beyond this, you can have a single pattern for all users across all organizations. Figure 5-4 illustrates the hierarchy Oracle Engineering uses to automatically number the new ECOs. When you create an ECO, it will be numbered using your specific

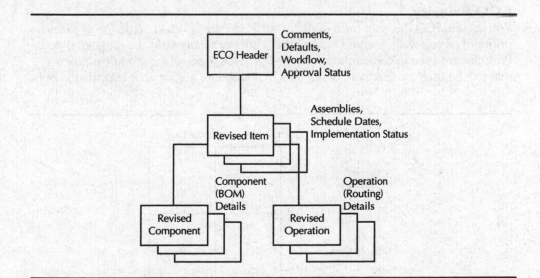

FIGURE 5-3. *Structure of an ECO—Items, Components, Operations, and Resources*

prefix in the current organization. If the you/current organization combination doesn't exist, the prefix at the next combination in the hierarchy—you/all organizations—will be used.

CAUTION
ECO Autonumbering always requires a prefix from this hierarchy. If a prefix is not found, you will have to manually define a number. If you plan to use autonumbering, it would be safe to define a prefix for the combination all users/all organizations.

The system administrator can set the profile option ENG: Change Order Autonumbering at the user level. If this is Yes for a user, that user can define the autonumbering prefix for all users. If this is No, those users can only define prefixes for themselves. If you don't want users to define their own prefixes, you should give them a responsibility that has the function Change Order Autonumbering excluded.

You define the autonumbering prefix in the ECO Autonumbering form. There are two sections in this form. In the first section, you identify the user(s) for whom you want to define a prefix for autonumbering. In the second section, you identify the organization(s) and specify the prefix and also the next number in the sequence for this prefix.

ECO Priority
You use the ECO Priorities form to define an ECO Priority. You can define as many priorities as you want, but you assign each a priority sequence in the range of 0–9. Priorities are used in conjunction with the ECO type to select the workflow process that will be used for approval. Other than that, priorities are for your information only.

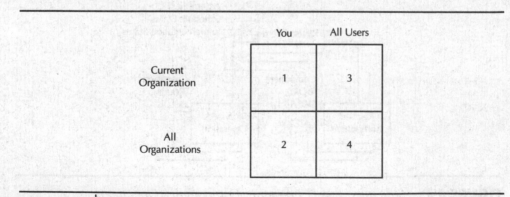

FIGURE 5-4. *The hierarchy of ECO autonumbering options*

ECO Type

You define ECO Types in the ECO Types form. ECO Types are useful in classifying your engineering changes. Secondly, an ECO Type identifies the type of information that is changeable by an ECO—Manufacturing and/or Engineering. Finally, ECO Type identifies the workflow process that is to be used for approval. You associate a workflow to an ECO Type in the Change Type Processes form.

You can optionally specify an ECO Priority for each workflow that you associate with the ECO Type. When you define an ECO, if a workflow is associated for an ECO Type/ECO Priority combination, that workflow will be used for the approval of that particular ECO. You can associate a workflow without specifying the ECO Priority, in which case that workflow will be used in cases where the ECO Type is specified and the ECO Priority is left blank. Another important fact is that, since ECO Priorities are organization-specific whereas ECO Types are not, if you associate a workflow to an ECO Type along with the ECO Priority, the combination will be valid in only the organization where the ECO Priority is defined.

ECO Reason

If you want to track and report on ECOs based on the reason they were proposed and implemented, you can define reason codes in the ECO Reasons form. You define a unique reason code and a brief description for each reason; you can assign these reasons to your ECOs for classification purposes.

ECO Approval List

You can predefine approval lists in the Approval Lists form. When you define an ECO, you can select one of these approval lists, which will then be used by engineering to get the approval from the individual people in the list.

NOTE
Approval List is used for sending notifications using Oracle Alert; this field will be disabled if you select a workflow to manage your ECO.

Profile Options

In your business, you may want to impose a rule that you should assign a new revision to an item, whenever the item is included in a change order. You can do this by appropriately setting up the ENG: Require Revised Item New Revision profile option.

You can control if you want to implement an ECO when the ECO has been superceded by higher revisions by appropriately setting up the ENG: ECO Revision Warning profile option. If the value is Yes, you will be able to implement a lower-level ECO revision. If the value is No or Blank, the implementation process will error out and the ECO cannot be implemented.

Defining ECOs

You define ECOs in the Engineering Change Orders form. If autonumbering is enabled, you will get a default number automatically, which you can change. The ECO Type you choose determines the types of items that you can include in this ECO (Manufacturing items only or Engineering/Manufacturing items). The ECO Type and ECO Priority combination is used to default the workflow process, and in this case, you cannot enter an Approval List. An ECO Department will be defaulted from the profile option ENG: ECO Department. Choose an ECO Reason to classify this ECO into one of your reason groupings.

If a workflow process is associated with the ECO, you start the workflow process using the Submit button. Once the workflow is started, you can view the approval history.

If you don't associate a workflow with the ECO, you can associate an approval list with the ECO. When you change the status to Ready to Approve, Oracle Alert will send notifications to the people on the approval list. If you use an approval list, the ECO approval status can only be changed manually.

If you don't specify an approval list or a workflow process, the ECO approval status will be set to Approved without being subjected to a formal approval process.

Choose a status for the ECO using the ECO Status window from the Tools menu. If the status is Scheduled or Cancelled, the Scheduled Date or Cancelled Date will also be displayed. You can provide an estimate of the implementation cost (both engineering and manufacturing) for the proposed change, by accessing the Enter Costs window through the Tools menu. This information can be used to calculate the payback period for the change, by comparing the current costs and future savings.

Choose the items that are included in the ECO in the Revised Items window that is shown in Figure 5-5. If you check the MRP Active flag, MRP will consider the change in components when exploding the revised item during the planning process. You can add or disable components in the Revised Components window. When you want to replace a component, you explicitly disable a component and add the new component.

Starting from Release 11i.5, you can create ECOs for tracking and implementing routing changes. You can revise a routing to add, change, and disable its operations or events, by specifying the appropriate details in the Routing Details tab. You can also add or disable Operation resources.

The logical data model presented in Figure 5-6 will reinforce your understanding of ECOs and the related entities.

The security function Engineering Change Orders: Update secures the ability to update engineering change orders, and Engineering Change Orders: Approvals secures the ability to submit an ECO for approval, while Engineering Change Orders: Release secures the ability to release engineering change orders.

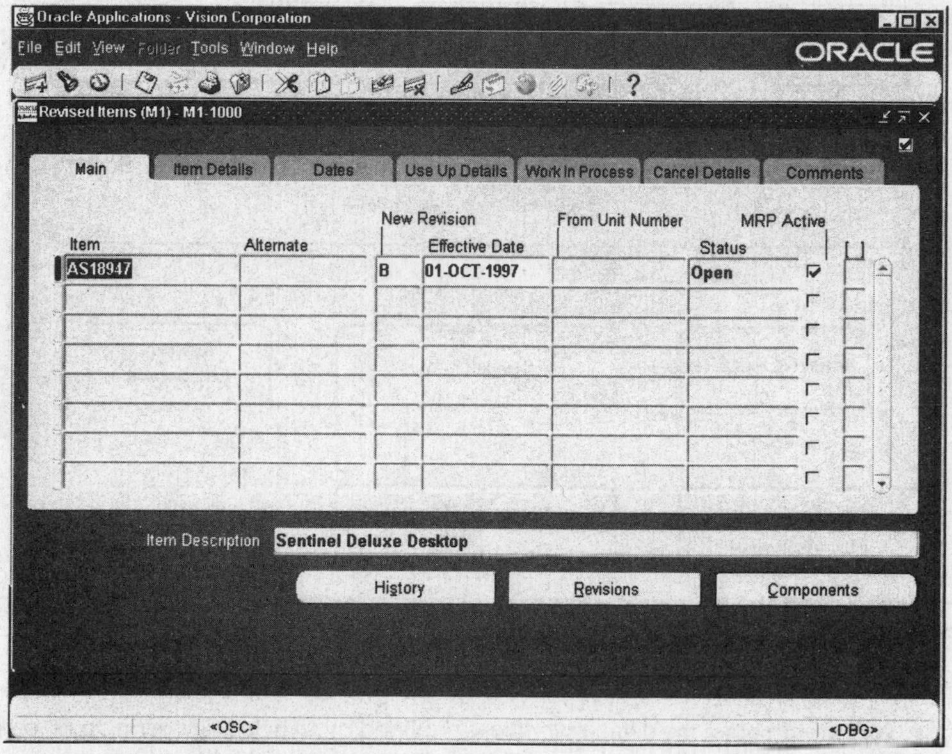

FIGURE 5-5. *The Revised Items form enables selection of items to include in the ECO*

ECO Approval

In an enterprise setting, you'll typically have an engineering board or a change review committee that will review the engineering changes proposed and either approve or reject the proposal. Oracle Engineering lets you model these engineering boards and change control committees using ECO approval lists.

If an approval list is used for approval, the ECO status should be modified manually to reflect the current status. When an approval list is used, all the users in the list are notified using Oracle Alert. Users can respond to the alert notification with their approval/disapproval. Based on the responses, you set the approval status manually.

On the other hand. if you use a workflow to manage the approval process, the workflow will modify the status to Approved programmatically, when all the approvals have been received. Workflow needs to know how to select the necessary approvers; one way to do this is to associate an approval list with the seeded workflow. In this

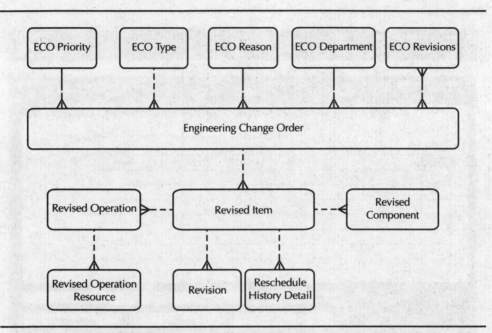

FIGURE 5-6. *ECO Logical Data Model*

case, you should open the default workflow provided by Oracle Engineering and load an ECO approval list as a role to the approval process using the following steps:

1. Open the workflow builder and connect to the applications database.

2. Open ECO Approval.

3. File I Load Roles from database.

4. Load the approval list that you want to use in the ECO workflow.

5. Click Processes and open Standard Approval Process.

6. Open the property window of the node Standard Approval and click the Node tab.

7. Select the role that you loaded in step 4 as the performer.

8. Save your changes to the database.

You should recognize that this is a static assignment. So, if this process is selected, the approval list that you assigned here will be used always. If you wish, you can define additional workflows with different approval lists, then assign the appropriate workflow to the combination of ECO Type and ECO Priority, as discussed earlier.

If you want to use the same workflow, but a different approval list for each ECO, you must configure the workflow to select the correct approval list. One simple method is to identify the desired approval list on a Descriptive Flexfield (DFF) on the ECO, and then design the approval workflow to get the approval list from the DFF. Use the following steps to customize your workflow:

1. Open the workflow builder and connect to the applications database.

2. Open ECO Approval.

3. Click Processes and open Standard Approval Process.

4. Open the properties window of the node Standard Approval and click the Node tab (shown in Figure 5-7).

5. In the Performer section, set the type to Item Attribute.

6. Set the performer to ATTRIBUTE1 (or any descriptive flexfield column that you enable to store the ECO approval list for each ECO).

7. Save your changes to the database.

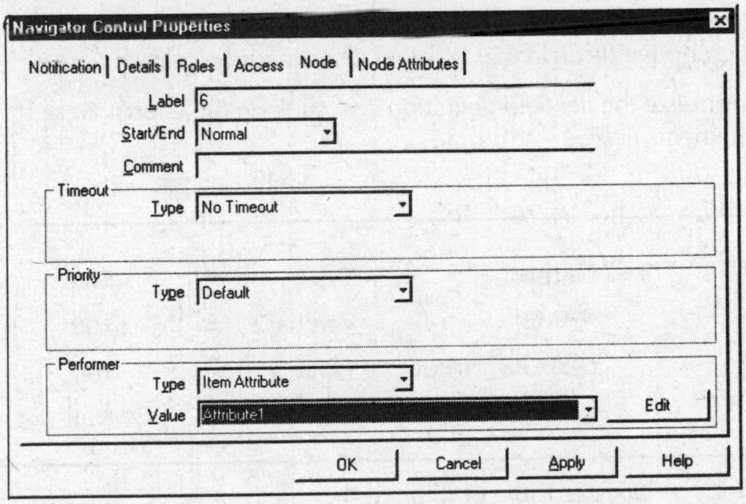

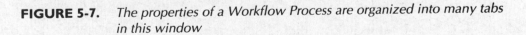

FIGURE 5-7.   *The properties of a Workflow Process are organized into many tabs in this window*

To create an approval list value set, follow these steps:

1. Navigate to the Value Sets form.

2. Enter a name for the value set with the following settings:

   ■ **Format Type**   Char

   ■ **Max. Length**   100

   ■ **Validation Type**   Table

3. Navigate to the Validation Table Information by clicking the Edit Information button and fill in the following information:

   ■ Table Application: Applications Object Library

   ■ Table Name: WF_ROLES

   ■ Uncheck Allow Parent Values

   ■ Table Columns (see Table 5-1)

   ■ Where/Order by clause: where wf_roles.orig_system='ENG_LIST'

4. Save the value set.

To enable an ECO Descriptive Flexfield, follow these steps:

1. Navigate to the Descriptive Flexfield Segments form and find the descriptive flexfield that is called Change Order Information.

2. Unfreeze the flexfield definition and click on the Global Data Elements field.

	Name	Type	Size
Value	NAME	Varchar2	100
Meaning	DISPLAY_NAME	Varchar2	100
ID	Null	Null	Null

TABLE 5-1.   *Value Set Table Columns*

3. Click the Segments button and fill in the following information:

- **Number**   1 (the sequence in which you want this field to appear in the flexfield form)

- **Name**   Specify a name (e.g., Approval List)

- **Window Prompt**   Specify the prompt

- **Column**   ATTRIBUTE1 (or other unused attribute)

- **Value Set**   Select the value set that was created before

4. Freeze the flexfield definition; compile and close all the forms.

When you define your ECO, you should select an approval list in the descriptive flexfield and save the ECO. When you submit the ECO for approval, the workflow process will use the approval list that was selected in the descriptive flexfield.

Accessing ECOs

Access to ECOs is controlled using two filtering mechanisms: the ECO Department and the BOM Item Type (an item attribute covered later in this chapter) of items. Figure 5-8 illustrates the access control provided by ECO Departments. The profile option ENG: ECO Department, which can be specified at all the levels, determines the department that will be defaulted if a user creates an ECO. This profile option is also used to determine whether the user has access to ECOs from either one department or all departments.

CAUTION
If a user doesn't belong to any ECO Department (the user's ENG: ECO Department is not specified), that user can access all the ECOs in the system. So you should make sure that users are not provided with this level of authority unintentionally.

If you want to strictly enforce department-wide security to your ECOs, specify the ENG: Mandatory ECO Departments profile option as Yes. This will ensure that all ECOs belong to ECO Department. The profile options in Table 3-2 control access to ECOs at the item level, depending on the BOM Item Type of the item.

Product Family items are not controlled using this security mechanism. Additionally, you can control the ability to create ECOs for engineering items using ENG: Engineering Item Change Order Access.

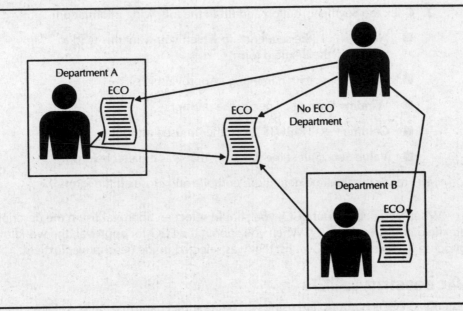

FIGURE 5-8. *The ECO department controls who can access an ECO*

Rescheduling ECOs

You can reschedule all the revised items that are pending in the ECO together or one by one, using the Reschedule window from the Tools menu. If you reschedule from the ECO form, all the revised items will be rescheduled. If you reschedule from the revised items window, only the current revised item will be rescheduled.

Profile Option	BOM Item Type
ENG: Planning Item Change Order Access	Planning item
ENG: Model Item Change Order Access	Model and Option Class items
ENG: Standard Item Change Order Access	Standard item

TABLE 5-2. *ECO access control using BOM Item Types*

CAUTION
Just specifying the effectivity date (by rescheduling) doesn't mean that the changes will be implemented on the effectivity date. You should make sure that you change the ECO status to Scheduled and run the autoimplement manager daily, if you want this to happen.

The security functions Engineering Change Orders: Schedule and Engineering Change Orders: Reschedule secure the ability to schedule and reschedule engineering change orders, respectively.

Implementing ECOs

Once the proposed changes are approved, you can implement the changes. You can implement an ECO if the approval status is not Rejected and if the status of the ECO is not Hold or Cancelled.

There are two ways in which you can implement an ECO: manually, using the Tools | Implement option, or automatically, using the concurrent program AutoImplement Manager.

When you implement an ECO manually, you can implement all the revised items together or individually in different dates. The security function "Engineering Change Orders: Implement" secures the ability to implement engineering change orders manually. If you want to implement all the revised items in an ECO, choose Tools | Implement when you are in the ECO form. On the other hand, if you want to implement only one revised item, choose Tools | Implement from the revised items window.

You can schedule an ECO for implementation by changing the ECO status to Scheduled. The AutoImplement Manager will implement this ECO on the scheduled date. AutoImplement Manager is a concurrent program that will automatically implement all the ECOs whose schedule dates are on or before the current system date. It's a good practice to have the AutoImplement Manager running on a daily basis, at the start of the day. Once an ECO or a revised item is implemented, all changes to the revised item are prohibited in the ECO.

Canceling ECOs

You might want to cancel an ECO or a few revised items in the ECO, or even further down, a few component changes on a revised item. If you choose Tools | Cancel when you are in the Engineering Change Order form, the ECO will be cancelled. If you choose Tools | Cancel from the Revised Items window, the selected revised item will be cancelled. If you choose Tools | Cancel from the Revised Components window, the selected revised component will be cancelled.

If you cancel an entire ECO, you will not be able to perform any action on the ECO, other than merely viewing it. Component cancellations can be viewed in the Cancel Details tab on the Revised Components window. The security function Engineering Change Orders: Cancel secures the ability to cancel engineering change orders.

Using ECOs for Mass Changes

When a component that is used in many assemblies is to be replaced, you can use the mass change capability that is available in Oracle Engineering or Oracle Bills of Material. It is always a good idea to use the mass change capability in engineering, since engineering provides more control through a two-step process. You define the mass change order first and then later implement it. The other benefit is that this change could be tracked with an ECO number, whereas the implementation through the Bills of Material applications is immediate and there is no tracking ability in bills of material.

In a mass change, you can add, delete, or replace a component or modify component information across all or a subset of parent items. You can use item categories and item types as a mechanism for selecting a subset of affected assemblies. This will be particularly useful if you can identify the pattern of occurrence of your mass changes.

Unlike ECOs, when you want to replace a component with a mass change, you don't have to explicitly add and disable a component. When you choose update as the action, another row is added with the action of New, and you should update the new row with your new details, including the new component.

Use-up ECOs

Use-up dates are calculated during every planning run for all the items in that plan. The use-up date for an item is the date on which the on-hand quantity for the item will be exhausted, considering the gross requirements calculated by that plan. Figure 5-9 illustrates how the use-up date is calculated during every planning run. In the illustrated example, the use-up date is the fourth day.

When you define an ECO, you can base the effective date of the revised item on the use-up date of either the revised item or one of the components of the revised item. You can select the use-up date of either the revised item or one of its components

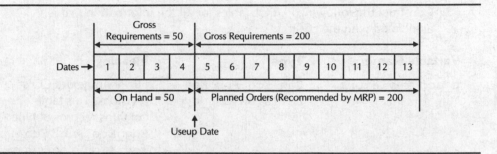

FIGURE 5-9. *How the use-up date is calculated*

in the main tab. Navigate to the Effective Date field in the Main tab and bring up the LOV, to select a use-up date. In this list of values, you will see the use-up date of the revised items and all its components, in each of the current MRP plans for the item. This way, the use-up item and the MRP plan will be defaulted and the revised item's effective date will be linked to the use-up item and the corresponding plan.

If the use-up date changes in a subsequent MRP run, the results vary depending on whether the use-up item is the revised item itself or one of its components. If the use-up item is the revised item, the effective date will be changed automatically. But if the use-up item is a component, the ECO Use Up Alert will be triggered to notify the items' planner of the date change; the effective date on the ECO will not be changed automatically. The rationale is that you might want to base the schedule on a different component, particularly if you are replacing components in a matched set. In this case, you must manually reschedule the revised item's change.

ECO Business Object API

You can use the ECO business object API to integrate with other software systems. In a nutshell, the ECO business object API can be used to create or update an ECO in Oracle Applications by calling a PL/SQL procedure directly instead of using the open interface.

1. Initialize the system. Follow the initialization guidelines in the section "BOM Business Object" in Chapter 4.

2. Construct a PL/SQL Record for the ECO header information, for example, p_eco_header of type Eng_Eco_Pub.eco_rec_type.

3. Construct the following PL/SQL tables for all the information that is associated with the ECO:

Variable Name	Type	Meaning
p_eco_revisions	Eng_Eco_Pub.Eco_revision_tbl_type	History of your ECO's revisions. This table contains records of type Eng_Eco_Pub.Eco_revision_rec_type
p_eco_revised_items	Eng_Eco_Pub.Revised_item_tbl_type	List of revised items that are to be included in the ECO. This table contains records of type Eng_Eco_Pub.Revised_item_rec_type
p_rev_components	Bom_Bo_Pub.Rev_component_tbl_type	List of the components for each bill. The record type for this table is bom_bo_pub.rev_component_rec_type
p_ref_designators	BOM_Bo_Pub.Ref_designator_tbl_type	List of reference designators for each component. The record type for this table is bom_bo_pub.ref_designator_rec_type
p_sub_components	BOM_Bo_Pub.Sub_component_tbl_type	List of substitute components for each component. The record type for this table is bom_bo_pub.sub_component_rec_type
p_rev_operations	Bom_Rtg_Pub.Rev_Operation_Tbl_Type	List of revised operations for each revised item. The record type for this table is Bom_Rtg_Pub.Rev_Operation_Rec_Type

Variable Name	Type	Meaning
p_op_resources	Bom_Rtg_Pub. Rev_Op_Resource_ Tbl_Type	List of operation resources for each revised operation. The record type for this table is Bom_Rtg_Pub.Rev_Op_Resource_Rec_Type
p_sub_resources	Bom_Rtg_Pub. Rev_Sub_Resource_ Tbl_Type	List of substitute operation resources for each resource. The record type for this table is Bom_Rtg_Pub.Rev_Sub_Resource_Rec_Type

4. Call the procedure process_eco, with the parameters that you constructed in step 3. You don't have to supply all the parameters in every case. If you browse through the signature of this procedure in the manual, you would note that most of the parameters have a default value. So, if you were inserting a whole new ECO, you would provide all the information. On the other hand, if you are modifying an ECO header attribute, you just provide the new header record.

```
PROCEDURE Process_Eco
(p_api_version_number
-- IN API version for compatibility checking
,p_init_msg_list
-- IN Should the message list be initialized?
,x_return_status
-- OUT Return status, indicates success or failure
,x_msg_count
-- OUT Number of messages during the process
,p_bo_identifier
-- IN Type of business object
,p_ECO_rec
-- IN PL/SQL Record for header info
,p_eco_revisions
-- IN PL/SQL Table for ECO revisions
,p_revised_items
-- IN PL/SQL Table for revised items
,p_rev_components
-- IN PL/SQL Table for revised components
```

```
    ,p_ref_designators
    -- IN PL/SQL Table for reference designators
    ,p_sub_components                  .
    -- IN PL/SQL Table for sub components
    ,p_rev_operations
    -- IN PL/SQL Table for revised operations
    ,p_rev_op_resources
    -- IN PL/SQL Table for operation resources
    ,p_rev_sub_resources
    -- IN PL/SQL Table for sub resources
    ,x_ECO_rec
    -- OUT PL/SQL Record for header info
    ,x_eco_revisions
    -- OUT PL/SQL Table for ECO revisions
    ,x_revised_items
    -- OUT PL/SQL Table for revised items
    ,x_rev_components
    -- OUT PL/SQL Table for revised components
    ,x_ref_designators
    -- OUT PL/SQL Table for reference designators
    ,x_sub_components
    -- OUT PL/SQL Table for sub components
    ,x_rev_operations
    -- OUT PL/SQL Table for revised operations
    ,x_rev_op_resources
    -- OUT PL/SQL Table for operation resources
    ,x_rev_sub_resources
    -- OUT PL/SQL Table for sub resources
    ,p_debug
    -- IN Toggle to indicate debug mode
    ,p_output_dir
    -- IN Debug file dump directory
    ,p_debug_filename
    -- IN Debug file name
    );
```

5. Check completion status by processing the OUT parameters and commit, if everything was fine.

CAUTION
Business Object APIs will not issue commits or rollbacks. You have to do that explicitly in your calling code. The API will return the state of the business object and the process completion code (success or error). You can decide to commit or rollback the changes in your code.

Summary

In this chapter, we covered the features related to prototyping your engineering concepts and managing engineering changes during the product development phase. You can define engineering items, bills, and routings and use them to prototype your new product ideas. Once your product is proven, you can release the product to manufacturing.

Engineering Change Orders allow you to define, track, and implement changes to your items, bills, and routings. You can create engineering changes for both manufacturing and engineering items. If you want to mass replace a component across many using assemblies, you can use Mass Change ECOs.

CHAPTER
6

Assemble to Order
and Pick to Order

ssemble to Order (ATO) and *Pick to Order* (PTO) are stocking strategies that are used by manufacturers, when they can produce a variety of finished products from a relatively small number of subassemblies and components. This stocking strategy is widely known as the "hourglass" strategy, where you maintain your inventory at the narrowest level in your bill structure. This maintains inventory in a more flexible state and helps minimize your inventory investment. An ATO environment is where you wait until you have an actual sales order before you begin manufacturing the finished product. PTO implies that you will pick multiple items based on one line item on a sales order.

Configure To Order Environment

In both ATO and PTO environments you might actually configure products based on the customer order, or simply manufacture or ship standard products or predefined configurations. A configure to order environment is where you allow your customers to configure the finished product that they intend to buy. Typically you will offer a variety of choices to your customer from which they can choose the best options that suit them.

Market Orientation versus Stocking Strategies

Whether you offer configurable products depends on your market orientation; but if you do, you cannot follow a Make to Stock strategy. You will potentially follow one of the three possible stocking strategies—*Make to Order* (MTO), ATO, or PTO, depending on the complexity of your products (how configurable your products are). On the contrary, you can operate with an MTO/ATO/PTO stocking strategy but still choose not to offer configurable products. The difference between MTO and ATO is the level at which you stock your components. So, from here on, when we mention ATO we really mean both ATO and MTO because the business processes are similar albeit the stocking levels are different.

ATO/PTO Scenarios

In a configuration scenario, a model bill of material is used to represent the list of choices; if there's no need to offer choices, a standard bill of material is used. The difference between models and items is essentially the ability to configure an item while creating an order. Beyond this creation of the configuration item, the manufacturing and distribution processes are the same for both models and standard items. These scenarios are summarized in Figure 6-1.

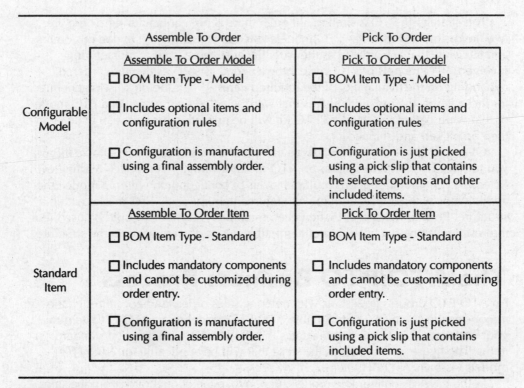

	Assemble To Order	Pick To Order
Configurable Model	**Assemble To Order Model** ☐ BOM Item Type - Model ☐ Includes optional items and configuration rules ☐ Configuration is manufactured using a final assembly order.	**Pick To Order Model** ☐ BOM Item Type - Model ☐ Includes optional items and configuration rules ☐ Configuration is just picked using a pick slip that contains the selected options and other included items.
Standard Item	**Assemble To Order Item** ☐ BOM Item Type - Standard ☐ Includes mandatory components and cannot be customized during order entry. ☐ Configuration is manufactured using a final assembly order.	**Pick To Order Item** ☐ BOM Item Type - Standard ☐ Includes mandatory components and cannot be customized during order entry. ☐ Configuration is just picked using a pick slip that contains included items.

FIGURE 6-1.   *ATO/PTO scenarios*

In an ATO environment, the strategy is to forecast, build, and stock the subassemblies and parts that are used in the model. Oracle offers two flavors of ATO—the first one is the ATO model in which the customers can configure the product to their liking, and the other one is the ATO item that is preconfigured. Once the customer order is received, the subassemblies and components are assembled, according to the instructions in the routing, and shipped.

For configurable models, the subassembly/component list will vary with respect to each order and so will the manufacturing instructions (routing). So, a notional item is created for each unique combination of options using an automatic process. This item can be numbered and named according to your business needs. For example, when a model called MD45890 is ordered with a set of chosen options, the system will create a notional item to represent the chosen options, and numbers the new item as MD45890*99, based on your BOM parameters. This item is referred to as the configuration item in Oracle Applications.

The strategy in PTO is similar, although there is no manufacturing. There are two flavors of PTO as well—PTO models that can be configured by the customers and PTO kits that are ordered as they are. Because there is no manufacturing involved, PTO models or PTO kits can be shipped as soon as they are ordered, depending on the availability of the required items. When the pick list is generated for these items, the individual items that were selected (in the case of a PTO model) or that were part of the standard PTO kit will be printed in the pick list, which can then be picked and shipped.

Over and above the vanilla flavors that are shown in Figure 6-1, Oracle allows you to have hybrid items such as an ATO model within a PTO model. Starting with Release 11i5, Oracle supports multiple levels of configuration within a model; the applications will generate a unique configured item for each ATO model within a structure. Prior to Release 11i5, however, multiple ATO models could be used, but the result was one flat bill of material for all levels of configuration in the structure.

The ATO/PTO Business Process

An ATO/PTO process flow starts with entering sales orders and goes through the major steps in shipping a configurable ATO/PTO model or an ATO/PTO item to your customer. Figure 6-2 demonstrates this flow for both models and standard items. The figure also highlights the steps that will be applicable for ATO/PTO models vis-à-vis ATO/PTO items.

In the case of configurable models, you invoke the configurator from the sales order; choose appropriate options, and save the configured item sales order. Once the sales order is booked, you can create the configuration item, configuration item bills, and configuration item routing in the appropriate inventory organizations automatically. For ATO/PTO items, and PTO models, these two steps are not necessary because you order and use standard predefined items.

When using ATO models/items, you create a final assembly order (a discrete job or a flow schedule) to fulfill the sales order. The item is manufactured using the designated items and then shipped to the customer.

With PTO models/items, a pick list is generated for the sales order; the subassemblies and components are picked and optionally packed, before shipping to the customer.

Setup for ATO/PTO

Oracle enables you to define various business rules that support these business processes, so that your day-to-day operations will be easier to manage. For example, in a configurable ATO environment, the system will define a new item for every order, if a matching item is not found. This section will cover the setup for using Oracle Applications in an ATO/PTO environment.

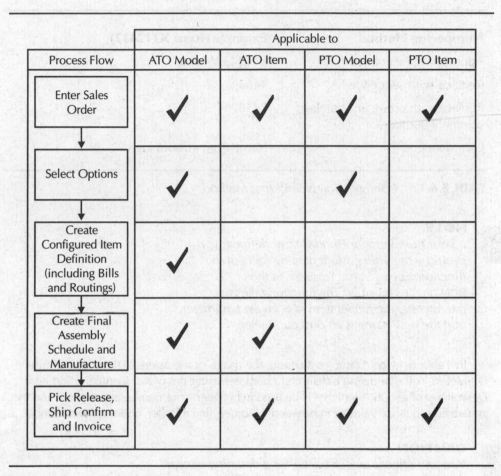

Process Flow	Applicable to			
	ATO Model	ATO Item	PTO Model	PTO Item
Enter Sales Order	✓	✓	✓	✓
Select Options	✓		✓	
Create Configured Item Definition (including Bills and Routings)	✓			
Create Final Assembly Schedule and Manufacture	✓	✓		
Pick Release, Ship Confirm and Invoice	✓	✓	✓	✓

FIGURE 6-2.   *ATO/PTO flow*

BOM Parameters and Profile Options

Almost all the information in this section applies, only if you are planning to operate with configurable ATO/PTO models.

The factory floor that produces the products doesn't have to concern itself with the model bills, because there is a lot of additional information in the model bills. For this reason, a configuration item is created for each order that includes the options that were selected by the customer. The values in the fields Numbering Segment and Numbering Method in the BOM Parameters window are used to create a number for the new configuration item. You identify one of the segments from your item key flexfield as your numbering segment. Let's say you use only one segment from the Item key flexfield. Your numbering segment would be SEGMENT1.

The numbering method can take one of the four values as illustrated in Table 6-1.

Numbering Method	Example (Item X112432)
Append with sequence	X112432*4463
Replace with sequence	4463
Replace with order, line number, shipment number	74587*4*5
User defined	Name from custom logic

TABLE 6-1. *Configuration Numbering Method*

NOTE
If your numbering method is User defined, you should write your custom naming logic in the function `user_item_number` in the `BOMCFGIB.pls` file. The function takes two parameters: the model item id is an `in` parameter, and the new name is an `out` parameter.

In Table 6-1, the examples illustrate the usage of the asterisk (*) as the delimiter character. You can define a delimiter character using the BOM: Configuration Item Delimiter profile option which will be used in between your numbering segment and the generated sequence value or in between the order, line number, and shipment number.

CAUTION
You can choose any character for a delimiter except the one you chose for the Item key flexfield delimiter, if you use a multi-segment item. If in fact you have the same delimiter for both the Item key flexfield and the configuration item delimiter, the Create Configuration Item process will fail.

You can specify the default User Item Type for every configuration item that is automatically created using the BOM: Configuration Item Type profile option.

Before creating a new configuration item, you can check for existing configurations that match with the selected options of the new sales order. You can control this using the BOM: Match to Existing Configurations profile option. If the value is Yes, a check for matches will be performed before a configuration is created through the AutoCreate Configuration concurrent program or the Create Configuration Item workflow activity.

The standard matching logic checks for the existence of another configuration that has the same options with the same quantity as the one that is being ordered. If you want to use a custom logic for matching instead of the standard matching logic, you can indicate that using the BOM: Use Custom Match Function profile option.

NOTE
If you want to use custom matching logic, you should implement that logic in the function find_matching_config *in the* CTOCUSMB.pls *file. The model line id from the table* oe_order_lines *should be passed as an* in *parameter, while you have four* out *parameters – the matched item id, error message, message name, and table name.*

When you enter orders in Oracle *Order Management* (OM), OM verifies that the items exist in the organization that is pointed by QP: Item Validation Organization. The value of this profile option should normally be the item master organization for the install, unless there are good reasons to do otherwise. As in the case of items, OM uses the same item validation organization to get the model bills of material that is to be configured. It's a very good idea to define all your configurable model bills in your item validation organization. If you have to maintain your bills from a different organization, define common bills of material in your item validation organization, so that you always maintain your bills of material from one organization.

CAUTION
MO: Operating Unit and QP: Item Validation Organization are definable at the responsibility level. You must ensure that responsibilities that share a common operating unit should also have a common item validation organization. Otherwise, AutoCreate Configuration might not work properly, because:

■ *It attempts to enable the configuration item in the organization identified by QP: Item Validation Organization and*

■ *It uses the numbering method from the BOM Parameters in QP: Item Validation Organization for numbering the item.*

Item Templates

There are various types of items that are used in an ATO/PTO scenario. The templates for the top-level items are outlined in Figure 6-3, with the appropriate attribute settings.

The seeded templates include ATO Item, ATO Model, PTO Model, ATO Option Class, and PTO Option Class.

We discuss some of the attributes that are important for ATO/PTO operations next. The models, items, and components should all have the BOM Allowed flag enabled.

	Assemble To Order	Pick To Order
Configurable Model	**Assemble To Order Model** ☐ BOM Item Type = Model ☐ BOM Allowed = Yes ☐ Planning Method = MPS PLanning ☐ Forecast Control = Consume ☐ Build in WIP = Yes ☐ OE Transactable = Yes ☐ Check ATP = Yes ☐ ATP Components = Yes ☐ Assemble to Order = Yes	**Pick To Order Model** ☐ BOM Item Type = Model ☐ BOM Allowed = Yes ☐ Planning Method = Not Planned ☐ Build in WIP = No ☐ OE Transactable = Yes ☐ Check ATP = No ☐ ATP Components = Yes ☐ Pick Components = Yes
Standard Item	**Assemble To Order Item** ☐ BOM Item Type = Standard ☐ BOM Allowed = Yes ☐ Planning Method = MRP PLanning ☐ Forecast Control = Consume ☐ Build in WIP = Yes ☐ OE Transactable = Yes ☐ Check ATP = Yes ☐ ATP Components = Yes ☐ Assemble to Order = Yes	**Pick To Order Item** ☐ BOM Item Type = Standard ☐ BOM Allowed = Yes ☐ Planning Method = Not Planned ☐ Build in WIP = No ☐ OE Transactable = Yes ☐ Check ATP = No ☐ ATP Components = Yes ☐ Pick Components = Yes

FIGURE 6-3. *Item templates for top-level items*

For PTO models/items, the Pick Components flag is enabled, whereas for ATO models/items, the Assemble to Order flag is enabled. These two attributes are mutually exclusive.

Ship Model Complete is applicable only for PTO models, PTO items, and PTO option classes. Enabling this attribute will mean that all the components in the model, kit, or option class ship together.

You can enable Available To Promise (ATP) checking for the model/components using the Check ATP and ATP Components attributes. ATP is covered in detail in Chapter 12.

You have to enable the Forecast Control appropriately for ATO models, ATO items ATO, and option classes. Forecast Control is not applicable to PTO models, PTO kits, and PTO option classes; forecasts are always exploded for PTO models/kits/option classes.

The MRP Planning Method determines the type of planning that you intend to use on your ATO models, ATO items, and ATO option classes. PTO models, PTO kits, and PTO option classes are not planned using MRP; their components are always exploded while loading the forecasts. Forecasting and Planning are covered in detail in Chapters 8–11.

Setup for Configurable ATO/PTO Models

The first step is to define your ATO/PTO models as items with a BOM Item Type of Model and one of the two attributes—Assemble to Order (for ATO models) or Pick Components (for PTO models)—enabled. You should then define the bills for these models with appropriate option classes and options. The last step is to define a generic routing for ATO models, which can then be used as a template routing. You can define your model routing in such a way that your configured items will get a routing that inherits the appropriate operations automatically. Routing is not applicable to PTO models.

Item Setup   Define your model in the item master organization, and enable it in the organization(s) from where the model will be manufactured and shipped. You should then define your components, apply the appropriate template, and enable them in the organization(s) from where the model will be manufactured.

The model, option classes, and options should be added to a price list in Oracle Order Management. Thus there is a price for the basic and standard features and the price adds up as each option is selected.

You should have your model bill defined in the manufacturing organization(s), because the configuration bill of material is created using the model bill defined in the manufacturing organization. The configuration item will be enabled in the item master organization, the organization pointed by the responsibility's QP: Item

Validation Organization, the shipping organization, and the manufacturing organization(s). As described earlier, if BOM: Match to Existing Configurations is Yes, the auto-create process checks for matching configuration items in the system. The standard matching logic tries to find a match in the whole system and is not organization dependent.

Bill of Material Setup   A configurable model can potentially contain four types of items—additional models, various option classes, the options within each option class, and the standard included items. An ATO/PTO model can have option classes, options, and standard items as components. An ATO model can have another ATO model as a component. A PTO model can have both ATO models and PTO models as components.

If the parent item has its item attribute ATP Components enabled, the cases where a component's ATP will be performed is indicated in Figure 6-4.

You can enter the Minimum Quantity and Maximum Quantity for each option (not for mandatory components), defining a quantity range that is enforced during order entry. These quantities must be a multiple of the particular component's quantity in the bill. The Optional attribute is applicable only in model and option class bills and is used to indicate if a model, option class, or option is optional.

The Mutually Exclusive attribute is only applicable to option class items. If the option class is flagged as mutually exclusive, you can only select one option from that option class. For example, if you are a car manufacturer, you can have an option class called Audio System with three options—Bose, Sony, and Sharp. These

	Bill attribute: Check ATP = Yes	Bill attribute: Check ATP = No
Component's Item attribute: Check ATP = Yes*	ATP is checked	ATP is not checked
Component's Item attribute: Check ATP = No	ATP is not checked	ATP is not checked

* Yes = Material only, Remove only, or Material and Resource

FIGURE 6-4.   *Component ATP*

options are mutually exclusive; but the decision is indicated at a higher level, which is the option class.

In the case of PTO option classes, you can set the Basis to Option Class to prevent modification of the extended order quantity on the option class item. This determines if the extended order quantity on an option class can be modified during order entry. Extended order quantity of options within an option class can be modified irrespective of the value of the Basis field.

NOTE
Extended order quantity is calculated by multiplying order quantity of the model and the component quantity in the bill.

You can assign item catalog descriptive elements to models and option class bills, if the descriptive element is also listed in the catalog for the item. The auto-create process will generate an item description based on the option's values for models and if the item has one or more descriptive elements that have their Description Default enabled. You can use this feature to generate meaningful item descriptions. For example, Neptune uses this feature to include the memory in the description among other things. So, if a customer selects 256MB as the RAM option during his order, the value 256MB will be included in the item's description.

Routing Setup   You can specify if a routing step is option-dependent while defining routing operations. During the auto-create process, all the operations that are not option-dependent are copied over to the configuration routing. But, an option-dependent operation is copied only if an option referencing that operation is selected during order entry.

When the configuration item is created, you might want your chosen options to inherit the operation sequence number from their option classes. You can achieve this using the profile option BOM: Inherit Option Class Operation Sequence Number. When this profile is set to Yes, all the option items whose operation sequence numbers are 1 will inherit the operation sequence numbers from their parent option classes.

The inheritance logic goes all the way up to the top of the model structure, until it finds a sequence that is not 1. For example, the options (Celeron, Pentium III, Athlon, and K6) shown in Figure 6-5 have an operation sequence of 1. The option classes AMD and Intel also have an operation sequence of 1. The next level option class, which is CPU, has an operation sequence of 45. The chosen option will inherit the operation sequence number from the CPU option class as 45, when the configuration item is created.

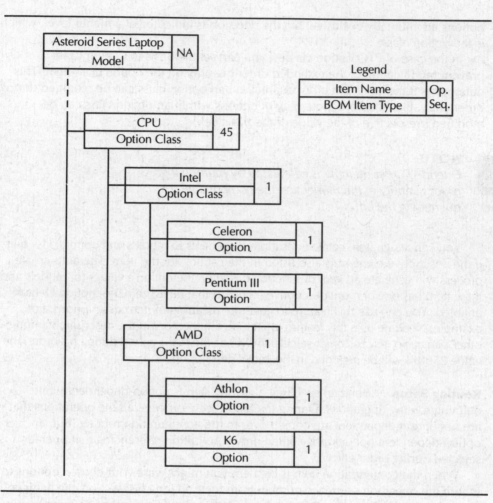

FIGURE 6-5. *Operation sequence inheritance*

This is a convenient feature if multiple option choices will use the same routing operations. For example, Neptune offers a choice of several CD-ROM and DVD-ROM drives on its machines. Regardless of the drive chosen, the same routing operation is used to install it. But the drive is not required, so the operation is option-dependent. (If an option were mandatory, e.g., the choice of processor, you would not have to make the operation option-dependent at all.)

Making the Auto-Created Configurations Orderable   If you want to accept customer orders for the configured items that are created by the auto-create process, you should enable the following item attributes for that item:

- Shippable

- Customer Ordered

- Customer Orders Enabled

- OE Transactable

You should also add the item to the appropriate price lists.

Setup for Standard ATO/PTO Items

You can create a standard ATO/PTO item, by enabling the Assemble to Order or the Pick Components attributes of the item appropriately. Alternatively, you might want to predefine standard configurations, which are based on a model and use them directly during order entry, instead of picking option by option. The idea is to save time and effort during order entry, especially for frequently sold configurations. We'll take a look at the steps in defining standard configurations.

Item Setup   Define the configuration item with your desired name and apply either the ATO Item or PTO Kit template, depending on the type of standard item that you're defining. In the Bills of Material section of the item attributes, select the base model for this item as the model on which you are basing this new item.

TIP
In most cases, you can copy the item attribute values from your base model and change the base model attribute and the BOM Item Type attributes.

You can catalog the configuration item using the same catalogs established for the base model, so that this item will also appear in catalog searches like all the configuration items that were created automatically and are based on the same model. The ATO item should be added to a price list in Oracle Order Management.

Bill of Material Setup   If you want to define the bills of an ATO/PTO item from scratch, you can do that just like you would do for any normal item. Alternatively, if you want to define the ATO/PTO item bill that is based on another item (the item's Base Model), navigate to the Bills of Material window and select the item for which you want to define the configuration bill. Navigate to the Configurator window using Tools I Configure Bill menu and select the various options that are available in the model.

> **NOTE**
> *You should identify the configurator engine URL*
> *using the BOM:Configurator URL of UI Manager.*
> *This URL will be used to invoke the configurator*
> *from the Bills of Material form.*

Once you complete your selections, Oracle Bills of Material creates a single level bill for the configuration item that includes the model item, selected option classes, selected options, and all the mandatory/included items. You can roll up lead times and cost for the configuration item by running the appropriate concurrent programs.

Routing Setup   Routings for ATO items can be defined in the same way that you do for any normal item. If you created a configured bill, using Tools I Configure Bill, the routing is not created for you automatically. However, this feature always assumes that your BOM: Inherit Option Class Operation Sequence Number is Yes and shares the routing from the Base Model; the Op Seq number in the configuration bill will be inherited from the Base Model.

Ongoing Activities

The ongoing activities in managing an ATO/PTO environment relate to almost every module in Oracle Applications. Because all these modules are covered in detail in various parts of the book, we attempt to mention only the aspects that are relevant to ATO/PTO in this chapter.

Because ATO/PTO is a stocking strategy, it affects almost every part of the business from planning to invoicing. In this section we cover all the features in the various modules of Oracle Applications that support the ATO/PTO business process.

Forecasting and Master Scheduling ATO Models/Items

You can create aggregate forecasts for the ATO models/items and option classes and generate forecasts for your options and mandatory components by exploding these aggregate forecasts. Depending on the value of the item attribute Forecast Control, the item's forecasts will be exploded and consumed.

Forecasts for the ATO model will be consumed once the sales order is entered. Once the configuration item (covered in the section "Managing the Configuration Item") is created, the configuration bill is exploded and the forecast(s) for model, option class, option and mandatory items are consumed again, if their Forecast Control is Consume or Consume and Derive.

You can master schedule your ATO models and later on assemble your ATO items and configuration items using a final assembly schedule. Forecasting and Master Scheduling are covered in detail in Chapters 8–11.

Enter Sales Order

Enter a sales order from the Sales Orders window. You can start entering the sales order by specifying the customer. Most of the information could be defaulted based on the customer that was selected.

For ATO/PTO models, the options that are selected will be included in the sales order as separated lines. This is covered in detail in the next section, "Select Options." In the case of ATO items, only the ATO item appears in the sales order.

You can mix ATO models, ATO items, PTO models, PTO items, standard items, and non-shippable items in a single sales order. You can ship each line to a different ship to location, and you can source each line from a different warehouse. You can also create customer shipment schedules from a line so customers can get volume discounts, but still manage to maintain their inventory levels to match their plans.

Order Management is covered in detail in Chapter 12.

Select Options

Navigate to the sales order line that contains the ATO/PTO model and invoke Oracle Configurator using the Configurator button. In the Configurator window that is shown in Figure 6-6, you can choose the options that are to be included in the item. When you select an invalid option, the configurator explains the rule violations in the rules window. You will be allowed to save the selections partially, but you cannot proceed to create the configuration item, until you complete all the required selections.

The Configurator window that is used throughout Oracle Applications for creating configured products is the runtime engine of Oracle Configurator. We discuss Oracle Configurator briefly, in the section "The Oracle Configurator," later in this chapter.

When you finish choosing your options and save your configuration, all the chosen options and their respective option classes will be included in the sales order, as separate lines along with the automatically included (mandatory) items.

If you know that a configuration item with similar options exists already, you can link that item to the ATO/PTO model line using Actions/Link Config Item, after you book the order line.

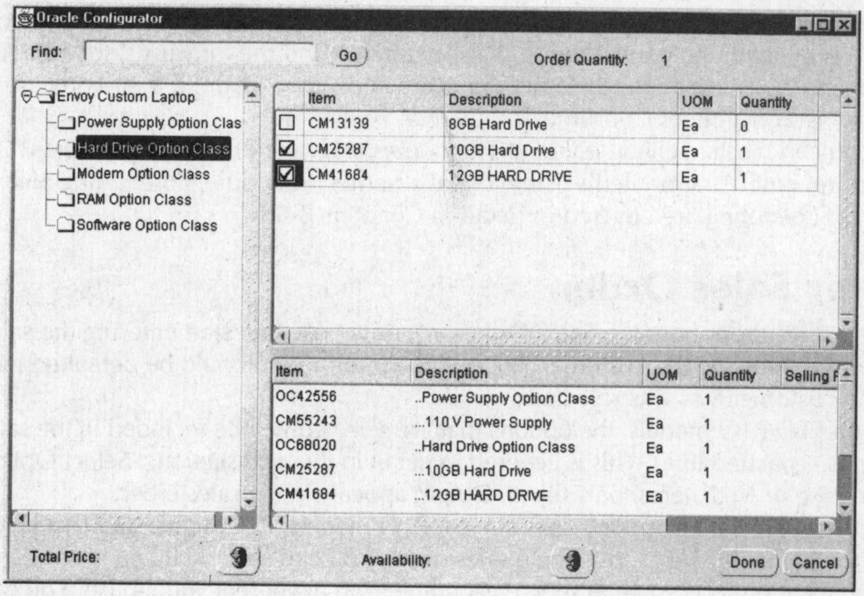

FIGURE 6-6. *Configurator runtime engine*

Managing the Configuration Item

This step is applicable only for configured (CTO) items. As mentioned before, the system creates a configuration item, if it doesn't find a matching configuration during the auto-create process. In this section, we will discuss how to create and deactivate a configuration item.

Creating the Configuration Item

Once the sales order line becomes Create Configuration Eligible, you can proceed to create the configuration item. You can create a configuration item either by running the AutoCreate Configuration Items concurrent program or by using the Progress Order action from the Sales Order Line. Figure 6-7 shows the sales order after the configuration item is created. As you can see, the configured item is inserted as a separate line with a ".0" appended to the line number that contains the ATO model. The selected options and option classes are also included in the sales order with increasing lines numbers appended to the line number that contains the ATO model.

When you create the configuration item using the AutoCreate Configuration Items concurrent program, you can specify the sales order number to create

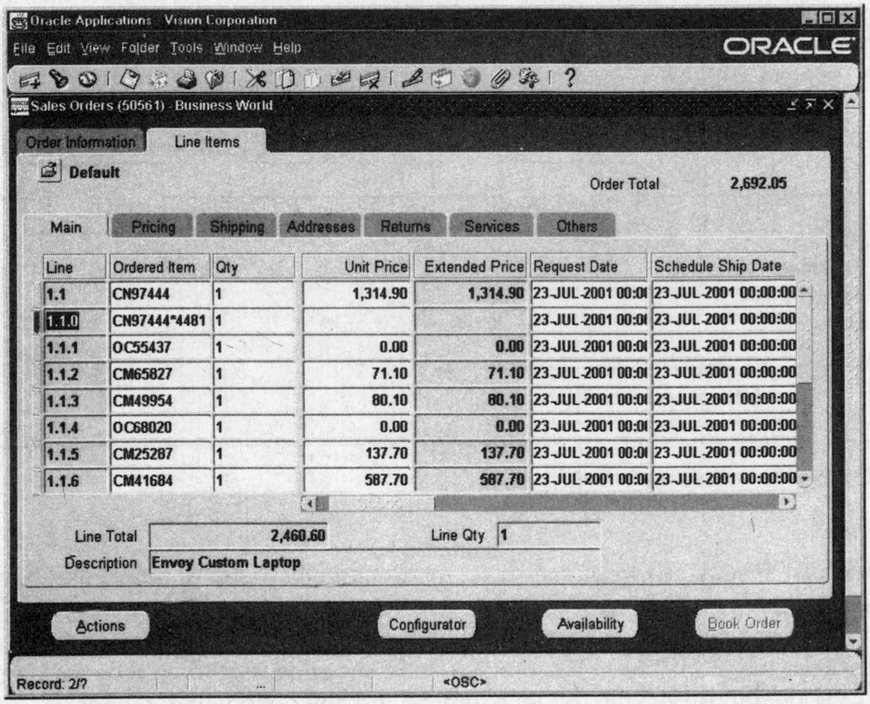

FIGURE 6-7. *Configured item in the sales order*

configuration items for a sales order. If you leave the sales order field blank, all the
eligible sales orders will be considered.

When you specify Release Offset Days, all the sales orders whose latest start
date falls within the range of today (the date on which the concurrent program is run)
and the date of (today + release offset days), adjusted for non-workdays, will be
processed. For example, let's say the scheduled shipment date is 24-DEC-2001 for an
order. The order has a configuration item ConfigItem in line 2 with a quantity of 10.
The fixed lead-time for ConfigItem is 2 days, and variable lead-time is 0.30 days.
The latest date on which this order needs to be started (or the expected release date
for final assembly) is calculated as 24-DEC-2001 - (2 + (0.30 * 10)+1), and adjusted
for non-workdays. The expected release date is 14-DEC-2001. If you run the
AutoCreate Configuration Items program on 11-DEC-2001 with a Release Offset
Days of 5 days, this sales order will be processed. If the Release Offset Days is 3
days, the sales order will not be processed. This is illustrated in Figure 6-8.

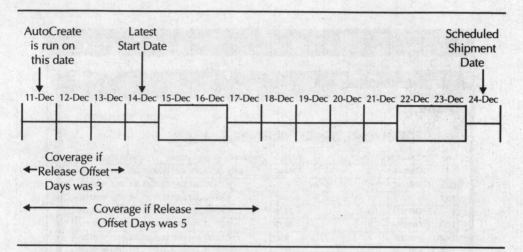

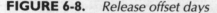

FIGURE 6-8. *Release offset days*

You can specify an Organization, in which case, all the sales orders that have the specified organization as the shipping warehouse will only be processed.

When a configuration is created, many item attributes, including lead-time, are copied from the model item. The configuration's routing is generated by picking all required operations from the model's routing and any optional operations corresponding to selected options. You need to decide if the optional operations will significantly change the configuration's lead-time from the lead-time of the model; if it will, you should calculate the item's lead-time during the auto-create process. The concurrent program will calculate the lead-times for the configuration item if the Perform Leadtime Calculation parameter is Yes. If this parameter is No, lead-times will be copied from the model. This parameter is defaulted from the profile option BOM: Perform Lead Time Calculations.

During the auto-create process, you can calculate various flow manufacturing parameters such as the Total Product Cycle Time, Yield, Net Planning %, and Operation times, by setting the parameter Perform Flow Calculation to Yes. If Perform Flow Calculation is No, these values will be copied from the model. The auto-create process performs a single level cost rollup.

As mentioned earlier, you can create configuration items from the sales order pad as well. In this case, you will create configuration items for one sales order line at a time. When you create configurations from the sales order pad, lead-times will always be calculated for the configuration item.

Characteristics of the Configuration Item

The configuration item that is created by the AutoCreate process has a BOM Item Type of Standard. The Base Model attribute points to the model item from which this configuration is created. The item attributes Customer Orders Enabled and Internal Orders Enabled are set to No.

When you view the bills of material for the configuration item, you'll see a single level flattened bill. In addition to the included items and the selected options of the model, the model itself and the chosen option classes are listed as components, as shown in Figure 6-9. This is because for configuration items, the forecast consumption logic explodes the configuration bill and consumes forecasts for the model, option classes, and options. The auto-create process replaces the sales order demand for the model, option classes, options, and mandatory components with a sales order demand for the configuration item. After this, forecast consumption first unconsumes and then reconsumes (by exploding the

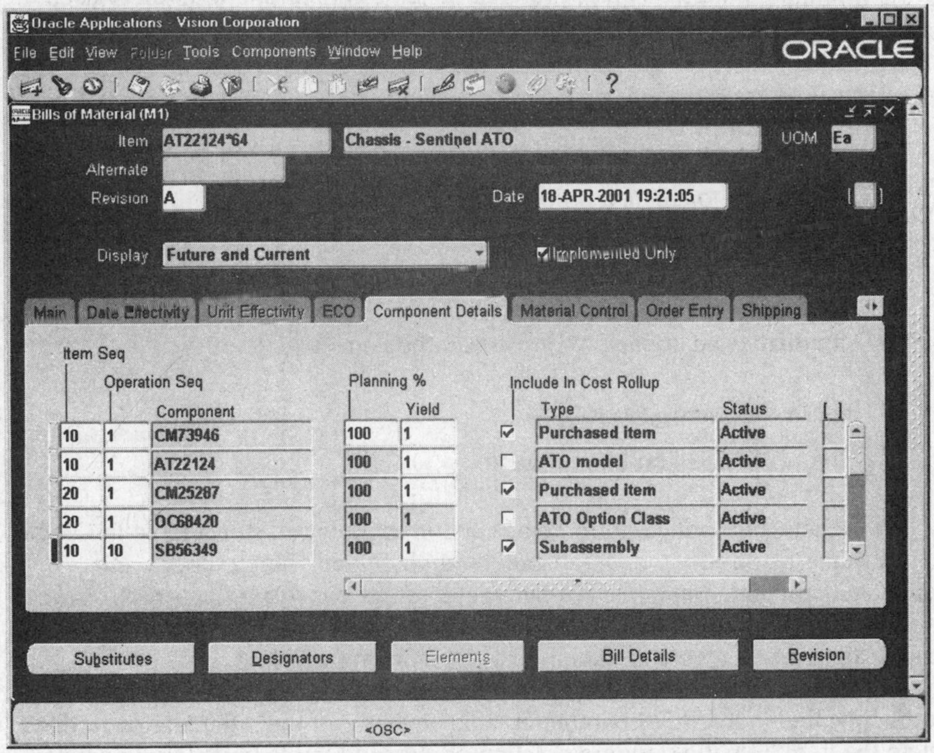

FIGURE 6-9. *Configuration item bills*

configuration bill) forecasts for the model and its components which have their Forecast Control as Consume or Consume and Derive.

The included items and the chosen options inherit the component attributes such as supply type, supply subinventory, and the locator details from the base model and option class bills. The model and option class items that are included in the configuration item bill are assigned with the supply type of phantom automatically.

A routing for the configuration item is created automatically during the AutoCreate process. Option-dependent operations are dropped if the corresponding option was not chosen. The completion subinventory and locator are derived from the base model's routing. The resources for each operation are copied from the base model routing operations.

Deactivating Configuration Items

In a high-volume configure-to-order environment, you can generate a large number of configured items, bills, and routings. Over time, you might want to deactivate your configuration items if you don't intend to use that item in the future. You do this by running the Deactivate Configuration Items concurrent program. This concurrent program will change the item status to whatever you specify in the Inactive Status field in BOM Parameters window. You can choose any one of your item statuses as your inactive status.

TIP
You might want to create a unique status to differentiate obsolete configurations from items that are obsolete for other reasons.

You can deactivate configuration items if the items are

■ Not in any open sales order

■ Not available as on-hand inventory

The Deactivate Configuration Items concurrent program is available in Oracle Bills of Material. Specify the Organization in which you want to check and deactivate configuration items as a parameter to this concurrent program. You can also specify the Shipped Number of days ago parameter, and the system will only deactivate items that were last shipped before these many days.

The deactivation process only sets the status of the configuration to the status that is specified in the BOM parameter Inactive Status of the organization; it doesn't delete the item. Use the standard deletion process in Oracle Inventory to define a group of obsolete configurations and delete them. If you have used a unique status to identify obsolete configurations, you can use it as the search criterion to populate the delete group.

Manufacturing

For configured ATO models and standard ATO items, you create final assembly orders once your sales orders are booked. Depending on the type of manufacturing method you follow, you can either create a discrete job or a flow schedule to manufacture the configured item. Although Discrete Manufacturing and Flow Manufacturing are covered in detail in Chapter 16, we are covering the features relevant to ATO in this section.

Discrete Manufacturing

You can create a discrete job automatically using the AutoCreate Final Assembly Schedule concurrent program or using the Progress Order action from the sales order pad for configured sales order lines. In these cases, a work order created for the full line quantity and is reserved to the sales order automatically.

Finally you can create a discrete job manually and include an ATO item in the job. In these cases, the jobs are not reserved to any sales order automatically. However, you can reserve them manually by navigating to the Sales Orders window that is shown in Figure 6-10, in the Discrete Jobs form.

Once a final assembly order is reserved to a sales order, you cannot make changes to the sales order without unreserving it from the WIP job. You can instruct WIP how to respond when you unreserve the WIP job from the sales order using the parameter Respond to Sales Order Changes in the WIP Parameters window. If the value is Never, there won't be any effect on the existing work orders. If the value is Always, all the work orders that are reserved by a particular sales order will be put on hold. If the value is When linked 1 to 1, the work order will be put on hold if it is the only supplying work order for a sales order (the sales order is not linked to any other work order).

When you complete the discrete job, the sales order reservation is transferred from the discrete job to the completed quantity. When you return a completed assembly back to the job, the on-hand inventory is unreserved from the sales order.

CAUTION
In the case of assembly returns, the reservation is not transferred back to the job. You have to explicitly create a reservation between the job and sales order, if necessary.

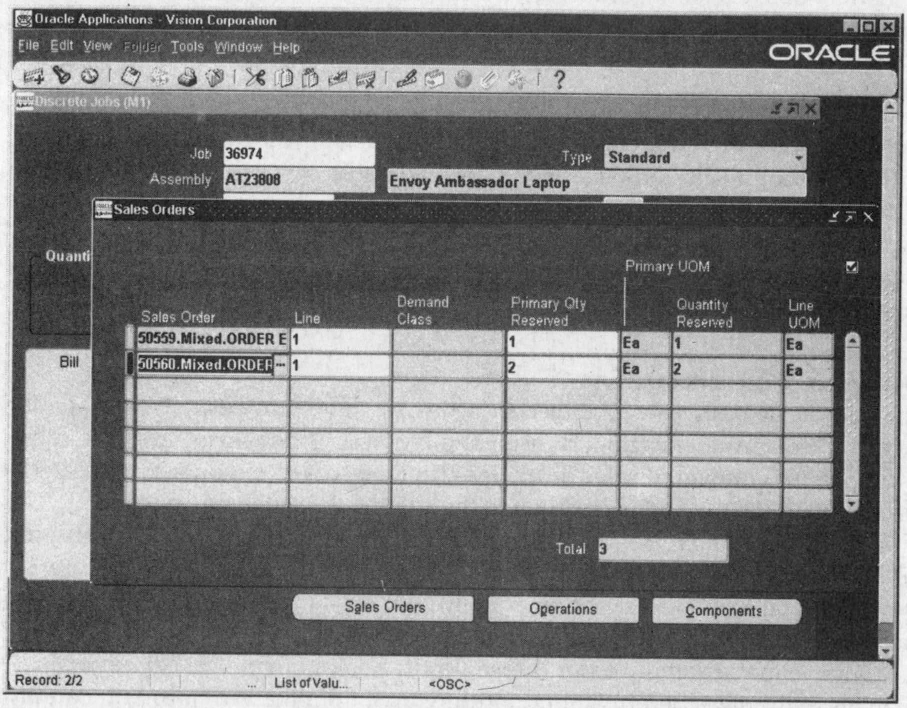

FIGURE 6-10. *Sales Order window in the Discrete Jobs form*

Flow Manufacturing

You can create a flow schedule from the Line Scheduling Workbench or using the Progress Order action from the sales order pad. In the Line Scheduling Workbench, you can create fresh flow schedules for unscheduled sales orders by selecting the Unscheduled Orders and implementing them.

Pick Releasing and Confirming Shipments

The Pick Release process releases only eligible sales order lines that meet the release criteria. However, what gets released depends on the type of the item. For ATO items, the process releases the sales order for shipment, if there's enough inventory to fulfill the quantity required by the line. The ATO item is printed on the pick slip.

For ATO models, the process doesn't release the sales order line until the finished items are received into Oracle Inventory from the job/schedule that was reserved to the sales order line. If you allow partial shipments, the pick release process releases the sales order line as and when inventory becomes available from the reserved job/schedule. If you don't allow partial shipment, the process waits until the entire line quantity is produced by the reserved job/schedule. Only the ATO configuration item is printed on the pick slip.

For PTO kits and PTO configuration items (created from a PTO model), the process explodes the kit and prints all the shippable components on the pick slip. If the item attribute Ship Model Complete is enabled, pick release will wait until the whole set of configuration components become available. Otherwise, pick release would release a partial release component, depending on availability of components.

You can confirm individual pick slips, in the Confirm Shipments form. If you want to confirm an entire batch of pick slips you can do that from the Confirm Shipment Batches window. You can view the details about your shipment in the View Orders form, from the Shipping Lines region.

The details of the Pick Release and Ship Confirm are covered in Chapter 17.

Invoicing

Although Invoicing is part of Oracle Financials, the features relevant to ATO/PTO models are briefly mentioned here for completeness. ATO/PTO items are treated just like regular items, as far as invoicing is concerned. You can create invoices for all shipped, invoiceable items using the Receivables interface.

Only order lines are invoiced—included items and mandatory standard components are not invoiced. In addition to being in an individual order line, the item attributes Invoiceable and Invoice Enabled must be enabled for the invoicing process to pick up an order line containing the item.

So, if the item attribute Invoice Enabled is not enabled for a ATO/PTO model, neither the model nor the options are invoiced. If the item attribute Invoice Enabled is enabled for an ATO/PTO model, the model and all options with the Invoice Enabled attribute enabled are invoiced, because the selected options and option classes are included as separate order lines.

All the Invoice Enabled components of a PTO kit will be invoiced (the components of a PTO kit are listed as separate order lines). Because an ATO item is ordered as it is, only the ATO item appears on the invoice to the customer.

The Oracle Configurator

Oracle Configurator is a user-friendly tool for implementing guided selling applications. The configurator has a runtime engine that is embedded in using modules such as Oracle Order Management, Oracle Sales Online, Oracle Bills of Material, etc. The runtime engine uses the model information that is available in Oracle Bills of Material, while checking for constraints/rules.

Oracle Configurator has a developer tool, which can be used by implementers or developers to develop configuration models and user interface customizations. You can test your configuration models from within Oracle Configurator Developer.

You can use Configurator Developer to create and verify configuration rules such as automatic inclusion or automatic exclusion, etc. A complete coverage of Oracle Configurator is beyond the scope of this book.

Summary

In this chapter, we discussed the detailed business flows that are applicable in Assemble To Order and Pick To Order environments. We discussed the setup for ATO/PTO including BOM parameters, items, bills and routings.

This chapter also looked at the day-to-day activities in the ATO/PTO environment in the later part of the chapter. The ongoing activities included planning, entering orders, choosing options, creating configuration items, manufacturing configured items, picking and shipping ATO/PTO items, and finally invoicing ATO/PTO items.

CHAPTER
7

Manufacturing
Engineering

anufacturing Engineering facilitates the manufacturing function. In other words, Manufacturing is the executor, whereas Manufacturing Engineering is the enabler. The relationship between Manufacturing Engineering and Manufacturing is analogous to the relationship between Marketing and Sales. Typical Manufacturing Engineering activities include designing production lines, reducing the manufacturing cycle time of existing products, manufacturing tooling, reducing setup time, improving process capability, etc. The focus for Manufacturing Engineering features in Oracle Applications has increased in recent releases, especially in the areas of flow line design. This chapter presents the theoretical background in the beginning and then describes the features in Oracle Applications that support the Manufacturing Engineering function.

Process Layout

A process layout organizes production resources by processes. The products that are being produced in the process layout are moved to the appropriate process in a predefined sequence. For example, if an automobile wheel needs to go through the grinding, plating, and painting processes, wheels will be moved to these processes one after the other in an appropriate batch size.

In Oracle Applications, you can model these processing centers or work centers as departments, and assign the individual resources to these departments in the appropriate number. These departments and resources are then included in the routings of the assemblies that need to be processed in those departments. Departments and Resources are covered in Chapter 4.

Product Layout

A product layout organizes production resources by the production sequence of a family of products. The resources are organized in such a way that all the products that are being produced follow a flow pattern before reaching the final state. Generally, it is not very economical to have a product layout for just one product—so typically, a product layout is designed for a family of products.

In Oracle Applications, you can model a product layout as a repetitive production line or a flow line. Repetitive lines can be defined using the Production Lines form. Although there are many features in planning and manufacturing execution that support repetitive manufacturing, there aren't many manufacturing engineering features. The bulk of the manufacturing engineering features that Oracle provides deals with designing lines for flow manufacturing; it is flow line design that is the focus of this chapter.

Line Layout

A flow line is a collection of machines and/or assembly workstations. The resources in a line are arranged to address one or more constraints—for example, distance traveled by the product or the space occupied by the machines. Some lines might be U-shaped, whereas another might be organized as a straight line to satisfy these constraints.

Final Assembly Line

A final assembly line produces the assembly that is shipped to the customer. The demand for the final assembly is independent in nature. In a pull-based system, the final assembly line is communicated with the change in demand scenarios. The final assembly line reacts to this change, whereas the feeder lines and the replenishment processes react to the change in requirement from the final assembly line.

Feeder Lines

A final assembly line can potentially have many feeder lines. Although there is not much difference in the way they are designed, feeder lines produce subassemblies or components that continuously feed the final assembly line that produces the final product at the required rate and time.

In Oracle Applications, there are two types of feeder lines, attached and detached. An attached feeder line produces first level components or phantom items. A detached feeder produces subassemblies that have second-level BOM on the parent assembly.

Product Synchronization

Product synchronization shows the relationship between the individual production processes that produce a product. This final assembly line forms the trunk of this tree diagram, while the various feeding lines connect to this final assembly line at various points of the tree. In the world of flow manufacturing, a finished assembly is viewed as a pile of parts and a sequence of steps. Establishing the product synchronization enables you to get a high-level view of the manufacturing process flow and is one of the very first steps in designing a line.

Line Design Process and Factors

Each production line is unique. Even within a production line, one product might undergo a significantly different set of operations from another product. Yet, it is possible to follow a standard set of steps in building a highly flexible and responsive line. Figure 7-1 outlines these high-level steps. The rest of the chapter talks about

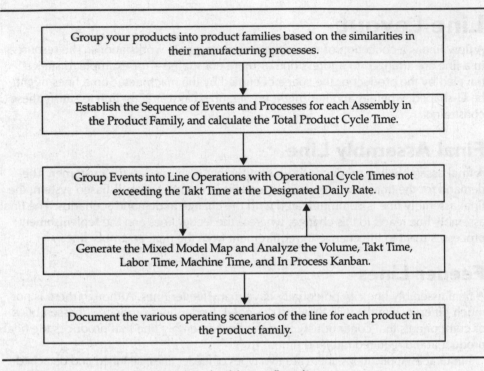

Group your products into product families based on the similarities in their manufacturing processes.

Establish the Sequence of Events and Processes for each Assembly in the Product Family, and calculate the Total Product Cycle Time.

Group Events into Line Operations with Operational Cycle Times not exceeding the Takt Time at the Designated Daily Rate.

Generate the Mixed Model Map and Analyze the Volume, Takt Time, Labor Time, Machine Time, and In Process Kanban.

Document the various operating scenarios of the line for each product in the product family.

FIGURE 7-1.   *High-level steps in building a flow line*

these steps in detail and explains the various features within Oracle Applications that can be applied at these steps.

The first step in building your line is to identify the set of products that can be potentially produced by this line. Product families were covered in detail in Chapter 4. When you have identified your product families and the individual products within each product family, define all the process steps and events for each product. You can also calculate the approximate total product cycle time (covered in the section "Total Product Cycle Time") after you define the various processes for each product.

Define a set of events from the manufacturing viewpoint and group them into line operations in such a way that the operation cycle time doesn't exceed the takt time (covered in the section "Takt Time"), at the designed daily rate (covered in the section "Designed Daily Rate") of the product. As a rule of thumb, you can calculate the minimum number of line operations before you proceed with the design process (the formula is presented in the section "Number of Line Operations"). While establishing the sequence of events, the thought process should follow the natural flow of the product. But also keep in mind that it's important to look at the flow creatively to gain maximum benefit. For example, one auto manufacturer reportedly installs one tail light at one point on the line, and the other much farther downstream—the movement of that unit of work (installing one tail light) was found to produce a better balanced line than installing both at the same time.

After defining an approximate grouping, generate the mixed model map and analyze the output (mixed model map is covered in section "Mixed Model Map"). Continue to regroup the work events until the desired results are achieved. When you are satisfied with the results, you have to document the different output levels of the line for each product within the product family and the number of labor resources that are required in each of those scenarios.

Before delving deep into the line design process, let us examine some of the important factors that have an impact on the line design process. Some of these factors are not calculated by Oracle Applications currently. They are mentioned here because they have a great deal of influence to the line design process.

Designed Daily Rate

The Designed Daily Rate (DDR) represents the designed capacity of a line. DDR represents the maximum output levels of the line at any time. It is very hard to operate at an output level that is higher than the DDR for an extended period of time. DDR is calculated using this formula:

$$\text{Designed Daily Rate} = \frac{\text{Targeted Monthly Volume}}{\text{Workdays per Month}}$$

The DDR is part of the contract that is established between Marketing and Manufacturing. Currently, the DDR for each product has to be calculated manually.

Flow Rate

Flow Rate represents the rate at which production should progress on an hourly basis. Flow rate can be calculated using this formula:

$$\text{Flow Rate} = \frac{\text{Designed Daily Rate}}{\text{(Effective work hours per shift) X (\# of shifts)}}$$

The effective work hours are the shift work time that is adjusted for allowances, such as breaks, maintenance, or efficiency. Flow rates are useful in line design as well as monitoring line performance on an hourly basis. Currently, the flow rate for each product has to be calculated manually.

Takt Time

Takt is a German word that implies "drumbeat" or "rhythm." In the context of flow manufacturing, Takt Time represents the ideal time for each operation during the production of a product. The line (and each operation) must complete one assembly when one unit of takt time elapses to satisfy the market requirements; if each operation takes exactly the takt time, the line will be perfectly balanced. If some operations take longer than the takt time, you'll be building bottlenecks; if some operations take less than the takt time, you won't be fully utilizing those resources.

Takt time is the inverse of flow rate multiplied by 60 to get the time in minutes. Takt time can be calculated directly using this formula:

$$\text{Takt Time} = \frac{(\text{Effective work hours per shift}) \times (\# \text{ of shifts}) \times 60}{\text{Designed Daily Rate}}$$

The Mixed Model Map calculates takt time for a group of products, using this formula:

$$\text{Takt Time of a Component} = \frac{(\text{Effective work hours per shift}) \times (\# \text{ of shifts}) \times 60}{(\text{Designed Daily Rate of Assembly}) \times (\text{Component Quantity})}$$

In principle, the takt time represents the targeted work content time at each line operation. So, the work events are grouped into line operations that are approximately equal to the takt time, but should never exceed the takt time. Note that this is the takt time at the DDR. If you operate at a rate that is lower than the DDR, your takt time will increase.

Number of Line Operations

When you have the takt time and the work content, you can calculate the approximate number of line operations that are required in order to meet the daily demand using this formula:

$$\# \text{ of Line Operations} = \text{Round Up} \left[\frac{\text{Work Content}}{\text{Takt Time}} \right]$$

The # of line operations gives you an idea as to how many workstations might be required in the line. For example, if the manufacturing lead-time is 120 minutes, and if the takt time at the designed daily rate is 6.7 minutes, the number of line operations is approximately 18. Currently, the number of operations has to be calculated manually.

Operation Times

The operation times can be calculated for the events, processes, and line operations that are available in your flow routings. The operation time calculations are based on the resources that are available in each of the events.

The calculated labor time for an event is the sum of scheduled and unscheduled labor usage rates in the event. The calculated labor time for a process or a line operation is the sum of the calculated labor times of all the events that form the process or line operation. Events with a lot basis will temporarily be converted to item basis for this calculation. The calculated machine time is similar to calculated labor times, except that the system includes the scheduled and unscheduled machine times in the calculation.

The calculated elapsed time for each event is the sum of the non-overlapping scheduled labor and machine usage rates for each event. The calculated elapsed time for a process or a line operation is the sum of the elapsed times of all the events that form the process or line operation.

The resources that will be included in these three lead-time calculations are illustrated by Figure 7-2 (resource type of L indicates labor resource and M indicates machine resource).

NOTE
Elapsed time will not include scheduled resources that overlap with other scheduled resources. For example, if you have an operator who spends 1.5 minutes of scheduled time in an event, which also has a machine that runs for 4 minutes after the operator, the elapsed time for the event is 5.5 minutes. On the other hand, if the machine doesn't have to wait for the operator, the elapsed time would be 4 minutes.

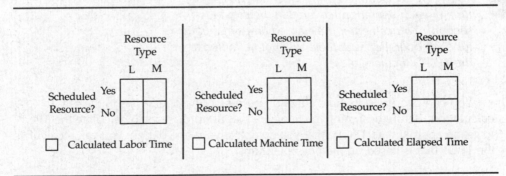

FIGURE 7-2. *Resources that are included in Operation Time calculations*

To calculate the operation times for an assembly, choose Tools | Calculate Operation Times.

Total Product Cycle Time

When you design an item, you identify the steps in manufacturing the item as processes in the flow routing. The processes in turn are a collection of events. Using these processes, you can calculate the Total Product Cycle Time (TPCT) of an item. The TPCT is the longest lead-time through the production process, considering all the feeder lines.

If you create subassemblies on a detached feeder line (standard subassemblies in the second level of a BOM), you would use feeder line sync and perform a work order-less completion at the end of that line. This is covered in detail in Chapter 16. The work content on the feeder line would not be part of the TPCT for the final assembly.

An attached feeder line (single level on the BOM or a second-level phantom) is counted in the TPCT. This is illustrated by the example in Figure 7-3. The feeder's feeding operations 10 and 30 are attached feeders and will be included in the TPCT calculation of the assembly, whereas the feeder that feeds operation 20 is a detached feeder and will not be included in the TPCT calculation.

The system always calculates TPCT from the back. For example, in Figure 7-3 the two paths that will be considered for TPCT calculations are 40-30-301-302-303-304 (Path #1) and 40-30-20-10-101-102-103 (Path #2). The path 40-30-20-DF30-DF20-DF10 will not be considered since that path includes a detached feeder line. The lead-time for Path #1 is 140 minutes, and the lead-time for Path #2 is 120 minutes. So the TPCT for the assembly is 140 minutes.

To calculate TPCT for an assembly, choose Tools | Calculate Total Cycle Time. Alternatively, you can enter a Total Cycle Time manually as well.

CAUTION
The TPCT is calculated using the rolled up elapsed time of each operation (covered in the previous section). You can enter the elapsed times manually for each operation, but these will not be included in the TPCT calculation.

You can choose to include either processes or line operations in the TPCT calculation. Before designing the line, you can use processes to calculate the TPCT to get an approximate TPCT. After you complete your line design, you can recalculate the TPCT that is based on the line operations.

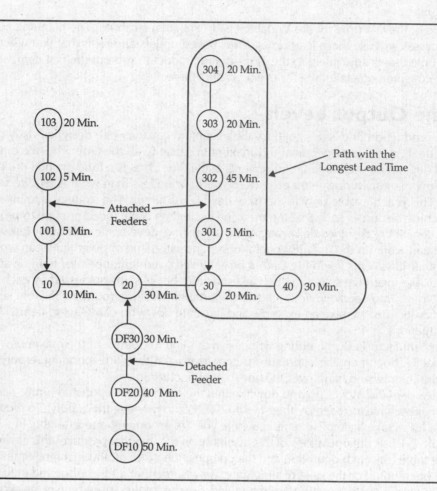

FIGURE 7-3. *TPCT calculation with attached and detached feeders*

 NOTE
When you make changes to your flow routing by adding or removing events, processes, and line operations, the lead times and total cycle time are not recalculated automatically. You have to use Tools | Calculate Total Cycle Time and Tools | Calculate Operation Times to recalculate these times.

After you calculate the TPCT in the flow routing and the Takt Time in the mixed model map, set the value of TPCT for the Fixed Lead Time item attribute and the value of the takt time for the Variable Lead Time item attribute. The planning processes will use these lead-times. The implied understanding is that you will take the time that is equivalent to the TPCT of the product to roll out the first item, and it will consume one takt time for every product thereafter.

Line Output Levels

The production line is designed for the maximum capacity (the designed daily rate). But the line will not operate at this maximum capacity all the time. The line output will depend on the market requirements at the time. This is a fundamental principle of flow manufacturing—you produce no more or no less than what is required.

This is achievable only if you have flexible resources. The strategy is to invest in machine resources such that the machine cycle time is balanced enough to produce the item at the designed daily rate. At the same time, develop flexible labor resources that can work on the different operations in the same line or potentially can work in other lines. This flexibility cannot be achieved overnight; operator training and a flexible incentive system (which takes the number of skills possessed by each employee into consideration) are two important means in producing flexible labor. In this section, we take an example and illustrate how you can react to demand fluctuations.

Manufacturing Engineering will design the line to operate at the maximum capacity, document the alternative output levels and the corresponding resource requirements, and hand over the line to manufacturing.

As demand moves up and down within the previously negotiated limits, line managers have to redeploy their labor resources to manage the supply. To illustrate this, let us take a simple example, where you are producing one assembly in a line. Table 7-1 lists the operations of this assembly on the line that produces this assembly. The table lists each operation and the composition of labor and machine time in the operation. For the sake of simplicity, we assume that all the labor and machine resources in each operation are scheduled. So, the total elapsed time is the sum of the labor and machine times. With this background, let us investigate two demand scenarios with which this line might be operated.

Scenario 1

In this scenario, the line is required to produce 260 assemblies per day. The takt time for this output level is 5.54 minutes. Figure 7-4 shows one possible way of deploying your labor resources to achieve this level of output. The first resource handles operations 10, 20, and 30; the second resource handles operations 40, 50, and 60; the third resource handles operations 70, 80, 90, and 100; and the fourth resource handles operations 110, 120, and 130.

To analyze the output levels of this line, you need to consider two factors—the operational cycle time for each operation and the load on each labor resource. If

Op Seq.	Scheduled Labor Time	Scheduled Machine Time	Operational Cycle Time (Total Elapsed Time)
10	1.4	4.0	5.4
20	1.5	3.9	5.4
30	1.5	3.8	5.3
40	1.5	4.2	5.7
50	1.5	3.6	5.1
60	1.3	4.0	5.3
70	0.8	3.5	4.3
80	1.5	4.0	5.5
90	0.9	4.0	4.9
100	1.5	3.8	5.3
110	1.4	4.0	5.4
120	1.5	3.6	5.1
130	1.5	4.0	5.5

TABLE 7-1. *Summary of Line Operation Times for the Example*

you quickly skim through the operational cycle time column in Table 7-1 and the total time taken by each labor resource in Table 7-2, you'll notice that except operation 40, all the times are either equal to or less than the line takt time. To balance this line, you might place some in process kanbans after operation 40 to act as a buffer between operations 40 and 50. With this configuration, the line can deliver approximately 262 assemblies per day under normal operating conditions.

Scenario 2

In this scenario, you are required to produce 240 assemblies per day. That works out to a takt time of 6 minutes. Figure 7-5 shows one possible way of deploying your labor resources to achieve this level of output. Note that this layout only uses three labor resources as compared with the layout in Figure 7-4, which uses four labor resources. The first resource handles operations 10, 20, 120, and 130; the second resource handles operations 30, 40, 100, and 110; and the third resource handles operations 50, 60, 70, 80, and 90. In this scenario, the labor resources are flexed

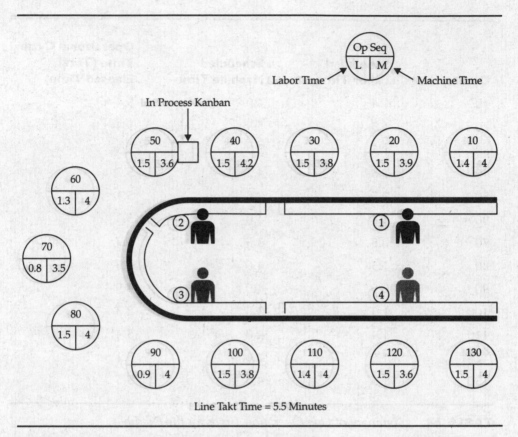

FIGURE 7-4. *The Line operated with four persons*

Labor Resource	Number of Operations Covered	Total Time per Assembly
1	3	4.4 minutes
2	3	4.3 minutes
3	4	4.7 minutes
4	3	4.4 minutes

TABLE 7-2. *Labor Resource Deployment Details for Scenario 1*

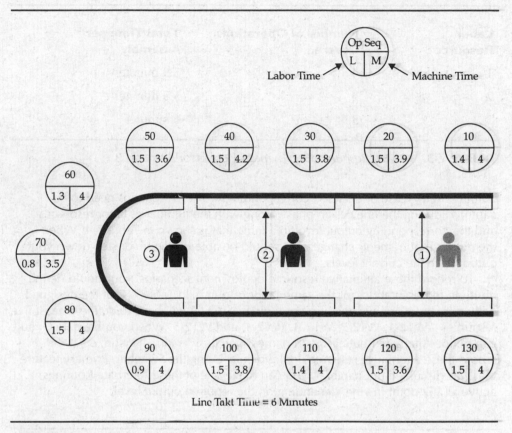

FIGURE 7-5. *The Line operated with three persons*

across a higher number of operations and this might involve additional fatigue. This fatigue will have to be factored into the operation cycle times appropriately.

On quickly skimming through the operational cycle time column in Table 7-1 and the total time taken by each labor resource in Table 7-3, you'll notice all the times are either equal to or less than the line takt time. With this configuration, the line can deliver approximately 240 assemblies per day under normal operating conditions. Also note that the in process kanban after operation 40 is no longer necessary, since the operation cycle time is now less than the takt time.

The mixed model map (covered in the section "Mixed Model Map") provides you with the capability to analyze the operation times and identify the bottleneck operations; it also calculates the in process kanban that is needed as a buffer. The actual resource deployment is not known at the time of designing the line. As you increase or decrease the number of labor resources deployed in the line, the line

Labor Resource	Number of Operations Covered	Total Time per Assembly
1	4	5.9 minutes
2	4	5.9 minutes
3	5	6 minutes

TABLE 7-3. *Labor Resource Deployment Details for Scenario 2*

output will increase or decrease correspondingly. These scenarios need to be captured during the line design phase along with the number of labor resources and the corresponding output level in a table that is shown in Table 7-4. When the output requirements change, you should be able to step up or step down your output from the current levels.

To record these alternative resource deployment scenarios, you should define multiple representations for the same labor resource. In Table 7-4, at the designed daily rate, there are five operation groupings. So, you will have to define at least five resources—W12-1, W12-2, W12-3, W12-4, and W12-5. When you have this, you can define Alternate Routings, with names such as 5Person, 4Person, etc., and record these alternative resource deployments. Using the Switch to Primary feature that was discussed in Chapter 4, you can make one of these Alternate Routings active at any point in time, depending on the required output level.

Scenario	Output Level	Resource W12-1	Resource W12-2	Resource W12-3	Resource W12-4	Resource W12-5
1	300	10, 20	30, 40	50	60, 70	80, 90
2	260	10, 20, 30	40, 50	60, 70, 80	80, 90	
3	220	10, 20, 30, 40	50, 60	70, 80, 90		
4	150	10, 20, 30, 40	50, 60, 70 80, 90			

TABLE 7-4. *Labor Resource Deployment Scenarios*

NOTE
The multiple representation of the same labor resource need not be product or line specific. For example, W12-1...W12-5 can be used in other products that are produced in other lines as well.

Using the line designer (covered in the section "Graphical Line Designer") and the mixed model map, you can create alternative scenarios that meet the two important objectives of a flow line—to achieve a takt time for an output level that is equal to the designed daily rate and to design the operations in such a way that you can change the output levels easily by flexing your labor resources.

Designing Lines

A highly responsive line should be designed after taking the peak demand into consideration. The designed daily rate thus represents the peak demand that is agreed to by everyone. Although the line is designed for this peak demand, the line is not required to operate at this peak demand. Typically, the line can operate anywhere between the peak capacity and 50 percent of this peak capacity, by flexing the resources. In certain cases, the line might be flexible enough to operate at significantly lower capacities, but it might not make economical sense to operate a line at these levels for long. During the line design process, you will have to consider these alternative capacity scenarios and plan alternative resource deployments. For example, if you operate the line with five labor resources, you might be able to achieve a flow rate of 20 per hour, whereas if you use four labor resources, you might achieve 15–17 per hour. These different scenarios can be modeled as Alternate Routings during the line design phase. With sufficient notice, manufacturing can step up or step down the line output. In this section, we discuss the features in Oracle Applications that can be used for designing and balancing your flow lines.

Defining Flow Lines

You define flow lines in the Lines window, which is shown in Figure 7-6. Name the line and specify the line start time and stop time to indicate the hours of operation of the line. For 24-hour lines, set the stop time equal to the start time. Set the line lead-time as routing based, so that the line lead-time can be dynamically calculated based on the product routings.

The Maximum Hourly Rate and Minimum Hourly Rate enable you to specify the boundary conditions for the line. The maximum hourly rate is equal to the designed daily rate divided by the effective hours of operation of the line, if the line produces only one product.

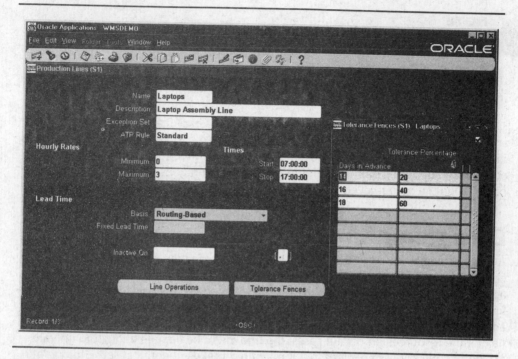

FIGURE 7-6. *Define flow lines and specify flex fences*

The minimum hourly rate can be equal to 0, although that might not be economical in reality. If the line produces more than one product, you should estimate the rates for the line considering the demand for all the products.

Tolerance Fences

Marketing and Manufacturing establish an agreement that details the extent to which manufacturing can either step up or step down their output levels and the amount of notice (in terms of days) for the change in output level. This agreement is represented as tolerance fences in Oracle Applications. Tolerance fences provide the marketing team with the flexibility to quickly respond to customer demand fluctuations. If the line produces more than one product, you should estimate the tolerance fence for the line considering the demand for all the products.

You can specify these tolerance fences in the Tolerance Fences window that you can access by clicking the Tolerance Fences button in the Production Lines form. The scheduling tool will use the flex fences to consider excess demand, based on dates and the corresponding expanded capacity. For example, you can go over 20 pecent of the standard capacity with 15 days notice.

Graphical Line Designer

The Graphical Line Designer enables you to visually design a flow line. You can add standard operations, processes, and events to an item's routing by dragging and dropping the appropriate icons. The designer consists of two panes—the tree hierarchy pane and the graphical network pane, as shown in Figure 7-7.

The Tree Hierarchy Pane

The tree hierarchy pane (left pane) enables you to switch between two views—Item Routings view and Template Routings view using the tree tabs on the left side of the pane. The Item Routings tab displays all the items that are associated with the line. The Template Routings tab displays all the product families that can be used as a template for creating new routings.

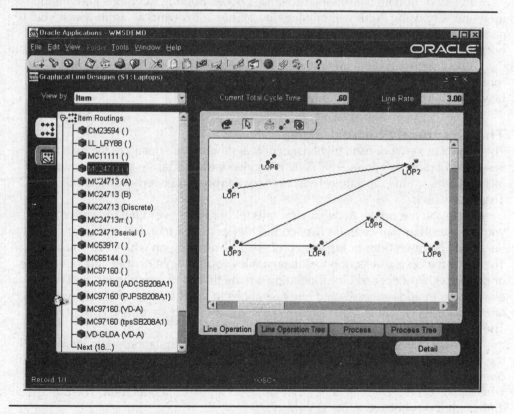

FIGURE 7-7. *Design lines using the drag and drop of features of the Graphical Line Designer*

When the graphical line designer is first brought up, the Item Routing tree tab is selected on the left pane and the tree is collapsed. When you select an item on the left pane, you will see a graphical network of line operations on the graphical network pane (covered in the next section). The View by drop-down list enables you to view the line items either as a list or as a list that is organized by product family.

Select the top-level node Item Routings and press the right mouse button on the node. Choose New from the pop-up menu to create a new routing. This will bring up the Add Item Routing window. From this window, you can create a new routing, copy the routing from another item or a template, or assign a common routing for this item.

If you want to access the routing details of an item, navigate to that item and press the right mouse button. Choose Routing Details from the pop-up menu to bring up the Routing Details window. From here, you can view or update the routing information.

To view or update the routing revisions, choose Routing Revisions from the pop-up menu. Choosing Items will bring up the Master Items window, from which you can define new items. You can also view the bills or indented bills of the selected node by choosing the appropriate menu option.

If you are on an Alternate routing in the tree navigator, you can make that routing the Primary routing by choosing Tools | Switch to Primary. Switching between alternates and primary was covered in Chapter 4.

The Graphical Network Pane

The graphical network pane (right pane) displays the routing details of the item that is selected on the left pane. This pane is divided into four tabs—Line Operation (network view), Line Operation Tree (tree view), Process (network view), and Process Tree (tree view).

When you are on the network view tabs (either Process or Line Operation), you see a toolbar that contains five icons. The Connector icon lets you create links between line operations or between processes, depending on which tab you are in. The second icon is a selection tool that enables you to move existing line operations or processes. Process and Line Operation are the third and fourth icons, and they enable you to add processes and line operations in the Process and Line Operation tabs, respectively. These icons will be enabled only if you are on the correct tab. The fifth icon enables you to add events to the routing.

To create a line operation, process, or event, choose the appropriate icon in the toolbar and click on the graphical network canvas. If you have selected the operations icon, clicking on the canvas will bring up the Line Operation window, where you can either create a new one or select an existing operation. The process and event icons behave in the same way.

To define a network connection, select the Connections icon. Click the first operation or process and drag onto the target operation or process to create a network connection between them. This will bring up the Network Connection window, where you can identify the Transition Type and the Planning Percent. The possible values for transition type are Primary, Alternate, and Rework. The planning percent is the percentage of product that follows this network path.

When you are on the Tree View tabs (Line Operation Tree and Process Tree), you see another toolbar that has four icons and two drop-down menus. The first three icons enable you to view the line operations/processes in three tree styles—Vertical style, Organizational Chart style, and Interleaved style. The fourth icon toggles the view of the event/line operation/process times in the tree view. The first pull-down menu enables you to switch between viewing system calculated operation times and user entered operation times. The second pull-down menu enables you to view the current, future and current, or all events on the routing.

When you are on the tree views, the last node will be named as Un Assigned Events. This node will enable you to access all the events that are available in the routing, but haven't been assigned to any process or line operation in the routing.

You can explode the nodes of a tree and assign events to each process or line operation by dragging and dropping events from the Un Assigned Events node. This feature is useful during line design. Potentially, you will have to iterate between generating the mixed model map and dragging and dropping events between line operations several times.

On the graphical network pane, you can right-click any of the icons (in the network views) or any of the nodes (in the tree views), which will bring up a pop-up menu with five choices: Cut, Paste, Delete, Properties, and Standard. Cut enables you to remove an operation, process, event, or connection and store this information on the clipboard. Paste enables you to paste an icon that has been previously put in the clipboard. Delete permanently removes an operation, process, event, and the associated connections. The Properties menu takes you to the details window of the relevant operation, process, or event. Standard enables you to access the Standard Line Operations, Standard Processes, or Standard Events window, depending on the type of icon on which you're right-clicking.

While designing lines, you will try out various combinations of resources and events to achieve your design objectives. When you change the operation compositions, you generate the mixed model map and review the composition of each operation in terms of the machine and labor time and the total time. You can generate the mixed model map from the line designer using Tools | Mixed Model Map.

Mixed Model Map

The Mixed Model Map (MMM) is a powerful tool that can help you in identifying imbalance problems. The MMM takes a form of demand and a product mix and provides you with a recommendation for smoothing your line operations or processes.

Mixed Model Map Parameters

To generate the MMM, you provide a demand source which can be one of four demand types—Forecast, Master Demand Schedule, Master Production Schedule, or Flow Schedule. You also optionally provide the product family that will be produced by this line; this will restrict the calculations to only the specified product family in the demand stream and is useful if your demand includes products not produced on the designated line. Specify the start date and end date of the demand period. The Demand Days will be calculated as the difference between the start date and end date. The effective work hours per day can be specified in the Hours per Day field. Use the boost percentage to increase or decrease your demand during the MMM generation.

The MMM can be generated either for line operations or processes. The output can be sorted by the Display Sequence or the Operation/Process Code using the Sort Order field. You can choose to include either the rolled up time or the manually entered time in the MMM calculations. The process can recommend the in process kanban either for the process/operation or for each machine. Specify the IPK recommendation level using the IPK Value field. The Time UOM enables you to view the time information in the map in hours, minutes, or seconds. When you specify the appropriate values in the MMM parameters form, press the Generate button to generate the MMM output.

Mixed Model Map Output

This MMM generation process takes these inputs and identifies the total demand for all the products in the family. For this total demand, the resources required for each of the line operation is calculated. Additionally, the process also calculates the in process inventory that is required to keep the line in balance. Figure 7-8 shows a mixed model map output.

Resource Recommendations

The MMM calculates the process volume for each operation/process. This is the number of units that will pass through the operation or process. For example, an operation that is used by only some products on the line will have a lower process volume than an operation that is used by all products; an operation that is repeated in rework loop will have a higher process volume than one that is not repeated. The MMM uses this process volume to weight the operation times that were covered earlier to calculate the three weighted times—Machine Weighted Time (MWT), Labor Weighted Time (LWT), and Elapsed Weighted Time (EWT). The machines and labor that are needed at each operation or process are calculated by dividing the MWT and LWT, respectively, by the operation takt time.

The machines and labor assigned in each operation are the total number of resources in the department that the events are assigned to. For example, an operation LO1

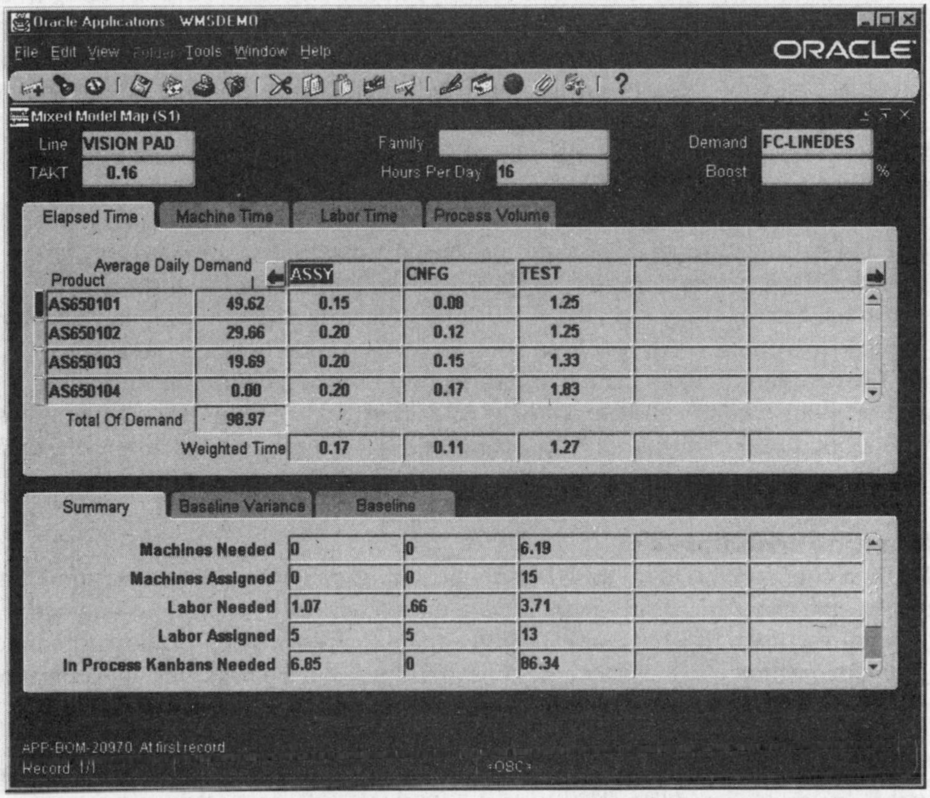

FIGURE 7-8. *Generate mixed model map for the line and compare it with the baseline*

comprises events E1 and E2. E1 uses a machine resource called M1 from department D1, and E2 uses a machine resource called M2 from department D2. D1 contains four M1s, whereas D2 contains five M2s. The machines assigned for LO1 will be the sum of M1s and M2s in departments D1 and D2—in this case, 9.

CAUTION

If the same resource (machine or labor) is used in multiple events, the assigned resources will be overstated. In the previous example, if E2 also used the machine resource M1 from department D1, the machines assigned for LO1 would have been 8.

The in process kanbans needed at each operation depend on the extent by which the EWT of the operation exceeds the line takt time. For example, if the line takt time is 6 minutes and the EWT is 8 minutes for an operation, the amount of inventory that is required after this operation is approximately 25 percent of the day's requirement.

Takt time for assigned (ATAKT) gives you an idea as to how much time will a process / line operation consume if it utilizes all the assigned resources. ATAKT is equal to the EWT divided by the number of people assigned to the operation.

Because absolute synchronization between all the operations is not likely, the next step is to identify the operations that cause line imbalances and solve the imbalance problem. The first time you generate the MMM, the likelihood of seeing fractional resource requirements in every operation is very high. As already noted, line balancing is an iterative process. In MMM, you have a tool, with which you can iterate faster.

The first steps in reducing the imbalances is to regroup your events using the graphical line designer and generate the MMM again. When you reach a point where further optimization might not be practical, you have a few alternatives in solving the remaining problems, depending on the type of resource—machine or labor.

Machine Imbalances

The first alternative is to try to reduce the machine cycle time at the operation that is causing the imbalance. You might reduce the cycle time using various engineering techniques, or you might be able to shift certain processing steps to downstream or upstream machines. In the latter case, you would regroup the respective line operations with the new set of events using the line designer.

The second option is to invest in new machines that can meet the additional requirements, although they give rise to questions on where will they be positioned in the line and the additional space requirements before going through a rigorous capital expenditure review process.

The third option is to build in process inventory after the constrained resource called *In Process Kanbans* (IPKs) by operating the constrained resource for extra time or shifts.

Labor Imbalances

Labor imbalances can be adjusted by moving some of the labor-intensive events to downstream or upstream operations. In cases where this is not possible, you have to build IPKs by overtime operations of the constrained labor resource or hire additional resources and increase the resource count in the appropriate department.

Another option is to evaluate converting the labor time to machine time if possible.

Operating with Baselines

When you generate the MMM, you can save the results as a baseline for future comparison. You can have one saved baseline for each line or product family combination. To save the generated map as a baseline, choose Tools | Save as Baseline. To query a saved baseline for comparison, choose Tools | View Baseline.

Operational Method Sheets

A standard operation within Oracle Applications typically contains all the events that would be available in the operational method sheet(s) for the operation. Create an operational method sheet for each of the line operations and attach the method sheet as an attachment to the line operation.

In operations involving multiple events, each of the individual pages within the operational method sheet typically corresponds to an event. In such cases, you can attach the page(s) to the corresponding event. Figure 7-9 shows a sample operational method sheet.

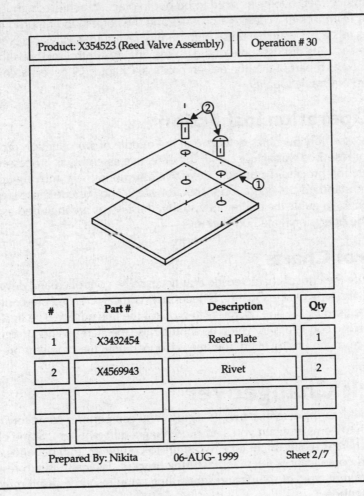

FIGURE 7-9. *Operational method sheets*

NOTE
Operational Method Sheet is also referred to as Operation Standard or Standard Operation in some manufacturing text books. In Oracle Applications, standard operation is different from the operational method sheets.

Building Quality into the Process

It takes a lot of effort to produce quality parts all the time. Stringent quality control and assurance methodologies need to be put in place to achieve high levels of quality. It is important to design a product and the corresponding production processes in such a way that these high quality levels are easily achieved. The following sections discuss some of the online quality control methods that can be designed as a part of the line design process. Chapter 19 covers a complete discussion of Oracle Quality.

Pre-Operation Inspection

When an assembly becomes defective in the middle of a production process, significant resource wastage occurs if the defective assembly is processed farther in the production process. To prevent defective assemblies from moving upstream, you can define standard pre-operation inspection steps and include these steps in your work events. To guide the operators visually, these steps are included as inspection steps in the operational method sheets.

Control Charts

You identify the critical characteristic that needs to be controlled and develop a control chart using Oracle Quality. If necessary, you can create a pre-control chart that can be used by the line operators to monitor the line quality. The line operator is advised on the conditions in which he should raise the alarm. When irregularities are identified from the control chart, the line is stopped until the problems are corrected.

Quick Changeover

Most manufacturing activities involve setup. You can perform some form of setup for a batch of items or when you start producing a different item. Some changeovers are fast, whereas others might take two shifts to complete. It all depends on the nature and complexity of the manufacturing process. Typically, setup resources handle different types of setups and scheduling setup resources itself might require special attention.

From Setup Type	To Setup Type	Penalty
Setup Step 1	Setup Step 2	0
Setup Step 2	Setup Step 3	0
Setup Step 2	Setup Step 1	4 (Some waste)
Setup Step 3	Setup Step 1	10 (Worst)

TABLE 7-5. *An Example of Resource Sequence Relationships*

When you define a resource (Resource was covered in Chapter 4), you can assign various setup types to the resource. This feature is available as a part of Manufacturing Scheduling. When you identify the setup types for a resource, you can establish the resource sequence relationships and the penalties associated with each sequence as illustrated in Table 7-5.

Line Performance

When a line is laid out, the line performance must be at an acceptable level to justify the investment. Even after laying out a flow line, if a line doesn't produce to demand, it's only as good as a highly efficient process layout. Flow lines should produce what is required of them—both on an hourly basis and over a period of time. The two important factors that gauge the health of a flow line are Line Flow Rate and Line Linearity. Line Flow Rate is used to gauge the hourly performance of a line, whereas Line Linearity is used to gauge the performance of a line over a period of time.

Line Flow Rate

Line Flow Rate is monitored by comparing the actual line output per hour against the planned output per hour. Currently there is no standard report that does this for you, but a custom report that plots the actual completions in an hour against the planned completions will be very useful and not hard to build. You can have a standard display board in each of your lines (the important ones that you want to monitor) that will display the flow rate in the form similar to the one that is shown in Figure 7-10.

Line Linearity

Comparing the planned production to the actual production at the end of the production period conceals most of the problems. For example, let's say that your line is supposed to produce 10 widgets everyday and the actual production is 5, 6,

Reed Valve Line										Total
Hour	1	2	3	4	5	6	7	8	9	9
Flow Rate	23	23	23	23	23	23	23	23	23	207
Actual Rate	22	23	9	14	22	23	23	23	23	182

Cell Leader - Sam Edwin   Date: 7-JUN-2001   Shift #: 2

FIGURE 7-10.   *Monitoring Line Flow Rate*

6, 7, 7, 13, 13, 14, 16, 13. The difference between planned and actual production on each of these days is –5, -4, -4, -3, -3, 3, 3, 4, 6, 3, which represents the deviation from plan. At the end of the 10-day period, if you measure the total deviation by summing up these deviations, you will get a value of 0. This might appear to indicate that the line performed quite well during the period, when in reality you did not produce the correct number of widgets on any day. The process is out of control, yet the simple comparison of total planned to actual masks this fact.

Using a measure such as the Line Linearity Index will help uncover such problems. The Line Linearity Index considers the absolute deviations. The formula for line linearity is shown here:

$$\text{Line Linearity Index} = \left[1 - \left(\frac{\text{Sum of Absolute Deviations}}{\text{Total Planned Production}} \right) \right] \times 100$$

In the previous example, the sum of all the absolute deviations is 38 and the total planned production is 100. The Line Linearity Index for your line is therefore 62 percent for the period. The goal is to improve the Line Linearity Index by minimizing the deviations from the planned production rate.

The Flow Workstation has a tab called Linearity and enables you to monitor the trend online. You can also create a visual control chart such as the one that is shown in Figure 7-11 that tracks the actual linearity against the target linearity, with a lower limit that prompts for management actions.

You can use the Flow Line Linearity report that is available in the Productivity Reports window to plot these values in the visual control chart. The report shows the planned production rate, actual production rate, variance, and linearity index for the selected lines.

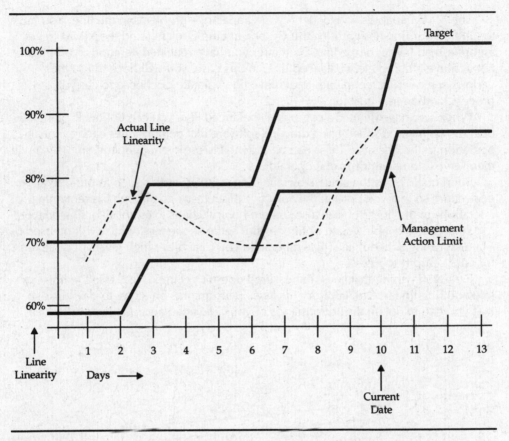

FIGURE 7-11. *Visual control chart to monitor linearity trend with management action limit*

Summary

This chapter has discussed the types of layout supported by Oracle Applications and the suitability of these layouts to various business needs. Takt time, Operation Times, and the TPCT were discussed in detail.

The Graphical Line Designer enables you to define your routings using an easy-to-use graphical user interface that supports drag and drop of operations. The information in the Graphical Line Designer is presented in two panes—the tree hierarchy pane and the graphical network pane. You can drag and drop events between operations or processes in the graphical network pane.

The MMM enables you to identify the imbalance problems in the line. You have to iterate your line design using the Graphical Line Designer and the MMM to get an optimized layout of the line. Even after you have repeated iterations, you might not achieve a completely balanced line. In this case, you will have to use the various engineering techniques to achieve line balance or choose to carry in process kanban as a cushion.

When you have defined a completely balanced line, you can optionally generate operational method sheets using drawing software that demonstrates each event and operation to the operator. These can be attached to the event or operation, which will then serve as a reference for the operator.

Build quality into the process by including standard events such as pre-operation inspection, so that you don't allow defective products to go through the remaining operations in the line. You can also use pre-control charts to establish online quality.

Setup types enable you to optimize your setup sequences, which will be used by Manufacturing Scheduling. This will enable you to achieve high levels of utilization for your setup resources.

Finally, anything that goes unmeasured doesn't get improved. Use the line flow rate and line linearity to monitor your lines performance on a day-to-day basis so that you can maintain the performance of your line at an acceptable standard.

PART III

Supply Chain Planning

CHAPTER
8

Planning Fundamentals

he Oracle Applications suite currently offers two products for material and capacity planning in a manufacturing or distribution environment: Master Scheduling/MRP and Advanced Supply Chain Planning. Master Scheduling/MRP offers single-organization, unconstrained planning of material and resources. We'll use the term *MRP* to refer to this planning tool. Advanced Supply Chain Planning (ASCP) is the next-generation planning tool; it offers multi-organization planning and the option of constraint-based and optimized plans.

This chapter describes the basic logic common to both planning methods and details the common setup needed by both methods. Subsequent chapters describe the unique characteristics of MRP and ASCP.

NOTE
In past releases, Oracle sold a product called Supply Chain Planning, which provided the capability of planning across a supply chain, but without the constraints, optimization, and variable granularity of the Advanced Supply Chain product. With Release 11i, this is no longer sold as a separate product, so it will not be explicitly covered in this book. However, much of material describing Advanced Supply Chain planning applies to the older supply chain planning; notable exceptions are the constraint and optimization capabilities of ASCP and the treatment of sourcing rules, which are described in Chapter 11.

Basic Planning Logic

The basic logic of both MRP and ASCP is time tested and well documented in numerous sources. Though not a comprehensive discussion of basic MRP logic, what follows is a brief overview of the process. The process is illustrated in Figure 8-1. It involves the recognition of demand or requirements, the netting of those requirements against available and scheduled quantities, and the generation of recommendations to meet those requirements. In a manufacturing environment, the process proceeds top-down through the bill of material, so that recommendations at one level form the basis of the requirements on the next level of components, and so on.

Recognition of Demand

Demand initially starts as a statement of what a company expects to sell or ship. This type of demand represents what you know or think you are likely to sell outside

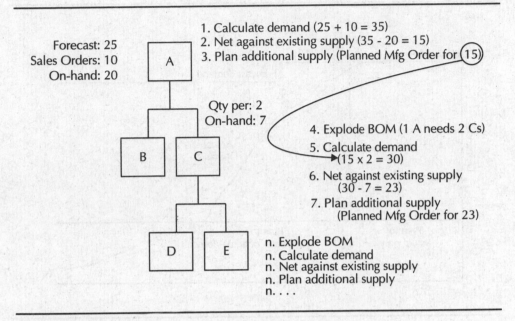

Forecast: 25
Sales Orders: 10
On-hand: 20

1. Calculate demand (25 + 10 = 35)
2. Net against existing supply (35 - 20 = 15)
3. Plan additional supply (Planned Mfg Order for 15)

Qty per: 2
On-hand: 7

4. Explode BOM (1 A needs 2 Cs)
5. Calculate demand
   (15 x 2 = 30)
6. Net against existing supply
   (30 - 7 = 23)
7. Plan additional supply
   (Planned Mfg Order for 23)

n. Explode BOM
n. Calculate demand
n. Net against existing supply
n. Plan additional supply
n. . . .

FIGURE 8-1. *Basic netting, planning, and explosion logic*

your company and is traditionally called *independent demand* because it is to some extent outside of your control. In a manufacturing business, the independent demand for your finished goods determines the demand on the component parts; this is called *dependent demand*, since it depends on, and can be calculated from, your bills of material.

Independent demand is typically some combination of forecast and actual (Sales Order) demand. Depending on the stocking strategy you employ for a particular product, the mix of forecast and actual demand will vary; in a make-to-stock strategy, you will rely heavily, perhaps exclusively, on forecast demand. In a make-to-order strategy, you will rely heavily on actual sales orders. Furthermore, the ratio of forecast to actual will likely vary over the time horizon, as shown in Figure 8-2—in the near term, you might rely most heavily on actual demand, while using forecast demand at the mid- and long-range points of the time line.

Oracle Applications allow you to have alternate forecast scenarios, so the forecasts you want to use to plan, as well as the actual demand you want to recognize, are stated in a Master Demand Schedule (MDS). The MDS is discussed in more detail, in the "Master Scheduling" section.

Dependent demand is demand calculated from the explosion of your bill of material. An important premise of MRP planning is that you should calculate, not forecast, dependent demand. For example, one automobile requires four tires; if you forecast or sell one auto, you know you will need four tires to build it. There's

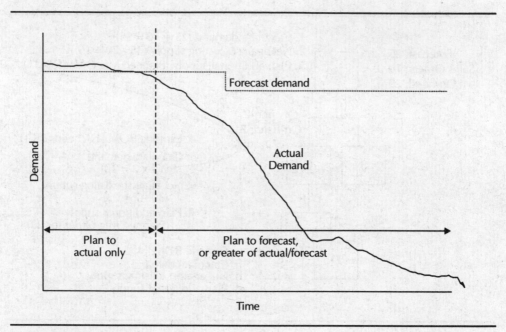

FIGURE 8-2. *Actual and forecast demand*

no point in forecasting tires; you can calculate the requirements from the bill of material. Because they represent an attempt to predict the future, forecasts are notoriously inaccurate; forecasting what you can calculate can only compound problems.

It is possible that one item can have both independent and dependent demand. If you were to sell tires as service parts, in addition to including them on a manufactured auto, you would want to forecast the independent *portion* of the demand on tires while calculating the dependent demand.

Gross to Net Calculation

Once the demand is known, the next step is to determine how much of that demand can be satisfied from existing stock or existing orders. It's simple arithmetic; if you have gross requirements (total demand) for 100 units of a product, and you have 25 on hand, the net requirements are 75.

Time-phasing makes this arithmetic a little more interesting. If that same demand were spread out over four weeks (25 per week), your 25 on-hand would satisfy the first week's demand. If you had an existing order (e.g., a manufacturing order) to build 25 more in week 3, the system would expect you to reschedule that order to satisfy the demand in week 2 and would then see net requirements for 25 each in weeks 3 and 4.

Recommendations

In the scenario described earlier, the planning process would recommend that you reschedule the existing order from week 3 to week 2 and would recommend that you create new orders to satisfy the demand in weeks 3 and 4.

In this process, planning will respect any order modifiers you've attached to the item, such as minimum or maximum lot sizes. It will look at any anticipated shrinkage factors you've associated with the product and inflate the planned orders to compensate. And it will respect time fences to allow you to stabilize your production or procurement schedules in the short term. It is the application of all these factors that makes planning beyond the scope of paper and pencil for all but the simplest scenarios. Order modifiers, shrinkage, and time fences are described later in this chapter.

Bill of Material Explosion

In a manufacturing environment, once the top-level demands are known, the component demands are calculated based on the explosion of the bill of material. The component demand (plus any independent demand for the component) constitutes the gross requirements at the next level. The planning process then continues to calculate net requirements and plan orders at each level in the bill of material.

Planning Cycles

You can use Oracle's planning products in numerous ways to generate distribution plans, master schedules, and manufacturing (MRP) plans for your enterprise. The possibilities are almost endless, but we'll discuss two typical examples here.

Figure 8-3 shows the traditional planning cycle. In this cycle, you create forecasts and book sales orders, load the selected forecasts and orders into a Master Demand Schedule, use the MDS as input to planning a Master Production Schedule, and submit that MPS to MRP. This cycle separates master scheduling and MRP so that you can firm up a master schedule before submitting it to MRP. You must synchronize these plans by carefully considering the timing of the running of each plan.

Figure 8-4 shows a *holistic* planning cycle; in this cycle there is only one plan that satisfies the needs of distribution planning, master scheduling, and manufacturing. You still generate forecasts, book orders, and load demand schedules, but you use one or more demand schedules from multiple organizations to generate one complete supply chain plan.

As noted earlier, numerous variants of these cycles are possible. A company that does not need to separate the Master Production Schedule from the MRP Plan can run MRP directly from the MDS. Within the supply chain plan, master schedules can be used to introduce some stability and local control into the plan. But all plans require some initial statement of demand, usually a combination of forecast and

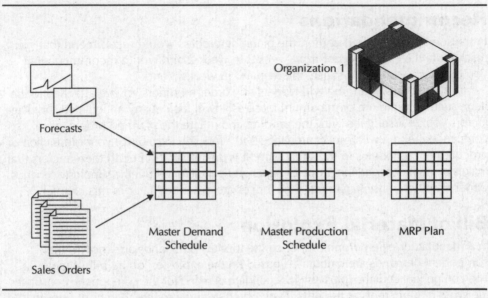

FIGURE 8-3. *Traditional planning*

sales orders. All plans require some sort of master schedule to identify the demand that drives the plan. They will plan for effectivity date changes in your bills of material and plan for both discrete and repetitive production. These common elements are described in the following pages.

Forecasting

For most businesses, forecasts are necessary at some point in the time horizon. Even a company with a pure make-to-order strategy (if such a company exists) will probably want to use forecasts of future demand for long-range planning. Forecasting is at least as much art as science, and the art of forecasting is beyond the scope of this book. But we will describe how forecasts are represented, generated, and used within the manufacturing and supply chain planning process.

Oracle Demand Planning (described in Chapter 9) generates forecast data. In addition, the Oracle Inventory and Master Scheduling/MRP applications provide basic methods to generate forecasts from historical data, described in the section titled "Generating Forecasts from Historical Information." Forecasts can also be entered manually; imported through an open interface, described in the "Open Forecast Interface" section; or loaded via an API, described in the section titled "Forecast Entries API."

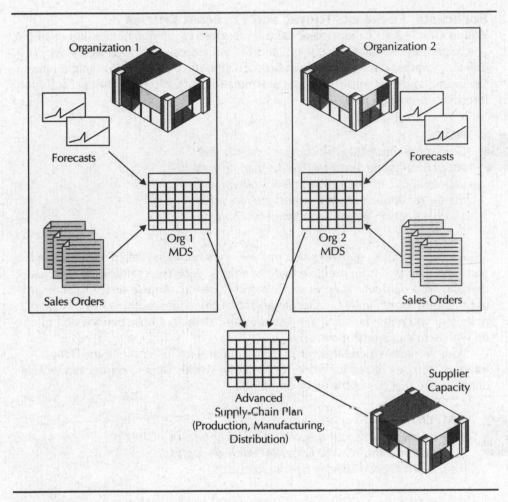

FIGURE 8-4.   *Holistic planning*

Forecast Terminology and Structure

To understand the use of forecasts in planning, it is helpful to understand the terminology and data structure Oracle uses to represent forecasts. One *forecast* typically contains multiple items; each item has multiple *entries* that represent a dated demand for that item. For ease of use and to control forecast consumption, forecasts are grouped into *forecast sets*.

Forecasts, Forecasts Items, and Forecast Entries

Within Oracle applications, forecasts are identified by unique names. For example, you might have separate East, West, and Central forecasts, or you might have different forecast names by product line or distribution channel. You might have Optimistic and Pessimistic forecasts or simulations of various scenarios. Each such forecast is identified by a name.

NOTE
Give some thought to the conventions you will adopt for naming forecasts. Unlike many names in Oracle applications, forecast names (along with master schedule and plan names) are limited to 10 characters in length and cannot be changed.

A forecast will typically contain multiple item numbers, called forecast items, and each item will have multiple forecast entries, each representing the forecast demand for a particular day, week, or monthly period. (Oracle seems reluctant to use the term *month* unless it refers to an actual calendar month; in the context of planning, you might be using a 4-4-5 or 5-4-4 calendar, whose periods don't line up with actual calendar months.)

Your workday calendar controls the valid dates for forecast entries. Daily forecasts can be entered for working days only; weekly or period forecasts will be dated on the first day of the week or period.

CAUTION
If your workday calendar specifies a Quarterly Type of "Calendar months," Oracle does not currently support the use of a "Period" bucket type for forecasts.

Forecast Sets

Oracle requires you to group forecasts into forecast sets, which are simply collections of forecasts. Forecast sets serve as both a convenience (you can refer to multiple forecasts by referencing their set) and a method to control forecast consumption, described in the following. This structure—forecast sets, forecast names, forecast items, and forecast entries—is illustrated in Figure 8-5.

NOTE
Forecast set names are defined in the same database table that defines forecast names, so they share the same size restrictions. In addition, forecast set names must be different from forecast names.

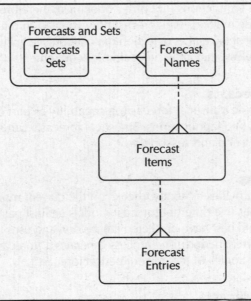

FIGURE 8-5. *Forecast data model*

Forecasts are always organization/item-specific; they represent anticipated demand for an item from an individual organization. But they may be defined at a more detailed level, if necessary. You can define a forecast at the customer level; such a forecast represents demand for an item from an organization to satisfy the orders of a particular customer. Or, you can define the forecast at the customer address level, where demand is maintained by customer ship-to address.

At the forecast set level, you define the default bucket size (day, week, or period) for the forecasts in the set, though this can be easily overridden for any forecast entry. You define the level (item, customer, or address) for which all forecasts in the set will be maintained. And you define certain controls that affect forecast consumption; these will be discussed later, when we discuss the forecast consumption process.

At the forecast level, you define the level identifiers (e.g., the customer name if the forecast is maintained at that level) and the optional demand class that will further control forecast consumption.

Generating Forecasts from Historical Information

The Oracle Master Scheduling/MRP and Inventory Applications provide two basic methods to generate forecasts from historical data: statistical forecasting and focus forecasting. While both methods use proven algorithms, they are basic in the level of control they provide. Unlike Oracle Demand Planning, they are based strictly on the history of issue transactions (not order bookings); therefore, if you have shipped late in the past, these methods will forecast how you can ship just as late in the future! And they offer none of the outlier detection or collaborative features of Oracle Demand Planning. Nevertheless, they may meet simple requirements.

Statistical Forecasts

Oracle provides basic statistical forecasting capability as part of the Inventory and Master Scheduling/MRP applications. Statistical forecasts can span multiple periods and can recognize trend and seasonality.

Focus Forecasts

Focus forecasting provides a "sanity check" on the current month's forecast. Focus forecasting examines five different forecast models against past history, determines the model that would best have predicted the history, and uses that model to generate a forecast for the current period. (The process generates a "forecast" for multiple periods, but they are simply copies of the current period forecast.)

Generating Forecasts

You generate a forecast by first defining a forecast rule that specifies a bucket type, a forecast method (statistical or focus), and the sources of demand. For the statistical forecast method, the forecast rule also specifies the exponential smoothing (alpha) factor, trend smoother (beta) factor, and seasonal smoothing (gamma) factor. Then, in the Generate Forecast window, you specify the following:

- Name of the forecast you want to populate.

- Forecast rule that determines the bucket, forecast method, and demand stream.

- Selection criteria to identify the items for which you want to generate a forecast. You can select all items, all items in a designated category set, items in a specific category within a category set, or an individual item.

- An overwrite option, which determines what happens to existing forecast information. All Entries deletes all existing forecasts before repopulating the forecast data. Same Source Only deletes only forecast entries that were previously generated from the same source that you are about to load. None does not delete any existing entries.

■ Start date and cutoff date for the forecast information that you are about to generate.

NOTE
Choose the Overwrite option carefully; if you do not explicitly delete existing information through your choice of the Overwrite option, you might duplicate information already in your forecast.

Open Forecast Interface

To populate forecasts using the Open Forecast Interface, you must first define your items, organizations, forecast sets, and forecast names. Then, load your forecast data into the table MRP_FORECAST_INTERFACE. Required data includes

■ INVENTORY_ITEM_ID

■ FORECAST_DESIGNATOR

■ ORGANIZATION_ID

■ FORECAST_DATE

■ QUANTITY

■ PROCESS_STATUS

Set the PROCESS_STATUS to 2 to designate data waiting to be processed.

The Planning Manager (described later in this chapter) periodically checks the MRP_FORECAST_INTERFACE table to determine if there is any new data to be processed. If the Planning Manager detects new data, it launches the Forecast Interface Load Program. This program validates the data in the interface table and loads valid data into the specified forecast. If the load program detects an error, it sets the PROCESS_STATUS to 4 and enters a text message in the ERROR_MESSAGE column in the interface table. Use SQL*Plus, or a custom program, to view and correct invalid date in the interface.

Forecast Entries API

You can use the forecast entries API to integrate with other software systems. This section describes the major steps in using this API.

1. Construct the following PL/SQL table for all the information that is associated with the forecast:

Variable Name	Type	Meaning
p_forecast_entries	A PL/SQL table that contains records of type mrp_forecast_interface_pk. mrp_forecast_interface	These are the actual forecast entries.
p_forecast_designators	A PL/SQL table that contains records of type mrp_forecast_interface_pk. rec_forecast_desg	These are the forecast designator information.

2. Call the function mrp_forecast_interface, with the parameters that you constructed in step 1. You don't have to supply both the parameters in every case. For example, if you are inserting new forecast entries or updating existing forecast entries, you would provide all the information. On the other hand, if you are deleting all the forecast entries, you need only provide the forecast designator.

```
mrp_forecast_interface_pk.mrp_forecast_interface
(p_forecast_entries
-- INOUT PL/SQL Table for forecast entries
,p_forecast_designators
-- IN PL/SQL Table for forecast designators
);
```

3. The function returns true if the API completed successfully and false if there were failures.

Forecast Consumption

In order to avoid overstating demand as actual orders are booked, forecasts are typically reduced by the amount of the sales order demand. The process is called forecast consumption. Then, when actual orders are combined with forecasts in a master schedule, the demand statement remains accurate. *Forecast consumption* also serves as a measurement of the forecast's accuracy—if you've sold less than you forecast, the forecast will not be fully consumed; if you've sold too much, the result will be reflected as overconsumption at the forecast set level.

Forecast consumption is one of the functions of the Planning Manager, described later in this chapter. At its simplest, forecast consumption reduces a forecast demand by the amount of the actual sales order demand in that period. The remaining forecast quantity is referred to as the current forecast; the original forecast quantity remains visible for comparison and analysis.

The first rule of forecasting is that the forecast will be wrong. It is highly unlikely that a customer order will exactly match your forecast quantities (although supply chain collaboration might help ameliorate this problem). So, to make the process yield usable results, a number of factors influence the supposedly simple process of forecast consumption.

Forward/Backward Days

To compensate for the discrepancy between customer orders and forecasts, you typically provide a "window" within which the forecast will be consumed. This window is expressed as a number of working days, as determined by the shop calendar. Within this window, forecast consumption will first look backward and then forward to match the forecast with the actual demand. You define this window as an attribute of each forecast set.

Consider this example:

Days	1	2	3	4	5	6	7	8	9	10	11	12	13	14	15	16	17	18	19	20
Forecast	5	5	5	5	5			5	5	5	5	5			5	5	5	5	5	
Demand										30										

☐ = Non-work Day

With no window for consumption, the sales order demand on day 10 would consume the entire forecast of 5 on that day and then "have no where to go." Thus, the total demand for the second week would be 50: 30 actual and 20 of the remaining, or unconsumed, forecast, as shown here:

Days	1	2	3	4	5	6	7	8	9	10	11	12	13	14	15	16	17	18	19	20
Forecast	5	5	5	5	5			5	5	5	5	5			5	5	5	5	5	
Demand										30										
Unconsumed	5	5	5	5	5			5	5	0	5	5			5	5	5	5	5	

Daily buckets; Backward Days = 0; Forward Days = 0   ☐ = Non-work Day

With forward and backward days set to 3, the actual demand would "search" for forecast if there was not sufficient forecast quantity remaining on the demand date. The process always goes backward first (assuming that you are late in realizing your forecast), and then forward if necessary. So the demand of 30 on day 10 would consume 5 on day 10, then search backward consuming forecast on day 9, 8, and 5 (day 6 and 7 are non-work days). Since the backward consumption only accounted for 20 of the 30 demanded, the process would then search forward and consume forecast on day 11 and 12. The result is shown here:

Days	1	2	3	4	5	6	7	8	9	10	11	12	13	14	15	16	17	18	19	20
Forecast	5	5	5	5	5			5	5	5	5	5			5	5	5	5	5	
Demand										30										
Unconsumed	5	5	5	5	0			0	0	0	0	0			5	5	5	5	5	

Daily buckets; Backward Days = 3; Forward Days = 3 ☐ = Non-work Day

Forecast Bucket Type

The bucket type of a given forecast entry allows an order anywhere within that bucket to consume forecast. If the forecasts in the previous example were expressed as weekly instead of daily forecasts, the order on day 10 would consume all the forecasts for the week starting with day 8, even with no backward/forward days:

Days	1	2	3	4	5	6	7	8	9	10	11	12	13	14	15	16	17	18	19	20
Forecast	25							25							25					
Demand										30										
Unconsumed	25							0							25					

Weekly buckets; Backward Days = 0; Forward Days = 0 ☐ = Non-work Day

Note that the consumption window is always expressed in days, regardless of the forecast bucket type. Thus, in the example above, a backward parameter of 2 days would not change the consumption, since 2 days backward only moves the consumption window back to day 8. A backward parameter of 3 days, however, would move the consumption window back to day 5, which falls in the previous week. Since the forecast bucket is a week, that week's forecast would then be consumed. Thus, a backward consumption parameter of 3 days (or more) would result in the following:

Days	1	2	3	4	5	6	7	8	9	10	11	12	13	14	15	16	17	18	19	20
Forecast	25							25							25					
Demand										30										
Unconsumed	20							0							25					

Weekly buckets; Backward Days = 3; Forward Days = 0   ☐ = Non-work Day

Forecast Level

As mentioned earlier, you can forecast at three levels: item/organization, item/organization/customer, or item/organization/customer address. Sales Order demand only consumes the appropriate level; i.e., if your forecast is maintained at the customer level, only a sales order for the customer associated with the forecast will consume that forecast. Likewise, if you maintain a forecast at the customer address level, only a customer order with a matching ship-to (or bill-to) address will consume that forecast.

Outlier Update Percent

The dynamics of your particular market will determine how much of a forecast you will want a single sales order demand to consume. For example, if you sell to major retailers or distributors, you might expect a single order to consume most or all of a forecast. But if you are selling computers directly to individual consumers, it might be highly unusual for a single sales order to consume more than a small fraction of a week's forecast. In this situation, an unexpectedly large order would be called an outlier because it represents demand that falls outside of the expected pattern. If you were to allow such an outlier to consume the entire week's forecast, you might be understating demand—you would show no remaining forecast, even though you might expect that your normal demand patterns would persist, and additional orders would eventually be placed according to expectations.

To prevent such unwanted forecast consumption, Oracle lets you specify an outlier update percent; this determines the percentage of an individual forecast that a single demand (i.e., a single order or shipment line) can consume. For example, if you had an original forecast quantity of 100, but had set an outlier update percent of 10, no sales order line could consume more than 10 percent, or 10 units, of the original forecast quantity. A sales order for 20 units, therefore, would only consume 10 units of the forecast, leaving an unconsumed balance of 90 units for that forecast entry. Note, however, that the forward/backward days would still be applied; the excess amount of the order could still consume other forecast entries based on your consumption window.

Consumption Within Sets

A given demand can consume multiple forecasts, but it will consume forecasts entries from only one forecast within a forecast set. For example, if you have an Optimistic, Realistic, and Pessimistic forecast, you should define them in different forecast sets; each forecast could therefore be consumed by your sales order demand so you could gauge the accuracy of each forecast. (You would, of course, use only one forecast for a given planning scenario, or you would be overstating demand.)

Demand Class

Forecast sets control forecast consumption because a given demand will consume (or attempt to consume) forecast entries in only one forecast within the set. Sometimes your forecast level will control which forecast is consumed within a set—if your forecasts are defined for each customer, the customer on the sales order will determine the forecast to consume. However, if you're forecasting at the item level only, and if you have the same item in multiple forecasts within a set, you will need to control which forecast should be consumed. You control forecast consumption with *demand classes*.

A demand class is simply a name you attach to a forecast and sales order demand; then sales order demands will only consume forecasts with a matching demand class. In the absence of a demand class, a sales order will consume the first forecast it finds (alphabetically) in a forecast set. Thus, if you had an Asia, Europe, and North America forecast in a forecast set, a sales order from New York would consume the Asian forecast, since Asia sorts alphabetically before North America. You can control the consumption by defining demand classes that correspond to each forecast—you might simply use the same name for the demand class and the matching forecast—and then apply the demand class to the appropriate sales order line.

Order Management lets you attach a demand class to an order type or to a customer address; defaulting rules would apply the desired demand class to a sales order line. If you forecast geographically, you would probably determine the demand class from the customer address; if you forecast by distribution channel, you might determine the demand class from the order type.

An order will normally consume only forecasts with a matching demand class; however, if there is no forecast with a matching demand class, the order will consume forecasts that have no demand class (i.e., the demand class is null). You might use this capability to maintain specific forecasts for some of your major sales channels, for example, while maintaining a generic forecast for all other demand.

Similarly, an order with no demand class will normally consume a forecast with a null demand class. If you prefer to have such orders consume from a specific demand class, you can specify the demand class as the Default Demand Class on the Organization Parameters form.

In some cases, there will be orders that you will not want to consume forecast. For example, you might have received an order that you know is due to production problems at a competitor or due to some other event that you did not anticipate in your forecast. Such orders (sometimes called "bluebirds") should not consume forecast; they represent excess or abnormal demand and should be added to the forecast. You can accomplish this with demand classes as well—define a demand class with a name such as Abnormal and assign it to the abnormal demands that you recognize. Create a dummy forecast for the Abnormal demand class. The Abnormal demand class and forecast will keep the demand from consuming another forecast; if you exclude the Abnormal forecast but include all sales orders (including the "abnormal" ones) in the master demand schedules driving your plans, you will properly recognize the abnormal demand in addition to your normal forecasts and orders.

Aggregate Forecasts

In some cases, it is easier to forecast at an aggregate level and use an anticipated distribution percentage to calculate the forecast for an individual item. Neptune Inc., for example, sells computers with a mix of processors, hard drives, CD drives, etc. Their sales and marketing staffs can forecast with some success the total number of computers they will sell, and they have a good idea of the relative mix of options. However, trying to forecast individual combinations of features is nearly impossible. In this case, the model and option bill of material that defines the options that customers can choose includes a distribution percentage on each component in the bill. This lets Neptune enter a forecast for the model item, and the forecast is exploded to calculate a forecast quantity for each option.

You can use a similar process even for items that you make to stock. You can group similar products in a product family or planning bill and enter an aggregate forecast for the family or top level of the planning bill. Both product families and planning bills let you aggregate forecast; additionally, product families can be used in the design of flow lines (discussed in Chapter 7) and to enable two-level master scheduling, described later in this chapter.

Forecast Control

Forecast control is an item attribute that controls the forecast explosion process. The attribute has three possible values:

- **Consume and Derive** This setting implies that the forecast can be calculated, or derived, from the explosion of an aggregate forecast; since the item will have a forecast, it is eligible to be consumed. Note that this setting does not *require* that forecast be derived, only that it is possible. It is a good choice as a default setting for your item templates, as it allows forecasting, consumption, and calculation from a model bill, planning bill, or product family.

- ■ **Consume** A forecast control setting of Consume implies that forecast will be maintained separately for the item, but not derived from explosion of an aggregate forecast. This might be useful if you have an item that you want to forecast separately, but want to include on a planning or model bill for completeness.

- ■ **None** None implies that no forecast is maintained for the item.

NOTE
To explode and derive a forecast through multiple levels of a planning bill or model and option bill, you must set the Forecast Control attribute for all intermediate levels in the bill to Consume and Derive. If you "break the chain," forecast explosion will stop.

Forecast Explosion

Forecast Explosion is the process that takes an aggregate forecast and generates individual item forecasts for the components of a planning bill, model and option bill, or product family. You can initiate the process at several points: when you copy a forecast or when you load a forecast into a master schedule.

Forecast Explosion takes each forecast quantity at the top level and explodes it through the bill of material, multiplying by the Distribution Percent and the Quantity per, if any. It continues down the bill of material until is has created forecast for the first standard item it finds down each branch. In other words, once Forecast Explosion finds a standard, stockable component, the explosion of that branch of the structure is finished; it does not generate forecast for components of subassemblies, for example.

Master Scheduling

The planning process always starts with a master schedule. Like forecasts, each master schedule is identified by a 10-character name. Oracle supports two types of master schedules: Master Demand Schedules and Master Production Schedules.

While the distinction between a Master Demand Schedule and a Master Production Schedule is unfamiliar to many people, it is a useful concept. In many businesses, especially for seasonal products, it is not feasible to produce exactly to meet the customer demand. In such cases in particular, it is helpful to separate demand from supply.

Master Demand Schedules and Master Production Schedules

A Master Demand Schedule (MDS) is an anticipated shipment schedule; it is the statement of demand you want to recognize for a particular planning run. A Master Production Schedule (MPS) is a production plan, a statement of how you plan to schedule production. It might also be called a production forecast.

You define master schedules with several forms within the Oracle Applications suite. Use the Master Demand Schedules form to define an MDS; all that is required is a name and description. You can optionally associate a Demand Class with an MDS and indicate if shipments should automatically relieve the MDS. You would probably want to enable shipment relief for the master schedule that represents the demand you actually plan for, but you might choose to turn off relief for an MDS that you use for simulation or historical purposes. (Master Schedule relief is discussed in more detail later in this chapter, in the section titled "Schedule Relief.")

The form you use to define an MPS depends on the type of plan you will execute. Use the Define MPS Names form for a master production schedule that you will use for single-organization, Master Scheduling/MRP plan. This form is found under the Material Planning menu seeded in Oracle Applications. If you're running the older supply chain plan, you must use the Define Multi-Plant MPS Names form, found under the Supply Chain Planning menu. Like an MDS, you can associate an MPS with a demand class and enable or disable relief. In addition, for an MPS, you must specify if it is to be considered in the calculation of Available to Promise quantities in Order Management and Inventory and whether or not it is considered a Production plan. Designating an MPS as a Production plan allows automatic release of orders during the planning process.

To define an Advanced Supply Chain plan, use the MPS Names form under Advanced Supply Chain planning; this will be discussed in greater detail in Chapter 11.

You can enter master schedule quantities manually, but most often you will use concurrent programs within Oracle Applications to populate your master schedules with the appropriate data. An MDS will typically contain a combination of forecasts and sales orders. You can also copy one or more master demand schedules into a new MDS; this can be useful for simulations or for retaining historical data.

As a statement of production, an MPS will represent your production plans. In an environment where you can produce exactly to customer demand, you might simply copy your MPS from your MDS and then modify it manually. Like an MDS, you can also copy one or more master production schedules into a new MPS for simulation or to retain history. But you can also plan an MPS using the planning process in either Master Scheduling/MRP or Advanced Supply Chain Planning to generate an MPS. This process applies the netting logic described earlier to calculate net requirements and plan orders for those items you have designated as Master Scheduled.

NOTE
It is possible to load an MPS with forecasts and sales orders; in this case, the MPS would function exactly like an MDS. However, this usage obscures the purpose and distinction of the two schedule types; we will assume throughout this book that you will use an MDS to represent independent demand and an MPS to represent a production plan.

Master Schedule Load

The process of copying data into a master schedule is called a *load*. Because the master schedule represents the demand that drives the planning process, you must reload the master schedule as often as you need to recognize changes in the demand. The process is simple, but it does provide a few options:

- Name of the schedule you are about to load.

- Source of the information (source type, source organization, and source name).

- If you want to include Sales Orders in the master schedule, you can choose to load All Sales Orders or Sales Orders from the Start Date Forward. Additionally, you can limit sales order lines to a specific demand class only.

- The treatment of the Demand Time Fence. You can choose to Load Forecast outside the demand time fence only. If you are including sales orders and have consumed the forecast, this is a typical choice; it results in sales orders only inside the demand time fence and the greater of sales orders or forecast outside the demand time fence. (The demand time fence is defined as an attribute of each item.) You can also choose to Load orders within and forecast outside demand time fence (ignoring any large orders outside the demand time fence) or to Ignore the demand time fence (loading all specified data regardless of the demand time fence).

- A start and end date, to limit the information you will load.

- You can choose to explode the forecast when you load a master schedule.

- You can load current (consumed) forecast quantities or original (unconsumed) forecasts, and you can consume the forecast if you have not already done so. These options are the key to utilizing two-level master scheduling, which is discussed later in this chapter.

- The overwrite option: All Entries, None, or Same Source Only.

NOTE
The Overwrite option first deletes any information that matches the overwrite criterion; the load process then re-creates the appropriate data. As with forecasts, you must choose the Overwrite option carefully, or you may duplicate existing data. Same source refers to data with the same type and name. For example, if you were loading a specific forecast into a master schedule, the Same Source Only option would delete any existing forecast data with the same type (forecast) and the same forecast name; any data from different forecasts would not be affected.

Several other options are useful primarily for simulations:

■ **Modification**   Modifies the loaded quantities by a positive or negative percentage.

■ **Carry Forward Days**   Shifts the quantities forward or backward in time. Enter a positive number to shift the quantities forward; a negative number to shift backward.

Source List

If you have many forecasts, master schedules, or plans that you will regularly consolidate into one master schedule, you can define a source list that identifies all these objects with a single name. Then, when loading a master schedule, you can specify the single source list name, rather than running multiple loads for each forecast, schedule, or plan you want to load.

Open Master Schedule Interface

You can populate master schedules using the Open Master Schedule Interface. Like the Open Forecast Interface, described earlier, you must first define your items, organizations, and master schedule names. Then, load your data into the table MRP_SCHEDULE_INTERFACE. Required data includes

■ INVENTORY_ITEM_ID

■ SCHEDULE_DESIGNATOR

■ ORGANIZATION_ID

■ SCHEDULE_DATE

- SCHEDULE_QUANTITY
- PROCESS_STATUS

Set the PROCESS_STATUS to 2 to designate data waiting to be processed.

This process is also controlled by the Planning Manager; it periodically checks the MRP_SCHEDULE_INTERFACE table and launches the Master Schedule Interface Load Program to process new data it detects. The load program validates the data in the interface table and loads valid data into the specified master schedule. Errors are handled just like the Open Forecast Interface; the load program sets the PROCESS_STATUS to 4 and enters a text message in the ERROR_MESSAGE column in the interface table. View and correct invalid data with SQL*Plus or a custom program.

Reviewing the Master Schedule

Oracle provides several forms and reports where you can review your master schedules. Online, you can use the Item Master Demand Schedule Entries and the Item Master Production Schedule Entries forms to view master schedule data; you can view the schedule details in the same form you entered them or consolidate the data into weekly or period buckets. The Master Schedule Detail Report provides detailed information, in a bucketed horizontal display, a detailed vertical display, or both. The Master Schedule Comparison Report lets you compare two master schedules.

NOTE
The Master Schedule Detail Report, and many other bucketed reports in Oracle's planning applications, let you control the level of detail reported. The reports are formatted to show multiples of 12 buckets; you choose the number of buckets (12, 24, or 36) that you want to see on the report. Then you specify how many of those periods are weeks; the remaining buckets will show "period" information. To ensure that the period buckets show data for a complete period, the number of weekly buckets you can choose is determined by your planning calendar and the number of weeks remaining until each period start date. For example, if you use a 4-4-5 calendar for planning buckets, and it is week 1, you could choose 4, 8, or 13 weeks; if it is week 2, you could choose 3, 7, or 12 weekly buckets.

Schedule Relief

Just as forecasts must be consumed to avoid overstating demand, master schedules must be reduced to prevent overstating demand or supply. If a sales order MDS entry remained after the sales order had been shipped, you would overstate demand. Similarly, if an MPS entry remained after you had created a discrete job or purchase requisition, you would duplicate supply. The process of removing this duplication is called *relief*, and it is another function of the Planning Manager.

Shipment Relief

Because an MDS represents a statement of expected shipments, it is relieved when the demand no longer exists (i.e., when a sales order has been shipped). As long as the Planning Manager is running, the process is automatic.

Production Relief

Master Production Schedules are relieved when a real statement of production replaces the plan that the MPS represents. Note that this is not when the product is actually produced; it is when the production order (a WIP discrete job or repetitive schedule) is created. While this strikes some people as unusual, it is quite sensible— if you had both an MPS entry and a WIP job, you would be doubling your statement of production. Again, the process is handled by the Planning Manager and is automatic.

Two-Level Master Scheduling

If you use Product Families to forecast, you have the option of utilizing two-level master scheduling. This technique lets you determine how remaining aggregate forecasts will be exploded and used in the planning process and further refines your control over the forecasting and planning process.

To understand two-level master scheduling, consider the following simple example in Figure 8-6. The bill of material structure illustrated shows an aggregate item, A, with components B and C, distributed at 50 percent each. A forecast for 100 A, therefore, generates a forecast for 50 each of B and C.

If A is a Planning Bill item, two-level scheduling is not supported, and the forecast is consumed only at the components, B and C. A Sales Order for 60 of item C will consume the entire forecast for C, actually overconsuming C's forecast. But the demand for B remains unchanged. Thus, if you were to run a plan with all the current demand data, the total demand is 110 units, even though the aggregate forecast was only 100.

In the two-level scheduling scenario, the forecast is consumed at both the aggregate and the component levels. You can choose to re-explode the remaining aggregate forecast, with the results shown in Figure 8-7. Note that this will keep the aggregate demand constant, until the entire aggregate forecast is oversold. Notice, too, that this dynamically adjusts the mix of B and C, based on the forecast consumption.

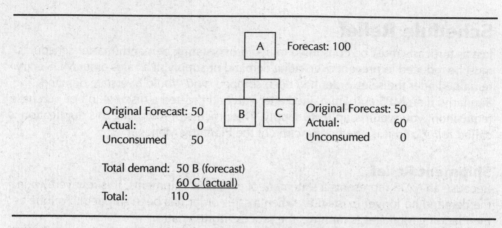

FIGURE 8-6. *Traditional forecast consumption and explosion*

The choice of forecast explosion methods is controlled by the explosion options used when you load the master schedule from a forecast. The Load/Copy/Merge Master Demand Schedule form lets you copy forecasts into your master schedule. Options let you choose whether to load the current (i.e. the remaining forecast, after consumption) or original forecast quantities, whether to explode the forecast, and whether to consume the forecast if consumption has not already occurred. If you explode the original quantities and select the Consume option, you will get the demand shown in Figure 8-6. If you explode the current quantities, you will get the demand picture that we've been calling two-level master scheduling (see Figure 8-7).

There are several potential pitfalls to be aware of in this process. If you explode original quantities, include sales orders, and do not select the consumption, you will inflate demand. The load process will do exactly what you ask—it will explode the

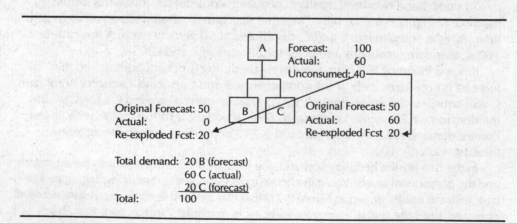

FIGURE 8-7. *Two-level master scheduling*

original quantities without consumption and add in sales orders that otherwise should have consumed that forecast. This will result in the very duplication of demand that forecast consumption is designed to prevent. (The load process does not allow you to consume if you are loading the current, i.e., already consumed, quantities.)

A second pitfall is loading a forecast that you have already exploded. This also results in duplicate demand—you will load the existing forecast for the components or family members and then create additional forecast by exploding the family forecast.

Capacity Planning

Oracle provides two types of capacity planning within its planning products: Rough Cut Capacity Planning (RCCP) for evaluating the high-level capacity requirements of a master schedule and Capacity Requirements Planning (CRP) for evaluating the detailed capacity requirements of an MRP (or ASCP) plan. Both types of capacity planning compare the available capacity with the calculated requirements. Available capacity comes from your resource definitions, as described in Chapter 4; what differentiates CRP from RCCP is the method of calculating the resource requirements.

Capacity Requirements Planning (CRP)

CRP calculates required capacity from the routings used to build your products. It is always run as part of running an MRP (or DRP) plan, since it needs to know the planned orders for its calculation.

In calculating resource requirements, CRP uses the primary routing for planned orders, but will use alternate routings if they have been specified for existing jobs. It recognizes modifications you have made to WIP resources (for example, specifying the use of an alternate resource). Because it is run as part of MRP, it benefits from the netting logic inherent in planning—if your on-hand quantities don't require planning of new replenishment orders, you won't generate capacity requirements. And if jobs on the shop floor are partially completed, CRP recognizes which resources have already been used and only plans requirements for the resources that remain.

Rough Cut Capacity Planning (RCCP)

RCCP lets you check your master schedule against critical resources that you identify in a bill of resources. RCCP can be used to evaluate either master production or master demand schedules. In a manufacturing environment, it is more typical to use RCCP to evaluate production schedules because the constraints are most often manufacturing resources. In a distribution environment (or for a quick check on distribution-related resources), you can use RCCP to evaluate master demand schedules.

What makes rough cut rough? Since it does not use detailed routings, it is inherently less detailed. Though it might seem obvious, a hidden implication is in the requirements for subassemblies. Because RCCP does not depend on the netting and explosion logic of MRP, it may show resource requirements for subassemblies even if a subsequent MRP plan will find that there are no net requirements because of on-hand quantities. And there is no visibility to the progress of WIP jobs.

Bills of Resource   RCCP calculates resource requirements simply by multiplying the master schedule quantity by the resource requirements expressed in a bill of resources that you define for the master scheduled item. In a manufacturing environment, you can construct a bill of resources by rolling up the routings; this process is called a bill of resource load. The result might be considered a kind of "aggregate routing" for the item; it lists all the resources you need to manufacture the master scheduled item and all its subassemblies. You can then modify the bill of resources by deleting noncritical resources or by adding resources that are not normally part of your routings—shipping capacity, for example.

Strictly speaking, a *bill of resources* is a listing of the resources you want to evaluate for a single item. But, to be useful, any evaluation of capacity must look at all the demands placed on your resources. It doesn't do much good to know that item A requires 20 hours of a resource, unless you also know the demands placed by items B and C—it's the total resource requirements that you must compare to the resource availability. For this reason, bills of resource are grouped into a bill of resource set; when you evaluate rough cut capacity planning, you must specify which bill of resource set you want to use to calculate resource requirements. Like so many objects in the Oracle Applications database you can have multiple bill of resource sets; this might be useful for simulations, or to evaluate distribution resources against your demand schedules and manufacturing resources against your production schedules.

Once you have defined a bill of resource set, you can view your rough-cut capacity plans on demand; the calculations are done when you perform the inquiry or run the report.

Use the Load Bill of Resource concurrent program to calculate bills of resource from your routings. Parameters include

- The bill of resource set you are loading.

- Whether you want to preserve any manual additions or modifications you may have made to the bill of resources, if it already exists.

- A resource group, to limit the creation of the bills of resource to items within a specific resource group. (Resource groups are discussed in Chapter 4.)

- Whether you want to create a bill of resource for all selected items or for Model and Option Class items only.

- How you want to deal with other master scheduled items that might be structured into bills of material at lower levels.

This last option, labeled Rollup MPS Items on the Parameters window, deserves explanation. Consider the example in Figure 8-8; if the only master scheduled item were A, you would typically want A's bill of resource to show two hours of labor—one hour to assemble C and one more hour to put B and C together to make A. But if C were also a master scheduled item, you would not want to roll its time up into A's bill of resource because you could be overstating the resource requirements. If your master schedule includes both A and C, a rough cut capacity plan would calculate one hour per unit for C and two more hours for A. This would overstate the capacity requirements—one of the two required hours was already planned for by C's bill of resource, and only one more hour of labor is needed to assemble product A.

You avoid this problem by setting the parameter Rollup MPS Items to No; this "breaks" the rollup process at each master scheduled item and ensures that a bill of resources does not contain resources that were already accounted for on other master scheduled items lower in the bill of material. Note that the parameter does default to Yes. While it's possible to construct a scenario where this could make sense (e.g., you plan to do rough cut capacity planning only against your top-level items), it would be inappropriate if you plan to do rough cut planning for all of your master scheduled items. Consider this carefully when loading bills of resources.

You can also build bills of resource "from scratch" by listing the resources you want to check in your RCCP plan. If you define bills of resource manually in a

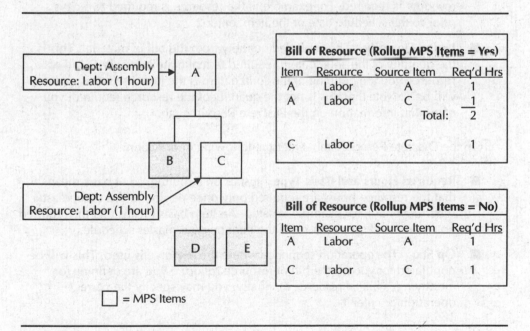

FIGURE 8-8. *MPS rollup options*

manufacturing environment, you may want to include the critical resources you need to build subassemblies of the master scheduled item.

A bill of resource for an item consists of one or more rows of data that specifies the following attributes for each resource you list. On the Main tab, enter the following information:

- **Department or Production Line and Resource critical to the production or distribution of the item** These are often the same departments and resources you use in your production routings, but you can also define other resources that might not traditionally be part of a routing. For example, if shipping capacity is critical to your business planning, you could define it as a resource within a department and use RCCP for a quick evaluation. The key thing to remember is that you must define these resources and assign them to departments, defining their available capacity just as if you were going to use them in a routing. This process is described in Chapter 4.

- **Source Item** That is, the item responsible for the demand. In a rolled-up bill of resources, this will be the item whose routing contributed the resource usage, either a subassembly or the item itself.

- **Setback Days** The number of days prior to the schedule date that the resource is required. For example, if the resource is required two days prior to the schedule date of the item, enter **2**.

- **Usage Quantity** The exploded quantity from the bill of material. This is the quantity of the source item required to make the item whose bill of resource you are defining; if the source item is the item itself, this quantity will be 1. Note that this is not the quantity of the resource required; you enter that information on the Discrete Resource tab.

On the Discrete Resource tab, enter the following information:

- **Required Hours and Basis Type** Just as on a routing, a Lot basis means that the resource hours are required only once per lot (in this case, master schedule entry); for example, a setup. An Item basis means that the required hours are need for each unit of the item on your master schedule.

- **Op Seq** The operation sequence where the resource is used. This will be populated for you by the bill of resource rollup; if you are defining (or modifying) a bill of resource manually, you may specify the correct operation or enter **1**.

The bottom of the form displays the source of the entry: Rollup means that the entry is the result of a routing rollup. Manual addition or Manual update indicates that you have created or modified this entry manually; this distinction allows you to re-roll routings and optionally preserve manual modifications to your bills of resources.

Planning for Engineering Changes

A key element of planning is the ability to recognize anticipated bill of material and routing changes. This allows you to phase in changes to the products you manufacture and have planning react appropriately—planning will stop generating orders for the obsolete components or resources and begin ordering the new components or resources.

Effectivity Dates

Both bills of materials and routings use effectivity dates, indicating when a component or routing operation begins to be effective, and optionally when the component or operation is disabled. Effectivity is determined by the start date of a planned order; planning (and WIP, if you manually create a job or schedule) will select only those components that are effective on the date the job is scheduled to start.

The effective date, labeled "From," defaults to the current date when you create a bill or routing; you can select a future date if the element is not yet effective. You cannot select a date in the past. If the ending date, labeled "To," is left blank, it indicates that there is no planned end to the effectivity of the component or operation.

Note that the To date is a disable date, the date (and time) that the component or operation is no longer used. This is important if you are replacing one component with another; you set the starting (From) date of the new component equal to the disable (To) date of the old component so that the new component becomes effective at the same time that the old component is discontinued. Unlike some systems that might term the end date an Effective Thru date, if you were to disable a component on the 15th, for example, but not start the replacement until the 16th, a job or planned order that started on the 15th would contain neither component.

When you're setting the effective dates for a new component, it's helpful to know its Total cumulative lead time. If you plan to add a component within its cumulative lead time, you might have to expedite orders in order to obtain the component in time.

Effective dates can be entered manually on bills or routings; effective dates on bills of material can also be maintained with Engineering Change Orders (ECOs). With Release 11i.5, you can also use ECOs to modify routings.

Engineering Change Orders (ECOs)

ECOs provide a more controlled environment for maintaining effectivity dates than the simple bill of material maintenance process. ECOs (described in Chapter 5) let you group multiple changes under a single control number. With an ECO, you set an effective date for all of the changes you want to make to an individual bill of material; this eliminates any possibility of "gaps" if you define a replacement component and lets you keep multiple component changes in synch with one another. ECOs allow the system to calculate the effectivity dates for a set of changes based on using up a component on a bill (or using up the assembly itself). ECOs let you control whether a set of changes is visible to the planning applications. And ECOs can base the schedule date of a change on the date on which an assembly or component is scheduled to be used up.

Schedule Date Changes

As you change effectivity dates, planning will replan accordingly. Moving a schedule date in (scheduling the change to occur earlier than originally planned) can result in expedite suggestions from planning; moving a date out could result in shortages of the old component, particularly if you have deactivated it.

If a pending change is driven by the use-up of the assembly itself, the schedule date of the change will be updated automatically if MRP calculates a new use-up date for the assembly. If the change is driven by the use-up of a component of the assembly, MRP will trigger the ECO Use Up Alert to notify the appropriate planner.

NOTE
At present, Use-Up planning is only integrated with MRP, not with Advanced Supply Chain planning.

Discrete versus Repetitive Planning Logic

Oracle Applications allow you to plan for both discrete and repetitive production methods in a single plan. Discrete production involves recording production against discrete jobs, sometimes called *work orders* or *production orders*. Discrete jobs represent production of a specific quantity of an item, completed on a specific date. Repetitive production records production against repetitive schedules, which represent a continuous rate production for a period of time. While much of the planning logic is the same, there are a few key differences between discrete and repetitive production that necessitate differences in the planning logic.

NOTE
Don't confuse repetitive production with flow manufacturing. Repetitive production *is designed for relatively high volume, continuous production of standard items.* Flow manufacturing *is designed for rapid production of individual items, even custom-configured products, at varying rates of production.*

Repetitive Production Concepts

A repetitive schedule represents continuous production over a period of time; it models an ongoing rate of production and ongoing consumption of components. Compare this with a discrete job that represents production of a specific quantity of a product on a specific date and models an individual requirement date for each component. Whereas a discrete job has a start date and a completion date, a repetitive schedule is defined by four dates:

- **First unit start**   The date that the first unit is started on a production line

- **First unit completion**   The date that the first unit is completed on the end of the production line

- **Last unit start**   The date the last unit on the schedule starts down the production line

- **Last unit completion**   The date that the last unit is completed

These dates are represented in the following diagram:

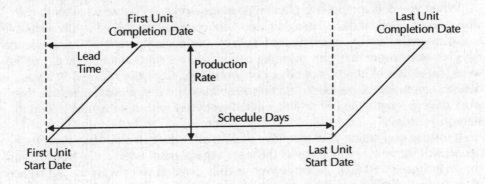

Discrete jobs have a total job quantity to be completed on a specific date. Each component on a discrete job is required on a specific date. Repetitive schedules, by contrast, represent a rate of production for a period of time (defined by the first and last unit completion dates). On a repetitive schedule, products are produced and components are required continuously over the duration of the schedule.

The nature of repetitive production requires slightly different planning logic than that described earlier; the following pages discuss differences between planning for discrete production and repetitive schedules.

Repetitive Planning Logic

The objective of repetitive planning is to calculate a smooth rate of production for a period of time. When planning repetitive production, the process calculates the rate of production by taking the average daily demand within user-defined buckets. This process requires some unique planning logic and uses some terminology that has not been discussed previously.

Planning Periods

You establish planning periods on the Planning Parameters form for each inventory organization. You define an Anchor Date, which marks the start of your repetitive planning periods. Initially, this should be the start date of the first repetitive planning period; after that, each time you run a plan the system will roll the anchor date forward, if necessary, to keep the anchor date consistent with the start of the first repetitive planning period. You also define two horizons as a number of days; this breaks up the planning horizon into three sets of periods. Within each, you define the size of the buckets. Smaller buckets are often used in the first set of periods, so that repetitive planning is more reactive to changes in demands, while larger buckets in the later sets of periods allow planning to generate smoother production plans.

When you define repetitive planning periods, you can choose whether to use workdays or calendar days. Though it seems counterintuitive, it is generally advisable to use calendar days to determine the length of your planning periods. Using calendar days lets you ensure that your planning periods always start on the same day of the week, regardless of holidays or other non-work days. Consider Figure 8-9; if you define your repetitive periods to start on a Monday and define each period as five work days in length, the first scheduled non-work day will shift the next period to start on Tuesday.

If instead you define your repetitive periods as seven calendar days long, each period will start on the same day of the week regardless of intervening holidays, as shown in Figure 8-10. Calculation of average daily demand will always use the number of work days within a period, even if the length of that period was determined by using calendar days.

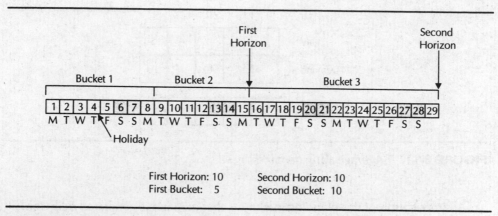

First Horizon: 10   Second Horizon: 10
First Bucket: 5   Second Bucket: 10

FIGURE 8-9. *Repetitive planning periods using work days*

Average Daily Demand

Consider the example in Figure 8-11. This example shows a weekly planning period, with demand of 40 on Wednesday of that week and demand of 10 on Friday. Since there are five working days in that weekly bucket, the average daily demand is 10 (50/5); consequently, planning will suggest a repetitive schedule with a daily rate of 10. Note, however, that this will not satisfy the demand of 40 on Wednesday; if you produce 10 per day, you will only have produced 30 by the end of the day on Wednesday and will not satisfy the total demand. To satisfy the demand, you may need to produce at a different rate than suggested, consider reducing the size of your repetitive planning buckets, or even consider if repetitive planning and production are suitable for a product with such an erratic demand pattern.

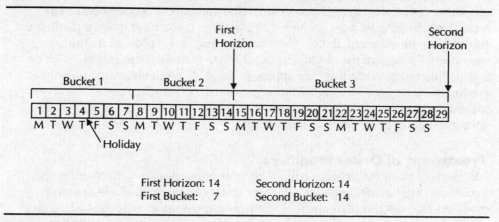

First Horizon: 14   Second Horizon: 14
First Bucket: 7   Second Bucket: 14

FIGURE 8-10. *Repetitive planning periods using calendar days*

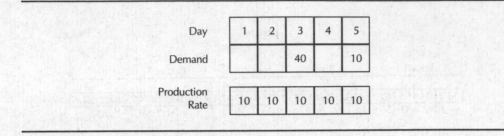

FIGURE 8-11. *Average daily demand*

An implication of this planning method is that demand is generated daily for the components of a repetitive schedule. This generally results in a large number of discrete demands. If you are not prepared to respond to these individually, you should consider adding order modifiers, for example, a minimum order quantity or fixed days supply.

Recognition of Existing Schedules

Perhaps the most unconventional aspect of repetitive planning is that it does not recognize, nor suggest changes to, any existing schedules. It always suggests new schedules. In part, this is because repetitive schedules have no identifying number (like a discrete job); they are identified by the rate and the four key dates. Suggesting a change to any of these parameters, therefore, means suggesting a new schedule. Thus, repetitive planning does not need to know the existing schedules; its job is to suggest the right rate of production.

Another implication of the fact that repetitive planning does not consider existing schedules is that any changes you made to the component requirements of a repetitive schedule are not considered in planning. If you have made a component substitution, for example, the planning process does not recognize it. Thus, you must carefully monitor the availability of substitute material (or excess plans for the original material). While this may appear problematic, remember that repetitive production is designed for high-volume production of standard items; if you are making frequent changes to component requirements, the product may not be a good candidate for repetitive manufacturing.

Treatment of Order Modifiers

Like discrete planning, repetitive planning uses order modifiers—minimum and maximum order quantities and fixed order quantity. While these are the same modifiers that discrete planning uses, they are interpreted as modifiers to the *daily rate*, not to the total schedule quantity. Keep this in mind if you use modifiers on repetitively planned items, or you can dramatically inflate your schedule rates.

NOTE
One exception to the use of order modifiers is the Fixed Days Supply modifier. Because repetitive planning inherently plans for a fixed number of days (as determined by your repetitive planning buckets), the Fixed Days Supply modifier is simply ignored for repetitive items.

Planning Controls

To allow you to build stability into repetitive plans, Oracle provides several controls that determine the maximum increase or decrease in repetitive schedules at different points in time. Oracle also allows you to specify how much overproduction you will tolerate, in order to reduce suggested changes to production rates.

First, within an item's lead time, planning will not suggest any new repetitive schedules. This reflects the fact that it is often difficult or impossible to change the production rate once an item has started down the assembly line.

Second, within an item's planning time fence, Oracle makes use of the item attributes Acceptable rate increase percent and Acceptable rate decrease percent. These attributes let you specify how much of a change is allowed within the planning time fence. These percentages are applied to the current rate of production and determine the maximum and minimum rates that planning will suggest for new schedules. For example, if the current production rate is 100 units per day, an Acceptable rate increase of 10 percent means that planning cannot suggest a new rate greater than 110 per day within the planning time fence. Similarly, an Acceptable rate decrease of 10 percent means that planning could not suggest a rate lower than 90 per day. Outside of the planning time fence, however, planning is free to suggest whatever rate is required.

Note that zeros and nulls are treated very differently in these attributes. A zero means the acceptable increase or decrease is indeed zero; no rate changes are allowed. Leaving the attribute blank (null) implies that there is no limit on the acceptable increase or decrease; planning can make whatever suggestions it wants.

To dampen minor fluctuations in repetitive schedules, planning uses another item attribute, Acceptable overrun percent. This is the amount that the current daily rate may exceed the optimal rate before planning will suggest a new rate. In other words, it is the rate of overproduction that is acceptable in order to avoid minor changes in scheduled rates. The overrun percent is applied to the optimal production rate, and the result is compared to the current aggregate rate. For example, if the optimal production rate is 100 units per day, and the Acceptable overrun percent is 10 percent, your current production rate could be as high as 110 per day before planning would suggest a new schedule with a lower rate.

Repetitive Schedule Allocation

Repetitive planning begins with the calculation of the total production required; this may be accomplished on multiple production lines, so the total required is referred to as the aggregate repetitive schedule. Once the aggregate rate of production is known, planning will allocate production across all the lines designated for the product. When you define production lines for an item, you specify the maximum rate the line can produce and assign a priority to that line and item combination; planning uses these rates and priorities to allocate production across lines.

The allocation process first attempts to assign production to the highest priority line (lowest number) for the item. Allocation will load the first line to its stated capacity, then load the second line to its capacity, and so on. If there is not enough capacity across all the designated lines for an item, allocation will load the excess production onto the first line. Note that while allocation will attempt to respect the maximum stated capacity of a line for an item, it does not consider the load placed by other items that may also be scheduled on the line. Also keep in mind that it will overload the primary line for an item, if necessary.

Repetitive Schedule Implementation

You can implement repetitive schedules from the Planner Workbench in much the same way that you implement discrete jobs; simply select the job or schedule for release, and initiate the load process from the Planner Workbench. This initiates the WIP Job/Schedule Interface program to load the job or schedule into WIP. But while a discrete job may be loaded in either a released or unreleased status, repetitive schedules are always loaded with a status of Pending – Mass Loaded.

This status avoids a restriction in WIP on the existence of overlapping repetitive schedules. WIP will not allow schedules for the same item on the same line to overlap, unless the schedules have a status of Cancelled or Pending – Mass Loaded. As mentioned earlier, planning always suggests the needed schedule and does not suggest changes to existing schedules. If you have already implemented a repetitive schedule for the same item, line, and time period, a new schedule would overlap. Thus, schedules implemented from the Planner Workbench always carry the status of Pending – Mass Loaded. You must release these schedules in WIP, respecting the restriction on overlapping schedules, before you can report production against the new schedule.

When you release a repetitive schedule, you have the opportunity of closing or canceling existing schedules; this lets you avoid overlapping schedules. Alternatively, you can simply modify the rate or dates of the existing schedule based on the suggestions of the new schedule; then you can cancel the new schedule. This is preferable if you have issued material or charged labor to the existing schedule, as it avoids misleading variances. The use of the Planner Workbench is discussed in detail in Chapter 11 and 12; repetitive production is described in more depth in Chapter 16.

Configuring Repetitive Planning

Repetitive planning requires the same setup as discrete planning. In addition, because of its unique requirements, it requires the following:

- Define production lines on the Production Lines form.

- Associate items and production lines using the Repetitive Line/Assembly Associations form.

- Define repetitive planning buckets on the Planning Parameters form.

- Designate the desired items to use repetitive planning logic on the Master Items or Organization Items forms.

- Set repetitive planning controls, also on the Master Items or Organization Items forms.

Kanban Planning

Another type of planning that Oracle Applications provides is kanban planning, part of Oracle's support for Flow Manufacturing techniques. As noted in Chapter 1, *kanban* is a Japanese word that suggests "sign" or "signal." From a manufacturing perspective, a kanban is a visual indicator—sometimes a card, sometimes an empty bin or rack— that triggers replenishment of an item. The intent is to streamline the manufacturing and procurement process; rather than relying on a computer simulation to suggest when to order, kanban replenishment triggers orders based on an operator actually signaling that more material is needed.

While kanban replenishment does not rely on MRP planning to launch the replenishment orders, effective use of kanbans does require appropriate sizing. If a kanban is too small, you might run out of material before it is replenished; if it is too big, you carry excess inventory. Oracle provides a kanban planner to size kanbans, and to resize them when necessary. In addition, though kanbans eliminate the launching of orders from MRP, MRP planning can still be valuable—it can provide calculation of usage over time, which can be useful in supplier negotiations or when deciding to expand manufacturing capacity.

Kanban Setup

You designate items as kanban-controlled through the item attribute Release Time Fence. Setting this attribute to Kanban Item (Do Not Release) prevents you from releasing orders from the Planner Workbench.

For the purposes of planning, kanban setup involves defining pull sequences, which specify the source of replenishment and planning parameters for kanban-planned items. For each item under kanban control, you define the subinventory and optional locator that you will replenish with the kanban. Then define the source of the replenishment (intra-org, inter-org, supplier, or production) and the appropriate source information. For example, for an inter-org kanban, you would specify the source organization, subinventory, and optional locator from which the material will be pulled.

The factors that control planning are the planning method, lead time, and lot sizing information for the specific kanban location. There are three planning methods:

- **Kanban size**   With this method, you specify the number of cards or kanbans you desire, and the planning process calculates the size of those kanbans, i.e., how much material must be replenished each time the kanban is signaled. For example, if you elect to employ a simple "two-bin" replenishment system, you would specify 2 as the number of kanbans; planning would calculate how much material is required in each bin to keep the line flowing smoothly and efficiently.

- **Number of cards**   Using this method, you specify the size of the kanban, and planning calculates the number of kanbans you need. For example, your kanban might be a rack or tote capable of holding a fixed amount of material, or you might determine the container size that an operator could move safely without assistance; planning determines how many of those containers you need.

- **Do not calculate**   With this method, you size your kanbans manually. This method excludes an item from kanban planning, while still letting you use the kanban to signal replenishment.

In addition, there are lead times and lot sizes defined for each pull sequence that affect the planning process:

- **Minimum order quantity**   This is defaulted from the item, but you can override for a specific pull sequence.

- **Lead time**   This is the lead time to replenish one kanban from its source.

- **Lot multiplier**   Use this if it makes sense to replenish in fixed multiples—for example, if the item has a natural lot size.

- **Allocation percent**   This represents the distribution of an item's demand across multiple locations.

- **Safety stock days**   The number of days of safety stock you want to maintain.

Additional detail on kanban setup is provided in Chapter 15.

Kanban Calculations

Kanban planning calculates the required number or size of kanbans, based on the planning method you specified for each pull sequence. Basically, the process looks at the average daily demand you supply and the planning parameters from each pull sequence and determines how much material or how many kanbans are needed to supply that demand. The details of the calculation program are described in detail in the Oracle Master Scheduling/MRP and Oracle Supply Chain Planning User's Guide, part of the Oracle documentation library provided with the software.

Average Daily Demand

A key to kanban planning is the calculation of average daily demand. When you define a kanban plan, you specify the source of demand—you can use a forecast, a master schedule (MDS or MPS), or actual production. For your initial kanban plan, you might want to use the same forecast or master schedule used for validating your line design on the Mixed Model Map (see Chapter 7). This forecast or schedule should be typical of the mix and volume of demand for which you are designing your line. On an ongoing basis you should check your kanban sizes against actual or planned production; this will give you early warning signs of changes in demand that might require intervention—perhaps the creation of a non-replenishable kanban to accommodate a one-time spike or a shift in demand patterns that might require a permanent change in your kanban sizes. This ongoing evaluation is often overlooked in flow manufacturing environments, but the simplicity of the Kanban Planner makes it easy to do.

Once the demand is identified, the kanban planning process performs an explosion much like MRP to determine dependent demands for your kanban items. The planner then applies the factors you defined in your pull sequences and uses the calculated yields from your flow routings to determine the optimal size or number of kanbans.

Effectivity Date Changes

It is important to note that kanban planning does not take into account effectivity date changes. The explosion process determines average daily demand using the effectivity date you specify when you run the plan; it does not see pending bill of material changes. Because kanban planning uses the average daily demand, recognizing pending bill of material changes would result in incorrect kanban sizes. For example, if you were replacing one component with another, the average demand would be too low for each component, and the kanbans would be sized inappropriately.

Generating and Implementing Kanban Plans

To generate a kanban plan, you first define one or more plan names using the Kanban Names window. The only parameter you need to specify is the source of the demand you want to use.

Then, launch the plan on the Launch Kanban form. Specify the effectivity date to use when exploding bills of material. You can optionally limit the plan to a range of items or item categories, and you can enter start and cutoff dates to restrict the demand data the plan considers.

When the planning process is complete, you can view the results on the Kanban Workbench, shown in Figure 8-12. The Details button shows the results of the planning process and the kanban parameters upon which that plan is based. You can view the demand used by the Kanban Planner with the Demand button.

If you want, you can rerun a portion of the kanban plan with new parameters—select one or more kanbans by checking the box to the left of each row on the Details window, and modify the desired parameters. You can modify the type of result you want to calculate (kanban size or number of cards), as well as source information, minimum order quantity, lead time, fixed lot multiplier, and safety stock days. For example, if you found that some kanbans were sized with odd quantities, you could specify the appropriate fixed lot multiplier. Save your changes, and click the Simulation Replan button. This will submit a request to run the Kanban Planner; when the planner completes, you can requery the form to see the new results.

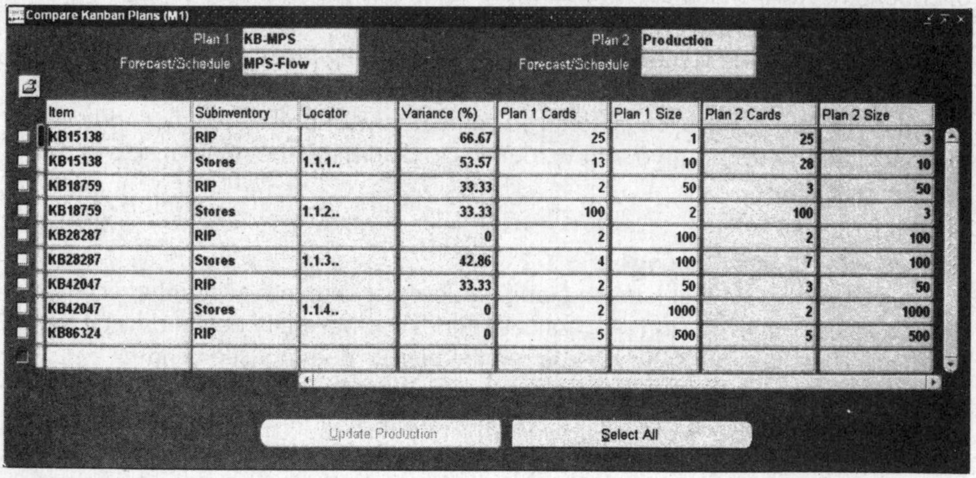

Compare Kanban Plans (M1)

Plan 1 **KB-MPS**   Forecast/Schedule **MPS-Flow**   Plan 2 **Production**   Forecast/Schedule

Item	Subinventory	Locator	Variance (%)	Plan 1 Cards	Plan 1 Size	Plan 2 Cards	Plan 2 Size
KB15138	RIP		66.67	25	1	25	3
KB15138	Stores	1.1.1..	53.57	13	10	28	10
KB18759	RIP		33.33	2	50	3	50
KB18759	Stores	1.1.2..	33.33	100	2	100	3
KB28287	RIP		0	2	100	2	100
KB28287	Stores	1.1.3..	42.86	4	100	7	100
KB42047	RIP		33.33	2	50	3	50
KB42047	Stores	1.1.4..	0	2	1000	2	1000
KB86324	RIP		0	5	500	5	500

Update Production   Select All

FIGURE 8-12. *View planning results on the Kanban Planner Workbench*

NOTE
Though Oracle calls this a simulation, there is no way to simply reset the plan to its state prior to the replan. To reset, you can either run the Kanban Planner again or change the parameters back to their original values and run the "simulation" again.

You can compare different plans, or you can compare the plan with the values that are currently driving your production execution system. When you press the Compare button, the Find window will ask for the name of the comparison plan; by default, it will select Production (i.e., the current definitions from your pull sequences), but you can select an alternative plan if you want.

TIP
To filter out trivial or nonexistent changes between plans, consider including selection on the Variance field in the Find window. For example, including the criterion Variance Greater Than 0 will show only differences between the plans.

You can implement suggested changes from either the Kanban Details or the Compare Kanban Plans window. To implement a change, select one or more kanbans with their selection check boxes (or use the Select All button), and click the Update Production button. This will update your current pull sequences with the information from the selected kanban plan. You will need to regenerate and reprint the kanban cards as described in Chapter 15; for convenience, the Tools menu on the Kanban Planner Workbench provides a link to the Kanban Cards form and allows you to print selected kanbans.

Planning Parameters and Profiles

A number of parameters, profiles, and item and bill of material attributes control the planning process. These are described in detail in the user guides for Master Scheduling/MRP, Inventory, and Bills of Material, part of Oracle's documentation library. A few highlights are noted here.

Planning Parameters

The Planning Parameters form lets you specify execution defaults and repetitive planning parameters for your MPS, MRP, and DRP plans in each inventory organization. These parameters are copied to each plan you define, but you can override them in the Plan Options window.

MRP Profiles

There are almost 100 profile options that control the execution and defaults of MRP plans (number of workers, debug mode, etc.). Most of these can be set at the site level, but several may be useful to set defaults for individual users. For example, the profiles MRP: Default Forecast Name, MRP: Default Plan Name, MRP: Default Schedule Name, and MRP: Default DRP Plan Name provide defaults for the forecasts, MRP plans, master schedules, and DRP plans that a user will work with on various inquiry and update forms. A default plan name will open automatically when you invoke the appropriate form; this saves you from having to find or query the plan you want to use (though you can override the default if desired).

Item and BOM Attributes

Much of the detail of planning is controlled by the various item and bill of material attributes. These attributes were mentioned briefly in earlier chapters, but several key attribute groups (corresponding to tabs on the Master Items and Organization Items forms) are especially important to the planning process. These are described in the following sections.

General Planning Attributes

The General Planning tab (shown in Figure 8-13) includes attributes that control MRP and ASCP planning, as well as the simpler planning methods provided in Oracle Inventory (Min–Max and Reorder Point Planning). Of special interest are the following:

- **Planner** This field identifies the planner responsible for the item. Besides being a mechanism to select items in the Planner Workbench and sort various planning reports, the planner is required for ASCP to generate recommendations. The planner also must approve any move orders requesting the item. Define planner codes with the Planners form; optionally specify their employee name and e-mail address.

- **Make or Buy** This field, along with sourcing rules (described in Chapter 11), controls the default order type planned for the item. If it is set to "Make," planning explodes the item's bill of material and suggests discrete jobs to satisfy demand; if it is set to Buy, planning will not explode a bill of material and will suggest purchase requisitions. You can override the suggested order type based on the setting of the Purchasable and Build in WIP

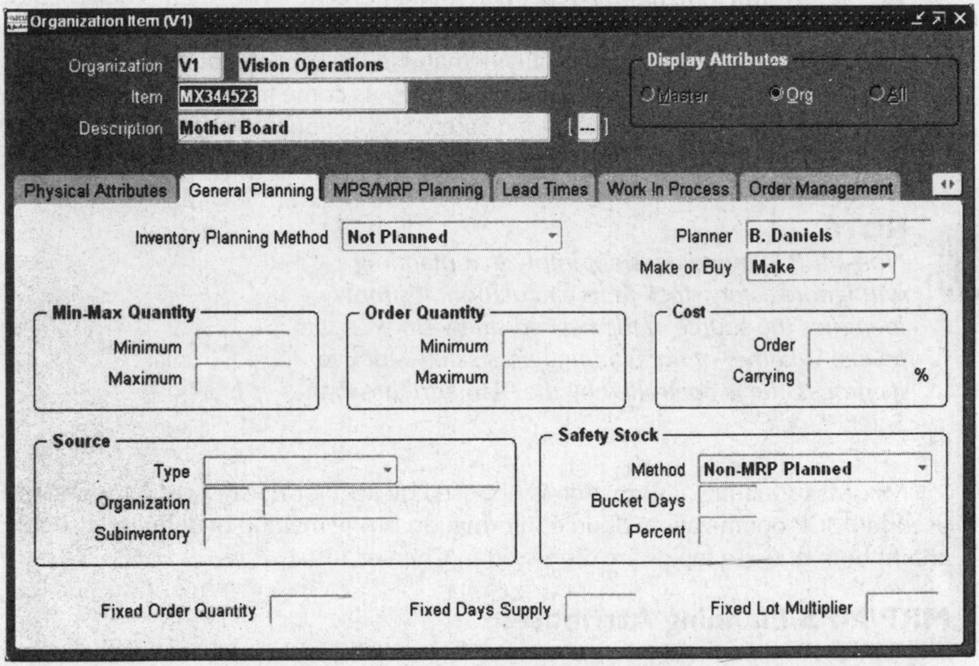

FIGURE 8-13.   *Item general planning attributes*

attributes. (This field also determines the default of the Based on Rollup attribute in Oracle Cost Management.)

■ **Order Quantity Modifiers—Minimum, Maximum, Fixed Order Quantity, and Fixed Lot Multiplier**   These attributes determine the quantity of the planned orders that MRP or ASCP can suggest; use them if there is a natural or economic lot size for the item (e.g. certain products are not practical to order in small or odd quantities; others might require a separate order if the order would be more than a full truckload, etc.). But use these with caution in a "lean" manufacturing environment; they can inflate order quantities and contribute to excessive inventory levels.

■ **Fixed Days Supply**   This attribute, sometimes called "period of supply," tells planning to generate planned orders to cover requirements for a certain number of working days. This will limit the total number of orders that are generated over time, but will result in overall higher inventory levels; consider using it for inexpensive items where the cost of ordering exceeds the carrying cost of the early inventory.

■ **Safety Stock Method, Bucket Days, and Percent** The safety stock method MRP Planned % tells planning to dynamically calculate safety stock as the percentage of the average daily demand in the buckets you specify. Non-MRP Planned means that safety stock levels come from Oracle Inventory, either calculated by the Reload Safety Stocks concurrent program in Oracle Inventory, or manually entered on the Enter Item Safety Stock form.

NOTE
Non-MRP Planned does not imply that planning will ignore safety stock in its calculation; it simply identifies the source of the desired safety stock levels. Whether or not planning uses safety stock in its processing is controlled by the plan attribute Plan Safety Stock.

Mix-Max Quantity information is not used by MRP or ASCP. Cost information is used in ASCP optimization; Source information is one method of defining a supply chain; both of these topics are discussed in Chapter 11.

MRP/MPS Planning Attributes

The MRP/MPS Planning Attributes tab (see Figure 8-14) includes the fields that pertain specifically to MRP planning. The following fields are important:

■ **Planning Method** The planning method determines the types of plans in which an item participates.

■ **Forecast Control** This attribute controls forecast explosion and consumption, as described earlier.

■ **Pegging** This determines the pegging information calculated by the plan. End assembly pegging maintains a "peg" or link to the end assembly responsible for the demand; Soft pegging maintains a link to the immediate source of the demand; Hard pegging is used for Project MRP. Various combinations of these values are allowed.

■ **Exception Set** The exception set controls certain types of exceptions. To define exception sets on the Planning Exception Sets form, give each set a name and set the sensitivity and time period for six types of exceptions: Shortages, Excess inventory, Overpromised inventory, Repetitive variances, Resource over-utilization, and Resource under-utilization. You may have different exception sets for different classes of items; for example, your definition of "excess" inventory will probably vary for inexpensive, fast-moving items versus expensive, slow-movers. Note that if an item has no exception set, the exceptions listed here will not be reported for the item.

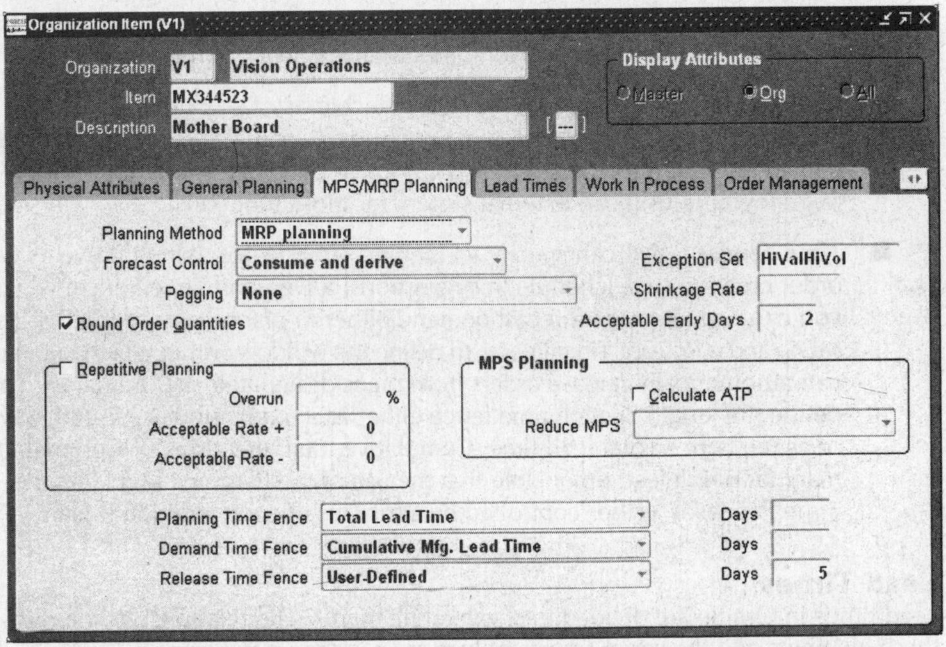

FIGURE 8-14. *Item MRP/MPS planning attributes*

■ **Shrinkage Rate** The shrinkage is a decimal factor, usually small, that reflects an anticipated loss of the item during its manufacture or procurement; planning will inflate order quantities to account for this expected loss. Compare this with component yield, discussed later in this chapter.

■ **Acceptable Early Days** This attribute filters out some "nervousness" in the plan. It suppresses "reschedule out" suggestions for existing orders if the order would be rescheduled by less than the number of acceptable early days. In other words, it defines how many days early an order can be before planning will suggest rescheduling it out.

■ **Round Order Quantities** If enabled, this check box tells the planning process to round planned order quantities up to the next higher integer. Note that this affects planned orders only; it does not directly affect the calculation of dependent demand or of WIP requirements, which may be fractional due to yield factors.

■ **Repetitive Planning attributes** Overrun % and Acceptable rate increase and decrease, as described earlier in the "Repetitive Planning" section.

- **Calculate ATP** This check box determines whether planning calculates and prints the available to promise on the Planning Detail Report; it does not affect the calculation of ATP for Order Management or Inventory inquiries.

- **Reduce MPS** This attribute lets you reduce master production schedule quantities based on the passage of time; use this only if you are not relieving the MPS through the creation of WIP jobs or purchase requisitions/orders (e.g., if you're using an external system for those functions).

- **Time Fences** You can specify a Planning Time Fence, which prevents new order creation or reschedule in suggestions; a Demand Time Fence, which you can use to ignore forecast demand either in planning or in loading an MDS; and a Release Time Fence, to define the window within which planning can automatically release orders from plans designated as Production. You define the length of each time fence either as a fixed number of work days or as the item's Total lead time, Cumulative total lead time, or Cumulative manufacturing lead time. Note that the use of the Planning and Demand Time Fences is further controlled by attributes of each individual plan.

Lead Times

Lead times in Oracle are divided into several elements. The relationship between these elements and the various types of lead time is shown in Figure 8-15.

- **Preprocessing** The time it takes to prepare an order for release; this might be the time it takes to prepare a shop packet for manufacturing or to prepare a purchase order. This is sometimes referred to as paperwork lead time.

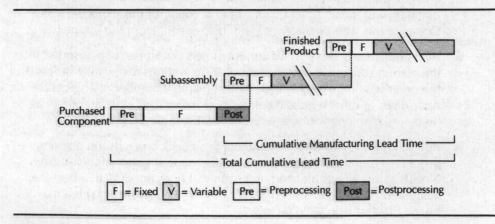

FIGURE 8-15. *Lead time elements and relationships*

■ **Fixed**   The portion of an item's lead time that does not vary with the order quantity. Setup time is a typical example; this is often a fixed amount of time, regardless of the size of the order. Planning uses fixed lead time to plan both manufacturing and purchase orders.

■ **Variable**   The portion of lead time that varies with the order quantity. Planning uses variable lead time to plan manufacturing orders only.

■ **Processing**   The time it takes for a supplier to fulfill your purchase order once released or the typical time it takes to complete a discrete job for the item. For manufactured items, this can be calculated from the fixed and variable lead times and represents the time it takes to manufacture the Lead time lot size quantity of the item; as such, it is an average. It is used to calculate the cumulative lead times. Planning does not use processing lead time at all for manufactured items; it uses the combined fixed and variable lead time. For purchased items, planning will use the processing lead time only if you do not specify a fixed lead time for the item.

■ **Postprocessing**   The time it takes to put away purchased material after it is received. Planning uses this for purchased material only; for manufactured items, you should include this in your routings if it is significant.

You can calculate fixed, variable, and processing lead times from your routing time, as described in Chapter 4. This process uses the lead time lot size, which you also specify on this tab.

The Lead Times tab also includes two types of cumulative lead time:

■ **Cumulative Total**   The "critical path" lead time, or the time it takes to buy the first piece of raw material, manufactures all the subassemblies and makes the item.

■ **Cumulative Manufacturing**   The cumulative lead time for manufacturing activities only; this is the cumulative total lead time, minus the purchasing lead time.

Cumulative lead times can be used to set the different planning time fences or the Infinite Supply Horizon in Oracle Inventory ATP rules. Using a cumulative lead time instead of a user-defined number of days means that these fences and horizons can shrink as you reduce lead times, without additional maintenance. Cumulative lead times are also helpful in reviewing proposed engineering changes; if you schedule a change inside an item's cumulative lead time, you may require expediting of material to satisfy the new demand. You can calculate cumulative lead times with the Rollup Cumulative Lead Times concurrent program after you have calculated or entered your item lead times.

Purchasing and WIP Attributes

The Purchasable and Build in WIP attributes control what types of orders you can release from the Planner Workbench. One or both of these must be enabled to allow you to release orders. The Make or Buy attribute and sourcing rules control the default type of order that is suggested, but you can override the suggestion with a different order type if the appropriate attribute is enabled.

BOM Information

The following component information from your bills of material is worth special mention in terms of planning:

- **Operation Seq** Identifies the routing operation at which the component is consumed. If you are planning by Operation Start Date, this information is used along with the Lead Time % from the item's routing to estimate when the component is needed. If your plan options specify planning by Order Start Date, this information is irrelevant for planning purposes; all material is planned to be available at the start of the job.

- **Planning Percent** Used in forecast explosion and in planning for Model, Option class, and Planning bills of material. The planning percent reflects the anticipated distribution of the component. Note that planning percents do not have to equal 100 percent. Certain optional components in a model will naturally total something other than 100 percent usage, and you can explicitly over- or underplan if you choose.

- **Yield** A decimal factor that represents the anticipated loss (or gain) of the component in manufacturing. Note that yield is expressed as a decimal factor and defaults to 1. A yield of .98, for example, represents that you expect to lose 2 percent of the component in the manufacturing process; planning will inflate the gross requirements of this component accordingly. Compare this with the item attribute Shrinkage; shrinkage represents an anticipated loss of the assembly in manufacturing or a purchased part during the procurement cycle. Planning will inflate the order quantity to account for shrinkage. It is expressed as a decimal quantity and defaults to 0. A shrinkage of .02, for example, indicates that you expect to reject 2 percent of the material during incoming inspection if it's a purchased part. These two factors, shrinkage and yield, are often confused. Though it is sometimes possible to manipulate the factors to give the same result, they are intended to model two very different events.

- **Material Control** For the most part, the material control attribute affects manufacturing execution, but two values have special significance in planning. A value of Supplier is intended to identify a part that is provided by your supplier as part of outside processing; you are not responsible for procuring this part, so planning will not plan it. A value of Phantom invokes planning's phantom-part logic; it will "blow through" these parts and plan for their components directly. (Internally, planning actually does generate orders for the phantom, but these orders are visible on the Planner Workbench only if you query them explicitly.)

Planning Manager

The Planning Manager is a concurrent program (*not* a Concurrent Manager, despite the name); its function is to manage many of the "housekeeping" activities required in the planning environment. For example, the Planning Manager performs forecast consumption and master schedule relief. It also processes the forecast and master schedule interfaces, validating the data and populating the forecast and master schedules tables.

It is important that the Planning Manager be active. If it is not, you might see some unexpected results in planning. For example, you will not see discrete jobs or purchase orders for master schedule item in your plans; the rationale is these might not have been reviewed for master schedule relief, and if that relief did not occur, planning might overstate the master schedule.

The Planning Manager typically runs continually in a production environment, though the program itself executes on a regular interval; during the day it will execute and then schedule itself (with the same concurrent request ID) to run again. The next day, a new concurrent request ID will be assigned.

You can determine if the Planning Manager is active by examining the Active check box on the Planning Manager form, by using the View Requests form (the program should be running or pending), or by examining its log file for recent activity. You start the Planning Manager on the Launch Planning Manager form; the only parameter required is the Processing Interval. Oracle recommends starting with the default interval of 30 seconds.

Summary

This chapter covered the common features of single-organization MRP and multi-organization Advanced Supply Chain Planning. It described the planning process and basic forecasting, master scheduling, and capacity planning terminology and activities. This chapter described engineering's impact on planning and the unique characteristics of repetitive planning and kanban planning. It also covered basic setup steps, including the critical item and bill of material attributes that control the planning process.

The following chapters provide details on Oracle Demand Planning and the unique features of MRP and ASCP.

CHAPTER
9

Demand Planning

n Oracle Manufacturing, Demand Planning is at the front end of the planning process. It is where you create and manipulate predictions of future demand. It gives these users an environment where they can "slice and dice" volume data. You can create these predictions yourself, or you can use the history created through the shipping system to create your time series data. You can combine calculated forecast data and adjust for events such as promotions, price increases, cannibalization from new product lines, etc. The responsibility for portions of the forecast can be assigned and then the aggregate forecast assembled for final review. It is a collaborative process involving internal and external participants. Information from several sources is collected and organized in order to estimate future demand based on market conditions. ODP provides exception-based forecast tracking and notifications. Figure 9-1 gives an overview of the demand planning collaboration.

Demand Planning Overview

Oracle Demand Planning (ODP) generates demand forecasts that form the basis of plans from long-term strategic business plans to forecasts that feed the master production schedule. ODP collects data from Oracle Applications into a central planning server. It comes with predefined collections for 10.7, 11.0, and 11i.

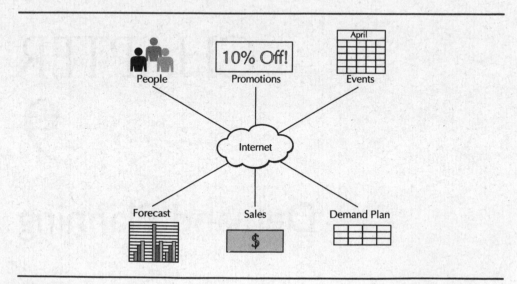

FIGURE 9-1. *Demand Planning in a collaborative world*

What Demand Planning Does

Demand Planning collects time series information from many data sources including shipments, bookings, opportunities, and other forecasts. Feeds into ODP can be time series data from Oracle Shipping, bookings from Oracle Order Entry, or a forecast from Oracle Manufacturing or a third-party application. ODP allows the data to be viewed at multiple levels of aggregation. It enables you to summarize the item, geographic, organization, and time hierarchies. When used with the Advanced Planning and Scheduling system, it creates the demand forecast that will drive the planning and scheduling systems.

ODP has capabilities to model promotions, product introductions with associated cannibalizations, and product phase outs. When making changes to the forecast, planners also associate change reasons with comments, creating an audit trail and knowledge base for future plans. Forecasts can be created at any level and later reconciled on a top-down or bottom-up basis.

Demand Planning User Interface

Demand Planning is used by professional analysts within the enterprise, as well as occasional users within the enterprise and in customer and distributor enterprises. Demand Planning provides interfaces for untrained users that are accessible through a Web browser, interfaces tuned for analytical processing as well as reports and notifications.

User Interfaces Available to Partners over the Internet

Oracle Demand Planning supports Internet collaboration, incorporating information from sales, marketing, operations, and customers. You can also manage multiple scenarios to develop a collaborative consensus demand plan. It is built on Oracle's Internet computing architecture, which enables all of the applications to be deployed over the Internet or your corporate intranet. ODP is also completely integrated with Oracle's Self-Service Web Applications. Any authorized person with a Web browser can verify and adjust forecasts based on local knowledge.

User Interfaces Tuned for Multidimensional Analysis

The *Worksheet* user interface provides drill and pivot capability. You can create a worksheet with selected measures and dimension values, adjusting the size of the columns to fit your data. You can arrange the dimensions on the page according to how you want to view the data. You can view a more detailed or higher level of data. You can view a different page of the worksheet.

Reporting and Alerting

ODP comes with a set of feedback and alerting mechanisms that range from preconfigured reports to user-defined alerts that will deliver e-mail when the defined condition is met. Such conditions might be significant forecast error for a particular region or low margin for a given product family. Both the preconfigured and ad hoc reporting tools come with graphing or export to Excel. The reports can handle currency and unit of measure conversions to ensure that the aggregate reports are expressed in common measures.

Demand Planning Technology

ODP imbeds state-of-the-art forecasting technologies from Geneva Forecasting. It supports level trend and seasonal exponential smoothing, linear and non-linear regression with outlier detection, and best fit analysis.

Oracle Express server is the database at the back end providing data manipulation and analytical capabilities.

Demand Planning Terminology

You should be familiar with the following terms that will be used throughout this chapter:

- **Scenario** A set of circumstances that might occur in the future, that you are creating a demand forecast for.

- **Measure** An attribute of the plan that determines its success as a plan. One such attribute might be forecast error. Another might be the profit yielded by the plan.

- **Forecast** A prediction of future demand in quantitative terms.

- **Baseline forecast** The forecast generated by the assigned forecasting method for a given scenario, before planners make any changes based on local knowledge.

- **Dimension** An attribute of the forecasts and planning data, that you might want to see quantities or measures aggregated by. For example, you might want to see the forecast error at various levels in the product dimension.

- **Hierarchy** A number of levels within a hierarchy. For example, the geography dimension can contain the location hierarchy. This extends from the customer location through countries and regions to "All Geographies."

■ **Time series data**   Any collection information about something varying over time. Demand or shipment information is an obvious example. Quality data or machine failure information might be others.

Understanding the Demand Planning Environment

ODP uses Oracle Express as the database that holds the forecast data. It is important to understand the distinction between the planning server, the demand planning consolidated database, and the individual planner databases. Figure 9-2 illustrates how the different pieces of the Express Server relate to each other.

The planning server holds all of the time series data, sales plans, and demand from internal or customer sources. The demand planning shared database holds the consolidated forecasts from all of the planners. Only the Plan Manager has access to this environment. Each planner has a personal database that holds the forecast for his or her portion of the aggregated forecast. Planners can manipulate plans and create histories and forecasts in their own private databases.

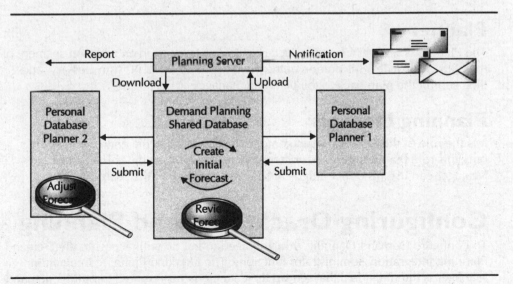

FIGURE 9-2.   *Demand Planning environment*

Understanding Demand Planning Roles

Your system administrator might have chosen different names for the roles and responsibilities in Demand Planning, but the following is a brief overview of the division of work. This division is delivered as different responsibilities.

Demand Planning Integration Administrator

The Demand Planning Integration Administrator is the individual who is responsible for a demand plan. You set up dimensions and hierarchies for Demand Planning and set up the ERP instances that Demand Planning will be working with. You set up demand plans with the express databases and run the collections from the source instances and publication of the forecasts. This work is done from within the Oracle Applications environment.

Planning Administrator

The Demand Plan Administrator assigns parts of the planning problem to individual planners. They track the progress of the Demand Planning cycle as well as defining and setting up planning alerts. This work is done from within the Express Server.

Planner

The Planner is responsible for the accuracy of the forecast in an assigned segment of the plan. You review his portion of the plan, make adjustments as necessary, and then submit the plan back to the planning manager.

Planning Manager

It is the role of the Planning Manager to review and adjust the entire forecast. It is only this role that gets this unrestricted view of the forecast data. The Planning Manager can use his or her judgment to adjust the plan in the shared database.

Configuring Oracle Demand Planning

To configure Demand Planning, you will need to log on with access to the Demand Planning Integration Administrator functions. The Demand Planning Integration Manager is the individual that sets up the data elements required to build a demand plan. These Data elements include Dimensions, Hierarchies, Planning Levels, Plan Names, Express set up data, Plans, and Output Scenarios. Oracle collects data into the planning server through a layer of views. As delivered these are collecting against the Oracle transaction systems, but the views provide an insulation should you need to integrate Demand Planning with other systems.

Demand Planning Dimensions

Dimensions are the ways that you "slice and dice" your data within the Demand Planning. You should think about the ways that your company assigns responsibility for tracking and achieving volume.

Oracle provides six predefined dimensions and two dimensions that can be user defined. You can also change the names and descriptions for the dimensions that Oracle delivers. For example, Oracle delivers a dimension for "Ship From Location." You might want to rename this to "Shipping Warehouse." Navigate to the Dimensions form in the Set Up menu.

Demand Planning Hierarchies

Hierarchies are the routes up the dimensions that you aggregate data. For example, you can aggregate data from customer site level up a geography dimension. To set up a dimension, navigate to the Hierarchies form in the Set Up menu. You will see the Oracle has seeded a number of hierarchies. For example, there are three hierarchies sharing the geography dimension: Customer Class, Customer Group, and Geography.

Demand Planning Levels

You might want to show projected volumes for a product grouping at various levels. Levels might include

- Customer site to plan distribution requirements, aggregated to

- Customer to verify with the account manager, aggregated to

- Customer class to verify with the sales manager, aggregated to

- All Geography to verify with the factory manager

To define the levels within a hierarchy you can either navigate to the Levels form in the Set Up menu, or you can create the Hierarchy Levels from the Hierarchy Definitions form. In the level definition you can state whether the level is Top, bottom or intermediate. This determines the navigation up and down the hierarchy.

Demand Planning Hierarchy Levels

To set up this hierarchy, click the Hierarchy Levels button in the Hierarchies form. You will see that levels within a hierarchy refer to their parent levels to form the hierarchy. Figure 9-3 illustrates how the hierarchies and hierarchy levels fit together.

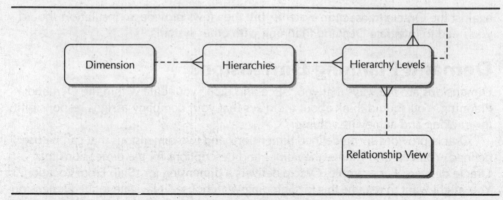

FIGURE 9-3. *Setting up Demand Planning herarchies*

You will also notice that the relationship between the parent and child levels is in a view. As delivered this view is over Oracle Applications, but if you are integrating to other systems, you can name a view that defines the relationship. For the form to work correctly the view that you define must return the following columns:

```
Name                       Null?  Type
--------------------------------- -------- ----
LEVEL_VALUE_PK             NUMBER
LEVEL_VALUE                VARCHAR2(4000)
PARENT_VALUE_PK            VARCHAR2(40)
PARENT_VALUE               VARCHAR2(4000)
ATTRIBUTE1                 VARCHAR2(0)
ATTRIBUTE2                 VARCHAR2(0)
ATTRIBUTE3                 VARCHAR2(0)
ATTRIBUTE4                 VARCHAR2(0)
ATTRIBUTE5                 VARCHAR2(0)
```

Defining Events

You can define marketing promotions, new product introductions, and phase outs to be considered within a demand-planning scenario. Navigate to the Promotions and Other Events form. Enter the name of the promotion. You can promote an individual product, a product family, a category, or all products. Enter the Start Date and End Date for the promotion. Click the Details button to record the effects of the promotional activity. The promotion will affect demand in different ways for different periods during the promotion. For example, if the promotion is a retail promotion and the retailers fill the shelves, there will be an initial peak followed by a plateau in demand at a higher level than unpromoted demand. The promotion will be running within a portion of the plan identified by the dimensions and levels. For example, the promotion might be running on the West Coast, through the Direct Sales Channel, in the Major Accounts Sales Organizations, serviced from the Nevada Distribution Center. Events are used in the definition of the Demand Plan scenario.

Defining Introductions

New Product Introductions enable you to use history of the Base Product to calculate forecast for the new item. It enables you to specify the Cannibalized Items whose demand is likely to fall due to the new product being introduced. For example, a manufacturer of communications equipment may move into the PDA market. The sales of PDAs will be based roughly on the sales of the smaller cell phones. The older cell phones will be unaffected by the PDAs as the buyers are likely to be early adopters who will choose between the high-end cell and the PDA.

Defining the Instances and Organizations to Be Collected from

Demand Planning is designed to get time series data from many data sources. These data sources could be on many instances. An enterprise might be running some divisions on one instance of Oracle Applications and other divisions on another. You can define the instances to collect from and the Organizations within those instances by navigating to the Instances form in the Set Up menu.

NOTE
You will have to run the Demand Planning Setup Data Collection once to collect the organization and item category information.

Defining Demand Plans

With the Demand Planning system configured you can start to define demand plans. Demand plans consist of a header that defines the dimensions that the demand plan will be analyzed by, the inputs that the demand plan will be based on, and the scenarios that the demand plan will attempt to forecast. The scenario has a set of events beyond the time series data to be considered, such as promotions and product introductions. The scenario is also defined by the levels at which the output of the planning scenario occurs. Figure 9-4 is a sample of a completed demand plan ready to start its cycle.

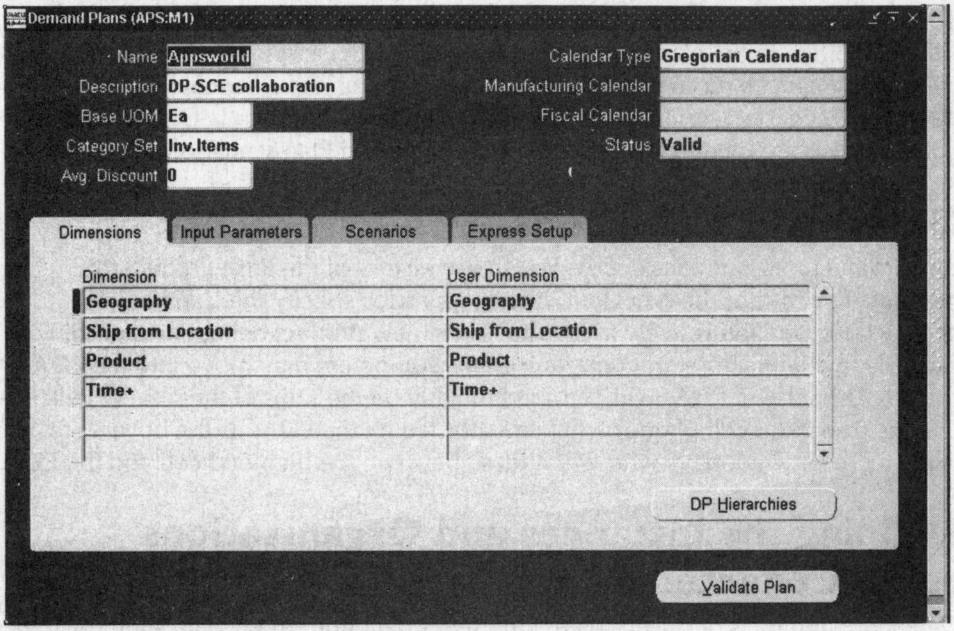

FIGURE 9-4. *A sample demand plan*

Defining Demand Plan Headers

As delivered, the demand plans are defined using the Demand Planning Administrator responsibility. Navigate to the Demand Plans form in the Demand Plan Definitions menu. Figure 9-5 illustrates how the demand plan is assembled from Inputs, Scenarios, and Outputs.

Your demand plan could be for any portion of the business. Decide on a name and description. You might need to decide on a common unit of measure to express volumes, if you want to show aggregate measures volume for items that have difference primary units of measure in their time series data.

NOTE
Unit of measure conversions are collected from the source system.

You will need to choose the item category set that represents the product hierarchy used for Demand Planning.

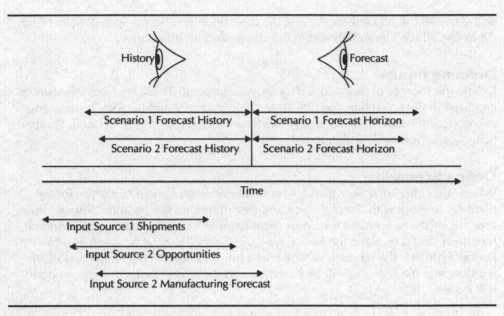

FIGURE 9-5. *Setting up a demand plan*

NOTE
Item Categories are a multi-segment key flex. As at time of going to press, Oracle does not support multiple levels in this hierarchy. For more information on item categories review Chapter 3 which covers engineering and product management.

You can also define the Average Discount to assume from the list price for calculating the future revenue stream. The volumes will be bucketed in time according to the type and name of the calendar that you choose.

Defining Dimensions

Define the Dimensions that you wish to use to analyze your data. Time and Product are mandatory. If you want to analyze by more than four dimensions, you will have to "collapse" those dimensions into "user dimension." For example, you might want to analyze by "Sales Representative" and can "Collapse" Sales Representative into Geography. The leaf node of the hierarchy will then be location and sales representative, rather than location. To be able to analyze the data using hierarchies within these dimensions you will need to click on the DP Hierarchies button. This will show all the hierarchies that use the dimension you have selected. Select Copy All to use all the hierarchies within this dimension for this plan.

Defining Inputs

Define the sources of time series data for your forecast. These are from the sources captured in the collection and pull stages. For shipment and booking history, you can choose the date that you would like to use as the time series: Booked, Shipped, Scheduled, Promised, or Requested.

Define Scenarios

When you choose the Scenarios tab, you are defining possible outcomes for the planners to work with. Enter a name and description for the scenario. For example, you might have a scenario for a new competitor entry, a scenario for an economic recession, and a scenario for a price war. Define the Forecast type and Forecast Period Type that the scenario will be based on. You need to define the historical window that the scenario will be based on and the future period that the scenario will cover.

Associate Events   You can associate events that you have defined in the Define Events and Promotions. Click the Events button and choose from the list.

Define Output Levels   Click the Output Levels button. You should think about the level that will be appropriate to generate the forecast at. If you generate the forecast at low levels, it can overwhelm the audience with too much detail. However, if the output is at too high a level, it will be forced down through allocation rules to lower levels. This can force local conditions to be "spread" across your plan. For example, if you output at "Region" level, but have a large demand from a particular "Customer," this local variation will be spread across all customers for that region.

Defining the Express Setup

The last tab is where you define the Express Setup. This is a highly technical function that you will need knowledge of the network topology to complete. The EAD (Express Applications Database) name is the name of the express database instance. The Express Port is the name and port number of the machine. The Shared Database Prefix defines how the shared Express databases will be named when it is created. If you leave this blank, the shared database will be created as *OPD<Demand Plan Name>*. The Express Connect String is how the information is passed to and from the express environments. The Shared Database Location is where the shared database will get created. The OWA (Oracle Web Agent) Virtual Path is the virtual directory path defined in the Oracle Express Web Agent cartridge.

Demand Planning Administrator Functions

The Demand Plan Administrator performs his work in the Express environment to administer and monitor the demand plan. The functions of the Demand Plan Administrator include

- Setting up the Express system parameters
- Managing predefined reports
- Managing Demand Plan Assignments
- Setting scenario properties
- Tracking progress of the demand plan

Setting Up Oracle Express System Parameters

You will need to specify the location of the public, shared, and private databases for Demand Planning. In the Navigator, go to Database Information. You can also change the appearance of the demand-planning page for the users with a background image and welcome text. If you leave this blank, the standard message will greet users.

You also specify how the application will handle Java foundation classes on this page. You can opt to install Oracle Jinitiator, enable users to access Java foundation classes remotely, or enable local install of Java Foundation classes. Jinitiator is Oracle's Java program for running its applications.

NOTE
The default setting is Local Cache Install of Jinitiator.
Check to ensure that users' PCs meet memory
requirements for the installed version of Jinitiator.

The Jinitiator properties are only relevant if you have chosen the Jinitiator option as the installation type.

Managing Predefined Reports

As Demand Planning Administrator you can select the predefined reports to make available to the planners and plan managers. You can specify the dimensions for which the reports can be generated and determine certain default report parameters. Default settings for predefined reports are Time Levels, Comparison Measures, and Review Document Dimension.

Dimension Selection Options

Single or multiple dimensions can be selected for each report. For example, if you select the Growth report and choose the Geography and Product dimensions, users will see a Growth folder with both Product Growth and Geography Growth documents.

Dimension Selection Restrictions

Restrictions for multiple dimensions apply to Mix Comparison Report and the Sales Trend reports. For Mix Comparison Report, only the Product dimension is available. For the Sales Trend and Cumulative Sales Trend Reports, the Analysis Dimension must be one of Time. Time cannot be an Analysis Dimension for any other report. Dimensions selected for reports must have a hierarchy defined. See the section "Configuring Oracle Demand Planning" for information on hierarchies.

Managing Demand Plan Assignments

Demand Planning responsibilities might be any combination of item, geographic, or customer characteristics. If you log with a responsibility with Demand Plan Administrator functions, you will be taken to the Web-based planning environment of Express. In the Navigation list, choose Demand Planner Assignments. The window for maintaining assignments appears in the workspace. Scroll to the bottom of the page and choose New. A row for "New Assignment" is inserted in the grid. Your Oracle ID is displayed as the default owner. Create a name for the assignment. Assign it to the proper planner using his or her Oracle ID. Choose Edit to assign the values for each dimension for this assignment. For example, Neptune might have a planner assignment for Server Products in Corporate Accounts on the West Coast. To check that there are no conflicts in the assignments, choose Refresh. A red flag will be displayed if conflicts are detected.

NOTE
To check for segments of data not yet assigned to any planner, scroll to the bottom of the Demand Planner Assignments list and choose Unassigned. An Unassigned dialog box appears with the unassigned data.

Setting Scenario Properties

In the Navigation list, choose Output Scenarios. The scenarios for the demand plan are displayed in the grid. Select a scenario and choose Properties. The Scenario Properties dialog box appears. The Forecast Method, Forecast Levels, and Allocation Rule tabs display the current settings for the scenario.

Specifying the Forecast Method

The forecasting engine that is included in Oracle Demand Planning offers a range of forecasting methods. A brief explanation of some of them follows:

- **Linear regression**   A forecasting method in which a linear relationship is determined from historical data. An example of a linear relationship might be a direct relationship between ice cream sales and sun tan lotion.

- **Polynomial regression**   A forecasting method of the nonlinear type in which a linear relation is fitted to a transformation of the original data. For example, the number of pairs of sunglasses is not directly related to the sales of ice cream. As the sales of ice cream increase the sales of sunglasses will also increase. But whereas people might buy ice cream every day, they are unlikely to buy sunglasses every day.

- **Exponential fit**   A forecasting method of the nonlinear regression type in which a linear relationship is fitted to a transformation of the original data between one variable and the log of the other variable. An example might be the correlation between time and Internet capacity, which doubles every six months.

- **Single exponential smoothing**   A forecasting method used where the volume is relatively fixed over time. Exponential smoothing gives an "average" of all the previous data, but will allow the average to "react" to the more recent data. It applies a proportion of the forecast error back to the forecast to come up with the new estimate. By setting a *Smoothing Coefficient* you can make the system react quicker. However, by following the random movements of the actual volumes too closely you can increase the degree of error over time. This needs to be balanced with the need to react to structural movements in the forecast.

- **Double exponential smoothing**   A forecasting method that extends the single exponential smoothing. It is appropriate where the rate of increase is stable over time. The smoothing technique applied to level demand is applied to both the level and trend.

■ **Holt winters** A forecasting method that extends exponential smoothing to the problem of seasonality. The volume in a given period is first determined as the exponentially smoothed level. The exponentially smoothed rate of increase or decrease is then applied. The new level is then adjusted up or down by a seasonality factor. For example, you might consider that there are 12 periods in the cycle. You might expect that the sales in June should be adjusted up by 120 percent. The observation in any given period will give forecast errors for Level, Rate, and Seasonality factors that are used to determine the new estimates. An example of a highly seasonal commodity might be ice cream. It would be expected that sales of ice cream would be greater in summer months than in winter.

If the Parameters box appears, you will need to provide the smoothing coefficients for the method you have chosen.

As an alternative to selecting a specific forecasting method, you can allow the system to automatically determine the best method to use. This is referred to as the automatic method. An expert system checks the forecast performance of each algorithm based on historical data.

Specifying the Forecast Level

From the Forecast Levels tab, double-click a dimension to view its levels and select a level. Forecast errors will tend to be less as you forecast at a higher and higher level. For example, for Neptune there will be a higher forecast error for the forecasts by distribution center and desktop product family than there will be for the desktop range as a whole. The errors higher up the hierarchy tend to cancel each other out. However, the local nuance can be lost if the aggregate forecast is allocated down.

Specifying the Allocation Rule

Allocation rules specify how volume data that has originated at different levels of aggregation are allocated upward or downward in the hierarchy when forecasts are changed or combined. You can choose from among the following allocation rules:

■ Allocate based on forecasted weights aggregated from the lowest level. Volumes are allocated based on the volumes at the lowest level or aggregated from the lowest level.

■ Allocate based on a forecast at each level. A forecast is done at each level below the level specified. Allocations from higher levels are based on the forecast at the lower level. The allocation is stepped through the levels downward. Allocations above the specified level are done by aggregating the forecast at the specified level.

■ Allocate based on historical weights for a user-specified period.

Tracking the Progress of a Demand Plan

Demand Planning is a workflow-driven application. The Demand Plan Administrator can track the progress of a demand plan through its lifecycle.

■ Downloading data from the Planning Server initiates the forecast cycle by loading data from the Planning Server into the Express database.

■ Forecasting data and distributing to planners creates the baseline forecast in the shared database and distributes data to planners, based on their data assignments.

■ Collecting forecast data from planners consolidates the forecasts that have been submitted by planners to the shared database.

■ Uploading the final forecast to the Planning Server loads the finalized forecasts from the Express shared database into the Planning Server.

To review the progress of a plan choose the name of the demand plan from the navigation list. The list of Workflow activities will be displayed. You can initiate the activities from this list by selecting the activity in the stage column and choosing Apply.

A batch log is also created when any of these tasks are performed. You can review the batch log by choosing Batch Log from the navigator.

Understanding the Demand Planning Cycle

Now that a demand plan has been defined you can push it through its lifecycle. The cycle starts by running a collection to gather the time series data. The data is gathered into the Planning Server and stored in the shared database. When the forecast is distributed to the planners, they can review baseline forecast, make adjustments, and submit their forecasts back for the planning manager to review. He or she can then review and adjust the forecast before publishing it to the planning server. Figure 9-6 illustrates the lifecycle of a demand plan.

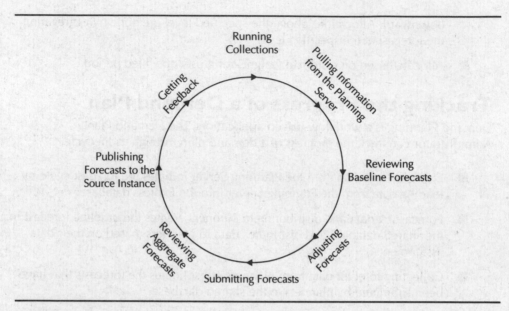

FIGURE 9-6. *The planning cycle*

Understanding Where the Source Data Comes from

Before the demand plans are available for use, you need to collect the data from the source systems into the Planning Server. As delivered, Oracle Demand Planning can collect data from Oracle Applications, Releases 10.7, 11, 11i. However, the collections are made through a set of insulating views. These views are listed in the following table.

View Name	Description
MSD_SR_SHIPMENT_DATA_V	Shipment source view
MSD_SR_BOOKING_DATA_V	Booking source view
MSD_SR_SALES_FCST_V	Sales forecast source view
MSD_SR_MFG_FCST_V	Manufacturing forecast source view
MSD_SR_OPPORTUNITY_V	Opportunity source view
MSD_SR_CURRENCY_CONVERSIONS_V	Currency conversion source view
MSD_SR_UOM_CONVERSIONS_V	Unit of measure conversion source view

View Name	Description
MSD_SR_ITEM_LIST_PRICE_V	Item information source view
MSD_SR_MFG_TIME_V	Manufacturing time source view
MSD_SR_FISCAL_TIME_V	Fiscal time source view

Running Collections

This will take the data and place it into the staging tables. Users will still need to run the pull programs to get the data from the fact tables into the destination tables on the Planning Server. To collect the data, navigate to the Collect Data function in the Collections menu.

NOTE
There is a profile option that enables you to collect all the data at once—this profile is MSD One Step Collections.

Choose the type of data you wish to collect. You will be taken to a concurrent submission screen. You can collect from Shipping Data, Booking Data, Manufacturing Forecasts, Sales Forecasts, and Sales Opportunities.

When you pull time data, you have the choice of Financial, Manufacturing, and Gregorian calendars. You will have to run the program once for every manufacturing calendar you have defined and once for every financial calendar you have defined.

This will have placed the data in the staging tables and you need to run the pull programs before you can define or generate a demand plan.

Pulling Information from the Planning Server

The Demand Planning Integration Administrator submits the jobs that collect data from the source systems into the Planning Server. They also submit the jobs that pull from the Planning Server into the shared database. To submit these jobs, sign on as Demand Planning Administrator. Choose Collection to get from source systems. Choose Pull to get from the Planning Server to the shared database.

The Planning Server stores the collected time series data from many sources, including

■ Historical shipment or booking data from transactional systems at the lowest level.

■ Forecast data from Sales, Manufacturing, Supply Chain, or third party at any level of aggregation.

- Scenario definitions. A scenario is a different forecast and costing outcome for potentially overlapping time horizon.

- The Levels and Dimensions by which you will be "slicing and dicing" your forecast data.

You could also collect from other data sources. You will need to write to the staging tables in the Planning Server. Other data sources might include non-Oracle Applications or syndicated sources such as Nielsen or IRI.

Reviewing Baseline Forecasts

Demand Planning sits on top of the Express Technologies. These are a set of multidimensional Online Analytical Processing (OLAP) tools. You can compare your plans with the constraint-based plans from Oracle Advanced Planning and Scheduling. From within the Documents folder in the Navigator, open the Forecast report. You can change the column widths. You can drill down by clicking a detail row and drill up by clicking the parent row. You can pull variables from the table to the page variables where they act as selection criteria. You can rotate the data by dragging the variable icon (the plate with raised bumps) to the column bar.

The baseline forecast serves as the initial estimate of is demand. A forecast is created for each scenario downloaded, and a set of forecast rules downloaded from the Planning Server. The forecast rules are a combination of forecast method, level, calendar, and horizon. You might decide to create a scenario for a new competitor entering the market and another for a new technology making one of your product lines obsolete.

Adjusting Forecasts

Individual planners have a worksheet interface to review and adjust the forecast. The Express worksheets are highly tuned to analyzing data at different levels of aggregation. Adjustments can be made by changing forecasting parameters or moving forecast volumes. These adjustments enable the planner to simulate possible changes. There are predefined reports available to check results as well as the capability to create ad hoc reports. Figure 9-7 is an example of the worksheet.

To access the demand-planning environment, log in and choose the demand planner responsibility. The application will appear with a list of demand plans. Choose a demand plan and start demand planning. You will be in the Demand Planning page. The Demand Planning page consists of a Report and Graph workspace and a Worksheet workspace. By choosing Modify Data from the toolbar or clicking on the cells in the worksheet the planner can edit the forecast. Forecasts can be entered in units or currency. You can increase or decrease by an amount or percentage. You can update a block of cells by selecting the cells and selecting the Modify Data button from the Documents toolbar. You can specify a value or increase or decrease by a specified percentage. You can create rich history of the changes by clicking the Change Reason icon on the toolbar, represented as a notepad. The activity log will show all changes to the forecast quantity. Forecast changes can be made at any level in the hierarchy and will be spread down and rolled up.

NOTE
If you make a change at a high level in a hierarchy and then make a change lower down that hierarchy, the system will prompt you to recalculate to ensure there are no conflicts in the data.

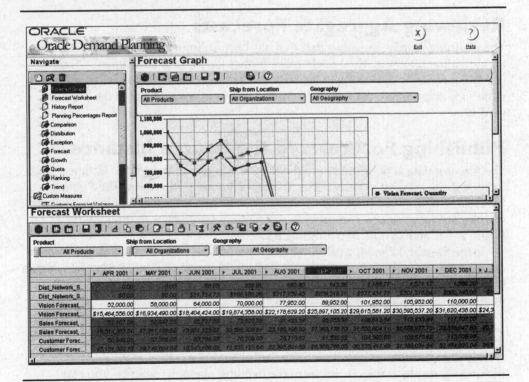

FIGURE 9-7. *Working with forecasts in Demand Planning*

You can lock one or more cells so that their values do not change when data is recalculated. Locking a cell protects the value in the cell as well as the values in all cells that are its children. To lock a cell or cells, highlight the area that you want to lock and click the LockCell/Unlock Cell button on the Document toolbar or right-click and choose Lock Cell from the pop-up menu. You can cut and paste between cells and between worksheets, if the selected block is of the same shape as the destination and the cells are not protected.

Submitting Forecasts

When a forecast is ready, the planner submits the final values to the shared database. If a demand plan includes multiple scenarios, planners submit a forecast for each scenario. To submit a forecast, the planner selects the worksheet that represents his best estimate of future demand and chooses Submit from the Documents toolbar. The forecast is then posted through to the shared database. If you are submitting forecasts for a given scenario, you will need to choose a scenario from the list box.

Reviewing Aggregate Forecasts

The planning manager reviews data that has been submitted to the shared database by individual planners. They might make further judgmental adjustments. The planning manager is working in the shared database. When the planning manager makes his submission, the forecast for the scenario is posted back to the planning server.

Publishing Forecasts to the Source Instance

The forecast data is published from the Planning Server to the source instance. This integrates the final estimate of demand into the transaction system. The Publish Forecast window specifies the parameters for publishing. You can publish an entire forecast scenario, or you can use optional filtering parameters to limit the data. Figure 9-8 is an example of publishing a forecast.

In the Demand Planning Administrator responsibility, choose the Publish Forecast option. You can publish from a scenario within a demand plan into a forecast within a forecast set in the source system. You can restrict the level of the forecast that is published to the source system.

Getting Feedback

Oracle Demand Planning includes a variety of tools for getting feedback and monitoring results at various stages of the demand planning process. You can

- Generate exception reports based on a variety of parameters

■ Run reports to check forecast accuracy, or set up alerts that will notify them of specific events

■ Compare actual results against forecasts, or compare forecasts for various scenarios against one another

■ Refer back to reports, graphs, and forecast worksheets that they have saved in their personal database

Predefined Reports

Demand Planning comes with a set of predefined reports. Predefined reports are selected and set up by the Demand Planning Administrator. Reports include

■ **Comparison**   Highlight similarities or differences between products, periods, or geographies.

■ **Distribution**   Focus on sales operations information such as slow moving items or items not selling.

■ **Exception**   A set of Pereto reports to focus attention on the top 20% of your products or to highlight your problems.

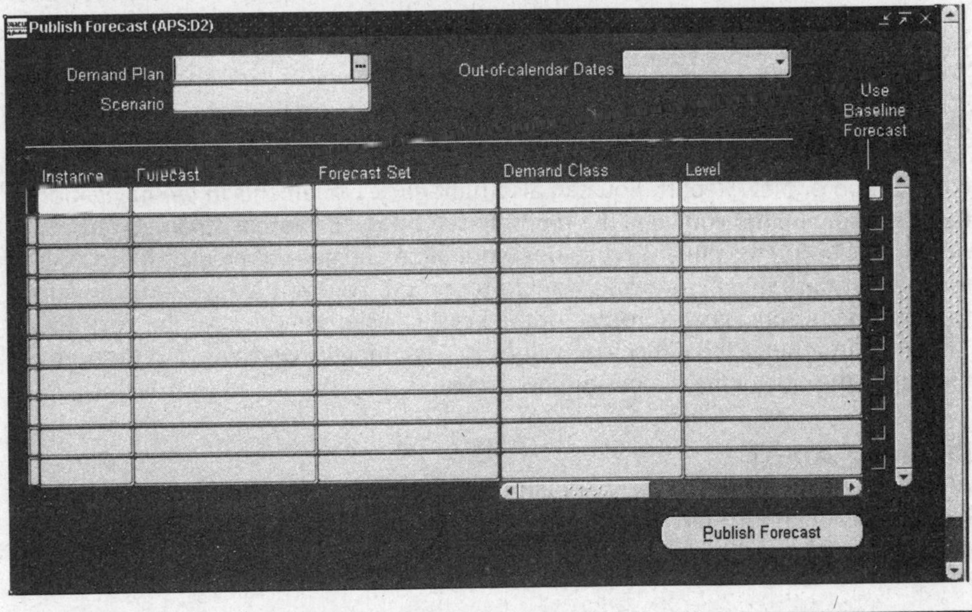

FIGURE 9-8.   *Demand plan publication*

- **Forecast**   Used for reporting forecast accuracy.

- **Growth**   Shows the difference in a selected measure between two time periods.

- **Quota**   Shows performance against a sales target.

- **Ranking**   Shows top dimension values such as products or geographies for a specified measure.

- **Review**   Sales operations focused report or account and quota review.

- **Trend**   Shows activity over time for a specified measure. This can be smoothed using a moving average.

The documents are grouped into folders that appear in the Navigation list below folders that you have created to store your personal documents. If there are no user-defined folders, the folders for predefined reports appear below individual documents.

To use a predefined report, double-click the Document Type after navigating to the correct folder. The document is displayed in the Report and Graph workspace. The data that it contains and the type of view (report or graph) are determined by the current settings. You can change the values displayed in the report by choosing Settings in the report heading. This displays the settings script that is close to natural language that you can use to select new values or change the type of view from report to graph.

Ad Hoc Reports

To generate an ad hoc report, click New on the Navigation toolbar and then choose New Graph or New Report. You can also right-click Documents in the navigation list. Choose whether you want the report based on the default or a named report or graph. Choose the dimension values (your slice of data) and measures (history, forecast, or custom measure) you want to report on. For example, you might want to report on history versus forecast for the West Coast of America for the year 2000.

You can arrange the dimension values for reporting by dragging and dropping the bar to the side of the dimension level name.

Defining Alerts

Alerts can be set up by planners or plan managers. To set up an alert, click the New icon and select New Alert. The Alert Wizard will be displayed. Define an exception condition such as:

```
"Select Geography within Geography:Country by Value
where Difference between Sales and Customer Forecast
is greater than the value 100"
```

Click the Next button and complete the selector form. First select Geography. Click the Selector button and select a value or select all by clicking the double-arrow button; then click OK. Repeat for Ship From Location, Product, and Time. Finally, define who will receive the messages.

Summary

This chapter explained the purpose of Demand Planning and the differences in the technology that underpins Demand Planning, covered the division of responsibilities in Demand Planning and the seeded roles, and looked at setting up Demand Planning—including planning dimensions, hierarchies, and levels—and explained how to define a demand plan, its inputs, and scenarios. The chapter then reviewed the administration of demand plans and how they are tracked, from pulling information from source systems to publishing the results back. Finally, the user environment for demand planners and how they get feedback on their plans was covered.

CHAPTER
10

Single Organization
Planning

or businesses with straightforward planning needs, Oracle has provided basic MRP for many years, in the form of its Master Scheduling/MRP application. This provides unconstrained, single-organization planning of material and capacity. It is this planning methodology that is the subject of this chapter.

The basic setup for planning is described in Chapter 8. For details on Advanced Supply Chain planning, see Chapter 11.

Types of Plans

Prior to Release 11i, Oracle supported three types of material and capacity plans: Master Production Schedules, MRP plans, and Distribution Requirements plans (DRP). From an Oracle perspective, the plan type simply determines the items that will be considered in the plan, based on the setting of the item's *Planning Method.* Simplistically, items designated as *MPS Planned* are planned in an MPS plan; items designated *DRP Planned* are planned in a DRP plan. An MRP plan will include items of all types. In addition, a plan might include intervening items of a different type, if it's necessary to correctly calculate dependent demand on lower-level items in the plan. For example, an MPS plan would plan the MRP item C in the following illustration because it is necessary to plan C to calculate the dependent demand for E.

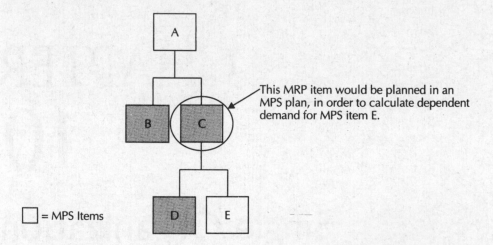

The different plan types enable you to control the planning process; for example; you can plan a Master Production schedule, adjust the schedule to level production, and then use that schedule as input to an MRP plan.

However, all these plan types use the same planning engine, and there is very little difference in the planning logic or execution activities. For all practical purposes, any of the plan types can provide the same result within a single organization. For simplicity, as we have done throughout this book, we will continue to refer to this single-organization, unconstrained planning as *MRP planning.* Any specific differences based on the plan type will be noted.

Although Distribution Requirements Planning is intended for use across multiple organizations, this plan type also uses the same planning engine as MRP For users of DRP plans, the basic setup and execution are the same as for an MRP plan. Defining the supply chain is covered in Chapter 11.

Defining Plan Names

The planning process starts with the definition of a plan name. You can have many different plans, for comparison or simulation purposes; each one is identified by a unique 10-character name. Define an MRP plan with the MRP Names form, Master Production schedules with the Master Production Schedules form, and DRP plans with the DRP Names form. Give each plan a name and description, and set the following options as appropriate:

- **Feedback**   If checked, this gives the planning visibility to the implementation status of planned orders.

- **Production**   This option enables a plan for the auto-release of planned orders.

- **Relief**   For MPS plans only, this enables production relief of the master schedule, as discussed in Chapter 8.

- **Inventory ATP**   For MPS plans only, this option determines whether the planned orders from this master schedule can be considered when calculating available to promise quantities. You would enable this function only for the production schedules that represent what you currently plan to produce; if you enabled it for schedules that reflected alternate scenarios or simulations, you might overstate availability because the quantities are added from all enabled schedules.

You can purge plans you no longer need using the same forms where you defined them. Use the Delete function (the red X icon on the toolbar) on the name of the plan you want to purge; when you save your changes, this process will submit a concurrent program to delete the plan and all its associated information. If the plan is not disabled, you will be asked to confirm that you want to purge it.

Plan Options

For each plan, you define the options that control its execution. The Options window is accessible from the Names form using the Options button or can be accessed directly from the menu. A sample Plan Options window is show in Figure 10-1.

Plan options include the following:

- **Schedule**   This is the master schedule that represents the demand that will drive the plan. If the plan you are launching is an MPS, the input schedule will be an MDS; if your plan is an MRP, the input schedule might be either an MDS or MPS.

- **Overwrite Option**   This option controls the treatment of existing *firm planned orders* in the plan. You can specify All, Outside planning time fence, or None. Existing firm planned orders will be deleted according to the option you specify before new orders are suggested. Actual orders (discrete jobs, purchase requisitions, and purchase orders) are never deleted in the planning process.

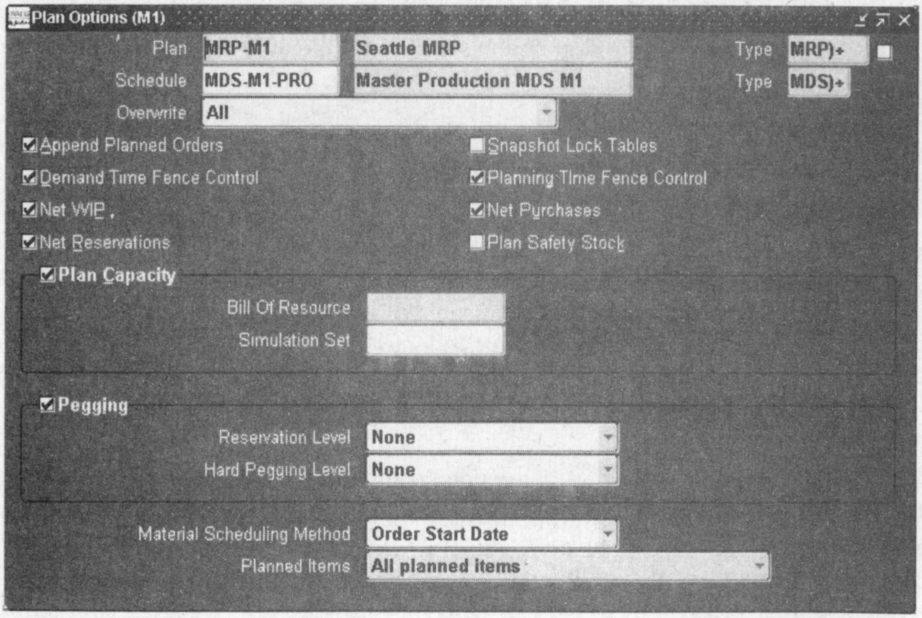

FIGURE 10-1.   *MRP Plan options*

NOTE
An important difference between MRP and MPS items is that planned orders for MPS items are automatically firmed, whereas orders for MRP items are not. Thus, to regenerate an MPS, you must specify the scope of regeneration in the overwrite option. When you run an MRP plan, it is always regenerated; the overwrite option controls only the treatment of planned orders that you have explicitly firmed.

- **Append Planned Orders**   This controls whether new planned orders will be generated in the plan. If you run a plan but do not append planned orders, you will get exceptions and recommendations for existing orders in the plan, but no new orders.

- **Snapshot Lock Tables**   This option determines whether you will lock tables during the snapshot process. Although this guarantees absolute data consistency, it prevents other users from performing transactions against those tables during the brief period that the snapshot has the tables locked. If you don't require absolute consistency—for example, while running a simulation—you might elect not to lock the tables during the snapshot.

- **Demand Time Fence Control and Planning Time Fence Control**   These options control whether these time fences will be used. Demand time fence control will ignore any forecast demand for an item inside its demand time fence; planning time fence control prevents planning from creating or rescheduling orders inside the planning time fence. Both time fences are set as item attributes.

- **Net WIP and Net Purchases**   These options control whether planning will view existing WIP jobs and purchase orders or requisitions as supply. Netting of WIP and Purchases should normally be enabled, though for some simulation scenarios, you might want to ignore existing WIP jobs or purchases.

- **Net Reservations**   Unlike the previous options, the Net Reservations option determines how planning treats existing sales order reservations. If this is enabled, MRP will respect existing reservations; if on-hand material is already reserved for a sales order and a new demand occurs earlier, MRP will plan a new order to satisfy the earlier demand. This is because you have indicated that MRP was to leave existing reservations as they are. If the Net Reservations options is not enabled (unchecked), MRP will assume you will adjust the reservation to use the existing material to satisfy the order that must be shipped first, and create a new order, if necessary, to satisfy the later demand. Note, however, that this only affects planning's assumptions; if planning recommends using previously reserved material to satisfy a new demand, you will have to cancel the reservation in Order Management to make the material available to the new order. Also, note that this only pertains to sales order reservations; inventory reservations (e.g., to an account number or alias) have no effect on MRP.

- **Plan Safety Stock**   This option determines *whether* MRP will include safety stock demand in its calculations. If enabled, MRP will plan for each item's safety stock, based on the Safety Stock Method specified for each item. If this option is not enabled, MRP will not plan for safety stock at all.

- **Plan Capacity, Bill of Resource, and Simulation Set**   These options enable and control capacity planning. For MPS items, you can identify the bill of resource to be used for rough cut capacity planning, as described in Chapter 8. For planning to recognize capacity modifications, specify the simulation set that defines those modifications (see Chapter 4).

- **Pegging, Reservation Level, and Hard Pegging Level**   The Pegging check box enables pegging for the plan, as specified in each item's pegging attribute; Reservation Level and Hard Pegging Level are used with Project Manufacturing.

- **Material Scheduling Method**   You can set this option to Order Start Date, which will date dependent requirements to coincide with the start date of the parent order, or set it to Operation Start Date, which calculates dependent demand based on the estimated date of the operation where the component is consumed. If lead times are short, or if your routings are not accurate (or nonexistent), use Order Start Date. But if your products lead times tend to be long, scheduling material to arrive on the operation start date can help to reduce inventory levels.

- **Planned Items**   The option has three values: All planned items, Demand schedule items only, or Supply schedule items only. For a production plan, the safe choice is All planned items. This will ensure that all items with the appropriate planning method will be considered. Choosing Demand schedule items only or Supply schedule items only will limit the plan to the items that appear on the master schedule and their components. These options can be helpful in testing, but in a production environment, they could result in ignoring other valid demands, e.g., a discrete job that had been created manually to build a prototype. Such an order might have components used by other products on the master schedule. If you ignore such a job, you could have an incorrect picture of total component demand, and therefore an incorrect plan.

The Subinventory Netting button on the Plan Options form takes you to a window where you can modify the netting attribute for each subinventory in the organization. When you first create the plan, the Nettable attribute is copied into the plan for each subinventory. If you want to change MRP's view of inventory, you can modify the Net check box in this window. This capability is useful primarily for simulation; for example, you might want to run a plan assuming you have no on-hand inventory at all. Note that setting the subinventory's Net attribute here changes it only for the *specific* plan; when changed, the setting is preserved with that plan until you change it back.

Generating the MRP Plan

You generate and regenerate MRP plans with the appropriate Launch form for the plan type. The Launch form is accessible from the menu or from each of the plan name forms. Generally, the default parameters will be appropriate, but you can override them if necessary. Parameters include

- **Launch Snapshot**   The snapshot is the portion of the planning process that collects current inventory and order information and explodes your bills of material. You must run this the first time you launch a given plan name, and you will normally run this process for any plan you will use to plan actual production. This ensures that planning is working with current data. However, for simulations you might choose to skip the snapshot. In this case, you will use the inventory levels, orders, and bills of material from the last time the snapshot was run for the plan.

- **Launch Planner**   The planner performs the netting and order planning functions of MRP; you will normally run this process, or no real planning will occur.

- **Anchor Date**   If you need to specify a new anchor date for repetitive planning, enter it here. As noted in Chapter 8, planning will automatically roll the anchor date forward, if necessary, with each planning run.

- **Plan Horizon**   The default plan horizon is calculated by adding the value of the MRP:Cutoff Date Offset Months profile to the current date. You can override this default if you wish.

Controlling Plan Generation

The Overwrite option and each item's Planning time fence are two key factors that control the scope of a plan's regeneration.

The Overwrite option of a plan determines how much data from a previous run of the plan is preserved when the plan is rerun. As mentioned earlier, this option determines if firm planned orders are deleted prior to replanning. And, because planned orders for MPS-planned items are automatically firmed, this option effectively controls the regeneration of the entire MPS plan.

The item's Planning Time Fence sets a portion of the planning horizon off limits to MRP. If you enable Planning Time Fence Control for a plan, MRP cannot plan new orders inside of each item's time fence, nor can it suggest rescheduling orders inside the fence. (It can still suggest canceling existing orders inside the time fence or rescheduling orders from inside the fence to outside.)

In conjunction with the planning time fence, the profile option MRP:Firm Planned Order Time Fence effectively moves out the item's planning time fence to the date of the latest firmed order.

Reviewing the MRP Plan

There are a number of reports you can use to review the results of a plan. Detailed reports, such as the Master Schedule Detail Report and the Planning Detail Report, are typical planning reports and include many of the factors used in the planning process. These reports show the traditional bucketed, horizontal display, and offer the option of a vertical display. Other reports, like the Late Order Report, Order Reschedule Report, and Planned Order Report, are more action-oriented; they highlight actions you should take or exceptions identified by the planning process.

Planner Workbench

The primary online form for reviewing, modifying, and implementing planning suggestions is the Planner Workbench. Oracle has designed the Planner Workbench (PWB) as a "one-stop shop" for a planner. From this form, you can view planning information, view exceptions and recommendations from planning, implement suggestions to create new orders, or reschedule or cancel existing orders. You can accept the recommendations as is, or you can modify the suggested dates and quantities. You can also simulate changes to the plan and immediately view the results.

The Planner Workbench has been part of Oracle Applications since the early versions of Release 10, and Oracle is continually enhancing its functionality. The following pages describe the Planner Workbench provided with Oracle's Master Scheduling/MRP Application and with the earlier Supply Chain Planning product. There are dramatic differences in the Planner Workbench provided with Advanced Supply Chain Planning; that version of the Planner Workbench is described in Chapter 11.

There is a separate Planner Workbench for each plan type (MRP, MPS, or DRP), each defined as a different function of the planning product. But they all use the same form and have virtually the same capabilities; unless noted, the following discussion applies to the Planner Workbench for any of the plan types.

Planning Information

The first window of the Planner Workbench shows the completion dates and times for the Snapshot and Planner processes (described later in this chapter). It provides buttons to access various detailed windows and a "launchpad" for running online or batch simulations of the plan. Only plans that have completed successfully are visible in the PWB. A default plan name will be populated based on the value of the profiles MRP:Default Plan Name, MRP:Default Schedule Name, or MRP:Default DRP Plan Name.

Reviewing Planning Exceptions

As a planner, your first selection on the workbench will probably be to view the exceptions and recommendations generated by the planning process. The Exceptions button first opens the Find Exceptions window, where you can enter selection criteria for the messages you want to view. A typical selection criterion is to find exceptions only for your Planner Code; because most of the windows of the PWB are folder forms, you might want to save one or more folders including this selection criterion. Clicking the Find button will access the Exception Summary window.

The Exception Summary window displays the unique messages generated by the plan and the Exception Count, the number of occurrences of that message. You can select one or more messages in this window by checking the box to the left of each message, and click the Exception Details button to view each occurrence of the selected message.

TIP
The MRP Planner Workbench provides only one default folder for the Exception Details window. You might want to define different folders for each type of message, to show the important details for that message with a minimum of scrolling.

Exceptions include item exceptions, order exceptions and recommendations, and resource exceptions. Item exceptions are those that apply to the items themselves, without reference to any specific order:

■ Items with excess inventory (as defined by the item's Planning Exception Set)

■ Items with negative starting on hand

■ Items with no activity—items included in the plan by virtue of the Planned Items option on the plan, but for which there is no demand

Order exceptions relate to specific orders. From the Exception Details window, you can drill directly to the order that is referenced:

■ Orders to be cancelled.

■ Orders with compression days—orders that are planned to start within the item's lead time. Oracle's planning process will never recommend a start date in the past; if the order should have started earlier, planning will recommend a start date of today, and then show how much you must compress the lead time (expedite) in order to meet the due date.

■ Past due orders.

Resource messages are generated only if capacity planning is enabled; they include

■ Resource overloaded

■ Resource underloaded

From the Exception Details window, you can select one or more messages and drill to detailed planning information utilizing the buttons provided. For order-based exceptions, a typical choice might be the Supply/Demand window.

Supply and Demand

The Supply/Demand window, shown in Figure 10-2, provides the most complete picture of the planning process. It shows all the requirements (demands) for each item and all the planned and scheduled replenishments (supply). Demands are shown as negative quantities; supplies are shown as positive numbers. You can access this window from a number of points on the Planner Workbench, and the selection criteria is based on the current row from which you invoked the window. For example, if you access this from the Exception Details window, you will see just the order referenced in the exception; if you access it from the Items window, you will see all the supply and demand for the item.

There are also separate Supply and Demand windows, which show just supply or demand data, respectively. These windows, like most of the windows within the Planner Workbench, are folder forms, and there are many additional fields available that are not displayed in the default folder that Oracle provides. You might want to add these fields to your folder definitions based on your manufacturing requirements;

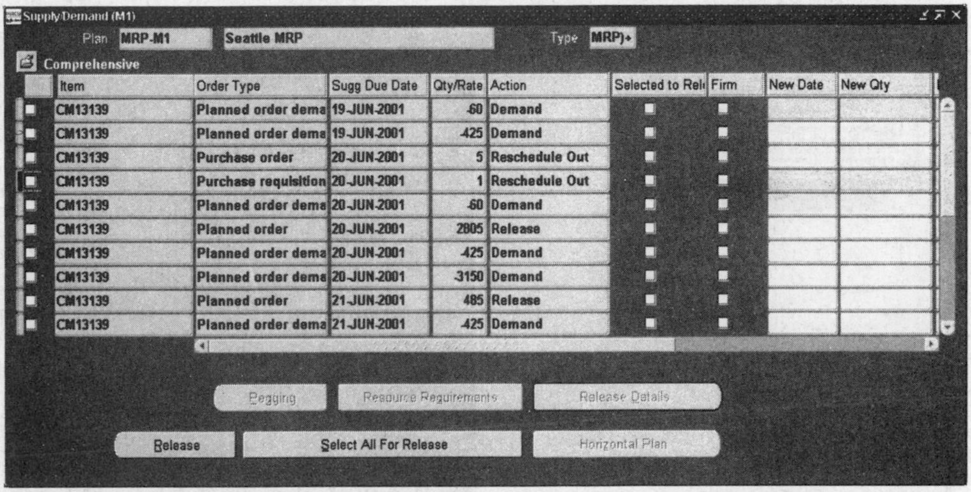

Item	Order Type	Sugg Due Date	Qty/Rate	Action	Selected to Rele	Firm	New Date	New Qty
CM13139	Planned order dema	19-JUN-2001	-60	Demand				
CM13139	Planned order dema	19-JUN-2001	-425	Demand				
CM13139	Purchase order	20-JUN-2001	5	Reschedule Out				
CM13139	Purchase requisition	20-JUN-2001	1	Reschedule Out				
CM13139	Planned order dema	20-JUN-2001	-60	Demand				
CM13139	Planned order	20-JUN-2001	2805	Release				
CM13139	Planned order dema	20-JUN-2001	-425	Demand				
CM13139	Planned order dema	20-JUN-2001	-3150	Demand				
CM13139	Planned order	21-JUN-2001	485	Release				
CM13139	Planned order dema	21-JUN-2001	-425	Demand				

Plan MRP-M1   Seattle MRP   Type MRP)+   Comprehensive

Pegging   Resource Requirements   Release Details

Release   Select All For Release   Horizontal Plan

FIGURE 10-2. *Planner Workbench Supply/Demand window*

for example, you can add Project and Task information in a project manufacturing environment, or the various repetitive schedule dates if you utilize repetitive manufacturing.

Pegged Supply and Demand

Sometimes to make better planning decisions, you must understand the source of a supply or demand. For example, a late order that is satisfying a forecast demand might be less of a problem than a late order needed to satisfy a sales order. For MRP planning, pegging information is displayed in the Object Navigator window, shown in Figure 10-3.

You can access the Object Navigator from the Supply/Demand, Supply, or Demand windows; select a *single order* by checking the selection box at the left of the row, and click the Pegging button. This opens the Object Navigator for the selected order.

NOTE
Because the Object Navigator window displays only a single tree at a time, it is accessible only if you have selected a single order.

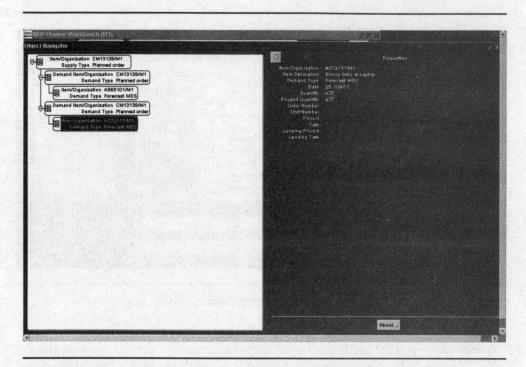

FIGURE 10-3. *Object Navigator, showing pegging information*

The left-hand pane of the window provides a graphical representation of the pegging tree. You initially see only the object you selected; you can expand it one level at a time by clicking the plus sign (+) on the right of the selected node. The right-hand window displays text information about the current node of the pegging tree.

Implementing Planning Recommendations

On the Supply/Demand or Supply window you can respond to the suggestions from planning. You can implement new orders and cancel or reschedule existing discrete jobs or purchase requisitions. As you implement planning's suggestions, you can change dates, quantities, or order types; and you can firm the orders you implement.

NOTE
The default label uses the term "Release" for orders you implement; this does not imply that orders you select are given a Released status. Purchase requisitions are always released in an Approved status, but the status of discrete jobs depends on the preferences you have set for the implementation of planned discrete jobs; you set this preference using the Tools | Preferences selection on the Menu bar. (The Preferences window also lets you select a default job class, determine grouping for purchase requisitions, choose whether to release phantoms or configurations, and select the types of demand and supply that are displayed.) As noted in Chapter 8, repetitive schedules are always given a status of Pending – Mass Loaded.

To implement planning suggestions, check the Selected to Release box for the orders you wish to implement; save your changes. When you have finished, click the Release button; this will launch the appropriate interfaces—the WIP Job/Schedule Interface for discrete jobs and repetitive schedules, and Requisition Import for internal or external purchase requisitions.

CAUTION
Because the information is based on a common database, all committed selections will be released when any user clicks the Release button, including orders selected for release by other users. Unless Oracle has changed this process since this book went to press, you should keep this in mind; if you have selected an order for release, another user could complete the implementation of that order, and you would have no opportunity to change your mind.

To firm a planned order, or to firm an order as you implement it, check the Firm check box for the order. To change the date or quantity of a planned order, use the Implement Date or Implement Qty/Rate fields. You can also change the type of order using the Implement As field. This field defaults based on the item's Make/Buy attribute (Discrete Job for a Make item, Purchase Requisition for a Buy item). If you need to change the type of a planned order (e.g., you need to make an item that you normally buy or buy an item you normally make), you can if the item's Build in WIP or Purchasable attributes allow.

NOTE
If both the Build in WIP and Purchasable attributes are disabled for an item, you will not be able to implement planned orders; the Implement As field will have a value of None.

The Horizontal Material Plan

The Horizontal Material Plan window, shown in Figure 10-4, provides the traditional, bucketed view of your plan. This window is accessible from a number of places within the Planner Workbench. The horizontal plan gives you the choice of viewing either Snapshot Data (i.e., the data that was gathered when the plan was run), or Current Data, on-hand and on-order quantities taken from the current data in the database tables.

The horizontal plan can display 22 different rows of data for each item; these are shown on the Preferences window, Figure 10-5. You access the Preferences window from the Tools option on the Menu bar. You can select the rows of information you want to see, as well as choose the Bucket Type (Days, Weeks, or Periods), the Display Factor (to scale the numbers, if they tend to be unusually large in your environment), the number of Decimal Places to display, and the Field Width of the buckets in the horizontal plan. The Preferences window also lets you select information for the Supply/Demand and Horizontal Capacity Plan windows.

Item Information

For information about the planning attributes of an item, select the Items window, as shown in Figure 10-6. This window displays items with their descriptions and the planning-related attributes that were effective when the plan snapshot was run.

Walking Up and Down a Bill of Material

From the Items window, you can view the components of a single item by selecting the item and clicking the Components button. Separate tabs in the Components window show effectivity and quantity information, use-up information, and

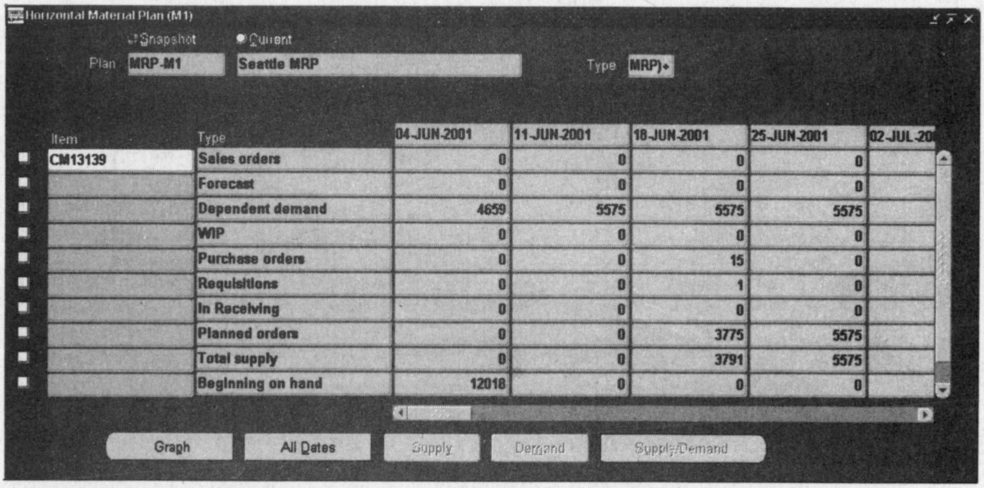

FIGURE 10-4.   *Planner Workbench Horizontal Material Plan window*

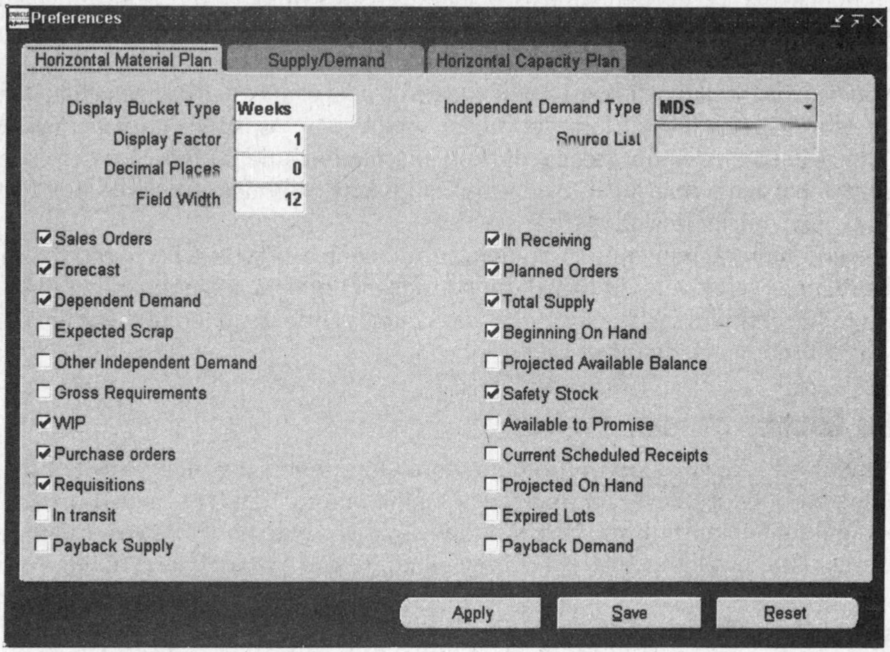

FIGURE 10-5.   *Preferences for the Horizontal Material Plan*

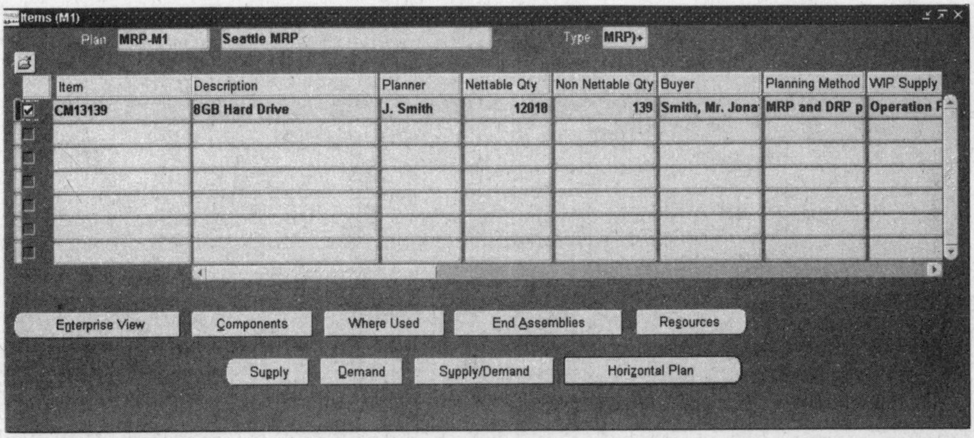

FIGURE 10-6. *Items window, showing item planning details*

summarized item details. From the Components window, you can select one or more component items and access their item details (the Items window) by clicking the Items button. From there, you can view that item's components and continue the process; in this way you can walk down the entire bill of material.

You can also walk up through a bill of material a level at time by selecting an Item on the Items window and clicking the Where Used button. As in the component view, you can select an assembly, access its item information, and perform a where-used inquiry for that item. You can also view the End Assemblies where an item is used with that button on the Items window.

It is important to remember that item, component, and where-used information on the Planner Workbench is based on the snapshot of data taken when the plan was run. This lets you see the data that was actually used to generate the plan, even if it was subsequently changed.

The Enterprise View

The Enterprise View window is useful primarily for users of the older Supply Chain Planning product; it shows summarized planning information for selected items across multiple organizations. This window also gives you the choice of snapshot or current data. A sample Enterprise View window is shown in Figure 10-7.

Capacity Planning

You can request detailed Capacity Requirements Planning (CRP) to be performed when an MRP or a DRP plan is run, using the Plan Options form shown in Figure 10-1.

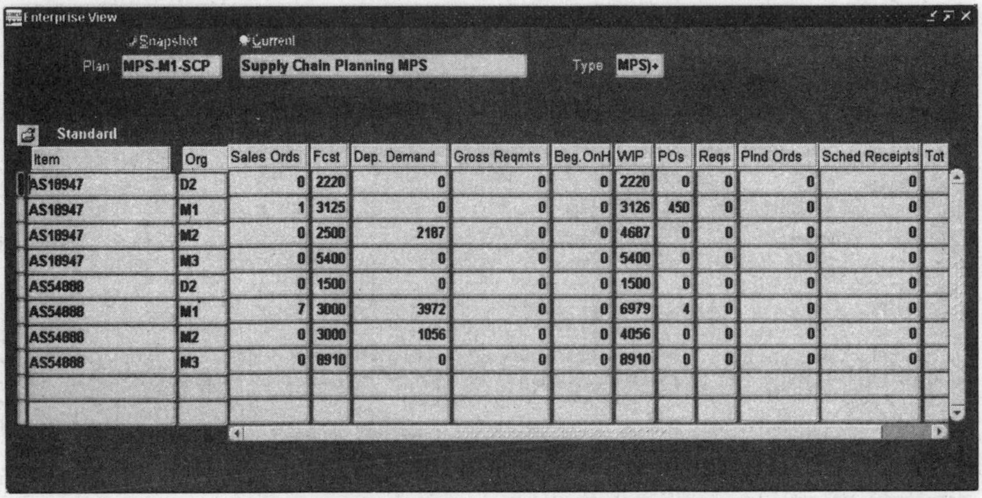

FIGURE 10-7. *Planner Workbench Enterprise View, showing summarized planning data for multiple organizations*

You check the box to enable capacity planning and optionally provide the name of a Simulation Set to reflect planning changes in capacity. As noted in Chapter 8, CRP uses detailed routing information to calculate load on your resources and compares that load to the defined capacity of those resources.

You can also perform Rough Cut Capacity Planning (RCCP) for an MPS plan type by including the name of a Bill of Resource on the plan options form. Although it lacks the detail of CRP, RCCP lets you check capacity for resources that might not be part of your routing by adding them to your bills of resource before you run RCCP. As noted in Chapter 8, you can also run Rough Cut Capacity Planning inquiries and reports against any master schedule, whether or not you included the bill of resource in your plan options.

Resource and Capacity Information

If you have requested capacity planning in your plan, you can view resource capacity information in the Planner Workbench. As noted earlier, MRP provides exception messages to identify over- and under-loaded resources. You can also view the Horizontal Capacity Plan window, shown in Figure 10-8. This window shows bucketed capacity information and can be tailored to show the data you want using the Preferences window, accessible from the Tools option on the Menu bar. You can also see detailed information about your resources on the Resources window.

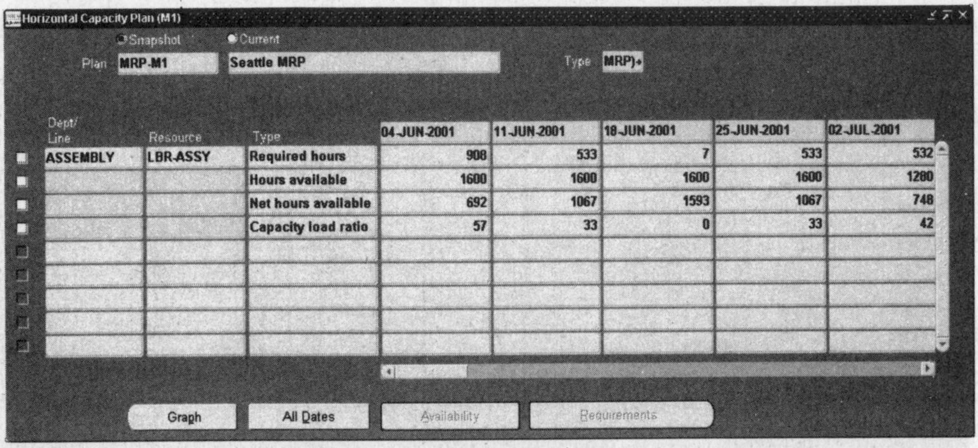

FIGURE 10-8. *Horizontal Capacity Plan*

Simulations

Since the introduction of the Memory Based Planner in Release 10.7, Oracle has provided the capability to simulate various changes to supply, demand, or capacity. Although sometimes referred to as "Net Change Replan" or "Net Change Simulation," the terms can be somewhat misleading.

First, process only responds to *net changes* you make on the Planner Workbench itself. To many people, true net change planning means reacting to the net changes made anywhere in the ERP system—changes in inventory levels, changes to bills of material, changes to customer orders, or unplanned scrap on the shop floor. MRP net change planning does not respond to these types of changes.

Second, to the extent that changes you make on the workbench are not automatically reflected in the execution systems, the process is indeed a simulation. For example, if you simulate a change to a sales order's schedule date, that change is not reflected on the sales order itself; it's only stored within the specific plan you change. However, there is nothing to prevent you from implementing and executing changes you make in a "simulation" session—if you change a date on a discrete job, for example, and implement that change, it *does* affect the actual job.

Finally, there is no simple way to "reset" a simulation with MRP planning. You can rerun the plan and overwrite *all* planned orders, though that plan will then react to any subsequent changes made in the execution systems, so it will not necessarily restore the plan to its pre-simulation state. Or, you can make simulations in a copy of the plan, but depending on your planning cycle, it can be clumsy to use the simulated plan in place of the original one—if you make changes to an MPS plan, you can replace the original plan with the simulation when you run your next MRP, but if you make changes to an MRP, you must disable the old plan and procedurally determine to use the latest copy for execution.

NOTE
These issues have been addressed with the enhanced simulation capabilities of Advanced Supply Chain planning; see Chapter 11.

Copying a Plan

Rather than making changes to your production plan directly, you might want to make a copy of that plan for simulation purposes. To copy a plan, you must have a current plan to copy from (the Source Plan), and you must define a new plan name of the same type (MRP, MPS, or DRP). This is the Destination Plan. Then, using the Launch Copy Plan form, submit the concurrent request that copies the plan.

The process runs by loading data from the flat files (operating system files) generated in the planning process under the new plan name. This has several implications:

■ If you have purged the flat files from the source plan, there is no data to copy, even though the source plan might still exist in the database. In this case, you can rerun the source plan and then copy it before you purge its intermediate flat files. (The mechanics of plan generation are discussed later in this chapter.)

■ You can only copy plans that have been generated by the planning process. This means you cannot copy an MPS that you have loaded manually with this method. For such a schedule, you could use the Load/Copy/Merge function.

Also, your destination plan must be empty; you cannot copy into a plan after it has been populated. You can create multiple plan names to accommodate multiple copies, or you can purge a plan when you've finished a simulation scenario and then re-create a new, empty plan with the same name.

For simulation purposes, you should consider the Planning Time Fence Control, Overwrite, and Append Planned Orders options of the destination plan. Normally, you will want to use the planning time fence and set the Overwrite option to Outside Planning Time Fence. This enables you to create new, firmed orders inside the planning time fence and tells the replanning process to preserve those changes. (If you did not use the planning time fence and told planning to overwrite *all* planned orders, you would not be able to introduce new supply in the simulation; it would be overwritten by whatever the planning process calculated as necessary.)

Simulation Scenarios

You can make the following types of changes on the Planner Workbench:

- Adding new demand (shown as a *Manual MDS* entry)

- Adding new supply (firm planned orders)

- Modifying due dates or quantities of existing demand entries or firm planned orders

- Modifying due dates of work orders or purchase orders

- Firming or unfirming existing discrete jobs and purchase orders

- Canceling existing work orders and purchase orders

- Modifying capacity for a specific resource

- Modifying alternate BOM and alternate designators for firm planned orders

You make these changes in the Supply/Demand, Supply, or Demand window of the Planner Workbench.

Simulation Modes

You can run planning simulations online or in batch mode. Online simulation gives you immediate feedback. It enables you to simulate multiple sets of changes, without increasing database traffic. However, online simulation does not allow you to change plan options, and it locks other users out of the plan while the online planner is active.

Batch replanning does take into account changes in plan options and enables other users to access the plan while you are entering your changes.

For either type of simulation, you might first want to establish a "baseline" by saving the exception message counts from the original version of the plan. To do this, navigate to the Exception Summary window of the Planner Workbench and click the Save Exceptions button. This will save the total number of exception messages in the plan with a unique version number; you can then compare the number of exceptions from the saved version(s) with the number of exceptions generated by your current simulation.

Online Simulation

To begin an online simulation session, select the Online mode in the Net Change Replan section of the Planner Workbench. Click the Start button; this launches a concurrent process that loads existing planning data into memory. You will see a status window that shows the progress of this process. Figure 10-9 for an example.

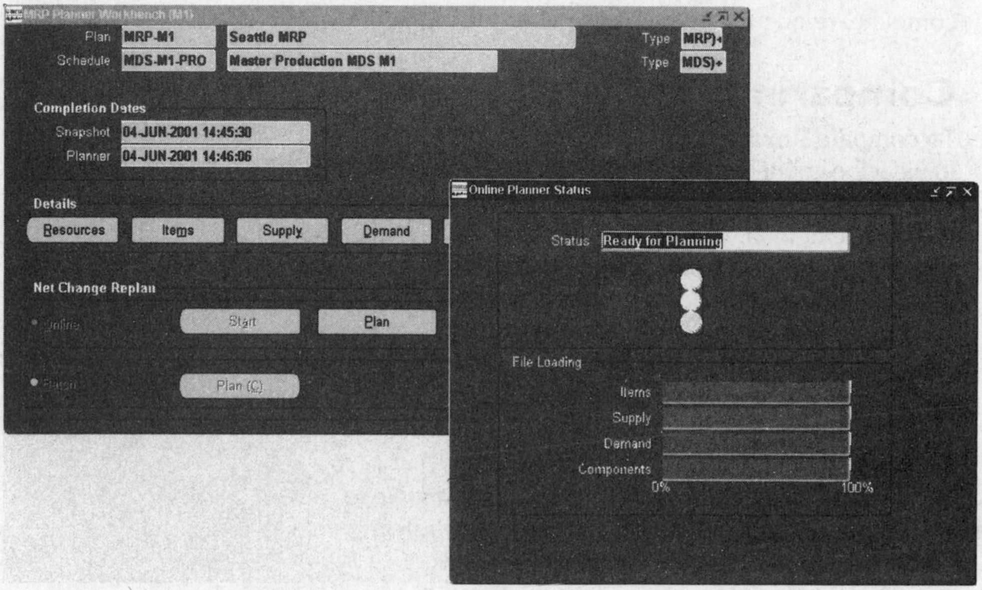

FIGURE 10-9. *Online Planner Status, ready for planning*

When the process completes, you will see the status Ready for planning. At this point, you can make your changes. Enter the data you want to change and save your changes. When you have completed a set of changes and want to see the results, return to the first window of the Planner Workbench and click the Plan button.

The status window will again show you the progress of the replanning process. When the status shows Ready for planning, you can view the results—new exception messages, new planned orders, or new recommendations—on the appropriate windows.

You can continue making additional changes and replanning as necessary. When you have finished, return to the first window of the Planner Workbench and press the Stop button. This will terminate your online planning session and make the plan accessible to other users.

Batch Simulation

To perform a batch simulation, simply make the changes you want on the appropriate windows of the Planner Workbench. When you have entered all the changes you want, return to the first window of the Planner Workbench. Select Batch mode in the Net Change Replan section. Click the Plan button; this launches the concurrent process that performs the replanning. This will clear your screen; when the process is complete, re-query your plan to see the results.

Comparing Simulated Scenarios

To compare simulated scenarios in MRP planning, the only online tool available is to view the count of exception messages. If you have saved the earlier message counts, you view the number of messages by version on the Exception Summary window. Using this method, you can quickly determine whether the number of late orders has increased or decreased due to the changes you made, for example. However, you can only see the *details* of the current set of exceptions; you cannot see the details of the earlier versions of your exception messages.

If you have maintained separate copies of different simulation scenarios, you can compare those with the Master Schedule Comparison report.

NOTE
Simulation capabilities, and the tools available to compare various simulations, are greatly improved in Advanced Supply Chain planning, described in the next chapter.

Technical Overview of the Planning Process

At a high level, the planning process involves two types of activities—the *Memory Based Snapshot* copies all appropriate ERP data, and the *Memory Based Planner* performs the netting and planning. Since Release 10.7, Oracle has utilized its memory-based planning engine to generate MRP plans. This technology offers significant efficiency improvements over the previous planning engine—all snapshot data is read into memory before netting and order planning, and both the deletion of data from a previous plan and the loading of data from the new snapshot have been moved out of the critical path.

In reality, these two major activities are broken into a number of subprocesses; this section provides a brief overview of these processes.

Memory-based Snapshot

The overall snapshot process copies the appropriate data from the transaction systems into tables used by planning. This data includes items, bills, safety stock levels, discrete jobs, purchase orders, sales orders, etc.

The Memory-Based Snapshot program (MRCNSP) begins the process; its job is to prepare a list of planned items. While the snapshot is reading the items for the plan, a separate Snapshot Delete Worker (MRCSDW) is deleting data old snapshot data. Performing these two tasks in parallel improves performance. When the old data is deleted, the new data is loaded into the table MRP_SYSTEM_ITEMS.

At this point, the memory-based snapshot launches the Snapshot Monitor (MRCMON), which controls the remaining snapshot processes. The snapshot monitor launches one or more Snapshot Workers (MRCNSW) and the first of several Snapshot Delete Workers. This delete worker will, in turn, launch additional delete workers to delete other existing planning data, while the snapshot workers are gathering the current data. As with the memory-based snapshot itself, the deletion of old data is performed in parallel with the snapshot of the new data. The snapshot workers write data to flat files in the operating system and store the filename and location in the database table MRP_FILES.

When the old data has been deleted and the new data collected for a given planning database table, the snapshot monitor launches a Loader Worker (MRCSLD) to load the data from the snapshot files back to the database. One loader worker is launched for each planning table to be loaded. The loader workers use SQL*Loader to load the flat file data to the database. The profile MRP:Use Direct Load Option controls whether SQL*Loader will use the direct path load or the conventional path load. The conventional path load builds standard SQL INSERT statements to update the database and can be used while other plans are running. The direct path load bypasses the standard SQL processor; it is therefore much faster, but requires exclusive write access to the table that it's loading, so that no other plans can be generated or executed.

Memory-based Planner

The Memory-Based Planner (MRCNEW) performs the planning calculations. It reads the data from the snapshot files into memory, performs planning for the list of planned items, and writes its results to another set of flat files in the operating system. At the completion of the planning process, it launches loader workers to load the final plan data back to the database.

Inter-Process Communication

The snapshot monitor uses the database table MRP_SNAPSHOT_TASKS to communicate with the snapshot delete workers. First, the snapshot monitor populates this table with a list of all the delete tasks. Each row in this table initially has a null value for START_DATE and COMPLETION_DATE. The delete workers look for the next task with a null START_DATE; a delete worker sets the START_DATE to show that it has begun to process the task and sets the COMPLETION_DATE when it is finished.

To communicate with memory-based snapshot and snapshot workers, the snapshot monitor uses database pipes. This type of communication includes requests for new snapshot tasks, task completion messages, lock requests, etc.

Concurrent Manager Requirements

With so many processes running in parallel, it is important that the concurrent manager that will run your plan can handle the number of processes your plan requires. If you run the plan as a single-threaded process, at least four concurrent processes must run simultaneously:

- Memory-based snapshot
- Snapshot monitor
- Memory-based planner
- All other snapshot workers, delete workers, and loader workers

The first three processes will all be running simultaneously for some period of time; they cannot complete until the loader workers and snapshot workers complete their processing. Therefore, if there are only three slots (target processes) available in the concurrent manager, the process will hang.

As described earlier, you can improve performance by running the snapshot processes in parallel. You control the number of parallel processes with the profile MRP:Snapshot Workers. Setting this profile to zero runs the plan as a single-threaded process; increasing the number of workers determines the degree of multi-threading. Each snapshot worker uses a simultaneous delete worker, so two processes can be running at the same time for each snapshot worker launched. Therefore, the *minimum* requirements on the concurrent manager can be calculated with the following formula:

```
Target processes = 4 + (2 * <number_of_snapshot_workers>)
```

Keep in mind that these are minimum requirements; if you are running other programs in the same concurrent manager, planning can easily fill up available concurrent manager slots and impair the performance of other requests. You might want to create a separate concurrent manager for planning, or at least ensure that the concurrent manager you will use has sufficient Target Processes to accommodate planning as well as other programs you anticipate running at the same time.

Summary

This chapter discussed the unique features of unconstrained, non-optimized planning. It described the different types of plans (MRP, MPS, and DRP) and discussed how to set up and generate those plans. It also covered the factors that control the scope of a plan's regeneration. The chapter described the available reports. The functions of the Planner Workbench for reviewing and implementing planning suggestions, viewing item and pegging information, and simulating changes to a plan and assessing the results were also covered.

This chapter has also provided a brief technical overview of the planning process. The next chapter discusses the capabilities provided by Oracle Applications to model multiple-organization, multiple-enterprise supply chains, and discusses the unique features of the newer Advanced Supply Chain Planning process.

CHAPTER
11

Advanced Supply
Chain Planning

tarting with Release 11, Oracle has offered Advanced Supply Chain Planning (ASCP) as an alternative to the single-organization planning discussed in Chapter 10. As its name suggests, ASCP plans across your supply chain and can incorporate customer preferences and supplier capacity. Some of these capabilities are also present in the earlier Supply Chain Planning (SCP) product, available since Release 10.7.

This chapter highlights the differences between SCP and ASCP. It describes the tools to define your supply chain; for the most part, these tools apply to both SCP and ASCP, but differences are noted. Additionally, this chapter discusses constraint-based and optimized planning, the mechanics of defining and running plans, and the tools to view and implement the resulting recommendations. Finally, the chapter describes the integrated performance measurement tools.

What's Different?

ASCP offers a number of enhancements to traditional planning: It offers the option of planning to material or capacity constraints; it provides automatic *optimization* of plans to meet explicit and implicit objectives; and it features built-in performance measurements to help you judge the effectiveness of the plan. As noted in Chapter 1, ASCP supports the concept of *holistic planning*—one plan can support all the functions traditionally provided by different plan types, planning all time periods, all manufacturing methods, and all organizations across the entire supply chain. This single-plan approach eliminates the synchronization of multiple plans, and it helps improve manufacturing flexibility and velocity.

As part of the holistic concept, ASCP can consolidate data from multiple instances—different instances of Oracle applications since Release 10.7, and even non-Oracle ERP systems—and provide a single, unified plan. This capability requires a much different architecture than the MRP planning (described in Chapter 10).

Multiorganization Planning

ASCP and SCP allow you to model complex supply chains and provide a unified plan for the entire supply chain. Your model can include customer preferences (for example, which organizations can supply which customers), multiple manufacturing and distribution organizations within your enterprise, and your suppliers. In simple cases, you might be able to model your supply chain using item and organization attributes. For more elaborate supply chains, you can define *sourcing rules* and *bills of distribution* and apply different sets of assignments of those rules.

The tools for defining your supply chain are described later, in the section titled "Modeling the Supply Chain."

Constraints

Unlike Oracle MRP planning, ASCP can respect various constraints on your production and distribution capabilities. This capability, sometimes called *finite planning* or *constrained planning*, enables you to generate a plan respecting material constraints, capacity constraints (including both manufacturing resource and transportation capacity), or both. You can plan for detailed or aggregate resources, and you can use item routings or bills of resource to control the granularity of the planning process.

You can enforce constraints selectively across the planning horizon. It may be important, for example, to recognize material and capacity constraints in the near term to avoid creating a plan that you can't execute. But at the far end of the horizon, it may be more important to generate an unconstrained plan to determine how much additional capacity you might need to meet the anticipated demand.

Constraint-based planning is a prerequisite for optimized planning—if there are no constraints, the assumption is that you can do anything; there's nothing to optimize.

Optimization

ASCP includes the option to generate an *optimized* plan. In an optimized plan, the planning process determines the relative cost of the different options available to it and chooses the "best" alternative based on those costs. Some of those costs are naturally present in your ERP data, such as the cost of using a substitute item or an alternate resource. Other costs are computed in planning by applying penalty factors to different events. For example, you might assign a penalty factor of 50 percent to exceeding resource capacity (reflecting that you would pay time-and-a-half if you had to work overtime); you might assign another penalty factor to satisfying a late demand, to artificially add cost to late production. In addition, optimization is influenced by the weight you give to each of three explicit planning objectives: Maximize Plan Profit, Maximize On-Time Delivery, and Maximize Inventory Turns.

Holistic Planning

The term *holistic planning* was coined by Oracle to suggest that one plan could meet all the needs typically addressed by multiple plans in more traditional planning scenarios. Holistic planning eliminates or reduces the need to keep multiple plans in synch. Specifically, holistic planning accommodates three dimensions of the planning problem:

- One plan can accommodate the entire planning horizon, with the appropriate level of granularity at different points along the horizon. This capability is determined by the definition of your plans, discussed in the "Aggregation" section.

- One plan can accommodate the entire supply chain, from your customers, through the distribution and manufacturing organizations within your enterprise, and down to your suppliers. The section titled "Modeling the Supply Chain" describes the tools available to define your entire supply chain, from customer through suppliers.

- One plan can accommodate all manufacturing methods: discrete, repetitive, process, flow, and project- (or contract-) based manufacturing. This capability is a function of the organizations included in your plan, discussed in the "Plan Organizations" section, and the architecture and instance definition, described in the section titled "Defining Instances."

Plan Types

ASCP uses basically the same plan types as traditional MRP, but uses slightly different names:

- **Distribution Plan**   equates to a DRP, or Distribution Requirements Plan.

- **Manufacturing Plan**   equates to an MRP, or Material Requirements Plan.

- **Production Plan**   equates to a Master Production Schedule, although there are significant differences between the earlier MPS and a Production Plan defined in ASCP.

Integrated Performance Management

ASCP incorporates performance management features from Oracle's Business Intelligence System (BIS). The Planner Workbench for ASCP displays four *Key Performance Indicators* (KPIs) for each plan:

- **Inventory Turns**   The inventory turns you could achieve if you executed the plan as suggested

- **On-Time Delivery**   The percentage of ontime delivery, to customer orders or to internal orders, that the plan projects

- **Margin Percentage**   The anticipated margin (profit) that would be generated by following the suggestions of the plan

- **Resource Utilization**   The utilization of resources projected by the plan

Release 11i.5 ASCP provides additional KPIs; right-click the workbench to select the following indicators:

- **Margin**   The margin amount (i.e., currency) that would be generated by following the plan suggestions

- **Cost Breakdown**   A comparison of four separate costs—Production Cost, Inventory Carrying Cost, Penalty Cost, and Purchasing Cost

You can use BIS to define targets for each of these KPIs. The Planner Workbench displays a graph for each of these KPIs and their targets so that you can easily assess the effectiveness of a particular planning strategy.

ASCP also provides enhanced exception messages and uses Oracle Workflow to provide notification and response processing for all those exceptions. See the sections titled "The ASCP Planner Workbench" and "Performance Management" for examples and more details of both KPIs and exception messages.

Architecture

ASCP is able to run on a separate server from your ERP system. This architecture eliminates any performance degradation on your transactions systems when a plan is running, and it enables you to run plans more often and more quickly than with traditional planning systems. (If you will run your plans overnight or at nonpeak hours, you can use the same server for both ASCP and ERP.)

The separate-server architecture also facilitates planning for multiple ERP systems; you can define multiple ERP instances to plan, collect their data to the planning server, and then run one single, consolidated plan with the aggregate data.

Because planning is designed to run on a separate server from ERP, you must explicitly publish the planning data back to the source instance to perform certain activities in your ERP system. The Push Plan Information concurrent program provides this function. For example, if you want to create flow schedules (described in Chapter 16) from an ASCP plan, you must run this program.

Whether you run ASCP on a separate machine, a single machine, or the same database instance as your ERP system, the process of setting up and running ASCP plans is unchanged—you must still define the source instances that planning will use (described in the section titled "Defining Instances"), and you must still collect data from those instances to the planning server (described in the "Data Collection" section).

Modeling the Supply Chain

ASCP (and earlier SCP) offers several methods of representing your supply chain. For the most part, these methods are identical whether you use them with ASCP or SCP; differences are noted.

Very simple supply chains—where one product is always supplied by a single plant and where there is no need to split purchase orders between suppliers—can be modeled with the item and organization attributes discussed in Chapters 2, 3, and 8. An item's Make/Buy attribute, for example, determines if the item is manufactured or purchased. The item's Source Organization identifies a single source of supply within your enterprise, for example, a manufacturing plant that might supply the item to a distribution center.

To model more elaborate supply chains, where one item may have multiple or alternate sources of supply, see the section "Multiple Sourcing Options" later in this chapter.

Multiple Organization Model

Central to any form of supply chain planning is the ability to model multiple organizations within your enterprise. This topic has been discussed in Chapter 2. A single plan can accommodate one, multiple, or all the organizations in your ERP system.

When you define the ERP instances from which you will collect planning data, you must identify the organizations in those instances for which you will plan. See the section "Defining Instances," later in this chapter. Then, when you define your plans, you define the organizations that participate in a given plan. See the "Defining the Plan" section.

NOTE
Whether your organizations use multiple sets of books or a single set of books, there is absolutely no effect on the planning process.

Multiple Sourcing Options

Oracle provides sourcing rules and bills of distribution to model multiple sources, including splitting production or purchases across plants or suppliers. These sourcing rules and bills of distribution are assigned to items, organizations, or categories using *Assignment Sets*. These tools allow you to model very complex supply chains; they are discussed in the following sections.

Both sourcing rules and bills of distribution use effectivity dates to let you project changes to your supply chain over time. The effectivity date initially defaults to the system date; like effectivity dates in routings or bills of material, a "null" ending date means that the effectivity of the rule has no projected end.

For each effectivity range, you define the sourcing options associated with the rule. There are three possibilities:

- **Make At** This option specifies that you will make any items associated with the rule at the receiving organization.

- **Buy From** This option indicates that you will buy any items associated with the rule from a specified supplier. With the Buy From option, you must enter the appropriate supplier, and optionally, the supplier site.

- **Transfer From** This option specifies a different organization within your enterprise as the source of items associated with this rule. With the Transfer From option, you identify the source organization; you must have already defined the shipping network between the source and receiving organization, as described in Chapter 2. You can also select a ship method from the shipping methods you defined in your shipping network; this will determine the in-transit time and shipping cost, which planning will use in its calculations.

Though the mechanics of defining sourcing rules and bills of distribution are much the same whether you're running ASCP or SCP, they operate very differently based on your planning method and options.

For ASCP, you assign each option a priority code. A priority code serves as a method for defining multiple sourcing scenarios—all the options within a single priority code will be considered as a unit. Within a priority code, you assign a percentage to each sourcing option. For example, if you have a group of items that you plan to buy from two different suppliers, you might define a sourcing rule with two "buy from" options within the same priority, specifying 50 percent for each supplier. If an alternate scenario for the same set of items is to buy from a single supplier, you would define a second scenario (priority) within the same sourcing rule, assigning the single supplier 100 percent of the purchases. Within a single priority code, the percentages must total 100 percent, or the group of options will not be considered by planning.

For SCP, the entire rule is treated as a single scenario; each option typically has a different priority code, which is used to "break a tie" if two options have identical planning percentages.

NOTE
This is a big difference between 10.7 SCP and ASCP. In SCP, each sourcing option typically has a different priority code, and the total of all percentages need to equal 100 percent for the sourcing rule to be active for planning.

You can define sourcing rules, bills of distribution, and assignment sets in your ERP instances; they will be collected with other planning data in the data collection process, described later. This approach makes sense if you have only one source instance, or if you want to use the same sourcing rules for other functions within your purchasing system. For example, you may want to use the same sourcing rules in your supplier item catalog that you use for planning.

You can also define sourcing rules, bills of distribution, and assignment sets on the planning server itself; this approach is useful if you will be planning for data collected from multiple ERP instances.

Sourcing Rules

A *sourcing rule* is a statement of planned sources of supply. Sourcing rules can be global (available to all organizations) or local (available only to the organization in which they are defined). You might use a local sourcing rule if the sourcing for a group of items varies based on the receiving organization. You might use a global sourcing rule for a set of products you buy from the same mix of suppliers, regardless of the receiving organization. A typical global sourcing rule for Global Order Promising might specify all sources of supply to your customers as "Transfer From" organizations.

Define sourcing rules on the Sourcing Rules form, shown in Figure 11-1. For each sourcing rule, specify a name and a description and choose whether the rule will be global or local.

TIP
Because you can use sourcing rules (and bills of distribution, discussed later) for many items, choosing descriptive names for the rules is helpful. For example, if you have a sourcing rule that you plan to use to identify the sources for fasteners, it might be helpful to name it something like "Fastener SR."

In the second region of the window, specify a range of effectivity dates for the rule.

For each effectivity date range, define the sourcing options (make, buy, or transfer) and their appropriate percentages. Depending on the option you choose, enter the additional information required, as described earlier, in the section "Multiple Sourcing Options."

Bills of Distribution

A bill of distribution is basically a collection of sourcing rules; in fact, there is nothing you can do with a bill of distribution that you could not do with a collection of sourcing

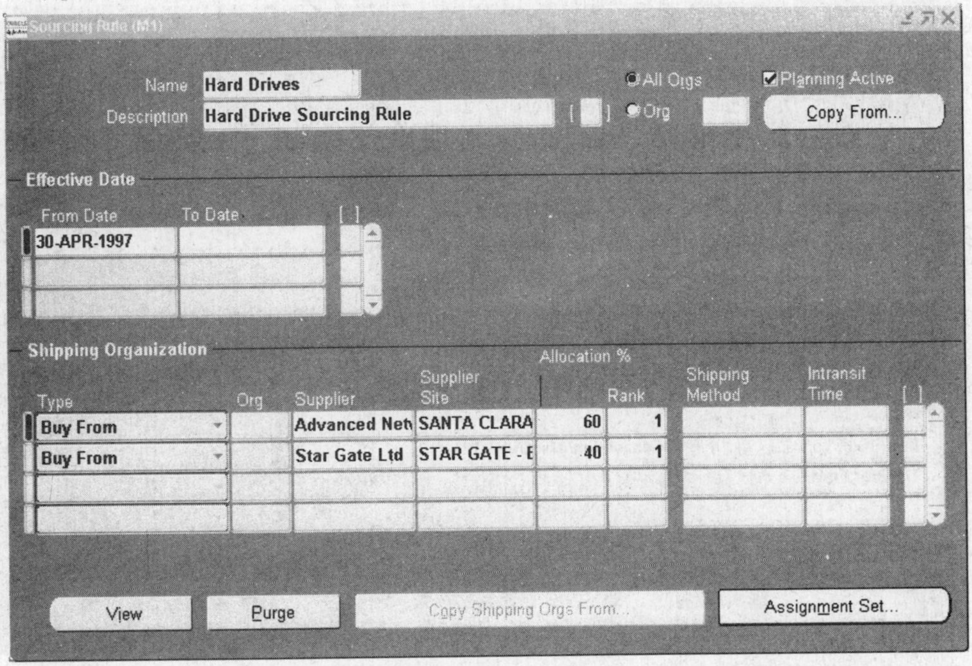

Sourcing Rule (M1)

| Name | Hard Drives | ○ All Orgs | ☑ Planning Active |
| Description | Hard Drive Sourcing Rule | [ ] ● Org [ ] | Copy From... |

Effective Date

| From Date | To Date | [ ] |
| 30-APR-1997 | | |

Shipping Organization

Type	Org	Supplier	Supplier Site	Allocation %	Rank	Shipping Method	Intransit Time	[ ]
Buy From		Advanced Net	SANTA CLARA	60	1			
Buy From		Star Gate Ltd	STAR GATE - E	40	1			

| View | Purge | Copy Shipping Orgs From... | Assignment Set... |

FIGURE 11-1. *Defining sourcing rules*

rules. But based on the definition of your supply chain, using bills of distribution rather than sourcing rules may be more convenient. For example, if the same set of sourcing rules apply to a group of items regardless of their organization, it may be simpler to define one bill of distribution and assign it to the item, rather than assigning a separate sourcing rule to each item/organization.

Bills of distribution are inherently global. For each bill of distribution, you define each receiving organization and effectivity date range, then the sourcing options for each organization and date range entry, as shown in Figure 11-2.

NOTE
Because bills of distribution and sourcing rules perform the same functions, the term "sourcing rule" is used in subsequent sections to refer to either a sourcing rule or bill of distribution.

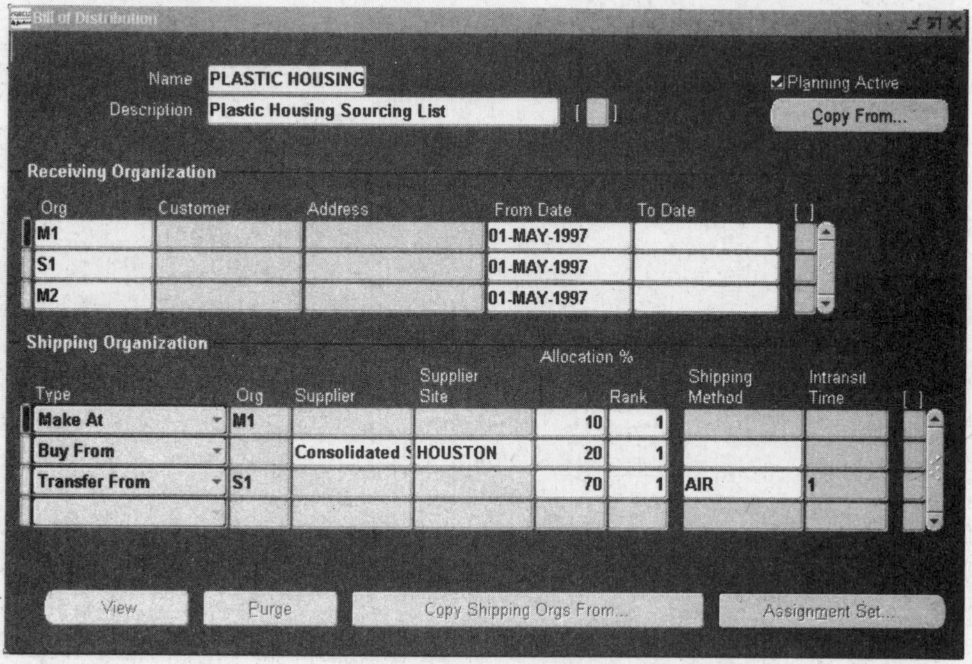

FIGURE 11-2. *Defining a bill of distribution*

Assignment Hierarchy

As noted earlier, sourcing rules themselves do not specify the items for which they will be used. This is the function of the *assignment set* and is one of the keys to the simplicity and flexibility of Oracle's ASCP model. An assignment set is literally a set of assignments that will be used in ASCP and for the purposes of Global Order Promising. You can define multiple assignment sets and use them for different purposes. For example, you might create one assignment set for your production plan, another for a simulated plan, and another for Global Order Promising. The capability to define multiple assignment sets lets you define multiple scenarios easily and use those scenarios in different plans.

Assignment sets also simplify the process of assigning sourcing rules to your items; rather than assigning a specific rule to each item, you can assign a default to an organization or to a category of items. Assign a sourcing rule to an individual item or item/organization only to deal with exceptions. You can further qualify these

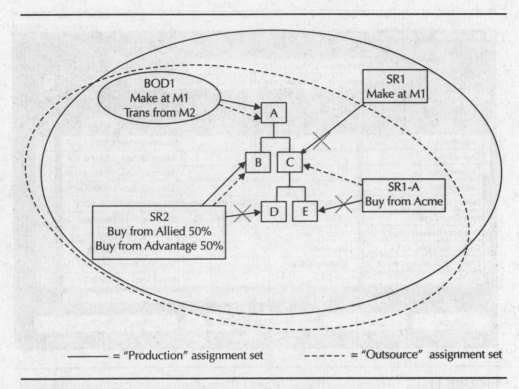

= "Production" assignment set   - - - - - = "Outsource" assignment set

FIGURE 11-3. *Assignment sets provide flexibility*

assignments by customer and address (site). Figure 11-4 shows the Sourcing Rule/ Bill of Distribution Assignments form.

For planning, you need to define one or more assignment sets that will determine the sourcing *within your enterprise.*

Assignment sets simplify the setup process by allowing you to assign sourcing rules at different levels of aggregation. Assignment sets defined within your ERP instance allow the following level of assignments:

■ All organizations within the instance.

■ A category of items, or a category of items within an organization. (You will have only one of these options, depending on the level at which you control the categories in your Planning category set.)

■ A specific item across all organizations.

■ An item in a specific organization within the instance.

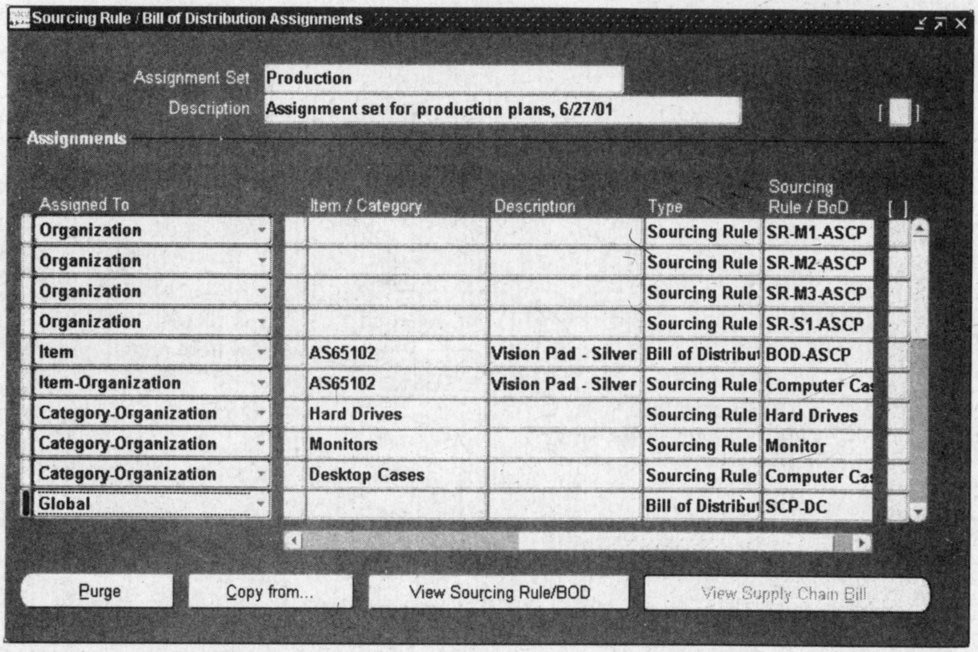

FIGURE 11-4. *Assign sourcing rules and bills of distribution in an assignment set*

Clearly, you can reduce the setup if you can assign sourcing rules or bills of distribution by category of items, rather than assigning sourcing rules to individual items.

Assignment sets that you define on the planning server offer the following levels of assignments:

- Instance

- Instance – Organization

- Item – Instance

- Category – Instance (available in Release 11i.5)

- Category – Instance – Organization (available in Release 11i.5)

- Item – Instance – Organization

It's possible that several assignments might apply to a given item; for example, you might have one assignment for the item and another for the category to which the item belongs. For planning purposes, the most specific assignment will be used. You can check all the assignments that exist for an item by using the View Sourcing Assignment Hierarchy, shown in Figure 11-5. This can be a good tool for troubleshooting your supply chain definition; you may find that sourcing for the item is coming from an unexpected source.

To use this form, enter the Assignment Set, Organization, Item, and effectivity date; then click the View Sourcing Hierarchy button. The resulting window shows all the levels at which you can assign sourcing information and the sourcing rule or bill of distribution that is assigned at that level. The levels are arranged in order of priority. The highest level at which sourcing information is present will be checked as Active, which indicates the sourcing information that will be used if you run a plan with this assignment set.

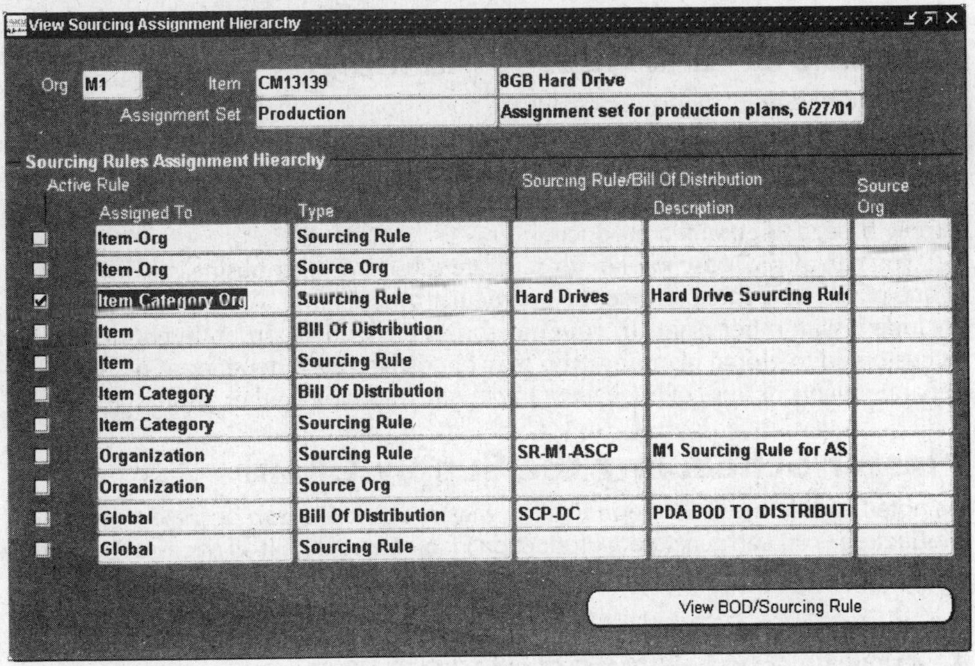

Active Rule	Assigned To	Type	Sourcing Rule/Bill Of Distribution	Description	Source Org
☐	Item-Org	Sourcing Rule			
☐	Item-Org	Source Org			
☑	Item Category Org	Sourcing Rule	Hard Drives	Hard Drive Sourcing Rule	
☐	Item	Bill Of Distribution			
☐	Item	Sourcing Rule			
☐	Item Category	Bill Of Distribution			
☐	Item Category	Sourcing Rule			
☐	Organization	Sourcing Rule	SR-M1-ASCP	M1 Sourcing Rule for AS	
☐	Organization	Source Org			
☐	Global	Bill Of Distribution	SCP-DC	PDA BOD TO DISTRIBUTI	
☐	Global	Sourcing Rule			

FIGURE 11-5.   *Troubleshoot your supply chain definition with the View Sourcing Assignment Hierarchy window*

NOTE
The View Sourcing Hierarchy Assignments window, shown in Figure 11-5, shows that the item attribute Source Org has the second rank among all of the possible levels of source information. It overrides even sourcing rules assigned to the item across all organizations. Be careful if you set this item attribute during item maintenance because it will have a strong impact on the sourcing of the item.

Sourcing and Assignment APIs

Oracle provides two APIs to create sourcing information—the Sourcing Rules/Bill of Distribution API and the Sourcing Rules/Bill of Distribution Assignment API. Their use is described in the Oracle ASCP and Global Order Promising Technical Reference Manual, available as part of the Oracle documentation library.

Global SCP and Subset Planning

Part of the holistic planning concept is the ability to run a single, global supply chain plan. This planning strategy results in no plans to synchronize, and can greatly shorten the planning cycle. It is especially well suited to an enterprise with a centralized corporate structure, interdependence among manufacturing facilities, a common supply base, and common products.

You can also choose to plan for separate subsets of your business. For example, if one plant is the sole producer of a particular product line, you may not need to include it with other plants in your enterprise. Or if your corporate culture isn't accustomed to global planning, you may choose to run independent plans for separate plants or lines of business; Oracle ASCP supports either approach.

Master Scheduling the Supply Chain

As noted earlier, the Production Plan, or Master Schedule, can be used to smooth production. You can generate a Production Plan, manipulate it as necessary, and then use it as input to another plan type (either a manufacturing plan or distribution plan).

Constraint-based Planning

A big difference between ASCP and earlier planning methods is the option of planning to constraints. Although Oracle has supported simultaneous material and capacity planning for a long time, the planning engine has always planned to meet due dates; capacity planning has been unconstrained, or *infinite*. ASCP provides the option of constraint-based planning, or *finite* capacity planning.

Furthermore, you can choose to plan to capacity (including transportation capacity) constraints, material constraints (including modeling the capacity of suppliers to provide material), or both; and you can specify different constraints and different levels of granularity in the different periods of the planning horizon.

Enabling Constraint-based Planning

There are two parts to enabling constraint-based planning: selecting the *hard constraint* and specifying the desired constraints and level of granularity across the planning horizon.

You select the hard constraint on the Options tab of the Plan Options form, shown in Figure 11-6. For each plan, you must select one of the following options:

■ **Enforce Demand Due Dates**   This sets the due dates of your demand as the hard constraint. Planning will always satisfy the demand on time unless you are using a planning time fence that prevents generation of planned orders in the near-term portion of the planning horizon. It will load primary resources to capacity, use alternate resources if available, and overload resources if necessary to meet the due dates. It will assume that material can be made available as necessary.

■ **Enforce Capacity Constraints**   This option sets capacity constraints as the hard constraint in the plan. Planning will load resources to their limits, schedule orders to be produced earlier than their due dates, and satisfy demand late, if necessary, to avoid overloading capacity. (You identify the type of capacity on the Aggregation tab of the Plan Options form.)

Types of Constraints

On the Aggregation tab of the Plan Options form, shown in Figure 11-7, check the Plan Capacity box. Then, identify the types of constraints and level of granularity for each portion of the planning horizon.

For each portion of the horizon, you can choose to plan to Resource Constraints, Material Constraints, or both. Each constraint, in turn, allows you to specify the desired level of granularity by using the Items, Resources, and Routings selection on the upper section of the form:

■ **Items**   Choose either Items, to plan for individual items; or Product Family, to aggregate item planning by product families. You would typically plan at the item level for near and mid-term requirements and plan at the family level only at the far end of the planning horizon.

■ **Resources** Choose either Individual, to plan each resource as defined on the Resources form; or Aggregate, to plan aggregate resources. You might use this if you have multiple resources that are not identical yet perform the same basic functions. For example, you might have several different machining centers with limited interchangeability; certain products might require specific centers, while other products might be able to use any center. For some types of planning, it may be more valuable to plan at the aggregate level.

You define aggregate resources as a function of each resource within a department. Define one resource to represent the aggregate resource, and specify its name in the Aggregate Resource field of the Department Resource Information descriptive flexfield to identify it as the aggregate. Then, specify this aggregate resource in the Aggregate Resource field for each of the "real" resources in that department that make up the aggregate. This is shown in the Figure 11-8.

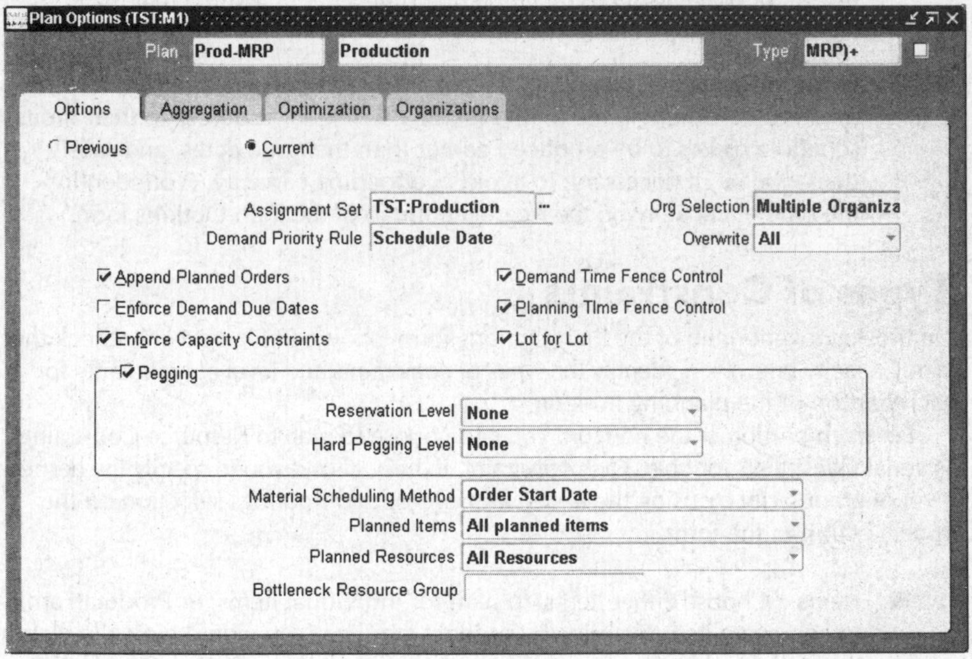

FIGURE 11-6. *Enable constraints on the Options tab of the Plan Options form*

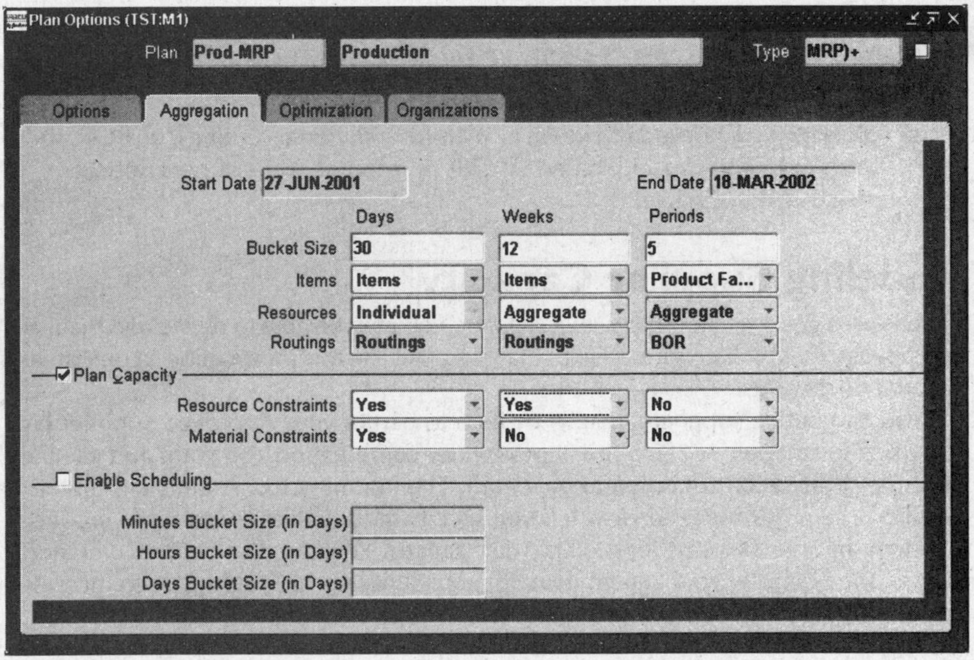

FIGURE 11-7. *Identify constraints and their granularity on the Aggregation tab*

Resource	Description	Aggregate Resource
MC-AGG	Machining center aggregate	MC-AGG
MC-1	Machining center 1, Mazak	MC-AGG
MC-2	Machining center 2, Cinc. Millachron	MC-AGG

FIGURE 11-8. *Aggregate resource definition*

CAUTION
Take care not to use the aggregate resource itself in your routings, or capacity planning will fail.

■ **Routings**   Choose Individual, to plan for individual routings; or BOR, to plan resource capacity based on bills of resource. Bills of resource were discussed in Chapter 8.

Modeling Supplier Capacity

If you have a good relationship with a supplier, you may be able to define and maintain the capacity they will commit to you. Planning will use this information to determine material constraints.

You can define supplier capacity by item as part of your Approved Supplier List, described in Chapter 13. Find the item/supplier combination you want and use the Attributes button to drill down to the detail. The Planning Constraints tab on the Supplier – Item Attributes window lets you specify the supplier's capacity to produce that item, in units per day, for multiple date ranges. You can also define Tolerance Fences; for example, your agreement with your supplier may allow you to increase demand by 10 percent if you provide at least 20 days advance notice.

Workflow can route supplier capacity exception messages directly to the supplier; the supplier's response can modify their capacity.

Optimized Planning

In addition to constraint-based planning, ASCP offers the option of optimized planning. As described earlier, an optimized plan will pick an "optimal" solution, based on the relative cost of the alternatives available. Enable optimization by checking the Optimize box on the Optimization tab of the Plan Options form, shown in Figure 11-9.

The optimization process considers the costs of the various options and chooses the best overall alternative. As a simple example, consider the following: Suppose you have an order priced at $100. If you have assigned a penalty factor of 25 percent to a late demand, each day that you are late in meeting that demand will "cost" $25 (25 percent of the $100); thus if you're a day late, the order will only be worth $75; if you're two days late, the order will be worth only $50, and so on. Against this artificial cost, planning weighs the cost of various options to satisfy the demand. For example, if you could use an alternate resource to meet the demand on time, the incremental cost of that resource would be considered—if the resource

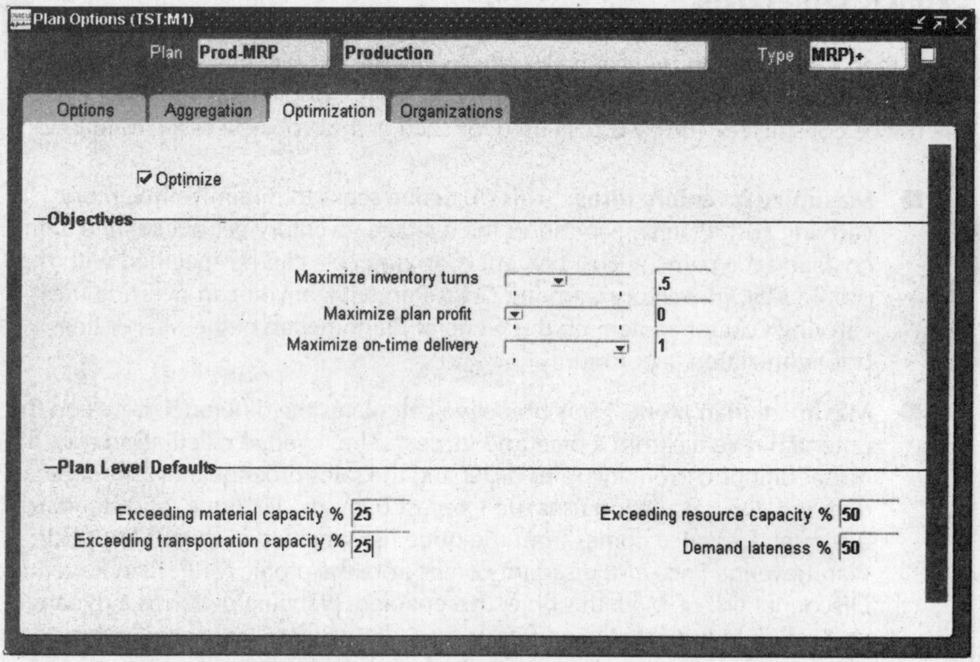

FIGURE 11-9. *Enabling an optimized plan*

cost more than $25 extra, planning might decide to ship the order one day late because the cost of the resource was greater than the penalty cost of being late.

Of course, this is a very simplistic example. Planning considers numerous other factors and many different scenarios; these factors are described briefly in the following sections, but the best advice is to test optimization carefully, changing only one factor at a time to evaluate its effect.

Optimization Objectives

Optimization uses both explicit and implicit objectives. Currently, Oracle supports three explicit objectives: inventory turns, plan profit, and ontime delivery. Implicit objectives are to minimize the costs of the following: late demand; resource and material exceptions; safety-stock violations; use of alternate sources, resources, routings, or items; and inventory carrying cost. These explicit and implicit objectives are discussed in the following sections.

Explicit Objectives

You enable each of the explicit optimization objectives on the Optimization tab of the Plan Options form (see Figure 11-9). To enable an objective, you assign a relative weight greater than 0 to the objective; a weight of 0 means the objective will not be considered. The basic data used for each of these objectives are as follows:

■ **Maximize inventory turns**   This objective seeks to minimize inventory carrying cost. Planning considers the average inventory per bucket, the item cost, and the carrying cost percent. Carrying cost can be specified with the profile MSO: Inventory Carrying Costs Percentage; you can override the carrying cost for an item on the General Planning tab of the Master Item or Organization Item form.

■ **Maximize plan profit**   This objective calculates the difference between the potential revenue from a plan and its cost. The revenue calculation uses the actual unit price from the sales order and the sales order quantity; for forecast demand, the calculation uses the forecast quantity, list price, and standard discount. List price comes from the price list specified in the profile MRP: Plan Revenue Price List; discount comes from the profile MRP: Plan Revenue Discount Percent. With this objective enabled, planning performs a dynamic cost rollup to evaluate the cost of various alternatives—for example, the cost of using substitute components, or alternate bills, routings, or resources.

■ **Maximize ontime delivery**   This objective minimizes the penalty cost for late demand. This penalty cost is calculated by applying a penalty factor to the order's value per day late, times the quantity of the demand. The penalty factor can be specified in the profile MSO: Penalty Cost Factor for Late Demands. It can also be specified for a plan on the Optimization tab of the Plan Options form (see Figure 11-9), in the Late Demands Penalty descriptive flexfield on the Organization Parameters form, or in the Late Forecasts Penalty descriptive flexfield on the forecast detail. Planning uses the most specific value it finds.

Implicit Objectives

Implicit objectives are to minimize a number of penalty costs. Implicit objectives each have a weight of 1, though you can control the cost by the way you choose your penalty factors. The penalty costs that planning considers include the following:

■ Cost of late demand

■ Cost of resource, material, and transportation capacity violation

- Safety stock violation

- Alternative sources

- Alternate bills, routings, and resources

- Substitute components

- Carrying cost

These penalty costs are calculated from existing ERP data or by applying a penalty factor to a cost. The data used includes the following:

- Resource cost

- Item standard or average cost

- Carrying cost percentage

- Selling price

- Transportation cost

- Sourcing rank

- Priorities for alternate bills, routings, resources, and components

- Penalty factors for exceeding resource, material, and transportation capacity

ASCP Setup

To generate an Advanced Supply Chain Plan, you must define your supply chain, as described earlier. You must also create the flexfields used by ASCP and define the application instances for which you will plan, the demand priority rules, and the plan names and their options. The following pages describe these activities.

Create Planning Flexfields

Many of the penalty factors used by ASCP optimization are currently provided as descriptive flexfields; when you prepare to use ASCP on an existing instance, you must run the Create Planning Flexfields concurrent program to enable these flexfields. The parameters for this program allow you to choose which attribute column in each table you want to use for the appropriate penalty factor. This avoids "collision" with existing descriptive flexfields you may already be using.

Defining Instances

Because ASCP can collect and plan data from multiple instances, you must define the instances for which you will plan. You define instances on the Application Instances form.

Identify each instance with a three-character code; this code will be prepended to organization codes, sourcing rules, bills of distribution, and assignment sets that you collect to the planning server. For each Oracle instance, specify the instance type: Discrete, Process, or both. Specify the version of each Oracle instance; versions starting with 10.7 are supported. If you will collect data from a legacy system, specify its instance type as Other.

If you run the planning server in a separate instance, you must specify the Application Database Link and the Planning Database Link; these links allow communication between the application database and the planning database. Your DBA can provide these values. You can also specify a default Assignment Set for the instance.

For each instance, you must specify the organizations within the instance from which you will collect data. Click the Organizations button; you will see a list of the inventory organizations defined in the instance. Select the organizations you want to plan by checking the Enabled box next to each organization.

Demand Priority Rules

Use the Define Priority Rules to define the way ASCP should rank your demands. This will determine which demands will be given priority in an optimized plan.

For each rule, assign it a name and description; then select one or more criteria in the order in which they should be applied. Available criteria are Schedule Date, Sales Order and MDS Priority, Request Date, Promise Date, and Gross Margin. Neptune, for example, tries to satisfy its schedule dates; if multiple orders have the same schedule date, Neptune will next use the Order Priority to break a tie, followed by the Gross Margin the order will generate.

You can define as many priority rules as you want and use different rules on different plans. The Default check box lets you specify one rule as your default.

Defining the Plan

Defining an ASCP plan involves defining a plan name for the appropriate plan type and specifying the desired options. As with single-organization planning, described in Chapter 10, there are separate forms to define each plan type. Regardless of the type of plan, you give each a name and description and identify scope of organizations for which it will plan—All or Multiple. (If you select Multiple, you will identify the organizations in the plan options.) You also indicate if the plan will be used for Global Order Promising calculations and whether it is a production plan. (A production plan enables auto-release of planned orders, as described in Chapter 10.)

Basic Options

For each plan, define its characteristics on the four tabs of the Plan Options window. The Options tab was shown earlier, in Figure 11-6. Many of the options on this tab are the same as for single-organization planning and were described in Chapter 10. Options that are unique to ASCP include the following:

- **Assignment Set**   This identifies the sourcing assignments to be used for the plan, as described in the "Assignment Hierarchy" section.

- **Demand Priority Rule**   This identifies the order in which demands will be prioritized; see the section "Demand Priority Rules" earlier in this chapter.

- **Enforce Demand Due Dates or Enforce Capacity Constraints**   This chooses the hard constraint for the plan, as described in the section titled "Enabling Constraint-Based Planning."

- **Lot for Lot**   This option enables true lot-for-lot planning, that is, it prevents the consolidation of planned orders for dependent requirements when multiple demands occur on the same day. With lot-for-lot planning, each individual demand will generate a separate planned order.

- **Planned Resources and Bottleneck Resource Group**   These options let you determine the resources that are planned. If you select All Resources, you will plan all the resources within the scope of your plan. If you select Bottleneck resources only, you identify those resources by means of the Bottleneck Resource Group; only resources within that group will be planned.

Aggregation

The Aggregation tab was shown in Figure 11-7. Here you set the number of daily, weekly, and period buckets for the plan; the window displays the end date of the plan based on your selections. For each bucket type, you specify the level of aggregation for that portion of the horizon. This was described earlier, in the section "Types of Constraints."

On the Aggregation tab, you also specify whether you are planning capacity, and you select the type of constraints—resource, material, or both—that you want to recognize within each bucket type.

At the bottom of the screen, you can enable detailed scheduling for the Daily buckets within the horizon. Check the Enable Scheduling box, and then specify how many of the days within the first portion of the plan will be scheduled to the minute or hour; discrete jobs and planned orders within this portion of the horizon will be scheduled using routing information. Jobs and planned orders in the remaining portion of the daily horizon will be scheduled by day.

Optimization

The Optimization tab, shown in Figure 11-9, lets you enable optimized planning. Here you specify the weight of each explicit optimization objective and plan-level default for the following penalty factors: Exceeding material capacity percent, Exceeding resource capacity percent, Exceeding transportation capacity percent, and Demand lateness percent. Optimization objectives and penalty factors were discussed earlier, in the section titled "Optimized Planning."

The combination of factors on the first three tabs yields a number of different classes of plans that you can define: unconstrained, resource constrained, material constrained, material and resource constrained, or optimized. But the number of options and factors that influence these plans allows for nearly infinite variety.

Plan Organizations

The Organizations tab lets you specify the scope of your plan by identifying the organizations that participate in that plan. An example of this tab is shown in Figure 11-10.

For each organization, specify the netting and safety stock options, the same as for a single-organization plan (see Chapter 10). Include a Bill of Resource name, if

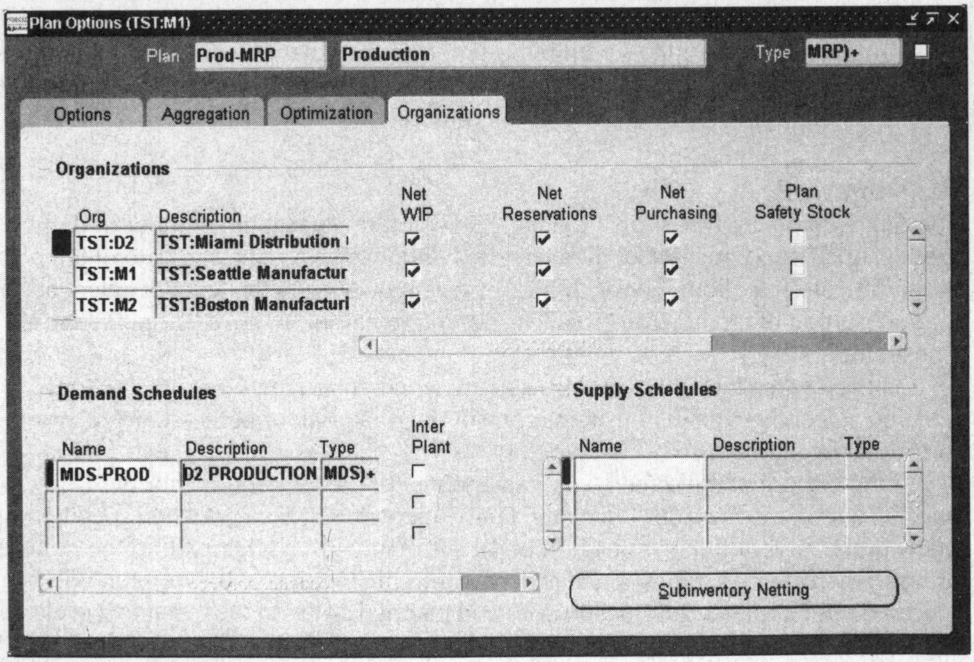

FIGURE 11-10. *Planning organizations*

you are using bills of resources (instead of detailed routings) at any point on the planning horizon. Also specify a Simulation Set if you want to recognize capacity changes as described in Chapter 4.

Specify the demand and supply schedules to be used at each organization. As described in Chapter 8, demand schedules identify independent demand. Supply schedules are used to smooth or manipulate production schedules by defining planned production for a particular organization; see "Master Scheduling the Supply Chain," earlier in this chapter.

Data Collection

The ASCP architecture requires that data be collected from your ERP system(s) to run a plan. After a plan is generated, the appropriate data can be published back to the appropriate source instances in the form of order releases, reschedules, and cancellations.

Data collection gathers data from the organizations of your defined instances; this data is referred to in Oracle documentation as the *Application Data Store* (ADS). The collection process consists of two concurrent programs: Planning Data Pull and Planning ODS Load. Oracle provides a report set, called Planning Data Collection, to run these two programs sequentially.

Data collection is a two-step process to accommodate the situation where you need to perform additional data cleansing to consolidate data from various instances. Oracle automatically consolidates the following data, based on the criteria listed in Table 11-1.

Data Object	Consolidation Criteria
Items	Matching concatenated item segments
Categories	Matching concatenated category segments
Category Sets	Matching category set names
Suppliers	Matching supplier names
Supplier Sites	Matching site codes
Customers	Matching customer names
Customer Site Uses	Matching customer name, site, use code, location, and operating unit
Units of Measure	Matching UOM codes

TABLE 11-1.   *Data Consolidation Criteria*

If data from multiple instances should be consolidated, even if the specified criteria do not match exactly, you can write your own programs to cleanse the data before running a plan. For example, if one source instance refers to a customer as "Oracle," and another uses "Oracle Corporation" to identify the same customer, you might want to incorporate additional data cleansing so that both customer records are represented as the same entity.

Types of Collection

When you run data collection, you can request the categories of data you want to collect. You can run data collection as a *complete refresh* or in an *incremental* mode. Requesting a complete refresh will delete data that you have already collected for the specified instance before populating new data. Thus, if you request a complete refresh but do not request to reload a certain category of data, you will effectively remove that data from the planning process.

Running Collections

Run data collection by selecting the Planning Data Collection report set from the menu. As noted earlier, this report set consists of the Planning Data Pull and Planning ODS Load programs. Enter the desired parameters for each program.

For the Planning Data Pull program, you must identify the instance from which you will pull the data, whether you are requesting a complete refresh, the number of workers, and the language. You also identify the categories of data you want to collect; Figure 11-11 shows many of the categories of data you can choose.

In addition to the specific categories of data, there are three additional parameters:

- **Recalculate NRA**   This option recalculates *net resource availability;* use this if you have made changes in the source instance that affects the availability of your resources.

- **Recalculate Sourcing History**   This option keeps your sourcing history up-to-date, so that sourcing decisions in planning are based on history as well as the current plan. If you utilize sourcing rules that regularly split sources (such as splitting purchases between several suppliers), you should select this option.

- **Analyze Tables**   This option helps maintain system performance; Oracle recommends its use.

When you have entered the parameters for the Planning Data Pull program, enter the following parameters for the Planning ODS Load program (most often, the defaults will be appropriate): Instance, Number of Workers, Recalculate NRA, and Recalculate Sourcing History.

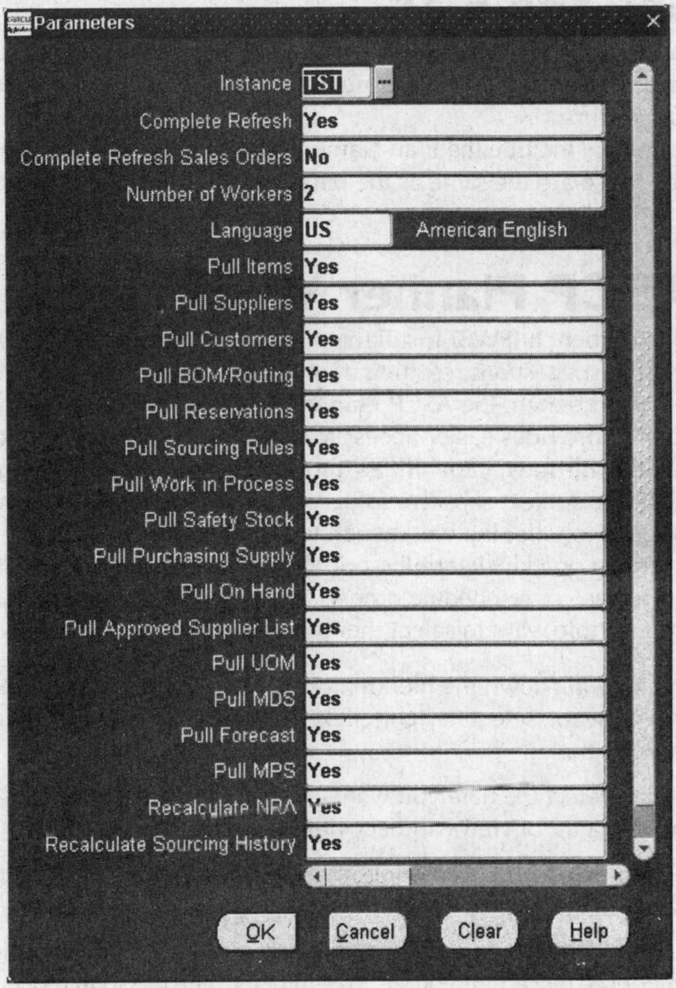

Parameters		×
Instance	TST	...
Complete Refresh	Yes	
Complete Refresh Sales Orders	No	
Number of Workers	2	
Language	US	American English
Pull Items	Yes	
Pull Suppliers	Yes	
Pull Customers	Yes	
Pull BOM/Routing	Yes	
Pull Reservations	Yes	
Pull Sourcing Rules	Yes	
Pull Work in Process	Yes	
Pull Safety Stock	Yes	
Pull Purchasing Supply	Yes	
Pull On Hand	Yes	
Pull Approved Supplier List	Yes	
Pull UOM	Yes	
Pull MDS	Yes	
Pull Forecast	Yes	
Pull MPS	Yes	
Recalculate NRA	Yes	
Recalculate Sourcing History	Yes	

OK   Cancel   Clear   Help

FIGURE 11-11. *Planning data pull parameters*

When the data collection process completes, you can view the collected data on the Collection Workbench. This is very similar to the ASCP Planner Workbench, discussed later in this chapter, but keep in mind that it shows only the data as collected from the source instances; no planning has taken place yet.

Running the Plan

Launching an ASCP plan is very similar to launching an MRP plan. You can access the appropriate launch form from the menu or from the Names form for the type of plan you want to run.

Plan parameters include the Plan Name, Launch Snapshot, Launch Planner, and Anchor Date. These are the same as the parameters for an MRP plan, described in Chapter 10.

The ASCP Planner Workbench

The Planner Workbench (PWB) is still the primary tool for viewing, modifying, and implementing the suggestions resulting from the planning process. Compared to the MRP Planner Workbench, the ASCP Planner Workbench has a greatly improved user interface—it provides easier access to data, a graphical view of each plan's KPIs, enhanced drill-down capabilities, more logical display of exceptions and related exceptions, context-sensitive folder forms to display exception details, and additional options to tailor the workbench to an individual user's preferences. It is designed to let you quickly determine priorities, view detailed information, simulate changes, and release or reschedule orders when you are satisfied with the result.

There are multiple ways to select the information you want to view:

- You can walk down the hierarchical display in the left pane to locate the data you want, select it, right-click, and select the view you want from the pop-up menu.

- You can select the data you want and use the Tools option on the menu bar to access a list of views and activities you can perform.

- You can expand the exception message summaries and drill down to the detail of a specific exception message.

- You can right-click an exception message to choose from multiple views of the detail or see related exceptions to help determine the source of a problem.

The PWB consists of two panes: the left pane (the Navigator) presents a hierarchical display of all plans and their planned objects (such as organizations, items, resources, suppliers, and projects); the right pane displays various detailed information about the objects selected in the left pane. An extensive set of preference settings let you tailor the display to your liking.

Left Pane (Navigator)

The left pane of the Planner Workbench, called the Navigator, displays all the planned objects for all plans, arranged in six different hierarchies. You select the view you want from the drop-down list at the top of the pane. An example, illustrating the Organization view, is shown in Figure 11-12.

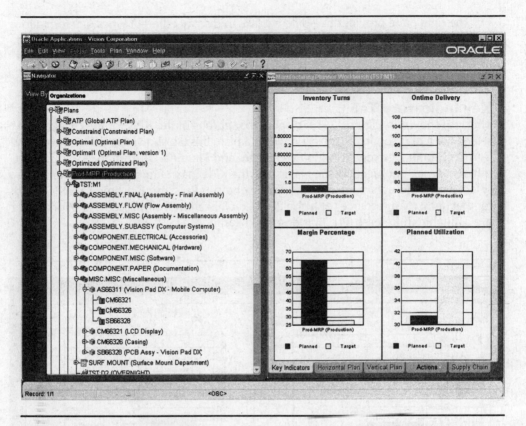

FIGURE 11-12. *Planner Workbench—Organization view*

The available hierarchies are Actions, Items, Organizations, Projects, Resources, and Suppliers. All views provide access to much of the same information, but the order in which it is presented differs; use the view that is most appropriate for the type of information you want. For example, if you are interested in a particular item across your enterprise, you might use the Items view; if you are interested in a group of items within an organization, you might use the Organization view; and if you are interested in items from a particular supplier, you might use the Supplier view.

Right Pane

The right pane of the PWB displays information based on the objects that you select in the Navigator. You can often select multiple objects of the same type (such as multiple plans, multiple items, or multiple resources) using standard Windows conventions (SHIFT-click, or CTRL-click); the right pane displays information for all the selected objects.

The right pane provides five different tabs to display different types of information: Key Indicators, Horizontal Plan, Vertical Plan, Actions, and Supply Chain. You can select the default tab that appears when you first open the workbench; this is described later, in the "Display Preferences" section.

Key Indicators Tab

This tab, shown in Figure 11-13, displays bar graphs of the KPIs for the objects you select. For a plan, or an organization within a plan, this tab shows four KPIs—Inventory Turns, Ontime Delivery, Margin Percentage, and Planned Utilization. As you select different types of objects in the Navigator, the KPIs may change for example, if you select items, the right pane displays the Inventory Turns and On-time Delivery KPIs for that item; for a resource, only the Planned Utilization is displayed. Additional KPIs are available in Release 11i.5, as described earlier.

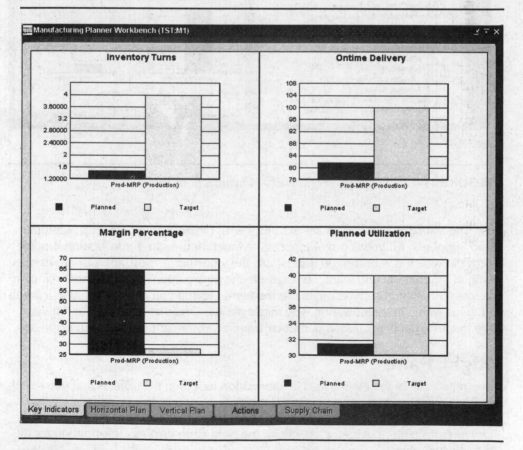

FIGURE 11-13. *Planner Workbench—Key Performance Indicators*

To best display the differences between the planned and target KPI values, the graphs do not necessarily start at the zero point on the Y-axis. You can expand an individual graph to the full size of the window by double-clicking; double-click again to return to the multigraph display. You can also see the precise data values by holding the mouse pointer over a bar on the graph.

For more information on the KPIs used by ASCP, see the section titled "Performance Management," later in this chapter.

Horizontal Plan Tab

This tab displays either a horizontal material plan (for organization items selected in the left pane) or a horizontal capacity plan (if you have selected one or more resources). A sample horizontal material plan is shown in Figure 11-14.

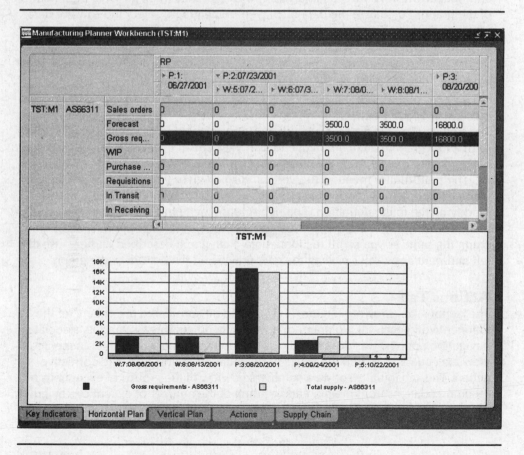

FIGURE 11-14. *Planner Workbench—Horizontal Plan*

The horizontal plan displays the rows of data and the time buckets you specify in your personal preferences, discussed later in this chapter. It also displays a graph of the information.

You can expand or contract time buckets by clicking the small triangle in the label of the appropriate time period, and you can change the width of the cells by dragging the cell boundaries, much as you would in a spreadsheet. To add or remove rows of data, right-click any row label and use the Show or Hide options in the pop-up menu to modify the display. These changes are effective only as long as you have the Planner Workbench open; to make permanent changes, use the Preferences window, which you can access from the right-mouse menu.

The right-mouse menu also lets you toggle between the Horizontal View and the Enterprise View and hide or show the graph.

To scroll through the graph, click in the graph window and scroll using the left and right arrow keys. Or, you can scroll by dragging the dark gray bar at the bottom of the graph. To change the data displayed in the graph, select the rows of data you want by clicking on the button to the right of the row label in the horizontal display; you can select multiple rows with SHIFT-click or CTRL-click.

The right-mouse menu in the graph section of the window lets you select either a bar graph or line graph of the selected data.

Vertical Plan Tab

The Vertical Plan tab displays a traditional, vertical material plan in a standard folder form and a graph of the cumulative totals. The Vertical Plan tab is active only if you have selected one or more organization/items in the Navigator.

The right-mouse menu in the vertical display gives you access to the Supply/ Demand and Items windows, as well as access to the standard Oracle tools for modifying the folder definition. The right-mouse menu in the graph lets you change the granularity of the display; you can choose days, weeks, or periods. Scroll this graph the same as you scroll the Horizontal Plan graph described earlier—use the left and right arrow keys or drag the dark gray bar at the bottom of the graph.

Actions Tab

The Actions tab, shown in Figure 11-15, might be considered the "heart" of the Planner Workbench for a planner or master scheduler. This tab, and its associated navigation options, was designed to make it as easy as possible for a planner to view exceptions, research the cause of potential problems, and take corrective action. This tab initially shows a summarized view of the groups of exceptions or recommendations from the plan and a graph of the number of exceptions by group. This tab is active for virtually any object selected in the Navigator and shows only the exceptions and recommendations for the selected object.

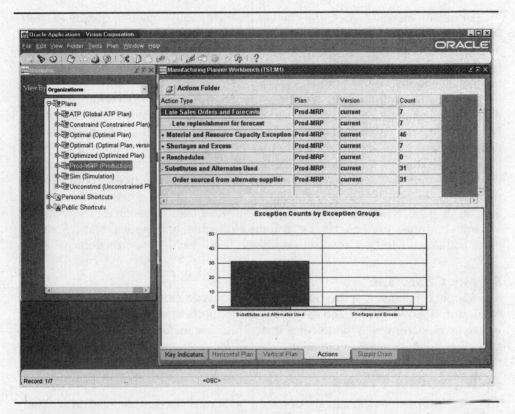

FIGURE 11-15. *Planner Workbench—actions*

Exception summaries are displayed in a standard folder form, which you can change as needed. The summary is arranged in order of importance—Late Sales Orders and Forecasts is at the top of the list because this is often the most serious condition; Recommendations (new orders to release) is at the bottom of the list.

Double-click a category to expand it to the specific message types within that category; a plus sign to the left of the category indicates where expansion is possible. Figure 11-15 shows the category Substitutes and Alternates Used expanded to show the specific message type, "Order sourced from alternate supplier," in that category. Double-click a category marked with a minus sign (–) to collapse it to the summary level.

Double-click a specific message type (or use the right-mouse menu) to display the details of each instance of the message. The resulting Exception Details window uses folders specific to each message type; this allows you to display data appropriate to each message type. Like all folders, you can easily tailor the display to your liking.

For certain message types, you can use the right-mouse menu to display Related Exceptions; these are intended to help determine the cause of a problem. For example, a "Late replenishment" message might be related to a material or capacity constraint; the Related Exceptions selection on the right-mouse menu would drill directly to these related exceptions.

From the Exception Details window, you can use a button on the form to access the Supply/Demand window, where you can take action on many of the exceptions. For example, you can firm planned orders, implement planned orders, and change their dates and quantities, just as you can on the Supply/Demand window in the MRP Planner Workbench, described in Chapter 10. You can also use buttons to access the Suppliers, Items, or Resources window, based on the type of exception. The right-mouse menu lets you access additional windows for the exception, including Supply, Demand, Resource Availability, Resource Requirements, Sources, Destinations, a Gantt chart showing the schedule, and the Horizontal and Vertical Plans. Some of these additional windows are discussed in the "Additional Views" section.

Supply Chain Tab

The Supply Chain tab is active only for a single organization item selected in the Navigator. It shows you a graphical picture of the supply chain bill or a supply chain where used, starting with the selected item. This view includes sourcing information as well as bill of material information.

Additional Views

The ASCP Planner Workbench provides many additional views of planning data; a few of the most useful windows are described in the following pages.

Supply and Demand

The Supply/Demand window, shown in Figure 11-16, continues to be the "workhorse" of the PWB. This window enables you to firm planned orders, implement recommendations for new orders, and reschedule existing jobs or purchase requisitions. As you release new orders, you can firm them, modify dates and quantities, change sourcing decisions, and change the order type.

The window is organized in a tabular format.

- **Order** Provides basic planning information and the For Release and Firm check boxes.

- **Release Properties** Lets you specify the revised date and quantity for orders you implement, as well as change their order types. A number of fields that are not shown on the standard folder provide additional options, including the capability to implement alternate bills or routings, change the source organization, specify or change a recommended supplier and site, or change project and task, among others. You can include these fields in your folder if you need to perform these types of activities.

- **Sourcing** Displays sourcing information—source organization, supplier, and supplier site. (You can override this information on the Release Properties tab, as described earlier.)

- **Line** Displays information about repetitive schedules.

- **Project** Displays project manufacturing information. As mentioned earlier, you can override this information using additional fields on the Release Properties tab.

To implement suggestions from the Supply/Demand window, check the For Release box; make any modifications using the Release Properties tab, and save your changes. Then, select Plan | Release from the menu bar. This will show a summary window of the number of jobs, schedules, requisitions, and reschedules, along with the concurrent request IDs that will implement these actions. Click OK to confirm. The Plan selection on the menu bar also includes the option to select all planned orders for release.

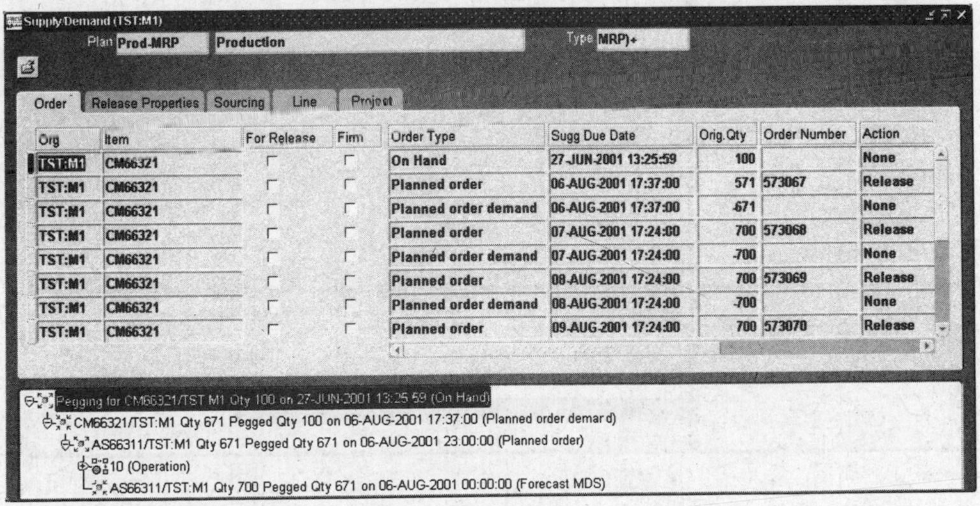

FIGURE 11-16. *Planner Workbench—supply and demand*

The Supply/Demand window includes graphical pegging information for each item if you selected pegging in your item attributes and plan options. You can access the Supply/Demand window from many places on the PWB, including the action messages, the Tools selection on the menu bar, or the right-mouse menu from the Navigator. As in the MRP Planner Workbench, individual views of Supply and Demand are also provided.

Gantt Chart

The Gantt chart provides a graphical view of your schedule. This window, shown in Figure 11-17, consists of four panes. The upper-left pane is similar to the Navigator; it lets you organize the orders or resources you want to see. The upper-right pane displays the schedules; you can reschedule jobs by dragging them to the desired

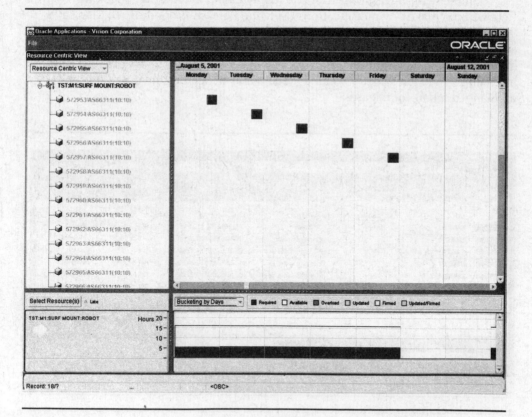

FIGURE 11-17. *The Gantt chart provides graphical scheduling*

point on the chart. The lower-right pane shows load and available capacity for the resources you select using the lower-left pane. Color-coding identifies resource requirements, availability, and overload, as well as resources or operation that have been updated or firmed.

You can access the Gantt chart from the Supply/Demand window. Select one or more jobs or planned orders using SHIFT-click or CTRL-click; then use the right-mouse menu to access the Gantt chart for the selected orders.

Other Windows

Other windows accessible on the PWB include Item Information, Resources, Resource Requirements, and Resource Availability. These windows are accessible from the Tools selection on the menu bar or from the right-mouse menu at various places in the workbench.

You can also view the options used for a plan with the Plan | Plan Options selection on the menu bar.

Display Preferences

To access the Preferences window, select a plan on Navigator. Then select Tools | Preferences from the menu bar.

The Preferences window contains five tabs. The Other tab lets you choose the default display format for the left and right panes of the workbench. It is where you specify the default Job Status, Job Class, and Firm flag for discrete jobs you release and the grouping method for releasing requisitions. Here you can specify whether you want to release jobs for phantom or configured assemblies. This tab also lets you specify the category set you will use and filter the recommendations you see—you may want to view only recommendations for the next week or two, as opposed to viewing all the recommendations over the entire planning horizon. Finally, this tab shows the date of the snapshot and plan.

The Material Plan, Capacity Plan, Supplier Plan, and Transportation Plan tabs let you control the formats of the respective horizontal plans. You can choose the number and type (days, week, or periods) of the display buckets, the display factor (to adjust for very large or very small numbers), and the rows of data displayed.

Typical Scenarios

The possible scenarios for different exception conditions and possible resolution are virtually endless. This section lists just a few types of exception and messages and discusses possible resolution activities. The Release 11i.4 User's Guide, part of Oracle's documentation library, lists each exception message and possible actions.

Late Replenishment for Sales Order

This exception is generated only for constrained and optimized plans when the Enforce Capacity Constraints option has been selected. The message details show the potential late orders. You might sort the details in descending order of Days Late to identify the most urgent orders.

You can drill to related exceptions (using the right-mouse menu) to see if the delay is the result of a combination of constraints—material, capacity, or transportation. If so, you might want to attempt to relieve these constraints, by expediting material, adding additional capacity (such as working overtime) or outsourcing production if possible. Performing a simulation of these possible solutions can help determine if they will resolve the problem.

You would perform similar actions for a "Late replenishment for Forecast" exception, although the situation is not usually as critical as a late sales order.

Constraints

Material constraint and Resource constraint messages are generated for constrained and optimized plans. You should determine the impact of the constraint; drilling to related exceptions can help. For example, if the constraint would result in a late replenishment for a sales order, it is most likely a higher priority than if it would simply delay replenishing safety stock.

You can deal with constraints in a number of ways—you might consider alternate resources or materials, adding resource capacity, modifying sourcing rules (such as using an alternate facility that has excess capacity), or outsourcing. You can simulate some of these changes on the Planner Workbench to assess their effectiveness; on an ongoing basis, you should make permanent changes in your source instances.

Reschedules

This type of exception includes Reschedule in, Reschedule out, and Past due order messages; they are generated for all plan types. The exception details show the specific order for which the exception was raised.

From the Exception Detail window, you can drill to the item's Supply/Demand window; there you might look at the pegging information to determine what other orders are affected. (*Remember*: The planning process assumes that you will accept its recommendations, so if you do not act on a Reschedule in message, another order might experience a shortage.)

If you elect to reschedule the order as suggested, you can do this for most order types from the Supply/Demand window. You must reschedule purchase orders from the Purchasing application because they usually represent a contract with the supplier.

Simulations

Like single-organization planning, described in Chapter 10, ASCP allows for online simulations to evaluate the effects of changes to your plan, or different planning scenarios. For comparison purposes, you may want to make a copy of a plan before simulating changes; you can access the Copy Plan program from the main menu, or from the Planner Workbench itself, by selecting Plan | Copy Plan from the menu bar.

The ASCP Planner Workbench provides the capability to compare plans by viewing their KPIs or action messages. It also provides the capability to "bookmark" the plan at various points in the simulation process and easily restore a plan to its state at a specified bookmark.

Simulation Scenarios

As with single-organization planning, you can make a number of changes on the PWB and run a replan to see the results. The type of changes you can simulate include those listed in Chapter 10—you can add new demand or supply, modify dates or quantities, cancel orders, select alternate bills or routings, and modify resource capacity. With ASCP, you can also simulate changes to demand priorities, supplier capacity, and optimization objectives.

Simulation Modes

You can run simulations online or in batch mode, as described in Chapter 10. But unlike Oracle MRP, ASCP keeps track of the changes you make during a simulation; you can access this log by selecting Plan | Undo Summary from the menu bar. This selection opens a window that summarizes the changes you have made during a simulation session; you can view the details of a specific change with the Detail button in that window.

From the Undo Summary window, you can undo selected changes. Select one or more changes (using SHIFT-click or CTRL-click if necessary), and click Undo. You must then rerun the online planner to replan, based on the restored data. You can also create "bookmarks" at multiple points during the simulation process—select Plan | Add Undo Bookmark from the menu bar, or use the Add Bookmark button in the Undo Summary window. You will be asked to supply a name for the bookmark. You can undo all changes back to a specific bookmark by selecting that bookmark in the Undo Summary window and clicking the Undo button.

Comparing Simulated Scenarios

If you have performed your simulation in a copy of your original plan, you can compare the copy to the original, using both the KPIs and the specific action messages. This is intended to provide easier analysis of the simulation than the tools provided with older, single-organization planning.

To perform this comparison, select two or more plan names on the Navigator (left pane) of the workbench; the Key Indicators and Actions tabs will display data for all the selected plans. Figure 11-18 shows KPIs for two plans.

You can also compare the simulation results with the original plan by comparing the count of the exceptions messages generated from each scenario. Select Plan | Save Actions from the menu bar, or select Save Actions from the right-mouse menu on the Actions tab of the Planner Workbench.

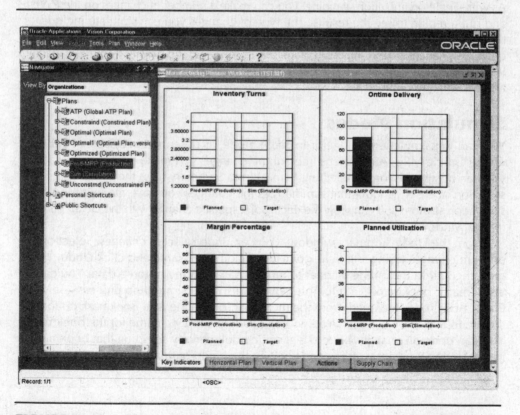

FIGURE 11-18. *Planner Workbench—comparing the results of a simulation*

Performance Management

As mentioned earlier in this chapter, ASCP is integrated with Oracle BIS. The performance measurements provided promote continuous improvement throughout your enterprise.

Exception messages are another indicator of performance; the capabilities of the Planner Workbench to drill to the cause of an exception and take corrective action when necessary also aid in performance improvement.

Key Performance Indicators

Four KPIs are displayed on the Key Indicators tab of the Planner Workbench; see Figure 11-13 for an example. You can set targets for each of these KPIs in the Performance Management Framework within the BIS application; within BIS, KPIs are referred to as *performance measures*. Set the performance measures at both the Total Organizations and Total Time dimensions for the following KPIs:

- **Inventory Turns** This indicator calculates inventory turns as the value of independent demand divided by the planned value of the averaged inventory. Set the target for MRP Inventory Turns.

- **Ontime Delivery** This indicator calculates ontime delivery as the percentage of the total number of orders that are planned to ship on time. Set the target for MRP Ontime Delivery percent.

- **Margin Percentage** This indicator calculates margin by calculating the price and discount of planned shipments, minus the cost of those shipments. Set the target for MRP Gross Margin percent.

- **Planned Utilization** This indicator calculates resource utilization as the average of the planned usage hours divided by the available hours, for all planned resources. Set the target for MRP Planned Utilization percent.

You can find detailed formulas for these indicators in the Oracle Advanced Supply Chain Planning, Oracle Risk Optimization, and Oracle Global Order Promising User's Guide—part of the standard Oracle documentation library.

Exception Messages

Release 11i.4 provides more than 40 exceptions and recommendations; these messages are described in great detail in the User's Guide, along with a suggested course of action for each message. Exceptions are displayed on the Actions tab of the Planner

Workbench, sorted in approximate order of severity. As described in the section titled "The ASCP Planner Workbench," many exceptions let you drill to the supporting detail and related exceptions to more easily determine the root cause of a problem.

In addition, Oracle provides five Workflow exception processes to route the appropriate information to the right people, including your trading partners. You can tailor these workflow processes to your business and trigger other workflow activities based on the responses to the notification that Workflow provides.

The seeded Workflow processes are the following:

- **Item Forecast Workflow** This workflow provides notifications of items that are overcommitted; below safety stock; or that have shortages, excess inventory, or expired lots. It also provides notification of past due forecast or late supply pegged to a forecast.

- **Sales Order Workflow** This workflow provides notification of late sales orders and late supply pegged to sales orders.

- **Rescheduling Workflow** This workflow provides notification of past due orders and orders to be rescheduled, cancelled, or that have compression days (that is, orders within lead time).

- **Project Workflow** For project manufacturing environments, this workflow provides notification of items with shortages or excess within a project and items allocated across projects.

- **Material and Resource Capacity Workflow** This workflow provides notification of material constraints.

Notifications are only generated from plans that are designated as "production." You launch these notifications from the Planner Workbench using the Tools | Launch Notifications selection on the menu bar. Planners can view their notifications from the Planner Workbench using Tools | Notifications.

Summary

This chapter has described what makes ASCP different from standard planning—the multiorganization capability, constraints and optimization, holistic planning, and a dramatically different architecture. It has explained the tools and processes for modeling your supply chain; those tools and processes apply to older SCP as well.

The options and setup for constraint-based and optimized planning, as well as the basic setup needed to make ASCP work, have also been detailed. Additionally, the process for collecting data and launching a plan, and many of the new features of the Planner Workbench, including enhanced simulation tools, have been described.

Finally, this chapter has outlined the performance management tools—KPIs and Workflow—that Oracle has integrated with the planning process. But this chapter has just scratched the surface—Oracle advertises the simplicity of ASCP and promises rapid return on your investment. Indeed, ASCP can deliver significant benefits with minimal setup, and in very short order; the tools are straightforward. However, becoming an expert on ASCP, totally understanding all the available options, and tuning it for your enterprise can require a good deal of experimentation. Be sure to allow sufficient time for testing when you implement ASCP for the first time.

PART IV

Supply Chain Execution

CHAPTER
12

Order Management

racle currently offers an Order Capture product in the CRM applications and an Order Management product in the Enterprise Applications of the E-Business Suite. With Release 11i, Oracle has also offered Advanced Pricing. The Order Management applications cover the order desk and commercial management activities of a company. The Order Capture products manage orders that originate in the Sales Force Automation systems, Web store, and Telesales environments until they are under the responsibility of the commercial management. One piece of terminology that is different in the Order Management applications is Inventory Organization and Warehouse. They are synonyms. The term "warehouse" is used within the Order Management application and is used in this chapter as well.

Basic Order Flows

Order Management supports a wide range of order management processes. Order Types can be configured to process as complex or as simple a sequence of activities as are needed. However, there are some fundamental pieces to the order management flow. Figure 12-1 shows the basic flow through the system for the main outbound order types for demand from customers. With Release 11, Oracle introduced support for drop shipments.

Order Management will also allow you to fulfill demand that has originated internally. This demand can be for internal use, such as samples, destructive testing, or engineering. It may represent replenishment through the supply chain created by the planning systems. Figure 12-2 illustrates the flow of supply and demand for internal requisitions and sales orders.

Setting Up an Efficient Order Desk

The first part of this chapter covers what you need to set up an efficient ordering environment with Oracle Order Management. It covers setting up items and ways to guide customers to those items and how to set up customer information and manage your credit exposure to those customers. This part of the chapter illustrates how to configure the order types and workflows to process orders in the manner you need, manage the exchange of longer-term planning and shipping schedules with your customer through release management, and set up tax information to determine tax liabilities for your orders and invoices.

Defining the Items You Sell

The first part of setting up the ordering environment is establishing the items that you are going to sell. Defining items for Order Management is much more than just

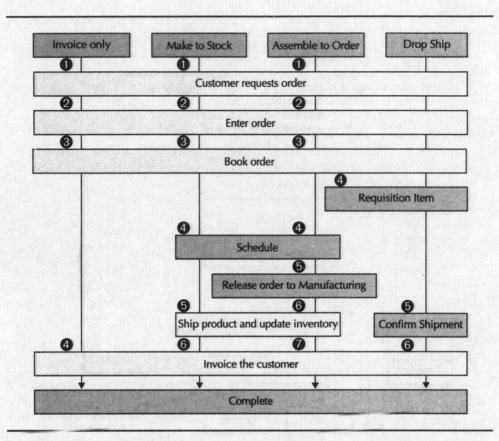

FIGURE 12-1. *Basic order flow for external demand*

the item definition. You need to let order management know the list of items that
the order desk is authorized to sell. Order Management has guided selling capabilities
through a hierarchy of options presented in a marketing bill of material and through
configuration rules in Oracle Configurator.

Identifying the Item Master

With Release 11i, the Item Validation Organization Profile option has been replaced
with an Order Management Parameter. The parameter defines the organization where
all of the item definitions for an operating unit are defined. Many operating units can
use the same Item Master organization. It is a simple way of authorizing an Order
Desk to a set of items. You can find an explanation of the terms organization and
operating unit in Chapter 2. To set the Item Master Organization, navigate to the
Setup | Parameters form.

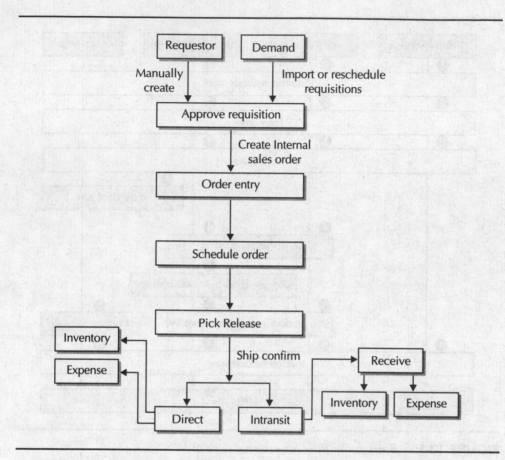

FIGURE 12-2. *Basic flow for internal demand*

Important Item Attributes for Order Management

The following are the important item attributes for Order Management. It decides how to process orders based on the values in these attributes. To set up item information, navigate to the Items | Master Items or Items | Organization Items form, depending on the control level you have selected for each attribute. You can find details on how to use the Items Definitions form in Chapter 2.

Main   On the Main tab the Primary Unit of Measure defines the unit that the item will be stocked and counted in.

Order Management Attributes   On the Order Management tab the following attributes are important:

- **Assemble to Order**   Flag set to Yes determines that the item is manufactured only when a sales order for the item requests it.

- **Available to Promise (ATP) Components**   Set to Yes determines that the available to promise date for the item is dependent on the availability of its components.

- **ATP Rule**   Determines the sources of supply and demand that influence the item's availability. For example, for items with a short shelf life you may choose to ignore internal demand when arriving at an availability date.

- **Check ATP**   Determines if the availability date for the order should be driven by material availability, resource availability, or both.

- **Customer Ordered Item**   Determines whether this item can be added to a price list and ordered through order entry.

- **Customer Orders Enabled**   Determines whether the item can be ordered on a regular sales order.

- **Default Shipping Organization**   Defines a warehouse that may be considered by defaulting rules when determining the default warehouse to ship the item from—for example, if the item is only manufactured in one location.

- **Internal Ordered Item**   Allows an item to be placed on an internal requisition.

- **Internal Orders Enabled**   Also allows an item to be placed on an internal requisition. You may want to define an item as internally orderable and enable it at a later date.

- **Over Return Tolerance**   Defines the amount that a customer can return in excess of the amount agreed on a Return Material Authorization (RMA).

- **Over Shipment Tolerance**   Defines by how much a scheduled shipment quantity can be exceeded when recording the shipment in Oracle Shipping.

- **Pick Components**   Defines the item as a Kit or Pick to Order model, where the components are stocked in the distribution warehouse and shipped to the customer. An example would be a computer that has the keyboard, monitor, and CPU stock separately shipped to the customer.

- **Returnable**   Along with the Stockable and Transactable flag, determines if this item can be returned into inventory from an RMA.

- **RMA Inspection Status**   Defines whether the item must be inspected or if it can be directly delivered into inventory when returned from a customer.

■ **Ship Model Complete**   Defines whether complete sets of a model that is picked to order must ship together. For example, if shipping replacement windows, you may need the windows, trim, closures, and sealers. If any of these are missing, you should not ship the order.

■ **Shippable Item**   Defines that the item is picked and shipped from Oracle Shipping.

Bill of Material Attributes   On the Bill of Materials tab, the BOM Item Type determines if the Bill of Material that is constructed for the item will be an option class or a model. An example of an option class for a car might be the sound system. Order Management will not allow the placing of an order for an option class.

Inventory Attributes   On the Inventory Attributes tab, the following attributes are important:

■ **Inventory Item**   Defines this item as one that you hold balances for. For example, a service contract would have this attribute set to No.

■ **Lot Control**   Defines that the item has quantities stored for each lot received. Whenever you transact the item, you must specify the lot you are transacting.

■ **Serial Number Control**   Defines when and if a serial number is assigned to a unit of inventory. It can be on receipt into inventory or on shipment to a customer.

■ **Revision Control**   Defines whether inventory is tracked by revision. If it is, all transactions for this item must also specify the revision of the item.

■ **Picking Rule**   Defines the order in which inventory lots and revisions will be allocated to the order as well as the subinventories and locators to pick from, greatly influencing inventory obsolescence.

■ **Transactable**   Defines that you place inventory transactions for this item.

■ **Reservation Control**   Defines whether a reservation can be made for this item. If you store a reservable item in a nonreservable subinventory, you cannot create reservations to that inventory.

■ **Stockable**   Determines whether the item is transacted and tracked in inventory.

■ **Subinventory Restrictions**   Determines if the item can be stocked anywhere in the warehouse or if it is to be restricted. For example, an item early in its lifecycle might be stored in a nonreservable quarantine location.

Invoicing Attributes   On the Invoicing tab, the following attributes are important:

- ■ **Invoice Enabled**   Defines this as an item that will be invoiced in Oracle Receivables.

- ■ **Invoiceable Item**   Also defines this as an item that will be invoiced in Oracle Receivables. You may choose to define that an item is invoicable and enable it for invoicing at a later time.

- ■ **Invoicing Rule**   Determines when the invoice gets cut for an order. You may choose to invoice on shipment or end of month.

- ■ **Payment Terms**   Defines one source of payment term that will be considered by defaulting rules to default to the order and pass to Oracle Receivables.

- ■ **Tax Code**   Defines the tax code and rates that will establish the tax schedule for the order line.

- ■ **Sales Account**   Defines one of the sources of the revenue account that will be considered by Auto Accounting when constructing the revenue account for an invoice.

Costing Attributes   The only attribute of significance to Order Management on the Costing Attributes tab is the Cost of Goods Sold Account. It is considered by Flexbuilder and Auto Accounting in its determination of the cost of sales account applied to the shipment.

Physical Attributes   A very important attribute on the Physical Attributes tab is Indivisible. It determines if the primary unit of this item can be transacted in smaller units. For example, if an item's primary unit is CASES, it may still be transacted as 1.5 Cases. However, if the item's primary unit is a CAN, it may be transacted only in whole units if the Indivisible flag is set.

Decimal Quantities

Anyone familiar with previous versions of Order Entry will know that the ordering environment had some challenges dealing with decimals. With the Order Management product, standard items can now be ordered in decimal quantities if the Item attribute Indivisible is set to No in the Physical Attributes tab in the Define Items form. It only applies to the primary unit of measure. For example, a manufacturer of breakfast cereal can now create a return for 4.5 cartons of granola. They can also prevent a return of less than one packet.

Defining the Marketing Bills of Material

The hierarchy of options that a customer is guided through is represented in Oracle in a Bill of Material. The top of this hierarchy is a Model. It could be assembled to order or picked to order. Within the model, the lowest level is either options, if you can choose them, or included items, if you get them regardless of whether you choose them. An example of an included item on a PTO model might be the cabling. An example of an option might be the monitor. Between the options and the model, options are grouped into option classes. Figure 12-3 shows the relationships between the various types of order lines.

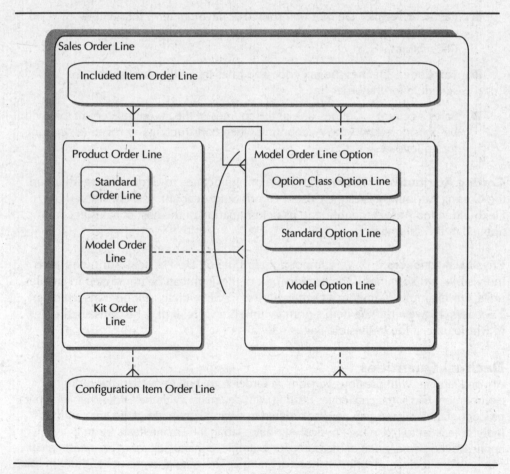

FIGURE 12-3.   *Relationships between model and option order lines*

Order Entry has some capability to guide the customer. To create the marketing Bills of Material, navigate to the Bill form. You can find details of how to use the Define Bill of Materials form in Chapter 3. A number of types of bills are important to Order Management:

- **ATO Model**   A hierarchical list of options, the configuration of which will be assembled to order

- **ATO Class**   A grouping of options under an ATO model

- **ATO Option**   An individual option under an ATO model

- **PTO Model**   A hierarchical list of items that will be shipped together as a unit

- **PTO Class**   A grouping within the hierarchy

- **PTO Option**   An individual item that is shipped as part of the unit

- **Included Item**   An item that the customer does not select but will be shipped with the rest of the options chosen under the PTO model

The following are the important Bill of Material attributes, from an Order Management perspective:

- **Basis**   Defines whether the quantity of an option is determined from the option class. For example, for a company selling cars, they may have a marketing bill that has an option for alloy wheels. The customer cannot choose to have other than four alloy wheels. They may also have an option for cup holders, where the customer can choose between zero and four cup holders.

- **Check ATP**   Determines whether the item must have projected availability at the date ordered for the demand to be placed on the planning systems.

- **Include on Shipping Documents**   Determines whether the components of the model should be printed on the shipping documents. For example, a computer system might be shipped with a monitor that you do want included on the shipping documents and an option for a network card that you do not.

- **Mutually Exclusive Options**   Determines for an option class if the options underneath it cannot be ordered together. For example, if the option class is for the sound system, the customer can choose either a CD changer or radio cassette.

■ **Required for Revenue**   Determines if the parent can be invoiced—for example, if a company sells a computer system where the system cannot be invoiced until the CPU ships to the customer.

Entering Orders Using other Item Numbers

Order Management allows you to enter orders using item numbers other than your own internal item number. Figure 12-4 explains the relationships between the various item identifiers within Oracle Order Management.

Supported item identifiers are as follows:

■ **Customer Item Number**   Defined in the Customer Item and Customer Item Cross-Reference forms.

■ **Item Cross-Reference**   Used to define generic item numbers such as UPC code, GTIN number, or EAN number. These are defined in the item cross-references form. Refer to Chapter 2 for details. There is a cross-reference type in the customer definition, but it is not currently used by Order Management.

Defining Configuration Rules

Oracle Configurator provides a rules definition environment that will allow a sales engineer to define the rules and relationships between the orderable characteristics

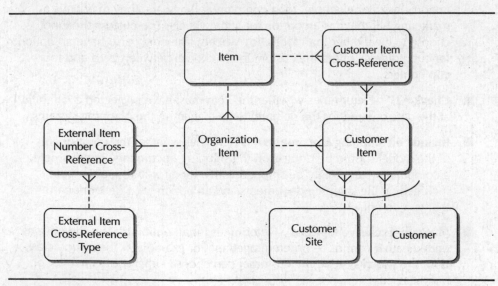

FIGURE 12-4.   *Understanding item number in Order Entry*

of a configurable item. Such rules might be incompatibility rules or options selected automatically because of previously selected options. You can express the rules in terms of both the items and the features of the item. For example, you can state that part number 1001 smoothing unit will not work with part number 1002, a 240-volt power source. You can also state that power consumed by the enhanced speaker reduces the battery life to two hours. It allows a customer to enter their requirements in terms of the features of the products being ordered rather than part numbers. It will reduce the selections based on what has already been chosen.

Oracle Configurator is an extremely flexible and robust product; a full description of its features is unfortunately beyond the scope of this book.

Defining the Customers You Sell To

Order Management shares the definition of customers with Accounts Receivable and with the CRM Applications. Figure 12-5 shows the Order Management information from the Define Customer form.

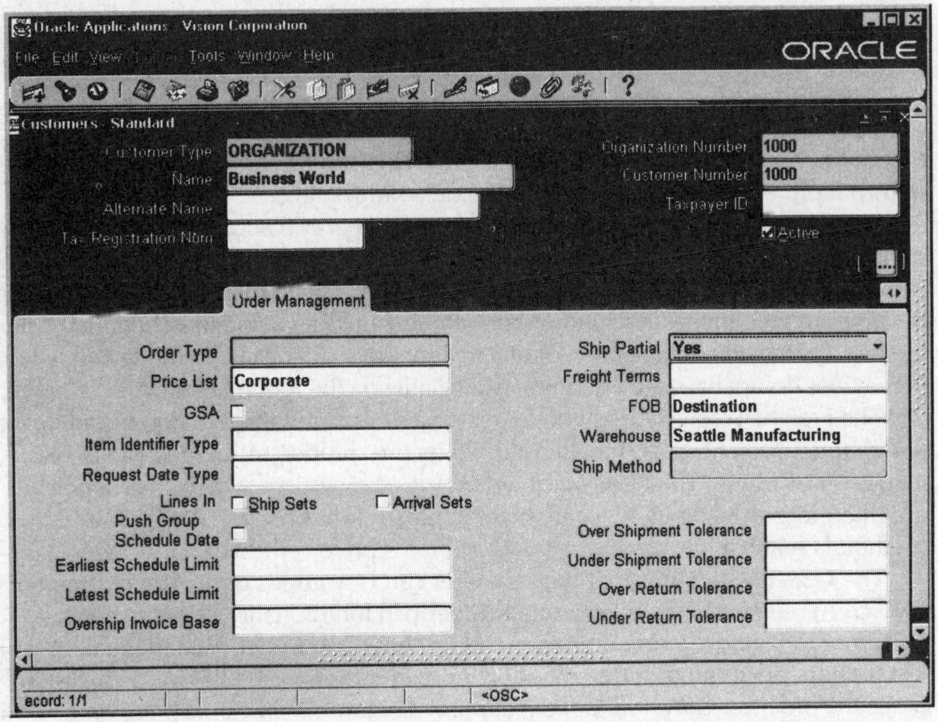

FIGURE 12-5. *Order Management information for customers*

Much information is agreed upon with a customer that will affect how an order and return should be processed. The agreement could be made for all sites that you ship and deliver to, or it could be specific to a given site. Hence, the information is defined for the customer and for the customer sites. You will need to understand the defaulting rules to know how your organization defaults this information to an order to control processing. You can define the customer organization as well as create "Accounts" with the customer. Accounts are created between an operating unit and the customer. For more information on operating units, see Chapter 2.

By defaulting the Order Type onto the order for the customer, you can define more of the processing. For example, Neptune has defined an order type for International Customers. These orders will always go through export compliance checking before the order is booked. Neptune has three major price lists: North America and Europe, South America and Middle East, and Rest of World.

NOTE
Order Types are defined for each operating unit.
Customers are not defined within an operating unit,
but customer sites and site uses are. You need to
default the order type for the customer from the site
or site use if you have multiple operating units.

The price list reflects the effort in doing business in these areas, and to some extent the AR risk. You can default the price list onto the order from the customer information. Again, this is subject to the defaulting rules.

The Ship Partial flag denotes whether the customer will accept a partial shipment of his order. Some industries consider the management of partial orders too expensive because many costs are tied to the receiving activity. The matching of the invoice also becomes more complex for the customer. By setting this flag to No, scheduling will find the first day that the full quantity for all the lines are available. Scheduling will fail if any of the lines do not have the full quantity available on the requested date.

The Freight Terms define who is responsible for paying the shipper and covering the charges. Freight costs may be prepaid by the shipper and added to the order value, for example. The FOB point determines the point at which the ownership, and therefore responsibility for insurance, passes for goods in-transit. The Ship Method is really a misnomer for the Customer's preferred carrier.

The GSA flag denotes that the customer can buy goods under a Government Service Agreement. This is very much American functionality. It entitles the customer to legally enforced preferential pricing. Oracle Order Management will test that the price on an order is not lower than an established GSA Price List. It will place the order on GSA hold pending approval. For GSA customers, the order would not be placed on hold. For those outside of the United States, this is an ideal way of setting up minimum pricing. You can let your sales force negotiate, knowing that if you have created a GSA Price List for your minimum prices, you will be alerted to any orders that violate this minimum price.

The Warehouse definition gives you some elementary distribution requirements planning capability. This warehouse may be considered by defaulting rules when defaulting a shipping warehouse for the order line. You may wish to define the closest warehouse or distribution center to the customer location here.

Request Date Type determines if the customer request date should be considered the requested shipment date or the requested arrival date. It is very likely that the date a customer requests will be the requested arrival date.

Ship Sets and Arrival Sets are groups of lines that must be considered together for scheduling. Ship Sets are a group of lines that must leave the warehouse together. For example, if a company is manufacturing kitchen units, that includes cupboard units, doors, and worksurface. The work cannot start unless all components arrive. The Schedule Date for the group of lines will be the latest date of all the lines in the group. The same company will also coordinate the delivery of the door furniture. These are stored and shipped from a separate warehouse. All the lines Cupboard Units, Doors, Worksurface, and Door Furniture must arrive at the same time. The scheduled arrival time considers the travel time between the source and destination. Having an arrival set that has lines from many warehouses will cause one ship set for each warehouse. The scheduled arrival date will be the latest date available at the destination for all ship sets within the arrival set. If a line is added to the order later, you may want to push the group schedule date by setting the flag of the same name.

Earliest Schedule Limit and Latest Schedule Limit affect the scheduling window for items that are defined as being ATP check items. You can set items to be ATP Check Yes or ATP Check No. If the item is set as ATP Check Yes, it is stating to the system that you must have availability to record the schedule date on the order line. This will basically mean that the scheduling attempt will fail, and the order will not progress. You will need to make another attempt to schedule the order. These schedule limits introduce a scheduling window that will allow the Order Schedule attempt to succeed.

The Overshipment Invoice Base determines whether a quantity in excess of the quantity ordered should be invoiced. Over and Under Shipment Tolerances govern when an overshipment quantity shipped in Oracle Shipping will trigger an error message to the operator confirming the shipment. Under Shipment Tolerances govern when the original order line should be considered completely fulfilled from an undershipment as opposed to creating a backordered shipment.

Over and under return tolerances govern if a customer would be allowed to return more than was agreed upon in the return material authorization. You can also set these values on an item-by-item basis for the customer by navigating to Shipping Tolerances.

A couple of properties are important on the Customer Details tab. The Demand Class partitions supply and demand through the supply chain. The demand class can be defaulted from the customer or customer site. It is one of the sources that can be considered by defaulting rules. (Demand classes are discussed further in Chapter 8.)

Customer Profiles

Customer profiles give you some way of defining your credit management policies. A profile class groups customers of like credit profile and the individual customer credit profiles.

Profile Classes   Customer profiles describe some common characteristics of a group of customers that all share a given profile. Most importantly they define whether customers in this profile class will be credit checked. You can also set up credit limits by currency for the profile class. This will be defaulted onto the customer profile.

Customer Profiles   Customer profiles carry much of the same information as the profile class, but are for the specific customer or customer site.

Deciding How to Process Outbound Orders

You can influence how orders are managed within Order Management in a number of ways. Workflow controls the activities in processing the order and when each activity becomes eligible. Defaulting rules determine the defaulting source for fields on the order entry form and for the API. This minimizes the amount of information needed by the person entering the order. Processing constraints prevent changes being made to order information when commitments have been made and communicated.

Order Workflows

Order Management leverages Oracle Workflow to control processing at the header and line. Oracle Workflow is a very broad tool, but the applicability to the ordering environment is very natural, making it easy to understand here. Figure 12-6 shows a standard order header process flow in the Workflow Builder.

Uses of Workflow   Workflow controls the processing of an order as follows:

■ **Ensuring prerequisites are met**   Where an activity should not proceed unless a prerequisite has been met, the transition between activities is managed by workflow. The workflow engine checks for subsequent activities when an activity completes and starts them, or it makes them eligible if all prerequisites have been met. For example, margin check may be something that the finance department needs to do before the order can be acknowledged to the customer.

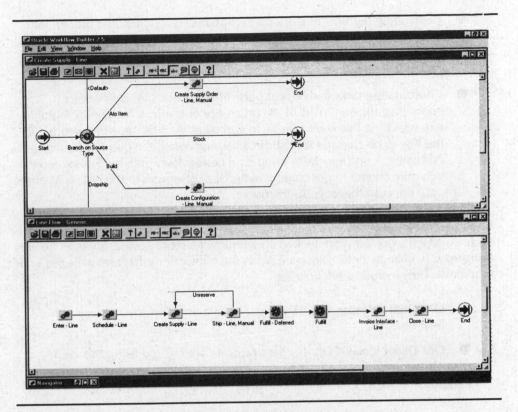

FIGURE 12-6. *The standard order process in the Workflow Builder*

- **Notifying individuals when their input or approval is needed** Oracle workflow comes with an e-mail notification engine, a Web-based notification viewing tool, and a forms-based notification viewing tool. You can notify anyone with access to a Web browser or e-mail, within and across companies. For example, you might want notify the credit manager before sending an acknowledgement for a large order.

- **Allowing individuals to state their approval or confirm an activity is completed** Anyone receiving a notification that requires a response can make that response in the e-mail they received, the browser they reviewed the notification in, or the form if they are an Oracle Applications user. For example, you may need the confirmation of the approval of the legal department before sending equipment to a foreign country.

■ **Controlling the flow of work on exceptions**   Workflow can branch the activity depending on the outcome. For example, if sales approval for a given order is not granted, the salesman may be notified that he has to renegotiate the order.

■ **Coordinating tasks in different parts of the order**   Workflow can coordinate different parts of the order. For example, a header level activity can wait for a line level activity to complete. A quote may be waiting for the line to be checked for margin tolerance before the quote is issued to the customer. A line may be waiting for a header level activity. For example, you may choose to not commit material or resources to the potential order until the customer accepts the quote.

Seeded Workflows   Order Management uses the following work item types. The Oracle seeded work items are locked up with low levels of access. It would be very dangerous to change these. These are really the transactions that are managed under workflow. They include the following:

■ **OM Order Header-OEOH**   Order header flows are created using this item type.

■ **OM Order Line-OEOL**   Order line flows are created using this item type.

Order header flows include the following:

■ **Generic order flow**   For orders and returns

■ **Generic order flow with header level invoicing**   If the order lines need to be coordinated for invoicing

■ **Return with Approval**   For returns or requests for credit that must be approved by someone other than the person entering the request

Line flows include the following:

■ **Generic**   Supports all basic item types except configured items.

■ **Generic with Authorize to Ship**   For use with standard items, approved before they are shipped from stock.

■ **Generic with Header Level Invoicing**   For use when the lines are coordinated for invoicing. For example, if a single invoice will be expected for the order, but the items have shipped on different dates. Credit management may be presented with a problem if the customer receives what they interpret as a duplicate invoice.

- **Generic, Bill Only**   For use where nothing will be shipped to the customer—for example, for a service contract.

- **Generic, Ship Only**   For use where the items will be shipped to the customer for free—for example, if you are shipping samples.

- **ATO Item**   For use with items that you build only when you get an order.

- **ATO Models**   For use with items that have many features and options that the customer can choose, and the assembly of the final configuration is not started until you get an order.

- **Configuration Line**   For use on the line for the final configuration of an ATO order.

- **Configuration with Authorize to Ship**   For use on a configuration line if you are using Release Management.

- **Standard Service**   For warranty and service agreements.

Line flows for returns and credit requests include the following:

- **Return for Credit Only**   For use where the customer is requesting credit for an item that they will not return. For example, if breakage occurs, the customer may dispose of the broken units without returning them.

- **Return for Credit Only with Approval**   For use where the customer is requesting credit for an item that they will not return, but the credit will be approved by someone other than the person recording the request.

- **Return for Credit with Receipt**   For use where the customer will return the goods they are requesting credit for. The person entering the order is approving the return.

- **Return for Credit with Receipt and Approval**   For use where the customer will return the goods they are requesting credit for, and the return is approved by someone other than the person entering the request.

Changing Workflows   If the workflows as seeded do not meet your needs, you can create new ones. Using one of the seeded workflows as a model, you need to copy it to a new process and then change its Internal Name, Display Name, and description in the Workflow Builder. You may wish to construct a new process using existing activities, or you may wish to construct new activities and link them into processes. There are standard functions and lookups available in the Item Type OM Standard-OESTD.

To make the workflow design environment easier to understand, you should follow the Oracle Naming conventions. On function definitions, you should state the execution mode in which the action will be taken. For example, you can book an order from the sales order form with BOOK_PROCESS_SYNCH. You can choose when to book the order and book it manually from the action button with BOOK_PROCESS_ASYNCH. You can defer booking and let booking pick up the order later with BOOK_PROCESS_DEFER. Activities in the process can be both the active function, as in purchase release, as well as a state, as in purchase release eligible or purchase release complete.

If you need to coordinate different parts of the order, you need the work items in workflow to converse with each other. Workflow provides a wait function, and Order Management creates the continue functions. For example, lines will wait for the header to be booked on a standard order, and the header will wait for the lines to be fulfilled before invoicing if you are doing header level invoicing.

Document Sequences

Order Management leverages the central document numbering systems provided within Applications Object Library (AOL). For the proper creation of an audit trail, some countries require that the order numbers be sequential and unbroken. AOL provides for automatic, gapless number sequences, and Order Management leverages this facility. A document category is created for each order type in Order Management. The document category can be assigned automatic, gapless, or manual order number assignments. For example, you may have an order type for requests for quotes that is manually assigned, an order type for quotes that is automatic, and an order type for standard commercial orders that is gapless.

Order Types and Line Types

Order Management provides for the definition of order types and line types in the Define Transaction Types form. Order types and line types provide certain defaulting and processing controls.

Main Information Tab   You can define the workflow that a line or header goes through. The header workflow is specified on the main window of the form. The workflow assignments are for an order type, a line type, or a combination of line type and item type. These are accessed from the Assign Workflows button. For example, an international order for an outbound Assemble to Order Model would need to go through export approval and release to manufacturing. A domestic request for quote order type for a standard item may go through sales approval.

For orders that you wish to capture a promotion code on for later analysis, you can enforce that an agreement code be entered. (See Chapter 20 for full explanation on how to set up promotions and agreements.) Your company policy may be to ensure that the customer's purchase order number is quoted on the sales order for easier collections.

You can specify a Price List for this Transaction Type. This is one of the sources for the price list that defaulting rules will consider for defaulting onto the order.

You can specify how to apply your credit policies at both booking and release for shipment.

Assign workflows used to process the order by clicking the Assign Workflows button. The workflows are assigned to a combination of the Line Type and Item Type for an Order Type. For example, you may process a standard line for an Assemble to Order item differently on an international order than you would on a domestic quote.

Shipping Information Tab　To explain what you can do in the Shipping Information tab, it is best to think of a few order types and how you might want them to behave from a pricing and allocation of inventory perspective. Neptune has decided to launch a targeted campaign to increase sales of the older line of laptops before the launch of its successor. To this end, it has set up a Laptop Discount Promotion Order Type. All the older laptops have been moved to the overflow warehouse as production of the new line ramps up. The units themselves will have a lower price if the customer quotes the promotion code, but the shipping priority on the low-margin older laptops will be lower. All the older laptops will ship FedEx ground. If customers order "Maine" external speakers, these will be drop-shipped from "Maine Acoustic Sciences."

The new line of laptops is available for priority customers only. To this end, Neptune has created a Priority Customer order type. This order type will always reserve inventory. Marketing allocates a portion of the forecast to priority customers so where inventory is not on hand for the Priority Customers, it is partitioned in the Priority demand class.

Financial Information Tab　The Financial Information tab defines how Oracle Receivables will create and process the invoice and cash applications. The Invoicing Rule defines when the invoice is created, and the Accounting Rule defines when the revenue from the sale is recognized.

Receivables may be the billing and collections system for many systems. You may have many Order Management organizations on different instances but have a single billing and collections organization. You can declare the Invoice Source for a given Transaction Type here, which allows you to trace from the invoice back into the system that created the order.

Credit Method Rules determine how credit memos get applied to invoices. This backs revenue out of General Ledger. It does not apply to all invoices, only those with revenue split across many periods. You can back revenue out on a LIFO basis,

Prorate across all periods, or back out for the number of units specified on the invoice line being credited.

The Receivables Transaction Type determines if the invoice that is created will be considered open and posted to GL. For example, Neptune creates proforma invoices for customers that have no Credit History with them. These proforma invoices allow the customer to create a payment voucher and deposit with Neptune before Neptune ships the goods.

The Cost of Goods Sold Account (COGS) is one of the accounts that receivable accounting will consider as a source for constructing the COGS account. You need to understand the receivable accounting setup to know how it will be used.

Order Holds

Order holds are a mechanism of stopping the progress of an order pending approval by someone with authority. You can apply holds to the following:

- **Customers** For example, if a customer files for protection from creditors, you may want to hold all orders for that customer.

- **Items** For example, if an item is in early release stages where supporting the early customers will be important. You may want to hold all orders for the item before shipment to ensure support is aware of the customer.

You define a hold source, and those holds are applied to an order line or to all lines in an order. You can define a hold to hold an order or line at a particular activity. For example, in the case of the customer filing for protection, you will want to apply the hold on the order as soon as it is entered. For the early lifecycle product, you will want to allow booking and acknowledgement but prevent the release for shipment.

In the case of the customer hold source, you can have the hold applied automatically. You will also want to apply the hold to all the orders that are on the order backlog to ensure that no product goes out the door to the customer.

In the Neptune case, if the new line of laptops has an overheating problem that was not detected in testing, it could cause unrecoverable disk errors and potential recall and warranty problems. They will also want to apply that hold to all orders currently on the order backlog.

Oracle Order Management provides several holds that are applied automatically for the following:

- Configuration validation errors
- Credit card risk
- Credit card authorization failure

- Accounts receivable credit check failure

- Government service agreement violation

Speeding Order Entry with Defaulting Rules

Defaulting rules allow you to speed the entry of orders. Defaulting rules are a very flexible tool. They allow the implementor to define a defaulting source for almost every attribute. Defaulting rules use the metadata (data about data) in Order Management. This metadata defines possible sources for the value of a given attribute. For example, the warehouse attribute for the order line exists on the Order Header, Item, Order Type, Customer, and Customer Address. Defaulting rules search through a list of sources for an attribute. Figure 12-7 shows the defaulting rules for defaulting the accounting rule onto the order header. The primary source of default is the accounting rule on the agreement. The secondary source of default is the accounting rule on the order type.

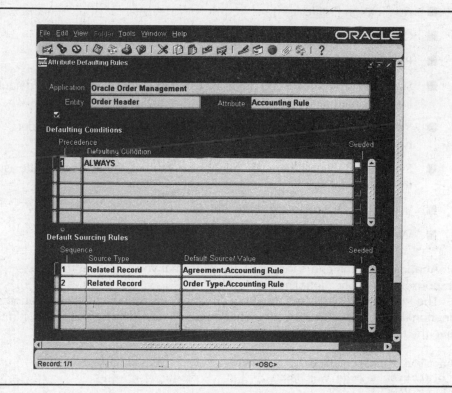

FIGURE 12-7. *Setting up defaulting rules*

Order Management allows you to define sets of defaulting rules and conditions under which the sets of rules should be invoked. For example, you may choose a set of defaulting rules for all orders that have come from the sales automation system and another set of rules for orders that originate at the order desk. You define a set of conditions and assign the order in which the sets of conditions are evaluated.

NOTE
You should set up a condition called "Always" that has no condition statements associated. It should be last in the list of condition sets so that the other sets of conditions are evaluated.

You also set up a sequence of default sources that should be evaluated. The system marches up this list of default sources until it finds a not null value to source from. You can choose from the following source types:

■ Application Profile

■ Constant Value

■ PL/SQL API

■ Same Record—Where you might be using the requested date as a default for scheduled date

■ Related Record—Where you might be using an attribute on the order type—for example, as a defaulting source for the price list

■ System Variable—Where you might be defaulting the requested date as the system date for Order Type of Emergency Shipment

■ Web Apps Dictionary Attribute Default

■ Web Apps Dictionary Object Attribute Default

Applications profiles are the set of constants that you can set at the User, Responsibility, Application, and Site levels.

The PL/SQL API single and multirow are a way of extending the application's functionality. You can create your own function to provide a default value. It must have the following signature:

```
function function_name (p_database_object_name VARCHAR2
, p_attribute_code VARCHAR2)
return VARCHAR2
```

Where *function_name* is the name of the new defaulting function, *p_database_ object_name* is the name of the object that the default is being gathered for, and *p_ attribute_code* is the name of the attribute that the value is being provided for.

Web Applications Dictionary (WAD) is the list of attributes and entities that form the data dictionary for the Self-Service Applications. It stores a default value for the attribute and for the attribute when it is part of an entity definition.

Processing Constraints

Processing constraints define whether a change is allowed to an order after certain activities have been completed, as well as the level of responsibility required to make the change. Figure 12-8 shows an example of the processing constraints setup.

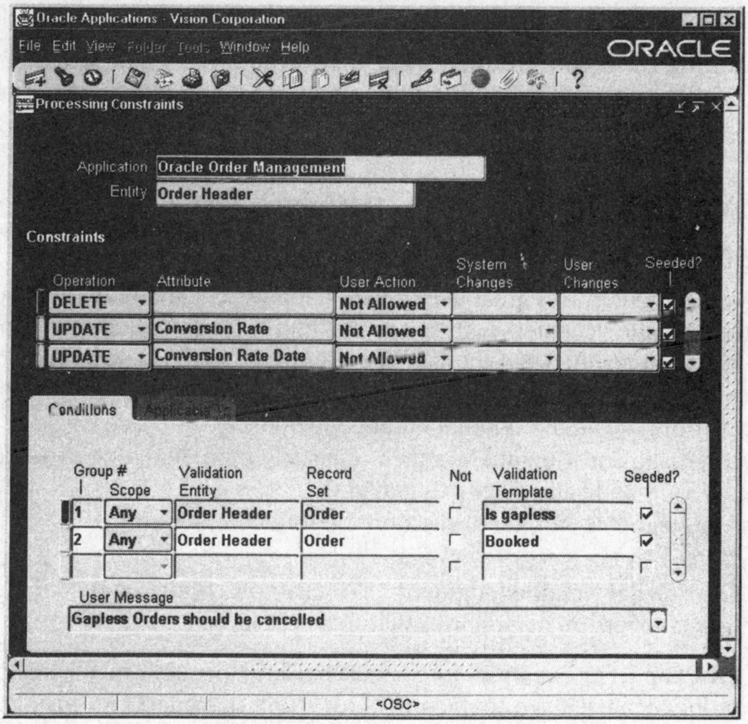

FIGURE 12-8. *Processing constraints*

For example, you might decide that the order entry operator can change the price and promised delivery date right up until the order has been acknowledged to the customer. After the order has been acknowledged to the customer, the order entry clerk can no longer make changes. The order desk administrator can, however, make whatever corrections are needed.

A processing constraint has two main parts. The first is the action that you would like to prevent from happening. The second is the condition or state after which you want to prevent it. You can detect the condition in three ways:

■ **Define the workflow activity and result** For example, you might want to prevent any updates to the cancelled quantity after any line within a ship set has been released to shipment.

■ **Define the condition as the value of a column in the table** For example, you might wish to prevent the ship-to location from being updated for an internal order.

■ **Define conditions through a PL/SQL package** For example, if you want to allow the credit authorization number to be updated only under very special conditions that are determined in a PL/SQL function.

Setting Up Standard Content for Order Documents

Order Management makes great use of the attachments capability of Oracle Applications. It allows you to embed content into the printed forms that move through the organization or to the customer. Figure 12-9 shows the relationships between the content, the forms from where the content is attached, and the forms and reports from where the content can be viewed.

You can make and view these attachments from the Attachments window in the Sales Order form and Sales Order Organizer.

These attachments will get printed on the following report:

■ **Sales Order Acknowledgment** For example, notifying the customer of special offers on accessories with his new laptop

■ **Pick Slip** For example, for special packing instructions for this customer's order because it is a replacement for a unit damaged in-transit

■ **Pack Slip** For example, for the packer to confirm the units have been packed in the shipment together

■ **Bill Of Lading** For example, for handling instructions to the carrier

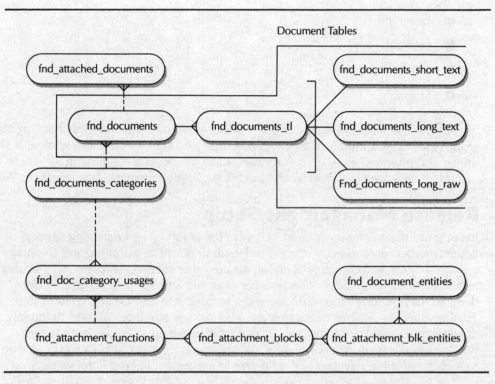

FIGURE 12-9.   *Understanding document attachments in Order Management*

You can set up attachments that can be simple text, such as "Thank you for purchasing from Neptune. Please phone our 24-hour hotline if you have any problems setting up;" files that might be graphics files (such as the company logo or customer's company logo); or URL references. Documents can be templates—for example, if you are going to use the template to record the inspector on the packing slip.

Documents can be one time. For example, you may want to inform the customer on the order acknowledgement that her computer is late due to quality problems on the components and you will ship as soon as components of the highest quality come in.

You can automatically apply attachments to the order or order line by specifying attachment rules. These apply the attachment if the conditions in the attachment rule are met. In the rules, you can state that a given attachment is to be applied to the following:

■ Customer

■ Customer PO

- Line type
- Line category
- Bill-to
- Ship-to

Rules in the same group number are considered AND conditions. By changing the group number, you introduce an OR condition. The automatic additions work in both online and imported orders. You can also attach the documents through the Tools menu. You will need to set the profile option OM: Apply Automatic Attachments to Yes.

Release Management Setup

Release Management allows you to connect the planning and receiving systems of your customer more directly into the order administration, planning, and shipping systems in your own company. It allows the customer to send you planning, shipping, and sequenced schedules of demand. For planning and shipping schedules, the demand may be forecast or firm demand. Firm demand may be approved to ship. To allow this high degree of automation, you can use a number of rules to identify changes in demand and when to ship that must be set up in advance. These are Release Management processing rules and shipment delivery rules. To set up Release Management rules, navigate to the Release Management | Setup Processing.

Matching Attributes

Oracle Release Management allows you to identify specific attributes used by the Demand Processor for determining if inbound schedules are new demand or changes to existing demand. To set up matching attributes, click the Matching Logic button of the same name in the Setup Processing Rules form.

Release Management Processing Rules

A program called the Demand Stream Processor looks at the incoming picture of demand and applies these rules to determine shipment dates and quantities. The rules themselves can be different for different items that the customer buys or different addresses that the items are delivered to. You can assign these rules at any level. The Demand Stream Processor evaluates the rules at the lowest level and works up to the customer level.

Demand Management Rules   Demand management needs several types of rules to process an inbound demand stream.

The Consume Demand Hierarchy determines the types of schedules that have precedence when different schedules have demand for the same time bucket.

The ATS Prehorizon Disposition/Cutoff Days determines the treatment of past due demand. This is demand that is dated before the horizon of the planning schedules.

Standard Packs Quantity is generally the quantity that is in a shipping unit. Neptune supplies an automotive electronics supplier with global positioning systems in a shockproof box with 24 units. Neptune spends as much time packing 18 as 24. Even if the quantity demanded is 18, a shockproof box of 24 will be packed. Release management will show that Neptune is 6 ahead of requirements.

Demand Tolerances are the limits of a change between any two demand streams. Demand will always be processed, but an exception will be raised

Demand Fences   The Demand Fences tab displays the frozen, firm, and forecast fences to Oracle Planning and forecast fence to Oracle Order Management for planning, shipping, and sequenced schedules. You cannot change demand within the Frozen Time Fence. If a demand stream includes a change within the frozen time fence, a warning is issued. Demand within the Firm Time Fence will be marked as shippable regardless of the status of the transmitted demand. Demand within the Order Management Forecast Fence will be marked as not shippable, regardless of the status of the transmitted demand. Demand within the Planning Forecast Fence will be updated as forecast regardless of the status of the transmitted demand.

Order Management Rules   Demand for Release Management is handled through a specified sales order and purchase order. The agreement between the customer and supplier is generally not in terms of quantities. They are much more likely to have established outline pricing (though shipments can be made and prices agreed and invoiced later). This can be recorded through the customer's purchase order or a pricing agreement within the Order Management systems.

CUM Management Rules   Cumulative quantities could be recorded at many levels, including by date only, by date and record year, CUM until manual reset, at item by date, and purchase order. The cumulatives could be for all quantities from a facility: for a given bill-to customer, for each ship-to site, for each intermediate ship-to site, or for all ship-to sites.

Shipment Delivery Rules

Shipment and delivery rules are a way of making the link between the days that your warehouses ship (or ship on a particular route) and the days that your customer's shipping dock will receive. Given that there is an in-transit lead time to be offset between your shipping dock and your customer's receiving dock, incoming demand must be offset by the in-transit time and pushed into a shipping day for the shipping warehouse. You set up Customer Receiving Calendar in shipping execution. Calendars can be specific to a customer site or shared. Oracle Release Management is seeded with industry-standard ship delivery pattern codes. You can view codes used by the ANSI X12 and EDIFACT standards, and you can modify some on the Maintain Ship/ Delivery Pattern Codes form. You can associate a receiving pattern to the customer site or customer item. To set up a delivery pattern for a customer address, navigate to the Release Management Processing Rules form and click Address Terms. On the Demand Management tab of the Terms At Address Level window, clear the Use Customer's Ship Delivery Pattern Code check box. The Calculate Scheduled Shipment Date program will look first at the Ship-From Customer Item level for a default. If no code is set at the Ship-From Customer Item level, it will look at the Ship-From/Ship-To Processing Rules.

Freight and Special Charges

Oracle Order Management uses the Advanced Pricing module to define charge types to cover freight and special charges. To define a new charge type, navigate to the pricing module and select modifiers. Modifiers are price modifiers—they can change a price up or down. In the case of special charges, they are being increased. Modifiers will be examined in greater detail in Chapter 20. The Modifier list is the schedule of freight charges. A customer, group of customers, or specific order may qualify for a schedule of freight charges through the Header Qualifiers. The lines on the Modifier list are the charges that will be applied to an order header or order lines. Charges can be applied automatically or manually to an order or order line. Charges are applied based on the line qualifications. Line qualifications might include item number, commodity, or customer. You can decide whether the customer is credited for the charge if the order is returned or charged for the freight costs of the return.

If the freight terms are prepay and add, the shipper (person requesting the goods to be shipped) will prepay the shipping costs to the carrier and then add them to the order. When the customer receives the invoice, it will include the shipping costs.

For freight charges that are prepaid and added to the order, pricing formulae can be set up to convert shipping costs to charges. These costs are converted to charges and applied to the order line after the order has been shipped.

Taxation

Explaining the full setup of the tax reporting system is beyond the scope of this book. A few vital things form part of the setup for Order Management. Oracle supports value added tax (VAT) and sales tax. Order Management allows you to credit check against the value of an order including the tax on the order. You can review the tax value for the order line and for the whole order in the order header. The main concepts to understand are

- Tax codes
- Locations

■ Exemptions

■ Tax profile options

Some important profile options control whether the tax treatment you define for the customer can be overridden at the time of order entry—Tax: Allow Override of TaxCode profile and Tax: Allow Override of Customer Exemption.

Setting Up Tax Codes

Navigate to the Order Management Set Up Tax Codes form. Create a tax code. Define whether you are creating a Value Added Tax, Sales Tax, or location-based tax. Define the tax basis. This defines whether the tax should be applied before of after discounts are considered, based on a previous tax value. Define the tax rate if the tax code is not location-based. Provide effectivity dates. You now have a tax code.

You can enter a tax code at the customer ship-to and bill-to business purpose level, as well as at the customer level. You can also assign tax codes to inventory items. If your tax method is VAT, you can include a tax code in the Tax Defaulting Hierarchy in the System Options window.

Setting Up Locations and Rates

Navigate to the Order Management Set Up Tax Locations. You are presented with the Elements of the Tax Location Flex Structure in the drop-down box. You can select an Address Element (State, County, City) and define the tax rate associated with a range of postal codes. Oracle also uses this table to automatically complete addresses. Postal Code ranges and dates cannot overlap. This is a great deal of data to set up and maintain, so Oracle provides a sales tax rate interface to some common tax providers, such as Vertex.

Setting Up Exemptions

Navigate to the Order Management Set Up Tax Exemptions form. You need to set a few profile options in order to use tax exemptions. They are Use Customer Exemptions and Use Product Exemptions. To create an exemption, enter the tax code that the customer or item (or range of items) is exempt for, and create the reason code and exemption certificate number.

Exemptions created automatically during invoice entry or import are recorded as unapproved. You may change exemptions with this status to any of the statuses listed here.

Setting Up Tax in the System Options

You need to set up a number of options in the Set Up | Customers | System Options form. These include what type of tax you operate under and the Location Flexfield Structure for Tax and Address Validation. It also holds the Tax Identification of your own organization. The Tax Defaulting Tab is where you can define the defaulting sequence for Tax Codes in much the same way as defaulting rules in Order Management.

Enforcing Credit Policies

Order Management provides for credit and risk management for both receivables accounts and credit card transactions. Your credit manager can set your credit policies up for groups of customers identified by a credit profile and assign customers to those profiles. Your risk management is somewhat different if the customer is paying with a credit card. The risk is more credit card fraud. The integration with iPayments means that the buying habits, locations, and amounts of the purchaser are considered before a transaction is authorized.

Credit Checking for Your Accounts Receivable Customers

Credit check may be triggered at booking and releasing for shipment for orders that

- Have a payment term that is checked for credit. For example, a Cash With Order payment term may be defined as requiring no credit check.

- Have an order type that has credit rules associated. For example, a company may have an order type for Proforma Invoice Required that it does not credit check because the order type is a hold source.

- For a customer that has a credit profile that allows credit checking. For example, Neptune is part of a conglomerate. Other companies within the conglomerate are exempt from credit check because the parent company underwrites the debt. Credit profiles can exist at the level of customer or bill-to site. Order Management will use the profile at the bill-to site if one exists. If one does not exist, it will use the credit profile for the customer.

NOTE
If the credit profile enforces credit check but there are no credit limits set up in the currency of the order, no credit check will occur. For example, if the customer is a Mexican customer who normally orders and pays in U.S. dollars but requests an order be expressed in Mexican pesos, you need to ensure that there are credit limits in this currency. There are multi-currency credit checking capabilities being delivered in an imminent release.

Credit check rules allow you to configure the open orders and invoices that will be considered against the credit limit for the customer. To define a credit rule, navigate to the Rules | Credit Check Rules form. If the credit limit is exceeded, either for the open balance or single total order amount, a hold is automatically placed on the order. Generally the credit manager will have the authority to remove that hold. You can choose to include uninvoiced orders, open receivables, or both. For open receivables, you can choose to include only receivables over a certain number of days overdue by specifying the open receivables days. If you have received payments that have not cleared through the banking system, you may wish to still regard the payment At Risk. By checking the Include Payments At Risk flag, you will include these values in your exposure calculation. You may wish to exclude orders that are not due to ship for some time. You exclude these by specifying a Scheduled Shipping Horizon Days range. You may wish to exclude orders that you are holding. If the order is on review for export compliance, you might want to exclude it from the exposure calculation. There is an option to exclude tax from the exposure calculation, although customers are liable for the tax on the order in most jurisdictions.

Orders will be placed on hold if the exposure exceeds the credit limit or if the value of a single order exceeds the maximum in the credit profile. Holds can be released manually by people with release authorized responsibilities. Holds can be released automatically if credit is reverified. This will happen every time you attempt to release for shipment. The verification will also happen from Order Entry if the order is revalidated because of date or price movements.

Credit Check for Credit Card Payments through iPayments

For payments with credit cards, Order Management integrates with the iPayments system. This is an authorization and risk management system. The payment server will obtain an authorization for both the amount and nature of the transaction going through the server. Risk factors and rules are set up in Oracle iRisk. If the card holder does not normally purchase at this time, have goods delivered to this address, order this value of transaction, or has a bad payment record, the payment server may flag it as a risky transaction and place a hold on the order. The threshold beyond which the order is placed on hold is OM: Risk Factor Threshold.

NOTE
The privacy of the credit card information is enforced through a profile option, OM: Credit Card Privileges. A value of None means that only the last four digits of the credit card are shown.

Compensating Your Salesforce

Order Management is integrated with the Sales Compensation Systems through sales credits. When you enter an order in Oracle Order Management, you also assign sales credit. The sales credit information can be passed directly to sales compensation if you compensate your salespeople on orders booked. Sales credits can be passed through to receivables if you compensate your sales folks on invoiced sales. Sales credits can be considered against a salespersons' quota, or they may be compensated without the order being counted against their quota. To set up the Sales Credit Type, navigate to the Sales | Sales Credit Type form. Neptune defines a sales credit type for Quota Sales Commission, Non Quota Sales Commission for its Salesforce, a Sales Credit type for Royalties paid to the supplier of preloaded software, and a Sales Credit Type for Rebates that it pays to its distributors.

Your salespeople are likely to be defined in HR. The Sales | Resource form is where you define salespeople if they are not defined in HR. For example, external distributors or agents would be defined here. Information relevant to the order entry process is in the Receivables and Compensation tabs. In the Receivables tab is a Territory Flexfield that is defaulted onto the order. The territories themselves are set up in the Territory Definitions form under the Sales menu. It governs very little processing, but some AR reports use this Key Flex Structure. It is typically set up to represent geographic regions.

CRM also has the notion of territories. These represent the sales responsibilities of the salespeople and govern a great deal of functionality. The Revenue, Freight, and Receivables accounts are also defined here. This is one of the sources that Auto Accounting in Receivables considers to construct the accounts. Neptune is very interested in customer profitability. It survives in a market where margins are very thin. The cost to serve a particular customer may make the customer unprofitable. Therefore, Neptune drives a Customer segment in its chart of accounts from the Salesperson.

Creating a Global Picture of Availability

Oracle Planning allows you to create a global picture of availability that can be shared by many systems. You can configure different sources of supply and demand to be considered when promising a date to a customer. The dates can be shipment or delivery dates. Both material and resource availability is considered for the promised date.

Global Order Promising

You can use Global ATP Server to support distributed order promising. Multiple Order Entry systems can access a global statement of availability. It is completely

Internet-based, allowing low-cost collaborative deployment with only a browser. You can deploy Oracle Global ATP Server either as a component of a complete applications system, or by itself on a separate distributed server. This lets you support any combination of centralized and decentralized order promising. Planning currently collects from prior versions of the ordering systems, back to Release 10.7.

Collecting Supply and Demand Information

Built-in collection programs let you collect data from any Oracle Applications instance and transmit the data to the planning or order promising server. You can also collect data from legacy applications via interface tables. This capability provides high availability and an extremely accurate statement of availability to all customers in your global supply chain. Non-Oracle applications' order entry systems can access global order promising via APIs. The Global ATP API Signature is as follows:

```
Call_ATP ( p_atp_rec              IN    MRP_ATP_PUB.ATP_Rec_Typ,
           x_atp_rec              OUT   MRP_ATP_PUB.ATP_Rec_Typ,
           x_atp_supply_demand    OUT   MRP_ATP_PUB.ATP_Supply_Demand_Typ,
           x_atp_period           OUT   MRP_ATP_PUB.ATP_Period_Typ,
           x_atp_details          OUT   MRP_ATP_PUB.ATP_Details_Typ,
           x_return_status        OUT   VARCHAR2,
           x_msg_data             OUT   VARCHAR2,
           x_msg_count            OUT   NUMBER
);
```

and the in parameter is

```
TYPE ATP_Rec_Typ is RECORD (
Inventory_Item_Id              number_arr,
Source_Organization_Id         number_arr,
Identifier                     number_arr,
Calling_Module                 number_arr,
Customer_Id                      number_arr,
Customer_Site_Id               number_arr,
Destination_Time_Zone          char30_arr,
Quantity_Ordered               number_arr,
Quantity_UOM                   char3_arr,
Requested_Ship_Date            date_arr,
Requested_Arrival_Date         date_arr,
Earliest_Acceptable_Date       date_arr,
Latest_Acceptable_Date         date_arr,
Delivery_Lead_Time             number_arr,
Freight_Carrier                char30_arr,
Ship_Method                    char30_arr,
Demand_Class                   char30_arr,
Ship_Set_Name                  char30_arr,
Arrival_Set_Name               char30_arr,
```

```
Override_Flag                  char1_arr,
Action                         number_arr,
Ship_Date                      date_arr,
Available_Quantity             number_arr,
Requested_Date_Quantity        number_arr,
Group_Ship_Date                date_arr,
Group_Arrival_Date             date_arr,
Vendor_Id                    number_arr,
Vendor_Site_Id                 number_arr,
Insert_Flag                    number_arr,
Error_Code                   number_arr,
Message                        char2000_arr
);
```

Order Promising Terminology

As Order Promising methodology has evolved, new terms have been coined to describe advanced order promising capabilities:

- **Available to Promise** Refers to the ability to promise availability based on a predefined statement of current and planned supply.

- **Capable to Promise** Refers to the additional ability to determine the availability of component materials and resources to meet unplanned demands.

- **Capable to Deliver** Refers to considering transportation resources as well as considering the transit time necessary to meet your customer's delivery needs.

Oracle Global ATP Server encompasses all of these capabilities.

Configuring Sources of Supply and Demand

You can control the list of potential sources to be considered in the availability check. An organization item, item, item category, or org can be assigned a set of sources through bills of distribution and sourcing rules. A global sourcing rule or bill of distribution may also be defined. Even though planning groups a set of bills of distribution and sourcing rules into an assignment set, ATP considers all available sources.

For example, assume that Factory1 has the following sourcing rule for assembly A. Table 12-1 shows a sample sourcing rule for assembly A.

	Source	Rank	Shipping Lead Time	Transportation Resource
Transfer from	Org 1	1	1 day	5 Units/Lot
Transfer from	Org 2	2	3 days	4 Units/Lot
Transfer from	Org 3	3	5 days	3 Units/Lot

TABLE 12-1.   *Sample Sourcing Rule*

You can also control the number of levels in your supply chain bill to be considered in your check. The level of checks performed by Global Order Promising is controlled by three flags:

■ **ATP flag**   An item attribute

■ **ATP Components flag**   An item attribute

■ **BOM Component Check ATP flag**   An attribute attached to each component of a BOM

At each level in the supply chain bill, you can specify the key components and bottleneck resources for which to check availability. The possible settings for the ATP_FLAG in the Items form are as follows:

■ None

■ Material Only

■ Resource Only

■ Material and Resource

You can also check the group availability of products that must ship together.

Setting Profile Options

You need to set some important profile options in order to get global ATP working. The first is INV: Capable to Promise. This is a site-level profile option. It can have the following values:

- Enable Product Family ATP and CTP
- Enable Product Family ATP
- Enable ATP

The second is a site-level profile option, MRP: ATP Database Link. This is a pointer to the database where the global picture of supply and demand resides.

For supply chain ATP (the consideration of multiple sources of supply), the sources to be considered are listed in an assignment set (see Chapter 11). The purpose of this assignment set is to define the portion of your supply chain from your enterprise *outward* to your customer; thus the sourcing rules typically use only the Transfer From sourcing option to indicate the plants or distribution centers that can ship material to your customers. Because you can have many assignment sets, you must specify the assignment set you use for Order Management (and for ATP inquiries within your ERP instance) in the profile MRP:ATP Assignment Set.

For multi-instance order promising, you must define your assignment set on the Planning Server and specify it in the profile MSC:ATP Assignment Set. This profile will govern ATP inquiries on the Planning Server; see Chapter 11 for a discussion of the Planning Server.

Entering and Managing Orders

Order Management provides two ways to get at the Order Entry form. One is to use the Order Organizer. You can click the New Order button from the List panel. The other is to navigate to the Orders form directly from the menu.

Using the Order Organizer

Order Management comes with an Order Organizer. It is the main place that a customer service representative would interact with the Order Management system. The Order Organizer gives you a way of

- Searching for orders
- Saving search criteria
- Accessing commonly used search criteria

To use the Sales Order Organizer form, navigate to Orders and Returns | Order Organizer. In the Order Organizer form's Find window, you can construct your search criteria from order header information, order line information, or order hold information. The Advanced tab allows you to expand your search into closed and cancelled orders. Once you have entered your search criteria and clicked the Find button, you will be taken to the search results and see a list of folders on your left. The folders show you today's orders. These are orders you have entered today. It shows you a folder representing your search results. You can save your search criteria if you think it is one you will use often.

Right-click is enabled in the Folder panel of the search results window. It will allow you to name and save the search. If you have the profile OM: Administer Public Queries set to Yes, you can save the search into the Public folder for others to use. The search results give you two tabbed regions: one for header information and one for line information. You can create a new order, open an existing order, or perform any of the actions available under the Actions button. If you are located on the Header tab, this includes viewing the order information; applying or releasing holds; applying document attachments; booking, canceling, or copying the order, pricing the order; and managing sales credits. The Progress Order option will display the list of workflow activities that are currently eligible. You can select the activity and execute it from the order actions list. You can notify someone, or all people, with a given responsibility about an order. For example, a particular order may need engineering verification. You can choose notification from the action list and notify engineering. The notification is recorded in workflow.

From the line, the list of available actions include all those at the header, as well as horizontal demand, installation details, release workbench for demand received through the demand stream processor, and the ability to split the line. You can see the tax details of a line.

The summary and the lines block are folders. You can choose the fields that are most important to you to place in the first panel.

Entering Sales Orders

Choosing the Orders form gets you to the heart of the Order Management system. From here you can view and modify both outbound orders and returns. You can check availability and schedule shipments, reserve inventory, assign credits to your salespeople, adjust pricing, and record payment information.

Although each field is validated as entered, the "Booking" process validates the completeness of the order information.

Entering Order Header Information

There are two tabs in the header. If you have set up your defaulting rules correctly, you should very rarely be visiting the other tab. You can also tune the folders for the tabs to give exactly the information needed for a given type of entry. For example, you might have a folder for recording quotes that includes the version and expiration date. A sample order header is shown in Figure 12-10.

Main Tab   The only information that must be entered in the header are the Order Type and the Currency. The customer in the Order Header is the sold-to customer. The trading community architecture allows the definition of a customer with many places of doing business, which Oracle terms customer sites. Each site can have many site uses. Site uses are user-defined, but different applications look for specific site uses. Order Management is interested in ship-to site uses and bill-to site uses. Accounts Receivable is interested in statement addresses and dunning letter addresses. A customer definition may be defined with a primary ship-to address. A ship-to address has an associated bill-to address. This gives the ability for pretty quick order entry; populating the customer can allow the system to populate ship-to and bill-to information. Each customer and customer site can have primary contacts. These can

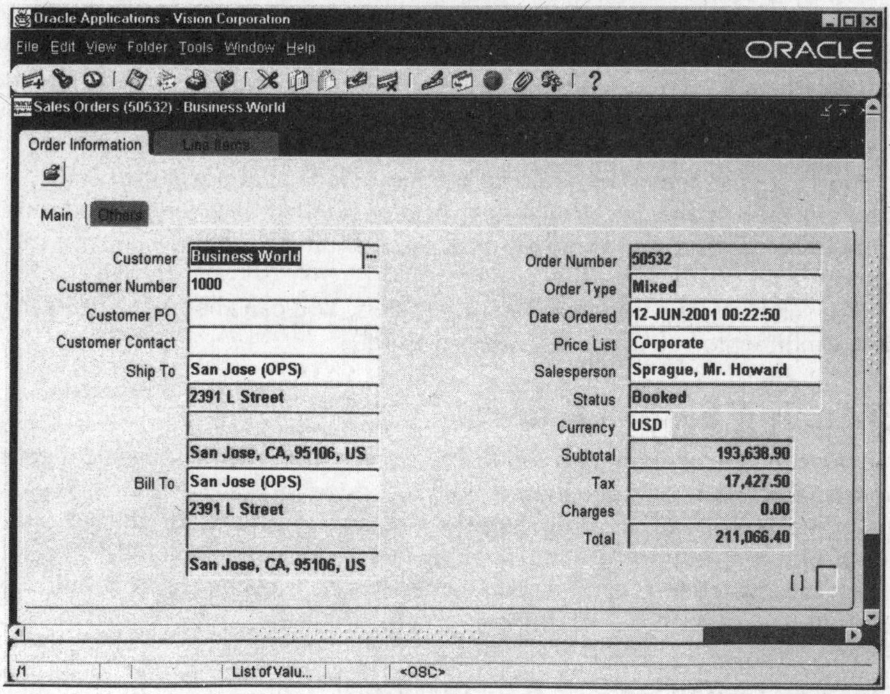

FIGURE 12-10.   *Sample order header*

be overridden at order entry, but again the order can be populated with pretty rich information with limited entered data.

NOTE
If you are entering an order for a new customer, Order Management provides a simplified customer entry form called Quick Customer Entry, which is available from the Tools menu.

You can set up an order type to require the entry of a customer purchase order. This gives some protection from AR risk if you can quote the customer's purchase order to their payables department. The system will alert you to a customer purchase order number that has already been used on another sales order. You can set up an order type to also require an agreement number. If you have set up an order type for promotional orders, you may want to capture the promotion code. For more information on agreements, see Chapter 20.

Other fields worthy of note on the Order Header Main tab are Price List, Salesperson, and Currency. There are many places from which you might default the price list, including; Customer, Customer Site Use, and Order Type, but you can override the defaulted price list here. There is a default salesperson defined for the customer. By default they get 100 percent of the sales credit that is fed to Sales Compensation. You can allocate the percentages to the sales team member in the Sales Credit window.

NOTE
If an order has come through Release Management, it will have customer item information in the order lines. If you change the customer at the order header, you will invalidate the customer items on the line. You must create a new order and cancel the old order.

Others Tab   The Others tab contains payment and freight terms for the order, logistics information to control the flow of the lines through the shipping system, and some tax information to be passed to the invoice.

You can choose a Payment Term for invoices handled through Accounts Receivable or a Payment Type if you are in a Payment with Order environment. Payment types can be cash, check, or credit card. If you select check, you can enter the check number. If you enter credit card, the credit card name, number, and expiration date will default from the primary credit card in the customer information, or you can enter them here. Enter the Approval Code for the credit card authorization.

NOTE
You can define the amount of the payment, but it is not transferred to Oracle Receivables. To enter receipts, deposits, and advances, you need to open the Receipts form in Oracle Receivables.

You define freight terms to define who is responsible for the freight. The F.O.B. point defines at what point ownership passes from the supplier to the customer. Generally, ownership passing will carry with it responsibility for insurance. The shipping methods are generally set up to represent common carrier charging tiers, such as two-day ground, overnight, and so on.

The warehouse can be defaulted onto the order from many sources. It also provides one of the sources of default for the warehouse on the lines. The line set drives some of the timing and reservation logic. You may want the lines to ship in a single shipment. If the lines are sourced from different warehouses, you may wish to have them arrive at the same time. The system ensures that all of the material is available at the same time before placing demand or allocating inventory. You can use shipment priority to allocate scarce inventory to orders during pick release. You can instruct warehouse staff on handling for a particular order by recording shipping instructions in the order header. Shipping instructions are printed on the pick slip—for example, "Pack Monitor in separate box on customer instruction." Packing instructions are printed on the pack slip. Packing instructions would be visible to the customer. An example might be "Monitor packed in separate box as per your request."

A bunch of tax handling information is exposed in the order header. Tax processing status declares how a transaction should be treated for tax. You can exempt a transaction that would normally be taxable, require tax for a transaction that is normally not taxable, or declare that the standard existing exemption rules should apply. If the customer has a tax exemption defined, Order Management displays any certificate number and reason for the exemption in the corresponding fields.

If you define the transaction as exempt, you must choose an existing certificate number for the ship-to customer, or enter a new, unapproved exemption certificate number. Unapproved exemption certificate numbers can be approved using the Tax Exemptions window. If you chose Standard in the Tax field, an existing exemption rule may display a certificate number in this field. The certificate and reason code must be supplied before the order can be booked.

The Order Source is for orders that may be imported from other sources or created through copy order. Sales Channel is defined on the customer, and customer site is commonly defined to be things such as Direct Sales, Distributor, and Web Site.

Order Header Actions   The Order Header Actions button allows you to perform many actions on the order that in previous versions of Order Management required you to navigate to other forms. The order header actions are as follows:

■ **Additional Order Information**   Gets you to a complete picture of what has happened to the order, including Holds applied and released, Deliveries scheduled and Trips in progress, Invoices billed and outstanding, and Quantities ordered and cancelled.

■ **Apply Automatic Attachments**   Allows you to add standard content to internal and external documents. See the section "Setting Up Standard Content for Order Documents" for more details.

■ **Apply Holds**   Enables you to hold the order line for a specified reason until a specified date.

■ **Cancel**   Enables you to cancel the outstanding quantity of all remaining line quantity for a stated reason.

■ **Charges**   Allows you specify freight or special charges for the order. Such charges might include documentation charges.

■ **Copy**   Enables you to copy lines to new or existing orders—for example, from a sales order to a return. You can choose to copy all the elements of the original order and order lines including holds notes and descriptive flex. You can choose to copy pricing or reprice for the new date.

■ **Notification**   Allows you to raise a notification to an individual or all people with a given responsibility. For example, you may wish to notify the Factory Manager that a large unplanned order has arrived.

■ **Price Order**   Reprices the order in background.

■ **Progress Order**   The Progress Order button presents a list of workflow activities that are currently eligible for the header workflow.

■ **Promotions and Pricing Attributes**   Allows you to record promotion codes and coupon numbers. These are modifiers in the pricing system. You can also record pricing attributes. Pricing attributes are discussed at length in the pricing chapter, but we briefly explain with an example. Neptune provides service coverage for its own and competitors equipment on customer site through its service division. Rather than recording all of the possible combinations of competitor and age of equipment as items, Neptune has an item that represents the size of machine and has pricing attributes for manufacturer and age of equipment. The price list is published for manufacturer and age of equipment.

■ **Release Holds**   Takes you to the Holds and Releases form where you can add, delete, and review holds.

■ **Sales Credits**   Takes you to a window where you can allocate the sales credits that drive your sales compensation. Sales credits can be counted against quota, counted as revenue credit, or be non-quota. For example, if Neptune's Education sales team needed help from the Industrial Equipment sales team to close a sale into school science laboratories, the Industrial Sales team might be compensated for the sale but still have their own quota to achieve. The quota or revenue credit needs to be completely assigned, so you must allocate 100 percent of the revenue credit. Sales credits can also drive revenue accounting. If you keep profit centers by customers or customer groupings, you may need to assign the revenue accounts to the salespeople. You set up salespeople in the Set Up | Sales | Salespeople menu. You can define Employees or Partners as receivers of commission or royalties.

■ **View Adjustments**   Allows you to create and review adjustments to the selling price. You can view the order-level adjustments in the Header tab. The Adjustments tab shows the adjustment to the selling price and the modifiers showing the discounts and promotions applied, and the Reasons tab records the reason when manual updates have been applied. Discounts can reduce the invoice, or they may be accrued and redeemed through credit memos or remittances at a later date. Accrued discounts do not affect the invoice value, but at the time of going to press there is no automatic remittance of accrued discount. The Accruals tabbed region is enabled only in Advanced Pricing.

NOTE
To modify a price in the Adjustments window, you must have the profile option OM: Discounting Privilege set to Yes, and the Order Type must not have the Enforce List Price Flag set to Yes.

Entering Line Information
The line information includes item, shipping, pricing, addresses, returns, service, project, and Release Management. To enter line information, click the Lines tab in either the Order Navigator or the Sales Order form. You can always see the order total as you enter order lines, so you can confirm back the order total to the customer as it is entered. Figure 12-11 shows an example of the Order Items tab.

Main Item Information   The line number is composed of the line, shipment, option, and service numbers; you can override the values. Select the ordered item for this order line. You can enter item information by using internal item numbers, customer item numbers, or any generic item number set up in Item Cross-References.

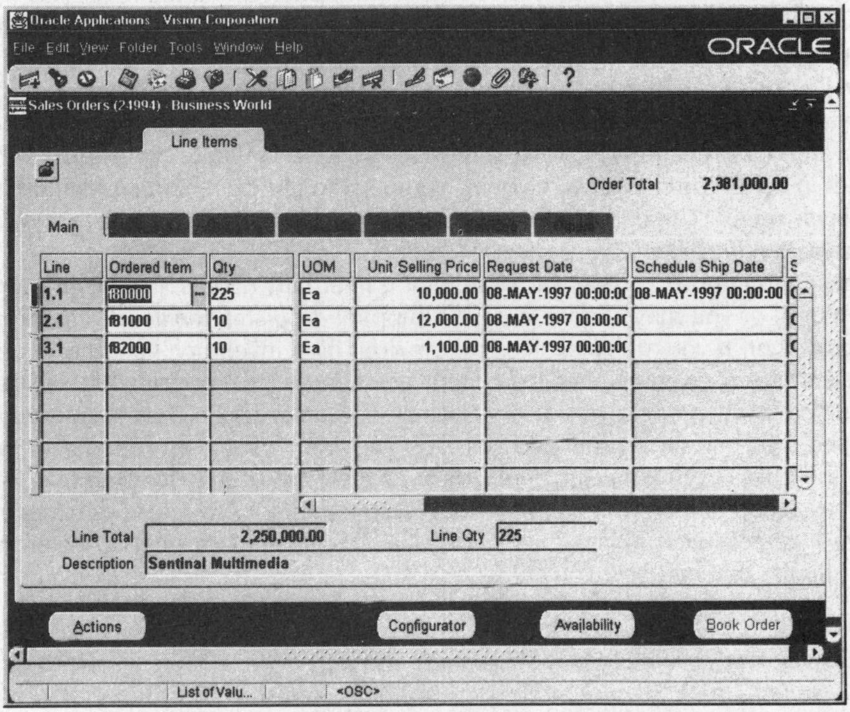

FIGURE 12-11. *Order Items tab in the Order Entry form*

NOTE
*If you expect to source the item directly from
a supplier in a drop shipment, you must set
the Purchasable attribute to Yes.*

When entering the unit of measure, you can enter only units of measure that the system can convert to its primary unit. The units of measure for models and kits are restricted to the item's primary unit of measure.

Pricing Information   You can select a price list. It is common to default the price list from the header to the lines. In any case, the price list currency must match the order currency. If you have the profiles option OM: Discounting Privilege set to Yes, you can adjust the price. You can also update payment term information here.

Shipping Information   You can specify information about the requested shipment as well as instructions to the shipping department on how to process the shipping of this order line. You will need to accept or override the default warehouse to be shipped from, and for internal orders, the receiving org or warehouse. The scheduled shipping date is offset by the transit time for the shipping method between the warehouse locations to arrive at the scheduled arrival date. You set up the offsets in the Shipping Networks form. You need to choose Shipping Method from the Tools menu. The dates requested by and promised to the customer are defaulted to the date entered and can be overridden here.

You can choose to source the transaction internally (that is, from your own inventory), or you may choose to have a supplier drop ship the goods directly to the customer. If you are going to ship from your own inventory, you may choose to reserve from inventory that is on hand. You can assign a priority that will be evaluated by planning for inventory allocation. If an order line has been partially shipped, you can see the shipped quantity. The line is "split" on partial shipment, with the lines moving independently through their workflows. The line may have been assigned to a Ship Set (all lines must ship together), Arrival Set (all lines must arrive together), or Fulfillment Set (all lines are considered together for determining the quantity that can be invoiced).

NOTE
Ship Sets will be created automatically when shipping a pick to order model with the Ship Model Complete flag set to Yes. Ship Sets must leave from the same warehouse. Lines within an arrival set can be dispatched from multiple warehouses. An arrival set may contain two or more Ship Sets.

NOTE
Customers familiar with the Release 10.7 Required for Revenue functionality should find the concepts of the fulfillment set easy to understand. The Required for Revenue flag is a component of a model that needs to be shipped in order to recognize revenue for the model or any part thereof.

Shipping method and shipping priority are ways of assigning and prioritizing work in the warehouse, including the allocation of inventory. You may override freight terms here, and you can give special instructions to warehouse staff and carriers through the shipping and packing instructions.

Address Information   You can specify address information by clicking the Addresses tab in the Sales Order form. The validation of the ship-to address is dependent on the value of the OM: Customer Relationships profile. If it is set to Yes, the shipping and billing addresses must be either for the order customer or for a customer that has a relationship defined with them. This might be appropriate if you are modeling a central buying department for a group of companies. If the profile is set to No, the shipping and billing addresses can be for the same customer. The Deliver-to addresses are for situations that do not warrant true "multi-leg" shipment capability but do get delivered to somewhere other than where you, as a supplier, ship them to. This is information for any subsequent carrier of the goods that will "deliver" after you have discharged your responsibility.

Return Information   To specify return information, navigate to the Returns tab. You can specify a reason code from the customer that is returning the goods and the line type to define the workflow for the line. You can specify a reference for the return, including Customer PO Number, Invoice Number, Order Number, or Serial Number. The Reference allows the system to correctly default the pricing and sales credits for the credit memo and commission clawback.

Service Information   To specify information on service items, navigate to the Service tab. Oracle Order Management allows you to order the service of an item at the same time as ordering the serviceable item. You could do this either through online or imported orders. Service coverage for the serviceable part will generally be a nonshippable item that will not need to be scheduled. The service lines will be linked to the serviceable lines. This reference is through the Service Reference Order Number, Line Number, and Shipment Number. They may also be linked to an entry in the install base via the customer product. This is where Oracle keeps a record of the items that are at the customer site and subject to service coverage. You specify the type of association in the service reference type. You could be selling service coverage for a group of items you have sold to the customer. This grouping is the system reference. Oracle pricing allows for pricing as a percentage of the sale of the serviceable line. For example, the service coverage for a $2,000 desktop unit might be 10 percent of the desktop price.

NOTE
The fulfillment of the service lines is generally through the fulfillment of the serviceable lines. This means that you invoice only for the service line when the serviceable product ships. You can also specify a service start delay on the service item when you set it up in Oracle Inventory. This will mean that the service coverage will be started and invoiced for a certain number of days after the serviceable line ships.

Project Information Oracle Project Manufacturing allows you to capture costs for a specific customer contract. Planning and reservations are also done at a project level to allow you to trace supply for a contract. You can record the project that will capture the costs for the contract in the Project tab. You can specify the project, task, and end item serial number. For example, if Neptune is supplying the flight computers for an aircraft manufacturer, the tail number of the aircraft might be recorded as the end item serial number.

NOTE
It is the warehouse Project reservation flag on the warehouse that defines whether the order line will require task as well as project.

Release Information Release Management information is used in automotive solutions, or anywhere that planning is highly coordinated between customer and supplier. The customer may give the supplier visibility into demand that is not authorized to ship. The customer will reissue their picture of demand for the same period many times, overlaying the supplier's picture. The demand may be on different schedule types, including planning schedules, shipping schedules, and sequenced schedules. The supplier needs to be able to determine the net change between transmissions. Deliveries from the supplier need to be in the correct sequence when unloaded at the customers' receiving dock to marry with the job on the production line. To enable this, the release information includes customer job, customer production line, receiving dock, and intermediate ship-to. The intermediate ship-to gives Oracle some capability to pool shipments. The release information also includes the unit identifier of the end item. For example, if Neptune is shipping onboard diagnostics to a car manufacturer, the diagnostic units will carry the vehicle identification number (VIN) of the car in which they will be fitted.

Line Actions Button You can do the following from the Actions button on the line:

- **Review Line Details** An audit of all activity for the order line, including deliveries, returns, and quantity changes.

- **Apply Automatic Attachments** Allows you to add standard content to internal and external documents.

- **Apply Holds** Enables you to hold the order line for a specified reason until a specified date.

- **Cancel** Enables you to cancel the remaining line quantity for all selected lines for a stated reason.

■ **Charges**   Allows you specify freight or special charges for the line. Such charges might include line haul cost.

■ **Copy**   Enables you to copy lines to new or existing orders; for example, from a template order to a shippable order.

■ **Horizontal Demand**   Takes you to a view of the demand, cast into the future. This format is widely used in the Release Management applications. It is really used where there is tight integration between the planning systems of the customer and the order management systems of the supplier. This is characterized by having many planned shipments of the order. In the automotive case, these shipments could even be within a day. It shows how far you are ahead or behind the current demanded quantity as well as the picture of demand cast into the future. The Release Management environment is also characterized by the management of the cumulative quantities. The total quantity requested and received is constantly reconciled between the customer and supplier. The cumulative, or CUM, details are also exposed in this screen, including how to identify the same demand between two transmissions of the demand stream. If you have standard blanket order requirements, you should also check out the Release Management capability.

■ **Installation Details**   Takes you to where you can update where the serviceable items are installed at a customer site for a serviceable item. Service coverage is applied to a system in the Oracle install base. A system for Neptune might be a server that it has sold to a customer with a specific hardware configuration. You can specify if the item is going into or coming out from the installation for outbound or inbound shipments. The Installation Details window also gives an audit trail of entries in the install base.

■ **Contract Details**   Applicable only to the sale of service coverage and extended warranty. You can specify how you want the details for the new service combined with the existing service contract.

■ **Notification**   Allows you to send electronic notifications to individuals or groups within the organization. For example, one of Neptune's salespeople has identified an opportunity to supply onboard computing to medical equipment manufacturers. You may want engineering to review a request for a modification to one of your standard products.

■ **Price Line**   Re-prices all the selected lines if any updates have occurred to the price or discount lists since the order was last priced. The order may also have accumulated enough volume to qualify for a volume price break.

■ **Price Order**   The equivalent of selecting all the lines and re-pricing.

- **Progress Order** Tests for all eligible workflow activities. If any activities are eligible and can be executed as functions within workflow, they can be executed from here. For example, you may have an export compliance system that can be invoked from a PL/SQL function and return a result of "approved" or "rejected." On a result of "approved," the function of print export documentation might become eligible. Another example might be to check the order line for profit margin compliance. These could be included in your workflow processes and then invoked from the form.

- **Promotions and Pricing Attributes** Allows you to record promotion codes and coupon numbers. These are modifiers in the pricing system. You can also record pricing attributes. (Pricing attributes are discussed at length in Chapter 20.) Neptune provides service coverage for its own and competitors' equipment on customer sites through its service division. Rather than recording all of the possible combinations of competitor and age of equipment as items, Neptune has an item that represents the size of machine and has pricing attributes for manufacturer and age of equipment. The price list is published for manufacturer and age of equipment.

- **Release Holds** Takes you to the Release Holds window. If you have authority through your responsibility to release the hold, the hold will be displayed and a release reason required. You can optionally explain your action with comments.

- **Release Workbench** Takes you to a navigator where you can see the release schedules. Release schedules are long-term planning schedules, medium-term shipping schedules, and short-term sequenced schedules. The release schedules will generally be received via Electronic Data Interchange (EDI) and will be netted before updating demand in the order backlog. The left panel is the series of shipping locations.

NOTE
Before you can use the Release Management workbench, you must use the Release Management Processing Rules form to associate ship-from warehouse with the customer locations from which you receive demand transactions and define how parties will track cumulative quantities between them. You will also need to define a pricing agreement that references the customer's purchase order and the customer items numbers.

The top-right panel has the item shipment information. Companies using Release Management will have coordinated production very closely so that the customer's manufacturing job is part of the demand stream received from the customer. There are many packing, shipping, and delivery terms that are agreed on an item-by-item basis in Release Management.

The lower-right panel is the shipments as they have been transmitted in the release schedule. The shipments could be firm or forecast for any time bucket: day, week, or month.

If the netting process had problems resolving demand in a given period, it will record exceptions, which you can view by clicking the Exceptions radio button.

- **Sales Credits**   Takes you to a window where you can allocate the sales credits that drive your sales compensation. The window behaves in the same way as the header sales credits. Sales Credits can be at either level. You should be aware that the sales credits at the header and line apply to all the order revenue. If no sales credits exist at the line level, the header sales credits will apply. If you apply sales credits at any level, you have to allocate 100 percent.

- **Split Line**   Allows you to specify other dates or shipping warehouses for part of the quantity in the order line. The order line in Order Management represents both the ordered line and the shipment of the ordered line. Lines may be split automatically by the system. For example, if a line is partially shipped, the line will split and the remainder of the line go through its own workflow. If you split a model line into shipments, Order Management duplicates everything beneath the model to each shipment schedule. With PTO configurations, you can change the options for that shipment schedule until the individual shipment schedule has been ship-confirmed. For example, your customer has a blanket order to ship 100 configurations each month for the next six months. After three months, you no longer support one of the options they chose, and they still have three months' worth of shipments outstanding. You can update the remaining three shipment schedules, removing the obsolete option.

- **View Adjustments**   Allows you to create and review adjustments to the selling price. You can view the order-level adjustments as they apply to the line and view the line-level adjustments. You can view the attributes that were priced and discounted by clicking the Attributes button. For example, Neptune's service department provides a full service coverage for backup and failover of their professional servers. The attributes that drive this price are environment controlled area, access restriction, and particulate count.

If the servers are in a poorly controlled area, the price is modified upward. Neptune does not keep combinations of these attributes as items. It has an item in its price list for Backup and Failover and modifies the price through pricing attributes.

■ **Tax Details** Takes you to a window where you can see the schedule of tax codes and rates for the order line. You assign specific tax rates to tax code in the Define Tax Codes and Rates window. Tax codes are used when calculating tax based on location and tax codes. You can group tax codes into tax groups where compound taxes apply.

Booking Sales Orders

You can book the sales order by clicking the Book Order button, which checks that the order is complete and valid. The validity check includes Credit Check Errors that will be returned in the Messages window. You can enter orders and not book them. Booking an order starts it on its workflow. You can set up the workflow to book the order automatically. Refer to the section "Order Workflows," earlier in this chapter. You would generally not want to have unbooked orders for too long. These are revenue opportunities that have not been responded to or orders that have validity problems. The workflow for the order will not be progressing. There are reports in the Order Management system to alert you to unbooked orders.

Managing Availability and Delivery Commitments

The management of availability and committing to deliver covers three areas: Available to Promise (ATP) inquiries, scheduling, and reserving supply. You can schedule order lines with multiple ship-to locations and shipping warehouses. You can specify which lines must be shipped together by using Ship Sets. You can specify which lines must arrive at the customer's dock together, even though they have shipped from different warehouses. You can request ATP and schedule dates for a single order line, a model with options, a ship set, a configuration, or an entire order. You can configure the sources of supply and demand to be considered by ATP. You can have orders scheduled automatically as they are entered.

ATP Inquiries

ATP inquiries will inform you of an available date without committing supply. You can check the availability of an order, order line, configuration, ship set, and arrival set. The ATP inquiry returns the first data after the requested schedule date that the requested quantity is available. For a group of lines, the date returned is the latest date of all the lines in the group. If the ATP flag is set to No in the item master, only the onhand and reservable quantities will be displayed. If the ATP flag is set to Yes, the warehouse, available quantity, available date, and request date are also shown. ATP check will be performed automatically if the OE:AutoSchedule is set to Y. ATP check will also evaluate sourcing rules to determine a warehouse to source the line from if one does not exist on the line. You can invoke the global ATP inquiry and see the approved sources, ship methods, and lead times if you would like to choose a source other than the primary. Table 12-2 shows the ATP behavior for each item type.

NOTE
Although Order Management allows you to specify times for requested and promised dates, ATP nets supply and demand at the day level.

If the Check ATP flag is set to Yes, the line cannot be scheduled unless the schedule date can be met with the current supply. By marking the item as ATP Check Yes, you are stating that the date promised to the order must have planned supply on the date scheduled. If the Check ATP flag is No, you can create unplanned demand in the system.

Item Type	ATP Behavior
Standard Line (not in any set)	ATP performed on line.
Standard Line (in ship or arrival set)	ATP performed on entire set.
ATO Model	ATP performed on all models, options, and classes under the ordered model line.
ATO Class	ATP performed on entire configuration.
ATO Option	ATP performed on entire configuration.
PTO Model (Non Ship Model Complete)	ATP performed on the model and its included items.
PTO Class (Non Ship Model Complete)	ATP performed on the class and its included items.
PTO Option (Non Ship Model Complete)	ATP performed only on the option.

TABLE 12-2. *Item Type ATP Behavior*

If you click the Availability button in the order header or select multiple lines, you will get the multirow availability window. From here, you can verify the availability dates for a set of order lines. If the shipping network has been set up in supply chain planning to include the customer site, the arrival date will be offset from the shipping date. If no shipping network is defined, the ship date and arrival date will be the same. You can choose to include or exclude the orders on hold from scheduling with the OM: Schedule Lines on Hold profile.

NOTE
The scheduling actions available on the order are dependent on the order type. You can restrict order types to ATP only, ATP and Scheduling without reservations, or all scheduling actions.

The Available to Promise formula is

ATP = on hand + supply – demand

where *on hand* = ATP–able quantity on hand; *supply* = planned orders, scheduled receipts (purchase orders, purchase requisitions, and discrete jobs), and suggested repetitive schedules; and *demand* = sales orders, component demand from planned orders, discrete jobs, and suggested repetitive schedules.

You can review the available dates down to the scheduled inventory receipt and issue documents. From the Availability window, click the Global Availability button. Choose an ATP source and click View ATP Results. You will see the ATP workbench. The left panel is the list of orders to be checked for availability. This workbench can also be called from the Schedule order backlog form, where many orders can be chosen. Within the order you will see the list of scheduling groupings: Ship Sets, Configurations, and so on, as well as independent lines. Click one of the groups, and the list of items will appear in the right-hand panel. You will see the earliest available dates and any errors encountered in scheduling. You can pick an item in the right-hand panel and see the list of available dates. The available dates are scheduled receipts into inventory. By clicking the Details button, you can see the validation of the available dates, transaction by transaction. Figure 12-12 shows an example of the ATP Details window.

If your ability to promise to customers is driven as much by capacity as having inventory, you can set the INV:Capable to Promise profile option. Capable to Promise (CTP) extends Available to Promise by taking into account capacity information. Whereas ATP considers only material availability and assumes infinite capacity resources, CTP considers availability of both materials and capacity.

Scheduling

Scheduling provides a schedule date and warehouse that will fulfill the customers request. If an item has Check ATP enabled, then the supply will be consumed from

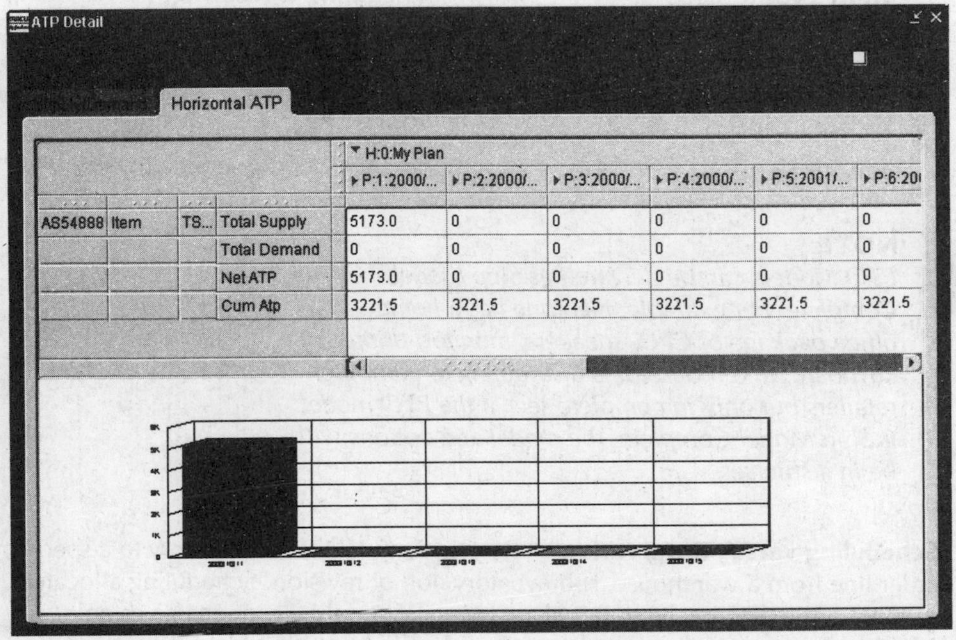

FIGURE 12-12. *Horizontal ATP results*

the pool of available supply for that item. If an item does not have Check ATP enabled, then the supply will not be consumed. Scheduling will behave differently for different types of items. The following table shows item types and scheduling results.

Item Type	Scheduling Outcome
Standard Line (not in any set)	Line is scheduled.
Standard Line (in ship or arrival set)	Whole set is scheduled.
ATO Model	Configuration is scheduled.
ATO Class	Configuration is scheduled.
ATO Option	Configuration is scheduled.
PTO Model	Model and included items are scheduled.
PTO Class	Option class and included items are scheduled.

Item Type	Scheduling Outcome
PTO Option	Option is scheduled.
Included Item	When scheduling the parent item, included items are scheduled.
Service Line	Cannot schedule service lines.

NOTE
PTO Models can be declared as Ship Model Complete. For example, Neptune has a home office package of CPU, speakers, monitor, printer, keyboard, and mouse. It is distributing to computer retailers but only in complete sets. If the PTO model is Ship Model Complete, the model and options will be in a ship set.

Scheduling versus Reservation   Reservations Allocates inventory to a specific order line from a warehouse, subinventory, lot, or revision. Scheduling allocates supply from a date bucket rather than a specific supply. Reserving gives an additional degree of certainty that the supply will be available, but it makes reallocation of supply much more difficult.

Scheduling Orders from the Order Entry Form   You can see the availability of the item ordered in the floating availability window. This window will show the requested and available dates, quantities, and scheduling exception messages for the warehouse on the order line. You can also use the schedule function from the Tools menu. This gives the full array of scheduling functions: scheduling, unscheduling, reserving, unreserving, and viewing schedule results.

Scheduling Orders in a Concurrent Program   You can also schedule orders in batch mode. Navigate to the concurrent program submission. The program will honor the OM: Schedule Orders on Hold profile. It will schedule only order lines that are eligible according to their workflow statues. Parameters include

- Order number range
- Request date range
- Ship-to location
- Order type
- Customer
- Item

Acknowledging Customers

Oracle Order Management provides printed acknowledgements and a mechanism to acknowledge customers electronically through the e-commerce gateway. To print acknowledgements, navigate to Reports and Requests concurrent submission form. The customer "sold-to" site must be set up to receive acknowledgements. There are two types of acknowledgment: original and order change. The order acknowledgement process picks up data from Order Management, writes it to acknowledgement tables in e-commerce gateway, and updates Order Management with the acknowledgment code and date. Acknowledgment codes exist at the header and lines level for automated processing of acknowledgements into purchasing systems. An electronic change order acknowledgement will be produced if there is a change to

- PO number, PO date, change sequence, bill-to location, and ship-to

- Location at the header level

- Customer line number, item, customer item, quantity ordered, unit of measure, unit price, ship-to location, request date, and promise date on the line

Or if the PO is cancelled, lines are cancelled and added.

Making Updates to Large Numbers of Orders and Lines

You apply mass changes by selecting the orders or order lines in the Order Organizer. Use the multiselect function to select the orders or order lines you would like to update. Choose Tools | Mass Update. You can select what you would like to set your orders or order lines to and click OK.

Invoicing Orders

Oracle Order Management provides a seeded workflow function to move the fulfilled order line shipments and authorized return lines, freight charges, and discounts to receivables. Receivables provides invoicing, revenue accounting, and collections capability. You can interface full or partial quantity of line shipments and RMA receipts, including PTO configurable items. Eligible priced option classes and options will also be invoiced with their model lines. Freight charges are invoiced as soon as at least one order line associated with the pick slip is interfaced. If associated order lines have been completely interfaced, the freight is interfaced as a separate transaction. Line and header charges and price adjustments, tax treatments, and payment information are interfaced. If customer item information exists, the customer item description is passed rather than the internal item description.

Important Profiles

The following profile options affect the operation of the invoicing interface:

- **OM: Invoice Numbering Method**   Determines whether the invoicing activity will generate invoice numbers based on the delivery name. Where a given shipment from your warehouse may be delivered to more than one destination for a customer, you can choose to create an invoice number that is equivalent to the delivery number. This makes the receipt matching task much easier for the customer. It is very common in the automotive industry.

- **OM: Show Discount Details on Invoice**   Determines whether discount information prints on the invoice.

- **OM: Non-delivery Invoice Source**   Transferred to Receivables if the OM: Invoice Numbering Method profile option is set to Delivery and the order line is non-shippable.

- **OM: Overshipment Invoice Basis**   Determines whether to invoice the ordered or shipped quantity for overshipments. This value also applies on credit memos for returns that are over received. This profile is superceded by the value at the customer and ship-to sites.

NOTE
Order Management does not currently create invoices for internal orders, even if there is an invoicing activity in the workflow.

Processing Returns and Requests for Credit

Order Management allows for the creation of RMAs and requests for credit in the Order Entry form. Returns could be for order placement or shipping errors, field failures, or return of samples. An RMA acts as an authorization for the receipt. The receipt is transacted in the Receiving form in the purchasing application. Credit may also be given for damaged or low value goods where no physical shipment of the goods will occur, but credit will be issued in AR. You can choose on an item-by-item basis those that you allow to be returned and those that must be inspected before going into inventory.

Setting Up Return Order Flows

We have discussed most of the setup for inbound orders under the "Deciding How to Process Outbound Orders" section, but the following pieces are worth special note.

Credit Transaction Types   Credit order types have an order type category of Return. A Mixed order type category can contain both sales order and return lines. However, you cannot enter return lines into an order with an order type category of Regular.

RMA line types have a line type category of Return. The following are examples of the basic line types:

- Return for credit without receipt of goods

- Return for credit with receipt of goods

- Return for replacement

- Return for rework and return to customer

- Free of charge issue of material in advance of material returns

Return Reasons   Accounts Receivable and Order Management share a set of return and credit reasons. If you generate credits from your RMAs, the return reason is carried through to the credit memo as the reason for the credit to provide a full audit trail. To set up return reasons, navigate to the Set Up Quick Codes Receivables menu.

Item Attributes   Physical items you expect to receive in Oracle Inventory must have the following item attributes: Returnable: Yes; Shippable Item: Yes; Transactable: Yes; and Stockable: Yes. To create credits for return items in Oracle Receivables, the item must have the item attributes Returnable: Yes and Invoice Enabled: Yes. Nonstockable items such as warranties will have the shippable and stockable flags set to No.

Entering Return Information

You can enter an RMA line in the Sales Orders form. You need to supply a line type in the line type category of "Return." You also need to provide information about the originating transaction, such as the order number, order line number, option number, and shipment number or invoice number and line number. For serial controlled items, you can also reference the serial number. You can choose whether to allow, reject, or warn the operator of mismatches between the RMA items reported by the customer and the related transactions through the profile OM: Return Item Mismatch Action. When you enter the quantity, you can enter positive or negative numbers. The quantity returned is displayed as a negative number and highlighted in red. The extended price of a return line is also displayed as a negative number and highlighted in red.

Pricing of Returns

If you use the copy order function to create a credit order, you can price the order at the current price list value, price the order as at the original pricing date, or create a new price and adjustments for the return.

Receiving and Returning Items under RMA

You can have inbound and outbound lines on the same order. Order Management allows you to enter lines on an order to receive the returned material and dispatch the reworked or replacement items. For example, a customer may make a return under warranty or trade in a prior model. For a lot and/or serial number–controlled item, the Sales Orders window allows you to enter the lot and serial numbers that the customer reports for a return line. This will allow you to verify warranty period, and so on, for the shipped product, but the actual lots and serials are recorded on receipt.

Special Order Flows

As of Release 11, Order Management allows for sourcing of an order directly from a supplier for delivery to a customer. Oracle also supports guided selling of configured products assembled to order. These more specialized order flows are discussed in the following sections.

Drop Shipments

Order Management allows you to define orders for which the default source type will be drop shipment. For this order flow, a purchase order is created "back to back" with the order line. For example, Neptune offers PDAs in its catalog to complement its line of personal desktop computers. However, it does not stock the equipment but instead has the PDAs delivered directly to its customers.

Benefits of Sourcing Externally   Most of the benefits in the drop shipments do not fall to the supplier. The company taking the order will have less inventory to carry and less of the costs that surround inventory: obsolescence risk, insurance, storage packing, and logistics. There are fewer steps in the delivery as the leg from the supplier to the company taking the order is eliminated. This should translate into shorter lead times.

Entering Orders   The transaction type has a default ship source type on it. This will be defaulted to the order line when it is entered. This determines that the line will be sourced by having purchase orders raised to fulfill the order line and not out of your own inventory.

Creating the Purchase Order   The creation of the purchase order goes through the requisition import process. To create requisition information available to purchasing, run the purchase release program. This picks up eligible externally sourced lines and creates entries ready for requisition import. Run Purchasing's Requisition Import program to create purchase requisitions based on this information. You can set the profile PO: Release During ReqImport to create releases each time you run the requisition import process. Ideally, you would construct a report set with the Create Purchase Release and Import Requisitions. After Requisition Import completes successfully, you can approve the requisitions to generate purchase orders.

You can verify sales order to purchase order correspondence in the Order Discrepancy Report to note any changes made after purchase release.

Recording the Receipt   When the drop shipment has been sent to the customer, the supplier can confirm the shipment through a phone call, an invoice, or an EDI document, such as an Advance Shipment Notice (ASN). You must process the receipt as if you were receiving into your inventory. This may be simply a ghost booking into inventory on the receipt and out of inventory on the shipment transaction. Navigate to the Receiving form in Oracle Purchasing. Though no physical receipt exists, a transfer of ownership and flow of costs does need to be recorded in your system. Once the order has been receipted, its shipment will be recorded, and it will be invoiced according to its assigned workflow.

Entering Configured Orders

Order Management comes with a graphical environment for the declaration of sales engineering rules and a graphical environment for the guided selection and validation of options. If the item being ordered is an ATO or PTO model, you can click the Configurator button to open the Configurator window and select options. You can view selected options along with their option classes from the Lines tab in the Sales Order form; however, you cannot modify the selections from the Sales Order form. To see (or hide) the configuration detail in the Sales Order form, click the Line Detail check box in the Tools menu.

Finding an Existing Item that Matches the Ordered Configuration

The default behavior of the system is to create a new configuration item for each model ordered. You can, however, search the system for an existing item that matches the ordered configuration. Once a match is found, the system will link the matched item to the sales order line. The order must be booked and scheduled, and a configuration item must not have been created for the order line. You need to set the profile BOM: Match to Existing Configuration to Yes. Oracle finds matching items using the descriptive elements in the item definition. If the way that you find existing configurations is different, you can set the profile BOM: Use Custom Match Function to the name of a PL/SQL function.

You can perform the match in a number of ways: From the sales order form, you can click the Actions button and choose Match or Create Configuration from the list of actions. Or, you can run the AutoCreate Configurations concurrent program.

If a match is found, the system links the matched item to the order line.

Processing Configured Orders

Processing a configured order goes through some additional steps. The configuration may be a unique specification, and the item information and supply need to be created. Functions needed in the configured order workflow are the following:

- Enter
- Schedule
- Create Configuration
- Lead Time Rollup
- Cost Rollup
- Create Supply (Work Order or Flow Schedule)
- Ship

These are all supported in the seeded workflow Line Flow – Generic. Appropriate subsets of the functions are supported in Line Flow – ATO Model and Line Flow – ATO Item.

Once a configuration item is created for an ATO model order line, Order Management creates a new order line for the configuration item. The configuration item line goes through manufacturing and shipping processes while the ATO model line waits for the completion of those processes.

Making Changes to Orders for Configured Items

When you order a configured item, the item and the work order to assemble the item are linked to the order. The work order is reserved to supply the sales order, and the configuration item is added to the order as a new line. Any changes that apply to an order that may have a unique item being assembled to order are going to be difficult to process automatically. There are questions of whether the changes can be applied to the existing work order, disposition of work in progress, and whether the changes affect a BOM unique to the order. Oracle requires you to remove the link between the order and the item before making changes to the order line.

Oracle has recently introduced capability for some of the changes to be handled automatically by the Configure to Order (CTO) products. When making changes for a configured order, CTO is notified and, depending on the type of change, they are either handled or the configuration item is de-linked automatically.

Delink Configuration Item   In Oracle parlance, when you remove the association between the sales order line and the configured item, you de-link the item. Once the item is de-linked, you can make adjustments to the supply and re-link if you choose. You can de-link a configuration item from an ATO model line through the Sales Order form Action button - Delink Config Item. Clicking Delink Configuration Item will automatically unreserve the supply to the sales order if any exists.

If discrete jobs exist for the configuration item, they may be put on hold automatically, based on the setting of the WIP parameter Respond to Sales Order Changes. This allows you to take whatever corrective action you want for those jobs—you may want to cancel the job, modify it, or continue to build the original configuration.

Link Configuration Item   You can manually link a configuration item to an ATO model line through the Sales Order form Action Button – Link Config Item. This is useful when you want to ship a near match item or need to relink a configuration item back to the original model line after you de-link the configuration item.

Order Management E-Commerce Capability

Order Management supports integration, both through well-defined PL/SQL APIs and through the e-commerce gateway. You can use these capabilities in application-to-application integration and in business-to-business integrations. There are a range of technologies further down the technology stack that are relevant to the integration problem. Workflow has been extended to include a business event definition. Applications can publish events, and consumers of the events can subscribe to them. Transformation and messaging services exist within the application server.

E-Commerce Gateway and Order Import   Transactions that are handled as standard through the e-commerce gateway include

- Orders
- Order Changes
- Acknowledgments

Transactions are handled for X12 and EDIFACT formats. The e-commerce gateway will load the order interface. To import orders, navigate to the import orders request and choose an appropriate order source to import. You can import orders in final or validate mode. You can review and correct orders in the import tables by navigating to the Orders, Import, Corrections form. If orders will not book, they can still be imported. You can correct booking errors in the Enter Orders form.

Order Management APIs   Order Management was one of the first users of the PL/SQL API standards. The user interfaces talk to the same API that the import program uses. The logic is centralized through three APIs: Get_Order, Process_Order, and Lock_Order. The Sales Order business object is comprised of several entities:

- **Header**   Corresponding to OE_ORDER_HEADERS_ALL
- **Header Sales Credits**   Corresponding to OE_SALES_CREDITS
- **Header Price Adjustments**   Corresponding to OE_PRICE_ADJUSTMENTS
- **Header Pricing Attributes**   Corresponding to OE_ORDER_PRICE_ATTRIBS
- **Header Adjustment Attributes**   Corresponding to OE_PRICE_ADJ_ATTRIBS
- **Header Adjustment Associations**   Corresponding to OE_PRICE_ADJ_ASSOCS
- **Lines**   Corresponding to OE_ORDER_LINES_ALL
- **Line Sales Credits**   Corresponding to OE_SALES_CREDITS
- **Line Price Adjustments**   Corresponding to OE_PRICE_ADJUSTMENTS
- **Line Pricing Attributes**   Corresponding to OE_ORDER_PRICE_ATTRIBS
- **Line Adjustment Attributes**   Corresponding to OE_PRICE_ADJ_ATTRIBS
- **Line Adjustment Associations**   Corresponding to OE_PRICE_ADJ_ASSOCS
- **Line Lot Serial Numbers**   Corresponding to OE_LOT_SERIAL_NUMBERS

These entities are passed to the API as a set of PL/SQL tables of records. It is not only the import action that can be performed through the process order API. Any action that you can perform in the user interface you can perform through the API. For example, you could book an order. One of the parameters to the OE_ORDER_PUB.PROCESS_ORDER. API is

```
p_action_request_tbl IN PL/SQL Table default G_MISS_REQUEST_TBL
```

The structure of the table would be

```
request_type := OE_GLOBALS.G_BOOK_ORDER
entity_code := OE_GLOBALS.G_ENTITY_HEADER as booking is an
order level action.
entity_id := Header ID of the order to be booked. If the order
is also being created in the same call to process order, then
the user does not need to provide this value.
```

Summary

This chapter discussed the management of orders through the sales administration department in a company. It covered the main capabilities to enter and schedule orders. This chapter covered the ordering environment extending from manual entry of orders, to processing orders through EDI transactions, to tying together the planning systems of your customer into your ordering environments with Release Management.

The chapter reviewed how to manage delivery commitments. It reviewed how different types of items are treated by the promising systems and how Order Management works in a global ordering environment to give accurate available dates.

The multitude of systems that the ordering systems touch and feed, including the receivables and sales compensation systems, were examined. The chapter reviewed some special ordering flows to cover drop shipments and configurations. Finally, it reviewed the APIs that are the core of how Order Management works.

CHAPTER
13

Procurement
Management

racle Purchasing is the procurement and supply management solution. It has functionality to serve the requisitioner who needs a pencil as well as the procurement manager who is sourcing a component supplier through Request for Quotes (RFQs) and negotiating long-term agreements. The procurement system is also fed from the planning systems that request material for production. It is tightly integrated with Oracle Workflow, routing requisitions and purchase orders up an approval chain. Purchasing has embedded alerting mechanisms that will inform purchasing managers when long-term agreements are coming to an end. Oracle Purchasing includes the flip side of the Release Management product in Supplier Scheduling. It gives access to suppliers through the Internet Supplier Portal and provides ways of reducing manual processing through Pay on Receipt self-billing functionality and procurement card capability. Figure 13-1 gives an overview of the components and the flow through the sourcing and purchasing system.

Solutions for Requisitioners

Oracle Purchasing requisition capability allows you to do the following:

- Direct the buying activity to professional buyers

- Pool the demand into fewer purchase orders, minimizing ordering costs

- Channel demand into long-term agreements

- Ensure that purchases are approved and funded

Requisitions can be manually created but are also fed from other systems. Master Scheduling/MRP, inventory planning, and outside processing in Work in Process all create requisitions. Requisitions can be sourced from suppliers or could be sourced from inventory. When the requisitions are sourced from inventory, an internal sales order is also created to ship the requisitioned item.

Oracle Purchasing has two modes of entering requisitions: forms-based requisitions in the professional forms and Web-based requisitions in Internet Procurement. The Web-based requisitions are built to be usable with zero training by an occasional user.

Internet Requisitions

From a self-service menu or Personal Home Page (PHP), you can choose the Internet Procurement option. The look and feel of the Web pages are the same as Oracle Exchange Marketplace and will be familiar from many consumer-oriented Web sites.

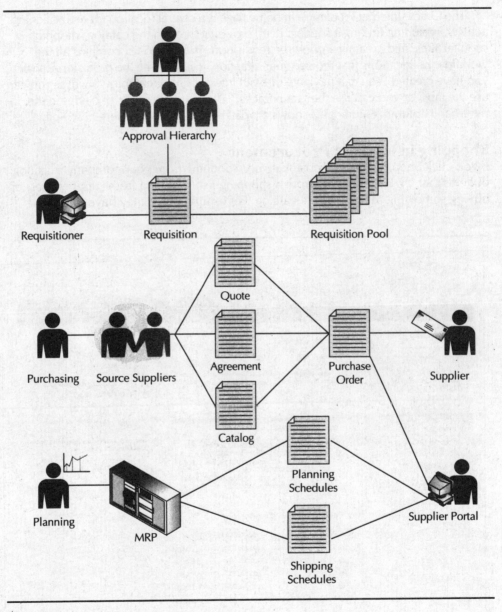

FIGURE 13-1. *Purchasing overview*

The Oracle Internet Procurement home page is a central location for requisitioning activity, including finding a specific item, browsing through the catalog, shopping at supplier sites, and creating a one-time requisition. The To Do list contains all the workflow notifications that require your attention. You can see the requisitions that you have created. You can navigate through Internet Procurement two ways. You can use the tabs, or you can use the "train tracks." These are the series of circles in the right-hand column. Figure 13-2 shows a typical Internet Procurement home page.

Shopping in Internet Procurement

If you click Shop, you can choose between shopping from your company's catalog of items that it buys, shopping from a shopping list, shopping from supplier sites, or buying something that is not in a catalog. For example, you may have to buy the

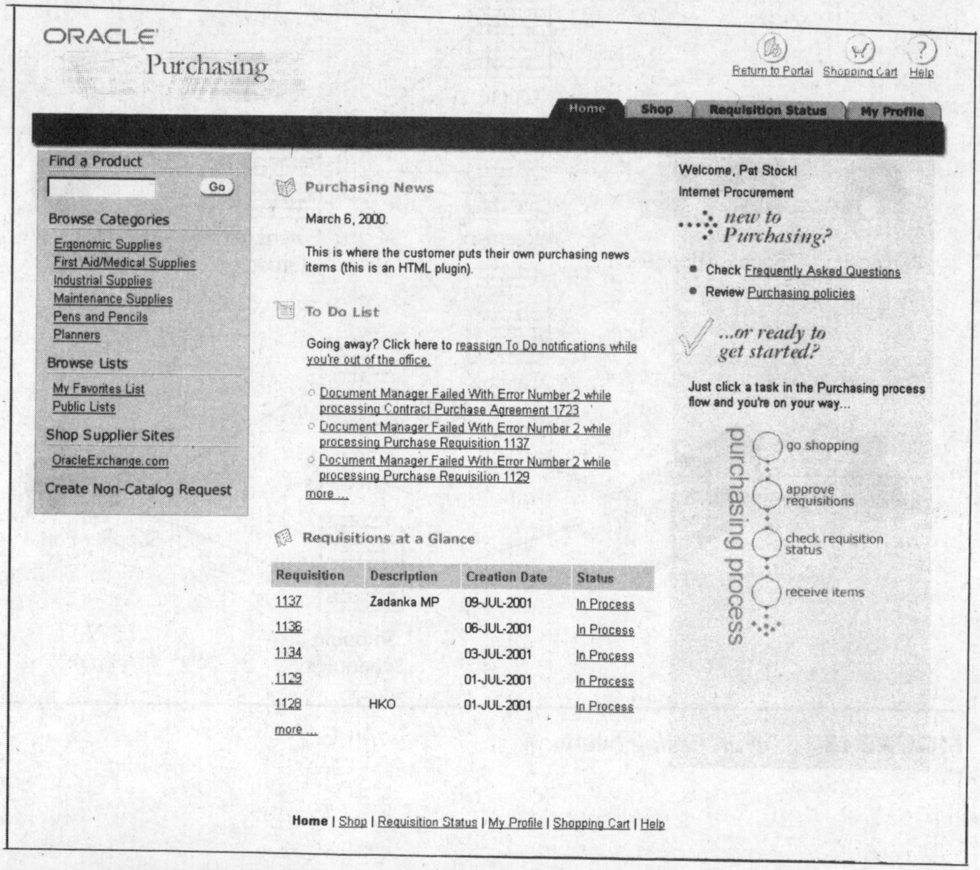

FIGURE 13-2. *Internet Procurement home page*

services of a waste management company to deal with a chemical spill. This service is unlikely to be any catalog. The administration of catalogs is described in the "Administering Catalogs" section. You can create lists from the catalog that you regularly buy. When shopping through the internal catalog, you can search directly for the item or browse through categories to locate the item. From either the catalog search results or the shopping list, you can select the items and click the Add To Cart button. You will always be able to review the contents of the shopping cart by clicking the global icon at the top right of the browser. When a shopping cart is active, the icon will be displayed in reverse video. When checking out the shopping cart, the train track symbols guide you through the process.

A core feature of the catalog in Internet Procurement is the searching capability using the Intermedia index. Although a full explanation of the Intermedia index is beyond the scope of this book, it gives the capability to very efficiently search a text string. That string could be the item description, the category that the item is classified within, or attributes that describe the item.

Shopping at Supplier Sites
You can set up links to other sites, such as TPN Register. You can select items from their catalog and return the selected items into a shopping basket in Internet Procurement.

Finding Requisition Status
To find the status of requisitions, you can review the Requisitions at a Glance section of the home page, or you can click the Requisition Status tab. The second-level tabs from here are Notifications, Receiving, Requisitions, and Approvals. You can cancel or withdraw the requisitions from the Notifications tab. You can also receive approved requisitions from here.

Reviewing Notifications
Any workflow activity can send a notification to an individual. This may be just a "for your information only" (FYI), such as a batch load finishing, or a process may be awaiting your input (To Do). An FYI notification may be that a particular purchase order had been approved. A To Do notification may be that a batch load has failed and may need to be resubmitted. You can respond to To Do notifications from within this tab.

Receiving
The Receiving tab allows you to notify the system that your ordered items have been received. The payables invoice submitted from the supplier will be matched against this receipt.

■ **Receive**   You can receive from the list of approved PO lines in the "My Items to Receive" area, or you can click the Receive link on the train track on the left-hand side.

- **Return** You can notify the system that you are returning received items to the vendor (RTV). The RTV will be let the Payables department know the quantity that should be paid for when the invoice arrives.

- **Correct Receipts** If you make a mistake in the receiving of the purchase order items, you can correct the receipt quantities by clicking the Correct Receipts link.

- **View Receipts** You can view items that you have received in My Receipts at a Glance area, or you can click the View Receipts link on the train track on the left-hand side.

Approvals

If there are any requisitions or purchases orders for which your approval is pending, you will see them listed in this tab.

Setting Your Profile

When setting your profile within Internet Procurement, you can specify your preferred date format, the number of rows returned in a page, and the location that goods you order should be delivered to.

Administering Catalogs

Oracle provides a Web-based environment for managing the catalogs. The catalogs can be built from internal information, or suppliers may publish their catalogs to you. Administering the catalogs includes creating the structure or classification scheme for the catalog, deciding how items in the catalog should be described, and loading the content.

Creating the Catalog Structure

The e-Content Manager responsibility, delivered with Internet Procurement, includes a schema editor. The *schema* is the classification scheme of the catalog. You can modify this classification scheme by adding categories in the schema editor. Oracle also provides a bulk load capability. You can define the catalog structure in a spreadsheet or XML file and upload it. To get the files for upload, you can click the Download Bulkload Resources.

Categories Categories can come from Oracle Applications Category definitions, they may come from supplier catalogs when they are loaded into Internet Procurement, or they may be added in the schema editors. To be able to process a requisition into Oracle Applications, the catalog category needs to be a category in the Purchasing functional area. The definition of categories is explained in Chapter 3

As you define Genus categories in the catalog, you can associate the Oracle Applications category.

Descriptors   There are two types of descriptors: local and global. *Global* descriptors describe all items. An example of a global descriptor might be an item number. A *local* descriptor describes all items within a category. For example, all electrical products must have wattage, voltage, and phase as descriptors. To add a new global descriptor, click the Schema Editor page. Ensure that you have no category selected and click Edit Base Descriptors. You can define the descriptor as numeric or string, and you can control whether the descriptor will be visible when selecting items. To add a local descriptor, click a category to make the descriptors specific to the category.

Table of Contents   The table of contents is how you navigate through the catalog. The table of contents is a list of item categories. These categories are arranged in a hierarchy. Each category in the hierarchy either may contain lower-level categories or cataloged items. Oracle uses the term "Master category" to describe the first level in the hierarchy, "Intermediate category" to describe the categories that you navigate to, and "Genus category" to describe the categories that have items associated with them. To maintain the category hierarchy, click the Table of Contents page. If you click the New Entry button, you will create a new master-level category. If you click the Edit button next to the category, you can add additional categories to it.

Loading Content into the Catalog

You can upload items and their descriptors by using XML files or spreadsheets. If you download a spreadsheet for a specified category, the category descriptors will be included in the downloaded spreadsheet. The files you download also contain examples of how to load items and descriptors. You can choose to load just the catalog items, the items with their associated prices, or prices and discounts.

When you have prepared your catalog content, you can load it by clicking in the Load Items and Price Lists. You can browse the file system to locate the file. The Catalog Authoring home page shows you the status of your most recent jobs. You can review the status of all your jobs by clicking the View Bulk Load Status page.

Building Catalog Content from Oracle Applications

When building the Internet Procurement catalog from internal sources, it includes the following:

- Item from the item master
- Requisition templates

- Blanket purchase orders
- Catalog quotation information
- Approved supplier list

To load the catalog you need to create a directory to store the extracted files. You must also set the UTL_FILE_DIRECTORY parameter in the ora.init file and the profile option ECE: Output File Path to point to that directory. You set up the extraction parameters in the Define Catalog Server Loader Values form in the Internet Procurement Setup menu under E-Catalog Admin. You need to run two concurrent programs to extract the data and load it into the unified catalog: Catalog Data Extract - Classifications and Catalog Data Extract – Items. Set the parameter Perform Load to Yes to automatically load the catalog with this submission.

Forms-based Requisitions

The professional forms environment also has requisitioning capability. These forms might still be accessible outside of the Purchasing department, but they have capabilities beyond Internet requisitions, such as creating multiple accounting distribution, encumbrance, and outside processing details. These additional capabilities require additional details and options on the forms; the added complexity may be less suitable for an occasional user than the self-service, Internet requisitions.

Finding Requisitions

You can locate existing requisitions using the Find Requisitions form. You can specify search criteria in the requisition header, such as Buyer, Requestor, or Requisition Number; requisition lines such as Internal Item and Revision or Supplier Item; and requisition distributions such as G/L Data, Charge Account, or Budget Account. Search criteria are grouped onto the following tabs: Item, Status, Date Ranges, Deliver To, Sourcing, and Related Documents. You can choose to return a set of headers, lines, or distributions. You can also create a new requisition from any window of the form by clicking the New button. Once a requisition has been approved, it is visible on the summary window, but you can't open it to change it.

Requisition Preferences

This is a way of setting up defaults for the entry of many requisitions. You can set defaults that will apply for the session. You can override defaulted values at time of entry. You can set defaults for an array of attributes, including Need by Date, G/L Date, Justification, Notes, and Delivery Location.

Entering Requisitions

You can create requisitions from the Requisition Summary form, from the Supplier Item Catalog, and from the Requisitions form. You can enter, edit, and approve requisitions from these forms.

Requisition Headers   The requisition number uniquely identifies the requisition. You can choose to number the requisitions automatically in the Purchasing Options form. You can enter a description for the requisition. You must enter a requisition type. There are two types of requisitions: Purchase Requisitions and Internal Requisitions. The requisition is destined to become either a purchase order or an internal sales order. The internal requisition cycle is explained in the "Internal Requisitions" section. The preparer is defaulted from the user information. The total value of all lines entered in the requisition is expressed in the base currency on the header. Requisition headers are stored in the table PO_REQUISITION_HEADERS_ALL.

Requisition Items   The item information includes a defaulted line number. The line type will be defaulted from the Purchasing options. You can choose a line type. The line types are user-defined, but are all quantity-based, representing the purchase of a quantity of a product; amount-based, representing the purchase of a dollar amount of a service; or outside processing. Outside processing represents value-added services you purchase from a supplier who performs manufacturing operations for you.

If the line type is quantity-based, you may specify a purchasable item, or you may enter a category within the Purchasing category set and identify the product you're requisitioning in the description field. You must also specify a quantity and unit of measure. For inventory items, you must specify a need-by date. If the item attribute Allow Override Of Item Description is set to Yes, you can override the defaulted description. For quantity-based lines, the price will default to the list price for the item but can be overridden.

If the line type is amount-based, you need only specify the category. For amount-based lines, the unit of measure defaults to your base currency, and price defaults to 1 and cannot be overridden. In this case, the quantity represents the dollar amount of the service you're buying.

Outside processing line types require an item number (identified as an outside processing item), unit of measure, quantity, and need-by date. They also require additional details, accessible with the Outside Processing button—job number, operation, and resource sequence for which you are purchasing the outside processing service. See Chapter 16 for additional discussion of outside processing.

If you only have one distribution for this requisition, you can enter it here. The charge account entered in your requisition preferences will be defaulted here. The tax code will be defaulted here from tax defaults in the Purchasing options. Details are in the "Purchasing Options" section later in this chapter. You can override the tax code if the profile Tax: Allow Override Of Tax Code is set to Yes. Requisition Lines are stored in the table PO_REQUISITION_LINES_ALL.

Source Details   In the Source Details, you can give instructions to the buyer. For example, as an engineer for Neptune you might be ordering gold-plated connectors and give instructions to the buyer that the plating needs to be at least 50 microns and the connectors must be in use at a top electronics manufacturer. The Buyer and Request for Quote (RFQ) required flags are defaulted from the item. You can override the default here. You can choose a supplier item number, source document, and line number. Source documents are blanket orders and quotations.

Details   The Details tab includes notes to the receiver, the UN number, the hazard classification, and a flag to denote that a requisition is urgent. The transaction nature and hazard classification are defined in PO lookups.

Currency   The Currency tab is where you enter conversion rates and dates, as well as the conversion into base currency. Base currency is the currency of the set of books where the operating unit for the responsibility posts transactions.

Delivery Information   The requisition may be destined for inventory, may be delivered to a point of use on the shop floor, or may be expensed on receipt. For an inventory destination, an inventory organization is required. For a delivery to a point of use, an inventory org and location are required. For a delivery that will be expensed on receipt, a requestor and delivery location are required.

Source Information   The sources that are available are dependent on the profile PO: Legal Requisition Type. It could be supplier, inventory, or both. You can mix supplier-sourced and inventory-sourced requisitions on the same requisition. If you are sourcing from a supplier, you enter the supplier and supplier site here. You can (optionally) enter a contact and phone number. If you are sourcing from inventory, you enter an inventory org and subinventory.

NOTE
Even if you are restricted to a single source type, Oracle Purchasing will not allow you to enter an invalid combination of source type and item. For example, if the item has Purchased Item set to No and Internally Ordered Item set to Yes, you will not be able to create a supplier-sourced requisition.

Distributions   If you are charging to more than one account, or wish to specify a budget account to encumber with the requisition value, you will need to invoke the Distributions window. For each line on the requisition, you can specify many of the following:

- **Charge Accounts** Charged when the goods are received

- **Budget Accounts** Encumbered when the requisition is approved

- **Accrual Accounts** Credited when the goods are received

- **Variance Accounts** Charged or credited with the difference between the invoice and the purchase order costs

The accounts are built automatically using rules implemented in workflow. To modify these rules, you should talk to both your financial accountant and your system administrator. You can apportion the charges across the distribution lines automatically using partial quantities of the requisition line. You can also specify the project and task that you would like to charge with this requisition. Distributions are stored in the table PO_REQ_DISTRIBUTIONS_ALL.

Outside Processing Information   An outside processing item is an item that represents the service provided by an outside processor in conversion or processing material that you supply to them. If you have requisitioned an outside processing item, the Outside Processing Information button will become enabled. This button opens the Outside Processing window, where you can identify the job, operation, and resource that requires the outside processing service.

NOTE
Outside processing requisitions are typically generated by work in process; see Chapter 16 for further discussion.

Accessing the Supplier Item Catalog   You can search for your required item on the Supplier Item Catalog. You can base your search on the following:

- Commodity codes or categories within any other category set

- Requisition template

- Item number, revision, and description

- Supplier, supplier site, or supplier item number

Or attributes on sourcing documents, such as

■ Deliver to organization and location

■ Line type

You can select from negotiated sources, such as quotes and blanket agreements, prior purchases, sourcing rules, or requisition templates.

See Chapter 3 for details of how to set up category sets and assign items to them. For details on the sources for the documents, review the sections "Requisition Templates" and "Sourcing Rules." Blanket agreements are explained in the "Purchase Orders" section later in this chapter.

Funds Check If you have enabled encumbrance accounting, from the Tools menu you can check that this requisition will not commit you to expenditures that will cause you to overspend your budget. Choose Funds Check, and the message window will pop up to show the funds check status.

Tax Summary From the Tools menu, you can review the Tax Schedule for the requisition. You can see the tax and taxed values for each tax code on the invoice. You can see the tax that will be recoverable (i.e., offsettable against output and sales taxes), and nonrecoverable (i.e., to be treated as an expense). Details on setting up tax for purchasing are laid out in the "Tax Defaulting Hierarchy" section later in this chapter.

Internal Requisitions

Internal requisitions are requisitions that are to be fulfilled from inventory. When a requisition is created, it may be sourced from a supplier, in which case it goes to a requisition pool, or it may be sourced from inventory, in which case an internal sales order will be created to ship it. Internal requisitions can be created because a requisitioner chooses the source type, because Inventory Planning has run and created replenishments from another inventory location, or because MRP has run and the item and facility being planned are replenished from another facility. The internal requisition could be fulfilled from inventory within the same warehouse. For example, Neptune's QA department keeps its own supply of units to be tested in an expense subinventory replenished from finished goods. It could be fulfilled from a different warehouse. For example, Neptune has three distribution warehouses in the United States that are replenished from the manufacturing warehouse. It could be fulfilled from another operating unit. For example, Neptune has a European distribution center that is owned and run by the European subsidiary incorporated in Holland. The Dutch distribution center is replenished from the Boston distribution center. Figure 13-3 shows the sources of supply and demand represented in the Order Management and Purchasing systems for internal requisitions.

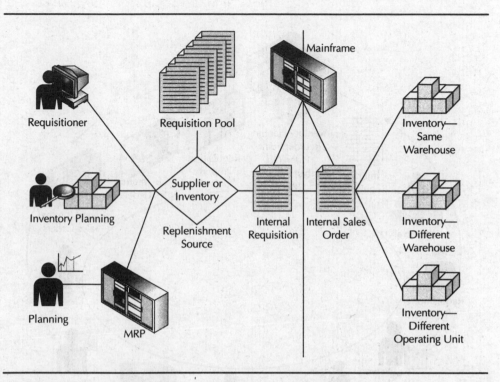

FIGURE 13-3. *Sources of demand and supply for internal requisitions*

The internal sales order is really a mirror of the internal requisition that is used by the Order Management and Shipping systems. An overview of the flow for internal requisitions is laid out in Figure 13-4.

Internal requisitions may originate in other systems. They interface to the purchasing systems through the Requisitions interface. You run the requisitions interface from the Submit form in the Requests menu. Internal requisitions are interfaced into the Order Management interface tables by running Create Internal Sales Orders requests from the Purchasing responsibility. You run the Sales Order import from the Requests menu in the Order Management responsibility. In the Order Management and Shipping systems, you can manage the internal sales order in the same manner as a regular sales order. Movements between warehouses can be direct shipments. A direct shipment is moved into the receiving location in the ship-to warehouse immediately on shipment. A movement may be an in-transit movement. When the shipping warehouse ships the internal sales order, Oracle puts the inventory into in-transit in the table RCV_SHIPMENTS. The shipment is placed into inventory when it is delivered at the receiving warehouse. The shipment may also go through receiving and inspection if the item's receiving routing requires it in the receiving warehouse.

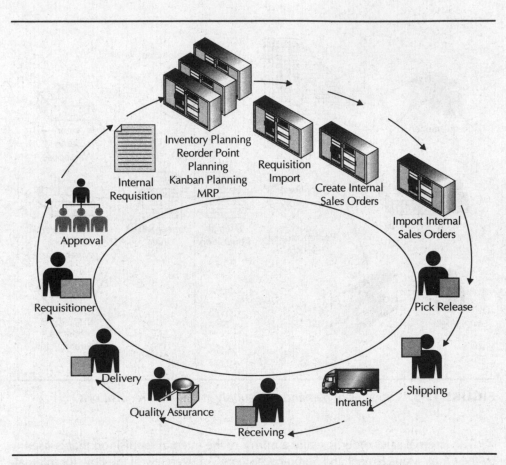

FIGURE 13-4. *Overview of internal requisitions flow*

Requisitioner Setup   The requisitioner must be authorized to create requisitions that are sourced internally through the profile PO: Legal Requisition Type.

Item Setup   The item must be set up to have Internal Orders Allowed set to Yes on the Order Management attributes. The Item must have a Source Type of Inventory on the General Planning attributes. The requisition will be created in the Unit of Issue defined in the Purchasing attributes.

Inventory Setup   Sourcing information is defined at the item, subinventory, and organization levels. The source is evaluated in the following sequence:

- **Item/Subinventory**   Defined when you create subinventory items
- **Subinventory**   Defined in the subinventory sourcing options

■ **Item**   Specified in general planning attributes

■ **Organization**   Defined in the organization setup

How internal requisitions are transacted between organizations is defined in the Shipping Network in MTL_INTERORG_PARAMETERS. You define the shipping network from the Inventory Organization form in the Tools menu. You need to define the following:

■ **Internal Order Required**   Defines whether transfers between organizations can happen without paperwork being generated.

■ **Transfer Type**   Defines whether the inventory will be moved into in-transit or will be immediately available in the destination warehouse on shipment.

■ **Receipt Routing**   Defines whether the goods need to be moved through a receiving pipeline, directly delivered into inventory, or inspected when received in the destination organization. Inspection might be needed due to possible damage in-transit or transfer of management responsibility for the inventory on receipt.

■ **FOB Point**   Defines the point at which responsibility for the goods in-transit passes to the destination organization. Responsibility may pass on shipment or on delivery.

■ **Transfer Charge Type**   Defines how the costs are uplifted in the destination organization to reflect carriage costs: percentage or amount.

Strategic Sourcing and Supply-based Management

Oracle Purchasing comes with a set of tools to locate, approve, and manage sources of supply. The overall flow through the strategic sourcing and supply management solution is illustrated in Figure 13-5.

The process starts with creating requests for quotes. The requests can be addressed to many suppliers.

Supplier Lists

The suppliers can be identified with a supplier list. Neptune has a supplier list for electronic components—one for plastic moldings and one for sheet aluminum casing. To create a supplier list, navigate to the Supplier Lists form in the Supply Base menu.

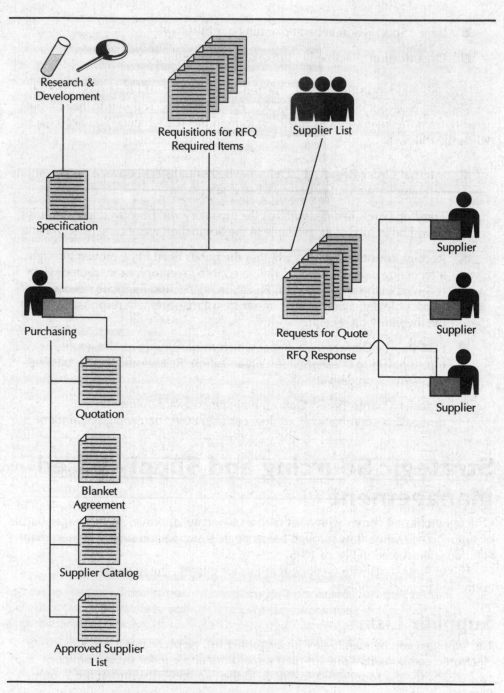

FIGURE 13-5. *Strategic sourcing and supply management flow*

Requests for Quotations

Items may be defined as requiring a request for quotation. For example, you may want to ensure that every time a requisition for artwork is issued, an RFQ is sent to four different graphic design houses. You may also have a new specification coming in from research and development, for which reliable suppliers, capable of delivering the appropriate quality of material, must be sought. The mechanism Oracle Purchasing provides for sourcing suppliers is an RFQ. To create an RFQ, navigate to the RFQ form in the RFQ and Quote menu. You can also create RFQs from the Autocreate form. The Autocreate form can show a list of requisitions that may require an RFQ. You can select the requisition items you would like added to the RFQ. For more detail about how to create an RFQ using Autocreate, see the "Autocreate" section later in this chapter.

RFQ Headers

You can set the RFQ to be automatically numbered, or you can enter your own numbers by setting the document numbering in Purchasing options. Purchasing supports three types of RFQ:

■ **Catalog**   Used for items that will be ordered regularly

■ **Standard**   Used for one-off items or items that are ordered infrequently

■ **Bid**   Used to source a specific quantity of an item to be delivered at a certain site on a certain date

Oracle prints the due date on the RFQ. The RFQ must be received by the due date. The medium for communication of the RFQ response is specified in the reply via. It can be e-mail, mail, or fax. Oracle Purchasing also provides a close date. If you enter a quote from an RFQ that is closed, Oracle will give you a warning alerting you to the status of the RFQ. The RFQ status can be any of the following:

■ **In Process**   Or being created.

■ **Active**   Or ready to print.

■ **Printed**   At least one copy.

■ **Closed**   When you change the status to closed, the system will delete all follow-up notifications. Change the RFQ to this status when you do not want any more responses to the RFQ.

By checking the Approval Required box, quotes can only be created from approved RFQ responses. By default, the user creating the RFQ is assigned as the buyer. The buyer will be notified of any RFQ responses via workflow notifications. The effectivity dates are those required of the quotes.

You can set payment and freight terms and set FOB point by clicking the Terms button.

You can address your RFQ to any number of suppliers by clicking the Suppliers button. This shows you suppliers and the status of their RFQ responses. You can add suppliers directly in this window, or you can add them from a supplier list.

RFQ Lines

You can specify a quantity or amount-based line type for the line. An amount-based line might be to produce the artwork for the badging of the new palmtop product line. The category will be defaulted from the item if entered and cannot be overwritten. If you choose an amount-based line type, you must choose a category. You can let the suppliers know the price you are looking for in the Target Price. If you click the More tab, you can define order quantities that are needed.

You can refine your target prices by defining price breaks. Price breaks are implemented in the same tables that Purchasing uses for defining shipments. You define price breaks by clicking the Price Breaks button. You can specify the quantity, price, effectivity dates, and delivery location. You can also refine the payment and freight terms and specify the lead time if suppliers specify different prices for immediate shipment of small quantities. You can also define tax codes and matching criteria at this level. Match levels can require that a supplier invoice have a corresponding purchase order (two-way match), purchase order and receipt (three-way match), or purchase order receipt and approved inspection (four-way match).

Quotations

Oracle Purchasing allows you to copy from the RFQ and create a quotation. From the Tools menu in the RFQ form, you can copy the following:

- Entire RFQ
- Just the header
- The header and the lines

You can choose to include or exclude the RFQ attachments when you create the quote. You must specify the supplier and the supplier site that you have received the quote from. The quote has the same structure as the RFQ. The header will be prepopulated with the RFQ that the quote was created from, but you can overwrite it. There is a quotation number from your own company's document sequencing as well as the supplier's quote number. Quotations are of the same three types as the RFQs. The effectivity dates for the quotation are in the header. The quotation is always from one supplier. The supplier information is populated in the header. You will only be able to create a quote if the supplier is one of the suppliers on the RFQ. If you copy an RFQ to a quotation for a supplier that has already quoted against this RFQ, you will receive a warning message but be able to process. You can also create quotations manually and create the reference to the RFQ by hand. You can approve the quotation for use as a sourcing document in the creation of purchase orders by clicking the Approve button. This will start a workflow approval process. Approval hierarchies, security hierarchies, and approval workflows are explained in the section "Approval Groups and Their Assignments." You can also approve quotations in a dedicated approval form. To approve quotations in this form, navigate to the Approve Quotations form in the RFQs and Quotations menu. You can locate quote lines by item and revision, item category, RFQ and RFQ line, supplier, quotation number, and project. The results are a set of shipments. You can approve the shipments individually, or you can select a single shipment and approve all shipments in the quotation by clicking Approve Entire Quotation.

Sourcing

When reliable sources have been established, you can allow those sources to default onto requisitions and purchase orders as they are created. Figure 13-6 illustrates how sources are determined and how they influence the creation of supply.

Oracle Purchasing allows for an approved supplier list, sourcing rules, and a bill of distribution to define approved sources for an item, item category, or inventory organization.

Defining Suppliers

You define suppliers in the Suppliers form in the Supply Base menu. For a supplier, you can define the following:

■ **General Information**   Such as name, taxpayer ID, and parent company. You can also specify a customer number for payables receivables netting functionality.

■ **Classification Information**   Such as Type (employee for expense payments, distributor for commission payments, etc.) or Standard Industry Classification (SIC Code).

■ **Accounting Information**   Such as Accounts Payable Control and Prepayment accounts.

■ **Control Information**   For matching basis and order limits.

■ **Payment Information**   Including the payment terms and aging basis.

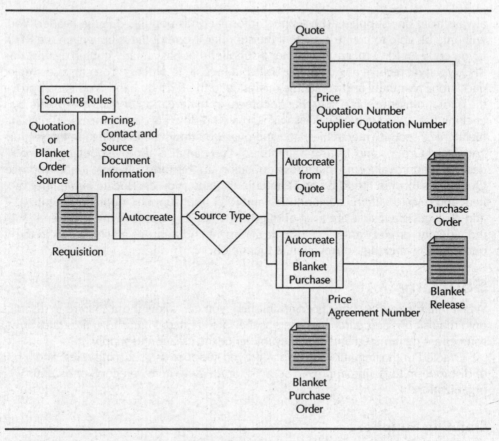

FIGURE 13-6. *Automatic sourcing flow*

- ■ **Back Account** For direct deposit information.

- ■ **EDI Information** For funds transfer.

- ■ **Purchasing Information** Including ship-to and bill-to addresses for RTV transactions. You can define the preferred Carrier, the FOB point (the point at which ownership passes), and freight terms (defining who is responsible for freight costs). You can also specify a purchasing hold here and give it a reason. New purchase orders will then be held.

- ■ **Receiving Information** Including receipt routing (which defines whether receipts are to be inspected before delivery), tolerances for early and late delivery, and receipt quantity. You can allow or disallow substitute receipts and unordered receipts. You can allow or disallow or warn when planned shipments are received at other locations.

Supplier Sites   Many of the terms defined for the supplier can be refined for each supplier site. A supplier site has a name, an alternate name, and an address. Each supplier site can have site uses of the following:

- **Pay**   Location to address payments.

- **Purchasing**   Location to address purchase orders.

- **RFQ Only**   Location to address RFQs.

- **Procurement Card**   Means that the supplier accepts procurement card payments. Procurement cards are like credit cards that are issued to the employee for corporate purchases. The purchase orders are sent to the supplier with a procurement card number. The supplier informs the card issuer of the fulfillment of the order. The credit card issuer then sends the transaction file to Oracle Purchasing for the creation of payables invoices, remittances, and distributions.

You can specify communication methods with the supplier site for phone, fax, and telex. You can also specify contacts; accounting information; matching criteria; and bank account, EDI, and tax information. In the Purchasing information you can specify pay on receipt information.

Managing Supplier Statuses

When an entry is made in an approved supplier list, the entry is assigned a status. The status controls the activities allowable for a supplier through the supplier status. You can create statuses and assign allowable actions by navigating to the Supplier Statuses form in the Supply Base menu.

Sourcing Rules

To define a sourcing rule, navigate to the Sourcing Rules form in the Supply Base menu. Give the sourcing rule a name and description. You can make it apply for all organizations or for a specified organization. You can make planning evaluate it when planning a supply chain. You can copy it from an existing sourcing rule. Sourcing rules can have many effective date ranges. For example, you might switch preferred suppliers of plastic resin during high demand for fuel oil in mid-winter and late spring.

In the Shipping Organizations, you can choose to

- **Transfer From**   Another facility's finished goods (specified by the org code)

- **Make at**   Another facility (specified by the org code)

- **Buy From**   A supplier and (optionally) a supplier site

You can specify allocation percentages. The allocation must total 100 percent. Oracle Purchasing will request from sources in order of rank. You may have two sources defined for the same shipping org with two different shipping methods and lead times.

You can assign sourcing rules to an item, a category of items, an organization, or an item in an organization, or you may use it globally.

NOTE
You can only define sources for an item category if the profile option MRP: Sourcing Rule Category Set has been set.

Planning uses a set of Sourcing Rules and Bills of Distribution (BODs) to choose the source for any given requirement. This set of sourcing rules is called an *assignment set*. A bill of distribution is similar in nature to a sourcing rule, but specifies sourcing for a number of destination organizations. They are explained fully in Chapter 11. You can assign the sourcing rule to an assignment set by clicking the Assignment Set button, or you can go to the Assignment Set form.

Assignment Sets

As explained in the preceding section, you associate a sourcing rule with an item, category, customer warehouse, and so on through assignment sets. To create an assignment set, navigate to the Assign Sourcing Rules form in the Supply Base menu. Give the assignment set a name and description. When you make the assignment, you make it to an assignment type. For example, you can assign a sourcing rule to the following:

- **Item** For example, resistor RS11452 might come from RS Components.

- **Item Category** For example, electronic components might come from Philips Components.

- **Item in Warehouse** For example, speakers for the U.S. manufacturing plant might come from Boston Acoustic Research. Speakers for the U.K. assembly plant might come from Celestion.

- **Item Category in Warehouse** For example, all monitors in North America will be sourced from Sony. All monitors in Northern Europe will be sourced from Philips.

- **Organization** For example, everything for the Austin final assembly facility is sourced from the Austin manufacturing facility.

- **Global** If only one sourcing rule exists.

You can assign the organization, customer, and customer site if sourcing for a customer organization, item, or category depending on the assignment type chosen. You can choose to assign a sourcing rule or a bill of distribution. The assignment set name Purchasing uses is specified in the profile option MRP: Default Sourcing Assignment Set.

Approved Supplier Lists

The orientation of the *Approved Supplier List* (ASL) is a list of items and commodities that have approved sources from a list of suppliers. You can specify the quotes and blanket orders to source from, or you can set the profile option PO: Automatic Document Sourcing to default the latest approved sourcing document rather than specify one on the ASL.

To create an ASL, navigate to the Approved Supplier Lists form in the Supply Base menu. You can review a list of ASLs from the ASL Summary form. You can specify the manufacturer of the product, the distributor of the product, or a company that both sells and distributes. You must specify the name of the supplier; you can optionally specify the site that you purchase from. You can specify the approval status of this supplier to supply the items. In the Details tab, you can record a Review By Date. If this is a distributor, you can specify the manufacturer they must source from. For example, if Neptune is purchasing handheld multimeters for bench work, they may specify RS Components as the distributor and Fluke as the manufacturer. You can also specify that this ASL applies to your entire enterprise or a single facility. There is, however, always an organization that is responsible for negotiating on behalf of subsidiaries and operating units. This is denoted by the owning organization. You can create sourcing documents, supplier scheduling information, and planning information by clicking the Attributes button.

You must specify the unit of measure that will be used when creating purchase orders and the method of creating releases against blanket orders, which could be any of the following:

- Manual release through Autocreate

- Automatic release in complete status

- Automatic release in incomplete status

You can specify the maximum amount that a supplier can issue a price increase for without generating an exception. You can specify a country of origin to be defaulted onto purchase orders. Country of origin is the country where the majority of the value was added. For example, Neptune imports completed assemblies from Malaysia. The final badging and testing is done in the Austin plant. When Neptune supplies its product to its customers, the country of origin will be Malaysia. You can create a local approved supplier list based on a global one by clicking the Create Local button. A sample ASL is shown in Figure 13-7.

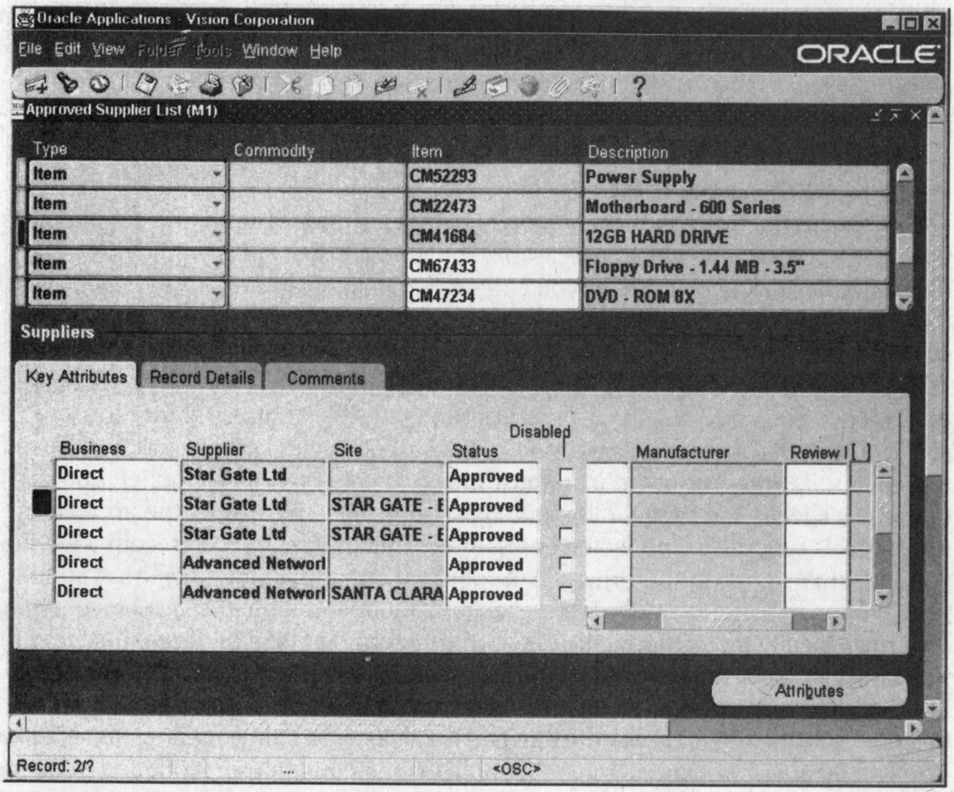

FIGURE 13-7. *A sample approved supplier list*

Source Documents   Source document types are blanket orders or quotes. You can specify many source documents and lines on those documents. Blanket orders will be used over quotes. The source document may be in an active or inactive status, and items may be sourced from these documents between their effective dates.

Planning Constraints   You can specify order modifiers. These will change the quantities requested by planning by rounding up to a minimum order quantity or a fixed order quantity. You can specify the lead time the requirements should be offset to arrive at the Purchase release date. You can also specify the delivery calendar that the supplier uses to ensure that the materials are scheduled to arrive on a delivery date before the need-by date. You can specify the capacity of the supplier over different date ranges. Tolerance fences record the percentage that demand issued to a supplier can change within the time fence days. For example, you may be able to change the demand placed on a supplier by 50 percent if the supplier has 60 days to react, but you can only change by 5 percent if the supplier has only 2 days to react.

Supplier Scheduling   In the Supplier Scheduling tab, you can enable the supplier for planning and shipping schedules. You can assign a scheduler to this particular item and supplier. You can automatically create shipping and planning schedules by checking the Enable Autoschedule box. You can specify the bucket pattern code for planning and shipping. These are the sequenced time buckets (days, weeks, months, and so on) of declining granularity as the time buckets get further into the future. You can specify the schedule type to use for planning and shipping. This defines whether to include forecast, forecast and orders, or material plans in the schedule. You can enable the authorization of raw material procurement or conversion within a number of days of your demand in the Authorizations section.

AutoCreate

AutoCreate allows you to create different target documents from the requisition pool. You can consolidate requirements onto purchase orders, lowering the ordering and administration costs. AutoCreate can also create an RFQ if the requisition is for an item that must have an RFQ raised. An overview of the AutoCreate function and the different document types that feed it and are created by it, is illustrated in Figure 13-8.

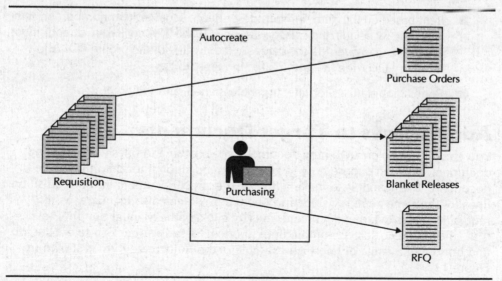

FIGURE 13-8.   *Automatic creation of documents with Autocreate*

Finding Requisitions in the Requisition Pool

To minimize the cost of creating and communicating purchase orders, requisitions are "pooled." A purchasing agent then gathers requisition lines to consolidate onto a single Purchase Order. You can find requisitions based on a number of criteria, including the following:

- Requisition approval status.

- Requestor and preparer.

- Requisition number and emergency requisition number (assigned only in self-service requisitioning).

- Supplier sourcing of sourced or unsourced.

- Suggested sourcing from a supplier or supplier site, document type, and document number.

- Assigned to a particular buyer (defaulted as the person logging into Purchasing, unless the value of the profile PO: Allow Buyer Override In AutoCreate Find is set to Yes).

- To be shipped to a particular delivery location. The working location of the buyer from their assignment in the Human Resources System is used as a default.

- Item based on the item number, description, supplier item number, or item category. By default, the category assigned to the buyer will restrict requisitions. The buyer can override the category if the value of the profile PO: Allow Category Override In AutoCreate Find is set to Yes.

- Requisition statuses for late, urgent, assigned, and RFQ required.

Adding Lines to Target Documents

You can choose to create a new document, or you can add lines to an existing document. You can choose how to group the requisition lines onto the created document. The default is to make a line on the target document for all requisition lines for the same item, revision, and line type. You can also manually assign requisition lines to target document lines by clicking the Manual button. Press CTRL-click a line to select multiple lines at once. Press SHIFT-click to select the top and bottom of a range of lines. An example of the Autocreate form is shown in Figure 13-9.

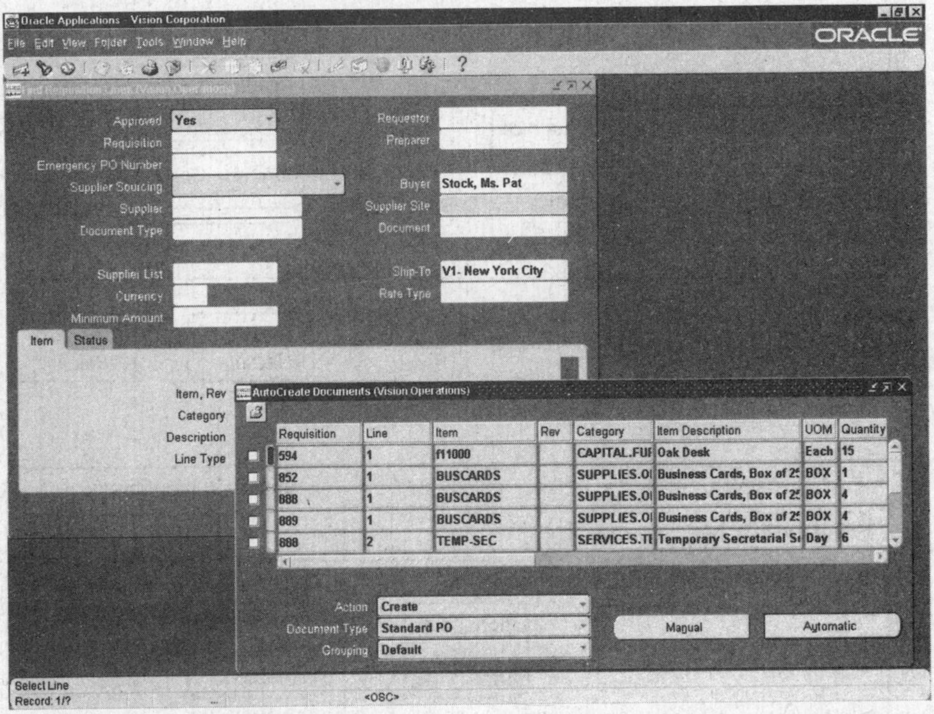

FIGURE 13-9. *Autocreate purchase orders form*

Purchase Orders

Purchase orders in Oracle are documents with a header, lines, shipments, and deliveries. An overview of how the purchase order tables are structured is given in Figure 13-10.

This structure is used to implement many types of purchase orders, including the following:

- **Standard purchase orders** These are orders for specific quantities of goods or services to be delivered on a given date or dates.

- **Blanket purchase agreements** These are agreements set up to cover a long period. They provide some security of supply and price to the customer and some certainty of demand for the supplier. They specify goods and services to be supplied, but no obligation to take delivery and compensate the suppler is established.

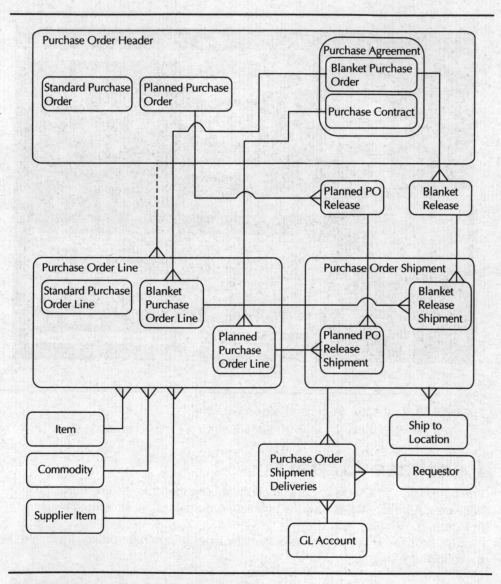

FIGURE 13-10. *Purchase order structure*

■ **Blanket releases** These are the purchase orders released against a blanket order. They inherit the terms, conditions, and prices of the blanket order. Delivery schedules are established for the releases. The release establishes obligations to compensate the supplier.

■ **Contract purchase agreements** A contract purchase agreement can establish terms and conditions of supply without specifying the goods or services to be supplied. Purchase orders that specify this agreement will inherit the terms and conditions of the agreement.

■ **Planned purchase orders** A planned purchase order is similar to a blanket order, but requires a tentative delivery schedule.

■ **Scheduled releases** These are purchase orders released against a planned purchase order. They inherit the terms, conditions, and prices from the planned purchase order.

Major Purchase Order Features

The purchase orders are the core of the purchasing system. To understand the purchase order system, you need to understand features that let the purchase order interact with the rest of the purchasing system and the rest of Oracle Applications. These features are explained in the following sections.

Workflow-Driven Automatic PO and Release Creation

You can let workflow create releases and purchase orders for approved requisitions where sourcing has been defined or can be determined. The workflow for creating purchase documents is called *PO Create Documents*. It is initiated at the end of the requisition approval workflow if the Attribute Is Automatic Creation Allowed is set to Yes.

Budget Checking

You can reserve funds when you enter a requisition and purchase order. You can choose to encumber a budget at requisition or purchase order. Planned purchase orders can reserve funds and have the encumbrance reversed when a release is generated against the planned purchase order. To use encumbrance accounting, you must enable the budgetary control flag for a set of books. When you enable the budgetary control flag, the system automatically creates encumbrances from requisitions and purchase orders. You define a set of books in the Setup menu in the General Ledger responsibility.

Purchase Order Approvals

Purchase orders can go through their own approval cycle. For example, a new supplier of important components may require the approval of Engineering and Manufacturing before the purchase order can be issued. Approvals are workflow-driven. They can be delivered in the universal work queue, or they can be delivered in e-mail. You can assign approval limits and authorities for commodities and ranges of expenses. Approval limits are explained in the "Approval Groups and Their Assignments" section later in this chapter.

Purchasing Notifications

Purchasing will alert buyers to other conditions requiring action, such as blanket orders nearing expiration date or order quantities not released. You can establish notification conditions that specify the number of days before the condition is met. You set the Notification Controls from the Tools menu on the Purchase Orders form.

Revision Control and Change History

Purchase orders are revision-controlled documents. Changes to certain attributes of the purchase order will cause the purchase order to have to be reapproved. Changes to attributes will cause the revision number to be incremented. A history is kept of the changes and person making the change. Attribute changes at the header, line, shipment, or distribution may cause a document revision. Attributes at the header that cause a document to be revised include (but are not limited to) payment terms, expiration date, buyer, ship-to, and bill-to. Attributes at the line that cause a document to be revised include item, revision, supplier item, quantity, and price. Attributes on the shipment that cause a document to be revised include quantity, promised date, need-by date, and latest acceptance date.

Shipment Schedules

You can request the quantity on a purchase order line to be shipped to many places and at many different times. You can see the quantities ordered, received, invoiced, and cancelled for each line shipment. On creating a shipment, Purchasing will create a distribution or delivery for the shipment. For more information, see the "Distributions" section.

Acceptances

The supplier's acknowledgement of the purchase order is recorded as a supplier acceptance on the purchase order. You enter and view acceptances from the Tools menu when reviewing a purchase order.

Print Purchase Orders

Purchase orders can be printed or faxed if you have any facsimile software that is compatible with the Commerce Path Fax Command Language. You can choose to print all, new, or changed purchase orders. Purchase orders print with attached text notes; they can also be printed in multiple languages. To print purchase orders, navigate to the Submit Requests form and choose Purchase Order Report.

Copy Purchase Orders

You can copy purchase order documents to other documents from the Tools menu in the Purchase Order form. You can copy from

- One standard purchase order to another

- A standard purchase order to a standard or planned purchase order

- A quote to a standard purchase order or blanket purchase order

Finding Purchase Orders with Purchase Order Summary

Purchasing has a search capability that allows you to enter search criteria, including supplier, ship-to, deliver to, item, purchase order, and related documents, and to see resulting headers, lines, shipments, or deliveries. To find purchase orders, navigate to the Purchase Order Summary form in the Purchase Orders menu.

Entering Search Criteria

You can search based on order number and release, type, supplier and supplier site, ship-to organization and location, bill-to organization and buyer, line number, type, and shipment. If you are interested in documents for an item, you can search on internal item number, item category, description, and supplier item number. If you're interested in date information, you can use the dates ordered, approved, promised, needed by, or closed. You can search on approval status, control status, and hold status, as well as whether the order is frozen or firmed. If you have found a document that references a purchase order, you can use related contract, internal, or supplier quote number; line number, paper, or system requisition number; receipt; or invoice number as selection criteria. You can search based on the delivery organization, subinventory, and location, as well as the requestor. You can search based on the actual or budget account or project and task to be charged. You can also create a new purchase order or release from the search criteria.

Viewing Search Results

You can choose to view the headers, lines, shipments, or deliveries resulting from your query. You can choose to review all of the releases for the blankets you have selected.

Headers Search Results

The headers results window is a folder form, meaning that you can customize the columns of the purchase order header that are displayed. You can include any column, including purchase order number, revision number, release number, supplier and supplier site, buyer, and amount. You can open the PO you have selected, and you can move to a line inquiry for the order or orders you have selected. You can create a new PO or a new release of the selected PO.

Lines Search Results

The line results window is also a folder form. You can include any column, including purchase order number, line number, item number and category, line description, and quantity. You can open the PO that the line is on for review, and you can move to a shipment inquiry for the line or lines you have selected. You can create a new PO or a new PO release of the selected line's purchase order.

Shipments Search Results

The shipments results window is another folder form. You can include any column, including purchase order number, line number, release number, item number, ship-to organization, location, and quantity. You can open the PO that the shipment is on for review and maintenance, and you can move to a distribution inquiry for the shipment or shipments you have selected. You can create a new PO or a new PO release of the selected shipment's purchase order.

Distribution Search Results

Like the other windows, the distribution results window is also a folder form. You can include any column, including purchase order number, release number, line number, shipment number, distribution number, item number, quantity, amount, and account to be charged. You can open the PO that the shipment is on for review and maintenance. You can create a new PO or a new PO release of the selected distribution's purchase order.

Entering and Maintaining Purchase Orders

You can create and maintain purchase orders either from the Purchase Summary form by clicking the Open button, or you can navigate to the Purchase Order form in the Purchase Order menu. An example of the Purchase Order form is shown in Figure 13-11.

Purchase Order Header Information

The purchase order header information includes the purchase order number and revision number, purchase order type, supplier, supplier site and contact at that site, buyer (defaulted to the person creating the purchase order), status, total amount, and (optionally) a description.

Approvals

You can start the validation and approval process by clicking the Approve button. Validation errors will be shown if the purchase order cannot start the valid approval process, due to missing data, for example.

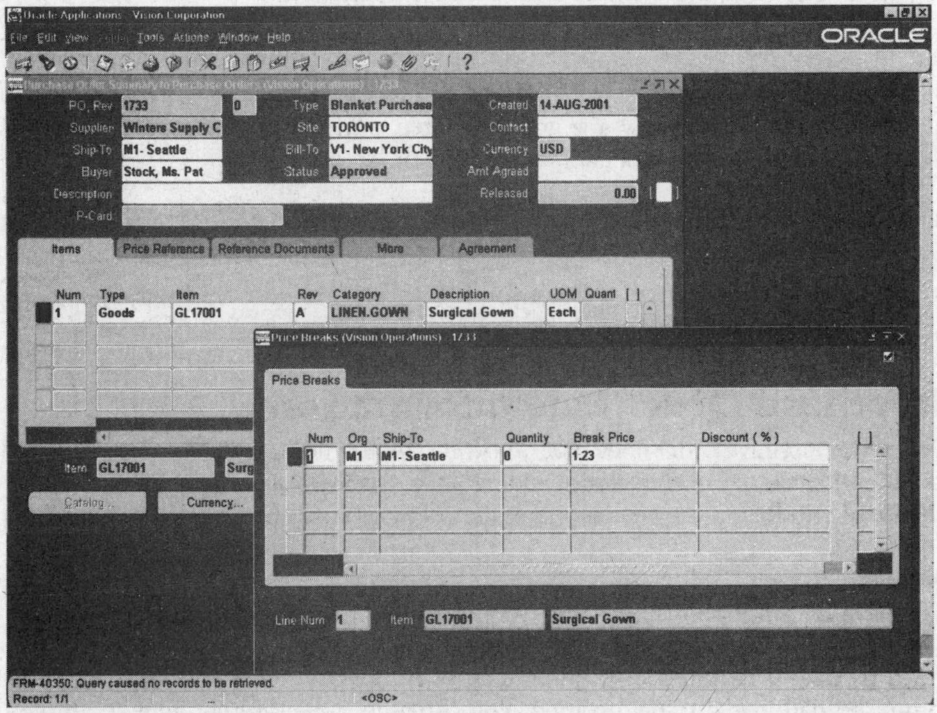

FIGURE 13-11. *Blanket purchase order with price break*

Terms

By clicking the Terms button, you can specify payment and freight terms, the preferred carrier, FOB point, and whether the purchase order is pay on invoice or receipt. You can identify the order as firm, which will suppress "reschedule-in" messages in the planning process. You can declare that an acceptance is required and specify a date by which it must be received. If you mark this order as a supply agreement, you can specify agreement controls. You can specify the effectivity date for the order, the minimum value order that will be released at any one time, and the maximum amount that the prices on the order can be uplifted by.

Tools Menu

There are many useful functions available on the Tools menu when maintaining a purchase order, including the following:

■ **Preferences**   Sets up defaults for many fields to speed entry

■ **Acceptances**   Shows the responses from a supplier in acknowledging the order or issuing change orders

- ■ **Action History** Shows a list of approval actions

- ■ **Copy Document** Allows you to copy from one purchase order document to another of the same type or different type

- ■ **Tax Details** Shows the goods, taxable, and tax (both recoverable and nonrecoverable) for each line on the order

- ■ **Tax Summary** Shows a summary of the goods, taxable, tax recoverable, and nonrecoverable by tax code

- ■ **Convert Currency** Allows you to convert prices to the ordering currency based on the order exchange rate

Purchase Order Line Information

From the purchase order lines block, you can define item, price reference, related documents, hazard classification, and notes to suppliers. The lines are displayed in the same window as the header information. The line number is displayed in all tabs.

Items

The item information includes line type (defaulted from the purchasing options), item, revision, category, and description purchase UOM quantity and price. The need-by date is required for MRP/MPS or inventory planned items, and the promised date can also be recorded. You can record the supplier item and the account to be charged for encumbrance. The extended price is displayed. You can attempt to reserve funds by clicking the Reserve check box.

Price References

The price references include list price defaulted from the line type, item, or document specified in the supplier item attributes, and market price from the item definition. It can be overridden here. It is used for the analysis of cost savings. You can allow prices to be different on releases against this PO by checking the Allow Price Override flag. If you check this flag, you can also set a maximum price.

Reference Documents

You can refer to the contract, quotation line number, and type as well as the supplier's quotation number. These will be automatically populated if you have used copy order to create the document.

More

You can annotate purchase orders with notes to supplier recorded here. You can overwrite the UN number and the hazard class of the material, which are defaulted from the item definition. You can mark that this is a capital expense. If it is a capital expense, the transactions will be moved to Oracle Assets.

Agreements

You can refine the terms agreed for the order as a whole at the line level. You can specify the minimum release quantities and total amount of the agreement, as well as review quantities already released.

Price Breaks

When entering blanket agreements, you can define price breaks by clicking the Price Break button. You can define the price break to be specific to a ship-to location. Enter the price break quantity and amount. The system will display the percentage from the order line price that this represents. You can also input the percentage, and the system will display the amount as you exit the field.

Shipments

If you click the Shipments button in the Purchase Order form, you can split the line into multiple shipments with different dates and locations and see the shipping status of the shipments.

Main

You can see the ship-to organization and locations, quantities, and dates both needed by and promised by the supplier. You can vary the tax code for each shipment if the value for the profile Tax: Allow Override of Tax Code is Yes. If you create a new shipment line, the fields will be defaulted from the previous line, leaving only the quantity to be adjusted.

Receiving and Matching Tolerances

In the More tab, you can see the matching and receiving tolerances. You can specify the percentage of the expected amount within which the receipt will be closed for receiving and billing. You can specify two-, three-, or four-way matching for the shipment. You can specify that the invoice must match the purchase order quantities or receipt quantities. You can choose to accrue the liability on receipt. Items destined for inventory are always accrued on receipt. Expensed receipts may be accrued on receipt or at period end, based on your purchasing options. You can mark the shipment as firm to suppress reschedule-in suggestions by planning.

Receiving Controls

You can review the receiving controls for the shipment by clicking the button of the same name. You can set tolerances for early and late delivery and overshipment, and you can determine whether the system should warn on receipt or prevent entry. You can allow the receipt of substitute items from the supplier. You can set how the receipt should be routed on delivery. It may be delivered directly into inventory, held in the receiving dock before delivery, or sent for inspection.

Distributions

If you click the Distributions button in the Shipments window, you can split the shipment into multiple deliveries with different destinations and Charge Accounts. For example, you might have ordered many copies of a handbook for manufacturing and supply chain applications. The books will be received in one receipt but delivered to six supply chain professionals in the building, each working for a different cost center.

Destination

You can choose a destination type of inventory, expense, or shop floor. The destination is specified as the requestor and their location. For inventory destination types, a subinventory is also required. You can specify any quantity of the shipment to be delivered to this destination. The balance will be created as a new distribution. You can specify the G/L date when the transactions should be reflected in G/L. Recovery rate is the tax recovery rate. You reserve funds by checking the Reserve check box.

Accounting

Under the More tab, you can define the requisition that this order is supplying. If you have used Autocreate to create the purchase order, it will be automatically filled in. The online flag denotes that this is from an online requisition as opposed to a paper requisition system. The accrual, charge, budget, and variance accounts will be built by the Account Generator. You can override accounts here, apart from for outside processing items. The resource is a determinant of the accounts for outside processing items.

Project

You can charge a project or task within a project and specify the expenditure type to be reflected in the project. The quantity can be further allocated between different unit numbers. For example, if Neptune is purchasing specialized optical sensors for auto placement equipment for two different customers, it can record the unit numbers of the Auto Placement equipment.

Outside Processing Information

As covered in requisitions, an outside processing item is an item that represents the service provided by an outside processor in conversion or processing material that you supply to them. If you have ordered an outside processing item, the Outside Processing Information button will become enabled.

Supplier Scheduling

Supplier scheduling allows you to communicate longer-term plans to your suppliers. You can include demand from the Purchasing systems and the Planning systems. You can have sourcing determined by planning and purchasing sourcing. You can communicate using discrete quantities or cumulative quantities ordered since a given date for delivery to a ship-to organization. It also allows you to commit to the raw material costs and conversion costs for your suppliers, as well as the price of the finished goods. You can communicate the schedules using standard X12 and Edifact transactions, printed reports, and supplier self-service transactions. The main flows of the Supplier scheduling system are shown in Figure 13-12.

Defining Bucket Patterns

You need to define how demand will be grouped as you issue the schedule to your suppliers. In the near-term, your supplier will need to know demand day-by-day. Further out in the time horizon, there is less need for that level of detail. To set up a time bucket pattern, navigate to the Bucket Pattern form in the Setup menu. You can give the pattern a name and description and list the number of days, number of weeks, number of months, and number of quarters in the planning horizon.

Defining Schedule Options

You must define how the schedule will be built for each ship-to organization. The organization can be enabled for CUM Management. CUM Management means that the demanded quantities are expressed to the supplier in terms of the cumulative quantity since a date agreed by both parties. This is very important where demand is issued to the supplier very frequently, and there is a danger of counting the demand twice if discrete quantities are issued. CUM Management will be further examined in the section "Managing Cumulative Quantities." You can also state that goods returned to the vendor on an RTV transaction should update the CUM quantity.

In the Defaults section, you can define the sources of demand for the planning and shipping schedules. A central theme here is firm demand and forecast demand. *Firm* demand is a request for the materials to be delivered. *Forecast* is guidance on future demand. A typical planning schedule covers between 4 and 24 months. A typical shipping schedule covers between three and four weeks. An overview of the firm and forecast horizon is illustrated in Figure 13-13.

For the Planning schedule, you can specify it as the following:

■ **Forecasts All** Defining blanket releases; approved requisitions; and unimplemented MRP, MPS, and DRP planned orders as forecast. No firm section of the schedule.

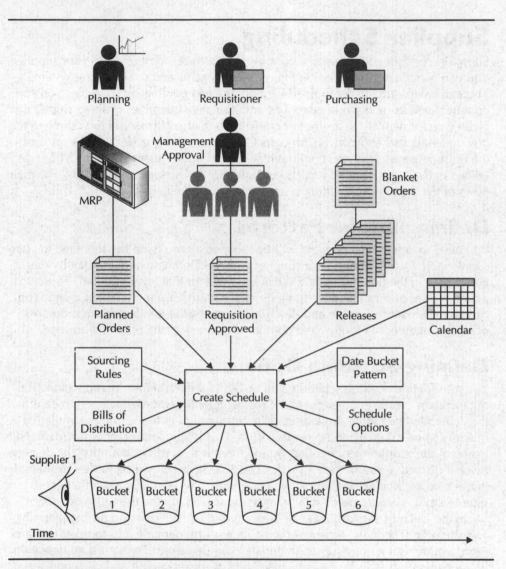

FIGURE 13-12. *Supplier scheduling overview*

- **Forecast Only**   Defining approved purchase requisitions and unimplemented MRP, MPS, and DRP planned orders as forecast.

- **Material Release**   Defining approved supply agreement releases as firm; approved purchase requisitions and unimplemented planned orders as forecast.

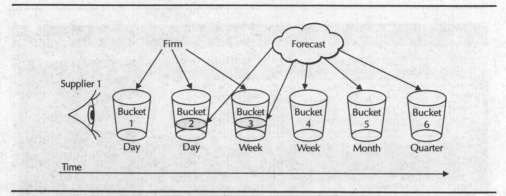

FIGURE 13-13. *Firm and forecast entries in the schedule*

For the Shipping schedule, you can specify it as the following:

■ **Release Only**   Defining just releases as firm demand.

■ **Release and Forecast**   Defining approved supply agreement releases as firm; approved purchase requisitions and unimplemented planned orders as forecast.

You can assign a default Material Requirements Plan (MRP), Master Production Schedule Plan (MPS), and Distribution Requirements Plan (DRP) to use to drive the automatic creation of the schedule.

Creating the Schedule

You can build, rebuild, review, confirm, and print schedules using the Find Supplier Schedules form in the Scheduler Scheduling menu. You can revise a previously issued schedule and simulate what a schedule would look like without actually sending it. You can make changes to the underlying blanket releases and then rebuild the schedule. If authorizations are enabled in the ASL, you can view the highest authorized quantities for an item within the schedule. If CUM Management is enabled for the ship-to organization, the authorized quantity will be the cumulative quantity from the start of the CUM period. If CUM Management is not enabled, the authorized quantity is the quantity since the start of the schedule horizon. An example of the Supplier Scheduling Workbench is shown in Figure 13-14.

Scheduling Options

To build a new schedule, click the Build radio button at the top of the form and click the New button. You must specify the schedule type you are building, the bucket pattern you are creating it into, and the start of the scheduling horizon. If

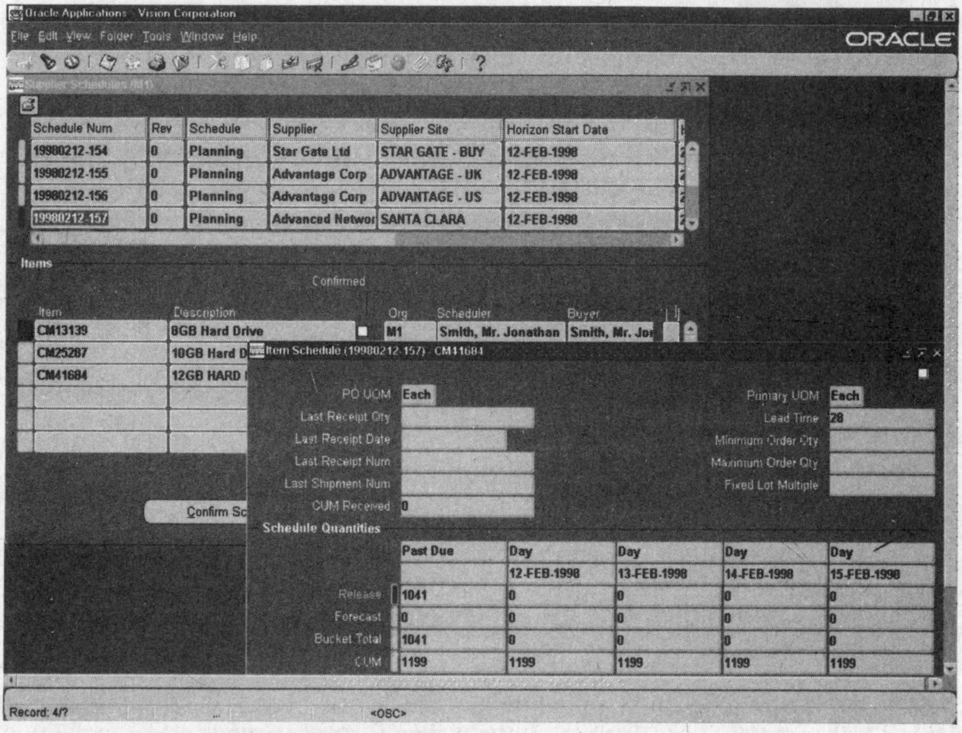

FIGURE 13-14. *Supplier Scheduling Workbench*

your schedule type includes forecast data, you must include an MRP, MPS, or DRP schedule name. You can build the schedule for a combination of the following:

- Supplier

- Ship-to organization

- Category set, item category, item, and description

- Buyer, planner, and scheduler

Schedules and Schedule Items

In the Supplier Schedules window, you can review the schedule information, including schedule number, revision, type, supplier, supplier site, horizon dates, and ship-to org; and the information about the items on the schedule, including number, description, buyer, planner, and scheduler. You can confirm your schedule by clicking the Confirm check box.

Item Schedules

If you click the Item Schedules button, you will be taken to the window of the same name. You can see the schedule for the item displayed in the date buckets of the pattern used by this schedule. You can see the primary UOM and the order modifiers from the planning system, including minimum, maximum, and fixed lot multiple and lead time offset. You can see the Purchasing UOM, last receipt, and shipment information from the shipping system, as well as the cumulative quantity received. The scheduled quantities are broken down into release quantities, forecast quantities, and cumulative quantity.

Autoschedule

If the attributes in the approved supplier list have a supplier site specified and have Autoschedule set to Yes, you can create the schedules with a concurrent program, Autoschedule. You must set the bucket pattern and schedule type for both planning and shipping.

Managing Cumulative Quantities

Much of the functionality in supplier scheduling rests on the communication of cumulative quantities. You set a counter running over a defined period. Receipts add to the cumulative, and Return to Vendor (RTV) transactions subtract from it. The period might be a model year in the automotive industry or a quarter in the electronics industry.

CUM Periods

To set up a CUM period, navigate to the Find CUM Periods form in the CUM Management menu. Choose CUM Periods from the radio group and click the Find button. You define the CUM Period for a given ship-to organization. You can review and adjust the cumulative quantities for the items shipped to this organization by choosing CUM Period Items from the radio group in the Find window or by clicking the button in the CUM Periods window.

CUM Period Items

From the CUM Period Items window, you can review the item, CUM quantity, and UOM for the CUM period, supplier, and supplier site being reviewed. The High Authorizations section of the window shows the current and highest authorization quantities for each authorization type. Authorization types are the following:

- **Finished Goods** Authorization is to procure and convert material. Liability is for finished product at list price.

- **Labor and Material** Authorization is to procure and convert material. Liability is for labor and material cost.

- **Labor** Authorization is to convert material.
- **Raw Material** Authorization is to procure raw materials. Liability is for material cost.

You can make adjustments to the CUM quantities and authorizations by clicking the Adjust button.

Communicating the Schedule to Suppliers

You can communicate schedules to your suppliers in a number of ways, including standard EDI transactions, printed reports, and supplier self-service in the Oracle Internet Supplier Portal. The EDI transactions offer a high degree of automation between supplier systems and your own systems but are expensive to set up. You can communicate long-term planning schedules and shorter-term shipping schedules.

EDI Transactions
The X12 transactions that support the supplier scheduling process are the 830 Planning schedule and the 862 Shipping schedule.

Planning Schedules The planning schedule is of three types: forecast only, forecast with authorizations, and forecast with release. If you use an 830 Forecast with Material Release, you may eliminate the need for a shipping schedule, but the planning schedule becomes the system of record for release information and must be archived.

Shipping Schedules The shipping schedule is more typically used for near-term requirements. Daily buckets are generally used to gather blanket release and purchase order information.

Reports
You can print both the Planning Schedule report and the Shipping Schedule report by navigating to the Report Submission form. Parameters include schedule number and revision, supplier number range, supplier site, and whether this is a test print or not. A test print allows you to print a schedule that is not confirmed.

Supplier Self-Service
The Oracle Internet Supplier Portal has secure self-service inquiry screens for both planning and shipping schedules. It does not offer the degree of automation of EDI, but it is available to any supplier with access to a Web browser without set-up or training costs.

Internet Supplier Portal

Oracle Purchasing also provides extranet access to key suppliers through the Internet Supplier Portal. This system is available over the public Internet and is designed to be usable by an occasional user. The system is built around the Web applications architecture. You can create a user in Oracle Applications and assign the supplier and supplier site to the user. When the supplier logs on, they are restricted to data for that supplier. The Supplier Portal integrates workflow notifications viewer, enabling cross-enterprise business processes, such as registration and order acknowledgement, to be managed at very low cost. It integrates data from four key supplier facing applications:

- Oracle Purchasing
- Oracle Supplier Scheduling
- Oracle Payables
- Oracle Inventory

The capabilities cover the same areas as the core purchasing product: Supply-Base Management, Purchasing, Supplier Scheduling, Outside Processing, Receiving, Invoicing, and Inventory.

Supply-based Management

In Internet Supplier Portal, suppliers can update supplier capacity on the ASL, specify supplier/item order modifiers such as minimum order quantity and lot quantity restrictions, define supplier/item lead times, and view RFQs.

Purchasing

In Internet Supplier Portal, suppliers can acknowledge purchase orders by an accept or reject action; change promise dates for delivery; and view purchase orders with related invoices, receipts, revisions, and order history. Suppliers can review blanket purchase orders and associated releases. They can review planning and shipping schedules. They can review outside processing orders, including quality specifications and attachments.

Receiving

Suppliers can review quality plans and record results for shipments. Suppliers can enter Advance Shipment Notifications (ASN) when goods leave their facility, and view the receipts, eliminating the need for proof of delivery tracking. Suppliers can review their open delivery schedules, any overdue receipts, and their on-time delivery performance.

Invoices

Suppliers can enter Advance Shipment and Billing Notifications (ASBN), confirm the receipt of an invoice, and confirm payment has run.

Configuring Oracle Purchasing

To configure Oracle purchasing, you need to define requisitioners; delivery, shipping, and billing locations; approval hierarchies; document routings; and security.

Locations

At the time of going to press, purchasing uses the standard location model provided by the Human Resource Applications. To set up a location, navigate to the Locations form in the Setup menu. You must give the location a name and (optionally) a description. You can provide a contact for the address and a ship-to site if the location is only a delivery address. For example, the mailroom may be a ship-to address for an office delivery location. You can mark the address as a combination of the following:

- **Ship-to** Making it valid as a ship-to on a purchase order. For example, Neptune warehouse 3.

- **Receiving Site** Making it valid as a receiving location, for receiving transactions. For example, Receiving Dock 1.

- **Bill-to Site** Making it valid as a bill-to printed on a purchase order. This is where the supplier will send his invoice. For example, Neptune Payables department.

- **Internal Site** Making it valid as a ship-to location on an internal requisition.

Buyers

Employees, once defined in the Human Resources system, can then be defined as buyers to the purchasing system. Only buyers can create purchase orders and use the Autocreate functions. The Define Buyers form is in the Setup menu. Buyers are associated with a purchasing category and ship-to location.

Approval Groups and Their Assignments

Approval Groups are a set of authorities to approve documents. Members of the approval group may be such through the jobs or positions assigned to the approval group. The approval group may be granted approval authority for a given document type over the following:

- Range of items
- Range of item categories
- Range of account numbers that the purchases will be charged
- Document value

A given approval group may be assigned approval authority or excluded from the approval of many ranges. For example, Neptune records all maintenance activity in the account range 7000–7999. Computer maintenance is in the account range 7800–7899. An approval group of "MRO Non Computer" is responsible for all maintenance, repair, and overhaul procurement except for computer equipment. This approval group is assigned to a job or position hierarchy for the approval of requisitions and purchase order document types. The Approval Group Definition and Approval Group Assignment form is in the Setup menu. Jobs and positions are part of the Human Resource setup. The approval routing of a document may follow the employee supervisor relationship defined when creating employees, or it can follow the position hierarchy. You make this choice in Financial Options.

Adding Notes to Purchasing Documents

Purchasing has the capability to add brief notes to lines in the More tab. These notes must be less than 240 characters. It also takes advantage of the standard attachments capability to add unlimited text. To add and review attachments, click the paper clip icon in the toolbar. These capabilities include the ability to review the catalog of standard content as a template. For example, you may have a standard terms and conditions template. You may attach this as a template and modify it for a specific order. The capabilities include the ability to attach many kinds of documents, including spreadsheets, graphics, or a reference to a URL. You may attach documents to an item and have these documents applied to all requisitions and purchase orders for this item.

Purchasing Documents Attachment Flow

You can attach text to purchasing documents and have the text flow through dependent documents:

- Requisition attachments are copied to purchase order lines through AutoCreate.
- Blanket order attachments can be reviewed from the release headers.
- Requisition attachments are copied to corresponding RFQ. You can choose to copy the RFQ attachments to a corresponding quote.

Attachment Usages and Printing Attachments on Documents

You can specify where the attached text will be viewable and printable through the assigned usage:

- **Supplier**   Means that the text will be printed on all documents.

- **Receiver**   Means that the text can be attached to RFQs, POs, quotations, receipts, and requisitions, and it will be viewable in the receiving forms and print on the receipt traveler.

- **Approver**   Means that the text can be attached to a requisition and will be displayed to approvers.

- **Buyer**   Means that the text can be attached to a requisition and will be displayed to buyers when POs are created.

- **Internal**   Means that the attachment will be viewable only from the creation form and not printed on documents. The exception is RCV Internal attachments that are visible to receivers and printed on receiving travelers.

- **Payables**   Means that the attachment is viewable in payables during receipt matching.

Purchasing Options

There are some options defined for the operating unit that is running purchasing. These include sources of default; how to accrue liabilities; what level of control you institute over purchase orders, invoices, and receipts; and how to create internal sales orders, document numbering, and tax. To define the purchasing options, navigate to Purchasing Options form in the Setup menu. The tabs are defined in the following sections.

Default Options

You can define the exchange rate type that defaults onto the orders. Purchasing helps you ensure that releases are economic by letting you restrict the minimum release amount. You can set price breaks to be per release or cumulative across orders. Prices can be defaulted as fixed, cost plus, indexed, or variable. You can set the default line type. The number of days that buyers will be warned before quotes expire can be set here. You can enforce that RFQs are required for all requisitions. Tolerances can be set within which a shipment will be considered completely received, within which the shipment will be considered closed for invoice matching, and within which the shipment will be considered completely matched.

Accrual Options

You must define whether to accrue expense receipts at period end or on receipt. Inventory must currently be accrued on receipt. You must also define a default expense accrual account.

Control Options

You can specify various controls and level of controls over orders, receipts, and invoices. And you can prevent orders that exceed the requisition price by a certain percentage from being approved. You might want to only order in full lot quantities. You may have defined an item that is less specific than what you actually require from a supplier. For example, if you defined an item for 1/4-inch threaded fasteners, but require a galvanized black fastener, you can overwrite the description of the item on the order line.

Price Tolerance   You can define the maximum percentage that a purchase order may be created for in excess of the requisitioned value. If you choose to enforce the price tolerance, the purchase order can be created, but it will not be able to be approved.

Lot Quantity   Defines whether requisition line quantities should be rounded into fixed-lot quantities or whether recommendations for such rounding should be presented to the user.

Receipt Close   This defines when a shipment from a supplier can no longer be received against—when it is received, passed inspection, or delivered.

Requisition Cancellation   This defines if purchasing should cancel a requisition when canceling a purchase order: always, optionally, or never.

The other option flags are as follows:

- **Notify If Blanket PO Exists**   To alert purchasing users to the existence of a blanket PO when creating any purchasing document for an item that is on a blanket.

- **Allow Item Description Update**   Allows an item description to be updated on a PO line when that line is created. For example, you may define an item for 1/4-inch threaded fasteners and update the description to include the color.

- **Enforce Buyer Name**   To allow only the buyer assigned to the category to create purchase orders for requisitions within that category.

- **Enforce Vendor Hold**   To prevent the approval of an order for a supplier currently on hold.

Document Numbering Options

You can define whether the document numbers for the purchasing document types are assigned and whether documents are identified by a number or an alphanumeric identifier. You can assign the next number in the numbering sequence for all of the purchasing document types.

Tax Defaulting Hierarchy

The tax defaulting hierarchy allows you to assign precedence to each place that a tax code is stored for defaulting onto an order. Places that you can default from are ship-to location, item, supplier site, supplier, and financial options.

Requisition Templates

Requisition templates are a way of guiding the requisitioner to the items and sources for those items without them having to navigate all purchasable items. If stationery supplies generally comprise 20 items, the user will have only the 20 items to choose from, and prices and sources can be predetermined. To create or modify a requisition template, navigate to the Requisition Template form in the Setup Purchasing menu.

When defining the template, you must give the template a name and description. You can (optionally) set an expiration date. The template type limits the use of the template to internal or external requisitions.

Template Lines

Give the template line a number and choose a line type. The line type will determine if the item number is mandatory. If the item is revision-controlled in the destination organization, you can choose a revision. If an item is not mandatory, choose a category and description. You can specify the source type of inventory or supplier, unit, and purchase price.

Line Sourcing Information

For supplier-sourced requisition lines, you can specify the supplier, supplier site, and contact. For inventory-sourced requisitions, you can specify the organization and subinventory.

NOTE
You can set the line sourcing even though it may be inconsistent with the sourcing type assigned at the header.

You can name the buyer and the supplier item number for the item. You can set the default for the RFQ required flag for all requisitions that are created from this template.

Document Types

You cannot define new document types, but you can create new subtypes of them. To update an existing subtype, or create a new subtype, navigate to the Document Types form in the Setup Purchasing menu. If you create a subtype of quotation, it is further classified as either a bid (specific order) or catalog (multiple orders).

You can limit the ability of the creator of a document to approve or modify it. You can disallow anyone from changing the approval routing through changing the forward-to, from, or approval hierarchy.

With the security level and access level, you can limit the maintenance and review of documents of this type available to the following:

■ Only those in the approval hierarchy

■ Only members of the Purchasing department

■ Only the owner of the document

■ All users

You can forward documents directly to the first person in the approval chain with sufficient authority to approve them, or you can forward them to the next person in the chain through the Forward Method. You can archive documents of the document subtype on approval or printing.

Workflow Settings

You can set an approval workflow for documents of this subtype. You can also set the startup process that will create the document in the workflow system. If the subtype you are defining is a subtype of requisition, you can define a workflow process to manage the Autocreate function.

Line Types

You must define line types by giving them a name and description. You must define whether the value basis of the line is based on the quantity. You can assign a default category, unit of measure, and price to the line type. You can define whether a receipt is required for shipments of this type of line. If you click the Outside Processing check box, only outside processing items can be added to a line of this time.

Periods

If you have enabled encumbrance, when you create transactions in Purchasing you will also create encumbrance entries. These entries are posted to a period balance defined in a G/L calendar. A period is defined by its name, start date, end date, fiscal year, and status. Statuses for purchasing periods are the following:

- **Closed**   Means that you can no longer accrue purchases in this period.

- **Future**   Means that you will be posting to this period in the future.

- **Never Opened**   Periods are created in this status by default.

- **Open**   Means that you can post entries in this period.

- **Permanently closed**   Means that you do not intend to open this period in the future, although this status is reversible.

Purchasing Workflows

Purchasing uses Oracle Workflow extensively for routing documents, automating activities, notifying users that their input is required, detecting out of tolerance conditions, and allowing an expert user access to change the application's logic in a supportable way.

Constructing Accounts

The name of this workflow in the workflow builder is PO Account Generator. Purchasing uses the account generator functions implemented in workflow to determine the accounting code combinations. Requisitioners and purchasing agents do not need to enter accounting distributions because they can be generated automatically. The workflow functions take segments from the code combinations that are defined for the application's objects used in the transaction. It uses them to assemble code combination to charge. For example, if a requisition is to be delivered to an expense subinventory, code combinations are associated with both the item and the subinventory that can be used. Segment 1 may be taken from the item, and segment 2 may be taken from the subinventory to construct a valid code combination. Be sure to work with your financial and systems administrator people when making changes.

The system builds accounts for the charge, budget, accrual, and variance account and can use segments from preceding accounts as a default. The following processes can be changed and the other parts of the installation still be supportable by Oracle:

- Generate Default Accrual Account

- Generate Default Budget Account

- Generate Default Charge Account

- Generate Default Variance Account

- Build Expense Charge Account

- Build Inventory Budget Account

- Build Inventory Charge Account

- Build Expense Project Accrual Account

- Build Expense Project Budget Account

- Build Expense Project Charge Account

- Build Expense Project Variance Account

- Build Shop Floor Charge Account

- Get Charge Account for Variance Account

Approving Requisitions

This work item type is displayed in the workflow builder as PO Requisition Approval. The requisition approval process is the one that routes a requisition up either the supervisor or approval hierarchy. When an approval is entered, either the next person in the hierarchy is notified of the pending approval or the prior approver has sufficient authority to approve the requisition. The requisition approval workflow contains the following functions:

- Reject Requisition

- Reserve at the Start

- Reserve Before Approve

- Return Requisition to Submitter

- Verify Approval Authority

- Verify Approval Authority for Approve Action

- Verify Approval Authority for Approve and Forward Action

- Verify Requisition

- Approve Requisition

- Approval List Routing

- Main Requisition Approval

- Notify Approver

- Response with Approve Action

- Response with Approve and Forward Action
- Response with Forward Action
- Response with Reject Action

Approving Purchase Orders

This work item type is displayed in the workflow builder as PO Approval. The purchase order approval process also takes into consideration interaction between the requisitioner and the supplier in its workflow. It is aware of changes in source documents. It is also aware of change order processing on the purchase order. The purchase order approval process contains the following functions:

- Do Document Changes Require Reapproval?
- Find Approver
- Get All Blanket PO Changes
- Get All Contract PO Changes
- Get All Planned PO Changes
- Get All Release Changes
- Get All Standard PO Changes
- Notify Approver
- Print Document
- Print Document (Change Order)
- Fax Document Process
- Fax Document (Change Order)
- Approve and Forward PO
- Approve PO
- Approve PO (Change Order)
- Forward PO
- Get All Document Changes
- PO Approval Process
- PO Approval Top Process
- Reject PO

- Reserve Before Approve
- Return PO to Submitter
- Verify Approval Authority
- Verify PO

Managing Change Orders

Whenever the document status becomes Requires Reapproval, it goes through the same workflow process as its approval. The document requires reapproval whenever its revision is incremented or any of its change tolerances are exceeded. Change tolerances are as follows:

- Change Order Header Blanket Total Tolerance
- Change Order Header Amount Limit Tolerance
- Change Order Header Purchase Order Total Tolerance
- Change Order Line Quantity Tolerance
- Change Order Line Unit Price Tolerance
- Change Order Line Quantity Committed Tolerance
- Change Order Line Agreed Amount Tolerance
- Change Order Line Price Limit Tolerance
- Change Order Shipment Price Override Tolerance
- Change Order Shipment Quantity Tolerance
- Change Order Distribution Quantity Ordered Tolerance

If the changes are within these tolerances the changes are reapproved automatically. These change tolerances are stored as Work Item Attributes on the PO Approval work item type.

Automatic Purchase Order and Release Creation

This process is displayed in the workflow builder as PO Create Documents. You can automatically create purchase orders or releases at the end of the requisition approval process if the attribute Is Automatic Creation Allowed is set to Yes. You can set the value of this attribute by opening the process in the workflow builder. You can also automatically submit the purchase order for approval by setting the value of the Work Item Attribute Is Automatic Approval Allowed to Yes.

Receipt Notification Requests

This process is displayed in the workflow builder as PO Confirm Receipt. This process tests for shipments that have passed their need-by dates that were routed for direct delivery to the requisitioner. The requisitioner is notified via e-mail, the forms-based notifications viewer, or the Web-based notifications viewer. The user can respond to the notification and update the received amount automatically.

Procurement Process Flows

Purchasing also delivers purchasing best practice business processes that can be navigated. You can access them from the Processes tab in the navigator. Purchasing delivers a procure to pay, sourcing, receiving, and PO creation. You can start the process in the process navigator and invoke the forms and processes that are needed to execute the process. Click the Launch button to start the process. An example of the purchase order create process is illustrated in Figure 13-15.

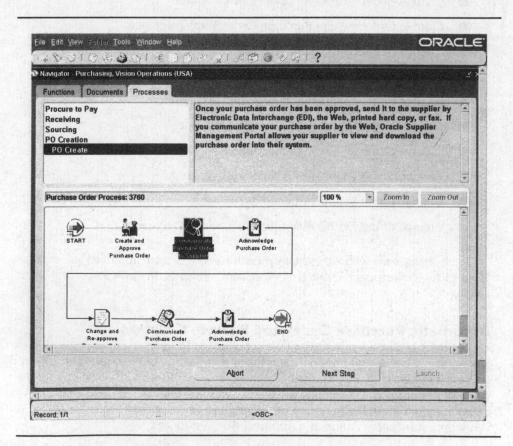

FIGURE 13-15. *Navigating through the PO creation process*

Universal Inbox

You can use a number of Web-based user interfaces for the management of notifications. You can see and respond to both To Do and FYI notifications in your notifications viewer. To review your notifications, navigate to the Worklist in the Workflow User menu. You can set up rules for delegation of notification due to absence. To set up notification rules, navigate to the form in the Workflow menu.

Important Item Attributes for Purchasing

To set up the item attributes for purchasing, navigate to the Master Items or Organization Items form in the Items menu. You can define an item to be a Purchased item, and you can separately set its current status to Purchasable. The Purchasable attribute can be status-controlled. You can mandate that an approved supplier must be used to purchase from. The item description can be updated when the purchase document is created if you set the Allow Description Update to Yes. You can mandate that RFQs must be issued when requisitions are raised. The Outside Processing Item flag defines this item as the service provided by an outside processing provider in converting material you supply to them. You can define the item to be taxable or not, and you can define the tax code that applies to it. The default buyer will be defaulted onto requisitions for this item, and a default purchasing unit of measure will be the unit of measure that you raise purchase documents in. The percentage of the shipment quantity—within which the quantity received will be deemed to completely fulfill the shipment line for receiving—is defined in the Receipt Close Tolerance. The percentage of the shipment quantity—within which the quantity received will be deemed to completely fulfill the shipment line for invoice matching—is defined in the Invoice Close Tolerance.

For invoice matching, you can define that the invoice line quantities will be matched against receipt quantities or inspected and approved quantities. You can define the hazard class for the item. You can define a list price for defaulting onto requisitions and a market price from which you can judge the performance of your buyers. You can define the price increase tolerance beyond which price increases on catalog updates will be flagged to buyers.

You can record accounts that may have segments used from them in the account generator processes for encumbrance account and expense account for noninventory items. If the item will be received into the asset register, you may define the asset category that it belongs to.

Importing Requisitions

The main way to get information into the purchasing system is through the requisition import process. Requisition import receives requisitions from Order Management for drop ship orders, Master Scheduling, and MRP for supply requisitions; Inventory for kanban replenishments; and Work In Process for outside processing requirements.

You can automatically source the requisitions, create purchase orders and releases, and submit them for approval all in the same run. Set the profile PO: Release During ReqImport to Yes. Requisition Import calls the Create Document Workflow for the Approved requisitions.

If you are using encumbrance, the status of the imported requisitions is set to pre-approved, and they will not show up as supply until approved.

Submitting Requisition Import

To submit the requisition import process, navigate to the submission form and select Requisition Import. You can specify an import source or leave it blank for all sources.

NOTE
Only import sources that are currently in the interface table will be rendered in the LOV.

You can specify a batch number to import, or you can import all batches. You can group requisition lines onto requisitions by buyer, item category, item, location, or supplier. Choose whether to launch the approval workflow for approved requisitions.

Requisition Import Interface Table

The Requisitions interface table is called PO_REQUISITIONS_INTERFACE_ALL. The interface table contains information about the source system, processing status, sourcing, requisition document, suggested vendor, approval, destination and delivery, encumbrance and account information, approval information, and line information. These are all in the single table.

Create Document Workflow Functions

Purchasing wraps a number of functions in wrappers to allows them to be called by workflow for the creation of requisitions. They are implemented in a package called PO_AUTOCREATE_DOC. The workflow activities call the functions within this package. The workflow wrappers themselves call other procedures. To call a function from workflow, it must have the following signature:

```
Argument Name                    Type                       In/Out ---------
-------------------- ------------------------ ------
ITEMTYPE                         VARCHAR2                   IN
ITEMKEY                          VARCHAR2                   IN
ACTID                            NUMBER                     IN
FUNCMODE                         VARCHAR2                   IN
RESULTOUT                        VARCHAR2                   OUT
```

Purchasing provides the following functions in the PO Create Document workflow:

- **Is Automatic Creation Allowed** Implemented in the function SHOULD_ REQ_BE_AUTOCREATED

- **Launch Process To Verify Req Line Information** Implemented in the function IS_SOURCE_DOC_INFO_OK

- **Is This An Emergency Requisition?** Implemented in the function IS_THIS_ EMERGENCY_REQ

- **Put All Requisition Lines On A Purchase Order** Implemented in the function INSERT_INTO_LINES_INTERFACE

- **Launch Process To Create/Approve PO or Release** Implemented in the function CREATE_DOC

- **Remove Processed Req Lines From Temp Table** Implemented in the function PURGE_ROWS_FROM_TEMP_TABLE

Summary

This chapter reviewed the applications in the purchasing and supply base management space. They cover applications to coordinate requisitions through both Web-based and forms-based interfaces. You also reviewed the applications used to find suppliers for a given product or service. These are the RFQ and Quoting systems. The applications that link suppliers to the items and commodities that they are approved to supply were also covered.

The chapter also covered the different types of purchase orders and how they are created with the Autocreate functions, how planning and purchasing demands are grouped and bucketed into schedules in Supplier Scheduling, and the extranet applications that allow suppliers to interact with your system in Internet Supplier Portal. How to set up and integrate the purchasing with other applications was also covered.

CHAPTER
14

Receiving

racle Receiving is the part of Oracle E-Business Suite concerned with the physical receipt of materials and acknowledging the receipt of services. It includes inspection capability to ensure that material is of appropriate quality before being delivered. You can receive against a supplier shipment, a shipment from another organization, and a shipment returned by a customer.

You are able to stage the inventory in a receiving location or route the receipt directly to central stores, a point of use on the shop floor, the requestor, or the WIP job or schedule awaiting outside processing. You can control at what point shipments are available to be received against and matched to invoices. You can receive unexpected shipments as unordered receipts. Receiving provides transactions to return substandard or late materials to suppliers with Return to Vendor transactions. In Oracle Warehouse Management (OWM), transactions can be received in a forms-based user interface or through RF devices in mobile receiving in WMS.

You can record the Advanced Shipment Notification issued from a supplier updating the expected quantity and time for the delivery.

Managing Inbound Shipments

The total receiving process consists of three main activities:

- **Receiving**   The process of recording the arrival of material at your location.

- **Inspection**   Accepting or rejecting the material.

- **Delivery (Putaway)**   Delivering the material to its requestor (for expensed items); moving the material to its stocking location, point of use, or intermediate location (for inventory items); or delivering outside processing directly to the WIP job.

The combination of activities you require for an item is called its *receipt routing*. A *standard* routing requires separate receiving and delivery steps; *inspection* adds the requirement for an inspection step to the standard process; and a *direct* routing performs the receipt and delivery in one step. The overall process is illustrated in Figure 14-1.

Oracle Receiving allows you to control your receiving process with a number of parameters, item and supplier attributes, and profiles. For example, you can use direct receiving for some items and require inspection for others; you can even require inspection for an item from one supplier, but waive inspection for the same

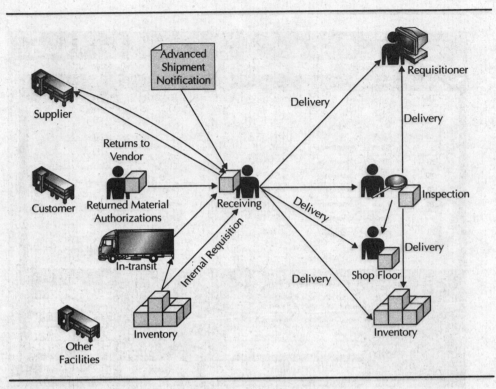

FIGURE 14-1. *Overview of Receiving in Oracle Purchasing*

item from another supplier. Integration with Oracle Quality lets you execute detailed collection plans as part of the inspection process.

Furthermore, you can set over-receipt and early/late tolerances at several levels and determine if a violation of a tolerance should be treated as an error or a warning, or if it should be simply ignored.

Receipts

If you need to enter quantities received and other shipment information, you will need to invoke the Receipts form. To navigate to the standard receiving forms, click the Find button from the Find Expected Receipts window. You can record receipt header information before being presented with a list of expected receipts. You can confirm the entire receipt by clicking the Express button or click Headers to return to the receipt header. An example of the Receiving Transactions window is shown in Figure 14-2.

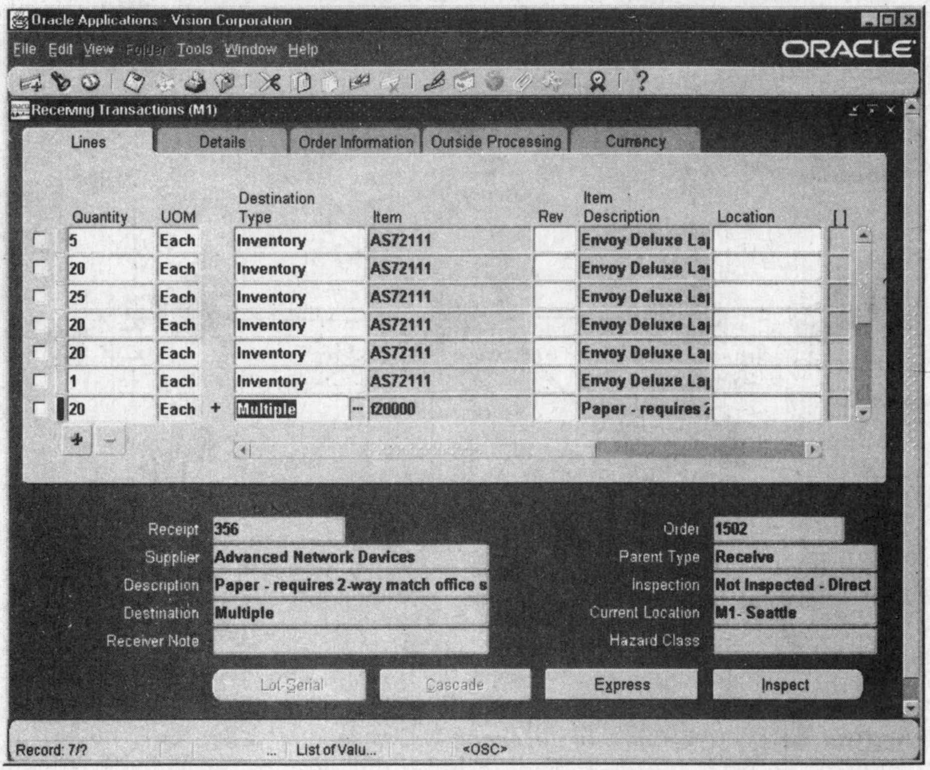

FIGURE 14-2. *An example of the Receiving Transcation window*

Finding Expected Receipts

You find expected receipts in the Receiving form in the Receipts menu. The form has two main tabs: Supplier and Internal, and Customer. Customer—visible only if Order Management is installed—will search for Return Material Authorizations to receive.

Supplier and Internally Sourced Receipts

To search for receipts, choose a source type of Internal, Supplier, or All. Enter the supplier. This is the source inventory organization for internal requisitions. For supplier-sourced shipment, you can enter the purchase order, line number, and shipment number. For internally sourced shipments, you can enter the requisition number and line number. The list of valid values for purchase orders is restricted to those that have at least one approved shipment. The list of valid values for shipments and requisition lines is restricted to those to be delivered to the organization you are currently transacting on behalf of. You can also search based on the supplier's shipment or ASN number.

Customer Returns

To search for customer returns to receive, enter the Return Material Authorization (RMA) number, customer number, RMA line number, customer item number, and line type. For example, line type might be Return for Rework and Reissue.

Line-Level Restrictions

You can further narrow your search to restrict for item, due date, and shipment.

- ■ **Item restrictions**   Are item number, category, description, and supplier item number.

- ■ **Date restrictions**   Can be to shipments due on the current date or any arbitrary date range. The due date is the promised date, if it exists. If no promise date has been entered, the need-by date is used for purchase orders and the request date is used for RMAs.

- ■ **Shipment restrictions**   Are container, truck, and bar code number.

Receipt Headers

In the Receipt Headers window, you can add to an existing open receipt or enter a receipt number if automatic receipt numbering is not enabled. Otherwise, a receipt number will be generated and the field will not be protected. You may enter a shipment number, packing slip number, waybill/airbill number, bill of lading, the number of containers received, and the person receiving the shipment. This header information is optional; you can also close the Receipt Headers window and proceed directly to the lines.

Receipt Lines

On the Receipts window, you can see order type and number, supplier or source inventory organization with the due date, item description, hazard classification, UN number, destination location, and receipt routing. You may see a plus sign (+)

indicating there are multiple distributions for the shipment line. The tabs described in the following sections show many other details of the shipment.

Line Information

Line information includes the quantity and UOM, destination type, (inventory, expense, or shop floor), item and revision if specified, delivery location, and requestor. If the destination type is inventory, the destination subinventory and locator may also be specified. The category of the item and ASN type is displayed. The country of origin for the receipt can be entered here. For example, Neptune may receive a shipment of optical assemblies from Malaysia, but it may receive the next shipment of the same item from Japan.

Line Details

Details of the shipment line include packing slip, supplier lot, and transaction reason. You might enter a transaction reason if you were receiving only part of a shipment because of quality reasons. The supplier lot gives you lot tracability back into the suppliers lot tracking system.

Currency

You can override the exchange rate on an order if you match invoices to receipts. The rate type must be User and you must have the profile PO: Allow Rate Override for User Rate Type set to Yes.

Order Information

Order information for the shipment includes order type, number, release number, order line number, shipment number, supplier, quantity ordered, UOM, due date, and supplier item number.

Outside Processing Information

Outside processing information includes job or schedule, production line, and operation sequence number. For example, Neptune manages the sheet cutting, drilling, and folding of the machine chassis in its machine shop but sends the folded work out to be anodized.

Shipment Information

The shipment information includes all the document references that are needed to track the material while in transit. These include the carrier, a reference to the truck and the container in the truck, bills of lading, freight and waybill, and the barcode label.

Express Receiving

You can select all lines and receive them either to a receiving location or to their final destination. If you have provided source information in the Find window, you can click the Express button from the Expected Receipts window. Purchasing then presents you with a choice of receiving or final destination and selects all the shipment lines. You can deselect them individually, or you can unexpress them all by clicking the renamed Express button. Purchasing will perform the following checks and report the errors to you:

■ Revision subinventory or locator is required and cannot be defaulted.

■ Lots or serials are required.

■ Receipt date tolerances are exceeded, and purchasing options are set to reject.

■ Ship-to location is missing for receiving location.

■ Delivery location is missing for expense receipts to final destination.

■ Receipt header and purchase order suppliers are different.

Unordered Receipts

Purchasing allows the receiving staff to record the receipt of materials for which an expected receipt cannot easily be located. You can later research these and match them to purchase order shipments and RMAs.

Receiving Unordered Shipments

To receive an unordered shipment, choose Unordered from the Find window in the Receipts form. Purchasing will present you with a receipt header. From there you can navigate to the receipt lines.

NOTE
Make sure that you choose the correct tab when you click the Unordered button. Unordered purchase receipts can later be matched only against purchase receipts, and likewise for unordered RMA receipts.

Matching Unordered Receipts against Expected Shipments

To match unordered receipts against expected shipments, navigate to the Match Unordered Receipts form in the Receiving menu. The form presents a Find window where you can locate unordered receipts based on receipt number, supplier (or customer for RMAs), item, item description, category or supplier item number, receiver location, and transaction dates. Enter your search criteria, and click Find to list the receipts you want to match. The Unordered Receipts window is split into the receipts section on the left and the expected shipments on the right. Enter the order (or RMA number), release, line, and shipment to match against. You can review the receipt and purchase order from the Tools menu.

Receiving Transactions

Purchasing provides a set of transactions to trace materials from the time of receipt to the time of final delivery. Movements within receiving and through inspection are recorded as receiving transactions. A receipt quantity may be split as it is stored and inspected in many locations.

Finding Receipts to Transact

To find receipts to transact, navigate to the Receiving Transactions form in the Receiving menu. Purchasing presents a Find window that is very similar to the Find window in the Receiving form. The main differences are in the tabs in the lower part of the window. There is a tab for Receipt Details that includes the receiver. The transaction Details tab includes Receipt Routing: Direct or Receiving.

When you click the Find button, Purchasing will present a list of receipts. The receipts listing is similar to the Expected Receipts window. You can enter a quantity up to the receipt quantity and transfer it to another location. Purchasing records the parent transaction on possibly many children.

Inspecting Receipts

Purchasing offers two modes for entering quality and inspection information. If Oracle Quality is installed and the value of the profile QA: PO Inspection is set to Oracle Quality, the quality icon will appear in the toolbar and as an entry in the Tools menu. You can invoke it by clicking the Inspect button. Oracle presents a collection plan from Quality. Only collection plans that have been associated with the receiving transaction will be displayed. If mandatory collection plans are used, the quality data must be entered and saved before the transaction can complete.

Delivery

If the receipt does not require inspection, it may be delivered. When you select a line to receive, you may be presented with shortage information for this item. You must enter a transaction quantity. The unit, destination type, and location will be defaulted from the receipt but can be overridden. In the Details tab, you can update the packing slip number, supplier lot number, and a reason code for the transaction.

Reviewing Receiving Transactions

You can review your receiving transactions from the Receiving Transactions Summary form in the Receiving menu. The Find window is similar to the Find windows in the other receiving transactions, except for being able to return headers or transactions as results.

Transaction Header Results

The Transaction Header Results window is a folder form. Any column from the receipt header can be chosen to be displayed in the window, including receipt number, date, supplier and supplier site, shipment number, and ship date. You can review the transactions for any receipt header by clicking the Transactions button.

Transaction Line Results

The Transaction results is also a folder window. You can choose or eliminate any column from the transaction. Transaction type is always displayed. Transaction types will include corrections, returns to vendors, receipts, transfers, and deliveries. Other columns include transaction quantity, UOM, transaction date, item, and destination.

Correcting Receiving Transactions

You can correct any receiving transaction you have recorded by entering the change to the existing transaction, positive or negative, in the Corrections form on the Receiving menu. The form has the same Find window as the Receiving Transactions form.

Returns to Vendor

Purchasing provides a way to return defective material to a supplier. If material has been received and in inspection is noted to be substandard, you can acknowledge that the material has been retuned to the vendor. The same transaction can be used to return returned material to customers. To enter a return, navigate to the Return form in the Receipts menu. The find criteria are similar to the other receiving functions. After you click the Find button, you will be presented with a list of receipts that may be returned. When you enter a return quantity for a purchase order, the open quantity on the line is increased by the return quantity. For returns against the RMA, the RMA received quantity is decreased.

NOTE
There is an RMA number in the transaction details region to record the RMA number issued by your supplier. It is not the RMA number that you issued to your customer.

Managing Shipments

You can define inventory movements between facilities to be direct or through in-transit. Direct movements move directly into inventory in the destination organization. For example, Neptune has defined an organization for the manufacturing facility and another organization for finished goods inventory stored within the same building. In-transit movements create a shipment that is received at the other facility. When a supplier submits an ASN, it also creates a shipment. The shipment can be updated by navigating to the Manage Shipments form in the Receiving menu. Purchasing presents you with the familiar Find window. You can update the expected receipt date, bill of lading number, freight carrier, packing slip, number of containers, and ship-to location.

Receiving Options

You can define many options to control the behavior of receiving for each operating unit. You can specify how early and late a shipment can be and whether the system should prevent the receipt or warn the receiver. You can control the quantity over the ordered quantity that is allowable and again whether the receiver should be warned or prevented from entering the receipt. You can allow or disallow receiving substitute items and unordered items. You can allow receivers to view expected quantities or allow blind receiving. The actions for shipping other than to the requested ship-to are specified here. Document numbering for receipt documents and the account code that stores the value of inventory in receiving is stored here. There are some options that can be set in many places. For example, Days Early Allowed can be set on the item, supplier, and purchasing options. Purchasing will default the Days Early Allowed onto the purchase order from the item first. If no value has been set for the item, it will look at the supplier. If no value has been set for the supplier, it will look to purchasing options.

Summary

In this chapter, you examined how inbound shipment are handled in Oracle Purchasing and Receiving and how to find expected receipts and the sources of those receipts. You also reviewed standard and express methods for receiving; how to handle receipts that are unexpected; how the received quantity is moved within receiving for storage, inspection, and delivery; how to correct receiving transactions; and how to reject material and send it on its way back to the vendor. The options that control the behavior of the receiving transactions were also covered.

CHAPTER
15

Inventory and Warehouse Management

lanning, replenishing, consuming, and shipping inventory in an optimal manner can save millions by reducing obsolescence and increasing the inventory turns. These business processes consume a lot of labor and equipment to store, retrieve, and move these materials. For example, to move a pallet, you may need a pallet jack or a fork truck and a employee who is trained to work with that equipment. To pick peaches, you might just need a peach picker and no specific equipment. Using these resources in an optimal manner is a very important objective for warehouse managers. Figure 15-1 shows the different types of material transactions that take place in a warehouse.

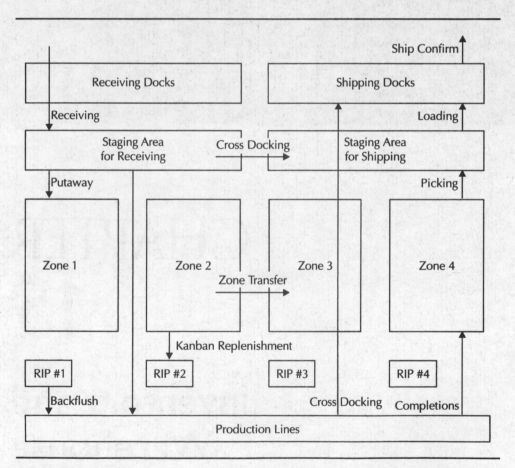

FIGURE 15-1. *Material handling tasks in a warehouse/manufacturing plant*

This chapter discusses the features provided by Oracle Applications to manage the material handling function in a manufacturing plant/distribution center. Most of these features are provided in Oracle Inventory and Oracle Warehouse Management (OWM).

Units of Measure (UOM)

Unit of measure (UOM) is used for all material transactions. UOM Classes define the high-level groupings of UOMs. The grouping is based on the nature of measuring. For example, you can have a class called Quantity that can have UOMs such as each, dozen, and so on. Another class could be weight, with lb, kg, and ton as UOMs. Each class contains one base UOM.

You can define conversions between UOMs. *Standard* conversions define conversions that are not specific to the item or the class. A dozen equals 12 each is a standard conversion. Item-specific conversions identify the relationship between two UOMs, with respect to an item. For example, you can put 12 EA of item X in the case BigBox. But, you might be able to put 24 EA of item Y in the same case.

The on-hand balance (covered in the section "On-Hand Balances") for each item is maintained in the primary UOM of the item, which is identified using the item attribute Primary UOM. You must define a conversion between a non-base unit of measure and the base unit of measure before you can assign the non-base unit of measure to an item.

When you define an item, you decide which type of unit-of-measure conversion to use—item-specific, standard, or both. If you specify item-specific, the system uses unit of measure conversions unique to this item. If none exist, you can transact this item in its primary unit of measure only. If you specify Standard, standard UOM conversions are used. If you specify Both, both item-specific and standard unit of measure conversions are considered. If both exist for the same unit of measure and item combination, the item-specific conversion is used. Unless you have a specific reason to exclude either standard or item-specific conversions, the system default of Both is almost always an appropriate choice.

NOTE
UOM definitions are stored in the table MTL_UNITS_OF_MEASURE. All the conversions are stored in the table MTL_UOM_CONVERSIONS.

During transaction execution, when you enter an item's quantity, the default is the primary unit of measure for the item. You can select a UOM that has either the standard or item-specific conversions from the primary unit of measure. Transactions are performed in the unit of measure you specify. The conversion happens automatically, and item quantities are updated in the primary unit of measure of the item.

Material Transactions

Material transaction is a general term that represents material movement in a warehouse or a manufacturing plant. For example, when you move material between zones or release material to the shop floor for production, you are performing a material transaction.

Material transactions have two aspects: change of physical location and the impact to material accounts. The two concurrent programs—Transaction Manager and Costing Manager—are responsible for processing these two aspects of each material transaction. You can also process your transactions online, instead of using the Transaction Manager.

Transaction Source Types

The transaction source type represents the type of entity in Oracle Applications that a transaction can originate from. For example, the source type of a PO Receipt transaction is a purchase order. A number of transaction source types are seeded as system-defined transaction source types. Additionally, you can define source types if you need to validate your transactions against a different type of entity. The User-Defined tab in the Transaction Source Types form allows you to do that. You can select the Validation Type as None or Value Set. If you want to validate against a dynamic list of values, you can define a SQL query–based value set if you want.

Transaction Actions

The transaction action identifies the nature of material movement. It is generic and not specific to any source. For example, the action Receipt Into Stores just means that some material is going to be received into inventory. With the transaction source type of Purchase Order, this action indicates a PO Receipt; with the transaction source type of an Account, this action indicates an Account Receipt. Oracle Applications comes seeded with many transaction actions.

Transaction Types

Transaction type represents a convenient way of representing a transaction source type and transaction action and offers a classification mechanism for classifying your transactions by using meaningful names.

In some cases, transactions happen behind the scenes—as it does with sales order issue, for example. When you ship an item, the sales order issue transaction happens behind the scenes. In certain other cases, you are allowed to specify the transaction types. For example, when you perform a miscellaneous receipt or a WIP completion, you are allowed to specify the transaction type you want to use. Based on this, you are allowed to define transaction types that include a subset of transaction source types and transaction actions. For example, you cannot use Sales Order as the source type for the transaction types that you define. But, you can use the transaction source type Inventory in your transaction types.

Transaction types that have actions—such as Receipt Into Stores, In-Transit Receipt, Direct Organization Transfer, Assembly Completion, or Negative Component Issue— allow you to specify whether you want to receive Shortage Alerts when those transactions happen. Shortage alerts communicate the receiver of any material shortage in some usage point.

Transaction Reasons and Corrective Actions

While performing an inventory transaction, you can choose a transaction reason to classify the transaction. From an OWM perspective, transaction reasons serve two purposes: identifying the reason for not performing the directed task and automatically initiate a corrective action. When a user is not able to complete a directed task, the user will be prompted to enter a reason. Based on the selected reason, the associated workflow will be launched. For example, if a picker cannot perform the task due to inadequate quantity in the suggested locator, the actions could be to generate a cycle count automatically, perform the adjustments, and then notify the warehouse manager about this discrepancy.

You define transaction reasons in the Transaction Reasons form. When you define a reason, you identify the reason type, which is used to restrict the reason list for each task type. For example, a reason type that you define for picking cannot be used during problems in putaway. You can optionally associate a workflow that will be launched when the associated reason is selected.

Cost Groups

In the pre-11i releases (and the 11i installations that don't enable OWM), subinventory is both a physical zone and a logical collection of accounts that tracked the value of the items in the subinventory.

When you install OWM, a subinventory is purely a physical zone. The logical collection of accounts is separated from subinventory and is provided using cost groups. To provide backward compatibility, the subinventory form will accept a cost group as the default cost group for the subinventory and the Accounts tab in the subinventory form will display the accounts in the cost group. The accounts in the subinventory form cannot be edited directly, although you can change the default cost group for the subinventory.

NOTE
Even in the installations where you don't enable OWM, a cost group is automatically defined in the name of the subinventory, with the subinventory accounts; the underlying cost group is used in the transactions behind the scenes.

You define cost groups in the Cost Groups form. The Cost Groups form allows you to define the various valuation accounts and variance accounts that are needed to handle standard costing, average costing, FIFO costing and LIFO costing. A complete coverage of these costing methods is dedicated to Chapter 18.

If you don't have OWM, you provide the subinventories and locators that are involved in the transaction; the system will determine the cost group from the subinventory or organization settings. OWM provides you with a rules framework that can automatically determine the cost group for a transaction based on numerous criteria. The rules engine will use only the default cost group at the organization level if it is not able to find a cost group. Cost Group rules are covered in the section "The Rules Framework."

OWM also provides transactions to change cost group, independent of physical movement.

Material Status Control

When you find material discrepancies in a zone, you may want to prevent all new transactions from and to this zone and perform an emergency cycle count. The Material Status Control feature allows you to do exactly this and helps you in managing similar situations with locators, lots, and serials.

You define material statuses in the Material Status Definition form shown in Figure 15-2. The status usage identifies to which entities this status can be applied. For example, you might want to apply a status to a subinventory to prevent the receiving transactions into the subinventory and not intend to use it for lots.

The Transactions Shuttle Region lists the allowed transactions and disallowed transactions in two text lists. You can move the listed transactions between these two lists using the Shuttle Control that is provided between the two text lists. When a status is applied to an entity, entity will be prevented from all the disallowed transactions. For example, if you find that a particular lot contained defective components, you can define a status called Hold that disallows all the transactions and apply that status to the lot in order to prevent that lot from being shipped or used in manufacturing. Once you segregate the defective pieces, you can change the status of the lot back to Normal.

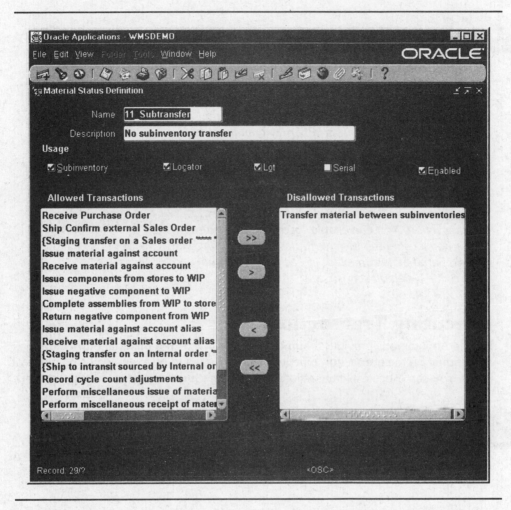

FIGURE 15-2. *The Material Status Definition form allows you to identify the allowed and disallowed transactions for each status*

NOTE
An item in inventory might get its status from the serial and lot to which it belongs and the locator and subinventory in which it currently resides. The transactions that are disallowed by these statuses will not be allowed for this item; it is a cumulative effect. For instance, consider a lot packed into an LPN. This LPN may contain other items packed into it that are not status controlled. If the lot packed into this LPN is assigned a status that prevents customer shipments, the shipment of the LPN to a customer will be prevented as the system applies a cumulative status while performing a transaction. You can enable lot and serial statuses for items using the item attributes Lot Status Enabled and Serial Status Enabled. In each case, you have to provide a default status.

Executing Transactions

Oracle Applications provides a number of ways to execute material transactions. Depending on the transaction type, transactions need to be executed using different forms. You can execute all transactions either using the desktop or mobile applications.

NOTE
The profile option INV:Transaction Date Validation allows you to decide whether you want to allow transaction dates to be a past date or a date in the past period.

Subinventory Transfers

You can execute subinventory transfers from the Subinventory Transfers form. The transaction results in the movement of material between two locations within an organization. The locations can be either subinventories or locators.

NOTE
The profile option INV:Allow Expense To Asset Transaction allows you to decide whether you want to allow transferring material from an expense subinventory into an asset subinventory.

Miscellaneous Transactions

Miscellaneous transactions are a way of issuing material to or receiving material from groups that are not inventory, receiving, or work in process, such as a research and development group or an accounting department. With a miscellaneous transaction you can issue material to or receive material from General Ledger accounts.

You can use your user-defined transaction types and sources to further classify and name your transactions. You can perform the receipts for items that were acquired by means other than a purchase order from a supplier. Miscellaneous transactions are very handy during the initial implementation phase for testing various transaction scenarios.

> **NOTE**
> *The Material Workbench (covered in this chapter)*
> *allows you to perform mass move and mass issue*
> *transactions where you can move all the material in*
> *a zone in one transaction.*

Inter-Organization Transfers

Interorganization transfers allow you to transfer material between inventory organizations. The transaction is available in two shipment modes: direct or in-transit shipments. You can use a single transaction to transfer more than one item. The items you transfer must exist in both organizations, although they can have different attributes and control level (locator, revision, lot, and serial number) settings. You perform interorganization transfers on the Interorganization Transfer form. The transfer type, in-transit ownership, in-transit accounts, and other details are defined on the Shipping Network Between the Two Organizations. Shipping networks are covered in Chapter 2.

Direct Shipment   Direct shipment results in the movement of materials to the destination organization immediately. The source and destination information are required at the time of the transaction. You cannot perform a direct transfer of items that are not under revision/lot/serial number control in the shipping organization if the destination organization requires any of these controls. For example, if an item is under revision control in organization A01, you cannot ship the item from organization A02 to A01 if the item is not under revision control in A02.

In-Transit Shipment   In-transit shipment is typically used when transportation time is significant or if you require separate shipping and receiving steps. The delivery location need not be specified at the time of the transfer transaction. Only the source and freight information is required. The interorganization transfer charge is specified when the shipping network was defined between the two organizations. Based on the interorganization transfer charge that applies between the organizations, a percentage of the transaction value or an absolute amount is used to compute transfer charges.

If the FOB point is set to Receipt in the shipping network, the destination organization owns the shipment after receiving the items. If it is set to Shipment, the destination organization owns the shipment when the shipping organization ships it and while it is in-transit. You can update the freight carrier or arrival date in the Maintain Shipments window.

At the time of shipment, the receiving parameters for the destination organization should have been defined. You can receive and deliver your shipment in a single transaction or receive and store your shipment at the receiving dock. Receiving was covered in detail in Chapter 14.

You can perform an in-transit shipment of items that are not under revision/lot/serial number control in the shipping organization even if the destination organization requires any of these controls. In the case of lot- and serial-number–controlled items, you will be required to provide a value during receiving. In the case of revision-controlled items, you can receive only the same revision that was shipped.

Move Orders

A *move order* is a mechanism for requesting, sourcing, and transferring materials within an organization. Move orders also allow you to track the movement of material within a single organization. They allow materials managers/planners to request and authorize the movement of material within a warehouse for purposes such as putaway, replenishment, and picking. You can generate move orders either manually or automatically depending on the source type you use. All the move orders created are automatically preapproved.

Subinventory Transfer Move Order Requisition

A subinventory transfer move order requisition and a regular subinventory transfer achieve the same end result: transferring material between subinventories or locators. However, the processes have significant differences, as highlighted in Table 15-1. Both subinventory transfer and move order are useful in different circumstances, and you should establish procedural control on using these two methods of transferring material between subinventories.

Pick Wave Move Order

A specific type of move order called the Pick Wave Move Order is used for managing the outbound logistics of the pick released materials. Wave picking is discussed in the section "Wave Picking." Pick wave move orders are automatically created by releasing sales order lines for picking, as described in Chapter 17.

Number	Subinventory Transfer	Subinventory Transfer Move Order
1	No tracking number exists for the transaction.	You can track the move order using the move order number.
2	The transaction is a single-step process.	The transaction has three steps: move order requisition, sourcing, and transaction.
3	Typically, subinventory transfer is performed after the material is physically moved—just for the sake of recording the material movement.	Move order allows you to move material with prior approval, source the material from all the stocked locations, and perform the transaction along with the physical movement of the material.
4	Because it is a single-step process and can't be tracked, it cannot be used as the transaction vehicle for processes such as pick release, replenishment, and planning.	Move order is used as the transaction vehicle by pick release, replenishment, and planning processes.

TABLE 15-1.   *Comparing Move Order Requisitions with Subinventory Transfer*

Replenishment Move Order

The planning processes, such as Min–Max planning and ROP planning, and the replenishment processes, such as replenishment counting and intra-org kanban can automatically create preapproved move orders of type replenishment. (Kanban is discussed in the "Kanban Materials Management" section later in this chapter.)

Pick Releasing WIP Requirements

Starting from Release 11i.6, you can pick release WIP requirements: requirements of discrete jobs, repetitive schedules, and flow schedules. If you use backflushing, the picked materials will be directed to the backflush subinventory and locator. If you intend to issue the material to the job/schedule, the appropriate WIP job/schedule will be indicated to the picker.

Creating and Using Move Orders

You create move orders in the move orders form. The header contains the move order number and description. Each line indicates a material requirement. The line contains the required item, quantity, and the destination details. You can optionally specify source information.

Once you submit the move order for approval, the item planner (specified by the item attribute Planner in the General Planning tab) for each line gets notified. When the planner approves the move order line, the move order line becomes eligible for transaction.

The Transact Move Order Lines form allows you to perform detailing and move order transactions. If the source information is not complete, you can click the Location Details button to request the system to suggest sourcing suggestions. This process is called *detailing*—it creates a pending reservation that will be consumed when you transact the line. It therefore decrements the available-to-transact (ATT) quantity.

The profile option INV:Detail Serial Numbers allows you to specify whether you want the detailing process to suggest individual serial numbers. When this profile option is turned on, each pick task asks the picker to pick individual serial numbers, which results in the picker searching for the serialized item. In most cases, you save a lot of time by turning this profile option off. When the profile is turned off, you can pick the items in whatever order you want and enter the serial numbers as you pick.

By clicking the Transact button, you can transact the move order lines that have been detailed.

Material Workbench

The Material Workbench provides a convenient user interface for performing the common material transactions. It also provides the ability to perform various queries such as availability. Figure 15-3 shows the Material Workbench. The tree navigator on the left pane allows you to navigate among the different warehouses and drill down to the various zones and locators within each warehouse.

The Material Workbench supports the Mass Move and Mass Issue transactions from the Tools menu. An example of a mass move transaction is to move all the items in a locator to a different locator. An example of a mass issue transaction is to issue all the items in a locator to an account alias, if, for example, the locator and all its contents were damaged.

In a future release of 11i, you can create location-based cycle counts from the Material Workbench. You can select a range of locators and schedule cycle count for the selected locators. You can also perform mass updates of statuses.

Movement Statistics

Movement statistics provides the capability for gathering, reviewing, and reporting statistical information associated with material movements in the enterprise. Movement statistics is an important part of the Intrastat reporting requirements of the European Union, which requires tracking material movements regardless of the countries involved in the material movement process.

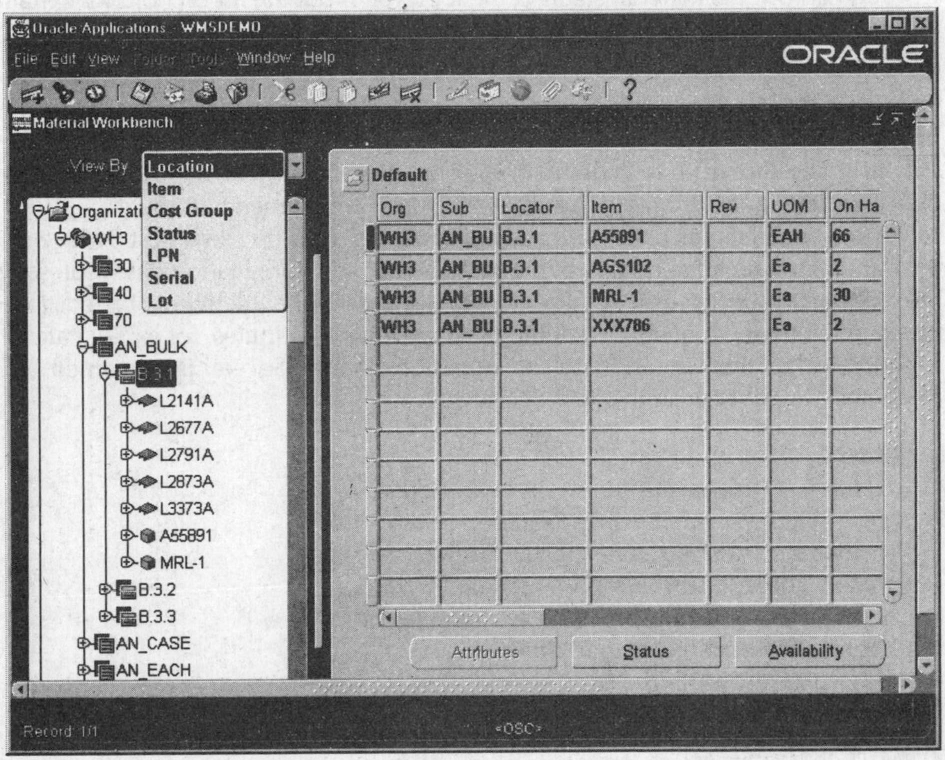

FIGURE 15-3. *The Material Workbench allows you to perform mass moves and issues*

NOTE
When you perform interorganization transfers, RMA receipts, RMA returns, supplier receipts, and supplier returns, you can invoke the Movement Statistics window from the Tools menu.

Managing Lots

Lots represent a group of on-hand items that generally have the same characteristics. For example, you can classify all the output from a production batch into three lots—each with a concentration of 90 percent, 80 percent, and 70 percent, respectively. The lot functionality in Oracle Applications supports lot attributes, lot splitting, and lot merging. For directed picking or putaway, you can use lot attributes as criteria in your rules.

You can use the material status at the lot level to put the lot on hold for certain types of transactions. For example, you can prevent sales order shipments on a particular lot.

Lot Attributes

Lot attributes allow you to capture lot specific information. The attributes have been classified into date attributes, character attributes, and numeric attributes.

Maturity date is the date a lot matures and is ready to be used. Best by date is the date after which the quality of the lot may degrade. Origination date represents the manufacture date of the lot. Retest date is the date on which the lot needs to be tested again to verify quality. In addition to these date attributes, lot expiry date is controlled by the item attribute Lot Expiration Control. Several other named attributes are available at the lot level as well.

NOTE
To track additional attributes, 20 date attributes (D_ATTRIBUTE1 .. D_ATTRIBUTE20,) 20 character attributes (C_ATTRIBUTE1 .. C_ATTRIBUTE20,) and 30 numeric attributes (N_ATTRIBUTE1 .. N_ATTRIBUTE30) are provided at the lot level. These attributes are stored in the table MTL_LOT_NUMBERS.

Lot Splitting

Lot splitting allows you to split a quantity of material that is produced in a single lot into multiple lots. Splitting may also be performed when a portion of a lot has different characteristics. Lot splitting can be of two types—full and partial lot splits. A *full lot split* is to split the entire quantity of a lot into new child lots, leaving the parent lot with no quantity. A *partial lot split* is to split a partial quantity of a lot into new child lots, leaving a remainder quantity in the parent lot. You enable an item for lot splitting using the item attribute Lot Split Enabled. During the lot-splitting process, the lot attributes of parent lot are defaulted to all the child lots. You can perform lot splitting by using the mobile transaction form Lot Split.

NOTE
Parent lot and starting lot mean the same thing, as do child lot and resulting lot.

Lot Merging

Lot merging allows you to merge multiple existing lots into a new lot as well as to merge multiple existing lots into an existing lot. Merging may be performed when you want to store lots together from multiple inventory locations or when the identity of each lot needs not be maintained.

Lot merging supports full and partial lot merges. A *full lot merge* is to merge the entire quantity of one or more lots into a new lot or an existing lot. A *partial lot merge* is to merge a partial quantity of one or more lots into a new lot or an existing lot, leaving a remainder quantity in the parent lots.

You enable an item for lot merging using the item attribute Lot Merge Enabled. During the lot merging process, the lot attributes of the resulting lot are defaulted from the starting lot with the largest quantity. If equal quantity lots are merged, the lot attributes will be defaulted from the first specified starting lot. You can merge lots using the mobile transaction form Lot Merge.

NOTE
Merging lots with different cost groups causes problems due to co-mingling. So, for a lot merge, the cost group of all starting lots must be the same.

A lot that has been reserved to a demand cannot be split or merged. Reservation is covered in the section "On-Hand Balances."

Lot Genealogy

When you split a lot to form multiple sublots or when you merge multiple lots into a single lot, Oracle keeps track of these transactions. Lot Genealogy stores the relationship between lots and sublots. The Lot Genealogy form that is shown in Figure 15-4 provides a tree navigator that you can use to navigate between lots and sublots.

The Job Lot Composition form allows you to view the component lot information for a discrete job. This form is covered in Chapter 16.

The profile option INV:Genealogy Prefix Or Suffix determines how the item number should be displayed along with the lot number in the genealogy tree structure. The two possible settings are Prefix (the lot number is displayed before the item number), and Suffix (the lot number is displayed after the item number). The profile option INV:Genealogy Delimiter determines what should be the delimiter between the item number and lot number.

CAUTION
Without setting the two profiles discussed in the previous paragraph, when the user views the lot genealogy, it will show NULL on the tree node instead of the lot number.

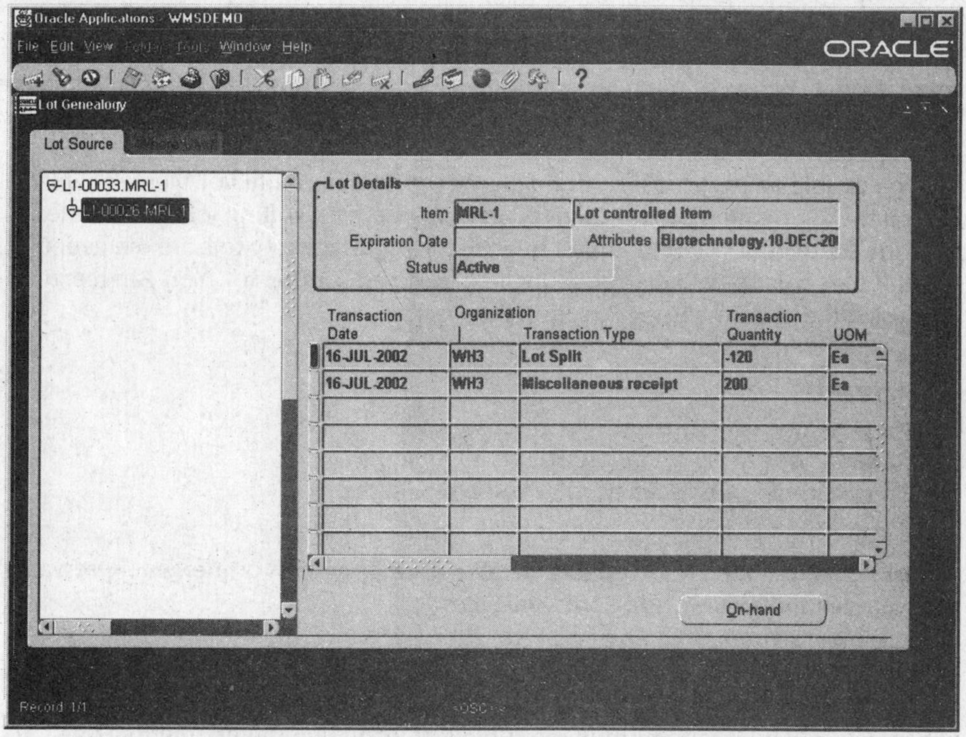

FIGURE 15-4. *The Lot Genealogy form allows you to view the composition of a lot and the related transactions*

Managing Serialized Items

You can use the serial number functionality provided by Oracle in a variety of situations. At a very high level, serial numbers provide you with the ability to track individual items. Additionally, if you want to track the characteristics or change in characteristics of each serialized item, you can use serial attributes. When you build items in manufacturing, you may want to keep track of the As Built configuration of the serialized assembly and all the serialized components. You can use serial genealogy to keep track of As Built configurations.

Serial Attributes

At the serial number level, you can capture the origination date and country of origin. A number of standard attributes allow you to track the life of the serialized item. For example, Cycles Since New allows you to track the number of usage cycles this item has gone through from the beginning of its life. Like lots, serial numbers are also provided with 20 date attributes, 20 character attributes, and 30 numeric attributes for tracking additional attributes. Several other named attributes are available at the serial level as well.

NOTE
To track additional attributes, 20 date attributes (D_ATTRIBUTE1 .. D_ATTRIBUTE20,) 20 character attributes (C_ATTRIBUTE1 .. C_ATTRIBUTE20,) and 30 numeric attributes (N_ATTRIBUTE1 .. N_ATTRIBUTE30) are provided at the serial level. These attributes are stored in the table MTL_SERIAL_NUMBERS.

Serial Genealogy

In certain industries, knowing the As Built configuration of an item is important. The As Built configuration is a multilevel structure that consists of the various lot/serialized components of a serialized assembly. Keeping a record of the As Built configuration allows you to serve your customers better. For example, you can send them periodic reminders for maintaining certain parts. You can also use serial genealogy to investigate customer claims. For example, assume that your customer replaces one of the components in the assembly with another component, which results in the assembly failing during operation. While investigating this failure, serial genealogy will come in handy.

Serial genealogy allows you to capture the As Built configuration of an item. When you build an item using Oracle Work In Process, you specify the serial numbers of the assembly that is being produced and the serial numbers of the components that are used in the assembly. Figure 15-5 shows the Serial Entry form that relates the assembly serial numbers to the component serial numbers.

Once you build your serial genealogy, you use the Serial Genealogy form to browse the genealogy of a parent item. You can access this form by clicking the View Genealogy button in the View Serial Numbers form.

On-Hand Balances

The On-Hand balance model keeps track of the inventory that is on-hand and inventory that has been committed to some type of demand, among other things. You can view the on-hand balance information of an item using the View On-Hand Quantities form. Based on the function security of your responsibility, you will be able to view the on-hand balances of your current organization or across organizations. You can choose to view the quantity by revision, subinventory, and locator.

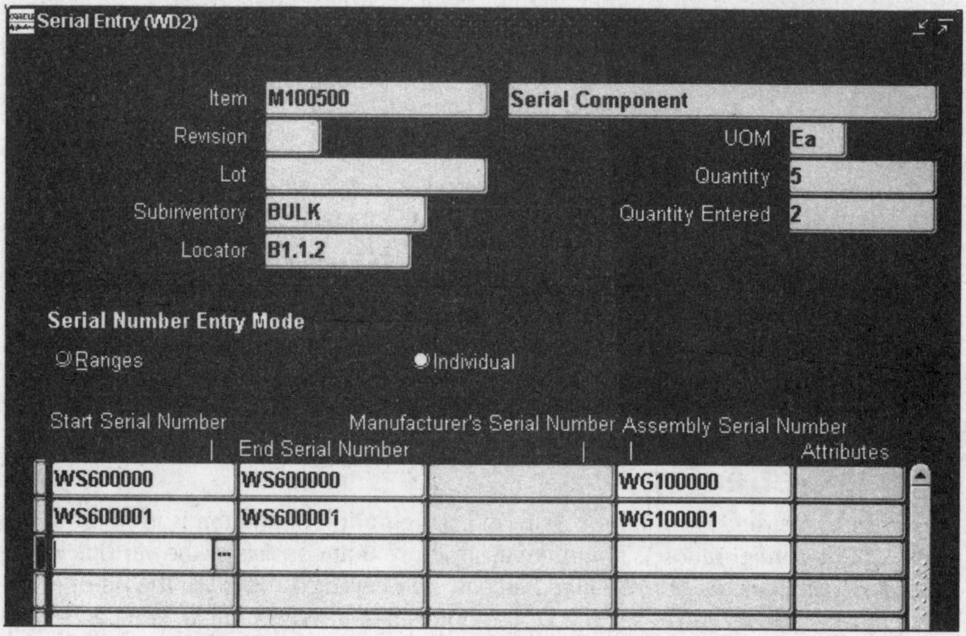

FIGURE 15-5. *The Serial Entry form allows you to build the As Built configurations during the WIP Completion transaction*

The Quantity Tree

The *quantity tree* is a memory structure that holds inventory information of each item in memory, in the form of a tree. This information will be stored in nodes at different levels that represent the inventory control levels of an item—revision, lot, subinventory, locator, and LPN. Figure 15-6 shows the node levels in the quantity tree. The tree is kept in synch with the underlying tables when information about an item changes.

The inventory information that is captured at each of these nodes includes quantity on-hand, reservable quantity on-hand, quantity reserved, quantity suggested, available to transact, and available to reserve. The value at each node is the sum of the values at all the child nodes.

While developing custom applications/reports, you can use the quantity tree to get accurate information about your on-hand quantities. For example, if you want to find the on-hand quantity for an item, use the public API INV_QUANTITY_TREE_ PUB.QUERY_QUANTITIES.

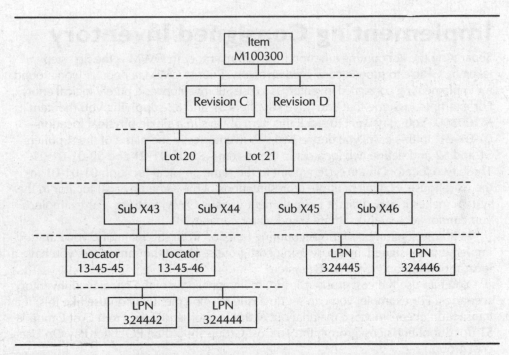

FIGURE 15-6. *The inventory control levels that form the nodes of the quantity tree of an item*

NOTE
The Global Inventory Position Inquiry form allows you to check the inventory position across inventory organizations in a single user interface.

Reservations

When a demand arises, a suitable supply is identified and reserved to the demand so that upstream processes, such as shipping, can fulfill the demand. In simple terms, a reservation is an association between a demand and a supply. The Item Reservation form allows you to define and view reservations in an inventory organization. Many demand types are supported by reservations, although all can be reserved only to on-hand quantity.

NOTE
Starting from Release 11i, the reservations model in Oracle Applications is architected to support reserving any supply to any demand, although some supply types such as WIP jobs, POs, and In-transit Inventory are not enabled yet.

Implementing Consigned Inventory

Separating the accounting function from subinventory in OWM is the first step taken by Oracle to support consigned inventory. Prior to OWM, a popular workaround for implementing consigned inventory is to use Subinventory as a purely logical entity. For example, assume that you have suppliers S1 and S2 supplying you the item M100500. You may want to stock this item always in a single physical location— 01-01-01. In this case, you define two subinventories in the name of the suppliers— S1 and S2 and define two locators in the system—S1-01-01-01 and S2-01-01-01. These two locators in the system point to the same physical location 01-01-01 in the warehouse. Having multiple representations of the same physical locator in the system makes it very difficult to implement various OWM features. For example, you cannot accurately estimate your locator capacity.

With the separation of the accounting function from subinventory, you can implement consigned inventory using cost groups, and at the same time, you have a locator defined only once in the system.

You can use the cost group rules to implement some of the consigned inventory scenarios. For example, you can set up a rule to implement pay on use like this: if a transaction occurs to move material out of this locator, and if the From Cost Group is S1 (for Supplier1's cost group), the To Cost Group should be POU (for Pay On Use cost group.)

The complete solution on consigned inventory that includes the following features is being developed, but the release schedule was not known at press time:

- Ability to establish various event points when the ownership is transferred

- Automatically notify payables about the receipt transaction and trigger the payment process

The Rules Framework

OWM comes with a flexible rules framework that is used by various OWM features to identify a target value based on a set of rules. For example, putaway uses the rules engine to identify the most optimal storage location considering factors such as case volume, case weight, and locator capacity among others. Almost all the essential data objects in Oracle Applications and their associated attributes are enabled for use in the rule definition, including the descriptive flexfield values for these entities. In this section, the OWM rules engine is discussed in detail followed by the various applications of the rules engine.

Business Objects

Business objects is a common name for all the entities in Oracle Applications that support your business. Examples of business objects are Organization, Item, Item

Category, Subinventory, and so on. You can use the attributes of these business objects as criteria while defining your rules. For the item business object, examples of attributes include Item Name and the item attribute Inventory Item, among others. You can also use all the enabled descriptive flexfields of the various business objects as attributes in the definition of rules.

The rules framework is seeded with a rich set of business objects. This framework also stores the relationship between the corresponding business object and the context-sensitive operation (that is, Pick, Putaway, Labeling, Cost Group Assignment, and Task Management). Thus, defining new business objects involves defining these complex relationships with the appropriate transaction, which is a technically involved step.

Rules

Rules consist of four key elements: restrictions, sort criteria, quantity function or return value, and (optionally) consistency. Restrictions are constraints that must be satisfied in order that the rule returns a valid dataset. Restrictions are applied on the superset to achieve domain reduction. Sort criteria identifies the order in which you present the reduced domain to the transaction process from a perspective of consumption.

Quantity function determines the formula by which you identify available stock or location capacity. In some rules, quantity function is not used; instead a direct return value can be specified. Consistency allows users to model the resultant set to be consistent within a batch or location. Figure 15-7 shows the OWM Rules form that is used for defining the various types of rules.

The rule type identifies the application for this rule. The rule types supported in the current release can be for picking, putaway, cost group assignment, task type assignment, and label selection.

The suggestion are directly specified or derived using a function. Picking and putaway rules use function-based suggestions. The quantity function for picking rules checks for the available quantity, whereas the quantity function for putaway rules checks for available capacity. Cost group assignment, task type assignment, and labeling rules use direct return values. Additionally, task type assignment and labeling rules can be assigned with a rule weight, which will determine the ordering of these rules during evaluation.

Rule assignment can be organization-specific or common to all organizations. Indicate this using the Common To All Orgs check box. For picking rules, you can indicate whether this rule should consider the pick UOM of the subinventory or locator before considering the locator. Pick UOM was covered in detail in Chapter 2.

Each row in the Restrictions tab is a restriction within a rule. A restriction is a logical expression. Consider the comparison A > B. This logical expression has three parts—two operands and a comparison operator. In the restriction, the left operand is a combination of a business object and a object parameter. The right operand could either be a combination of a business object and an object parameter or a constant value, or it could be derived from a value set as well. The value in the

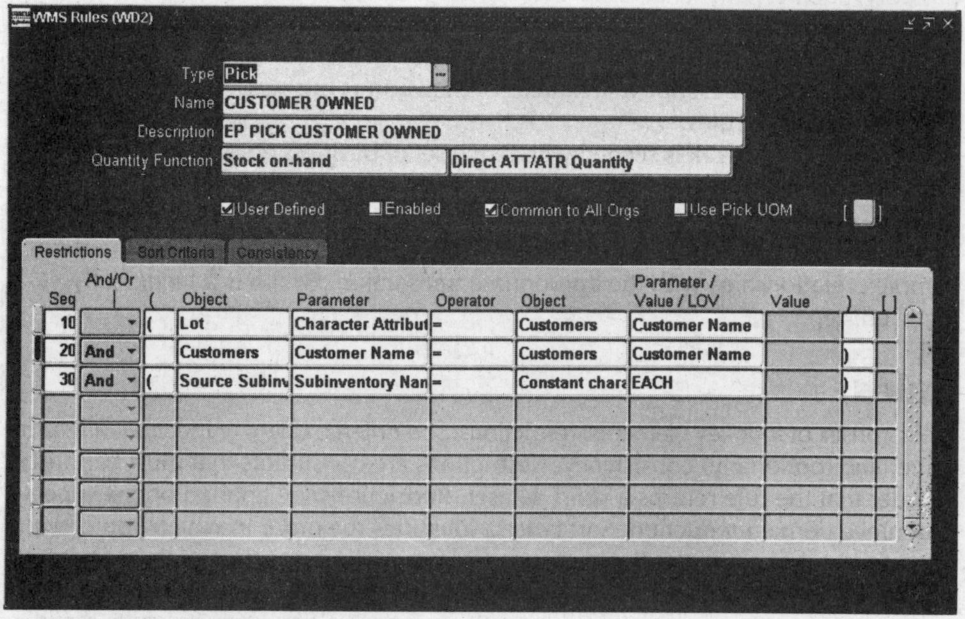

WMS Rules (WD2)

Type Pick

Name CUSTOMER OWNED

Description EP PICK CUSTOMER OWNED

Quantity Function Stock on-hand | Direct ATT/ATR Quantity

☑User Defined ☐Enabled ☑Common to All Orgs ☐Use Pick UOM [ ]

Restrictions | Sort Criteria | Consistency

Seq	And/Or	(	Object	Parameter	Operator	Object	Parameter / Value / LOV	Value	)	[ ]
10		(	Lot	Character Attribut	=	Customers	Customer Name			
20	And		Customers	Customer Name	=	Customers	Customer Name		)	
30	And	(	Source Subinv	Subinventory Nan	=	Constant chara	EACH		)	

FIGURE 15-7. *Configure your rules in the OWM Rules form*

operator column links these two sides. Each restriction is identified by the restriction sequence. Grouping restrictions within the rule is achieved by the AND/OR and (" "). These columns are useful for modeling complex logical expressions.

NOTE
If you want to use a dynamic list of values on the right side for comparison, choose the right hand object as Expression. For the Expression object, you can include a SQL statement in the parameter field, which should evaluate to your dynamic list of values during runtime.

The Sort Criteria tab allows you to sort the picking or putaway suggestions based on certain criteria. This sortation logic allows you to break the ties between two or more suggestions while generating a suggestion. For example, if your picking sort criteria is to sort the possible results in ascending order of the expiration date (FEFO—First Expire First Out), the lots that expire first are suggested first.

The Consistency tab is applicable only for picking rules, and it allows you to specify certain criteria that must be met by all the picks suggested by the rule. For example, you may want to specify that all the picked items should belong to the same lot. Another example might be to get all the items from the same locator. Thus, consistency can be used to establish certain business rules (picking from a single lot) and also for optimizing your warehouse activities (picking from the same locator.)

OWM is packaged with several seeded rules. To create user-defined flavors of these seeded rules, users can copy these rules and modify the content of the rules in their copy. Rules, once defined, may be edited before being enabled. When you complete your definition, enable the rule by using the Enabled check box. When you enable a rule, the rule verification process checks for the validity of your rule. Typical checks include proper usage of parentheses and appropriate data values (string, number, and so on). You cannot edit an enabled rule. To edit the enabled rule, users need to first disable it. This is done to prevent active rules from being modified.

Strategies

Strategies are collections of rules in a specific sequence. The rules within a strategy are evaluated one after the other until the required suggestions are generated. Figure 15-8 shows the Strategies form, which allows you to define strategies and associate rules with strategies.

TIP
Often, the flexibility offered by the rules engine results in different approaches in modeling the same constraint. As a norm, choose the approach that has fewer rules. This may result in improved runtime performance.

When you assign a rule, you specify whether the rule can return with partial success by using the Partial Success Allowed check box. This helps users model the "All or None" scenario.

Each rule that is assigned to the strategy can be assigned with an effectivity. This effectivity control allows you to set up time-dependent and seasonal rule assignments. For example, certain rules may not be applicable in the winter season, whereas certain others may become invalid during the summer season. You specify the effectivity by using the three fields: Date Type, From, and To. Table 15-2 lists the different date types that are available with a short explanation and example From and To values.

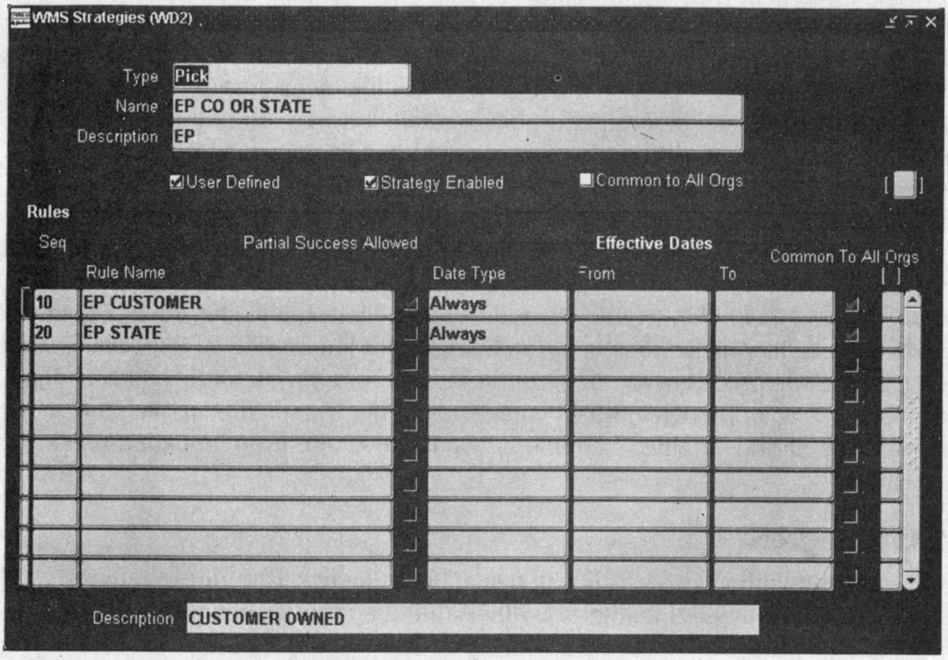

FIGURE 15-8. *Create strategies and assign rules in the OWM Strategies form*

Date Type	Description	Example Values	
		From	**To**
Always	The rule is not time dependent.	NA	NA
Full Date	Date with day of the month, month, and year. Rule will be applicable only within a specific period.	12-JUL-2000	30-JUL-2001
Date	Date without year. Rule will be applicable in a certain period within each year.	June 30	June 30

TABLE 15-2. *Date Type, From, and To Allow You to Set the Effectivity of Rules Within a Strategy*

		Example Values	
Date Type	Description	From	To
Month	Date without year and day of the month. Rule will be applicable in a certain month within each year.	June	August
Day	Days of the week. Rule will be applicable in a certain period within each week.	Monday	Thursday
Shift	Shift-dependent strategies. Rule will be applicable only within a shift on each day.	GraveShift	GraveShift

TABLE 15-2. *Date Type, From, and To Allow You to Set the Effectivity of Rules Within a Strategy* (continued)

TIP
Sequence the rules within each strategy considering the priority of evaluation. For example, a customer-specific rule should be evaluated before an item-specific rule and should be listed ahead of the item-specific rule. Always ensure that your last rule is broad enough to generate a suggestion.

Rule assignment can be organization-specific or common to all organizations. Indicate this using the Common To All Orgs check box.

Strategy Assignments

Strategies are assigned to instances of business objects. For example, the strategy HazMatPick can be assigned to the item M100300, which is a hazardous chemical. When you associate a strategy to an instance of a business object, you are essentially establishing a policy at that business object level. Figure 15-9 shows the Strategy Assignments form.

You can associate each business object with three strategies—one each for pick, putaway, and cost group assignment. When a picking suggestion is generated for this business object, the assigned pick strategy is used. Similarly the putaway and cost group strategies are used when the appropriate suggestions are generated.

Let's explain the strategy assignment process with an example. A strategy called STANDARD is considered applicable to all items in an organization and hence is assigned at the organization level. A zone that stores hazardous chemicals in this organization is assigned with a strategy called HAZMATZON. Within that zone are

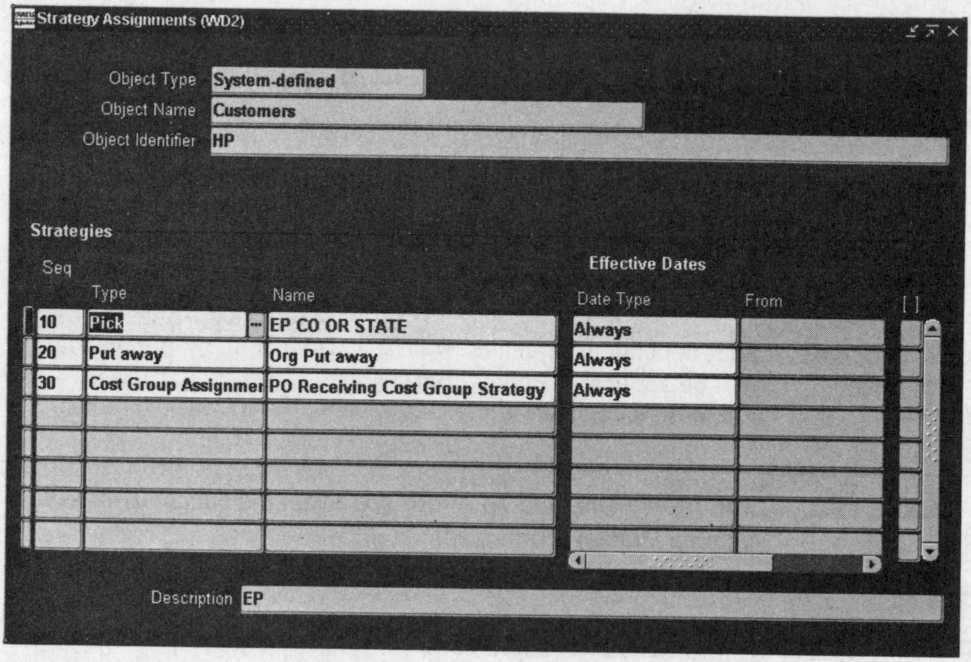

FIGURE 15-9. *Assign strategies to business objects in the Strategy Assignments form*

certain locators that store items that need a different way of handling. A strategy called HAZMATLOC is assigned to each of these locators. Finally, certain items require much more specialized handling. Strategies that satisfy those requirements are created and assigned to each of those items. The strategy search order for item, locator, subinventory, and organization is 1, 2, 3, and 4 respectively. In this example, strategies were established at four levels. Figure 15-10 illustrates the applicability of the four levels of strategy assignment.

When you assign strategies to business objects, assign strategies that are broader in nature to objects that have a wider applicability. Once you establish these broader strategies, you should concentrate on exceptions. Because every activity happens within the context of an organization, consider establishing a very broad policy at the organizational level.

TIP
You can find the rule and strategy that resulted in generating the suggestion in the Material Transaction History.

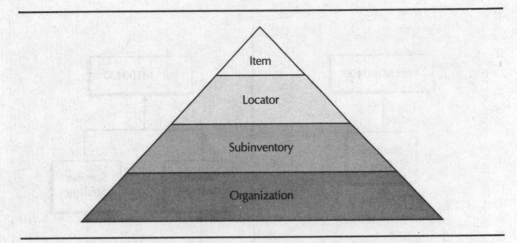

FIGURE 15-10. *Objects that have wider applicability should be assigned with strategies that have a broader perspective and should be accorded lower priority in the strategy search order*

You can assign strategies to business objects with effectivity. The effectivity options available at the rule assignment level (listed in Table 15-2) are available during strategy assignment as well.

Effectivity control during rule assignment and strategy assignment is offered for greater flexibility. In most cases, it is possible to achieve the same results using effectivity control at one of these levels as illustrated by Figure 15-11. If two or more currently effective strategies are assigned to a business object, the strategy with the lowest sequence number will be used.

The level of flexibility is often associated with ease of use. As the level of flexibility increases, the level of complexity increases. In areas where there's a lot of flexibility, it is better to establish some procedural controls. Because you have to test your rules for various conditions before releasing it for production, consider making a policy in your organization that your effectivity controls are used only at one of these levels. This way, if you get unexpected results, it's easier for you to troubleshoot at one place rather than going back and forth between two places.

Strategy Search Order

Strategy search order specifies the business object hierarchy within an organization, which is used by the rules engine to select the appropriate strategy. For example, you can associate the picking strategy OrgPickStrategy at the organization level and the strategy HazMatPickStrategy for a set of items. The intent for this is to use HazMatPickStrategy for certain items and OrgPickStrategy for the remaining items. In this case, you should specify the strategy search order as item and then organization.

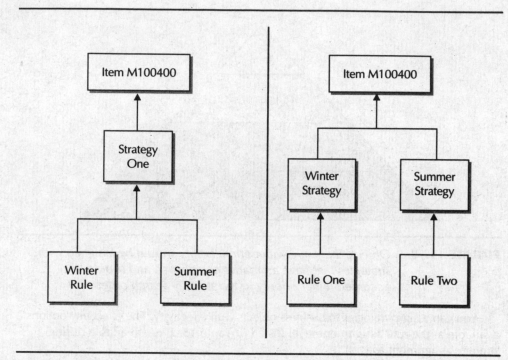

FIGURE 15-11. *You can establish date effectivity at both the rule assignment level and the strategy assignment level*

During strategy search, the business object with the lowest search order is accorded the highest priority.

NOTE
Strategy search order identifies the hierarchy of business object-level policies. Establishing the strategy search order is a one-time step that you perform as part of the implementation process. It is analogous to establish policies ahead of conducting business.

You specify the strategy search order using the Strategy Search Order form. When you establish your strategy search order, give higher priority to the objects that might need special handling. Item-level strategies, for example, would need to be accorded a higher priority than the organizational-level strategy.

Where Used Inquiries

OWM provides the strategy and rules Where Used forms to analyze the impact of modifying a rule or a strategy. The OWM Strategy Where Used form shows the object types and object identifiers to which a particular strategy is associated. The OWM Rules Where Used form shows the strategies in which a particular rule is used. When you want to modify a rule or a strategy that is used in production, use these Where Used forms to analyze the impact.

Rules Logical Data Model

The rules framework consists of four important entities: business object, strategy, rule, and restriction. The logical data model in Figure 15-12 highlights these entities and the relationships between them. It also shows the strategy search order that is established as a part of the initial implementation.

As shown in the figure, although the business objects are common across the framework, rules and strategies are designated for specific business purposes. For example, the Picking Rule and Picking Strategy address the business problem of picking within the rules framework.

Applications of the Rules–Strategy–Business Object Framework

The picking, putaway, and cost group assignment processes use the Rules–Strategy–Business object framework to generate suggestions. The suggestion generation process is shown in Figure 15-13.

NOTE
If after applying a strategy the rules engine is not able to come up with the required results, organization level defaults will be used.

The picking, putaway, and cost group assignment rules use this framework. Note that although you may have a number of strategies assigned to various business objects, only one strategy is used for a suggestion. Once a strategy is selected using the strategy search order, the rules within the strategy are executed to generate the suggestion. If even after applying all the rules, the suggestion cannot be completed, the rules engine does not go back to the strategy search order to pick the next strategy.

Applications of the Standalone Rules Framework

The task type assignment and labeling rules use the Standalone Rules framework. These rules have a rule weight that is used by the rules engine to sequence the rules before evaluating each of them.

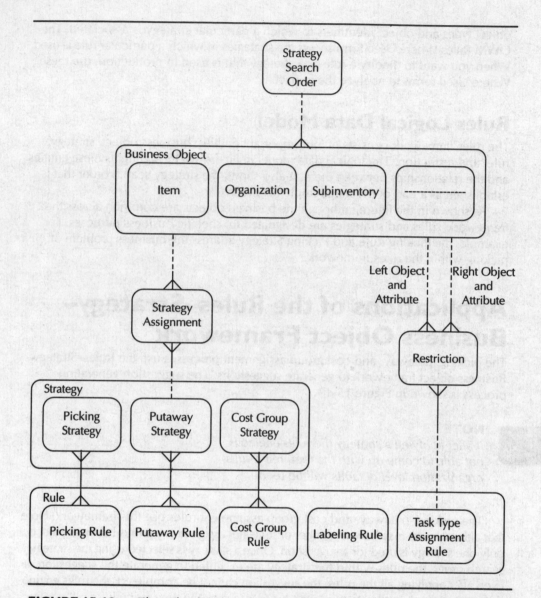

FIGURE 15-12. *The rules framework logical data model highlights the important entities in the rules framework*

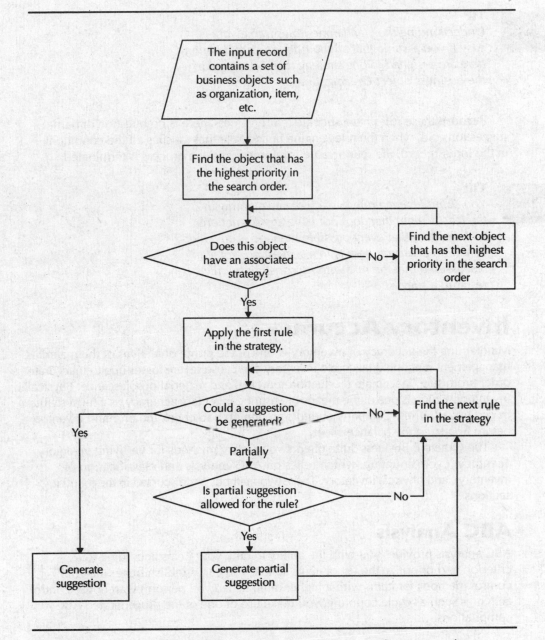

FIGURE 15-13.   *The suggestion generation process for applications in the Rules–Strategy–Business Object framework*

TIP
*Understanding the Standalone Rules framework is
easy if you assume that all the rules you are defining
here are assigned to one strategy that is assigned to
the business object Organization.*

Because these rules have specific return values, there is no question of partial
suggestions. So, when the rules engine finds a rule that satisfies all the conditions
in the input record, the return value is returned, and the process is terminated.

TIP
*You should have a rule in each organization with
the least weight that does not have any restrictions,
to make sure that every possible scenario is covered.
When no other rule results in a suggestion, you can
rest assured that the rule with no constraints will
result in a suggestion.*

Inventory Accuracy

Maintaining the accuracy of inventory is one of the prime objectives of the materials
management function. Inaccurate inventory can cause severe losses due to inaccurate
order promising, inaccurate production sourcing, and material obsolescence. Physical
inventory, which is one of the means of ensuring inventory accuracy, is a legal statute
in certain countries. Company auditors are required to check the on-hand inventory
before finalizing the balance sheet.

The Oracle E-Business Suite offers two primary methods for verifying inventory
accuracy: cycle counting (which relies on ABC analysis and classification of
inventory), and physical inventory. These two methods are discussed in the following
sections.

ABC Analysis

ABC analysis provides you with the ability to rank your items according to a
criterion and prioritize the list of items so that you can establish better material
control methods for items with a higher rank. When you perform warehouse control
activities such as cycle counting, you make use of one of the pregenerated ABC
compilations.

ABC Compiles

You define ABC analysis in the Define ABC Compile form. The Content Scope
allows you to decide on the items that you want to include in the analysis—all
items in the organization or only the items in the specified subinventory. If you use

Organization as the content scope, all the items that are enabled in the organization are included in the analysis; if the content scope is Subinventory, all the items that have a defined item-subinventory relationship with this subinventory are included in the analysis. As far as the content scope is considered, the current on-hand quantity and item cost are irrelevant. That is, items with zero on-hand quantity and zero cost are included in the analysis.

The Valuation Scope is used for ranking the items within the ABC compile. If your content scope is Organization, your valuation scope is automatically Organization. If your content scope is Subinventory, you can set the valuation scope to be either Organization or Subinventory.

If you set the valuation scope as Subinventory, the items that are included in the analysis are ranked based on their position within the subinventory, according to the chosen criterion. For example, assume that you have items M100000 and M100010 in the subinventory with a quantity of 5 and 20 respectively. When your compile criterion is Current on-hand quantity, item M100010 will be ranked higher than M100000.

NOTE
Compiles based on on-hand quantity is shown as a simple example only; most experts would recommend that a compile be generated on a basis that includes both usage (either historical or projected) and unit value. Oracle provides these methodologies as well.

If your valuation scope is Organization, the items that are included in the analysis are ranked based on their position in the whole organization, according to the chosen criterion. Extending the example from the previous paragraph, if the quantities of M100000 and M100010 at the organizational level are 200 and 100, respectively, item M100000 will be ranked higher than M100010.

ABC analysis is a very general term. The Compile Criterion allows you to rank your items based on various criteria. Some of the standard classifications that are used in the industry are discussed in the following paragraphs, along with the respective compile criteria.

FSN Analysis   The classifications fast moving, slow moving, and nonmoving (FSN) are used for ranking items so that you can stock the fast moving items closer to the shipping docks and periodically dispose of the non-moving items. If you create an ABC compilation with one of three material usage quantity criteria—Historical Usage Quantity, Forecasted Usage Quantity, or MRP Demand Usage Quantity—the resulting ABC compilation would be an FSN compilation.

Unit Cost Grouping   Classifying your materials based on their unit costs is currently not supported by any compile criterion. You can achieve the same results by setting up a new subinventory (non-nettable, non-ATP, and nonreservable). Using a custom script, load all the items into this subinventory with a quantity of one. Perform a subinventory level ABC compilation for this subinventory with the current on-hand value as the compile criterion. This will produce a compilation that is based on the unit cost of the item.

Once you finish generating a compilation, have a custom script remove all the items from the subinventory by transacting the material out. If you want to recompile your ABC assignments, you can reload all the items again and then perform the compilation.

Usage Value Analysis   When you want to classify your items based on their overall usage value, you choose one of the usage value criteria: Current on-hand value, Historical usage value, Forecasted usage value, or MRP demand usage value. Usage value analysis gives you the effect of considering both unit price (which is the criterion for unit cost grouping) and usage quantity (which is the criterion for FSN analysis).

Management by Exception   When you want to rank your items based on the problems encountered during the previous cycle count, use either Previous cycle count adjustment quantity or Previous cycle count adjustment value. This way, you can exercise more control over items that have problems during a cycle count.

Sometimes, the number of transactions that happen on an item is an indicator of the potential number of inaccuracies that can result on an item. If you want to rank your items based on the transaction volume, you use Historical number of transactions.

ABC Classes

ABC Classes are used for identifying the item groupings within an ABC classification. You can define the classes to suit the terminology in your company. For example, you can use the standard terms A, B, and C, or you can define High, Medium, and Low for ranking items by usage value. Similarly, fast, slow, and nonmoving would allow you to rank items based on usage quantity. Furthermore, you can have as many classes as you need.

ABC Assignment Groups

ABC assignment group links an ABC compile to the various ABC classes that are assigned to the assignment group. To assign items to the classes, click the Assign Items button. For example, you could assign the classes High, Medium, and Low to the ABC assignment group with the top 5 percent of items in the High class, the next 15 percent in the Medium class, and the last 80 percent in the Low class. To manually include items or update the item assignments, click the Update Items button.

Cycle Counting

Cycle counting is a procedure in which a selected list of items are physically counted to verify the on-hand quantities of those items. Unlike Physical Inventory, which typically counts *all* the inventory in an organization once a year, cycle counting normally involves continuous counting of a subset of inventory on a regular cycle, usually prioritized by ABC classification. For example, you will count your A items more frequently than your B or C items.

Cycle counting offers a number of advantages when compared to physical inventory:

- Fewer items are counted each day, so there is less disruption to normal production or distribution operations.

- Although all items are normally counted in the course of a yearly cycle, the high-value (A an B) items are counted more often, providing bigger "bang for the buck."

- More frequent counting of high-value parts offers a much better opportunity to identify and correct the *causes* of error, rather than just fixing the numbers.

- Cycle counting often relies only on the material handling professionals in an organization, and thus can be inherently more accurate. By contrast, physical inventory often requires that *all* personnel on the shop floor (and sometimes the front office) participate in the count. A wry sage once remarked, "There are three kinds of people in world—those who can count and those who can't." In a physical inventory, the mass mobilization of resources often involves the use of people who simply "can't count." This is not because of skill or intellect, but just because the office workers may not know proper item identification or the correct unit of measure. Physical inventory sometimes results in creating as many errors as it corrects.

In areas where physical inventory is not a statutory requirement, many companies have been able to satisfy their auditors with a good cycle counting program and thus can avoid the disruption of an annual physical inventory.

You can define and maintain an unlimited number of cycle counts. For example, you can define separate cycle counts for each of your zones.

You define a cycle count in the Cycle Counts form. The cycle count header contains a set of parameters including the cycle count name. The workday calendar is used to determine the days on which cycle count needs to be scheduled automatically. The general ledger account is used to charge cycle count adjustments.

The Control, Scope tab allows you to specify the last effective date after which the cycle count becomes inactive. Enter the number of workdays that can pass after the date the count request was generated before a scheduled count becomes a late count. Enter the sequence number to use as the starting number in the next count request generator. The count sequence number uniquely identifies a particular count and is used in ordering the cycle count listing.

Specify whether you can enter counts for items not scheduled to be counted and whether to display system on-hand quantities during count entry. Specify whether items with out-of-tolerance counts should be automatically assigned with a status of Recount and included in the next cycle count listing. If the cycle count is not for the current organization, you can navigate to the Subinventory region and select the subinventories to include in the cycle count.

The Count option in the Serial Control, Schedule tab is used to specify whether to exclude serialized items from the cycle count, create one count request for each serial number, or create multiple serial details in a count request. The Detail option allows you to specify if you want to capture serial numbers during the count process. If the detail option is Quantity Only, serial number entry is optional if the count quantity matches the system quantity. The Adjustment option allows you to specify if the discrepancies can be automatically adjusted or if every count needs to be reviewed by the approver.

You can enable the cycle count for automatic scheduling. If you turn automatic scheduling on, you should specify the Frequency of scheduling—daily, weekly, or by period. This information is used, along with the count frequency of each cycle count class, during automatic cycle count scheduling. The value you enter here dictates the amount of time that is available to complete the generated cycle count requests. The last scheduled date is displayed for informational purposes. The next scheduled date is also displayed, although you can enter a different date to override the automatically scheduled date.

In the Adjustments, ABC tab specify when approval is required for adjustments. If you choose Never, all adjustments are automatically performed. If you choose Always, all the cycle counts need to be approved before they can be adjusted. Only the counts that are out of tolerance need to be approved if the approval option is Out Of Tolerance. The Hit/Miss% is used for hit/miss reporting. A count is considered a hit if the count variance is within the Hit/Miss% from the system quantity.

The cycle count item initialization or update is based on the Group that is specified in the ABC initialization or update information. If the initialization option is None, the existing list of cycle count items is not changed. The (Re)initialize option deletes existing information and reloads the items from the ABC group. The Update option results in updating any ABC classification changes and allows you to indicate whether to delete unused item assignments that are no longer referenced in the specified ABC group.

Cycle Count Classes

You enter cycle count classes in the Cycle Count Classes window. You can enter ABC classes to include in your cycle count. You can also enter approval and hit/miss tolerances for your cycle count classes. For each class that is included in the cycle count, enter the number of times per year you want to count each item in this class.

You can enter positive and negative tolerances for each class, which will override the tolerances at the cycle count header level. The tolerances are of two types—quantity and value. The Hit/Miss% for the class overrides the Hit/Miss% of the cycle count header.

Including Items in a Cycle Count

You need to load items into your cycle count before you can schedule or count them. You can either enter the items manually in the Cycle Counts window or automatically include items based on an ABC group. You specify an ABC group from which to load your items and all items in the ABC group you choose are automatically included in your cycle count. The ABC classes for that ABC group are also copied into the current cycle count classes and the classifications of the included items are also retained.

Once you have generated your list of items to count from an ABC group, you can periodically refresh the item list with new or reclassified items from a regenerated ABC group. Using the Cycle Counts window, you can choose whether to automatically update class information for existing items in the cycle count based on the new ABC assignments. When you choose the items to include in your cycle count, you can specify which items make up your control group. The control group items can be included in a cycle count every time when you generate automatic schedules, regardless of their schedule frequency.

Cycle Count Scheduling

You can schedule cycle counts either automatically or manually. The number of items in each cycle count class, the count frequency of each class, and the workday calendar of the organization are used to determine the items that need to be included in the scheduled cycle count. In the case of automatic scheduling, the Cycle Count Enabled item attribute should be set to Yes for the items you want to include in the cycle count, and automatic scheduling should be enabled when you define your cycle count.

To generate automatic schedules, invoke the Cycle Count Scheduler from the Tools menu. In the Cycle Count Scheduler Parameters window, indicate whether to include items belonging to the control group. The auto scheduler schedules counts only for the schedule interval you defined for the cycle count header.

You can also manually schedule counts using the Manual Schedule Requests window. You can request counts for specific subinventories, locators, and items. You can manually schedule specific items or all items in a subinventory. If you enter an item and a subinventory, the item is scheduled only in this subinventory.

Count Requests

After you have successfully scheduled your counts, the process Generate Count Requests should be submitted to generate count requests. This process takes the output of the automatic scheduler and the manually scheduled entries and generates a count request with a unique sequence number for each item number, revision, lot number, subinventory, and locator combination for which on-hand quantities exist. These count requests are ordered first by subinventory and locator, then by item, revision and lot.

If OWM is enabled for an organization, these count requests can be dispatched as tasks to the users who are performing the cycle counting one-by-one.

Cycle Count Approvals

The Count Adjustment Approvals Summary window allows you to approve the count adjustments that require approvals. You can access this window by choosing Tools | Approve Counts. You can approve or reject the adjustment, or you might ask for a recount.

Physical Inventory

Physical inventory is the periodic reconciliation of physical inventory with system on-hand quantity. In some countries, performing a physical inventory of the legal entity's assets at the end of the fiscal year is a legal requirement. Oracle provides a fully automated physical inventory feature that can be used to reconcile system-maintained item on-hand balances with actual counts of inventory. Although physical inventory involves physically counting items, just like cycle counting, there are some major philosophical and technical differences:

■ Physical inventory takes a snapshot of inventory on-hand quantities at the beginning of the process; all adjustments are made against the snapshot quantity.

■ Physical inventory generates unique tag numbers for recording counts; missing tags can be identified, and "blank" tags can be generated to record quantities of unexpected material that turns up in the process. (With cycle counting, you'd need to use a miscellaneous transaction to report "found" material.)

■ Physical counts are reviewed, and either accepted or rejected, as a whole. In contrast, cycle count adjustments are performed as each count is entered, provided the count is within tolerance.

■ Physical inventory has no predefined tolerances; it is a user's decision to accept or reject the entire count.

See the Oracle Inventory User's Guide for details on running a physical inventory.

Inventory Planning

Material Planning (MRP and ASCP) was covered extensively in Part II. This section presents an overview of the inventory planning features that allow you to manage your inventory levels using two planning methods—Min–Max Planning and Re-Order Point Planning. Any planning algorithm is concerned with answering two questions—when to order and how much to order. Figure 15-14 shows how the two inventory planning methods handle these two questions.

You can use only one of the two planning methods for an item at the organization level. You select the planning method for an item by using the item attribute Inventory Planning Method in the General Planning tab. The choices are Min–Max Planning, Reorder Point Planning, and Not Planned. Depending on the planning method that is enabled for an item, additional attributes have to be set up. Optionally, you can enable an item for Min–Max Planning at the subinventory level.

Establishing sources at the organization level and at the subinventory level were covered in Chapter 2. Using the same methodology, you can establish the sources at the item level using the three item attributes: Source Type, Source Organization, and Source Subinventory. These sourcing attributes are available at the subinventory

	Min-Max Planning	Re-Order Point Planning
When to Order?	When the Current Quantity On Hand falls below the Minimum Inventory that is required	When the Current Quantity On Hand falls below the Re-Order Point
How much to Order?	The difference between Maximum Stockable Quantity and the Current Quantity On Hand	The Economic Order Quantity is calculated and used

FIGURE 15-14. *Min–Max Planning and Re-Order Point Planning handle when to order and how much to order*

item level as well. You can establish these sources in the Subinventory Item window. When you perform subinventory level planning, the program attempts to get the sourcing information in the following sequence—Subinventory Item, Item, Subinventory, and Organization. When you perform organization-level planning, the sequence is as follows: Item and Organization.

Min–Max Planning

Min–Max Planning allows you to specify the maximum and minimum inventory levels for your items and maintain on-hand balances between these two levels. Min–Max planning triggers a supply order when the quantity on-hand falls below the minimum inventory level. By default, Min–Max tries to restore the inventory balance to the maximum level. For example, if the minimum quantity is 25 and the maximum quantity is 100, Min–Max will create a supply request when the on-hand balance drops to 24. The requisition quantity will be 76. Although Min–Max takes the pending demand and supply into consideration, it does not take the lead time to source or fulfill those quantities into consideration.

TIP
Your minimum inventory level should be set considering the lead-time demand and safety stock requirements. You should also ensure that your Min–Max levels avoid too many orders being placed.

Min–Max does take the order modifiers into consideration while creating the supply request. Order modifiers were discussed in Chapter 8.

Min–Max Planning at the Organization Level

To enable an item for Min–Max planning at the organization level, choose Min–Max Planning as the value for the item attribute Inventory Planning Method. Specify the minimum and maximum inventory levels by using the item attributes Min–Max Minimum Quantity and Min–Max Maximum Quantity, respectively. Depending on the value of the Make Or Buy item attribute, the program will generate either work orders or requisitions as supply.

Min–Max Planning at the Subinventory Level

In the Subinventory Items window, specify the planning method as Min–Max Planning. Specify the minimum and maximum inventory levels using the attributes Min–Max Minimum Quantity and Min–Max Maximum Quantity, respectively. Subinventory-level planning generates only requisitions.

Min–Max Planning Concurrent Program

To perform Min–Max planning, run the Min–Max Planning report. Choose the planning level as Organization or Subinventory. If the planning level is Subinventory, you should select a subinventory. The parameter Restock allows you to specify whether you want to create supply orders. You can set Restock to No to print a report. If you set Restock to Yes, the program will create requisitions or work orders appropriately.

Reorder Point Planning

An item is enabled for Reorder Point (ROP) Planning by using the item attribute Inventory Planning Method. Once you enable an item for ROP Planning, provide the values for all the related attributes—Pre-Processing Lead Time, Processing Lead Time, Post-Processing Lead Time, Order Cost, and Carrying Cost Percentage.

Safety Stock

Safety stock provides the cushion that protects your consuming lines from fluctuations in the supply process. The safety stock level for each item can either be calculated automatically or be entered manually. You can also use MRP or ASCP to dynamically calculate safety stock, as was discussed in Chapter 8.

If you set the attribute Safety Stock Method to Non MRP Planned, you can calculate the safety stock using the methods that are available in the Enter Safety Stocks window. You can use the mean absolute deviation or a user-defined percentage of forecasted demand. Once you're in this window, select Tools | Reload to invoke the Reload parameters. The choice of methods are Mean Absolute Deviation and User-Defined Percentage.

If you select User-Defined Percentage, the safety stock is calculated as the gross demand for the forecast period multiplied by the value of the parameter Safety Stock Percent. If you select Mean Absolute Deviation, specify the service level. The safety stock is calculated using the following formula:

Safety Stock = Z×1.25×MAD

MAD is the average of the absolute deviations of the historic forecasts from the actual demand. Z is the probability value from the normal distribution that corresponds to the specified service level.

ROP Planning Calculations

When you run ROP Planning, the reorder point is calculated using the following formula:

Reorder Point = Safety Stock + Forecast Demand during Lead Time

The lead time is the sum of the Pre-Processing, Processing, and Post-Processing lead times. Because safety stock is controlled by date effectivity, it is possible to have different safety stock levels during the lead time. In such cases, the largest of safety stock during the lead time will be used. The demand from forecasts during the lead time is added to the safety stock to get the reorder point.

NOTE
ROP Planning uses forecasts as its source of anticipated demand. Because you can only establish forecasts at the organization level, ROP Planning is available only at the organization level.

The ROP Planning process creates a supply request for a quantity that is equal to the economic order quantity (EOQ), when the on-hand quantity is less than the reorder point. The EOQ is given by the formula that is shown here:

$$\text{Economic Order Quantity} = \sqrt{\frac{2 \times \text{Annual Demand} \times \text{Ordering Cost}}{\text{Inventory Carrying Cost Percent} \times \text{Unit Cost}}}$$

The annual demand is calculated by annualizing the current demand rate. The ordering cost and inventory carrying cost are obtained from the item attributes.

ROP Planning Concurrent Program
To perform ROP planning, you run the Reorder Point Planning report. The planning level is always Organization. The parameter Create Requisitions allows you to specify whether you want to create requisitions or not. You can set this parameter to No for simulation runs. If you set this to Yes, the program will create requisitions.

Replenishment Counting

In subinventories where you are not maintaining perpetual on-hand balances, you can use the replenishment counting system to plan your inventories. This may be ideal for replenishing free stock items that you don't intend to keep track of. You can only use the replenishment counting system at the subinventory level. To use replenishment counting, you must set up item-subinventory relationships using the Item Subinventories or Subinventory Items windows.

You create a replenishment count in the Replenishment Count Headers window. While generating the replenishment, you can choose to specify the order quantity or choose the maximum order quantity from the Min–Max planning settings. You enter the count details through the Replenishment Counts window. The Process

Replenishment Counts program processes the replenishment counts and creates requisitions for items that need to be ordered, or it creates move orders for items to be replenished from a subinventory.

Replenishment Tasks

A move order line is created for each item found to need replenishment where the supply source type is subinventory. The move order line is allocated based on the picking and put away rules. (Move order is covered in the section "Move Orders" and rules are covered in the section "The Rules Framework.") After the lines are allocated, the rules engine is invoked to assign a task type for each task. These tasks are then dispatched to qualified users. (Task type assignment and task dispatching are covered in the section "Task Management.")

Data Field Identifiers in Barcode Scanning

Barcoding speeds up data entry and avoids data entry errors. All the mobile transaction forms (also called *pages*) support barcoded data. Data field identifiers (DFI) are used for identifying the type of data that is embedded within a barcode while scanning them using a barcode reader. For example, the DFI for an item number is I+. DFIs allow you to scan data in an arbitrary sequence. That is, if your data entry page has item number followed by the transaction type, you are not constrained to scan these data in that sequence. If you use DFIs to identify these fields, the correct field will be populated regardless of the sequence of scanning. If you don't use DFIs, the current field will be populated with the scanned information.

NOTE
Oracle Applications comes seeded with industry standard DFIs.

Attribute-Level DFI

The AK Dictionary stores the DFI information. You can also configure your field labels in the dictionary. The Define Attributes form (available from the standard AK Developer responsibility) is used for defining DFIs at the attribute level. The DFI for each attributes is entered in the Default Varchar2 Value field.

Region-Level DFI

Instead of defining DFIs attribute-by-attribute, you can define DFIs at the region level. In the Define Regions form (available from the standard AK Developer responsibility), find the resource table for your application by using the Region ID. For inventory and OWM, the region ID is INVRESOURCETABLE. Once you find the resource table, click the Region Items button. On the Region Items window, locate your appropriate field(s) and specify the DFIs in the Default Varchar2 Value field.

The DFI String

The DFI string always takes the following format:

DFI=Q+, q+, Q, q REQ=N

This DFI indicates that four DFIs (Q+, q+, Q and q) may be used for this field. It also indicates that this field can take values without a DFI. To make the DFI required for a field, use the REQ=Y instead of REQ=N after the DFI list.

CAUTION
DFIs should be listed in the order they should be validated against. In your DFI sequence for a field, if you enter A before A+, this will result in data validation errors for data that have A+ as the DFI. For example, assume that the field is A+M493874. When the mobile server reads this value, it immediately resolves it based on the first character and identifies the field because there is a match for A before A+. So the field value would be +M493874. To avoid this, arrange your DFI list from most specific to least specific. In this example, A+ should come before A in the sequence.

Compliance Labeling

Customers might require you to ship your items with a label that suits them. Sometimes, you may be required to provide different kind of information in your labels to comply with the legal requirements of the state or countries in which the transaction takes place. The compliance labeling support provided by OWM allows you to handle these and similar requirements.

NOTE
*The tables WMS_LABELS and WMS_LABEL_FIELDS
store the information about labels.*

Label Types

Label types identify what information is applicable to a particular label format. Oracle
has provided eight label types: Material label, Serial label, LPN label, LPN Contents
label, LPN Summary label, Location label, Shipping label, and Shipping Contents label.
These label types are associated with a set of fields. When you define a label format,
the list of fields is restricted based on the label type that you choose.

Business Flows

Within OWM, business flows represent the various transaction points where a label
may be required. For example, Receipt is the business flow that represents receiving
materials. OWM has enabled 22 business flows for which you can automate label
printing.

Assigning Label Types to Business Flows

Once all the label types and the business flows are defined, assign the appropriate
label types to each business flow. The Assign Label Types to Business Flows form
that is shown in Figure 15-15 allows you to do that. As a part of executing each
business flow, Oracle will generate an XML file and write this to a specific directory.
The labeling software (third-party software) has polling processes that take each
XML file, generate the label, and direct it to the appropriate printer.

NOTE
*Not all the label types can be associated with every
business flow. For example, Location label types
cannot be associated with the Receipt business flow.
Please refer the product documentation for OWM to
check if a particular label type can be associated
with a business flow.*

Label Formats

You define label formats by using the Define Label Formats form. Each label format
is based on a label type. You can disable a label format by using the effectivity date.
The Default Label check box allows you to specify the default label for a particular
label type. If the rules engine is not able to suggest a label format based on the

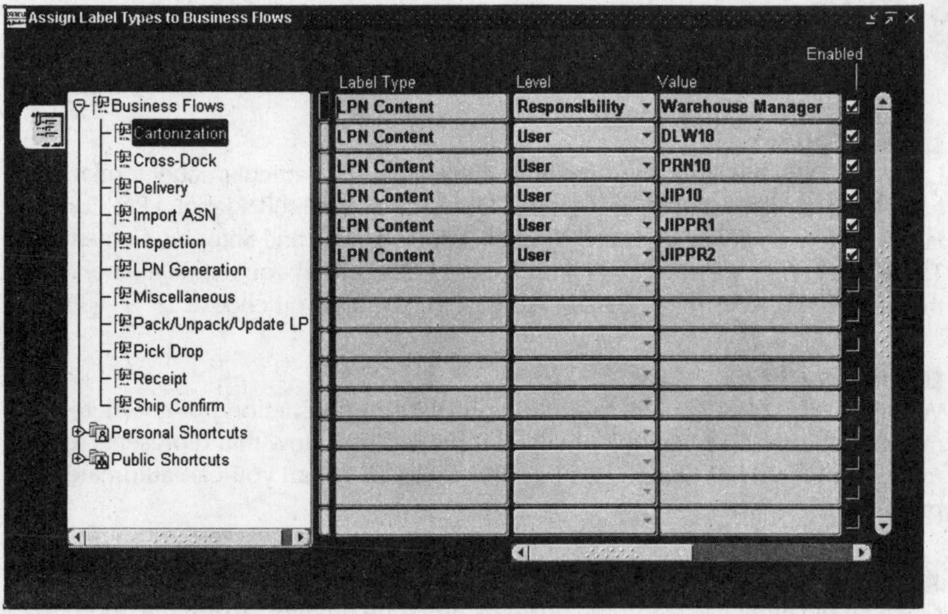

FIGURE 15-15. *Assign label types to business flows to indicate label usage*

available rules, the default label format for that type will be suggested. You can have only one label format as the default for each label type.

NOTE
Label format rules were covered earlier in the section "The Rules Framework." If you want a label format to be considered, you have to define at least one rule with that label format as the return value.

Once you define the label format, you can select all the fields that are applicable in that label format. The Label Fields button in the Define Label Formats form takes you to the Define Label Field Variables window, which allows you to select the appropriate fields for a format. For each field that is selected in a particular format, specify the Field Variable Name that is used for passing information on to the labeling software.

CAUTION
The XML file that is generated contains the name of the label format and the Field Variable Names as tags that identify each field. You should make sure that the labeling software understands these variable names.

Not all printers are capable of printing all the labels. So, once you have defined your label formats, associate each label format with the appropriate printers by using the Choose Document and Label Printers form.

The Label Generation Process

When a business flow is being executed, one label format per applicable label type will be returned based on the label format rules. For each label format, an XML file is generated, based on the label format definition. This XML file will be read by a labeling software, which interprets this information and prints the appropriate label.

Container Management

The Container Management feature in Oracle Applications allows users to define containers in and pack/unpack materials into these containers. Users have visibility to the contents of containers and can transact material by container instead of individually.

Containers are items. A container item is identified using the Container flag in the Physical Attributes tab of item attributes. The Physical Attributes tab that is shown in Figure 15-16 also contains other physical attributes, such as the container type, internal volume, maximum load weight, and the minimum fill percent of the container item. These capacities will not prevent the user from overpacking but will issue a warning if a user attempts to put more items in a full container.

The attributes in the sections Weight, Volume, and Dimensions apply to both container and contained items. This information is used as packaging constraints by the cartonization process while generating packaging recommendations.

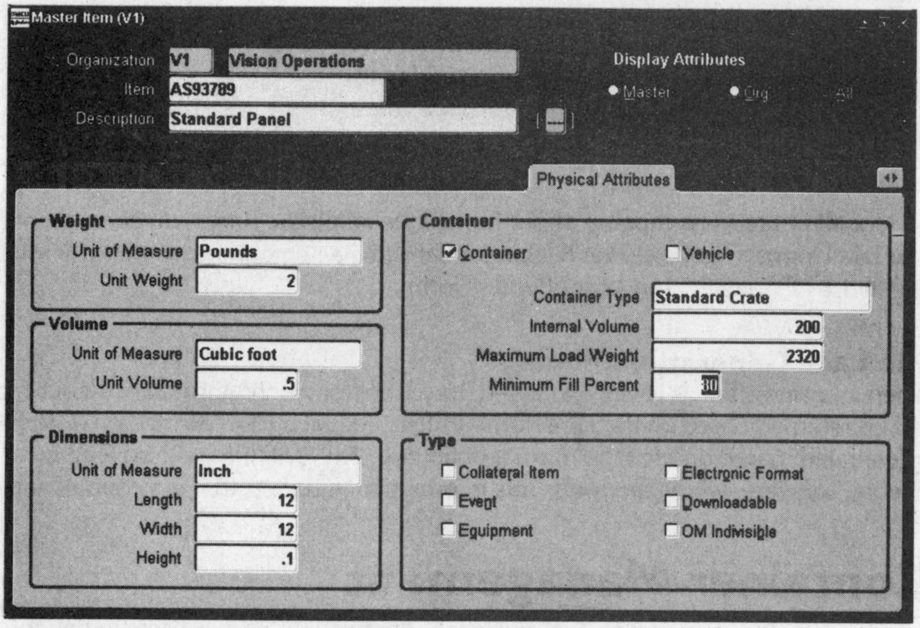

FIGURE 15-16. *Define the physical attributes of container items in the Items form*

CAUTION
Weight, Volume, and Dimensions should all be entered for each of the container and contained items. If any of this information is not defined, cartonization will fail. Cartonization is covered later in this chapter.

Because containers are items, they can be replenished through inventory replenishment mechanisms such as the Min–Max or ROP planning. Containers can be planned as other items if they are included on the bill of materials for the finished goods they are used to store. This enables users to forecast their container requirements. As with other items, a user can view the on-hand balances of containers in a particular inventory location.

Typically reusable container items are serial controlled. The serial number serves to identify the container instance during its life. Reusable containers will be supported in a future release of OWM.

License Plate Numbers

A License Plate Number (LPN) serves as a unique identifier for each individual container. LPNs can be pregenerated and associated with containers at a later time. So, an LPN need not be associated with a container item when the LPN is created. The pregenerated LPNs that are not associated with any container item do not have any container item's characteristics, such as capacity, dimensions, and so on.

You specify the default prefix, default suffix, and the starting LPN Number Revision, Lot, Serial, LPN tab of the organization parameters by using the Prefix, Suffix, and the Starting LPN Number fields in the LPN Generating options. You generate LPNs by using the Generate LPN concurrent program.

LPN is not the same as the container item serial number. The serial number of a container item is used to track the container during its entire life, whereas during the course of its life the container may be associated with many LPNs depending on the number of times the container was cycled through different warehouses and manufacturing plants.

NOTE
The tables WMS_LICENSE_PLATE_NUMBERS, WMS_LPN_CONTENTS, and WMS_LPN_ HISTORIES store all the LPN information.

At the LPN (container instance) level, OWM stores information about the contents and location, status, a history of all transactions, and whether the container has been sealed. Sealed containers cannot be packed, unpacked, or partially reserved. You can view the on-hand balances of LPNs of a particular container item as well as the balance of the unused container items that do not have an associated LPN.

The transaction history and current location of each LPN is stored by OWM at all times. They could reside in the following:

- Receiving

- Inventory (in a subinventory and locator)

- WIP (used for packing, as assemblies are completed)

- Transit (notice sent through an advanced shipment notice [ASN] or interorg transfers)

- Trading partner site

The LPN Contents form allows you to view the contents of a specific LPN. The top-right block provides information on the LPN itself, including location, associated container item, and LPN number. The left panel provides a tree view of the hierarchy of containers. In the lower-right block, the contents of the highlighted LPN on the left pane is displayed. Contents can be items or containers. If the item is lot- or serial-controlled, you can view that information using the Lot/Serial button. Figure 15-17 illustrates how you can use the mobile forms to view the contents and details of an LPN. You can also use the Material Workbench to view the contents of an LPN.

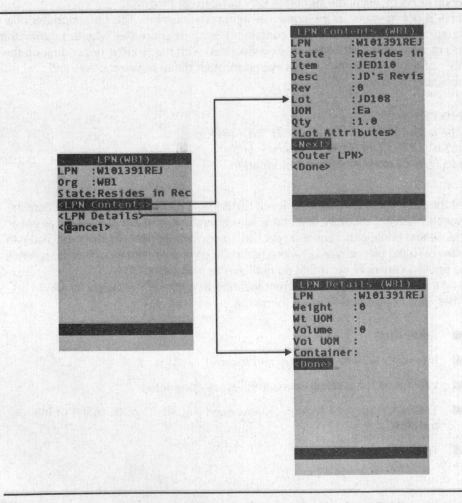

FIGURE 15-17. *You can view the contents and details of an LPN by using mobile LPN inquiry*

Cartonization

Cartonization simplifies the process of deciding which container to use for a particular packaging problem. The cartonization process automatically suggests packing configurations for groups of items considering various packing constraints. The category Set Functionality that was discussed in Chapter 3 is used for grouping container items and content items.

Cartonization Group Definition Using Category Sets

Container items and content items are classified into cartonization groups by using the two seeded category sets—container items and content items. Before defining categories and assigning them to these seeded category sets, decide on the control level of these category sets. If you want to follow a uniform cartonization scheme (centralized scheme) across all organizations, choose the control level as Master. If you want each organization to design their cartonization scheme (decentralized scheme), choose the control level as Organization. Figure 15-18 illustrates the concepts of container items and content items.

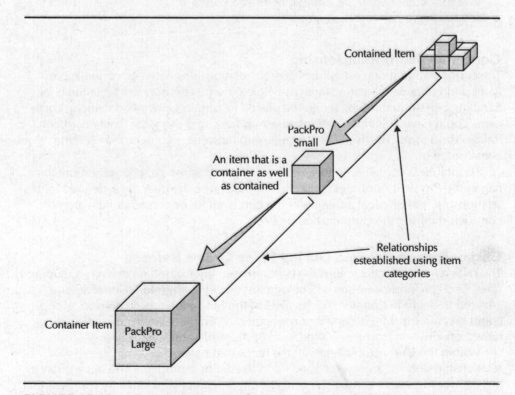

FIGURE 15-18.   *Container items and content items are linked using a cartonization group*

The container items and content items are matched using these seeded category sets. For this reason, both these category sets must have the same category codes. For example, you can have a category called HAZARDOUS in both of these sets. Assume that HCASE1 and HCASE2 are used for packing hazardous materials. HCASE1 and HCASE2 will be assigned to the HAZARDOUS category under the container items category set. If you have two items called Phenyl Alcohol and Sulphuric Acid, and if you want them to be packed using the hazardous packing material, these items will be assigned to the HAZARDOUS category under the Content Items category set. If the cartonization process has to find a suitable container for the item Phenyl Alcohol, it will look at all the suitable containers that belong to the category HAZARDOUS in the Container Items category set.

NOTE
The cartonization group is defined by the category code. All the container items that belong to a category code within the Container Items category set and all the content items that belong to the same category code within the Content Items category set form a single cartonization group.

Container Item Relationship

The cartonization group establishes generic relationships between cartonizable items and containers, treating them as whole groups. This may not be enough for handling certain items, which must be placed in certain kinds of containers. These items could have container load relationships specified using the Container Item Relationship form. This is a direct relationship between a content item and the container item.

To include a container in the container item relationships, check the Container flag in the Physical Attributes tab of the item. Because the quantity is defined in this relationship, the physical attributes of the content item or container item are not considered during the cartonization process.

Cartonization Process During Sales Order Release

The pick release process groups the pick-released lines based on delivery grouping rules. Each pick-released line will belong to one delivery group. (Deliveries are covered in detail in Chapter 16.) A subset of the lines within each delivery group could be cartonizable, depending on whether the Enable Cartonization flag is turned on either at the organization level or the subinventory level.

Within the cartonizable lines, all the items that have a container item relationship defined are selected and cartonized. For example, a line has a quantity of 1000 for the item M100200. A container item relationship exists for this item that says that this item can be packed in a container called C300, and the quantity of M100200 per container is 120. The cartonization process will suggest nine containers—eight containers with 120 each and one container for the remaining 40. This will result in nine pick tasks from one picking line. Nine LPNs will be generated automatically as the suggested LPNs. You can ignore the suggested LPN and use your own if you want. Tasks are covered later in this chapter.

NOTE
The cartonization process assumes infinite availability of container items.

All the remaining lines that have items without a Container Item Relationship are assembled into subgroups that have the same Cartonization group.

The cartonization process tries to fit the entire subgroup in one container, if possible. The containers in the group are ordered from the smallest before starting the comparison. The comparison starts from the smallest container to check if it fits the entire subgroup of items. If not, the next bigger container is checked until a container that fits all the items is found or the largest container is reached.

NOTE
Container volume is used for ordering the containers from largest to smallest. While actually assigning items to the container, capacity in terms of both volume and weight are checked.

When the largest container is not sufficient to hold every item in the subgroup, the cartonization process assigns the portion of items that will fit in the largest container. Before assigning each item, the dimensions of each of the items are compared with the dimensions of the container.

NOTE
During dimension comparison, the largest dimension (among length, width, and height) of a content item is compared with the largest dimension of the container item; the second largest with the second largest; and the third largest with the third largest.

The remaining items are cartonized using the same process, starting from the smallest container in the group.

NOTE
Cartonization using a container item relationship does not suggest mixing different items in the same container. Cartonization using Cartonization groups suggests mixing different items in the same container.

Container Transactions

Container transactions allow you to transact material in bulk without having to worry about the contents. You can create prepack requests for the cartonization process to suggest the appropriate container for your WIP job completions. Once you pack a container with your items, the LPN of the container can be used to move the materials around the warehouse. When you want to take materials out of a container, you can perform an unpack transaction to transfer material out.

Container Prepack

Container prepack is used to suggest appropriate cartons and LPN labels in advance of a WIP completion. You can prepack LPNs in anticipation of the WIP job or schedule completion. A request can be made to pack the finished goods into a container in order to generate labels for the container. During the container prepack transaction, the cartonization process will be used to estimate the container requirements for the items that are to be completed from the Job/Schedule.

The prepacked LPNs will not be included in on-hand inventory. Labels can be printed with content data. The completion transaction will then be performed automatically when the LPN is packed.

Bulk Pack

The mobile Bulk Pack form is used to suggest containers to pack a single item in a particular locator in the warehouse. This might be used if you find a large amount of loose material of an item that should be packed. By leaving the container field blank on the mobile form, the cartonization algorithm is called on the quantity of the item to pack.

Packing Consolidation and Splitting

The mobile forms Consolidate and Split allow you to consolidate multiple LPNs into a parent LPN or do the reverse respectively. Figure 15-19 shows these forms. When you consolidate, you specify a parent LPN and specify all the LPNs that need to be consolidated one by one, by clicking the More button. The Merge button will complete the consolidate transaction. When you split an LPN, you specify the source and destination LPNs and the item and quantity that you're moving to the destination LPN. The More button allows you to continue with the split transaction. Clicking the Split button will complete the transaction.

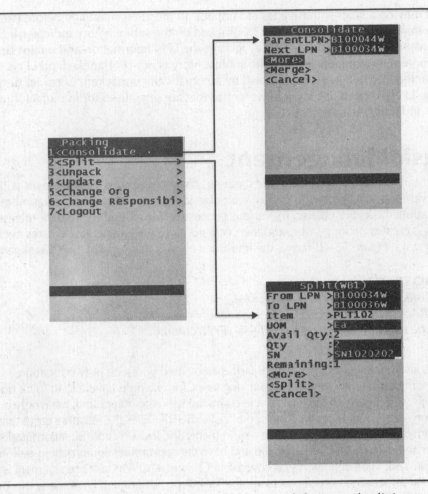

FIGURE 15-19. *The mobile UIs for packing consolidation and splitting a container*

Unpack Transaction

The unpack transaction results in putting the contents of an LPN into a locator as loose quantity or transferring it into another container (LPN). The Unpack mobile form allows you to perform this transaction.

Manufacturing Issue Transactions

Material is issued to Oracle WIP from only loose items and not from an LPN. All the LPNs that contain components that are used in manufacturing will have to be unpacked prior to the issue transaction—both backflush and push transactions.

It may be a labor-intensive task to unpack all the LPNs manually before issuing them to manufacturing. The flag LPN Tracked on the subinventory indicates if the subinventory keeps track of LPNs or ignores the LPN information and retains only the content information. Thus, if the subinventory is not LPN-tracked, all LPNs transacted into that subinventory will be automatically unpacked. Consider turning off the LPN Tracked flag for subinventories that are often used for manufacturing issue and backflush transactions.

Task Management

Task Management is the process of creating, dispatching, and tracking tasks within a warehouse. The objective is to maximize labor productivity and equipment utilization. Tasks are created by various processes. For example, the pick release process creates picking tasks, and the cycle count request generator creates cycle count tasks. Figure 15-20 shows the important entities that support Task Management.

NOTE
*Tasks are stored in MTL_MATERIAL_*
TRANSACTIONS_TEMP. You can identify the task
type for each from the WMS_TASK_TYPE column.

As shown in Figure 15-20, each task is associated with one or two locations depending on the type of the task. Picking tasks, for example have a load (pick from) location, and a drop off location. Cycle count tasks, on the other hand, have only one location—the count location. The type of tasks also identifies the resource requirements for each task. Based on the resource requirements and location considerations, tasks are dispatched to users who are qualified and have the appropriate equipment to perform the task. Task Type definition was covered in Chapter 4. OWM task management is built on top of two powerful processes: the Task Type Assignment Engine and the Task Dispatching Engine.

Task Type Assignment Engine

The task type assignment engine is called during the pick release process. Once the rules engine decides on the subinventory, locator, lot, and so on, the task type assignment engine is called and based on the task type rules, a task type is selected and stamped on the allocated line. Task type assignment rules were covered in the section "The Rules Framework." This engine also performs task splitting and merging based on certain conditions.

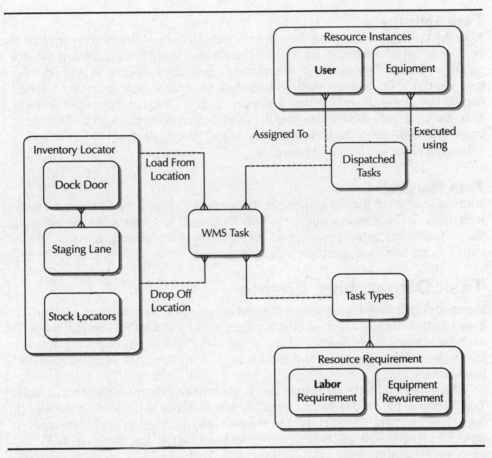

FIGURE 15-20. *The important entities in OWM Task Management*

Task Type Assignment

Prior to assigning a task type, the resource requirements of a task are not known. For example, you may want to perform task type assignment based on the pick UOM. If the pick UOM is PA (pallet), you may want to use the task type Pallet Picking, which requires a pallet picker and a forklift. Similarly, if the pick UOM is EA (each), you may want to assign Each Picking, which might have different resource requirements. Once the task type is assigned, the upstream processes know the resource requirements for that task.

Task Splitting

After the task type is assigned, the system knows all the possible equipment that can be used to perform the task. Equipment setup was covered in Chapter 4. If the task quantity exceeds the capacity of the smallest equipment available to perform the task, the task splitting engine will split the task into manageable units that can be handled by any equipment within the resource group. Each of those units will still have the same pick slip number and therefore cannot be dispatched to different users. The same user who picks the first unit will have to finish all the split tasks belonging to the same pick slip number.

Task Merging

If any of your items use the pick methodology Bulk Pick or if the lines were released with the pick slip grouping rule set to Bulk Pick, tasks for those items that belong to the same delivery, with the same picking and destination locators, are merged to form a single task for dispatching purposes.

Task Dispatching Engine

The task dispatching engine sequences and dispatches tasks. Tasks are sequenced based on task priority and then on the locator picking order/XYZ coordinates of each locator and the last pick location of the user. These were covered in detail in Chapter 2. The objective of task sequencing is to minimize the distance traveled by each user.

The sequenced tasks are dispatched to users when they press the Accept Next Task button in the mobile Tasks menu. The task is dispatched based on the user's role, the equipment currently used by the user, and the zone in which the user signed on. The task dispatching process tries to minimize *dead heading*, that is, users traveling with empty load.

Warehouse Control Board

The Warehouse Control Board is a managerial tool for warehouse managers. It provides a single window from which you can manage the tasks in your warehouse and also to gauge the performance of the warehouse. Figure 15-21 shows the Performance tab of the control board. It shows two pie charts—the first chart shows that all the tasks are completed and the second shows that out of all the tasks that were completed, 21 percent were picking tasks and the remaining 79 percent were putaway tasks.

The Task Details tab shows the task, task type, and the role required to perform this task, among many other details. This tab also shows the employees who are performing each task. You can assign/reassign tasks to users in this tab. For example, if the shift ends for a user in the middle of performing some tasks, you can reassign all the tasks that were pending in that user's queue to another user.

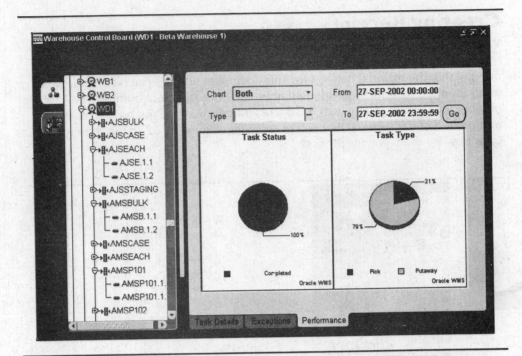

FIGURE 15-21.   *The Warehouse Control Board provides you a single UI from where you can manage your warehouse tasks and analyze warehouse performance*

All the tasks that had one or more problems during execution are shown in the Exceptions tab. For example, if a picker is asked to pick 10 items from a location and picks only 9 due to non-availability of material, an exception is recorded in the system. Similarly, if a user who is directed to put away the material in a particular location couldn't complete the task due to non-availability of space, an exception is recorded in the system.

Receiving and Putaway

Oracle supports receipts, inspection, and putaway for material from any source—suppliers, other organizations, and customer returns. You can easily configure if the material that is received needs to undergo quality tests before it hits your inventory balances through the receipt routings. The rules engine that was covered in the section "The Rules Framework" is used to determine the cost group for the received material and the optimal inventory storage location for a putaway. Receiving was covered in detail in Chapter 14 as provided in Oracle Inventory and Purchasing; it is mentioned here from the perspective of Oracle Warehouse Management.

Creating Receipts

When material reaches the receiving dock, the material is unloaded onto the receiving staging lanes and the receipt check-in is done against the document number that the material belongs to. This document number can be the purchase order number, internal requisition number, inter-org shipment number, RMA number, or an ASN. Along with the document information, you have to scan the information of the material that you're receiving. Figure 15-22 shows the mobile page flow for the receiving process.

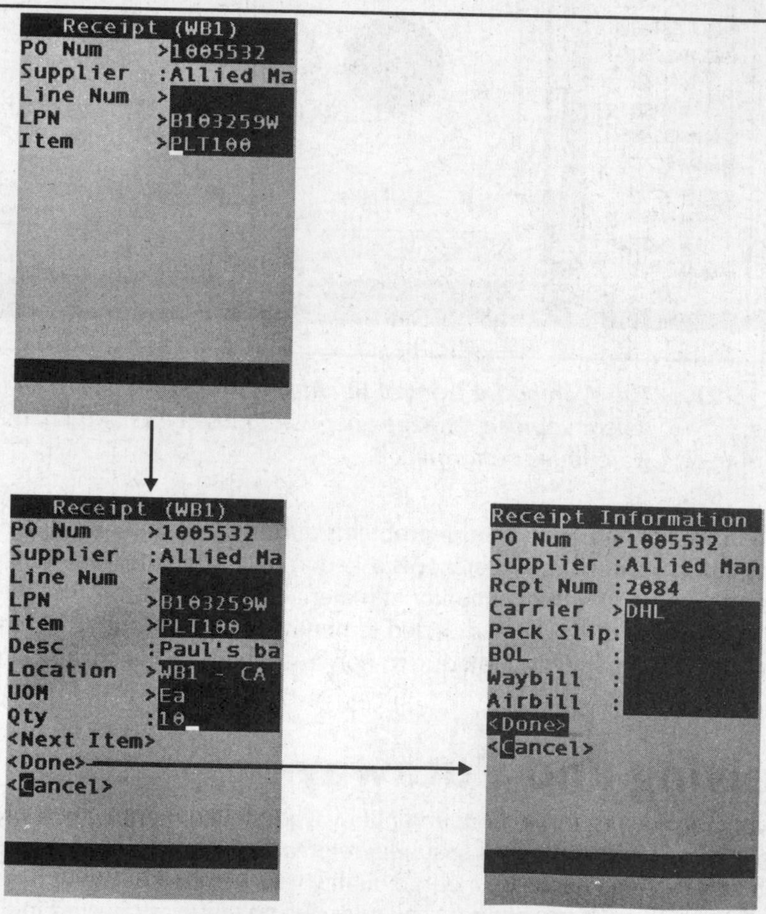

FIGURE 15-22. *Receipts using standard receipt routing can be received onto an LPN directly*

NOTE
CTRL+G *generates LPN, lot, and serial from the mobile device.*

Because putaways are always LPN-based, the material that is received should be associated to an LPN. You can use a pregenerated LPN, generate an LPN while performing the receipt, or receive material into an existing LPN. Material could be received into the LPN, and then put away from the LPN into your storage areas.

—If you don't want to use LPNs at all, you can model a transport cart as an LPN. If all subinventories were marked as non-LPN Controlled, OWM will force material to be put away loose, and the cart can be reused for putaways. Similarly, you could model an area on the receiving dock as an LPN and receive into that LPN. When you want to put away, you can specify the LPN that corresponds to the receiving area to take the material from there.

Putaway

When an LPN is scanned for putaway, the rules engine will be used to suggest an optimal putaway location for that material. During the process of the putaway, the user will be asked to confirm certain information about the material being put away, as shown in Figure 15-23. You can choose to accept the default LPN to drop off, generate a new LPN, enter an existing LPN, or leave the field blank. If an entire LPN is suggested to be put away in the same place, the To LPN field will be defaulted to the original LPN. You can leave the To LPN field blank for loose putaway.

NOTE
If the subinventory that the material is being putaway to is not LPN Controlled, the To LPN field will be hidden.

NOTE
If the receipt routing requires inspection, the LPN has to be inspected before putaway.

Once you choose an LPN, you can choose to drop it off immediately. Depending on the space in your vehicle, you can decide to load more LPNs by pressing the Load button. Once you've completed loading, you can go to the Current Tasks page (covered in the section "Currently Loaded Tasks") and drop off the LPNs one-by-one.

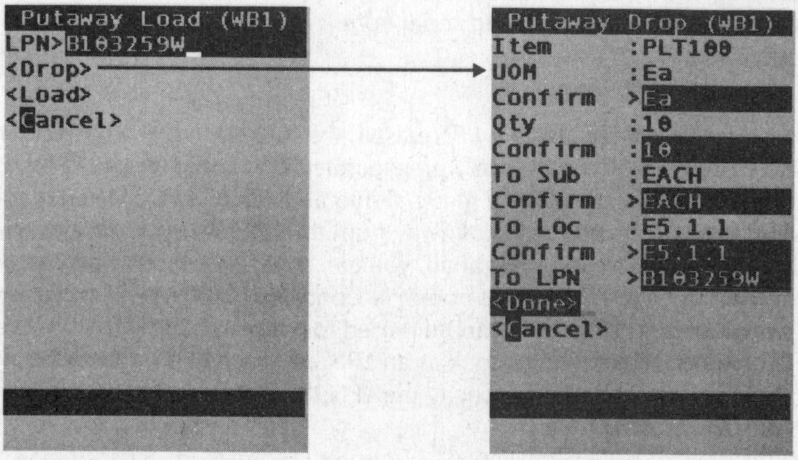

FIGURE 15-23. *Once you receive goods into an LPN, you can generate putaway tasks to put away the LPN using system-generated suggestions*

Implementing Opportunistic Cross-Docking

Cross-docking enables moving material directly from one process to the other without the need for stocking it. This can result in enormous savings in shipping and can also result in improved customer service. Cross-docking can be classified as two types: Opportunistic and Planned. Opportunistic cross-docking is available in the current release of OWM through the shortage handling functionality.

Cross-Docking from Receiving/WIP Completion to Shipping

If backorders exist for an item, Oracle will suggest that the material be put away directly to the outbound staging area for immediate shipment, if cross-docking is enabled for your organization. This happens when you receive items from your suppliers or when you perform assembly completions in Oracle WIP. This opportunistic cross-docking functionality is not available when you perform a direct receipt. Material that has been rejected at time of inspection will not be cross-docked but it can still be put away.

Cross-Docking from Receiving/WIP Completion to WIP Requirements

When shortages exist in WIP jobs, OWM directs the required material to the job/schedule, when you receive items from your suppliers or when you perform assembly completions in Oracle WIP.

If you check the warehouse parameter Prioritize WIP Jobs flag, WIP shortages are accorded a higher priority than sales order shortages. If this flag is not checked, sales order shortages are accorded higher priority. As long as material is available, OWM will try to meet all the shortages.

The Order Fulfillment Process

Order fulfillment is a very important function to the survival of any business. This function can make a huge difference in customer service. Activities in this process include scheduling your docks so that no conflicts arise in vehicle arrival/departure, pick planning, pick execution, staging and consolidation, loading the goods onto the vehicle, and finally, ship confirming. This section discusses these activities in detail.

Dock Scheduling

During trip planning, you can assign each trip to a dock door from which the truck will be loaded. You can create a dock appointment for this trip. You can schedule inbound unload activities or other activities to a particular dock door as well. If a trip has been assigned to a dock door and an appointment has been created for this trip, the pick release process will find the nearest staging lane that is either empty or is likely to become empty soon and direct all the picks for that trip to this staging lane. The staging lane to dock door assignments are performed at the time of setting up the warehouse. Figure 15-24 shows the Calendar form that allows you to schedule your docks for receiving and shipping.

Pick Methodologies

In some cases, it is optimal for a warehouse picker to perform multiple picks in each of his pick cycles. When he performs multiple picks, depending on the warehouse configuration and business conditions, in some cases picking the whole order in one cycle might be sensible; in other cases, splitting the order with respect to the zones from where the order has to be picked might make more sense. Pick methodology identifies how a sales order or a group of orders are handled in the warehouse.

NOTE
Internally, each pick task that is generated is stamped with a group ID that is generated based on the pick methodology. The PICK_SLIP_NUMBER column in MTL_MATERIAL_TRANSACTIONS_TEMP is used for storing the group id of each task.

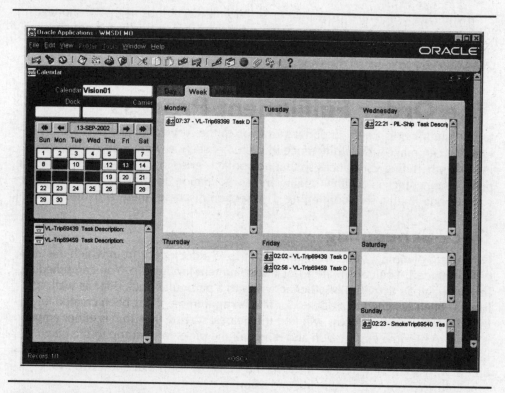

FIGURE 15-24. *The Dock Calendar form provides daily, weekly, and monthly views of your dock schedule*

Defining Pick Methodologies

The Pick Slip Grouping Rules form is used to define pick methodologies. The form supports defining four standard pick methodologies and a variety of user-defined pick methodologies. The field Pick Methodology is a drop-down list contains the four standard pick methodologies. Specify the rule name and (optionally) rule description and effective dates. The form also has a Group By section with 12 check boxes. For standard pick methodologies, the check boxes in the Group By region cannot be edited. Figure 15-25 shows the Pick Slip Grouping Rule form.

Order Picking   When this pick methodology is selected, the Order Number check box is automatically checked in the Group By region. Order picking involves picking one order by a picker, regardless of the number of zones the order needs to be picked from. All the tasks from a sales order are assigned to a single picker. The first eligible picker who accepts the next task gets all the tasks belonging to that order. This is typically used for managing emergency orders or orders from very important customers.

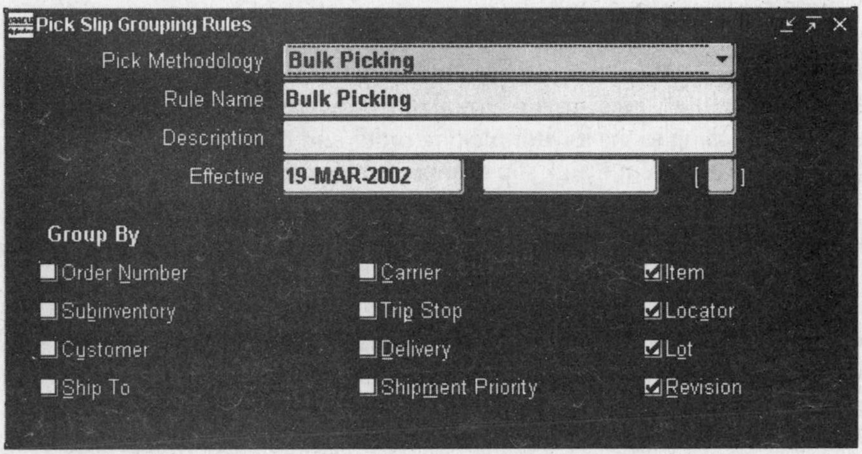

FIGURE 15-25. *The Pick Slip Grouping Rules form allows you to define the various standard and user-defined pick methodologies*

Zone Picking   Both the Order Number and Subinventory check box are automatically enabled in the Group By region for Zone Picking. Zone picking results in the splitting of the sales order by the zones from where the ordered items need to be picked. The pick tasks in each zone-order combination are dispatched to a picker who is assigned to the zone. The picker in this case will specify a subinventory during sign on.

Bulk Picking   An item may appear in a group of orders and instead of picking the item individually for each of the orders, it may make more sense to pick the item as a full pallet or a case and then split it (called the *sortation* process) across the orders, during the drop process or at the time of staging the material. This pick methodology is called *bulk picking.* This type of pick methodology is most suitable for high-volume items that need to be picked frequently. When this pick methodology is selected in the Pick Slip Grouping Rules Form, the Item, Locator, Lot, and Revision check boxes are automatically enabled. During the bulk pick process, the tasks are grouped if and only if they belong to the same delivery.

Bulk picks require an additional step—sortation. The picker brings the pallet or case and delivers the quantity required by each delivery in the appropriate staging lanes. At each staging lane, the appropriate quantity will be dropped off onto existing LPNs or new LPNs. Consider an example where a picker is asked to pick a pallet containing 12 cases of an item. Four orders needed this item in the quantity of 2 cases, 3 cases, 3 cases, and 4 cases each. If you used bulk picking, a pallet is picked, and the picker will deliver the required quantity in the four staging lanes that are handling the deliveries of these orders. The sortation and consolidation steps need to be performed manually, using the consolidation report that assists users to consolidate and sort the orders prior to loading them onto trucks.

Cluster Picking When this pick methodology is selected, none of the boxes are checked. The pick tasks are not grouped by any criteria. The tasks will be sequenced according to the locator picking order and dispatched to the pickers. Each pick task has a unique pick slip number in this case.

Assigning Pick Methodologies to Zones, Items, and Pick Waves

Because order picking and zone picking involve grouping by order, and cluster picking doesn't have any grouping, the only pick methodology that can be enabled at the item level is bulk picking. You can enable bulk picking for an item by checking the Bulk Picked attribute in the Inventory tab. You should scroll to the right to see the Bulk Picked attribute.

Depending on how you stock material in your zones, you may want to follow a different pick methodology in each of your zones. For example, in zones where you stock your pallets, you might want to follow bulk picking; in zones where you store individual pieces, you might want to follow cluster picking. From Release 11i.H, you can assign the bulk pick methodology at the zone level. If bulk picking is not turned on, cluster picking is assumed at the zone level. The zone level pick methodology, if assigned, overrides the item-level picking methodology.

A pick methodology can be assigned to a pick wave during pick release. Pick waves are covered in the next section "Wave Picking." If a pick methodology is assigned to a pick wave, this pick methodology will override the pick methodologies at the item and zone levels.

Wave Picking

Wave picking is the pull-based picking process. Sometimes, waves are associated with vehicle departures. For example, if three vehicles leave your warehouse every hour, one pick wave is released for each hour to fill the three vehicles that leave in that hour. The pick release process allows you to model different kinds of waves. You can create a wave that is based on a trip, delivery, carrier, customer, and so on. When you release your wave, you can select an appropriate pick methodology, if you want to override the methodologies assigned at the item level and zone level. Figure 15-26 shows the Inventory tab of the Pick Release form.

If you want to automatically source the material and create reservations, specify Auto Allocate as Yes. You can specify the subinventory and locator to pick from if you want to force a location. If you want to ignore the picking execution process and want to automatically confirm the picks of all the items that are detailed, specify the Auto Confirm option as Yes during pick release.

The pick release process creates a move order of the type Pick Wave. The move order is automatically detailed if the Auto Allocate option is set to Yes.

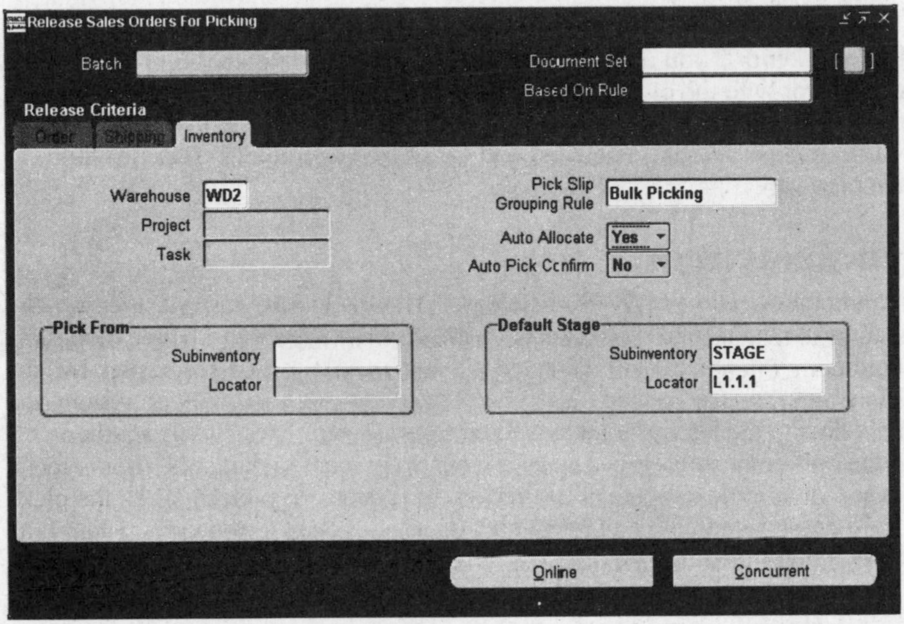

FIGURE 15-26. *The inventory options during pick release*

Staging Lane Assignment for Pick Tasks

Each line that is released for picking will have a staging lane as the destination for the pick tasks. The destination staging lane for each wave can be specified in the Pick Release window by using the Default Stage Subinventory and Default Stage Locator fields.

If a trip is associated with a dock door, the nearest available staging lane is suggested by the system, based on dock door-staging lanes assignment. Dock door to staging lane assignment was discussed in Chapter 2. If the dock door does not have any associated staging lanes, or if a dock appointment is not created, the staging lane that is specified during pick release is used. If a staging lane is not specified during pick release, the default staging lane is derived from the shipping parameters.

Enabling Cartonization

You can enable cartonization on the sales orders that are released for picking either at the organization level or at the subinventory level. This was covered in Chapter 2. After the lines are sourced during the detailing process they are grouped by destination. Cartonization is then performed to identify the optimal container for all the items in the group.

Cartonization is useful if you choose to route the container for picking along with the picker or if you use conveyor-based picking where you route the container in a conveyor with the pick slip in the container, and pickers in every zone complete the picks in their zone as the container moves along in the conveyor.

The move order that is detailed and cartonized becomes the task list for a particular wave.

Pick Execution

With the introduction of OWM in Release 11i, Oracle Applications offers a new set of features to manage the pick execution process in a warehouse. Three modes of pick execution are offered: system directed picking, manual picking, and pick by label.

In system directed picking, based on the conditions known to the system, the user is directed to various locations to pick items from. These items are then dropped off in the appropriate staging lanes. In manual picking, the user enters a pick slip number to indicate the priority to the system. In pick by label, the pick tasks are associated with an LPN, which dispatches tasks to the users. These three pick execution methods are discussed in detail in the following sections.

System Directed Picking

Choosing Task | Accept Next Task will give the user the next system directed task. The task dispatching engine evaluates the next task based on the roles assigned to the user and the equipment with which the user signed on. For example, if there are three pending tasks—a pallet pick, a replenishment, and an each pick—the user will not be given the pallet picking task if he did not have the required fork lift. The system will then give him either the replenishment or each picking task based on task priority. When the user completes the current task and chooses Task | Next Task, the next task is evaluated using the same criteria as before and also the user's proximity to the new task.

NOTE
Only picking, replenishment, and cycle count tasks are dispatched as system directed tasks. Putaway tasks are not system directed.

If a task has been explicitly assigned to a user through the control board, the user will get the explicitly assigned tasks first. The Task Dispatching Engine will not be called until all tasks in the user's queue have been exhausted. Figure 15-27 shows the steps in executing system directed tasks.

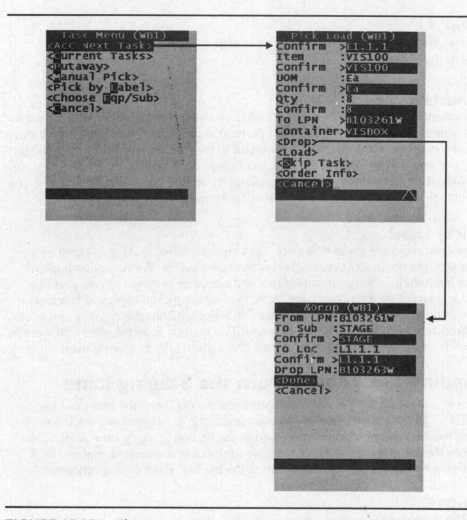

FIGURE 15-27. *The steps in executing a system directed pick*

The Accept Next Task button invokes the task dispatching engine to evaluate the next best task for the user. For picking tasks, the user is taken to the Pick Load page. After confirming the various details on the page, the user can either choose the Drop button to drop off the picked item or the user may decide to continue picking by choosing the Load button.

If the user clicks the Drop button, the user is taken to the Drop page. If the user continues to load more items, all the tasks of the user are tracked in the system and can be accessed using the Current Tasks menu. Executing current tasks is covered in the section "Currently Loaded Tasks."

NOTE
The Skip Task option allows the user to skip a system directed task.

Manual Picking

If you want to pick based on pick slip numbers, use manual picking. This is used for paper-based picking. Choosing Tasks | Manual Pick allows you to enter a pick slip and line number. The task(s) that correspond to the pick line id will be assigned to you, and you will be taken to the Pick Load page. After loading the picked item, you can drop it off or continue with your picking. If you don't drop off immediately, you can access the drop task from the Current Tasks menu.

Pick by Label

Cartonized picks are useful when you use conveyor-based picking (picking by passing a tote down a conveyor). You scan/enter the LPN; the corresponding task (associated during the cartonization process) would be assigned to you, and you will be taken to the Pick Load page. After loading the picked item, you can drop it off or continue with your picking. If you don't drop off immediately, you can access the drop task from the Current Tasks menu. This method is useful when you want to dispatch all the tasks that must be picked into a given LPN to a single user.

Loading the Vehicle from the Staging Lane

Once you stage all the items in the appropriate staging lanes, the items can be loaded on to the vehicle. During trip planning, a trip is assigned to a dock door. Using this and the associations discussed in the section "Staging Lane Assignment for Pick Tasks," the LOV of LPNs available for loading is restricted. Figure 15-28 shows the mobile UIs that are used during the loading and shipping processes.

NOTE
The dock door is used as a pseudo-location for the vehicle during the loading process.

You can use the LPN Ship page to load multiple items onto the vehicle. You can also use the Missing Items option to find out the items that are yet to be loaded based on the trip definition. Once you completed loading all the items, you can click the Ship option to ship confirm the trip. If there were missing items still, the Missing Items page will pop up with the details.

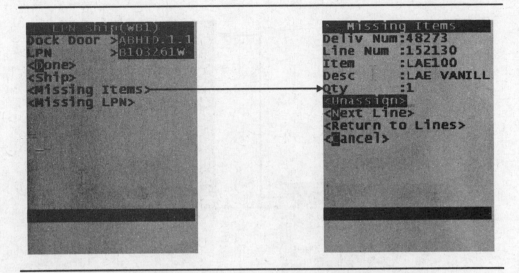

FIGURE 15-28. *Loading a vehicle using the LPN Ship page*

Currently Loaded Tasks

When a picker picks multiple items, the picker is essentially loading multiple items into the tote or equipment. This is the case when a user loads multiple containers from the receiving dock for putaway. These tasks are stored in the WMS_ DISPATCHED_TASKS table and can be accessed using the Current Tasks menu shown in Figure 15-29.

Choosing the Current Tasks menu option takes you to the Current Tasks page. The LOV for Current Tasks lists all the tasks that have been loaded by the user. The Task Type in the LOV shows the type of task. When the user selects a task, the Drop page comes up with the drop off details. The drop off subinventory and locator are displayed, and the user needs to scan these values for confirmation. If there is a discrepancy, the Reason page will pop up prompting for a reason. You can also choose a drop off LPN.

Kanban Materials Management

Kanban is a Japanese word that means "sign" or "signal." A brief introduction to kanban was given in Chapter 1. Kanban is a self-regulating, decentralized materials management system. Kanban system is generally used for managing items that have relatively stable demand and medium to high production volume.

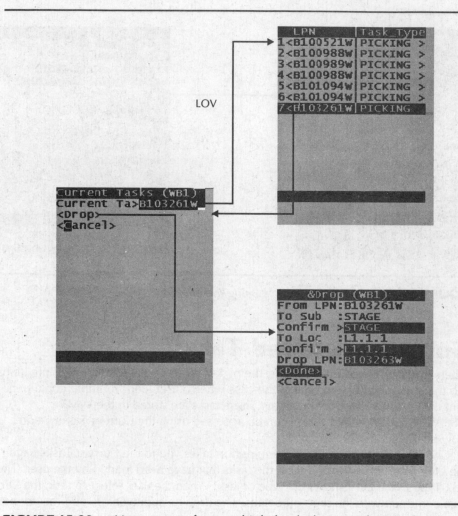

FIGURE 15-29. *Users can perform multiple loads during picking and putaway and use the Current Tasks menu to drop them off*

Interestingly enough, the inspiration behind this technique is the replenishment system used by the grocery stores in the United States. The quantity that is stored in the racks is calculated considering the forecasted demand and the replenishment interval. The racks are continuously replenished from the storage area at predetermined intervals. This section provides a detailed explanation of the features that are available in Oracle Applications to help you setup a kanban system.

Pull Sequences

Kanban items have many pull sequences that represent a series of supply points and usage points that model the actual replenishment network from the final consumption point to the original source of supply. In defining a pull sequence for a kanban item, you specify the supply source type for a kanban item at a specific location. You also specify what you want the kanban calculation program to calculate (kanban size or number of cards), the lead time for obtaining the kanban item, the allocation percentage, and other order modifiers that you want to affect the calculation program. This section discusses the concepts that are involved in a pull sequence. Defining pull sequences is covered in the section "Graphical Kanban Workbench."

Kanban Source Types

The kanban source type identifies the type of replenishment that is required to fulfill a material requirement that is generated by a kanban. The source types supported are Production, Intra-org, Inter-org and Supplier. Figure 15-30 illustrates the different kanban source types in Oracle Applications.

In Figure 15-30, the finished goods area stores the finished items on pallets, with a production kanban attached. When the pallet is emptied, the kanban card is sent to the assembly line. The assembly line restocks the pallet within the allowed lead time and sends it back to the finished goods area. Similarly, the assembly line sends signals to the various machining cells, for machined parts, and gets restocked. Note that the two kanbans—kanban from the finished goods area and the kanban from the assembly line—are not necessarily synchronized. That is, the assembly line doesn't necessarily wait until it gets the kanban from the finished goods area to send its kanban to the machining cell. This might happen if the lead time allowed for the machining cell is less than the difference between the lead time allowed for the assembly cell and the lead time for assembly. For example, let's say that the lead time allowed for the assembly cell is 36 hours per kanban quantity and the assembly lead time is 6 hours. If the machining cell needs less than 30 hours of lead time to deliver the kanban quantity required by the assembly cell, these two kanbans can be synchronized.

The assembly cell can pull purchased components from the RIP Store that serves this cell. This can either be through a backflush transaction or through an intra-org kanban. The RIP Stores can get the replenishments from the Central Store, which is an intra-org kanban. You can also communicate material requirements to other organizations or suppliers using an inter-org kanban or supplier kanban respectively.

Components of a Pull Sequence

You define a pull sequence for an item and a subinventory/locator combination. The subinventory/locator represents the usage point and is called as the kanban location. Figure 15-31 illustrates the important components of a pull sequence—usage

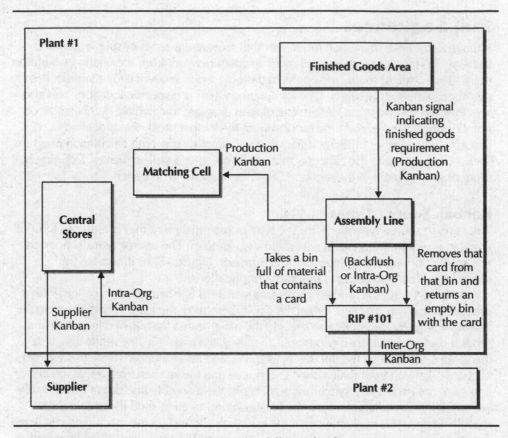

FIGURE 15-30. *Scenarios involving the different kanban source types*

point, supply point, and pull sequence attributes. As you can note from the figure, you should define a pull sequence for each usage point.

Once you identify the usage point, identify the supply point. Choose the source type from the four possible values—Intra-Org, Production, Inter-Org, or Supplier. Based on the chosen source type, you will have to provide additional information about the source type. The additional information that is applicable in each case is shown in Figure 15-31.

If the source type is production, enter the flow or discrete line that supplies to this location. If the source type is supplier, choose the supplier code and site. If you leave this blank, the requisition will be unsourced and Oracle Purchasing will attempt to find a sourcing rule for split sourcing. Sourcing rules were covered in Chapter 11. If the source type is Inter-Org, choose the organization from where you

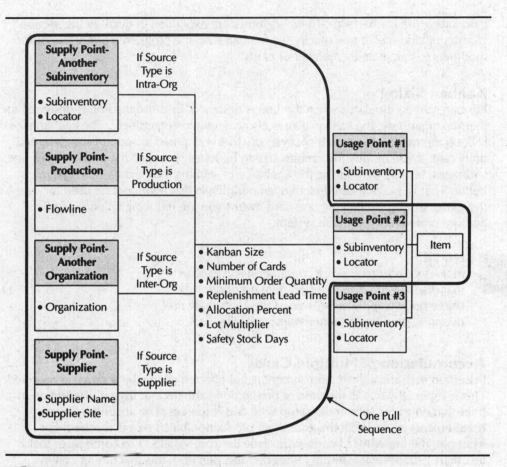

FIGURE 15-31.   *Information stored in a pull sequence*

want to replenish. If the source type is Intra-Org, choose the subinventory and locator from where you want to replenish.

Once you establish the usage point and the supply point, you identify the pull sequence attributes. You can specify either kanban size or the number of cards and have the kanban planning process calculate the other. If you specify both, the kanban planning process will not plan that pull sequence. If you want the kanban size to be calculated, the number of cards is mandatory. If you want the number of cards to be calculated, the kanban size is mandatory. When you choose Do Not Calculate for the Calculate option, both kanban size and number of cards are not mandatory.

Replenishment Lead Time, Allocation Percent, Safety Stock Days, Minimum Order Quantity, and Lot Multiplier are used by the kanban planning process while calculating the kanban size. These attributes are explained in detail in the section "Kanban Planning." If you specify the kanban size, the program will not use order modifiers to calculate the number of cards.

Kanban Sizing

Kanban size is calculated when the line is designed. Because the line is designed for the maximum rate, the kanban size is also calculated accordingly. The kanban size reflects the minimum amount of inventory that is required to support the designed daily rate. If you modify the kanban size to be lesser, you face the possibility of line shortages. Instead of reducing the kanban size, pulling a card out of the system is better. That is, make a card inactive temporarily so that it will not be used for triggering supply. Pulling out one card means you are reducing an equivalent amount of inventory from the system.

NOTE
In a kanban system, every container has a kanban that displays the item number, item description, usage point, supply point, size of the kanban (or pull quantity), and the sequence number of the card.

Accumulation of Multiple Cards

In certain scenarios, the replenishment is not effected even after a signal is received. This is especially true in the case of production kanbans that trigger production in lines that consume substantial setup time and resources. The accumulation of requirements occurs until the economic production batch size is reached. For example, the line MAC23 cannot produce the part M334533 in batch sizes that is less than 120. Several assembly lines pull this part from this machining cell in quantities of 30.

In these scenarios, accumulating the requirements and supply in batches is sensible. To aggregate demand before triggering replenishment, specify the minimum order quantity of the pull sequence to be an exact multiple of the kanban size. In the case of this example, the kanban size is 30 and the minimum order quantity is 120. The implication is that you will be accumulating four cards before triggering a supply order.

Kanban Planning

Kanban planning is a material-planning algorithm, which answers the two basic questions that any material planning algorithm tries to: When to order? and How much to order? You always reorder when your container or bin becomes empty. Every time you order, the quantity is equivalent to the kanban size. If kanban stopped here, it would have been just another material-planning algorithm. Kanban goes beyond answering these two questions and tells you how many such "kanban sizes" (in other words, cards) you need to support your material needs.

The kanban planning program doesn't calculate both the kanban size and the number of cards for a given pull sequence. You have to specify either the kanban size or the number of cards; kanban planning will calculate the other value for you. The formula shown here is used for this calculation:

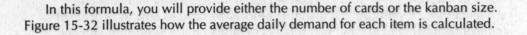

(Number of Cards − 1) × Kanban Size = Average Daily Demand × (Lead Time + Safety Stock Days)

In this formula, you will provide either the number of cards or the kanban size. Figure 15-32 illustrates how the average daily demand for each item is calculated.

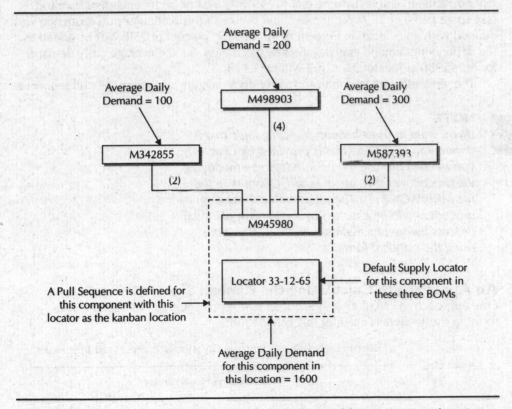

FIGURE 15-32.   *Calculating the average daily demand for an item in a location*

You provide a demand source to the kanban-planning program. For a given component, the average daily demand for each of the using assembly is calculated. This average daily demand is then multiplied by the component's quantity in the assembly to calculate the average daily demand for a component. This calculation is done based only on all the assemblies where this component has the specified kanban location as the default supply locator. In the example shown in Figure 15-32, M945980 is a component that is used by three assemblies—M342855 (Qty 2), M498903 (Qty 4), and M587393 (Qty 2). In all these three cases, the default supply locator for this component is 33-12-65. When a pull sequence is defined for M945980 with 33-12-65 as the kanban location, the average daily demand for M945980 will be 1,600.

The Allocation Percent allows you to specify the percentage of independent demand that is serviced from this kanban location. There may be many pull sequences for an item, and the planning process determines how to allocate this independent demand to these pull sequences based on the Allocation Percent. Extending the example, assume that M945980 also had an independent demand (say spare parts) of 250 from the demand source. If this particular pull sequence was defined with an Allocation Percent of 50, 125 (50 percent of 250) will be added to the dependent demand that was already calculated. So, the average daily demand for M945980 at locator 33-12-65 will be 1,725.

The replenishment lead time and safety stock days are taken from the pull sequence.

NOTE
If you want to use a kanban planning logic that is different from the one that is provided by Oracle, you have to provide the custom logic by modifying the procedure Calculate_Kanban_Quantity in the file MRPPKQCB.pls. The return values from this procedure will be checked by the kanban planning process before proceeding with the calculations using the standard formula.

An Approach to Calculating the Kanban Size

One approach to calculating the kanban size is presented in this section. The formula shown here is used for this calculation:

$$\text{Kanban Size} = \frac{\text{Designed Daily Rate} \times \text{Component Qty} \times \text{Replenishment Lead Time Hours}}{\text{Replenishment Hours per day}}$$

In this formula, the replenishment lead time in hours is divided by the replenishment hours to get the replenishment lead time in days.

Let's take an example to understand this formula. The designed daily rate of product M345432 is 100. Component M455332 is used in the production of M345432. The required quantity is one per assembly. The lead times for replenishment are

- RIP to Line: 1 Hour
- Stores to RIP: 1 Day
- Supplier to Stores: 5 Days

The plant operates for 20 hours in a day. Table 15-3 shows the kanban size as calculated using the kanban sizing formula for the three pull sequences.

The kanban size for RIP to Line is 5. The plant needs to build 100 assemblies per day, which translates into five per hour. Because the replenishment lead time is one hour between line and RIP stores, the hourly consumption rate itself is the kanban size.

Normally, the line has two bins to begin with, both containing components that is equivalent to the kanban quantity. The production operators pull the first bin, remove the kanban card from that bin and place it in the bin that they just consumed. This empty bin is placed in a marked place. Material handlers remove this empty bin and replenish it using the information that they find from the kanban. Thus, if you are operating a two-bin system, the number of cards that is required to support this scenario is two. This is exactly the way in which the standard formula provided by Oracle works. As you can see, when the kanban size is equal to the lead-time demand, you will be operating with two cards.

Pull Sequence	Kanban Size Calculation	Kanban Size
RIP to Line	$(100 \times 1 \times 1) \div 20$	5
Stores to RIP	$(100 \times 1 \times 20) \div 20$	100
Supplier to Stores	$(100 \times 1 \times 5 \times 20) \div 20$	500

TABLE 15-3. *Kanban Size for Three Different Pull Sequences*

Graphical Kanban Workbench

The graphical kanban workbench allows you to perform kanban setup, kanban planning, pull sequence definition, and planning simulations through a single user interface. A graphical view of the pull sequences allows you to get the complete picture between the various points of supply and points of usage. You can mass-add pull sequences for items in the workbench. You can simulate different scenarios and update the production pull sequence from the workbench. Figure 15-33 shows the Graphical Kanban Workbench.

The workbench is comprised of two panes. The left pane displays a list of items that can be viewed by Category, Buyer Code, Planner Code, Supplier, and Location using the View By drop-down menu. There are two tabs on the left side of this pane that allow you to toggle between Production and Planning views. Once you select a view, you'll see a list of items that are grouped according to the View By option.

Initially, the right pane displays a list of templates that can be used for creating new kanban networks. When an item is selected on the left pane, the right pane displays the data that is associated with the selected item.

The possible colors of the arrows in the replenishment chain are Black, Green, Blue, and Red. Black indicates that cards have not been generated.

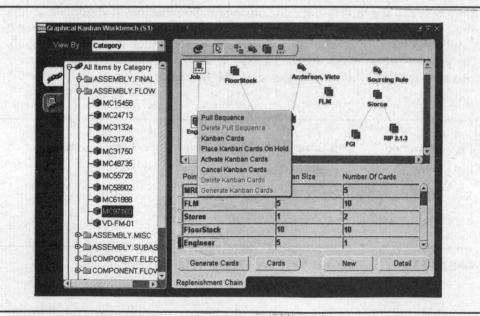

FIGURE 15-33.   *The Graphical Kanban Workbench provides a single UI for kanban setup, kanban planning, and simulations*

Kanban Execution

Once you define the various pull sequences, you generate kanban cards and use them for managing your replenishment process. You switch the status of kanban cards between full and empty during the life cycle of a card indicating that either the kanban container is either full or needs replenishment. When the status is changed to empty, a supply order is created depending on the minimum order quantity and the type of replenishment. Sudden spikes in demand are managed by creating one-time, non-replenishable cards.

Kanban Cards

Kanban cards are based on a pull sequence and are created for a combination of item, subinventory, and locator. The card is recognized by a unique identifier. You can generate kanban cards from the pull sequence, or you may create them manually in the Kanban Cards form.

The Replenishable flag identifies if the kanban card can be replenished or if it is created for satisfying some sudden spike in demand and hence doesn't require replenishment. Because your regular kanbans are designed for the daily rate, if you experience sudden spikes in demand, you can define non-replenishable cards to satisfy this excess demand.

You cannot override the quantity for generated cards. But you can control the inventory in the system by increasing the number of cards from the pull sequence. To reduce the inventory in the system, you can make a card inactive (covered in the "Card Status" section.)

For supplier kanbans, a supply source is defaulted if a sourcing rule is available for the item in the pull sequence. Based on the split percentage and the ranking in the sourcing rule, the primary supplier is defaulted. You can manually override this default supplier.

CAUTION
Changes to pull sequence are not reflected in the existing cards. Similarly, if you update the sourcing rule, it does not affect the existing cards. If the pull sequence is changed, you have to manually delete the existing cards and create new ones.

Card Status   The kanban card status allows you to manage the availability of the card. A card is available if the card status is Active. If you temporarily want to pull out a card from the system, set the card status to Hold. For permanently removing a card from the system, set the status to Canceled.

NOTE
Only canceled cards can be deleted.

Card Supply Status By default, a kanban card is generated with a supply status of New. The status needs to be switched to Empty to trigger replenishment. Figure 15-34 shows the different supply statuses during the replenishment process.

In the Figure 15-34, internal replenishment indicates intra-org and production kanbans, whereas external replenishment indicates inter-org and supplier kanbans. Once the supply status becomes Full, you can again signal replenishment by setting the card status to Empty again.

Signaling Replenishment

To signal replenishment, you set the supply status of the card to Empty. If the card is active, and if the accumulated quantity is equal to or greater than the minimum order quantity, a supply order will be created based on the supply type. There are two alternative UIs in which you can do this—the Kanban Cards form or the Replenish Kanban mobile UI. Table 15-4 explains the different supply types and what happens during the replenishment cycle of a kanban card.

Supply Type	What Happens When the Supply Status Becomes Empty?	When Does the Supply Status Become Full?
Intra-org	A Move order is created to move material from the source subinventory to the kanban location.	When the move order transaction is completed.
Production	A flow schedule/discrete job/ repetitive schedule is created.	When the flow schedule/ discrete job/repetitive schedule is completed into the kanban location.
Inter-org	An internal requisition is created.	The receipt of the material into inventory. The receipt needs to specify the kanban card number.
Supplier	A PO requisition is created.	The receipt of the material into inventory. The receipt needs to specify the kanban card number.

TABLE 15-4 *Supply Types and the Corresponding Replenishment Cycle*

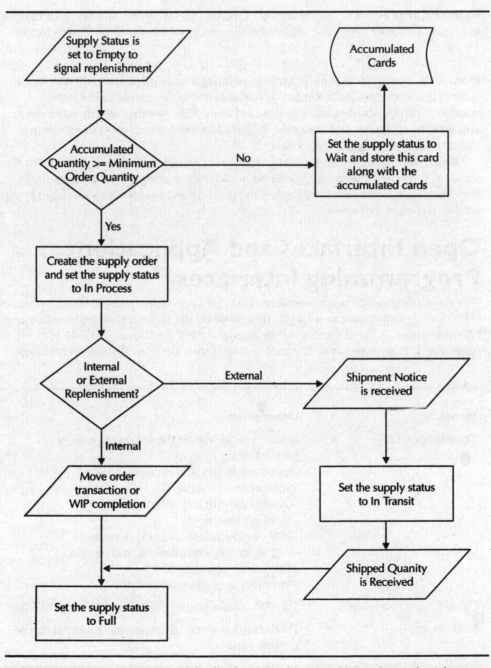

FIGURE 15-34. *Transition of the kanban supply status during the replenishment process*

Kanban Cards Form   In the Kanban Cards form, set the Supply Status of the card to Empty. This will trigger the replenishment process that was illustrated in Figure 15-34.

Mobile UI   In Oracle Mobile Materials Management, navigate to the Replenish submenu and choose Auto Replenish Kanban. In the Replenish Card Query window, scan the card number in the Card Num field. Verify that this is the card you want to replenish and select the Replenish option. If you want to cancel the transaction, select the Cancel option.

   If you want to replenish multiple cards, you can enter a partial number with the standard wild card characters (_ and %), which might bring up multiple cards. In these cases, you can select the Replenish/Next option to replenish a card and bring up the next card for review.

Open Interfaces and Application Programming Interfaces

There are a number of open interfaces (OIs) and application programming interfaces (APIs) for importing data that can be processed by the various Oracle Inventory and OWM features. A list of the open interfaces and APIs are shown in Table 15-5 for reference. Please refer to the Interfaces Manual for a detailed discussion on usage.

Name	Description
Transactions OI	Allows you to import the following type of transactions: –Inventory issues and receipts –Subinventory transfers –Direct inter-organization transfers –In-transit shipments –WIP component issues and returns –WIP assembly completions and returns –Sales order shipments –Inventory average cost updates
Cycle Count Entries API	This API allows you to process cycle count entries
Kanban API	This API allows you to update the supply status of kanban cards

TABLE 15-5.   *Open Interfaces and APIs in Oracle Inventory and Oracle Warehouse Management*

Name	Description
Lot API	This API allows you to create lots by inserting an entry into the MTL_LOT_NUMBERS table
Material Reservation API	This API allows you to do the following: –Query existing reservations –Create reservations –Update existing reservations –Transfer existing reservations –Delete existing reservations
Reservations Manager API	This API allows you to call the reservation manager online or submit reservation requests concurrently
Sales Order API	This API allows you to do the following: –Create a sales order in Oracle Inventory's local definition of a sales order –Update a sales order in Oracle Inventory's local definition of a sales order –Get a corresponding Oracle Order Management order header identifier given a sales order identifier and vice versa
Move Order API	–This API allows you to do the following: –Create a move order header –Create a move order line –Process a move order (create or update) –Lock a move order –Get a move order for a given header or header identifier –Process a move order line (cancel or update)
Pick Release API	This API allows you to release a set of move order lines for pick wave move orders. This API creates move order line details for the lines that are released, and, depending on the parameters passed in, runs the pick confirm process immediately afterward.
Pick Confirm API	This API allows you to perform pick confirmations on move order line detail records

TABLE 15-5. *Open Interfaces and APIs in Oracle Inventory and Oracle Warehouse Management* (continued)

Summary

The various transactions in a warehouse/manufacturing plant allow you to move and store materials. Material transactions allow you to transfer materials between inventory locations. You perform material transactions using the various transactions forms or the Material Workbench.

Lots and serial numbers allow you to identify and track your materials. There are various named and user-definable attributes at the lot and serial level. You can merge and split lots, and the Lot Genealogy form allows you to view the history of these merges and splits. Serial genealogy identifies the As Built configuration of an item. Material status allows you to identify subinventories, locators, lots, and serial numbers and prevent them from certain types of transactions.

Quantity tree is a memory structure that holds the on-hand quantity information in memory. You can view the on-hand information in the Material Workbench. Reservation is the process of reserving a supply to demand. The Supply Demand form allows you to view the reservation information.

The rules framework presents a flexible way of modeling execution constraints in a warehouse. The framework consists of business objects, rules, strategies, strategy assignment to business objects, and strategy search order. There are five applications of the rules framework in OWM: picking, putaway, cost group assignment, label format, and task type assignment.

Cycle counting and physical inventory help ensure the accuracy of warehouse inventory information. The inventory planning methods Min–Max, Reorder Point, and Replenishment Counting allow you to automatically trigger replenishment orders based on predefined conditions.

OWM provides complete support for barcoding. You can minimize data entry errors due to out-of-sequence scanning using data field identifiers. The various business processes in OWM are associated with a set of label types. When the business process is executed, one label per label type is generated and can be printed using a third-party label-printing software.

Containers allow you to store and transact materials in bulk. LPNs allow you to track these containers. Cartonization is the process of generating packing configurations considering various packing constraints. You can invoke the cartonization process on pick-released items to estimate the number/type of containers that are required.

Warehouse tasks are generated and managed by the Task Type Assignment Engine and the Task Dispatching Engine. Based on the various business conditions, tasks are split and merged by these engines before being dispatched to the appropriate resource.

Materials from suppliers can be received onto the receiving dock and inspected before putaway. The putaway process invokes the rules engine to identify the best location for putaway. The opportunistic cross-docking process allows you to cross-dock material from receiving/WIP to shipping and also from receiving/WIP to WIP.

You can maintain the carrier appointments in your receiving and shipping docks using the dock calendar. Pick methodologies allow you determine how the actual picking is carried out in the warehouse. The methodologies supported are order picking, zone picking, bulk picking, and cluster picking. The wave picking process allows you to release pick waves to suit your warehouse needs. For example, you can release a pick wave that contains all the items that are contained in a particular delivery.

Picking can be executed in three modes: system directed, manual, or pick by label. The picked items can be staged in staging lanes and can then be loaded onto the carriers using the Load form. Once the items are loaded, you can perform ship confirm. The Current Tasks menu allows you to complete the tasks that were started by you and await completion.

Kanban is a pull-based materials management system. You define pull sequences that represent the network of various supply points and usage points. The kanban planning process allows you to calculate either the number of kanban cards or the kanban size. Each kanban card has various supply status, and setting this status to empty triggers the replenishment process.

CHAPTER
16

Manufacturing
Execution

anufacturing Execution deals with the day-to-day activities of the shop floor—releasing jobs, issuing material, reporting progress, and recording production completion. In addition, it must handle events that are exceptions to the daily routine—scrapping material, substituting parts, and rework. And, it supports these activities across all manufacturing methods—discrete, repetitive, flow—and all manufacturing strategies.

Several Oracle applications provide the manufacturing execution functions described in this chapter—Work in Process (WIP) provides the basic functionality; Manufacturing Scheduling provides graphical, constraint-based scheduling; Flow Manufacturing adds the ability to create flow schedules; and Oracle Shop Floor Management (OSFM) provides enhanced functionality for lot-based production, such as semiconductor fabrication.

This chapter describes these activities. It starts with a high-level overview, describes each activity in detail, and then highlights any unique characteristics of an activity or transaction for each of the manufacturing methods or strategies.

Overview

The typical data flow for most manufacturing execution activities is shown in Figure 16-1. This shows the major activities associated with most production methods and strategies, though many variations are possible. The following sections describe the activities at a high level; each activity is detailed in this chapter.

Information Flow

In most environments, manufacturing is driven by the planning applications (MRP or ASCP), Order Management, or a combination of both. In addition, there are sometimes requirements for non-scheduled manufacturing—for example, rework of defective or outdated material, or production engineering prototypes.

The planning applications generate planned orders that represent recommendations to create repetitive schedules, discrete jobs, or purchase requisitions. Implementing these suggestions from planning, either manually or automatically, creates the corresponding jobs or schedules. (Implementing a planned order as a purchase requisition does not directly affect manufacturing.) Manufacturing based on planned orders is typical in companies employing a make-to-stock strategy and is often used to manufacture subassemblies in a make-to-order environment.

In a make-to-order environment, production of the finished products is initiated by the sales orders themselves. For configured products, the process includes a step that automatically creates the configured item; when the configured item is generated, Oracle provides a program to automatically create discrete jobs from the sales order demand for items identified as Assemble to Order, whether configured or predefined.

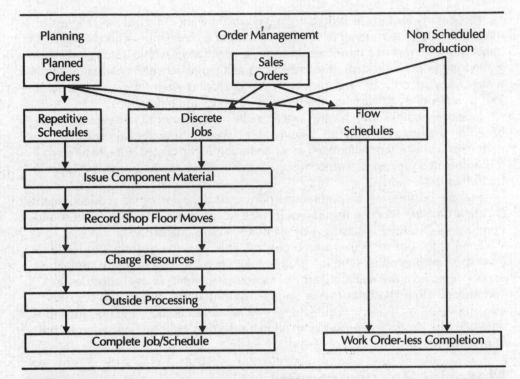

FIGURE 16-1. *Manufacturing execution flow*

Companies that employ a flow manufacturing strategy will typically generate flow schedules from the sales order demand. You can also create flow schedules from the planned orders coming from the planning process; this can streamline the manufacturing process, but it strays from the flow ideal of pure "demand pull."

Unplanned events, such as the need to rework defective material, or requirements not normally represented in planning or order management, such as building a prototype, also require manufacturing resources. These can be formally represented in the system by manually created discrete jobs (usually "non-standard" jobs), or production can simply be recorded using a *Work Order-less Completion* transaction, described later.

During manufacturing, the component material is removed from stock for use in the product being made. This material issue can be done with an explicit transaction, or it can be automated when the appropriate operation or entire job is completed. Oracle refers to the automated issue of components as *backflushing,* and the components to be backflushed as *pull* components. See the section titled "Material Requirements" for a full discussion. Figure 16-1 does not show the issue activity for a flow schedule; component material is *always* backflushed at completion.

Particularly for long lead-time items, you might want to record the progress of the job through the routing; this is the function of a *move* transaction. A move transaction can record a movement between different steps within a single operation (called *intra-operation steps,* discussed later) or a move between operations. Move transactions are only allowed for jobs or schedules that use routings, and for such jobs or schedules, at least one move is required prior to completion.

Jobs or schedules with routings will typically incur *resource charges* (e.g., labor), based on the routing definition. Like material issues, resource charges can be performed explicitly or automated as an operation is completed. Oracle refers to this automated process as *Autocharging*. (See the "Resource Requirements" section for further discussion.)

In some businesses, it is common to outsource all or part of the production; this is called *Outside Processing* and requires the integration of Work In Process and Purchasing. Outside Processing is detailed later in this chapter.

Finally, jobs or schedules are completed. This adds the quantity produced to inventory, and completes the job or schedule when the total quantity complete equals or exceeds the initial quantity of the job or schedule. Flow schedules are completed with a *Work Order-less Completion* transaction, which also backflushes all component material, and autocharges all resources at the standard rate and quantity. The Work Order-less Completion transaction can also be used to record unplanned production.

Material Requirements

When you create a job or repetitive schedule, the system takes a "snapshot" of the bill of material, extended by the job or schedule quantity, to identify the component material required. The snapshot uses the *start date* of the job or schedule to select the effective components, although you can override this by selecting a different effectivity by specifying a date or revision. The primary bill of material is used unless you select an alternate bill (or implement a suggestion from ASCP that uses an alternate bill).

Components designated as Phantoms are exploded to their non-phantom components during this process.

The resulting *material requirements* serve several purposes:

■ **Pick Lists and Pull Lists** The material requirements serve as the basis for the pick list (a document that identifies the material to be explicitly issued), and the pull list (a document that identifies material to be moved to replenish the location from which it will be backflushed).

■ **Material Control** The WIP Supply Type determines how the material will be supplied to WIP. A supply type of "Push" identifies material that will be issued; a supply type of "Operation Pull" identifies material that will be backflushed at the completion of an operation; and a supply type of "Assembly Pull" identifies material that will be backflushed upon assembly completion. The Supply Subinventory and Locator identify the location from which backflush material will be taken, or, in the case of Push material, the default location on the Material Issue transaction.

■ **Modification** Most attributes of the material requirements can be modified; for example, you can specify substitute or additional material to be used or change the supply type.

■ **Shortage Reporting** The material requirements serve as the basis for reporting shortages. Two types of shortages are reported: true shortages, indicating that insufficient material is available to meet the requirements within the organization, and shortages based on the supply subinventory/ locator, indicating that material needs to be moved to the point of use.

■ **Planning** Material requirements for discrete jobs are used in subsequent MRP or ASCP plans; i.e., any changes or substitutions you make are reflected in subsequent material plans. As described in Chapter 8, planning does not recognize modifications to material requirements for repetitive schedules.

Material requirements for flow schedules are not generated ahead of time, but calculated at the time of the Work Order-less Completion transaction. By default, these requirements use the primary bill of material effective as of the date and time of the transaction, although you can override the effective date, revision, or select an alternate bill.

Scheduling

Just as creating a job or repetitive schedule takes a snapshot of the bill of material, it also takes a snapshot of the routing. Based on the routing resources and the job quantity, the system *schedules* the job or repetitive schedule. For a discrete job, the schedule shows the anticipated start and completion date for each operation in the routing; for a repetitive schedule, the schedule indicates the start and stop dates for the first and last units at each operation.

Standard scheduling utilizes the capacity defined for a resource within a department. For example, if a resource is not available on the weekend, the operation where it is used will not be scheduled for the weekend. But standard scheduling does not consider the load placed on a resource by other jobs or schedules; that capability is offered by the Manufacturing Scheduling product, described later.

Operations

The operations for a job or schedule carry the scheduling information. They also serve as the basis for reporting quantities completed and drive the online dispatch list. Like the material requirements, you can modify the job operations to represent one-time changes in the process—use of alternate work centers or inclusion of additional operations, for example.

Resource Requirements

As part of the operations copied, creating the job or schedule copies the resources attached to each operation in the routing. These resources are used to generate the schedule and are the basis of resource charging. Like the operations themselves, the job resources can be modified.

NOTE
To delete operations or resources from a job or schedule, you must have no activity recorded against the operation or resource. If necessary, you can reverse any transactions you have performed and then delete the operation or resource.

Intra-Operation Steps

As you record the progress of a job or repetitive schedule, you can move the quantity to any of five *intra-operation steps:*

■ **Queue**   Quantities in the Queue step at an operation are available at the operation, waiting to be started. Releasing a job or schedule loads the job or schedule quantity to the queue at the first operation on the routing.

■ **Run**   The Run step represents quantities for which production has started.

■ **To Move**   This step indicates quantities that have been successfully completed and are ready to move to the next operation or quantities at the end of the job ready to move to stock.

■ **Scrap**   The Scrap step represents quantities that have been completed through the operation and then deemed unusable and scrapped. Scrapping is reversible, but while a quantity remains in the scrap step, it is assumed that it is "in the dumpster." If the scrap quantity of a job exceeds the anticipated scrap (represented by the item's shrinkage rate), the planning process will see less than it originally expected and might replan to cover the shortage, if necessary. The scrap operation also lets you remove the value of the scrap from the job by charging it to a scrap account.

■ **Reject**   The Reject step is similar to the Scrap step, but has no effect on planning or accounting. You might think of Reject as representing material awaiting disposition; you might decide to complete it, rework it, or scrap it. But as long as the quantity remains in the Reject step, it is assumed that it will be completed.

Figure 16-2 graphically depicts the relationship between these steps. A key concept illustrated in this figure is the notion of an *operation completion*. Any step past the Run step counts as a completion of the designated quantity at that operation. This is important because completion of an operation drives backflushing and autocharging. Operation pull components are backflushed, and WIP Move resources are charged only for quantities moved past the Run step. Note that Scrap and Reject indicate completion of the operation, implying that the material and resources at that operation were used; if material is delivered to an operation and determined to be defective before work starts, you should scrap it at the *prior* operation to avoid incurring charges from the current operation.

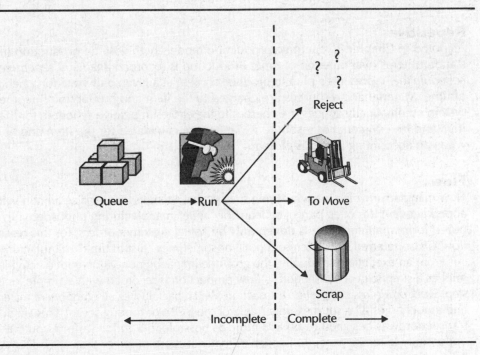

FIGURE 16-2.   *Intra-operation steps*

Production Methods

As noted earlier, manufacturing execution supports a number of production methods and stocking strategies—discrete, repetitive, flow, assemble to order, and configure to order. The next few sections highlight the key features of each method or strategy; later sections describe the various manufacturing activities as they pertain to each method.

Discrete

Discrete production records all production activities against a *discrete job,* sometimes called a work order, shop order, or production order. A discrete job represents a plan to produce a specific quantity of an item on a given date. All material issues, both manual and backflush, and all resource charges, automatic or manual, are charged to a specific job. Completion and scrap are recorded against the job, and detailed variances are calculated for each job when it is closed.

Besides standard production, discrete jobs can produce assemble to order (ATO) items and configure to order (CTO) items; both of these topics are discussed later. Additionally, you can define *non-standard jobs* for unplanned production like rework; non-standard jobs are discussed later in this chapter.

Repetitive

As noted in Chapter 8, repetitive production models high-volume production of standard items over a period of time. Production is recorded against a *repetitive schedule* that represents a plan to produce an item at a given daily rate for a period of time. Material and resources are charged to the item and production line; the system automatically applies the charges to the earliest repetitive schedule for that item and line. Material or resource variances are calculated for the item and line when an accounting period is closed.

Flow

Flow manufacturing is a manufacturing strategy that attempts to minimize all non-value-added activity; it is often part of a "lean" or "agile" manufacturing philosophy. In its purest form, manufacturing is driven only by actual customer orders; for this reason, flow is also referred to as "demand pull" or sometimes "just in time" manufacturing.

From an execution standpoint, the goal of eliminating non-value-added activities implies a simplicity of transactions—flow production is recorded with a simple, one-step, *work order-less completion* transaction, which backflushes all component material and autocharges all resources, regardless of the BOM or routing setup. This single transaction was designed to be as simple as possible, but it does afford you the opportunity to record exceptions, such as material substitution, or the use of alternate bills, routings, effectivities, or revisions.

Though sometimes confused with repetitive manufacturing, flow is quite different. It is designed for production of mixed products on a production line, one at a time, at the rate of production dictated by the demand; repetitive is intended for production of the same product at a standard rate for a period of time. And flow manufacturing can be used to produce ATO and CTO products as well as standard items; repetitive can only produce standard, non-ATO items.

Flow schedules can be generated from sales orders or planned orders, but they serve only as a means of communicating production requirements to the shop floor. They do not carry material requirements, operations, and resources like discrete jobs or repetitive schedules.

Assemble to Order

Assemble to Order is a stocking strategy where the products are built only in response to a customer order, rather than being built to stock in anticipation of demand. To utilize discrete jobs to produce on an ATO basis, you must explicitly define the item as an ATO item, using the Assemble to Order attribute found on the Order Management tab of the Master Items or Organization Items form. Discrete jobs for such items are created automatically and linked to the driving sales order; completed quantities are automatically reserved to the sales order.

You can also use Flow Manufacturing to fulfill customer orders; this, too, can be considered ATO. In this case, you do not need to set the item's Assemble to Order attribute, but you do need to link the item to a production line with a flow routing if you want to create flow schedules. (To simply record work order-less completions of standard items without creating flow schedules, no special setup is needed.)

Configure to Order

Configure to Order (CTO) is a variation of the assemble-to-order strategy. The difference is that the item must first be configured from a set of options before it can be manufactured. Options can be chosen using Oracle Configurator or simple model/option selection in Order Management; when chosen, the system automatically creates a unique item, bill, routing, and cost. This *configured item* is then manufactured like an ATO item using either discrete or flow manufacturing methods.

Configuring Oracle Work in Process

Configuring Oracle Work in Process requires setting parameters for each organization in which production will occur and defining *accounting classes* to identify the valuation and variation accounts to hold production values. Optional setup steps include creating shop floor statuses, which can be used to prevent move transactions at certain points in the routing; maintaining individual employee labor rates, to charge an employee's actual rate of pay to a job or schedule; and setting a number of profile options. These setup steps are described in the following sections.

WIP Parameters

The WIP Parameters form, shown in Figure 16-3, defines the basic rules and defaults for Work in Process for each of your inventory organizations. The form contains multiple tabs, each of which lets you define different defaults based on your manufacturing requirements:

- **Discrete** This tab defines defaults that apply primarily to discrete production—the Default Discrete Class, described later, which controls the accounting for jobs; lot numbering defaults; and the parameter Respond to Sales Order Changes. This parameter determines if WIP will put a job for a configured item on hold when you de-link the job from the Sales Order line.

NOTE
You must define and save the WIP Parameters record for an organization before you can define Accounting Classes for that organization. Thus, to add a default accounting class, you must first save the parameters without an accounting class, define the accounting class, and then return to the WIP parameters form to specify the accounting class as the default.

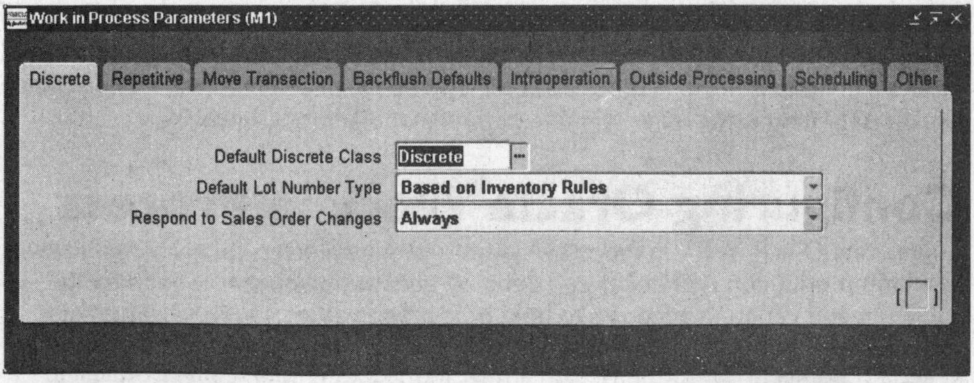

| Discrete | Repetitive | Move Transaction | Backflush Defaults | Intraoperation | Outside Processing | Scheduling | Other |

Default Discrete Class   Discrete
Default Lot Number Type   Based on Inventory Rules
Respond to Sales Order Changes   Always

FIGURE 16-3. *WIP Parameters establish many execution defaults*

■ **Repetitive**   The Repetitive tab contains two fields—Recognize Period Variances and Auto Release Days. The Recognize Period Variances field determines if you book variances for all repetitive schedules when you close an Inventory accounting period or only for repetitive schedules that are cancelled or completed with no further charges allowed. Generally, users choose to recognize variances only for cancelled or completed schedules; if you recognize variances for all schedules, a schedule that is in process might result in a large unfavorable variance in one period (for example, if you have issued all material but performed no completions) and a favorable variance in the next period. Auto Release Days specifies a window within which a subsequent unreleased schedule will be automatically released as you complete an earlier schedule.

■ **Move Transaction**   This tab lets you specify whether you *require* a scrap account when you move to a scrap intra-operation step or whether a scrap account is optional. You also control whether you can dynamically create new operations with a move transaction (by moving to a new operation) and whether you can move past a step that has a status that prohibits moves out of that step. (See "Shop Floor Statuses," later in this chapter.)

■ **Backflush Defaults**   On this tab, you can specify a default backflush subinventory and locator, used if the job or schedule's material requirements do not identify a subinventory/locator to backflush a component. Backflushing is the automated issue of specified components; it is discussed in detail later in this chapter. Unless your material control needs are very simple, you should probably specify a dummy location as the default; if that location is driven negative, it will indicate that you have not specified a real backflush location for one or more products. This tab also lets choose the selection method for backflushing lot-controlled components and the verification method—All or Exceptions Only. Choosing Exceptions Only requires verification only if there is a shortage of the component and might result in less stringent lot control and traceability.

■ **Intraoperation**   This tab lets you enable or disable intra-operations steps for the organization. The system will always use the Queue step at the first operation of the routing and the To Move step at the last operation; others are optional. For example, you might decide not to use the Run step or to disable either the Scrap or Reject steps.

■ **Outside Processing**   The Outside Processing tab lets you specify a default shop floor status for outside processing operations to prevent a manual move past or out of the operation. It also lets you choose the point at which requisitions are created for outside processing services.

- **Scheduling** This tab lets you enable constraint-based scheduling (discussed in the "Manufacturing Scheduling" section) and determine the constraints that will be considered.

- **Other** The Other tab lets you select a default ATP Rule for component ATP and a Default Overcompletion Tolerance.

WIP Accounting Classes

WIP Accounting Classes define groups of GL accounts that are used for valuation and variance reporting for different types of production. You define separate accounting classes for Standard Discrete jobs, Repetitive Schedules, Asset Non-Standard jobs, Expense Non-Standard jobs, and Lot-based Standard Discrete (used with Oracle Shop Floor Management).

For each class, you define the five valuation and four variance accounts to be used for production associated with the class. There is no separate account for material overhead variance because material overhead is earned only on completion to inventory. If there is a material overhead discrepancy (due to material substitution, for example), it is included in the Material Usage variance.

You can define as many of these classes as you need. The class you name as the default for discrete production will be used on standard discrete jobs and flow completions. Repetitive schedules get their accounting class from the production line/item association. You can override these as necessary when you create new jobs or schedules or when you perform a work order-less completion.

Shop Floor Statuses

Shop Floor Statuses are codes you apply to specific intra-operation steps in a job or schedule. They can be purely descriptive, or they can prohibit moves out of the specific step to which they are attached. Definition of a status is very simple—enter a status code, enter an optional description, and check the Allow Moves box if that status will allow moves out of the operation step.

These statuses work in conjunction with two WIP Parameters mentioned earlier in this chapter. The parameter Allow Moves Over No Move Shop Floor Statuses in the Move Transaction tab determines if you can move *past* a step that has a status that prohibits moves. And the parameter Shop Floor Status for PO Move Resources identifies a status that will automatically be applied to outside processing operations that include a PO Move resource. Such resources will generate an automatic Move transaction when the outside processing PO is received; in such a case, you do not want anyone performing a manual move transaction, or the automatic move transaction might fail. By applying a status that prohibits moves, you prevent this situation.

Labor Rates

If you want to charge *actual* labor rates in WIP, you must maintain the rates for individual employees. Employees are defined in Oracle's Human Resources (HR) applications, but HR labor rates are not currently used in WIP.

Use the Employee Labor Rates form to define employee labor rates. For an employee, define one or more labor rates with effectivity dates. These rates will be used only if you manually charge a resource defined as a Person and if you specify an employee when you charge the resource.

If the resource indicates that you will charge the actual rate, not the standard rate (i.e., the Standard Rate box is unchecked), the job or schedule will be charged for the employee rate times the hours reported; any variance that results will be booked to the *efficiency variance* account identified in the job or schedule's accounting class. If the resource indicates that you will charge the standard rate, the job or schedule will be charged at the standard rate of the resource, and the employee rate will be used to generate a *rate variance*. This rate variance will be booked to the variance account defined for the resource.

Profile Options

As in all applications, several profile options control manufacturing execution. A few of the more common options are as follows:

- **WIP:Discrete Job Prefix**   This enables you to specify a prefix that will be used with the system-generated number that identifies a job, called the *job name.* You might want to set this profile by user or responsibility, to identify the source of different discrete jobs.

- **WIP:Job Name Updatable**   This profile determines whether you can change the job name after you create the job.

- **WIP:Requirement Nettable Option**   This profile controls whether you can see component availability in all subinventories or only in subinventories identified as Nettable. If you want to restrict who can issue material from non-nettable subinventories (e.g., discrepant material), you could set this profile to "View only nettable subinventories" at the site level and set it to View All Subinventories for the users or responsibilities that can issue non-nettable material.

- **WIP:Move Completion Default**   The Move Completion Default profile specifies if a move transaction to the To Move step of the last operation for a job will automatically attempt to complete the quantity into inventory.

■ **WIP:Exclude Open ECOs** This profile determines how WIP views ECO revised items with an Open status. If you set this profile to Yes, WIP will exclude such open ECOs from affecting the material requirements of a job or schedule you create. You might want to set this profile by user or responsibility if you want certain users to be able to create a job for a pending ECO in an Open status, for example, to build a prototype of a pending revision.

■ **WIP:See Engineering Items** The See Engineering Items profile controls access to Engineering items, bills, and routings. Here, too, you might want to selectively set this profile at the user or responsibility level to control who can create jobs or schedules for products that have not yet been released from engineering.

In addition, a number of TP (Transaction Processing) profiles control the processing (online, concurrent, or background) for the various WIP transactions. For example, the profile TP:WIP Material Transactions Form determines the processing mode for component issues and returns; the profile TP:WIP Completion Transaction Form determines the processing mode for assembly completions or returns.

Several of the TP profiles let you specify the first field you typically enter on various transaction forms. For example, the profile TP:WIP Completion Transaction First Field specifies the field in which the cursor is positioned when you invoke the completion transaction. You can set the value to Job, Assembly, Line, or Sales Order. Job is the appropriate setting for discrete manufacturing because you will typically specify the job number. If you predominantly use repetitive manufacturing, you should set the profile to Assembly or Line because you will identify repetitive schedules by Assembly and Line. And if you use ATO, you might want to set the profile Sales Order and identify the job by the Sales Order to which it is linked. Similar profiles specify the first field for the Material Transaction, Move Transaction, and Resource Transaction forms. If you employ a variety of manufacturing methods, you can set these profiles at the user or responsibility level.

Defining Jobs and Production Schedules

The following sections describe the tools and methods for defining and maintaining the different production orders and schedules that Oracle provides—Discrete Jobs, Repetitive Schedules, and Flow Schedules.

Discrete

Discrete Jobs are perhaps the most versatile production vehicle in the Oracle E-Business Suite. They are used for multiple manufacturing strategies—make to stock, assemble to order, configure to order—and for non-standard production requirements such as rework and prototype production. Discrete Jobs can be created in several ways—by releasing planned orders from the planning application; by autocreating jobs based on ATO or CTO sales orders; through an open interface; or manually as needed. In order to create a discrete job, the item's Build in WIP attribute must be enabled.

Creating Discrete Jobs

As noted earlier, discrete jobs can be created when you release planned orders from the MRP or ASCP planner workbenches, described in Chapters 10 and 11. Normally, such jobs will be created using the bill and routing effective as of the planned start date of the job and using the default accounting class from the organization's WIP parameters. If necessary, you can override many of these defaults using the Release Properties tab on the Supply/Demand window of the Planner Workbench.

The process uses the open WIP Job/Schedule Interface; releasing the job loads the interface tables and submits a request to run the WIP Mass Load program; no user intervention is required.

You can create jobs manually, using the Discrete Jobs form, shown in Figure 16-4. The following information is required:

■ **Job (name)** More commonly called the job or work order number, this will automatically default, although you can override it manually. If you have set a prefix using the WIP:Discrete Job Prefix profile, the applicable prefix will be added to the system-generated number.

NOTE
Job Names are generated by an Oracle database sequence, WIP_JOB_NUMBER_S. There is only one sequence used across an entire installation; this implies that you will not have "gapless" numbering within an organization (other organizations' jobs will use numbers from the same sequence) or within a prefix. Also, because the job name is generated by the sequence before the job is saved, if you clear or exit the form without saving, you will have gaps in your job numbers.

■ **Type** This defaults to Standard, but you can change it to Non-standard to create a non-standard job; non-standard jobs are discussed later in this chapter.

■ **Assembly** This is the item number of the product you are building on this job; it is not required for non-standard jobs.

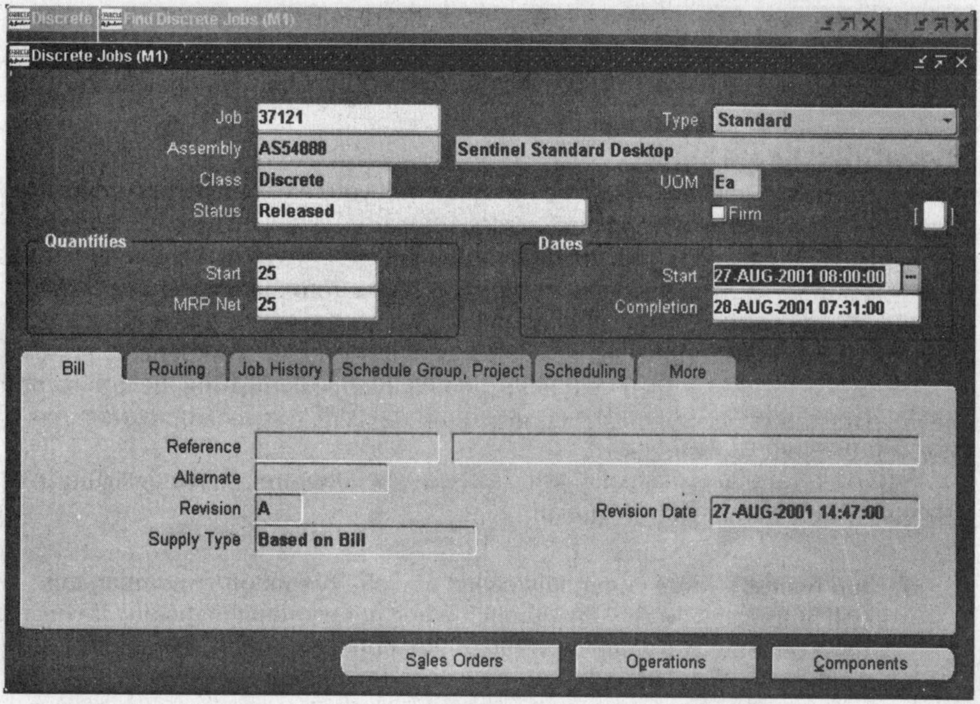

FIGURE 16-4. *Manually create and modify discrete jobs with the Discrete Jobs form*

■ **Class**   The accounting class of the job. This field defaults for Standard jobs based on your WIP parameters, but can be overridden. You must enter it manually for a non-standard job to determine the type of accounting performed.

■ **Status**   The status defaults to Unreleased, but you can specify Released or Hold when you create the job.

■ **Start (quantity)**   The quantity you plan to start for this job; this will determine the material requirements.

NOTE
The MRP Net quantity should be used only if you want to exclude quantities from being considered by planning, for reasons other than planned shrinkage.

■ **Start or Completion Date**   The date you plan to start or complete the job. If your assembly has a routing, the other date will be calculated by scheduling the routing operations; if the assembly has no routing, the item's lead time will be used. For non-standard jobs without routing, your must enter both the start and completion dates.

When you create a job, the system determines the effectivity of the bill and routing based on the anticipated start date of the job; if you enter a start date, the date you enter is used; if you enter only a completion date, the system estimates the start date by applying the item's fixed and variable lead time and estimating the start date.

The system explodes the assembly's bill of material to create the material requirements for the job, as described earlier. It also uses the routing to create a schedule for the job; if you enter a start job, WIP schedules forward from the start date; if you enter a completion job, WIP uses backward scheduling.

NOTE
If your item lead times do not closely reflect the item's routing, you might encounter some minor anomalies when backward scheduling—the system estimates a start date, selects the effective routing operations based on that estimated start date, and then backward schedules from your specified completion date. If the routing information does not correspond to the lead time, scheduling might result in a start date different from the date used to select the routing.

If the assembly has no effective bill or routing, you will receive a warning message, but the job will be created. If you want to prevent the creation of jobs for which there is no bill or routing, you can disable the item's Build in WIP attribute, either directly or through status control.

Other tabs on the Discrete Jobs form enable you to select alternate bills or routings, and the effectivities for those bills or routings, either by entering the effective date, or by specifying the corresponding item or routing revision. You can also enter or change the default completion location (this defaults from the routing), enter a description for the job, specify project and task information, and add Demand Class information. And you can view summary job history (quantities completed, scrapped, and remaining; and release, completion, and close dates).

Discrete Job Statuses

Discrete jobs will typically go through five different statuses:

- **Unreleased**   The job is awaiting release; no material, movement, or resource transactions can be recorded against the job, although you can modify the job or print paperwork.

- **Released**   The job is ready to start or in process. Releasing a job moves the job quantity to the Queue of the first operation. Releasing a job also sets the Release Date of the job to the current system date; this date is not modifiable.

NOTE
Although you can backdate WIP material, move, and resource transactions subject to the same rules defined in Inventory (e.g., the accounting period must be open), WIP imposes an additional restriction—you cannot date a WIP transaction prior to the release date of the job or schedule.

- **Complete**   The job is complete, and no further output is expected. WIP assigns this status automatically when you complete the total quantity for the job, or you can assign it manually. You can still charge material and resources to a complete job; this is especially useful if you do not record such charges at the time they are incurred.

- **Complete – No Charges**   This status indicates that no further charges or activity is permitted; you cannot issue or modify material transactions or charge resources. This status is always applied manually to discrete jobs; it is intended to signify that someone has reviewed the job and verified that all appropriate charges have been recorded.

- **Closed**   The Closed status books any job variances for the job; it is often an accounting function.

There are two additional statuses, intended to handle exceptions:

- **Hold**   This status prohibits further material or resource charges against the job, until the status is changed.

- **Cancelled**   The Cancelled status designates a job you no longer want to transact or use in planning.

All statuses are reversible, although Closed and Cancelled typically signify the end of production.

Updating Discrete Jobs

Most information on a discrete job can be modified before you close the job, but modifications are subject to some common-sense restrictions.

You can change most job header information on the Discrete Jobs form. A typical change is to release or hold a job. One notable exception is the Accounting Class— it cannot be changed after you save the job. You can change the start or completion date to reschedule the job, and you can change job quantities. You can increase the job quantity at any time, but you cannot decrease the quantity of a released job below the quantity that currently exists at the queue step of the first operation. (You can reverse move transactions to return the desired quantity to the queue, if necessary, and then reduce the job quantity.)

Though material requirements and job operations are visible from the Discrete Jobs form, you must use separate forms to modify them.

Use the Material Requirements form to add, modify, or delete material requirements. You can adjust requirements to any job that is not Cancelled or Closed with no charges allowed, but some restrictions apply to deleting or reducing requirement quantities—you cannot delete a requirement for which activity has occurred (but you can reverse the transactions, if necessary); and you cannot reduce a requirement to less than what was already issued or backflushed. However, you can reverse transactions, if necessary, to allow any modification to requirements.

You can also create material requirements "on the fly," by issuing material not required on the original job or schedule; this is described further in the "Material Control" section.

Use the Operations form to add, modify, or delete job operations or resource requirements. You can adjust operations on any job that is not Cancelled, Closed, or Complete with no changes allowed; you can only adjust operations for Repetitive Schedules that are unreleased. As with requirements, you can add operations, resources, or increase resource requirements at any time, but you cannot delete operations or resources, or reduce resource requirements, after activity has occurred for that operation or resource. Again, you can reverse transactions if necessary to allow modifications.

You can add operations "on the fly" based on the setting of the WIP parameter Allow Creation of New Operations. If this parameter is enabled, you can perform a move transaction to an operation sequence number that did not exist on the job; the operation will be dynamically created. This can be useful for in-line rework. For example, you might decide that all or a portion of the job quantity needs some additional processing. Operations created in this manner have little detail; you must use the Operations form to provide details, including resource requirements.

Simulating Discrete Jobs

The Simulate Discrete Jobs form lets you simulate a discrete job to determine if you have sufficient material and capacity before beginning production. Enter the assembly, dates, and quantity as you would for a job, and use the Operations and Components buttons to view the routing, resource information, and material requirements.

If the simulation is acceptable and you want to create a job, select Tools | Save Simulated Jobs from the menu bar. This opens a window where you can specify the job class, status, and description, and save the simulation as an actual job.

Non-Standard Jobs

Non-standard jobs (NSJ) are used for non-standard production activity, such as rework, prototype production, or even simple maintenance operations. You can create non-standard jobs on the Discrete Jobs form by specifying the Type as Non-Standard and selecting the appropriate accounting class to distinguish the NSJ as an Asset or Expense class. Asset jobs are customarily used for jobs that result in creation of a product, such as rework (creating a usable product from discrepant material), or prototype production. Expense jobs are used for activities where you simply want to charge material or resources to an expense account (e.g., maintenance).

Non-standard jobs differ from standard discrete jobs in that no bill of material or routing is automatically selected. You can create requirements and operations manually, as discussed earlier, or select *any* bill or routing when you create the job. For example, you might have a recurring upgrade or rework activity that you perform frequently; you might have an alternate bill that includes the standard components needed for the upgrade. Or, you might want to build a prototype of a new product, using a bill of material from an existing product as the starting point.

NOTE
Non-standard jobs emphasize flexibility; you do not have to select a bill or routing for the assembly you are building, so use caution that you do not inadvertently select the wrong bill or routing.

Subsequent processing of NSJs is the same as standard discrete jobs.

Repetitive

Repetitive Schedules are used to represent ongoing production of standard products over a period of time. They are used for standard products only; although you can modify their requirements or operations, the planning products do not recognize such modifications.

In order to define repetitive schedules, you must create at least one production line, using the Production Lines form; and associate your repetitive assemblies to the appropriate lines, using the Repetitive Line/Assembly Associations form.

Creating Repetitive Schedules

You can create repetitive schedules from the MRP or ASCP Planner Workbenches (described in Chapters 10 and 11), or you can create them manually with the Repetitive Schedules form shown in Figure 16-5.

To create a schedule manually, enter the production line and associated assembly. To specify the quantity to be produced, enter any two of the following: the *Daily Quantity* (i.e., rate) of production; the *Number of Days* of production, including decimals if necessary; and the *Total Quantity* desired; the form will calculate the missing element. Enter one of the four dates associated with the schedule: the *First Unit Start Date, First Unit Completion Date, Last Unit Start Date,* or *Last Unit Completion Date.* The system will calculate the remaining dates based on the item's lead time and number of days of production. Refer to Chapter 8 for further discussion of the various characteristics of a repetitive schedule.

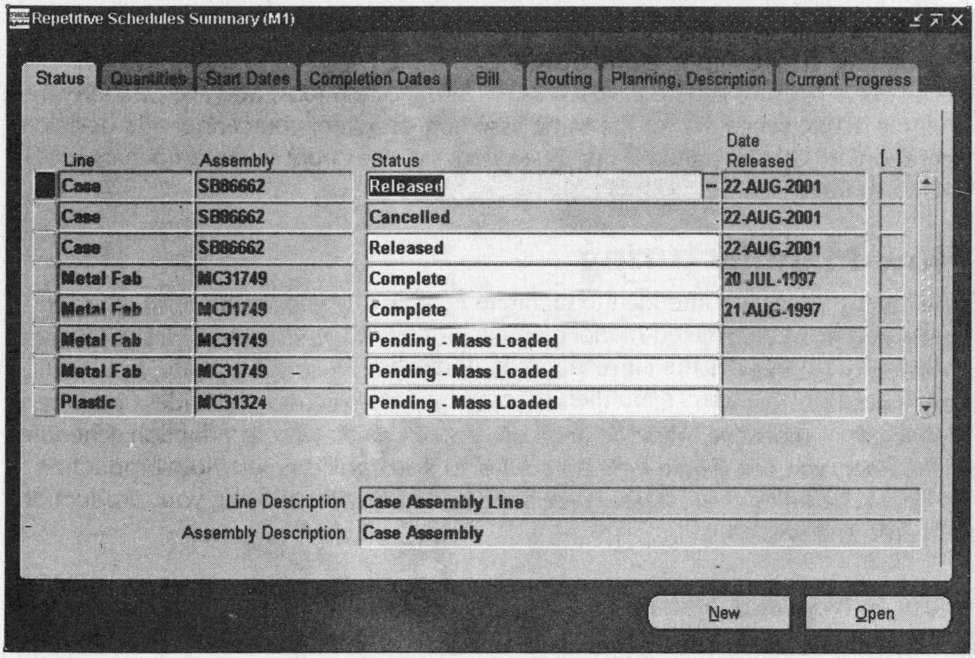

FIGURE 16-5. *Use the Repetitive Schedules form to create and modify repetitive schedules*

Repetitive Schedule Statuses

Repetitive schedules use many of the same statuses as discrete jobs, but there are a few differences in how the statuses are applied. Unreleased and Released are basically the same as for discrete jobs, although repetitive schedules can be automatically released based on the setting of the WIP parameter Auto Release Days.

Repetitive schedules are never closed; they use only the two Completed statuses. However, there are differences in how the statuses are assigned. If you complete the planned quantity on a repetitive schedule and there is another released schedule for the same assembly/line in the future (or if the next schedule is automatically released), the current schedule will be automatically assigned a status of Complete – No Charges. The assumption is that any additional charges can be applied to the next schedule. But if there is no released schedule in the future, the status will be changed to Complete, so that you can make any additional charges to the current schedule.

You can hold or cancel repetitive schedules just like discrete jobs. In addition, repetitive schedules that are created from the Planner Workbench are given a status of Pending–Mass Loaded as described in Chapter 8.

Updating Repetitive Schedules

Repetitive schedules can be updated much like discrete jobs; however, if there are multiple active schedules for the same assembly and line, you cannot add or delete operations or change standard operation codes or the count point, autocharge, or backflush flags.

Flow Manufacturing

Flow manufacturing is intended to facilitate flexible manufacturing of standard or configured items on a mixed-model manufacturing line. As discussed earlier, the flow philosophy emphasizes the elimination of all non-value-added activity; as a result, flow manufacturing offers simplified scheduling and execution activities compared to discrete or repetitive manufacturing. To communicate your production schedule to the floor, you can utilize *flow schedules*, or you can complete flow production without scheduling at all, if you have a method of communicating your production schedule and sequence.

Flow Scheduling Setup

Most setup for flow manufacturing is the same as for discrete production; however, there are two additional requirements if you want to create flow schedules—you must have your products associated with production lines by means of a flow routing (described in Chapter 4), and you must define *scheduling rules*.

Scheduling rules determine the priority in which demands will be selected for scheduling and the production sequence. You define scheduling rules on the Define

Scheduling Rules form. Give each rule a name indicative of its use. Choose one of the following scheduling methods to determine how mixed model production will be sequenced:

■ **Mixed Model**   This method provides the most detailed scheduling of mixed model production. It will suggest a production sequence that interleaves production of mixed models, based on the proportion of demand. Use this method if your line produces multiple products, with differing resource requirements but little or no setup differences. For example, Neptune builds several models of desktop computers on the same line; some include CD/RW drives, and others do not. Mixed model scheduling attempts to schedule alternating production of models to avoid creating a bottleneck at the operation that installs the CD/RW drives.

■ **Level Daily Rate**   This method attempts to schedule the same amount of mixed products each day, but does not sequence production of individual units.

■ **No Level Load**   The No Level Load method simply schedules production according to the priority criteria in your rule; it does not attempt to balance the production of multiple models. This makes sense if there is little difference in the resources required to product multiple models.

Figure 16-6 illustrates these different leveling methods.

In addition to the scheduling method, identify the criteria you want to use to select and prioritize the demands you schedule. Select one or more of the criteria

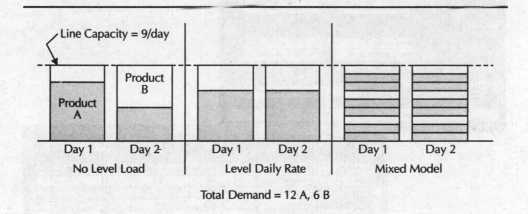

FIGURE 16-6.   *Line Scheduling Leveling methods*

for each rule and identify its order of priority. You can choose any combination of the following criteria:

- Order Due Date
- Order Entry Date
- Order Priority
- Order Promise Date
- Order Request Date
- Order Schedule Date

Line Scheduling Workbench

Create Flow Schedules on the Line Scheduling Workbench, by specifying the pool of demand you want to schedule, the scheduling rule to use, and the date(s) for which you want to create schedules. The Line Scheduling Workbench is shown in Figure 16-7.

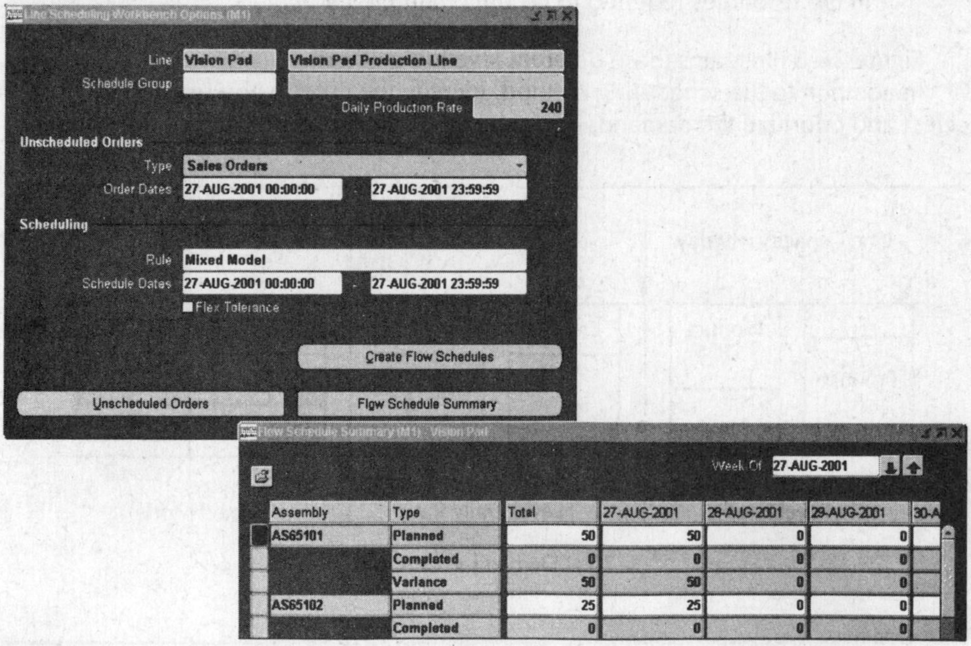

FIGURE 16-7. *The Line Scheduling Workbench lets you create and review flow schedules*

To create flow schedules, select the line you want to schedule. In the Unscheduled Orders region of the form, select the type of demand for which you want to create flow schedules—Sales Orders or Planned Orders from an MRP or ASCP plan. In this region, specify the demand due dates you want to consider for scheduling. Then, in the Scheduling zone, specify the scheduling rule and dates for which you want to create schedules. Click the Create Flow Schedules button, and the system will display the Flow Schedule Summary window for the schedules you are about to create. You can view the details, including the schedule sequence, by clicking the Details button. Save your work to create the flow schedules. Figure 16-8 graphically depicts this process.

You cannot modify or delete individual flow schedules; if you need to make changes to the overall production schedule, you can delete the schedules for a range of lines and dates and re-create the schedules. Select Tools | Delete Flow Schedules from the menu bar, and enter the desired parameters for the concurrent request.

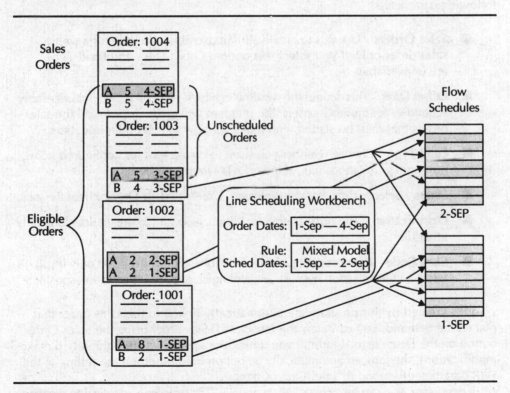

FIGURE 16-8. *Line scheduling process*

Assemble to Order

You can execute an assemble to order (ATO) strategy using either flow schedules or discrete jobs. In fact, flow manufacturing is, by its purest definition, an ATO strategy—you only build based on actual orders. However, Oracle documentation distinguishes between flow and ATO; when referring to ATO, it generally implies execution using discrete jobs, and the same convention is used in this book. If the item being built is a standard item with a predefined bill and routing, the overall process is very similar to standard discrete manufacturing, with one additional step—the automatic creation of the discrete job, linked to the sales order. Configure to order is a variation of this strategy, but generally involves the creation of a unique item; it is discussed separately.

AutoCreating Jobs

The AutoCreate Final Assembly Schedules program in WIP can automatically create discrete jobs for items identified as ATO items. This concurrent program accepts the following parameters:

- **Sales Orders** Use this to create a final assembly schedule for a single sales order only. If you select this option, Offset Days and Load Type are unavailable.

- **Offset Days** This defines the window in which you will create final assembly schedules for multiple orders; the program will create jobs for all the sales orders that must be started within this window to meet their due dates.

- **Load Type** Choose whether you want to create jobs for configured items, non-configured items (i.e., standard ATO items), or both.

- **Status** Select a default status (Released, Unreleased, or On Hold) for the jobs.

- **Organization** The organization for which you want to create final assembly schedules.

- **Class Code** The accounting class for the jobs. (This is available only if you select an Organization because accounting classes are organization-specific.)

Jobs created by this program are automatically linked to the sales order that placed the demand. You can view the associated sales order using the Sales Order button on the Discrete Jobs form. If you unlink the sales order from the job to make modifications, the job can automatically be put on hold based on the setting of the WIP parameter Respond to Sales Order Changes.

If necessary, you can also create jobs manually. The process is identical to creating a standard discrete job, but you have the option of linking the job to the sales order.

TIP
To link a job to the sales order, you must identify the sales order by the three segments of the sales order flexfield: Order Number, Order Type, and Order Source. There is no list of values provided for the individual segments, but using the Combinations button in the flexfield window can make it easier to find the sales order.

Configure to Order (CTO)

Configure to Order (CTO) is a variation of an ATO stocking strategy. It includes the additional step of automatically creating a unique item, bill, routing, and cost for the configuration being built and then follows the same flow as a predefined ATO item.

AutoCreating Configuration Items, Bills, and Routings

The program AutoCreate Configuration Items creates items, bills, and routings from the selections reflected in Order Management, as described in Chapter 12. The program is part of Oracle Bills of Material; it accepts the following parameters:

- **Sales Order Number, Release Offset Days, and Organization** These parameters perform the same selection function as they do in the AutoCreate Final Assembly Schedule program, described earlier.

- **Perform Leadtime Calculation** This parameter will calculate fixed and variable lead time for the configuration, based on the configured routing. If your routing times vary considerably based on optional operations, you should set this parameter to Yes. If you don't use optional operations, or if they have little or no effect on the lead time, you can set this parameter to No; in this case, the configuration's lead time attributes will be copied from its base model.

- **Perform Flow Calculations** Similar to the Perform Lead Time Calculation parameter, this parameter is used to invoke the flow calculations for configurations created with a flow routing. See Chapter 7 for more information.

AutoCreating Jobs

When the configuration has been created, the AutoCreate Final Assembly Schedules program, described earlier, creates discrete jobs for the configuration item. BOM includes a request set, named AutoCreate Configuration Items and Load Work Orders, that runs both programs together. In a heavy CTO environment, you might want to schedule this request set to automatically run at a regular interval.

You can also create flow schedules for these configurations, using the Line Scheduling Workbench, as described earlier.

Work Order Interface

You can also import discrete jobs and repetitive schedules from external sources using the Work Order Interface. You can also use the interface to add and change component requirements, add and change job operations and operation resources, and update operation resource usage.

In Release 11i, the interface consists of two tables—the WIP_JOB_SCHEDULE_INTERFACE and the WIP_JOB_DTLS_INTERFACE. Load header information in the WIP_JOB_SCHEDULE_INTERFACE table; load component, operation, or resource information in the WIP_JOB_DTLS_INTERFACE table.

Process data in the interface by running the WIP Mass Load program. You can view data in the interface table Pending Jobs and Schedules form; for jobs in error, use the Errors button to navigate to the Pending Jobs and Schedule Errors window. You can use this form to update failed rows and mark them for resubmission or delete them from the interface table. You can also choose to run the Work Order Interface report as part of the import process.

Material Control

Material Control deals with activities that involve material—either the component material that is issued or the assembly being produced that is ultimately received into inventory. Typical activities include the issue or backflush of components and the completion of assemblies into stock. This section discusses the issue activities and their reversal, as well as other types of material control, including by-product recovery and treatment of phantom assemblies. Completions are discussed later in this chapter.

Material Requirements

The material requirements for a job or repetitive schedule determine most of the material control activities for the components used. The requirements, created when the job or schedule is created, specify the quantity, supply type, and supply subinventory and locator for each component. And the table that maintains requirement information, WIP_REQUIREMENT_OPERATIONS, tracks the quantity issued to identify shortages.

The component's Yield Factor from the bill of material inflates requirement quantities; these quantities serve as the default for issue transactions and determine the quantities that will be backflushed.

NOTE
Backflushing will always use the component yield factor to adjust the quantity that is backflushed; there is no way to disable this behavior. Consider this carefully when assigning yield factors to backflush components.

WIP Supply Type

The WIP Supply Type determines how the component item will be supplied to WIP. You can enter a supply type for an item and override it in the Bill of Material, as described in Chapter 4.

Oracle provides the following supply types:

- **Push** Material is explicitly issued to a job or schedule, using the WIP Material Transaction. Material that is not issued is never relieved from inventory or charged to the job or schedule.

- **Assembly Pull** Material is automatically pulled (backflushed) as the assembly is completed into stock.

- **Operation Pull** Material is backflushed as the *operation* at which it is used is completed; see the "Intra-Operation Steps" section, earlier in this chapter, for a discussion of operation completion.

- **Phantom** A traditional phantom, or "transient," subassembly. Unless phantoms are explicitly transacted, they are never issued to WIP; rather, their components are added to the WIP requirements as if the phantom did not exist. See the "Phantom Assemblies" section later in this chapter. Oracle supports multiple levels of phantoms.

- **Bulk** Bulk material is never charged to WIP, unless you perform an explicit issue transaction for the specific bulk component. Items such as glue, sealant, shims, etc. that do not lend themselves to an exact quantity on the bill of material might be listed as bulk components. This provides documentation of the material to be used, but does not impact inventory or WIP valuation.

- **Supplier** Supplier material (called Vendor material in earlier releases) is intended to designate material provided by your supplier as part of their outside processing service. As such, this material is never issued to WIP and not planned in the planning applications.

Supply Subinventory and Locator

The supply subinventory and locator define the location from which the component is normally supplied to WIP. These attributes come from the bill of material or from the item master; if they are null for a pull (backflushed) component, the default value from the WIP Parameters is used.

These attributes are especially important for backflushed components, as they define the location from which material is backflushed. For Push material, they indicate the default location that will appear on the WIP Material transaction and the supply location that prints on the picklist. You can also run a variation of the shortage report to show material that is short in its designated supply subinventory/locator.

Component Issues and Returns

Components with a supply type of *Push* must be explicitly issued to a job or schedule, using the WIP Material Transactions form shown in Figure 16-9. To issue open requirements, select a transaction type of WIP component issue and select the radio button labeled Include All Material (the default). Click Continue, and you will open the WIP component issue window. This window shows all open requirements that meet your selection criteria, with the default quantity and supply location from the WIP requirements. You can accept all the defaults by clicking Done, or you can override the information as necessary. If one or more components are lot or serial controlled, use the Lot/Serial button to designate the correct lots or serial numbers.

The material transaction offers many options to reflect different types of material activity. You can limit the scope of the issue to material required at a specific department or operation by including these selection criteria on the first window of the form. You can issue excess material by overriding the quantity on the transaction window—for example, you might have a full reel, carton, or drum of material and want

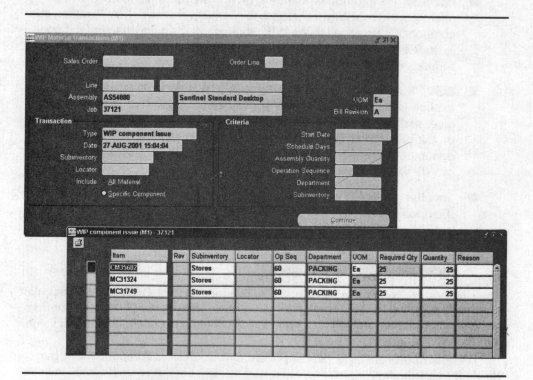

FIGURE 16-9. *Record component issues and returns with the WIP Material Transactions form*

to issue the entire amount (and return the excess later). Similarly, you can issue less than the default quantity, if you do not have sufficient quantity to fulfill the requirement.

For repetitive schedules, indicate the Start Date and number of Schedule Days for which you want to issue material; the material transaction will calculate the quantity needed for that many days of production. You can use a decimal quantity in the Schedule Days field if you want to issue material for less than a full day's production.

You can also perform material substitution with the material transaction. Select the Specific Component criteria in the first window, and enter *any* item in the transaction window; the new item will be issued to the job and added to the material requirements.

NOTE
You will receive a warning if the material is not on the bill of material or not used at the designated operation, but there is no restriction on the items you can issue in this manner. You can also issue material that is designated as pull (backflush) material; again you receive a warning, but will be allowed to proceed. Issuing backflush material will fulfill the requirements, and the material will not be backflushed in addition to the issue.

To return excess material, or simply to reverse an incorrect transaction, select a transaction type of WIP component return and proceed as before.

CAUTION
Be especially carefully when processing a return transaction with the Specific Component criterion. Just as there is no restriction on what material you can issue, there is no restriction on what you can return—you can return any item, whether it is on the bill of material for the assembly or it has been issued to the job. This capability can be helpful for "disassembly" types of work, but can play havoc with inventory accuracy if not carefully controlled.

Backflushing

To streamline manufacturing, many companies will employ backflushing for some or all of the components of a job or repetitive schedule. The assumption is that if a certain quantity has been completed, the correct components were used.

Backflushing, sometimes called *post-deduct,* automatically issues material based on completion of a quantity at an operation or completion of a quantity of a job into inventory. Material requirements with a supply type of *Assembly Pull* are backflushed as the finished assembly on the job is completed into inventory; requirements designated as *Operation Pull* are backflushed as a quantity is completed at the operation where they are used. See the section titled "Intra-Operation Steps," earlier in this chapter, for a discussion of what constitutes an operation completion.

NOTE
If you use operation-based backflushing, it is important that your bills of material accurately reflect the correct routing operation where the component is consumed; inventory accuracy and WIP costing are affected.

Backflush material is automatically deducted from the supply subinventory and locator specified in the material requirements; if there is no backflush location specified, the default from the WIP parameters is used. Backflushing may drive inventory negative in the supply location, even if your Inventory parameters prohibit negative inventory in the organization. The profile INV:Override Neg for Backflush controls this.

NOTE
If the component is under revision quantity control, backflushing will only backflush the current revision, based on the date of the transaction. If you backflush revision-controlled parts, review quantities in their supply locations carefully and decide how you want to handle parts at the old revision level. For example, you might decide to rework the old revision or manually issue the old revision to the work order to override the backflush logic.

Because backflushing is an automated process, there is no opportunity to override the quantity or location at the time of the transaction. However, you can modify the material requirements prior to backflushing, or you can still perform manual issue and return transactions as described earlier, to adjust backflushed quantities. For example, if a quantity of the component was damaged during assembly, you could issue extra material to replace it. Similarly, if you used less than the requirements indicated, you could return the excess material after it was backflushed.

A work order-less completion transaction *always* backflushes all required components—Push, Assembly Pull, and Operation Pull; it does not backflush components with a supply type Bulk or Vendor.

By-Product Recovery

You can represent by-products in your bills of material by including components with a negative quantity. This represents material that will be *recovered* from the job. MRP and ASCP planning will see these quantities as planned supply; this technique has been used with MRP systems for many years.

On the shop floor, you must receive this material back into stock. From a transaction standpoint, you can do this in several ways. If you designate the by-product as Operation or Assembly Pull, WIP will in effect perform a *reverse backflush* at operation or assembly completion and automatically return the material to the designated supply location. If you designated the by-product as a Push item, you must explicitly receive it back to stock, using the WIP Material Transaction. Select a transaction type of Negative component issue, and select the Include All Material radio button. Clicking Continue will show all the un-received by-products, optionally limited by additional selection criteria (operation, department, or subinventory). To reverse the recovery of by-products, select a transaction type of Negative component return.

> **TIP**
> *If you find the transaction types confusing, consider defining your own transaction types in inventory; for example, you could define a type called By-Product Recovery, with a source type of Job or Schedule and an action of Negative Component Issue.*

Phantom Assemblies

Phantom assemblies are collections of parts that are grouped together with a bill of material, but not normally built and stocked; rather, the phantom assembly serves as a convenient mechanism to attach the same set of parts to multiple bills and to centralized changes to those parts—if you change the bill of the phantom, you effectively change all the assemblies that use that phantom. Phantoms are sometimes referred to as "blow-through" or "transient subassemblies."

Although some will debate whether a true phantom *can* be built or stocked; in Oracle applications, both activities are possible. In fact, in Oracle applications, you can designate an item or a component as a phantom; this means that you can use an assembly as phantom in one bill but not another, or even on a specific discrete job.

When you create a job or repetitive schedule, WIP explodes any components designated as phantoms to their non-phantom components; these components become the material requirements for the job and drive the material control activities and shortage reporting.

NOTE
The planning products will net any on-hand quantities of the phantom assemblies before creating demand on their components, but WIP does not mirror this logic. If you want to use stock of a phantom that might be on-hand, you must explicitly issue it to the job or include it in the job's material requirements.

Open Transaction Interface

WIP component issues and returns, as well as completions and returns, are basically Inventory transactions. Like most Inventory activities, you can process these transactions with the Inventory Open Transaction Interface, described in Chapter 15. This might be particularly useful if you are using automated material handling or data collection equipment that can provide the needed data without additional operator intervention.

Shop Floor Control

Shop Floor Control activities are those that record the progress of a job or schedule on the production floor. Normally, these activities record the progression of a job or repetitive schedule through the operations on the routing; they might also include the scrapping or rejecting of the assembly during production, reflected by the intra-operation step to which you move all or part of the job. (See the discussion of intra-operation steps earlier in this chapter.) Shop Floor activities depend on the use of routings; although Oracle does not require routings to report production, routings are necessary to perform the shop floor activities described in this section.

Shop Floor moves can trigger backflushing of component material, as described earlier, and can also trigger *autocharging* of resources. Resource charging, whether automatic or manual, is discussed later, in the "Resource Management" section.

Dispatch Reports and Job Paperwork

In many environments, shop floor activity is driven by a *dispatch list*—a report or screen that shows scheduled work by department. The printed dispatch list can be sorted by operation start of complete date and is typically run for a range of dates. You can limit the output to a range of departments or a specific schedule group (to group similar products), and you can choose whether to show released jobs only or include unreleased jobs. In production, you might want to schedule this report to run every night; be sure to select the option *Increment date parameters each run* if you schedule this job to run at regular intervals.

Many businesses also employ a *job packet* or *job traveler*; this is a packet of information that contains routing and bill of material information and may also include other information, such as a drawing. In Oracle applications, the primary document for this purpose is the Discrete Job Routing Sheet (or Repetitive Routing Sheet); these reports list all routing and schedule information, as well as component information by operation. The routing sheet can be run for a range of jobs, schedule groups, or a range of scheduled start dates. In a production environment, you might want to schedule this request on a regular interval.

In a paperless environment, the functions of both the Dispatch List and the Discrete Job Routing Sheet are provided online, on the Discrete Workstation, discussed later in this chapter.

Move Transactions

The Move Transactions form, shown in Figure 16-10, lets you record movement between or within operations on the routing of a job or repetitive schedule. Move transactions can optionally charge resources, either automatically or manually. You can also view status information that you have assigned to an intra-operation step

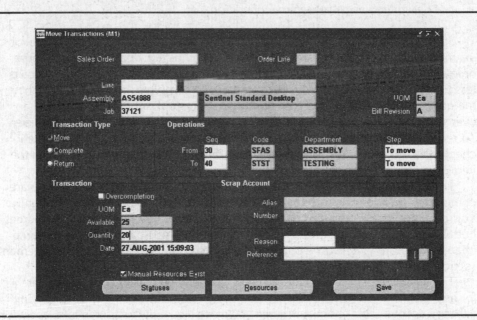

FIGURE 16-10. *Use the Move Transactions form to record shop floor moves*

and can optionally complete the quantity into inventory, given the proper setup. And, like other WIP transactions, the same form lets you reverse prior transactions.

To perform a move transaction, identify the job or schedule (assembly/line) you want to transact. Select a transaction type of Move, and identify the From and To operation and step for the move. In the Transaction region of the form, the Available field will show you the available quantity at the From step; enter the quantity you want to transact, and save your entry. The To operation defaults based on routing (as reflected in the WIP Operations); the next operation identified as a count point is the default To operation. You can override this if necessary to move to another step within the same operation, to reverse a previous transaction, or to move through multiple operations at once.

NOTE
"Skipping" an operation in a move transaction normally implies completing the skipped operation. This is determined by the operation's Autocharge flag; if you "skip" an operation designated as an autocharge operation, you implicitly complete that operation for the move quantity, appropriate material is backflushed, and resources are charged. In actuality, you can skip an operation only if it is not designated as an autocharge operation.

Some types of processes might not produce exactly the quantity expected; for example, stamping multiple small parts from a coil of stock can often yield more or less than expected, due to minor variations in the coil size. You can always record less than the operation quantity, but you can *overcomplete* (i.e., move more than the quantity that exists at the From operation and step) only if you specified an overcompletion tolerance (either a percent or amount) for the item or WIP parameter. To record an overcompletion with a move transaction, check the Overcompletion check box and enter a quantity greater than the available quantity, but within the item's Overcompletion tolerance.

The check box Manual Resources Exist indicates that the operations you are completing include resources that you have designated to be charged manually. You can enter these resource charges during the move by clicking the Resources button to access the Resource Transactions form, or you can enter the resource charges separately. Resource charging is discussed in the "Resource Management" section, later in this chapter.

The Move transaction also lets you enter a predefined reason code and reference for any transaction and optionally charge scrap to a scrap account, by specifying either an account alias or account when you move a quantity to a scrap intra-operation step. (A scrap account or alias can be required, based on the WIP parameter Require Scrap Account.)

You can reverse previous moves by simply moving backward; you reverse manual resource transactions by entering a negative quantity on an additional resource transaction.

Discrete Workstation

The Discrete Workstation offers a graphical dispatch list; a graphical, drag-and-drop interface to perform shop floor moves; the ability to charge resources to a job by entering a start and stop time (vs. entering the elapsed time); and links to the material, move, and resource transactions, if more options are needed.

The Discrete Workstation is intended as an operator's tool, more visually intuitive than the standard desktop forms. You open the workstation by specifying the department at which you are working and, optionally, the resource whose activity you are performing. The Workstation window, shown in Figure 16-11, consists of two

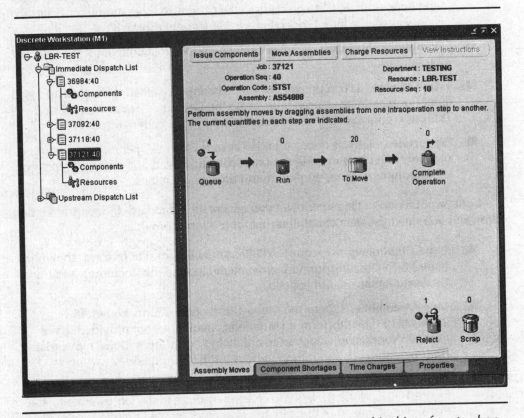

FIGURE 16-11. *The Discrete Workstation provides a graphical interface to shop floor activity*

panes. The left pane shows both an immediate dispatch list (job/operations already available to the specified department and resource) and an upstream dispatch list (job/operations at the previous operation). Each job shows the components and resources needed at that operation. You can change the view of the left pane using the buttons on the toolbar—the default is the vertical display shown in Figure 16-11, but you can also select an Interleaved style or Org-chart style. The Refresh button on the toolbar lets you refresh the display as the status changes on the shop floor.

The right pane of the Discrete Workstation shows information based on what you select in the left pane and lets you perform transactions. If you have selected a job/operation on the left pane, the right pane displays four tabbed regions:

- **Assembly Moves**   Provides drag-and-drop movement. The window shows the quantities available at each intra-operation step. To move a quantity, drag it from one icon (e.g., Queue) to the step you want. A window will open asking you to enter the quantity of the move. To move to the queue of the next operation, drag the quantity to the Complete Operation icon. This tab is only available for job/operations in the current dispatch list.

- **Component Shortages**   Displays any component shortages for the selected job/operation.

- **Time Charges**   Lets you enter resource charges by entering the start and stop times (instead of the elapsed time, as on the Resource Transactions form). This tab is only available for job/operations in the current dispatch list.

- **Properties**   Displays detailed properties for the job/operation, including assembly and operation descriptions, scheduled start and stop times, project and task information, and minimum transfer quantities.

Buttons at the top of the window let you access the standard desktop transaction forms, if you need the extra capabilities that those forms provide:

- **Issue Components**   Opens the WIP Material Transactions form, shown in Figure 16-9. Use this form to issue material to the job, including additional or substitute material, if needed.

- **Move Assemblies**   Opens the Move Transactions form, shown in Figure 16-10. Use this form if you need capabilities not provided in the Discrete Workstation, such as the ability to "skip" operations, move to a prior operation, or enter reason codes for the transaction.

- **Charge Resources**   Opens the Resource Transactions form, shown later in Figure 16-17. This form lets you charge resources to the job by entering the elapsed time instead of the start and stop times on the Discrete Workstation. You can also reverse resource charges (by entering negative quantities) and include reason codes on the transactions.

The View Instructions button shows any attachments for the job.

If you have selected the Components node on the left pane, the right pane displays the component requirements for that operation of the job. If you have selected the Resources node, the right pane displays detailed information about the resources required at that operation.

To see multiple windows of information, use the Pin Tab icon on the toolbar—click the pin icon to place the contents of the current right pane into a separate window, drag the window to the position you want, and open another window by selecting another node in the left pane. Figure 16-12 shows the result—the Assembly Moves, Component Shortages, and Time Charges windows are all visible.

Open Move Transaction Interface

You use the Move Transaction Interface to import move transactions from an external source; for example, you might want to perform shop floor moves based on input from a time and attendance system.

To use the interface, you must insert the appropriate data into the WIP_MOVE_ TXN_INTERFACE table; if you are using average costing and performing WIP completion or return transactions, you must insert data into the CST_COMP_SNAP_ INTERFACE table to calculate completion cost.

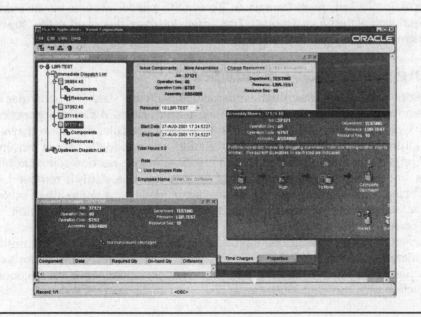

FIGURE 16-12. *Display multiple windows on the Discrete Workstation*

NOTE
You cannot create new WIP operations with this interface, regardless of the setting of the WIP parameter Allow Creation of New Operations.

The WIP Move Transaction Manager concurrent program, submitted from the Inventory Interface Managers form, processes data in the interface table. If you are using this interface regularly, you can schedule this program to run on a regular interval.

NOTE
Outside processing uses this interface to perform move transactions on receipt and delivery of purchase orders for outside processing; if you are using outside processing, you might also want to have this interface program running on a regular schedule.

You can review pending and failed transactions using the Pending Move Transactions form. You can correct failed transactions on this form and mark them for resubmission.

Move transactions processed through the open interface will autocharge appropriate resources, just like any move transaction. To perform manual resource transactions, see the description of the Open Resource Transaction Interface, described in the "Resource Management" section later in this chapter.

Using Shop Floor Statuses

Shop floor status codes, described earlier, can identify the state of a particular intra-operation step. For example, you might have a status called *Awaiting inspection* to simply indicate that material at the To Move step of a particular operation is awaiting formal inspection. In addition, shop floor statuses can optionally restrict movement out of or past that intra-operation step. If the Awaiting inspection status prohibits moves, you cannot move material out of the step until the status is removed. This can effectively put an operation "on hold" without holding the entire job or schedule; other activities on the job can continue, but the specific step of the operation is held until you remove the status code.

You attach status codes to operations using the Assign Shop Floor Statuses form; by restricting access to this form, you can control who can apply and remove status codes. Shop floor statuses also are used to prevent unwanted move transactions in conjunction with outside processing, as discussed in the next section.

Outside Processing

Outside processing is used when an external company does part or all of the work on a product. It is often employed for specialized activities, such as plating or conformal coating, that you do not have the capability or expertise to perform within your facilities or to outsource production during times of peak demand. Outside Processing (OSP), sometimes called subcontracting, relies on the integration of Work in Process and Purchasing—Work in Process drives the process using a standard discrete job, and Purchasing creates requisitions and purchase orders to procure the services of your supplier.

Outside Processing Setup

Setting up outside processing involves defining items and resources that represent the services you buy from the outside supplier and routings that utilize those resources. You might want to set up one or more departments to represent your outside suppliers, and you might want to define a shop floor status to prevent moves from an outside operation. You should also consider at what point in time you want to create the requisition for the outside services.

You must define one or more items to represent the services you will purchase from your suppliers. Although purchasing allows the creation of requisitions and purchase orders without a defined item, outside processing requires an item number—it provides a description of the service, unit of measure, and pricing information needed to support the automated creation of the OSP requisition and purchase order. The key item attributes for such an item are found on the Purchasing tab of the Master Items form:

- **Outside Processing Item** Check this box to identify this as an outside processing item.

- **Unit Type** Select either Assembly or Resource to indicate how the quantity of the OSP requisition and purchase order will be calculated—Assembly will create a requisition for the quantity of assemblies on the job, whereas Resource will create a requisition for the quantity of the resource on the job's routing. To make this decision, consider how you will specify the requested quantity to your supplier. For example, if you order assembly of circuit boards that you send to your supplier, then Assembly is probably the correct choice—you want a purchase order to request assembly of 50 circuit boards. However, if you are purchasing test time, you might want the quantity determined by the resource on the routing; choose Resource for this case.

If the OSP items simply represent the services you purchase, you don't have to define them as stockable inventory items. However, you can use the assembly itself as the OSP item; in this case, all the appropriate inventory attributes must be set. This case might be appropriate if your supplier does all the manufacturing of a product and you simply provide parts.

Next, you must define one or more resources to represent the outside processing in your routings and WIP. OSP resources have these unique characteristics:

- **Charge Type**   A charge type of *PO Move* or *PO Receipt* identifies a resource as an OSP Resource. The "PO" designation indicates that this is an outside service for which you will create a purchase order. The Move or Receipt portion of the charge type determines what will happen when the processed material is received back from the supplier. A charge type of PO Move will perform a move (through the open interface tables) to the next operation of a routing when the purchase order for the outside services is received; a charge type of PO Receipt will not perform a move when the PO is received. For this reason, you can have no more than one PO Move resource at any routing operation; if this were allowed, the receipt would attempt to move multiples of the quantity at the routing step. You can have as many PO Receipt resources as you need. For example, if you're ordering circuit board stuffing, you might pay the supplier a one-time setup charge, in addition to a per-unit price. You can reflect this with two separate resources (and two separate OSP items), but only one can initiate the move.

- **Outside Processing Enabled and Item**   Check either box to enable the resource for outside processing, and enter the outside processing item.

- **Basis Type**   The basis type (Item or Lot) has the same meaning as for internal resources. A one-time setup charge might have a Lot basis, whereas a per-unit service would have an Item basis.

When you use outside processing, you must consider one attribute of your Department definition: its Location code. This is an optional field for internal departments, but is required for outside processing. It is used to provide the Deliver-to location on the OSP requisition and purchase order, and the department to which the received material will be delivered depends on the resource's charge type. A PO Move resource will perform a move to the *next* operation in the routing. In this case, it is the department of the next operation that will be used as a deliver-to; that department must have a Location code. For a PO Receipt resource, it is the department that owns the OSP resource that must have a Location code.

TIP
*It doesn't hurt to define a location for all departments,
whether they are used in Outside Processing or
not. If you have a generic location code for your
manufacturing organization, you might want to use it
initially on all your departments; you can later change
this to a more specific location code if you choose.*

You might want to define one or more separate departments to represent your
suppliers, to help track material that has been sent out for processing, but this is
not necessary.

If you are using PO Move resources, you must ensure that you do not inadvertently
perform a manual move transaction outside the processing operation; if you do, the
automatically generated move transaction will fail when you receive the OSP
material. You can do this with a Shop Floor status. As described earlier, the WIP
parameter Shop Floor Status for PO Move resources will apply a status to operations
that use PO Move resources to prevent moves from the operation.

Another WIP parameter, Requisition Creation Time, controls the point at which
the requisition is created for the outside processing service. You can choose from
three values: At Operation, At Job/Schedule Release, or Manual.

Outside Processing Execution

Execution of outside processing activity is driven by WIP. You create and release a
discrete job or repetitive schedule as you normally would. If you have identified a
status code to be applied to OSP operations, based on your WIP parameters, it will
be applied to the Queue step of the OSP operation when the job is released. The
WIP parameter Requisition Creation Time controls the creation of the requisition for
the outside processing services; unless you have chosen to create OSP requisitions
manually, they will be created when you release the job, or when you move a quantity
into the queue step of the operation that uses OSP resources.

NOTE
*Requisition creation happens only when you perform
a forward move into the Queue intra-operation step;
a backward move or a move past the Queue step will
not create a requisition. If you are creating purchase
requisitions at the outside operation, the material
status described earlier can also prevent inadvertent
moves past the operation, which would bypass the
requisitions creation process.*

At this point, you can handle the creation of the purchase order for outside processing through any of the tools available in Oracle Purchasing—for example, you can automatically generate a release against an approved blanket order for the OSP item, or you can create the purchase order using the autocreate process.

NOTE
WIP loads the Requisition Import interface table to create the OSP requisition; you must ensure that the Requisition Import program is run, perhaps by scheduling it to run on a regular interval.

The move into an outside processing operation is meant to model the shipment of material to your supplier; however, no shipping documentation is produced.

When the supplier has provided their services and returned the material to you, receive the purchase order as you would any purchase order. You can perform a direct receipt, include inspection, or even incorporate a quality collection plan if you desire.

As noted earlier, if a resource with a PO Move charge type is used at the OSP operation, the receipt will move a quantity corresponding to the quantity of the receipt on to the queue of the next operation in the routing; if the OSP operation is the last operation, it will move to the To Move step of the current operation or complete the WIP job into stock if you have defined the appropriate defaults (discussed in the "Completions" section, later in this chapter).

NOTE
The move performed utilizes the Move Transaction interface. The receipt loads the interface table (WIP_MOVE_TXN_INTERFACE), but you must run (or schedule) the WIP Move Transaction Manager to actually execute the move from the interface data. You can view pending or failed move transactions on the Pending Move Transactions form.

Rework Production

Manufacturing operations offer frequent proofs of Murphy's Law—in spite of the best intentions and quality programs, there are still things that can and do go wrong in the production process. Sometimes you can correct the resulting problems by reworking the defective product; sometimes it must be scrapped. These activities—rework and scrap—are the subject of this and the next section.

If you discover a defect in the product during the production process, your first action might be to move the appropriate quantity to the Reject intra-operation step. This is optional, but it can indicate that the quantity does not meet quality standards. But note that, as discussed earlier, the quantity remains visible to the planning applications; the assumption is that rejected material will be fixed. You might also choose to use a shop floor status to further qualify the reason for rejection and possibly control who has authority to disposition the rejected quantity. (See the discussion of shop floor statuses, earlier in this chapter.)

In some cases, you might be able to fix a defect while the job is still in process. There are many options:

- Simply charge more time and/or material to the job.

- Add one or more routing steps to record rework activity.

- If you have anticipated such rework, you can use a "rework" step that you have already included in the product's routing.

- Choose to receive the product into stock; then rework it with a separate non-standard job.

The technique you choose will vary with the value of the product, the complexity of the repair, and the level of detail you need for current visibility and later reporting.

The simplest technique is to charge more time or material to the job or schedule to correct the problem. Charge material using the WIP Material Transaction, described earlier. Be sure to use the "individual component" transaction type, so that you can specify the extra components you are using. You can charge extra labor (or other resource time) to the job using the Resource Transactions, discussed later. Reason codes can be helpful to document the extra material issues, for later analysis.

Adding extra rework operations to the job can provide additional visibility to in-process rework—someone looking at the job can see that extra work is needed and track quantities queued or completed at the rework operation. You can add an extra operation with the Operations form and specify the necessary details, including the resources you expect to use. If some rework happens regularly in your operation (e.g., circuit board touch-up), you might find it helpful to define a standard operation to use as a template and either copy it (allowing modifications) or simply reference it as is. (See Chapter 4 for a discussion of standard operations.)

Based on the setting of the WIP parameter Allow Creation of New Operations, you might permit adding a rework operation on the fly. This technique is appropriate if your shop floor operators have authority to request rework. In this case, the operator simply performs a move transaction to a nonexistent operation sequence; this will dynamically create the new operation for the job or schedule. (If you use this approach, discipline is very important to prevent creation of bogus operations.) Note that operations created in this manner have no details; you must still use the Operations form to add the department, description, and resources. Also, keep in mind the completion criteria for the current operation—if you move a quantity to a new operation with a *higher* sequence than the current operation, you are effectively completing the current operation and incurring any designated material and resource charges; moving to a *lower* operation sequence does not complete the current operation.

If a given rework operation is simply a "fact of life," you might choose to include it in the standard routing for the product; in this case, it will always be available for use during production. However, consider the cost implications of such an approach—if you use the routing for a cost rollup, you include the *entire* cost of the operation in the product's cost. This might not be desirable if only a small percentage of items require rework.

In any case, rework operations are typically *not* identified as Autocharge operations. This means that "skipping" over the operation will indeed bypass the operation; it will not complete the operation, nor incur resource charges or initiate any backflushing at that operation.

Flow routings enable you to model rework loops. Such loops let you specify the anticipated percentage of their usage and are needed for accurate flow calculations. The planned percentage of rework will also affect standard cost calculations, as will the planned usage of alternate operations.

Another approach to rework is to complete the job into inventory and then rework using a non-standard job. This enables segregation of all rework charges. When you receive the defective product, use a non-reservable subinventory to ensure that the product is not accidentally shipped to a customer. And consider using a non-nettable subinventory if you want to "hide" the defective quantity from planning until it is repaired. However, this technique does imply the completion of the product at its standard cost, so it is most appropriate for products that are fully or nearly complete before they are reworked.

Assembly Scrap

When all else fails, it might be necessary to scrap the product. You can scrap an assembly by moving it to the Scrap intra-operation step at any operation in the routing, or you can complete the quantity into inventory and use a miscellaneous issue transaction to scrap it at a later time.

Scrapping material at an intra-operation step enables you to enter a scrap account; entering a scrap account (or alias) credits the job for the accumulated cost to that point and charges the scrap account. If you do not enter a scrap account, the accumulated cost remains in the job or schedule and normally generates an unfavorable *efficiency variance* in a standard cost environment—if the quantity remains in the scrap step, you will complete less material than originally planned, and thus less than the value of the material and resources expended. In an average cost environment, such a procedure will typically increase the average cost.

Completing a job to inventory and scrapping it from there is basically an inventory transaction. You will complete the job or schedule to inventory (typically a non-nettable, non-reservable subinventory) at standard cost. A scrap transaction (in the form of a miscellaneous issue to a scrap account or alias) will credit inventory at the standard (or average) cost and debit the scrap account.

Manufacturing Scheduling

Oracle Manufacturing Scheduling provides constraint-based scheduling and a graphical, drag-and-drop interface for rescheduling existing discrete jobs. For enabled organizations, the scheduling engine is invoked when you create jobs and can be used to reschedule individual operations, individual jobs, unscheduled (pending) jobs, or all jobs on the shop floor.

Configuring Oracle Manufacturing Scheduling

Manufacturing Scheduling requires little additional setup besides the normal WIP, BOM, and Routing definition. There is one set of WIP parameters you must consider and one profile that deserves special attention. In addition, you should understand the implications of resource scheduling in your routings. When you create jobs, you have the opportunity to enter a numeric *scheduling priority* and a *requested due date* (which might be different from the due date calculated by the scheduling process).

Manufacturing Scheduling WIP Parameters

The Scheduling tab of the WIP Parameters form (Figure 16-13) contains four fields that control Manufacturing Scheduling:

■ **Use Constraint Based Scheduler**   This check box enables Oracle Manufacturing Scheduling for the organization.

■ **Constraints**   The Constraints field enables you to choose the constraints you will recognize; you can select Resource Only (the default) or Resource and Material.

■ **Horizon**   The Horizon field defines the number of shop days for which you will use the scheduler. If you are using Advanced Supply Chain Planning, you can perform detailed scheduling as part of the planning process, and you should select a short scheduling horizon to avoid overriding the schedule planned by ASCP. You might also consider using ASCP for daily scheduling and perform detailed scheduling exclusively with Manufacturing Scheduling. Without ASCP, however, you should set a horizon at least as long as your longest lead time and allow extra time to consider future material receipts.

■ **Simulation Set**   Entering a simulation set here enables you to adjust resource capacity in Manufacturing Scheduling. Simulation sets are defined in Oracle Bills of Material and are used to define capacity changes for resources within a department; simulation sets designated to Use in Scheduling will be used when scheduling jobs. (See Chapter 4 for more details.)

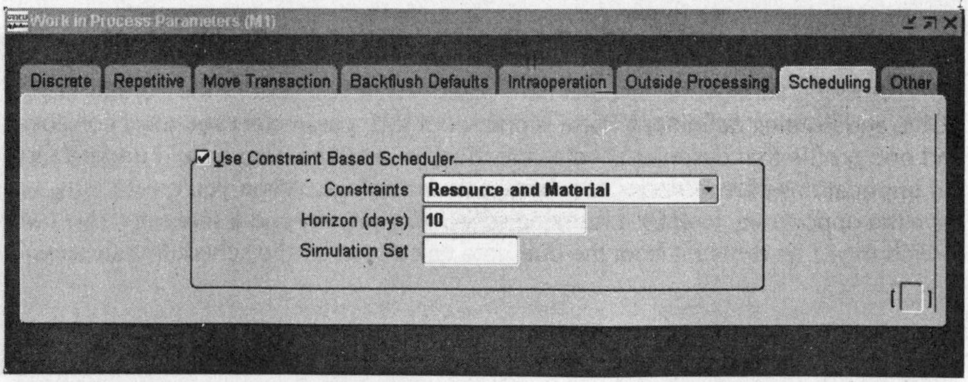

FIGURE 16-13.   *Enable Manufacturing Scheduling on the Scheduling tab of the WIP Parameters form*

Scheduling Profile Option

The WIP:Define Discrete Jobs Form profile option deserves special attention when using Manufacturing Scheduling. You can set this profile to *Interactive Definition* (the default) or *Concurrent Definition*.

Interactive Definition creates the material requirements and WIP operations interactively; your terminal is locked while these operations are proceeding. With manufacturing scheduling enabled, the status of the job is set to Pending Scheduling while waiting for the scheduling engine to run in the background. If scheduling is successful, the job is scheduled and the status is changed to Released. If scheduling is unable to schedule the job, you must determine the cause; see the "Scheduling Exceptions" section later in this chapter.

Concurrent Definition creates the requirements and WIP operations through a concurrent program, as well as running the scheduling engine. Control returns to you almost immediately, so this method is worth considering if you typically define multiple jobs at once.

NOTE

This profile can be set at all levels—Site, Application, Responsibility, or User—so you can tailor its setting to the type of activity an individual user or responsibility is likely to perform.

Resource Scheduling Options

Resources to be scheduled must be identified in the routing with a Schedule type of Yes, Next, or Prior, as described in Chapter 4. Resources with a schedule type of No are not scheduled.

Execution Options

Organizations that use constraint-based scheduling should consider two additional fields on a discrete job, as shown in Figure 16-14. These fields are found on the Scheduling tab of the Discrete Jobs form:

- **Requested Due Date**   The date you would like to complete the job. The requested due date will not be changed by the system.

- **Scheduling Priority**   The priority for scheduling the job. When scheduling multiple jobs, Manufacturing Scheduling schedules the highest priority jobs first to ensure that material and resources are allocated to the most important jobs. Within priority, jobs are then scheduled by the requested due date. The result is that the scheduled completion date might not match the requested date.

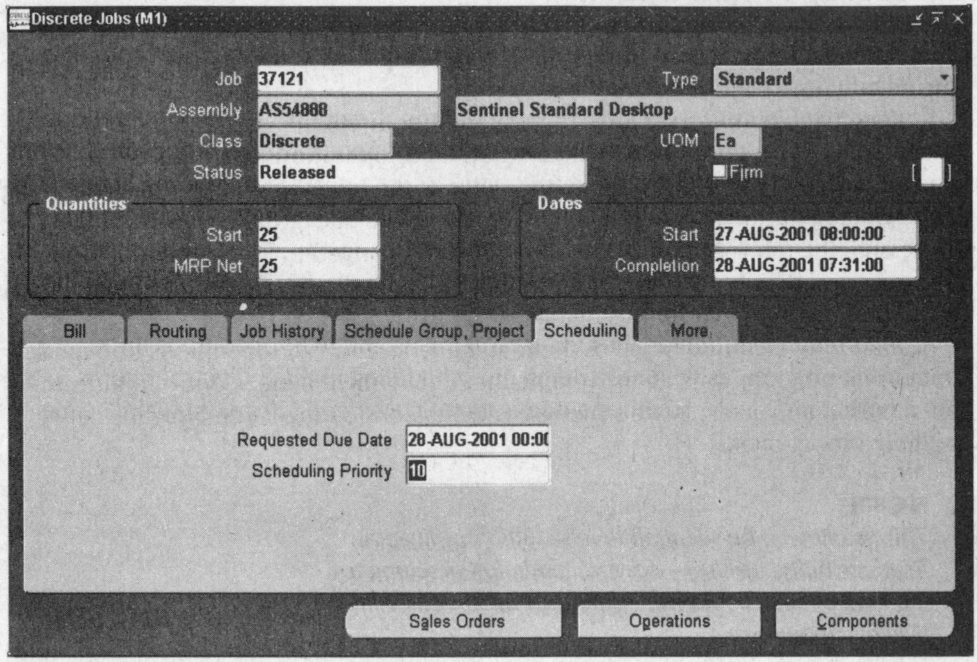

FIGURE 16-14. *Select Manufacturing Scheduling options for a job on the Scheduling Options tab*

Scheduler Workbench

The Scheduler Workbench, shown in Figure 16-15, provides a graphical view of all jobs on the shop floor. On the workbench, you can see a listing of all jobs, operations, and resources; a Gantt chart illustrating the schedule; and a graph of resource load versus capacity for selected resources. The workbench window consists of four panes—the Tree Hierarchy, the Gantt Chart, the Select Resources pane, and the Resource Load Versus Capacity pane. By default, only the Tree Hierarchy and Gantt Chart panes are displayed; you can show the additional panes by selecting Show/Hide Resource Load from the toolbar or by checking the Resource Load option on the View menu.

Using the Tree Hierarchy

By default, the Tree Hierarchy pane displays unreleased, released, and jobs on hold. You can expand each job to display its operations by clicking the plus sign (+) next to the job name; similarly, you can expand each operation to its resources.

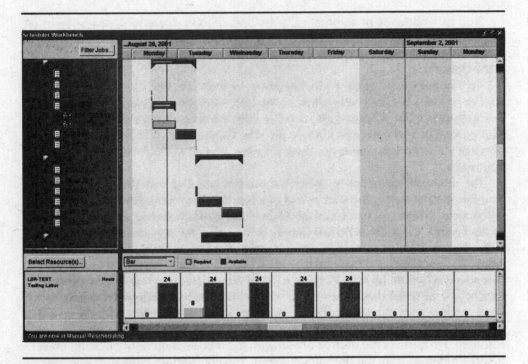

FIGURE 16-15. *The Scheduler Workbench provides a graphical view of your shop floor schedule*

The Filter Jobs button lets you limit the display by various criteria to help deal with different types of situations. For example, in cases of resource availability problems such as a breakdown or absenteeism, you might select jobs that use a specific department or resource. In cases of quality problems with a product or part, you could select jobs for a given assembly or component. And you can select jobs by status, including completed jobs if you want.

Using the Gantt Chart

The Gantt Chart pane shows the jobs, operations, and resources selected in the Tree Hierarchy, scheduled over time. You can change the scale of the timeline to view the appropriate level of detail—right-click the timeline, and select the appropriate increment from the drop-down menu (e.g. months, weeks, or days). You will typically want to adjust the timeline so that you can see at least one complete operation in the pane. The magenta vertical line on the Gantt Chart represents the current date and time.

You can manually or automatically reschedule jobs, operations, or resources on the Gantt Chart pane. Manual rescheduling does not respect constraints, whereas automatic scheduling will invoke the constraint-based scheduler. Manual scheduling is the default.

To manually reschedule a job, operation, or resource, you can grab and drag the start or end of a bar, or you can invoke the Edit Schedule window by right-clicking the appropriate bar. Choose Edit Schedule from the drop-down menu, enter the desired start or end date, and click Apply. The Gantt Chart will change to show the effect of your changes; however, these changes are just a simulation until you save your work.

For automatic rescheduling, select Automatic Scheduling from the menu or toolbar. You can grab and drag the start or end of a bar; the Automatic Reschedule window will appear, where you can verify the desired date and scheduling direction (forward or backward). Click the Schedule button; this invokes the scheduling engine, which will schedule the job, operation, or resource in the first available time slot where the necessary resources and material (based on your WIP Parameters) are available. You can also reschedule by right-clicking a job or operation and choosing Automatic Reschedule from the drop-down menu. With either method, choose Refresh Resource Load to view your changes and save your work if you are satisfied with the results.

From the Gantt Chart, you can view the details of a selected job, operation, or resource. First, select the desired object with the mouse; then right-click the object. Select Properties from the drop-down menu. The appropriate Properties window shows the details, including the scheduled start and end dates for each object and the progress (percentage of completion) for the total job and individual operations.

Scheduling Exceptions

Oracle Manufacturing Scheduling provides a range of messages to highlight conditions that need attention. Messages are categorized by severity—an *error* message indicates that a job was not scheduled; an *exception* message identifies a problem that should be corrected (e.g., a requested start date before the current date); a *warning* indicates an inconsistency, even though the job was scheduled (e.g., a job scheduled to complete before the requested date).

The Scheduling Exceptions form shows the messages generated by Manufacturing Scheduling. (See Figure 16-16 for an example.) The form is similar to the Scheduling workbench, in that it consists of two panes—a tree hierarchy on the left and the display window on the right, which shows the exception for the job selected from the tree. The display also includes the operation sequence where the exception occurred, and the severity of the message. Optionally, you can mark a message to indicate that you've read it (or might want to return for further review). Use the Properties tab to view details of the selected job.

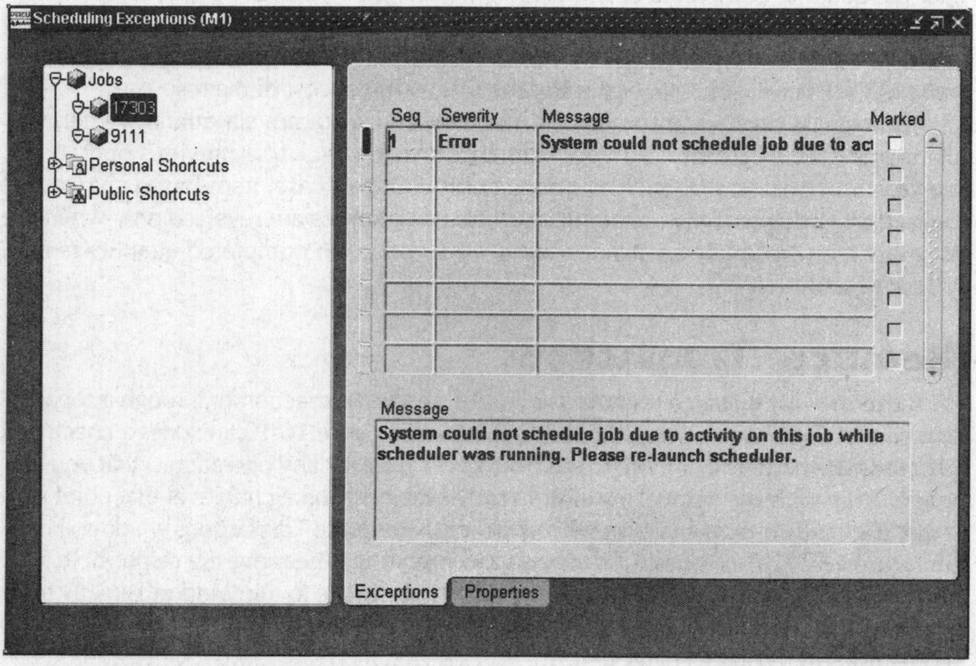

FIGURE 16-16. *The Scheduling Exceptions form lets you view scheduling messages*

You can view exceptions for a job from the Scheduler Workbench. Right-click any bar in the Gantt Chart, and select the View Exceptions option. Use the View All Exceptions form to see messages for all jobs and resources, in inquiry mode only.

Resource Management

Manufacturing involves the application of resources (usually labor) to materials to produce the finished product. Within Oracle Applications, resources can be charged automatically or manually. Resource charges might also generate overhead charges, based on your costing setup.

Auto-Charging Resources

Resources with a charge type of WIP Move are automatically charged, based on the completion of the operation where they are used. Lot-based resources are charged as soon as the first unit is completed at the operation; item-based resources are charged per the quantity completed at an operation. (See Figure 16-2 and the accompanying text for a discussion of operation completion.) Automatic item-based charges are calculated by taking the quantity completed, times the resource usage from the routing/WIP operations, times the standard (or average) cost of the resource.

Automatic charges are automatically reversed if you move a quantity when you "uncomplete" a quantity at an operation, by moving back to a previous operation or an intra-operation step such as queue or run. In this case, item-based charges are reversed per the quantity uncompleted; lot-based charges are reversed only when the last piece is uncompleted at an operation, i.e., when no completed quantity remains in the operation.

Resource Transactions

You can manually charge resources as part of a move transaction or through a separate transaction. The Move Transactions form, shown in Figure 16-10, includes a check box that indicates that one or more manual resources exist for any operation(s) that you are completing with your move. If you want to enter the resource charges at that point in time, click the Resources button, which opens the Resource Transactions window shown in Figure 16-17. This is helpful if the personnel reporting the move are responsible for entering their time as well. Alternatively, you can navigate to this window directly from the menu; this would be appropriate if time entry is a separate function or for subsequent corrections to resource charges.

On the Resources form, you can enter the following information:

- **Operation Seq**   The operation at which you utilized the resource.

- **Resource Seq**   The resource sequence that identifies the resource within the operation. If you are charging a resource that is not required on the job or schedule, you can enter a new, unique sequence to identify the resource within the operation.

- **Resource**   The resource you are charging. If you enter an existing Resource Sequence, the resource will be defaulted; if you are charging a new resource, specify it here.

NOTE
Resources charged must be assigned to the department for the designated operation.

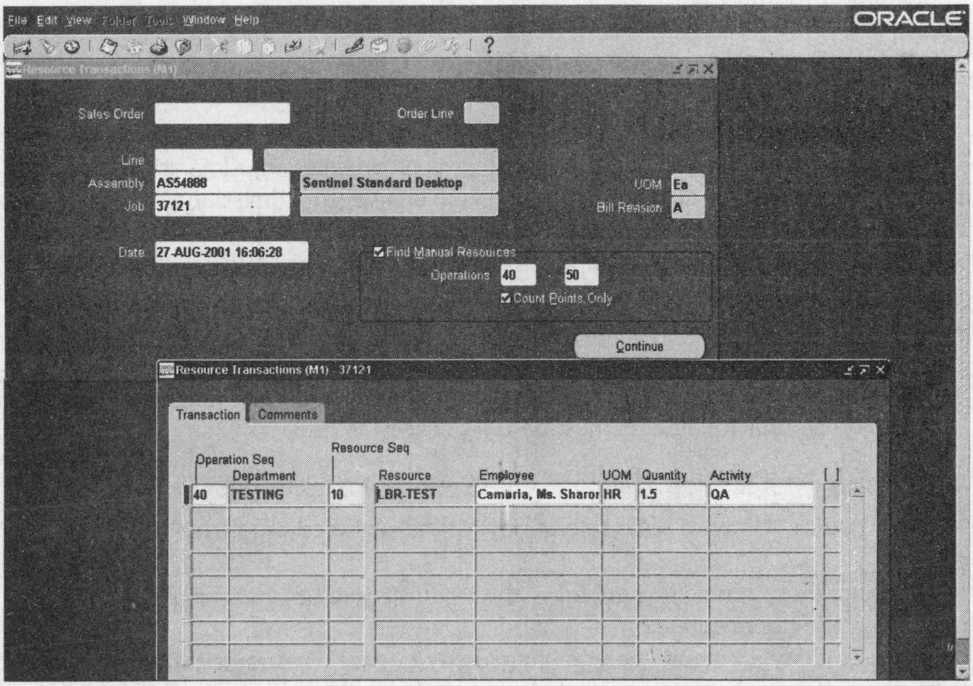

FIGURE 16-17.   *Use the Resource Transactions form to record manual resource charges and adjustments*

■ **Employee**   The name of the employee charging time. This field is optional and is accessible only if the resource being charged is identified as a Person. If an employee is entered, WIP will search for a pay rate associated with that employee. If no rate is found, you'll get a warning message, but if a rate is found, the actual rate will be used for valuing the transaction, as described later in this section.

■ **UOM**   The unit of measure of the resource quantity. This defaults from the resource definition, but you can enter any unit for which a conversion exists. For example, the default UOM of a resource is typically Hours, but you can enter Minutes if you have defined the conversion factor in Oracle Inventory.

■ **Quantity**   The quantity (e.g., the number of hours or minutes) of the resource charge.

■ **Activity, Reason Code, and Reference**   These codes can document the transaction.

Besides entering time for manual resources you can enter adjustments for resources that were automatically charged; for example, to charge extra time due to rework. You can reduce time charged by entering a negative quantity.

Manual resource charges can be charged at the standard rate or at the actual employee rate based on your resource definition. In order to charge at an actual rate, all of the following conditions must be true:

■ The resource must designate charging at the actual rate; i.e., the Standard Rate box must be *unchecked*.

■ You must enter an employee on the resource transaction.

■ You must have a valid rate of pay for the specified employee.

If any of these conditions are false, the resource will be charged at the standard rate, times the hours entered.

If you specify an employee with a valid pay rate for a resource that is designated to be charged at its standard rate, the job or schedule will be charged with the standard rate times the hours entered; the difference between the actual amount (actual rate times hours) and the standard amount charged will be written to the *rate variance account* defined for the resource. (See Chapter 4 for a discussion of resource definition.)

Open Resource Transaction Interface

The Resource Transaction Interface imports resource transactions from an external source. To use the interface, you must insert the appropriate data into the WIP COST_TXN_INTERFACE table. The Cost Manager concurrent program, submitted from the Inventory Interface Managers form, processes data in the interface table. This is the same program that costs your inventory and WIP transactions. Within a day, this program resubmits itself (with the same concurrent request ID) at the interval you specify on the Interface Managers form in Inventory; you will want to schedule this program to run on a daily interval so that it will restart each day with a new request ID.

Like the Resource Transactions form, you can charge person-type resources at either their standard or actual rates; you can also override the actual rate by specifying the desired rate in the USAGE_RATE_OR_AMOUNT column. You can also use the interface to charge non-person resources at a specific rate, using the same USAGE_ RATE_OR_AMOUNT column; this differs from the capabilities of the Resource Transactions form.

You can review pending and failed transactions using the Pending Resource Transactions form. You can correct failed transactions on this form and mark them for resubmission.

Outside Processing Charges

Outside processing resources are charged similarly to internal resources, but there are a few key differences:

- Outside processing charges are incurred when the purchase order for the OSP services is received and delivered to WIP.

- The actual rate for an OSP resource is the unit price on the purchase order. (The standard rate is defined for the resource itself, just like an internal resource.)

- The rate variance account for an OSP resource defaults to the organization's Purchase Price Variance (PPV) account, although you can change this if you want to segregate PPV for outside processing from PPV for material.

Oracle Shop Floor Management System

Oracle Shop Floor Management (OSFM) provides enhanced, lot-based production capabilities, compared to the standard capabilities of Oracle Work in Process. Specifically, it furnishes support for network routings (described in Chapter 4), complex lot transactions (including lot splits, merges, translation, and bonus lots), lot genealogy, yield-based operational costing, and enhanced co-product definition. These capabilities are typically required in semiconductor fabrication, but are applicable to other business processes as well.

While WIP tracks production by job or repetitive assembly, OSFM tracks production by lots. The process is illustrated in Figure 16-18. Raw materials are issued to WIP Lot; the lot moves through a series of operations and into inventory, where it is referred to as an inventory lot. At the next level of the bill of material, the inventory lot is issued to a new WIP lot, which again undergoes a series of operations and is received into Inventory, creating a new inventory lot. This process is repeated through all the levels of the bill of material. A *sector* consists of a level of the bill, the primary component at that level, and the routing of that component; it is identified by a unique extension to the original lot number.

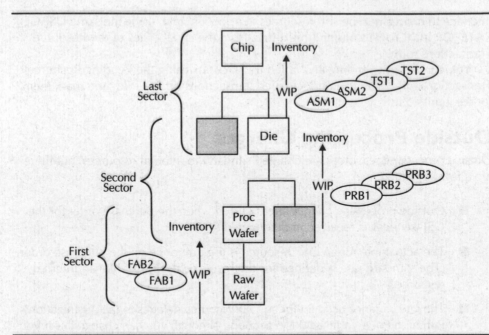

FIGURE 16-18. *Lot-based production flow*

Configuring OSFM

OSFM builds upon the basic functions of Oracle Inventory, Bills of Material, Cost Management, and Work in Process; you must first complete the appropriate setup steps for those modules. Then, you can complete the additional setup required for OSFM—parameters, standard operation details, lot sector extensions, and related profile options. These steps are described in the following sections.

OSFM uses network routings, built from standard operations. See Chapter 4 for a description of standard operation and network routings.

Parameters

The Shop Floor Management Parameters form provides additional parameters used by OSFM:

- **New Lot Separator**   When lots are created, split, or renamed, the resulting lot consists of the original lot number, concatenated with a sequential number. The character defined as the New Lot Separator separates the segments.

■ **Job Completion Separator** When a lot is completed, the resulting lot number consists of the original lot number, concatenated with this character and the appropriate Lot Sector Extension (described later).

■ **Undo Last Move** This check box lets you undo the last transaction in the Move Transactions form.

■ **Co-Products Supply Default** This check box enables planning to consider supply for co-products.

■ **Default Accounting Class** Similar to the default WIP accounting class, this is the default used for lot-based production.

■ **Miscellaneous Transaction Account** This is the account you will use for miscellaneous transactions when issuing or receiving material to locations other than Inventory, Receiving, or Work in Process.

Standard Operation Details

The Standard Operation Details form defines additional OSFM-related details for standard operations. Navigate to this window, select a standard operation, and enter the following details:

■ **Mandatory Intraoperation Steps** Check the intra-operation steps you require for this operation—Queue, Run, or To Move.

■ **Stocking Point** The Subinventory (and optionally, Locator) where material from this operation is stored.

Lot Sector Extensions

Define Lot Sector Extensions on the Sector Extensions and Item/Subinventory Associations form. These sector extensions will be used to identify the new lots resulting from a job completion.

Enter the Sector Extension Code and optional description and the Accounting Class. On the Item tab, select the items you want to assign to this lot sector; on the Subinventory tab, choose the subinventory for the items listed.

Profile Options

Two profile options are important to OSFM. The profile WSM:Allow Operation Jumps controls whether jumps (skipping of operations) can be performed in the Move Transactions form. The profile WSM:Complete Job Sector Lot Extension Level determines whether the item or subinventory lot extension is used to identify the new lot resulting from a job completion.

Lot Transactions

OSFM supports various lot transactions, including lot moves, splits and merges, update, and the creation of bonus lots (a lot that is entirely new or created from scrap).

The process typically begins with the use of the Lot Based Job form, shown in Figure 16-19, to define a job for the first sector. This form is used only if inventory lots for the raw components do not yet exist. For subsequent sectors, or if inventory lots exist for the components at the first sector, use the Lot Creation form shown in Figure 16-20.

The Lot Based Jobs form is very similar to the Discrete Job form, shown earlier in Figure 16-4. It uses the same table (WIP_DISCRETE_JOBS), offers most of the same options, and uses the same database sequence for generating job names—if you enter a job name manually, it must not conflict with existing jobs. However, for lot-based jobs, the job type will always be Standard.

To create lots for subsequent sectors in the production process, use the Lot Creation form (Figure 16-20). Select an existing lot number and subinventory; the system displays the available quantity for that lot. If you will create multiple lots from the starting lot, check the Multiple Resulting Lots box.

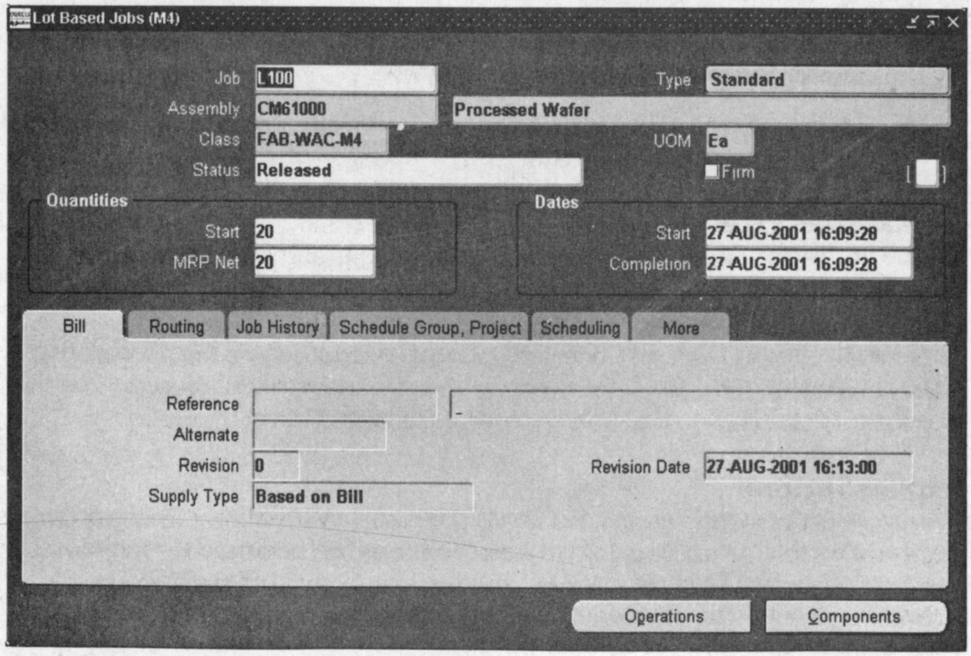

FIGURE 16-19. *The Lot Based Jobs form creates a job for the first sector of production*

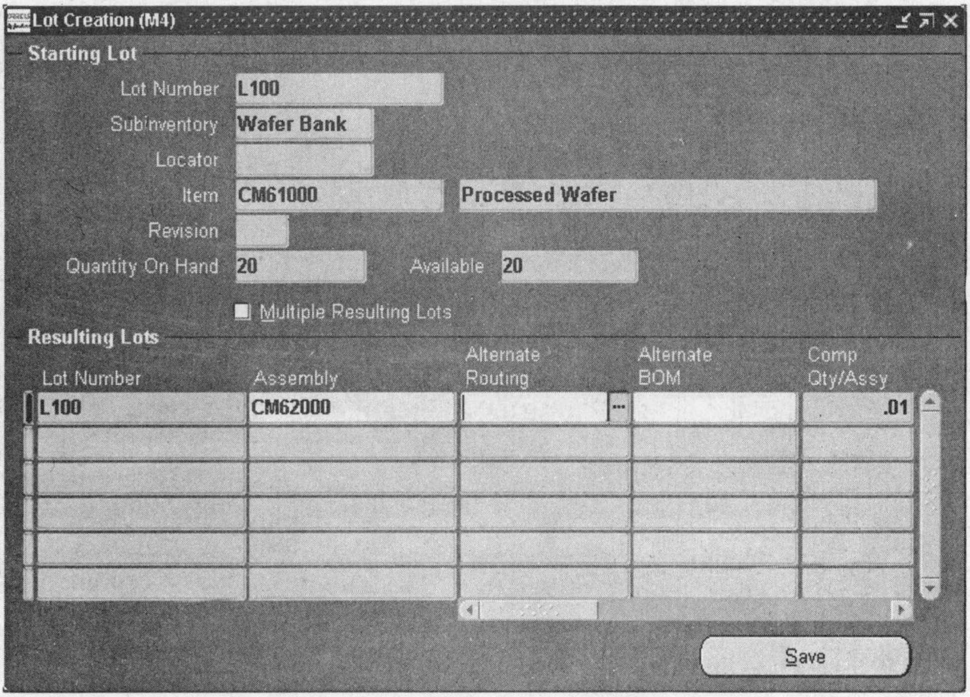

FIGURE 16-20. *The Lot Creation form creates subsequent sectors*

The Resulting Lots region will generate lot numbers for the resulting lot(s), identified by the original lot number, the New Lot Separator character (from the OSFM parameters), and a sequential number. In this region, you can assign an Alternate Routing, Alternate Assembly, Completion Subinventory, Accounting Class, Start Date, and Completion Date.

Lot Moves

The Move Lot Based Jobs form is used to record the progress of a lot-based job or subsequent sector through its operations. It is similar to the Move Transactions form, shown in Figure 16-10, but is more restrictive. Except for scrap transactions, Move Lot Based Jobs transactions are for the entire lot quantity, and the lot-based job is automatically completed when you move to the To Move step of the last operation. When a lot-based job is completed, the lot is automatically named using the appropriate lot sector extension, as described earlier. See Figure 16-21 for an example of the Move Lot Based Jobs form.

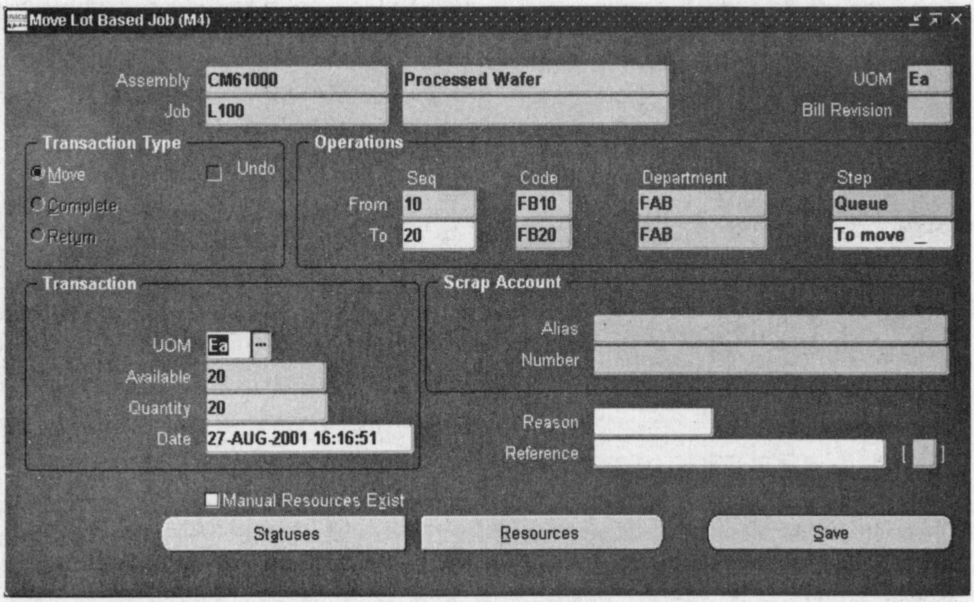

FIGURE 16-21. *The Move Lot Based Jobs form records lot activities*

NOTE
To open the Move Lot Based Jobs form, you must set the profile TP:Wip Move Transaction Quantity Default to "Available Quantity."

This transaction also enables you to "jump" operations, i.e., skip operations in the routing, or jump to any standard operation that is not included in the network routing. To perform a jump, select Tools | Toggle Jumping from the menu bar. Enter any operation sequence greater than the current operation, and select the operation code of the operation to which you want to jump. The word "Jump" appears to the left of the To operation, indicating that you are performing a jump.

Lot Splits and Merges
Throughout the production process, lots exist as either WIP lots (in process) or Inventory lots (in stock). For either type of lot, you can perform various actions.

WIP Lot Transactions

The WIP Lot Transactions form lets you perform the following tasks on WIP lots:

- **Lot Split**   Divides a WIP lot into two or more lots; each lot can have different operations, resources, and material requirements. This process can potentially create other assemblies from the original lot.

- **Lot Merge**   Combines multiple WIP lots into one lot. You can merge lots only for the same item and revision; with identical quality attributes; and at the equivalent intra-operation step at the same department, using the same resources.

- **Bonus**   Merges scrap quantities to create a new WIP lot or creates an entirely new WIP lot.

- **Update**   Updates the Assembly, Lot Name, Quantity, or Routing.

WIP Lot Transactions can be performed only for jobs at the intra-operation steps of Queue or To Move. The actual lot transactions are created by the WIP Lot Transaction Processor; make sure this is scheduled to run on a regular interval.

Inventory Lot Transactions

The Inventory Lot Transactions form lets you perform the following actions on lots in Inventory:

- **Lot Split and Lot Merge**   Splits or merges lots, similar to the WIP Lot Transactions.

- **Translate**   Changes the item, revision, or subinventory of an existing lot; this effectively translates one product to another.

- **Subinventory Transfer**   Moves a lot from one subinventory location to another.

Completions

Completion transactions increment inventory of the product and signal the end of production. You can complete discrete jobs or repetitive schedules with a completion or move transaction. You complete flow schedules or unscheduled production with the Work Order-less Completion form, shown in Figure 16-23.

Completing Discrete Jobs

You can complete discrete jobs or repetitive schedules with the WIP Completion Transactions shown in Figure 16-22. Alternatively, you can use the Complete option on the Move transaction to complete jobs or schedules.

Completing a Job or Schedule with a Completion Transaction

For jobs with a routing, only the quantity at the To Move step of the last operation is available for completion. (Overcompletions are allowed based on the Overcompletion item attributes or WIP parameter, as discussed earlier in the "Move Transactions" section.)

Identify your job on the WIP completion transaction; the first window will display the quantity eligible for completion. Click the Continue button, and enter the transaction details. The completion subinventory and locator defaults from the job (which defaulted from the routing), but they can be overridden if necessary. If you are completing an ATO or CTO item, and you have multiple Sales Order shipments linked to the job, the receipt will be allocated to the shipments in order of earliest schedule date; you can override this default by specifying the sales order, line, and shipment if desired.

To overcomplete a job, check the Overcomplete box on the WIP completion transaction, press Continue, and enter your quantity.

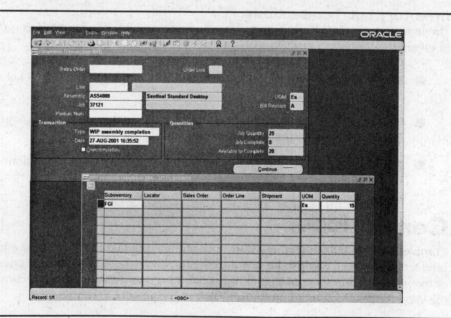

FIGURE 16-22. *Record completions of jobs or repetitive schedules with the WIP Completion Transaction*

When the total of the scrapped and completed quantity on a job equals (or exceeds) the quantity of the job, the status of the job is changed to Completed. This implies that no further production is expected from the job, but you can still charge material or resources to the job. When you are satisfied that there is no further activity to report for the job, you might want to change the status to Complete – No Charges. This status prohibits further charges and can be useful as a criterion for closing the jobs, as described in the section "Closing and Purging Jobs and Schedules."

To reverse a completion transaction, change the transaction type on the Completions Transaction window to Return Assembly to WIP; click Continue, and enter the location from which you are returning the material. The quantity will be returned to the To Move step of the last operation on the job's routing.

Completing a Job or Schedule with a Move Transaction

You can complete a job or repetitive schedule from a Move transaction, provided the following conditions are met:

- The job or schedule must have a default completion subinventory/locator; this normally defaults from the assembly's routing.

- If the assembly is lot controlled, the job or schedule must have a default lot number.

NOTE
*Serial controlled items cannot be completed
to inventory with a Move transaction.*

To complete an assembly into inventory with a Move transaction, identify the job or schedule on the Move Transactions form (refer to Figure 16-10). Check the Complete radio button; the "To" operation and step will default to the To Move step of the last operation of the job's routing. Enter the operation sequence and step from which you are moving the material, and enter the quantity you are completing. The quantity will be completed into the default subinventory and locator from the job or schedule.

To reverse such a transaction, check the Return radio button on the Move Transactions form and specify the operation sequence and step to which you are returning the entered quantity.

Completing Repetitive Schedules

You complete a repetitive schedule in the same way you complete a discrete job. There are two significant differences: If you complete the entire quantity on a schedule, the system might automatically release a future schedule; and the resulting status of the completed schedule might be set to Complete – No Charges.

The WIP parameter Autorelease Days controls the automatic release of future repetitive schedules. If you complete a schedule, and there is an unreleased schedule with a first unit start date within the number of days specified in the parameter, that schedule will be automatically released. (Overcompletions will be applied against that future schedule.)

Because repetitive schedules are charged by assembly and line, if there is another released schedule for the same assembly and line (or another schedule is automatically released by the completion of a schedule), the completion of the earlier schedule will change its status to Complete – No Charges. If there is no released schedule, the status will be changed to Complete, just like a discrete job. You must change the status to Complete – No Charges if you want to prohibit additional charges to a specific schedule.

Work Order-less Completions

The Work Order-less Completion transaction, shown in Figure 16-23, enables you to perform assembly completions without first creating a discrete job or schedule. It was initially introduced by Oracle as part of its Flow Manufacturing strategy, but is included with the Discrete Manufacturing package as well, so it can be used for light assembly (or disassembly) tasks, as well as reporting flow production.

In keeping with the flow philosophy of simplicity, the Work Order-less Completion transaction was designed to be as simple as possible. To record a basic completion,

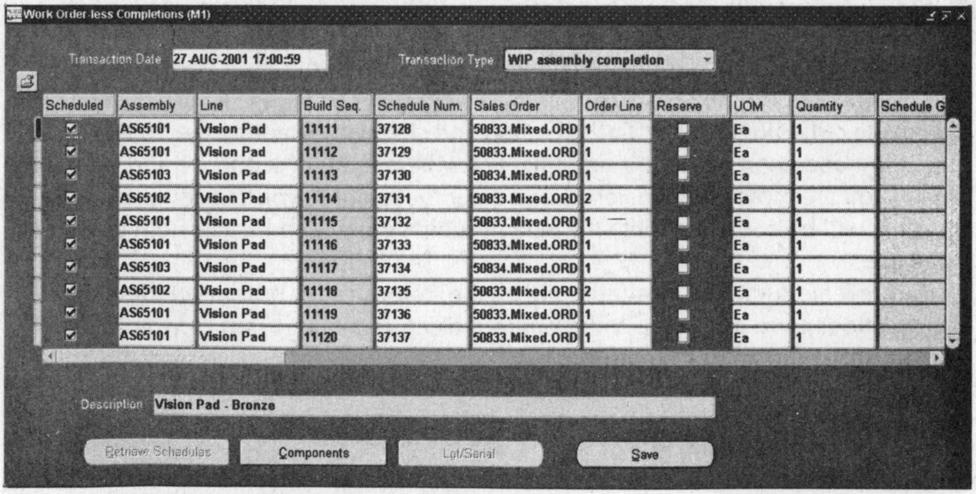

FIGURE 16-23. *Complete flow schedules or unscheduled production with the Work Order-less Completions form*

you must enter only a few fields: Assembly, Quantity, and Completion Subinventory/ Locator. The transaction backflushes all component material (except Bulk and Supplier material), based on the current primary bill, and autocharges all resources based on current primary routing. It will use the default accounting class from the WIP parameters.

NOTE
the Work Order-less Completion transaction is always processed in the background; make sure that the Material Transaction manager is scheduled to run on a regular interval.

To complete previously scheduled flow production, open the Work Order-less Completions form and click the Retrieve Schedules button. Enter the production line and any other selection criteria, as shown in Figure 16-24. The transaction

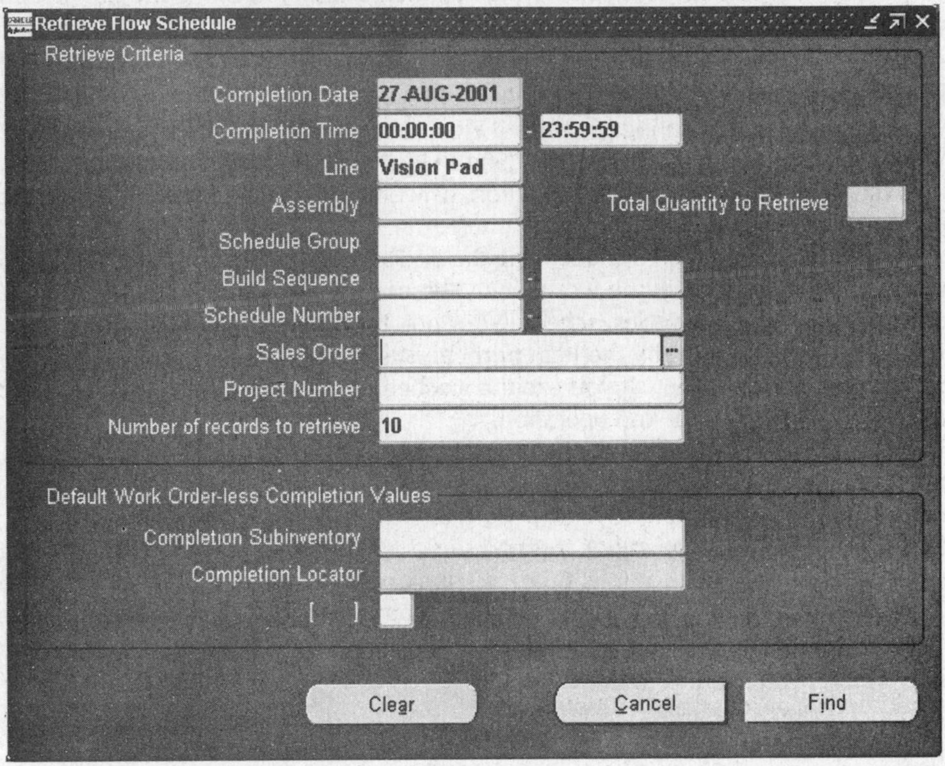

Retrieve Flow Schedule

Retrieve Criteria

Completion Date	27-AUG-2001
Completion Time	00:00:00 - 23:59:59
Line	Vision Pad
Assembly	
Schedule Group	
Build Sequence	-
Schedule Number	-
Sales Order	
Project Number	
Number of records to retrieve	10

Total Quantity to Retrieve

Default Work Order-less Completion Values

Completion Subinventory	
Completion Locator	
[ ]	

Clear   Cancel   Find

FIGURE 16-24. *Enter selection criteria on the Work Order-less Completion form*

defaults to the current day; you might want to limit the number of schedules you retrieve to represent the number of assemblies you normally complete at one time. For example, if you request only one record, it will show you just the first scheduled item for the line.

NOTE
The version of the Work Order-less Completion transaction accessible from the Work in Process menu does not activate the Retrieve Schedules button and does not show the Scheduled check box.

Although the transaction is simple, it offers a number of options to record exceptions to ordinary activity. You can choose an alternate bill or routing or specify a different revision or date for the bill or routing. You can choose a different accounting class, identify the kanban you are replenishing, and enter reason and reference information, like all material transactions. To record component substitutions, use the Components button and enter your substitute information.

Flow Workstation

Oracle Flow Manufacturing provides a Flow Workstation, similar to the Discrete Workstation described earlier, in the "Shop Floor Control" section. It displays the open schedules for a given line operation, as well as all the assemblies that use that operation. See Figure 16-25 for an example.

Open the workstation by specifying the line and line operation at which you are working. The left pane of the workbench shows open flow schedules for that line operation and the assemblies, scheduled or not, that use that line operation. Flow schedules are identified by the item number, schedule date, and build sequence created in line scheduling. If you expand a schedule or an assembly, you'll see the events that make up that line operation.

The right pane of the workbench shows various details—component requirements, resource requirements, or detailed properties—of the object you select in the left pane. For an event, you can view any instructions (attachments) associated with that event; these are typically the *operation method sheets* (OMS) for the event. If you select a schedule, you can note completion of the line operation to which you have signed on; this removes the line operation from the current operation's list of open schedules but does not generate any cost or material transactions. For either a schedule or an assembly, you can link to the Work Order-less Completion form to report scheduled or unscheduled completions.

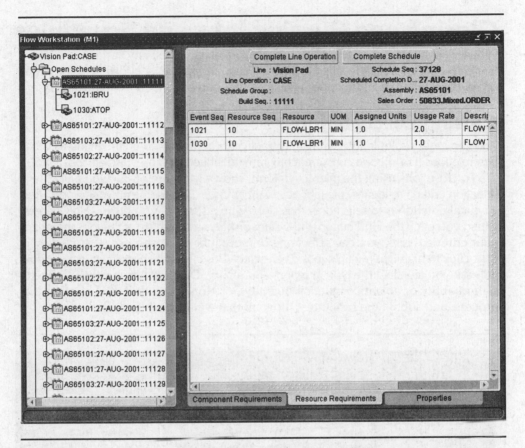

FIGURE 16-25. *The Flow Workstation shows flow schedules by line operation*

The toolbar of the Flow Workstation includes icons to change the view from the Vertical, Interleaved, or Org-chart display format, just like the Discrete Workstation. You can also use the appropriate icon to refresh the data and use the pin tab to display multiple windows of information from the right pane. In addition, you can signal a kanban for replenishment using the Replenish Kanban icon; this links you to the Kanban Card Summary form, where you can enter selection criteria, view activity, print new cards, as well as signal the kanban for replenishment.

Closing and Purging Jobs and Schedules

When discrete jobs are finished, they must be closed to post any variances to the General Ledger. As noted earlier, Repetitive Schedules are never closed; they are simply completed. Ultimately, both jobs and schedules can be purged from the database.

Closing Discrete Jobs

You can close multiple jobs with an interactive form (identified on the menu as Close Discrete Jobs [Form]) or a concurrent program (identified as Close Discrete Jobs [SRS]).

To close jobs using the interactive form, shown in Figure 16-26, you first enter selection criteria to identify the jobs you want to close. Depending on your procedures, a typical criterion is to select only those jobs with a status of Complete – No Charges. When you click the Find button, the system displays a summary of the jobs that meet your criteria. Here, you can select one or more jobs to close—use SHIFT-click or CTRL-click to highlight multiple jobs. Then select Close from the Tools menu; a window will ask you to select the type of report—Summary, Detailed (using either planned start quantity or actual completion quantity), or None. Choose OK to confirm the process, and submit the concurrent program that will close the selected jobs.

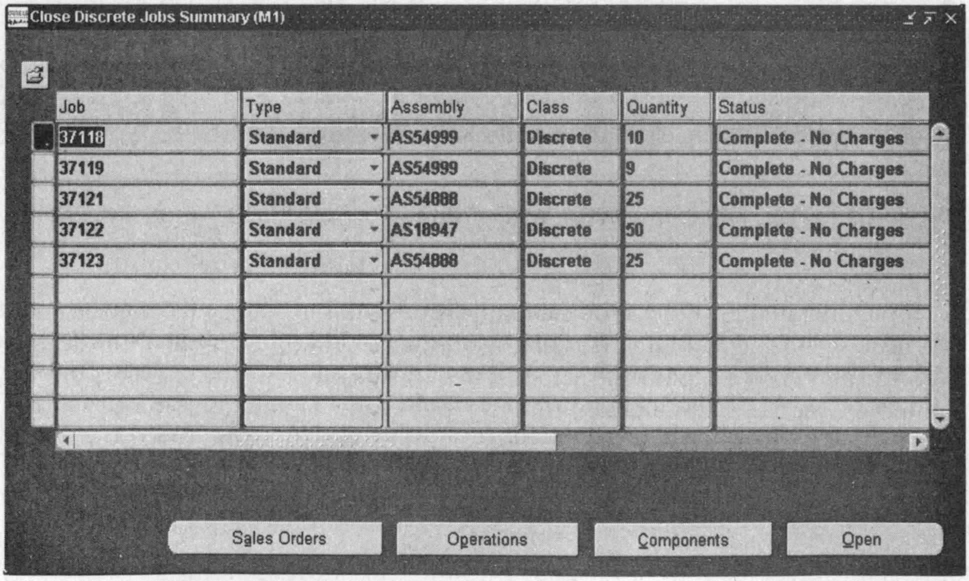

Job	Type	Assembly	Class	Quantity	Status
37118	Standard	AS54999	Discrete	10	Complete - No Charges
37119	Standard	AS54999	Discrete	9	Complete - No Charges
37121	Standard	AS54888	Discrete	25	Complete - No Charges
37122	Standard	AS18947	Discrete	50	Complete - No Charges
37123	Standard	AS54888	Discrete	25	Complete - No Charges

Sales Orders   Operations   Components   Open

FIGURE 16-26.   *The Close Discrete Jobs form initiates the close process*

CAUTION
The close process will close all selected jobs regardless of status; you can even close released jobs if you select them. Although the process will fail if there are unprocessed transactions in the Move or Material interface tables, it will not attempt to determine if you have entered all necessary transactions (e.g., material issues or resource charges).

Alternatively, from the Close Discrete Jobs Summary window, you can open an individual job to view its details. You can access the Close function from the Tools menu from the detailed view as well.

To close jobs using the concurrent program, enter the parameters to select the jobs you want to close. You can identify jobs by Class Type (Standard discrete, Asset non-standard, or Expense non-standard), a range of accounting classes, a range of jobs numbers, a range of job numbers, and a specific status. You also select the type of report to generate as part of the close process.

Purging Jobs and Schedules

When jobs or schedules are no longer needed for history, they can be permanently removed from the database with a purge program. The process is similar to the close process but is irreversible. As a safeguard, jobs or schedules can only be purged if they have been closed and the inventory accounting period is closed.

You can purge jobs using an interactive form or using a concurrent program (SRS). A separate online form is provided to purge repetitive schedules, but the same concurrent program purges both jobs and schedules. The interactive forms operate like the close form; you enter selection criteria and then select the jobs or scheduled you want to purge. Selection criteria include Assembly, start or completion dates, and accounting period. A selection criterion unique to the Purge Discrete Jobs form is the Include Configurations check box. This check box determines whether you purge jobs for configured items as well as jobs for standard items; it is checked by default, but you can uncheck it if you want to retain configured jobs for a longer period of time than jobs for standard products.

The WIP Purge concurrent program operates like the close program; you enter selection parameters, specify the report type, and submit the job to close all selected jobs and schedules.

WIP Costing

This section describes the primary costing methods for production: Standard Costing and Average Costing. It also discusses the unique characteristics of Flow and OSFM Costing and summarizes the process of transferring costs to the General Ledger. Additional details are contained in Chapter 18.

Standard Costing in WIP

For a standard cost organization, material costs are charged to WIP at their standard (Frozen) cost; resource costs can be charged at standard or actual (using either the standard rate of the resource or an actual employee rate); overhead is charged based on its definition. Material overhead in WIP is always the result of material overhead associated with components of a job or schedule; additional material overhead is earned only on the completion of a WIP job or schedule into Inventory.

Costs are relieved from WIP either by completions or scrap transactions. For a completion, the transaction relieves the standard cost for the number of assemblies completed; for scrap, the transaction (movement to the Scrap intra-operation step) relieves the standard cost that *should have been incurred* up to that point in the routing. (Costs are relieved by a scrap transaction only if you enter a scrap account or alias.)

NOTE
The scrap transaction will calculate the value of material and resources as defined by the requirements and WIP operations; if you have not issued the material or charged manual resources, that will not affect the value of the scrap.

WIP Transactions, like Inventory Transactions, are valued by the Cost Processor; this concurrent program should be running on a regular interval, and you must keep in mind that cost information will only be current as of the last run of the program.

The WIP Value Summary window, shown in Figure 16-27, displays a running total of the costs incurred and costs relieved from WIP.

When discrete jobs are closed, any residual value in the job is written off to the variance accounts designated in the WIP Accounting Class for the job. Variances for repetitive schedules are posted only when you close the Inventory Accounting period; based on your WIP Parameters, variances might be calculated only for schedules with statuses of Complete – No Charges or Cancelled or for *all* repetitive schedules (even those still active on the shop floor).

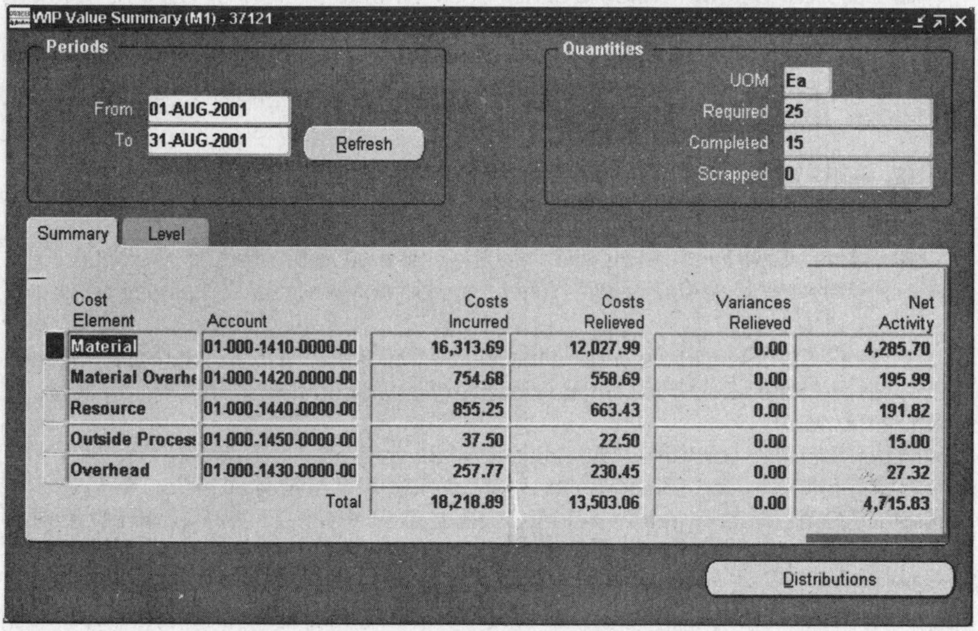

FIGURE 16-27. *The WIP Value Summary shows current job valuation*

Average Costing in WIP

Oracle supports Average Costing for Discrete Jobs and Flow schedules only; you cannot use Average Costing for Repetitive or lot-based (OSFM) production.

In an organization that uses Average Costing, material is charged to the job at its current average cost; resources are charged at a predefined rate, or at the actual rate, similar to the options with standard costing. When finished assemblies are completed, they are costed based on the setting of four parameters:

■ **Default Completion Cost Source**   Choose either User Defined or System Calculated. If you select User Defined, you must designate a cost type to be used and populate that cost type. If you select System Calculated, you must select a system option.

- **System Option**   Choose either Use Actual Resources or Use Pre-defined Resources. The option Use Actual Resources relieves actual cost from the job based on actual job charges, as each unit is completed. The option Use Pre-defined Resources relieves cost based on resource usage as specified by the job routing.

- **Cost Type**   This identifies the cost type used with the User Defined completion cost source described earlier.

- **Rates Cost Type**   This identifies the cost type to be used for overhead rates and for resource rates where you do not use actual employee rates.

Set the first three parameters on the Costing tab of the Work in Process Parameters form; set the Rates Cost Type on the Costing Information tab of the Organization Parameters form.

When units are completed, the unit cost of the assembly in inventory is recalculated if it is different from the unit cost of the completion. For Average Costing, the WIP Assembly Completion window includes a Final Completion check box that controls costing of the completed assemblies. If you check this box, WIP costs the completed assemblies by spreading the current job balances evenly over the units being completed or taking them to variance; if the box is unchecked, WIP costs the assemblies according to the Completion Cost Source method. The WIP parameter Auto Compute Final Completion determines the default value of the Final Completion check box.

NOTE
Under Average Costing, you may complete assemblies only to a single subinventory with the completion transaction; i.e., you may not enter multiple transaction lines on the WIP Assembly Completion window.

Flow Manufacturing Costing

Oracle supports both standard and average costing for flow manufacturing. The process is very similar to that described earlier, but it all happens when the Work Order-less Completion is reported. This means that the costs incurred, and the costs and variances relieved, are associated with each individual transaction. The net balance for flow schedules is always zero.

OSFM Costing

Oracle Shop Floor Management uses only standard costing, but it adds operation yield costing. This enables you to use operation yields in an assembly's cost rollup. Whereas a regular cost rollup (for a non-OSFM organization) uses the item shrinkage rate (from the item cost type), a cost rollup for an OSFM product utilizes the operation yield at each operation. Regular standard costing will simply inflate the total cost of the assembly based on the shrinkage rate; OSFM costing will inflate the cost of *each operation* by that operations yield factor.

OSFM costing also accounts for the lot-based transactions supported by OSFM— moves, scrap, split, merge, bonus, and update quantity. When you split a lot, the cost of the parent is reallocated to the resulting child lots in proportion to the split quantities. Merged lots inherit the cost of the component lots. The cost of a bonus lot is the standard cost of the assembly at the operation where you create the bonus lot.

You must run the Lot Based Transaction Cost manager to calculate costs in OSFM. This process also runs the Material Cost Transaction Worker, the Resource Cost Transaction Worker, the Overhead Cost Transaction Worker, and the Operation Yield Processor. In an OSFM environment, make sure this process is scheduled to run on a regular interval.

Cost Transfers

Like Inventory costs, costs from WIP transactions are transferred to the General Ledger when you perform an interim cost transfer (i.e., when you run the concurrent program Transfer Transactions to GL) or when you close the Inventory Accounting period. After you have transferred the costs from Inventory, you must run Journal Import in General Ledger. The journals will have a source of "Inventory." Then you can review and post the transactions as normal.

Summary

This chapter described the day-to-day processes to record manufacturing activity. It discussed the overall process, the key concepts of material requirements and operation scheduling, and the various production strategies—discrete, repetitive, flow, assemble-to-order, and configure-to-order.

WIP setup requirements were described in detail—parameters, accounting classes, shop floor statuses, employee labor rates, and profiles.

This chapter detailed the basic steps in all production—the creation of jobs or schedules, material issues, shop floor control, scheduling, resource transactions, and completions—and summarized the differences for each step because of differences in production strategy. It described the treatment of outside processing, scrap, and rework. The unique characteristics of Oracle Shop Floor Management for lot-based production were also discussed.

Closing and purging of discrete jobs and repetitive schedules were discussed in this chapter. Finally, it provided a brief overview of WIP costing and the "handoff" of cost information to the financial side of the Oracle E-Business Suite.

CHAPTER
17

Outbound Logistics

he Shipping Execution component of Oracle Order Management provides the basic transactions that deal with outbound logistics. These transactions include allocating material to sales orders; creating move orders to transfer the material from storage to one or more staging lanes; planning trips, stops, and deliveries; packing material; and confirming picking and shipping. These activities are the subject of this chapter.

Oracle Warehouse Management (OWM), described in Chapter 15, provides enhanced capabilities, including more flexible allocation rules, packing rules, task dispatching, compliance labeling, and a mobile interface.

Oracle Shipping Overview

The following section provides a brief overview of the terminology (Trips, Stops, Deliveries, Delivery Legs, and Delivery Lines) used in shipping execution. The next section summarizes the activities that the shipping process comprises: the major processes of Releasing Sales Orders for picking, Packing, and Confirming Shipments, and the discrete activities within each process.

Terminology

To understand Oracle's view of the shipping process, it's important to understand the following terms:

- **Trip**   The route traversed by a carrier to pick up and deliver items.

- **Stop**   A point along the route where material is either picked up or dropped off. A trip must consist of at least two stops (one pickup and one dropoff), but may include any number of stops.

- **Delivery**   A consolidation of sales order lines going from one location to the same customer location.

- **Delivery Line**   A shippable and booked sales order shipment line (order line detail).

- **Delivery Leg**   A Delivery Leg consists of two stops in which material is picked up and dropped off. Each delivery leg will typically correspond to a Bill of Lading.

The relationship between these entities is illustrated in Figure 17-1.

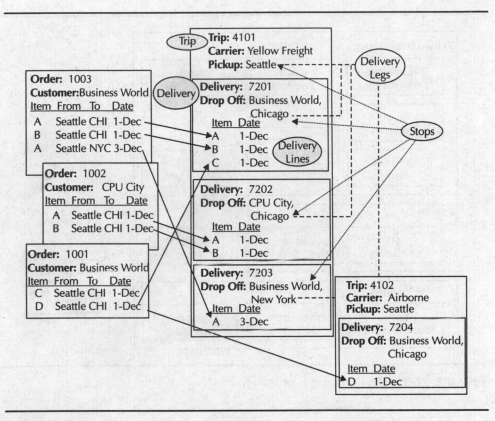

FIGURE 17-1. *Shipping-entity relationships*

Shipping Activities

In the Oracle E-Business Suite, the shipping process consists of a number of discrete activities, illustrated in Figure 17-2. Although most of these activities are required, if your process is simple, many of them can be automated in a single transaction. In the simplest case, all that is needed are two transactions: Pick Release and Ship Confirm. The pick release process can release orders for picking, create the staging move order, allocate material to the move order, transact the move order, automatically create trips and deliveries, and print designated picking documents. The shipment confirmation process for a trip decrements inventory, prints designated shipping documents, and updates the status of all the stops on the selected trip to Closed, indicating that all material has been picked up and delivered.

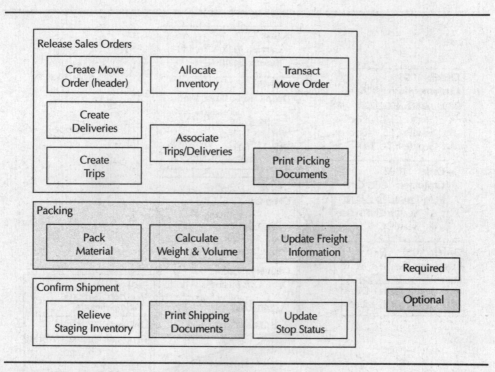

FIGURE 17-2. *The shipping process*

The overall process is almost infinitely flexible. Although you can automate many of the listed activities, you can also perform them separately if your business process warrants. For example, in many environments, picking is driven by a pick slip, printed as part of the picking documents. Pick slips are generated at one time, perhaps on a regular schedule; the actual physical inventory movement (transacting the move order) is performed later, by different personnel from those who generated the pick slip. In this case, it is appropriate to separate the release process from the move order transaction. As another example, if you need to plan complex trips of multiple stops, it might be appropriate to plan trips manually and later assign delivery lines, rather than combining or automating these activities.

Finally, there is no predefined sequence for many of the activities shown in Figure 17-2. You can print documentation at almost any point in the process; you can create deliveries and later assign them to trips, or you can create the trip first and then assign deliveries. The few dependencies that do exist should be apparent; for example, you cannot transact the staging move order before you've generated it. Typically, the process begins with releasing orders for shipment and ends with closing all the stops associated with a trip.

Configuring Oracle Shipping

In addition to setting up Oracle Inventory and Oracle Order Management, Oracle Shipping Execution requires a number of setup steps. Many of these steps are optional, based on the features you decide to use. These setup activities are described in the following sections.

Shipping Parameters

Use the Shipping Parameters window to set default shipping information for each warehouse (inventory organization). This window contains four tabs:

- **General**   This tab lets you specify the unit of measure class to be used for weight and volume calculations and the basis (quantity, volume, or weight) used for percent of fill calculations.

- **Pick Release**   The Pick Release tab defines defaults for the pick release process, including release sequence and pick slip grouping rules; whether to print pick slips at the end of the process or immediately; default picking document set; criteria for creating deliveries; default staging subinventory and locator; number of lines per pick slip; and whether to automatically allocate inventory as part of the release process.

- **Shipping Transaction**   This tab enables you to specify the default shipping document set, manual or automatic weight and volume calculation, packing controls, a default Goods Dispatched Account and category sets for freight class and commodity code.

- **Delivery Grouping**   The Delivery Grouping tab lets you specify the criteria for automatic delivery creation. Ship From and Ship To Locations are required criteria; you can also include Customer, Freight Terms, FOB Code, Intermediate Ship To Location, Ship Method, and Carrier.

Rules

Three types of rules are used within Oracle Shipping Execution: Release Rules, Release Sequence Rules, and Pick Slip Grouping Rules. All are optional, but can be convenient, depending on your business processes.

Release Rules

Release Rules establish defaults for the pick release process. Use the Release Rules form to define these rules. The form is very similar to the Release Sales Orders for Picking form, shown in Figure 17-3. On the Release Rules form, give each rule a name and range of effective dates; then enter the values you want to use when you invoke that rule during the release process. See the "Pick Release" section for a discussion of the available options.

Release Sequence Rules

Release Sequence Rules define the priority in which order lines are considered for allocation during the release process. A Release Sequence Rule consists of a priority for the following attributes, applied in ascending or descending sequence: Order Number, Outstanding Invoice Value, Schedule Date, Departure Date, and Shipment Priority. (Order Number and Outstanding Invoice Value are mutually exclusive.)

You can define multiple rules for different business purposes. For example, you might normally ship orders in order of schedule date, with shipment priority used to prioritize orders with the same schedule date. At month end, however, you might want to give a higher priority to high value orders, i.e., those with the greatest outstanding invoice value.

Using the Release Sequence Rules form, assign each rule a name and range of effective dates. Then select a priority from 1 (highest) through 5 for one or more of the available attributes, and select whether it should be considered in ascending or descending order.

Pick Slip Grouping Rules

Pick Slip Grouping Rules control how picking lines are grouped onto pick slips. Define these rules on the Pick Slip Grouping Rules form. Give each rule a name and effectivity range; then select the grouping criteria from the following: Order Number, Subinventory, Customer, Ship To, Carrier, Trip Stop, Delivery, and Shipment Priority.

Freight Information

In the shipping process, you might want to record freight information, such as the carrier, shipment method, and freight costs. The following sections describe the necessary setup steps.

Freight Carriers

Use the Freight Carriers form to define the carriers that you use for shipments between organizations, and shipments to and from customers and suppliers. For each carrier, enter a Name, Description, and Distribution account.

You must define freight carriers separately for each warehouse where you plan to use them. When you no longer want to use a carrier at a warehouse, deactivate it using the Inactive After field.

Carrier-Ship Method Relationships

Define the relationships between carriers and shipping methods on the Carrier-Ship Method Relationships form. These relationships establish the valid carriers for different ship methods. On the form, select the Ship Method (defined on the Ship Method Lookups form in Oracle Inventory), the shipping Organization (warehouse), and the Freight Carrier; check the Enabled box.

Freight Costs

On the Freight Cost Types form, you can define suggested freight costs that you can later apply to shipments. For example, if you have a Special Handling charge for hazardous materials, you can specify the default cost and later apply it to shipments using the Freight Costs window on the Shipping Transactions form.

To define a freight cost, specify a Name, select a Type (defined as a FREIGHT_ COST_TYPE on the Oracle Shipping Lookups form), select a currency, and enter the amount of the charge. When you apply a freight cost to a shipment, you can accept the information from the freight cost type or override it.

Documents

Although Oracle does not require you to print any documentation as part of the shipping execution, most enterprises still rely on paper documentation for some part of the process. Pick slips, packing lists, bills of lading, and shipping labels are typical examples. Bills of lading and packing slips are identified by a unique number; to generate these documents, you must set up three objects: document categories, if you need to establish different numbering sequences; document sequences, to establish the numbering rules for certain documents; and sequence/category assignments, to designate the numbering sequence for each document category. You can also define document sets to predefine groups of documents you will print at pick release or ship confirm.

Document Categories

The Document Categories form lets you define multiple subdivisions of a given type of document; you will later assign these categories to *document sequences,* described in the next section, to determine the numbering method for a given category of document. For example, if different carriers require different bill of lading numbers or formats, you can create multiple document categories for the bill of lading document and assign a different format and sequence to each.

To define a document category, give it a name and description and select the type of document (Bill of Lading or Packing Slip) to which it applies. In the Category Includes block, indicate whether it applies to one or all shipping methods and whether it applies to one or all shipping locations. In the Sequence block, you can specify an optional prefix, suffix, and delimiter; the Default Appearance provides a preview of the format.

Document Sequences

Document Sequences are used to determine the numbering method for a wide variety of documents in many different applications; in fact, the Document Sequences form is considered part of Application Object Library. Oracle Shipping Execution uses document sequences to generate numbers for bills of lading and packing slips.

You can define multiple sequences and assign each to a given document category. To define a document sequence, give it a name, select the application to which it pertains (e.g., Oracle Shipping), and select a range of effective dates. Select the sequence type—Automatic, Manual, or Gapless—and the Initial Value (starting number) for automatic or gapless sequences. Check the Message check box to have each document display a message to the user identifying the sequence name and value.

NOTE
Gapless numbering is supported only in certain localizations of Oracle Applications. Check the documentation for your localization before choosing this method.

Category/Sequence Assignments

After you have defined document categories and document sequences, assign the desired sequences to the corresponding category; this determines the number generation for documents within the chosen category.

Use the Sequence Assignments form (also part of Application Object Library). Select the application, Category, Set of Books, and Method; on the Assignment tab, provide an effective date range and select the Sequence. In addition to using separate sequences for different document categories, you can use separate sequences for the same document category with different effectivity dates; for example, you might want to use a different sequence for your packing slips for each calendar year.

Document Sets

You can define different sets of documents to print at Pick Release or Ship Confirmation steps in the shipping process. On the Shipping Parameters form, described earlier, you can choose one document set to Default on pick release and one to default on Ship Confirm; you can override these as necessary.

Define document sets on the Shipping Document Sets form. Give each set a Name and Description, and select its usage—either Pick Release or Ship Confirm. In the Documents block, select the application and the documents you want to print when you request this set.

Transportation Calendars

You can optionally assign a calendar to each of your organizations or trading partners (suppliers, customers, or carriers) to limit valid shipping days and times. If you do not assign a calendar to a trading partner, every day is considered a valid shipping and receiving day.

First, you must define a workday calendar that identifies the desired days and times; calendar definition is discussed in Chapter 4.

After you have defined the necessary calendars, assign them to the appropriate trading partners using the Assign Calendars form. On this form, select the trading partner type (Supplier, Customer, Organization, or Carrier) and name. Select the desired calendar usage (Shipping, Receiving, or, for Carriers only, Carrier), and enter the default calendar name.

For customers or suppliers with multiple sites, you can assign a different calendar to each site. Click Show Candidates, and the Site Calendars region will show all the sites for that trading partner; override the default calendar if necessary.

Shipping Exceptions

The Define Shipping Exceptions form lets you define exceptions that might occur during the shipping process. For each exception you want to track, define an exception name and description and specify the Exception type (Picking, Delivery, or Trip), the severity of the exception, and the method for handling the exception. Exception handling options are Manual, Workflow, or No Action Required. If you choose Workflow as the exception handling method, you must enter the Workflow Item Type and check the Initiate Workflow box. If you do not want to track specific exceptions, this step is optional.

Containers and Item Relationships

You can define containers as inventory items and define the relationship between shippable items and containers. This step is optional; use it only if you explicitly record packing during the shipping process. The process has been discussed in detail in the "Cartonization" section in Chapter 15.

Containers

Containers can be cardboard cartons, pallets, or airline shipping containers. You define containers as items using the Master Items form described in Chapter 3.

The key attributes that identify an item as a container are found on the Physical Attributes tab of the Master Items form: Container check box, Container Type, Internal Volume, Maximum Load Weight, and Minimum Fill Percent.

Container-Item Relationships

The Container-Item Relationships form lets you define how many of a shippable item, called the Load Item, can be packed into a specific Container Item. Specify the container item, the load item, and the maximum quantity of the load item that can be packed in the container. Check the Preferred Flag to identify the preferred container for a given item.

Because containers can be packed within other containers (for example, you can pack cartons into airline containers), container items can also be used as load items.

Pick Release

The shipping process generally begins with the release of sales orders for shipment. This can be done with the online form shown in Figure 17-3, through a concurrent program that you can schedule to run on a regular basis, or if you have predefined the deliveries, through the Shipping Transactions form. Releasing orders will create a Move Order (identified as a *Pick Wave Move Order*) and can optionally initiate any of the release-associated activities shown in Figure 17-2. It can allocate inventory, create deliveries and the associated trips, print specified picking documents, and even automatically transact the move order.

Online Pick Release

To release orders using the Release Sales Orders for Picking form, optionally select the document set you want to print and enter the criteria to identify the order lines you want to release. You can default this information by entering a Release Rule in the Based on Rule field on the form.

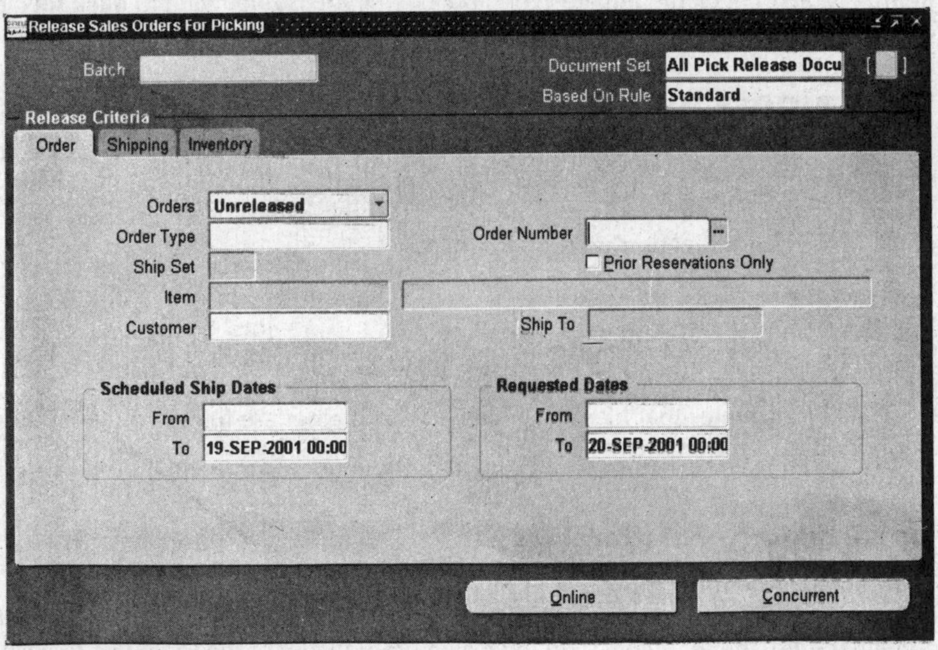

FIGURE 17-3. *Release orders on line with the Release Sales Orders for Picking form*

The form contains three tabs with different types of selection criteria. The Order tab lets you select lines for release based on order information. You can select order lines based on a range of Scheduled or Requested dates; you can also specify individual Orders, Order Types, Ship Sets (for a specific order), Items, Customers, and Ship To location. In addition, the form lets you limit the selection to order lines that are previously unreleased, only backordered lines, or all order lines, using the Orders field. And you can limit selection to lines that you have previously reserved.

On the Shipping tab, you can select order lines based on predefined trips, deliveries, or shipping attributes. Available criteria include Trip, Stop, Delivery, Ship From, Ship Method, Shipment Priority, or Line/Container. It is here that you specify the Release Sequence Rule to establish the priority for allocating inventory to lines; you can also choose to Autocreate deliveries and Include Assigned lines.

The Inventory tab lets you limit the inventory that is considered in the release process. You can specify a single warehouse, subinventory, and locator to pick from and restrict selection to a project and task if you want. On this tab, you can specify a Pick Slip Grouping rule to determine how your pick slips are created. Other options are to Auto Allocate (reserve) material, Auto Pick Confirm (transact the resulting Move Order), and the staging subinventory and locator to which the material should be moved.

When you have entered all the desired selection criteria, you can release the selected orders online or via a concurrent program. Click either Online or Concurrent. Releasing orders online will perform the process immediately, but your terminal will be locked until it completes; it might be useful for the occasional rush order. Releasing the orders using the concurrent process will submit a concurrent request to run as soon as possible and will unlock your terminal so you can perform other activities. If you have selected multiple orders, the concurrent method is usually preferable.

Concurrent Pick Release

If you want to automate the release orders on a regular basis, you can use the concurrent program, Pick Selection List Generation SRS. This submits the release request through the Standard Request Submission (SRS) form, so you can schedule the job to run on a regular interval.

The only parameter this program requires is a Release Rule, which specifies all the selection criteria and options; you can optionally provide a batch prefix if you desire.

Release Through the Shipping Transactions Form

If you have predefined deliveries, you can also release sales order lines using the appropriate window on the Shipping Transactions form. For example, you can select one or more deliveries and initiate the release process for those delivery lines; if you have associated the deliveries with trips, you can select one or more trips and run the release process for the delivery lines associated with those trips. These options are discussed later, in the "Shipping Actions" section.

Move Orders

The process of releasing sales orders creates move orders, identified as *Pick Wave Move Orders*. A pick wave move order is a request to move material from its location in inventory to a staging location for shipping. (Other types of move orders are discussed in Chapter 15.)

If you have selected auto allocation in the pick release process, the move order will be *detailed* at the time of creation, or you can postpone this activity until a later time.

Transacting the move order performs a subinventory transfer that moves the material from its stocking location to the designated staging location. This process is sometimes referred to as *Pick Confirm*. At this time, you can report missing quantities or change the transaction line if you have picked from a different subinventory, locator, lot, or serial number than the move order requested. If your inventory accuracy is high and your process is extremely simple, you might choose to automatically transact the move order as part of the release process.

Order Cancellations

Oracle Shipping execution allows cancellation or modification of sales orders or lines even after pick release. Canceling or reducing an order quantity will automatically reduce the detailed quantities on the Move Order and update any existing reservations to reflect the new order quantities.

Shipping Transactions

You can perform most shipping activities from the Shipping Transactions form. This form consists of two main windows: the Query Manager and the Data Manager. The Query Manager lets you find shipping-related entities, such as delivery lines, deliveries, LPNs (License Plate Number, or container identifier), stops, and trips. The Data Manager window lets you maintain information about those entities and perform the activities associated with shipping. The Query Manager is described in the next section; the Data Manager is described by type of data and activity in the following sections.

Query Manager

When you open the Shipping Transactions form, the Query Manager is the first window to open, as shown in Figure 17-4. In the left pane of the window, use the navigation tree to select the type of object you want to find; in the right pane, enter the selection criteria for the type of object you are seeking. Numerous selection criteria are available; Table 17-1 summarizes the available criteria for each type of object.

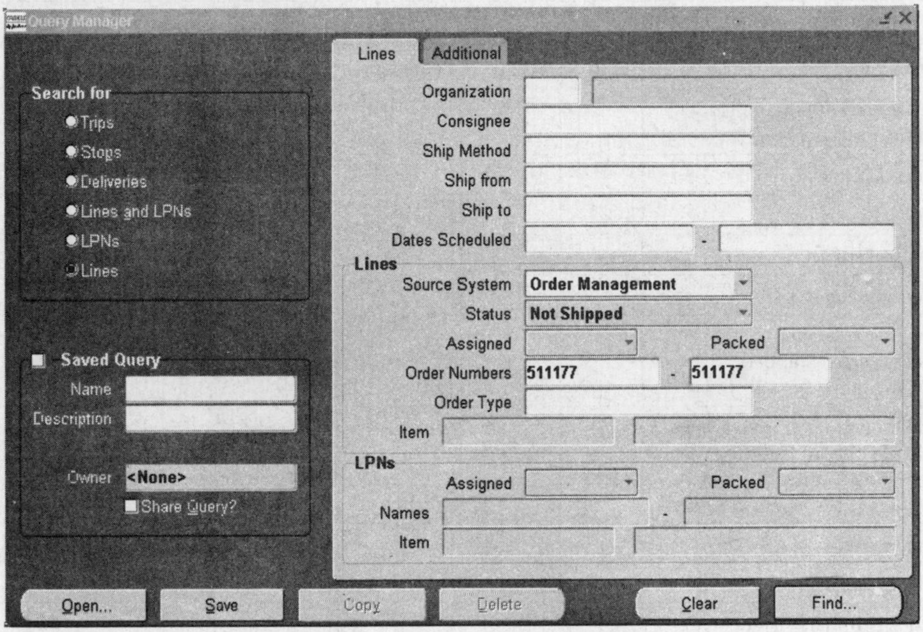

FIGURE 17-4. *Search for shipping entities with the Query Manager*

	Search Entities					
Criteria	**Trip**	**Stop**	**Delivery**	**Lines & LPNs**	**LPNs**	**Lines**
Arrival Dates		✔				
Assigned			✔	✔	✔	✔
Bills of Lading			✔			
Consignee			✔	✔	✔	✔
Deliver To				✔	✔	✔
Delivery Names			✔			
Delivery Status			✔			
Departure Dates		✔				

TABLE 17-1. *Available Search Criteria in the Query Manager*

| | **Search Entities** | | | | | |
Criteria	Trip	Stop	Delivery	Lines & LPNs	LPNs	Lines
Departure Fill (Empty, Under, Partial, Full, or Over)		✔				
Drop-off Dates			✔			
FOB			✔	✔	✔	✔
Freight Terms			✔	✔	✔	✔
Intermediate Ship To			✔	✔	✔	✔
Line Status (Staged, Backordered, Shipped, or Cancelled)				✔		✔
LPN criteria (Fill criteria, Use Shared Criteria, Include Immediate Contents, Include Containers for Selected Orders)				✔	✔	
LPN Names				✔	✔	
Order Lines				✔		✔
Order Numbers				✔		✔
Order Type				✔		✔
Organization			✔	✔	✔	✔
Packed				✔	✔	✔
Pick-up Dates			✔			
Planned	✔		✔			
Seal Codes		✔				
Scheduled Dates				✔	✔	✔
Ship Dates				✔	✔	✔
Ship From			✔	✔	✔	✔
Ship Method	✔		✔	✔	✔	✔
Ship To			✔	✔	✔	✔
Shipment Priority				✔	✔	✔
Source System				✔		✔
Stop Location		✔				
Stop Status		✔				

TABLE 17-1. *Available Search Criteria in the Query Manager* (continued)

Criteria	Search Entities					
	Trip	Stop	Delivery	Lines & LPNs	LPNs	Lines
Tracking Numbers				✔	✔	✔
Trip Status	✔					
Trip Names	✔	✔				
Vehicle Information (Organization, Vehicle Item, Prefix, and Number)	✔					

TABLE 17-1.   *Available Search Criteria in the Query Manager* (continued)

Enter your search criteria, and click Find. This opens the Data Manager window for the objects found by your query. You can return to the Query Manager at any time by clicking the Find icon (Flashlight) on the toolbar.

If you want to save a query for repeated use, give it a name and description in the Query Manager window; check the Share a Query? box to make the query public (accessible to others). You can reuse a Personal or Public Query by selecting it from the appropriate node in the left-hand pane of the Query Manager; within a session, you can reuse a previous query by selecting it from the Temporary Query node.

Data Manager

The Data Manager enables you to enter or maintain data for the entities involved in the shipping process: Delivery Lines, Deliveries, LPNs, Stops, and Trips. You can create or modify these entities in the Data Manager and perform activities on them. For example, you can launch pick release for trips, stops, or deliveries; associate delivery lines with deliveries; pack deliveries or individual delivery lines; and build trips selecting deliveries.

The Data Manager window consists of two panes, shown in Figure 17-5. The left pane is a tree-style navigator window, organized into Data Entry, Personal Queries, Public Queries, or Temporary Queries. The right pane is a folder form with multiple tabs that display information for the objects you have selected with the Query Manager or the object for which you are entering data. The type of information displayed is identified in the Context field at the top of the pane. You can rearrange the data in the folders to suit your preferences or business practices, or you can open a detail window with the Details button on the form. Use either the summary or detail window to change basic data for the object; perform additional actions by selecting the appropriate activity from the Actions menu at the bottom of the pane. The actions are described in detail later in this chapter, in the "Shipping Actions" section.

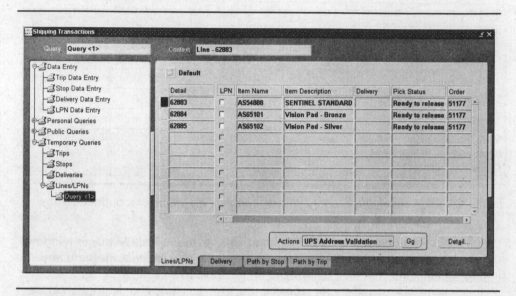

FIGURE 17-5. *The Data Manager lets you create or maintain shipping data*

Shipping Entities

As noted earlier, the shipping process utilizes the following entities: Delivery Lines, Deliveries, Stops, Trips, and optionally containers or LPNs. The relationship between these entities was illustrated in Figure17-1. The overall process is extremely flexible; you can model many different shipping processes with the tools that Oracle provides. Many activities are optional, and there are very few restrictions on the order in which you can perform the activities. The overall process flow was shown in Figure 17-2.

The following sections describe the basic data required for these entities; the "Shipping Actions" section and its subsections detail the activities you can perform for those entities.

Delivery Lines

Delivery lines are shippable Sales Order detail lines; they are created through Order Management and processed for shipment in a number of ways, as described in the "Shipping Actions" section later in this chapter.

Deliveries

A delivery is a set of sales order lines going from one location to the same customer location, on a specific date and time. You must assign deliveries to trips in order to ship them; you can optionally pack delivery lines into containers.

You can create deliveries automatically when you release sales orders for picking, as discussed earlier in the "Pick Release" section. Alternatively, you can use the Autocreate Deliveries action on the Shipping Transactions form to automatically generate deliveries for unassigned delivery lines. Finally, you can create deliveries manually and later assign delivery lines; this might be useful if you want to override the grouping defaults specified in the organization's Shipping Parameters.

Select Delivery Data Entry on the left pane of the Data Manager to manually create a delivery. This will open the Delivery window, shown in Figure 17-6. Enter a delivery name, or one will be automatically generated based on rules your system administrator can establish. The only other required information is the Organization from which the delivery originates and the Ultimate Ship To (typically, a customer location). The other information shown in Figure 17-6 is optional; you can specify it now or as it becomes known.

In addition, you can enter Bill of Lading (BOL) information or generate a BOL on the Legs tab and generate a packing slip for the delivery using the Packing Slip tab on the Delivery window.

Trips

A trip is a set of deliveries that is scheduled to be shipped on a specific carrier on a specific date. You can create trips manually and assign stops, deliveries, and

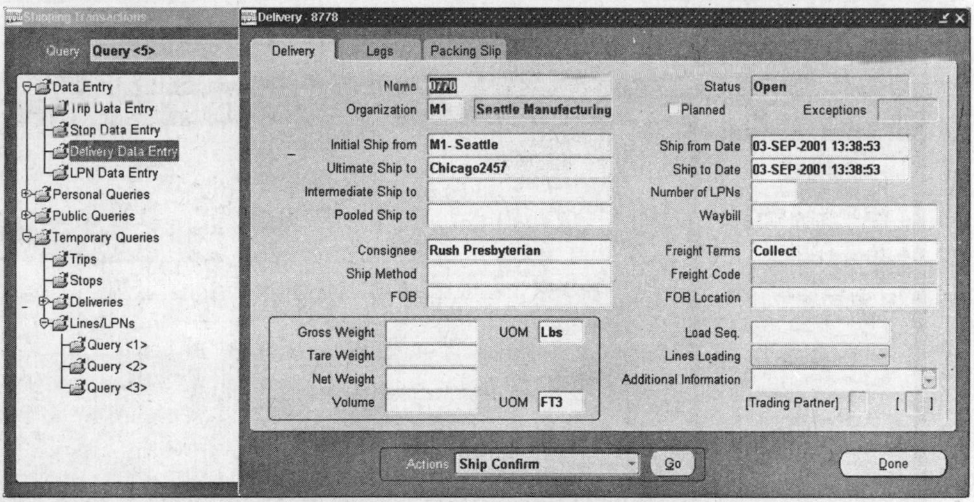

FIGURE 17-6. *Use the Delivery window to create and maintain delivery information*

delivery lines; or you can automatically create trips for existing deliveries, delivery lines, or LPNs.

To create a trip using the Data Manager, select Trip Data Entry on the left pane of the Data Manager. The only data required is a trip name. You can also enter the data shown in the detailed trip window in Figure 17-7.

Stops

A stop is a point along the route where material is either picked up or dropped off. Each trip must consist of at least two stops: one pickup and one dropoff. Stops are most commonly created automatically as part of trip creation, but they can be created manually for more detailed scheduling.

Select Stop Data Entry on the Data Manager to manually create a stop. This opens the Stops window, shown in Figure 17-8. Enter the Location of the stop (either an internal or customer location), the Trip to which the stop belongs, and Planned Arrival Departure dates and times. You can also enter weight, volume, and fill information for the stop and later record actual arrival and departure dates and times.

LPNs

A License Plate Number (LPN) is an identifier assigned to a specific container used to store or ship material, for example, a carton, pallet, or trailer. In the specific context of Oracle Shipping Execution, an LPN identifies a specific instance of a predefined *container item*, described earlier in the section "Containers and Item Relationships."

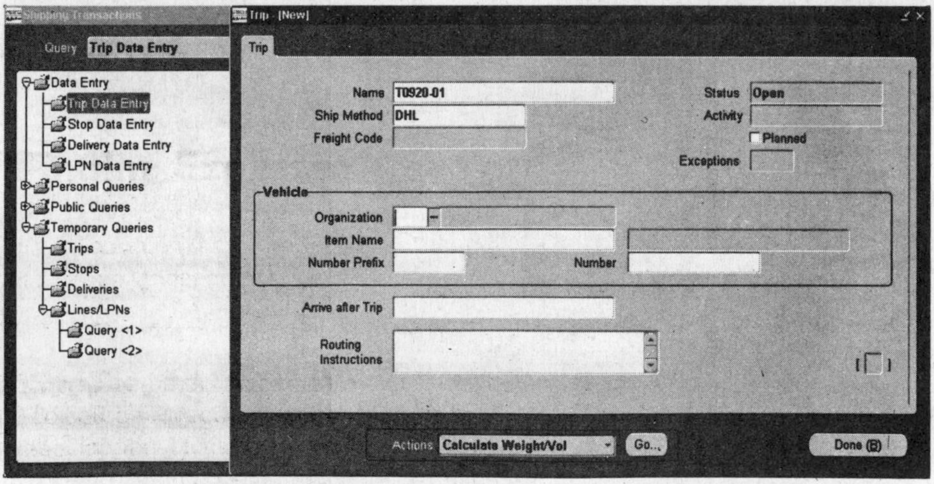

FIGURE 17-7. *Enter trip data in the Trip Details window*

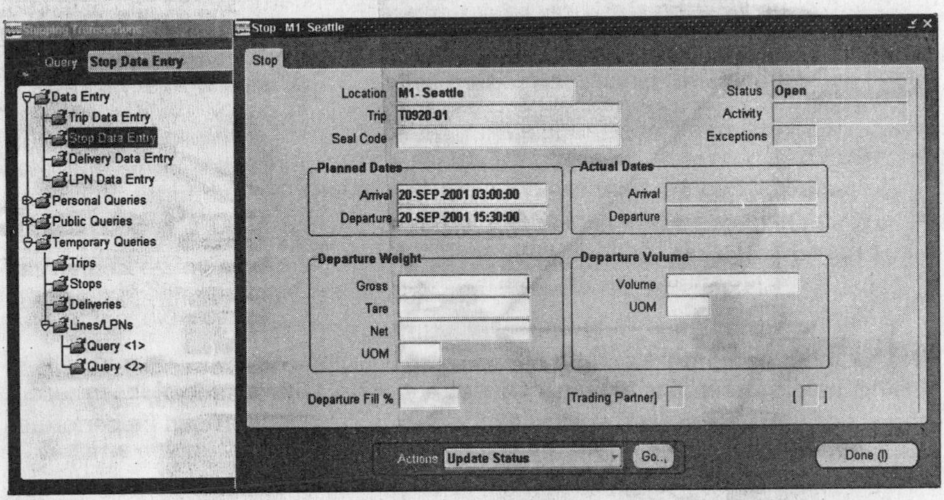

FIGURE 17-8. *Enter information about a stop in the Stops window*

To define an LPN in Oracle Shipping Execution, select LPN Data Entry on the Data Manager. This opens the Create LPNs window, shown in Figure 17-9. Enter the

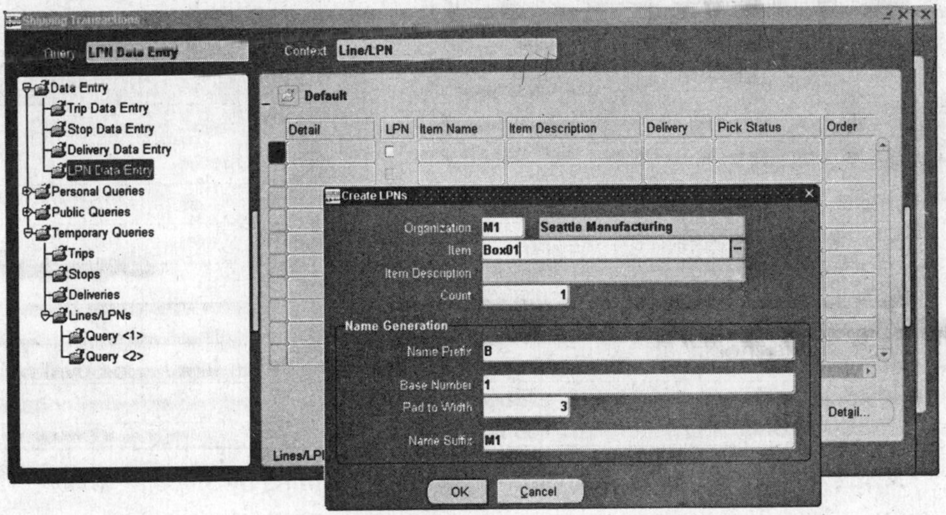

FIGURE 17-9. *Generate LPNs with the Create LPNs window*

Organization in which the LPN is located, the container Item for which you want to generate LPNs, and the Count (number) of LPNs you want. Optionally, enter the parameters to generate the identifiers: Name Prefix, Base Number, Pad to Width, and Name Suffix.

NOTE
Oracle Warehouse Management provides significant enhancements on LPN generation and use; see Chapter 15 for details.

Shipping Actions

Using the basic shipping entities, you can perform a number of actions to record the actual activities of your shipping process. Different actions can be performed for different objects, as summarized in Table 17-2.

Action	Entity				
	Delivery Line	**Delivery**	**LPN**	**Trip**	**Stop**
Assign/Modify Freight Costs	✔	✔	✔	✔	✔
Launch Pick Release	✔	✔	✔	✔	✔
Split Line	✔		✔		
Auto-create Deliveries	✔		✔		
Assign to Delivery	✔		✔		
Auto-create Trip	✔	✔	✔		
Create LPNs	✔		✔		
Packing Activities	✔	✔	✔		
Calculate Weight and Volume	✔	✔	✔		✔
Generate Loading Sequence		✔			
Assign to Trip		✔			
Plan		✔		✔	✔
Print Document Sets		✔		✔	✔
Update Status (Close or Reopen)		✔			✔

TABLE 17-2. *Shipping Actions That Can Be Performed by Shipping Entity*

Action	Entity				
	Delivery Line	**Delivery**	**LPN**	**Trip**	**Stop**
Ship Confirm		✔			
UPS Integration - (Rate and Service, Tracking, Time in Transit, and Address Validation)	✔	✔	✔		

TABLE 17-2. *Shipping Actions That Can Be Performed by Shipping Entity* (continued)

To perform any of these actions, use the Shipping Transactions form to locate (with the Query Manager) or create the desired entity. If your query retrieves multiple rows of data, select the specific entity in the Data Manager window. When appropriate, you can select multiple rows of data on the Data Manager using SHIFT-click or CTRL-click. Then choose the desired action from the Actions menu, and click Go. Each of these actions is described in the following sections.

Assign and Modify Freight Costs

You can add or modify freight costs for any of the shipping entities—delivery lines, deliveries, LPNs, trip, or stops. Find the entity you want using the Query Manager, and select Freight Costs from the Actions menu; click Go. In the resulting Freight Costs window, enter or modify the freight Cost Type, Currency Code, Amount, and optional Conversion type.

Launch Pick Release

In addition to releasing lines for picking using the online form or the concurrent program, described earlier in the "Pick Release" section, you can release lines from the Shipping Transactions form by selecting lines or any of the entities with which the line is associated—deliveries, LPNs, Trips, or Stops. Find the entities you want using the Query Manager, and select the desired lines on the Data Manager. Choose Launch Pick Release from the actions menu, and click Go.

This process launches a concurrent request to release the selected lines, as described earlier in the section "Concurrent Pick Release." No additional input is accepted; the release process uses the defaults established on the Pick Release tab of your organization's Shipping Parameters form.

Split Line

You can split delivery lines so that you can ship them separately. Find the lines individually, or find the LPNs with which they are associated. Select the desired lines in the Data Manager window, and choose Split Line from the Actions menu.

When you click Go, the system displays the Split Delivery Line window; enter the quantity you want to split from the original line, and click OK. This results in two separate delivery lines that you can process separately.

Auto-create Deliveries

To create a delivery for unassigned delivery lines or LPNs that are already packed, use the Query Manager to find the needed information. On the Data Manager, select the desired lines (use CTRL-click or SHIFT-click to select multiple lines) and choose Auto-create Deliveries from the Actions menu; click Go. A delivery is automatically created and attached to the selected objects.

Assign to Delivery

Another method of creating a delivery is to add or remove lines or LPNs from an existing delivery. Find the lines or LPNs you want, and choose Assign to Delivery from the Actions menu. When you click Go, choose the desired delivery from the list of values; the lines or LPNs will be assigned to the selected delivery.

To unassign lines or LPNs from a delivery, select the desired lines in the Data Manager window and choose Unassign from Delivery from the Actions menu.

AutoCreate Trip

To automatically create a trip for one or more deliveries, use the Query Manager to find the desired deliveries. This opens the Data Manager, displaying the designated deliveries; select the desired deliveries and choose the action AutoCreate Trip; click Go. Use a similar procedure to autocreate a trip for delivery lines or LPNs.

Create LPNs

In addition to creating LPNs from the LPN Data Entry node on the Data Manager, you can also create LPNs from Delivery Lines or LPN summary windows on the Data Manager. Choose Create LPNs from the Actions menu, and click Go. This opens the Create LPNs window, shown earlier in Figure 17-9. Enter the same details as noted in the "LPNs" section, and click OK.

NOTE
LPN creation from the Delivery Lines or LPN windows is provided as a convenience; the LPNs created are not associated with the selected line or LPN until you pack them.

Packing Activities

Packing is an optional activity in Oracle Shipping Execution that associates delivery lines with LPNs (containers). Oracle offers several options: the Packing Workbench, autopacking, and manual packing (and unpacking).

Packing Workbench   The Packing Workbench enables you to query multiple lines and multiple containers, compare the weight and volume of the items you want to pack with the capacity of the selected containers, and choose the mode of packing.

To access the Packing Workbench, use the Query Manager to locate both the lines you want to pack and the containers (LPNs) you want to use for packing. Select the desired combination of lines and LPNs, choose Packing Workbench from the Actions menu, and click Go. The Packing Workbench window contains two tabs. One displays the selected containers and their contents; the other displays the selected items. The left side of the packing workbench shows the available capacity of all the selected containers and the total weight and volume of the selected items.

Pack the selected lines into the designated containers by selecting the Packing Mode. You can choose either Equal packing or Full (sequential) packing. Equal splits the selected delivery lines equally across the selected containers. Full packing packs one container fully before proceeding to the next container. When you have selected the packing mode, click Pack.

Autopacking   You can automatically generate the required containers and pack them using the Autopack action. Autopacking uses the container-load relationships established in Shipping Execution or the preferred container item set up in Oracle Inventory.

To autopack, locate and select the desired lines; choose either Auto-pack or Auto-pack Master from the Actions menu, and click Go. The Auto-pack action creates and packs only the detail containers; Auto-pack Master packs the selected delivery lines into the detail container and then packs the detail container into the parent container.

Manual Packing and Unpacking   Manual packing of delivery lines verifies that the lines have been packed into containers. After you have packed a delivery line, you must unpack it to make any changes.

Verify packing by selecting the desired delivery lines (by searching for specific lines, deliveries, or LPNs). Choose Pack from the Actions menu, and click Go. To unpack a delivery line, LPN, or an entire delivery line, select the desired objects in the Data Manager window; choose Unpack from the Actions menu, and click Go.

Calculate Weight and Volume

The shipping parameter Weight/Volume Calculation specifies whether the weight and volume of various shipping entities are calculated automatically or manually. If you choose Automatic for this parameter, the weight and volume will be calculated when the delivery is packed, ship confirmed, or planned. If you choose Manual, you can calculate the weight and volume on the Shipping Transactions form.

Generate Loading Sequence

You can generate a loading sequence for lines within a delivery to support the customer's requested production sequence. To generate a loading sequence, you must specify the customer production sequence on the sales order line (found on the Others tab), assign containers to each of the delivery lines, and calculate the weight and volume of the delivery or trip.

Then, select the desired delivery lines using the Query Manager and Data Manager. Select the Lines Loading sequence (Forward, Forward Inverted, Reverse, or Reverse Inverted) for the delivery. Choose the Generate Loading Sequence action from the Actions menu, and click Go.

Assign to Trip

To manually specify the deliveries that are associated with a predefined trip, select the desired deliveries using the Query Manager and Data Manager; choose Assign to Trip from the Actions menu, and click Go. Enter the location where the items are to be picked up and the location where they are to be dropped off.

To unassign deliveries from a trip, search for the delivery lines or the delivery containing the delivery lines. Select the desired delivery lines, choose Unassign from Trip, and click Go.

Plan

Planning a trip validates certain characteristics of the trip to help ensure a successful shipment. When you plan a trip, the system validates the sequence numbers of deliveries within the trip and checks the weight, volume, and fill percent against the maximums for the containers in each delivery. Trip planning also verifies that the minimum fill percent is met and that the planned trip date is not past due.

After you plan a trip, you cannot add or delete delivery lines unless you first unplan the trip. You can also plan a delivery to prevent further changes.

To plan a trip or delivery, use the Query Manager to find the desired entities. Select the trips or deliveries in the Data Manager window, and choose the Plan action; click Go. To unplan a trip or delivery, select Unplan from the Actions menu.

Print Document Sets

After you have defined an LPN, trip, or stop, you can print picking or shipping document sets for that entity. Find it using the Query Manager, and choose the Action Print Document Set. Click Go, and select the desired document set from the Document Sets window.

Update Status

For the most detailed control of your shipping process, you can update Close or Reopen of individual deliveries or stops within a trip. Select the desired delivery or stop, and choose the appropriate action (Close or Reopen) from the Actions menu. Click Go.

Ship Confirm

Ship Confirm is the process that records whether items on a delivery have been shipped or backordered. To ship confirm a delivery, select the desired deliveries. Choose Actions | Ship Confirm | Go.

In the Confirm Delivery window, shown in Figure 17-10, use the following Ship Options to specify the activity that has occurred:

- **Ship Entered Quantities**   Confirms the quantities entered in the Shipped Quantity field for each delivery line.

- **Unspecified Quantities**   Used in conjunction with the Ship Entered Quantities option, this field determines what action to perform for unspecified (null) shipped quantities; you can Ship, Backorder, or Stage such quantities.

- **Ship All**   Confirms the entire quantity of each delivery line, regardless of what you enter in the Shipped Quantity field.

- **Backorder All**   Backorders the entire quantity of each delivery line.

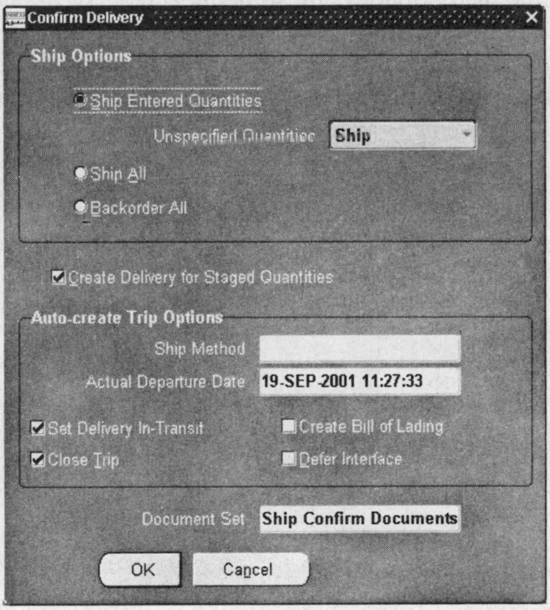

FIGURE 17-10.   *Confirm Shipments using the Confirm Delivery window*

As part of the ship confirm process, you can optionally create deliveries for staged quantities, auto-create a trip (specifying ship method and actual ship date), and print a set of documents.

UPS Integration

Currently, Oracle has an agreement with UPS and has developed APIs to provide UPS information by Delivery Line, Delivery, or LPN on the Shipping Transactions form. You can validate addresses, access rate and service information, track shipments, and view the time in transit. Oracle plans to add integration with additional carriers in the future.

Summary

This chapter described capabilities of Oracle Shipping Execution to manage outbound logistics. It described shipping terminology—trips, stops, deliveries, and delivery lines—and activities—release, move order transactions, trip creation and planning, and document printing. This chapter outlined the necessary setup steps, including shipping parameters, rules, freight information, documents, transportation calendars, exception definition, and container-item relationships.

The online and concurrent options for releasing sales orders have been described in detail. The available query options and shipping actions have been outlined. These actions include building trips, stops, and deliveries; packing; document printing; confirming shipments; and UPS integration. Additional capabilities, available with Oracle Warehouse Management, are detailed in Chapter 15.

PART
V

Support Functions

CHAPTER
18

Costing

osting is the application that keeps track of the value of items in the manufacturing and supply chain. You can assign accounts to manufacturing transactions. Costing keeps the value of raw material, work in process, and finished goods in line with the value in the Oracle General Ledger. You can use the bills of material and routings to roll up the costs of raw materials, manpower, machine resources, and other factory overhead. It reports many types of variances to help you judge the accuracy of your purchasing and manufacturing standards. It allows many cost types to enable you to judge the impact of a supplier's price increase and forecast standards for the next quarter. It supports many types of costing, including Standard, Average, LIFO, FIFO, and Periodic Average. It includes support for activity-based costing. The flow of cost through the factory is shown in Figure18-1.

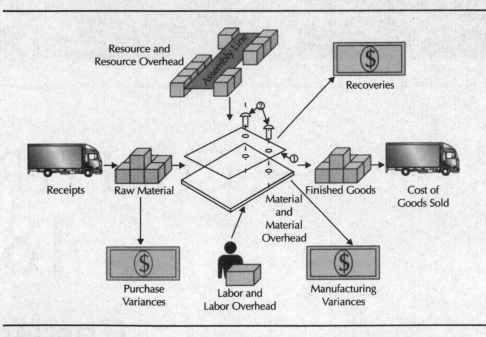

FIGURE 18-1. *Flow of costs through the manufacturing organization*

Setting Up Costing

To set up costing, you need to define the organizations within your enterprise. These organizations might be responsible for defining the costs for a number of facilities. For example, you might have a finished goods warehouse and a manufacturing warehouse located at the same address. You might wish for the costs defined in the manufacturing facility to be the same as the storage facility. You might also have a distribution facility at the other side of the country. The costs of transportation might be absorbed into the cost of inventory at the distribution center, meaning that the distribution center has its own costs. Item costs of any type are made up of a fixed set of cost elements and an unlimited number of sub-elements. The hierarchy of organizations for costing is shown in Figure 18-2.

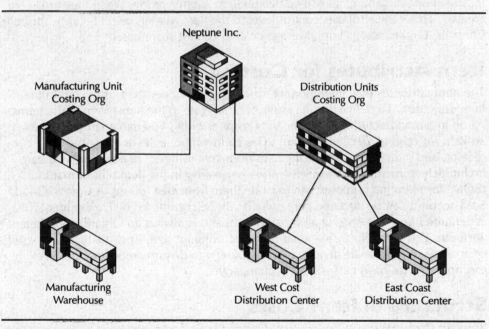

FIGURE 18-2.   *Costing organizations*

Costing Organizations and Children Organizations

When you define an inventory organization, you can specify both an item master organization and a costing organization. Child organizations of the costing organization can share the costs of the costing master organization if they are all using standard costs and are not manufacturing plants (i.e., are not WIP-enabled). The costing master organization can be a manufacturing plant. Items in each of these organizations will be stored at the same cost, provided they have the Costing Enabled and Inventory Asset Value attributes controlled at the item level rather than the item organization level. Defining inventory organizations is discussed in Chapter 2. To update the costing organization, select Organizations | Parameters | Costing Parameters. You can set the costing method, the default costing sub-element, and a set of accounts for inventory valuation that will be defaulted to subinventories when they are created. To set the attributes control level to the Item Master, select Setup | Attribute Controls. Organizations using average costing cannot share costs.

Item Attributes for Costing

The item attributes that are important for costing are under the Costing tab in the item definition. To define costing attributes, navigate to the Items form in the Items menu in a manufacturing or engineering responsibility. You can enable or disable an item for costing, declare the item to be an inventory asset or expensed on receipt, and include or exclude the item from cost rollups. For example, you can include cleaning materials for setup and changeover in the item bills of material (BOM) for planning purposes, but exclude them from cost rollups. A Cost of Goods Sold account can be declared here, which will be considered by Flexbuilder. This is defaulted from the organization parameters and is always an Organization Item attribute. You can define a standard manufacturing lot size. Costs that accrue based on manufacturing lot are divided by this quantity to determine the unit cost. An example of a lot-basis cost is tooling changeover.

Structure of Item Costs

You can store many costs for an item. Costs are of a cost type. A full history of item costs and how they have changed is kept. Cost types might include projected cost, current engineering cost, target cost, as well as the Frozen Standard cost. The data model that supports item costs is illustrated in Figure 18-3.

Each cost is made up of five cost elements. It is these cost elements that are posted to General Ledger. Each cost element can have an unlimited number of cost sub-elements. For example, Neptune separates packaging and costs from equipment costs in the material cost element. Figure 18-4 shows how the cost is structured from costing organization down to cost sub-element.

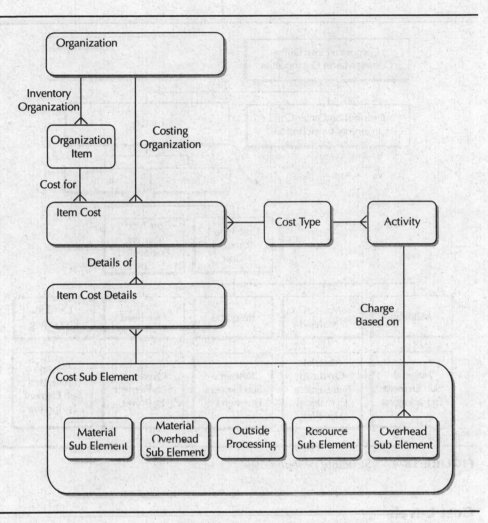

FIGURE 18-3. *Data model of item costs*

Cost Groups

Cost groups are a partition of costs that were first introduced to enable project
manufacturing environments. Cost groups ensure that the flow of costs for one
group of projects can be completely separated from the flow of costs for another.
Cost groups are now pervasive in the cost model. There are many other uses for cost
groups. For example, a given item might have both new and remanufactured units
in the same warehouse. Cost groups enable you to hold the remanufactured and
new units at different costs. To define a cost group, navigate to the Cost Group form.

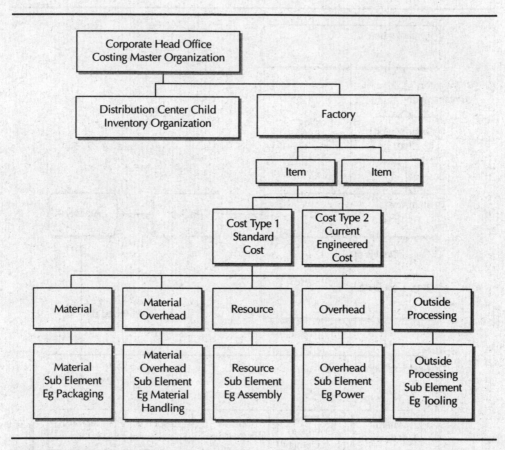

FIGURE 18-4. *Structure of item costs*

Cost Levels

Rolled up costs are captured for an item and stored by cost element for the current level and previous levels. For example, if the bill of material structure for a desktop computer is five levels deep, the assembly would have the sum of levels one through four stored as previous level costs and level five would be this level's costs. See Table 18-1.

Defining Cost Types

To define a cost type, navigate to the Cost Type. Give the cost type a name and description. For example, Neptune might have a cost type for target costs described as "Target costs to achieve corporate margin objectives." You must define a default

Level	Material	Material Overhead	Resource	Overhead	Outside Processing
This	75	12	30	8	
Previous	120	34	42	15	20
Total	195	46	72	23	20

TABLE 18-1. *Costing Levels*

cost type for components of an assembly that do not have costs of this type defined to be used during cost rollup. You can allow this cost type name to be shared among organizations by checking the Multi-Org box. Once the cost is created, you can prevent updates to the cost with the Allow Updates flag. The rollup options include the ability to account for component yield in the rollup. For example, if 5 out of 100 personal digital assistants (PDAs) fail because the screens break in manufacturing, the cost of a PDA should account for the extra material needed to make 100 good ones. You can take a snapshot of the BOMs that were used to derive the costs by checking the flag of the same name. The BOM product uses BOM alternates to denote different types of bills. You could define a BOM alternate called Costing to snapshot the bills into. There are a number of flags that affect the level of detail in the cost rollup. Figure 18-5 explains how they affect the costs that are rolled up from the material at a lower level to material costs at the higher level. You can also choose to keep the activity and operation cost breakdown from lower levels.

Cost Sub-Elements   Defining cost sub-elements involves material sub-elements and resource sub-elements.

Material Sub-Elements   Material costs can be broken down to further classify the material cost content. For example, you might wish to summarize the equipment and packaging costs of your products. Packaging costs might represent a significant opportunity for cost improvement for spares and consumables when material costs have been reduced. To define a material sub-element, navigate to the Material Sub-Elements form. Give the sub-element a name and description. You can associate the sub-element with an activity. This activity will be defaulted when the sub-element is used to define the item costs. The basis type defines how these costs accrue, on a per-item or per-lot basis. If the basis type is lot, the costs are divided by standard manufacturing lot size. If you are a Project Manufacturing user, you can associate the sub-element with an expenditure type.

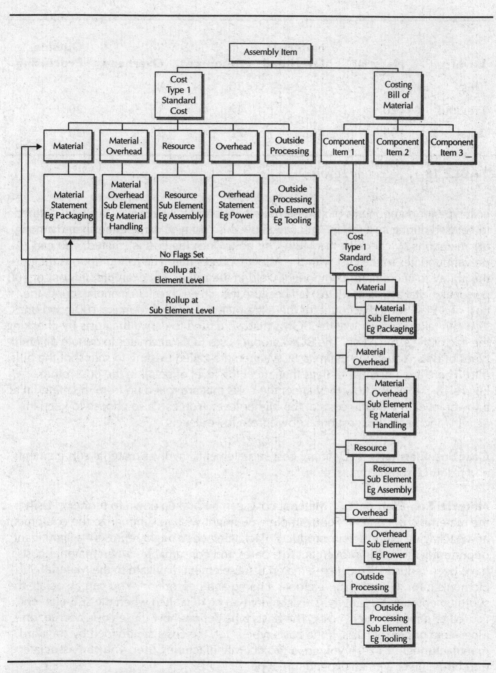

FIGURE 18-5. *Levels of detail in rolling up costs*

Resources   Define resources in the Resource form. You can name the resource and define its basis type: lot or item. You define if the resource is charged to the job manually, as you might have with time cards, or automatically, as you might have with power. The resource can be declared as costed, and if it is, rates and overheads can be associated with it. You define the resource recovery account and the efficiency variance account on the resource. You can define the resources that are allocated based on the resource. For example, you can allocate maintenance department costs on resource value consumed.

_If an outside party provides the resource, you define the item that you place on purchase orders (POs) when ordering the processing from them. The basis would then be on the transaction type of PO Receipt rather than WIP Move to accrue the charge. Outside processing costs are held in a different cost element.

Defining Overheads   The overhead definition adds indirect costs to the item. Material overhead is applied as product is completed or received. Resource overhead is applied as the job moves through the shop floor. Figure 18-6 shows how overheads are charged as work moves through the factory.

To define an overhead, navigate to the Overheads form. You must select a cost element of Material Overhead or Overhead. The absorption account is the recovery

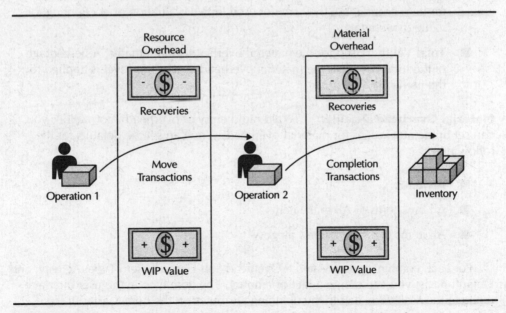

FIGURE 18-6.   *Overhead flow for resource and material overhead*

account for the resource that will offset the charge to WIP when the resource is used. You can choose the basis type for how this overhead is charged. Basis types are as follows:

- **Activity**   Used only for material overhead. The cost applied is the proportion of the cost pool for this activity that applies to this item.

- **Item**   Used for all sub-elements. For material and material overhead sub-elements, you can apply a fixed amount per item completed or received. For resource and resource overhead, you can apply a fixed amount per move operation on the shop floor.

- **Lot**   Used for all sub-element types. Costs are divided by the standard manufacturing lot size quantity.

- **Resource Units**   Used for overhead and material overhead sub-elements. A fixed amount is applied per resource unit used in the manufacturing routing and is applied to item cost.

- **Resource Value**   Used for overhead and material overhead sub-elements. A proportion of the resource value consumed in a manufacturing routing is applied to the item cost. Resource Units and Resource Values can be used for item costing, but they are not used in WIP valuation or accounting for value movements.

- **Total Value**   Used for the material overhead sub-elements. A percentage of the total costs less the material overhead cost at this level is applied to the item cost.

Material Overhead Defaults   To aid rapid entry of overhead information, you can set up default values for material overheads. You can set the defaults for the following:

- All items

- All buy items or All make items

- All items of a given Item Category

For each combination of Material Overhead Sub-Element, Item Type, Activity, and Default Basis, you can define a rate or amount. The item type in the user interface refers to the Make/Buy flag in the planning attributes on the Item Master. If the overheads are assigned on an activity basis, you can enter the number of occurrences of the activity and the number of units over which the cost pool should be allocated.

Defining Activity-based Costs

Activity-based costs are used where a high proportion of product cost is made up of the allocation of indirect costs. The more traditional approach of allocating these indirect costs is based on labor hours or material cost. It can unfairly burden profitable products that have high labor content and mask unprofitable products that are ordered in-small batches or have many engineering changes, high support costs, or other factors that drive costs. It lets you use nontraditional cost drivers to get a clearer picture of an item's true cost. For example, for service calls you can define an activity called "service," calculate a cost for a service call, and allocate that cost using an activity. To define activities, navigate to the Activities form in the costing Setup menu. You can define the Name and Description of the activity. You can use the same activity names across all organization units by checking the Multi-Org flag.

You can define the basis on which the costs are allocated: item, lot, or activity. If the basis type is lot, the activity cost is shared for all items in the lot, therefore, the activity cost is divided by the standard lot quantity. For item basis, the activity cost is charged per item for material and material overhead cost elements and per operation move for resource and resource overhead. For activity, the cost pool is allocated in proportion to the transactions affecting the item. For example, you might decide to allocate the costs of the manufacturing engineering department. You might decide that these costs represent $100 per item, $500 per manufacturing lot, or $12,500 per engineering change.

It lets you break down or aggregate traditional costs differently. For example, you can break down machine time into setup versus run time (and thus highlight potential opportunities for cost savings by a setup time reduction program). You will be able to see the same machine broken into setup and run components, or you can aggregate setup time for all resources for a product.

Click the Activity Costs button to set up the budgeted cost pool and corresponding number of transactions. This determines the cost per activity for each cost type.

NOTE

Oracle also has an activity-based costing product in the Business Intelligence Suite. That product is also useful for service-oriented companies that might not have a notion of product that they wish to cost. It has a more flexible notion of Cost Object to which cost will be applied.

Defining and Viewing Item Costs and Transaction Values

For all costing conventions there are some common basic activities. These include the ability to define the item costs, view the costs for an item, and review the transactions with their values under the prevailing cost conventions.

Defining Item Costs

Defining an item cost is done in three sections. You associate the item with the cost type, create the cost elements for the cost type, and define some details for the item–cost type combination.

Associating a Cost Type with an Item

The cost information is built from the Item Cost form. When you invoke the form, a Find window appears. From both the Find window and the Results window, you can click the New button. The Results window displays a list of Item Cost Types and their costs summarized to cost element level. When you click the New button, you are defining a new Item Cost Type association.

Defining Item Costs

When you create a new cost type association, you must click the Costs button to start to create the costs for the item in the new cost type. The Rolled Up costs will appear in the lower portion of the form. You can add user-defined costs in the top part of the form. As you add a cost element, the default sub-element and activity will appear. You can define the basis of item, lot, or activity for how the cost is accumulated. For lot basis, the cost is allocated over the standard manufacturing lot size. For activity basis, you must click the Activity tab and record the number of times the activity is expected to occur and the number of units of the item being costed that will be affected. This yields the proportion of the cost pool for this activity that accrues to the item being costed. You can define a rate per activity or an amount per item for this cost sub-element.

Defining Cost Details

You can define details and controls for the costs of this item under this cost type. You can declare that these costs are defaulted from the cost type definition. This means that the cost controls are defaulted and user-defined costs cannot be entered. There is a flag that defines the item is an Asset Item. This means that the cost for the item will be held in inventory. If the item is an expense item, its costs are recorded in Profit and Loss on receipt. An example of an expense item might be spares for the lathe. The Based on Cost Rollup flag determines if the costs will be overridden during cost rollup. Turning the flag off essentially freezes the costs. The flag is defaulted as Yes for items defined as Buy items in their item-planning attributes.

The manufacturing lot size to use for costing purposes can be set here. Costs accrued on a lot basis are divided by this quantity. An example of such a cost might be Setup costs. If left blank, it defaults to 1. The shrinkage rate defines the components wasted or reduced during assembly. The material used in those components still needs to be planned for and costed. For example, a supplier to Neptune manufactures ink cartridges for the printers. The technical spec for the ink well is 10 milliliters of ink. The ink well is overfilled to 11 milliliters in production to ensure that 99.5 percent of cartridges pass QA.

The cost information summarized to cost element is displayed here for reference, as well as the Sales and Cost of Goods Sold accounts that will be used by the Auto Accounting and Flexbuilder.

Viewing Item Costs

From the item details you can view a breakdown of the costs for the item and cost type. Many different views of the costs are available. The unit cost and percentage of the total cost are always displayed. An example of the Cost Summary form is shown in Figure 18-7. The cost sub-elements are summarized by Cost Element for the Frozen Standard Cost Type for Item AS18947.

Activity Costs Views

You can view cost-driving activities and the resultant costs for an item and cost type by department, level, and operation.

- **Activity by Department** Shows activity, department, and description

- **Activity by Level** Shows activity, costs at the current level, and costs at the previous level for the activities

- **Activity by Operation** Shows activity, operation sequence, and unit costs

- **Activity Summary** Shows each activity and a summary of its costs

Cost Element Views

The cost element views include analysis by activity, department, level, operation and sub-element.

- **Element by Activity** Shows element, activity, and activity name

- **Element by Department** Shows element name, department, and description

- **Element by Level** Shows element name, current level costs, and previous level

- **Element by Operation** Shows the element, operation sequence number, and unit cost

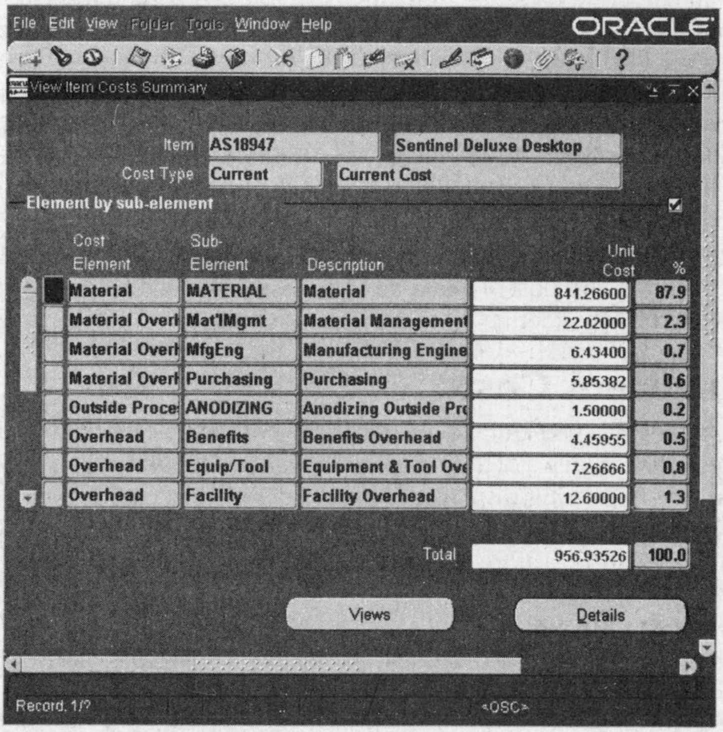

FIGURE 18-7. *A sample Cost Summary*

- **Element by Sub-Element**   Shows element, sub-element, and sub-element name

- **Element Summary**   Shows element and a summary of costs for that cost element

Sub-Element Views

The sub-element view includes analysis by activity, department, level, and operation. They are listed here:

- **Sub-Element by Activity**   Shows sub-element, activity, and description

- **Sub-Element by Department**   Shows sub-element, department, and department description

- **Sub-Element by Level**   Shows current level and previous level costs by sub-element

- **Sub-Element by Operation**   Shows sub-element, operation sequence number, and description

- **Sub-Element Summary**   Shows sub-element and description with a total cost for each sub-element

Summary Views

The operations summary view shows costs at the current and previous levels for each operation sequence. The Costs by Level view shows total costs for the Current level and Previews level. The Total Cost summary just shows the total cost.

Cost Details

When checking every view, you can click the Details button. The exact information shown in the Details window will depend on the view. You can see each element and sub-element, unit, basis factor, rate, and amount per unit and the resultant unit cost. For each activity cost, you can see the activity name, basis, and cost per resource unit.

Costed Bill of Materials

You can also review the costs of each item on the BOM for an item by reviewing the costed Bill of Material. To review the cost of components, navigate to the costed BOM. Click the Item Costs check box in the Display group and choose a Cost Type. You can review a costed bill down several levels. A Costing tab will appear in the results. Fields on the tab include Costing Quantity, Unit Cost, and Extended Cost.

Cost History

You can view how the costs of an item have changed over time and the transactions that caused them to change. Cost history is different for standard and average costing. The Standard Cost History form shows history from cost updates. The View Item Costs for Cost Group (or Item Cost History) is available only for average, FIFO, or LIFO. To review item costs, navigate to the Cost History form. You can search for a list of items for which you want to trace cost history. You can choose to inquire on the cost elements for this and previous levels, or you can choose to inquire on the transactions that moved the cost by clicking the History button. From the cost history page, you can see the transaction and inventory, costs, and quantities. You can choose to see the cost broken out by cost element by clicking the Details button. By clicking the Graph button, you can see the movement of costs plotted over time.

Mass Editing Costing Information

You can edit costing information en masse by navigating to the Request Submission form and choosing Mass Edit Costing Information. You can edit activity and shrinkage rates and create new costs from average purchase order, receipt, or invoice price. You can also apply percentage or absolute amount. To mass-edit costing information, select Cost | Mass Edit Cost Information.

Copying Costs

You can move costs from one cost type to any other cost type apart from the cost type being used for transactions in that organization; so you cannot move costs to Frozen Standard if you are using this costing method for the organization. You cannot move costs to the Average Cost Type if you are using this costing method. There are several concurrent requests that move costs between cost types and organizations. These are as follows:

- **Copy Item Costs**   Copies costs from one cost type to another

- **Copy Item Costs Across Organizations**   Copies the cost type to different organizations, where it can be separately maintained if necessary

- **Copy Overhead Costs**   Copies the overhead costs to the target cost type

- **Copy Resource Costs**   Copies resource costs to the target cost type

All these requests share the same parameters. You can merge new costing information with existing costs, update costs only where they are missing, or completely overwrite the target cost type with the source cost type. When moving costs between organizations, you can choose to create the same costing sub-element detail in the target organization, or you can summarize the sub-elements from the source organization into a single sub-element in the target.

Accounting for Value Movements

Within the costing system there are two main mechanisms for assigning accounts to value movements in costing. These are the category accounts for the inventory value and WIP Accounting Classes for the values in Work in Process.

Values in Inventory

As delivered, the e-business suite will value all inventory in a given subinventory using the same set of accounts for standard costing organizations and one set of accounts per costing organization for average costing. To define the accounting for a subinventory, navigate to the Subinventory form. You can implement product-line accounting by using the costing client extensions. Although you can set up category accounts for inventory and default WIP Accounting Classes for item categories, the defaulting of the accounts needs the client extension enabled. To define category accounts, navigate to the Category Accounts form. For standard costing organizations, the accounts are defined for a subinventory and item category. For average costing organizations, the accounts are defined for a cost group and a category. Accounts can be defined for Material, Material Overhead, Resource, Outside Processing, and Expense (for items that are expensed on receipt into this subinventory, for example, consumable floor stock such as wipes or lubricant).

Detailed examples on how to write client extensions to invoke product line accounting are found in the files CSTACHKS.pls and CSTACHKB.pls. These files are located in the Cost Management top, admin/sql directory. These are template packages for the writing of client extensions.

Values in WIP

Values in WIP are defined in WIP Accounting Classes. The default discrete accounting class is defined in the Discrete tab in the Organization Parameters form. You can further refine the assignment of the WIP Accounting Class by assigning it to item categories in the Default WIP Accounting Classes for item categories form. You can assign the WIP Accounting Classes for Discrete Jobs and Repetitive Schedules. In an average costing organization, you can refine your assignment to both item category and cost group. When defining a WIP Accounting Class for an average costing organization, you can also choose how the costs are relieved from WIP: to allocate a proportion of the material and resources actually used or an allocation of the values in the BOM and Routing. An example of the WIP Accounting Classes form is shown in Figure 18-8.

Other Account Assignments

You can also assign accounts to other entities that will influence the cost of an item and the value of its movements. These include the following:

- **Freight Carrier**   For shipping costs in interfacility movements.

- **Shipping Lanes**   Defined in the Shipping Networks form, hold the Transfer Credit for the shipper and Purchase Price Variance for the Receiver. It defines the intercompany payables and receivables accounts to allow intercompany balance sheet eliminations. It also defines the account that holds the value of inventory while in transit.

- **Receiving Dock**   Defined in the Receiving Parameters form, holds the value of inventory received but not delivered or put away in inventory.

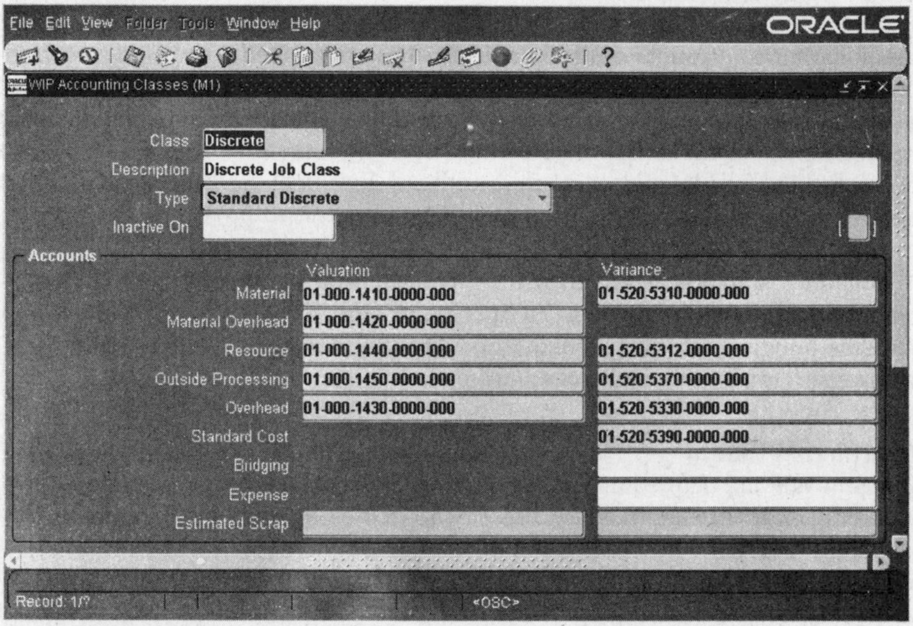

FIGURE 18-8. *WIP Accounting Class for a standard costing organization*

Viewing Transaction Costs

You can view the cost of the transactions from many subsystems. To review transaction costs, navigate to the View Transactions menu.

Receiving Transactions

From the Receiving Transaction form, you can choose to review the Header or the Transactions. When in the Transaction window, from the Tools menu you can review the accounting information: the transaction type, account, debit and credit amounts in the functional currency, the currency that the transaction was entered, the conversion rate, and the order and shipment that is the source of the transaction. You can also review these entries as T accounts and activity summary from the accounting detail.

Material Transaction Distributions

You can search for material transactions based on transaction information such as transaction dates, source type, source, transaction type, and quantity. You can also specify if you wish to see costed transactions. You can search based on item information such as item number, revision, description, and item category. You can search based on inventory information such as subinventory, locator, serial number, lot, and supplier's lot number. In the Results window, you can click the Distributions button.

The distributions show the date, account, transaction value, item, and transaction type, with the quantity and unit cost.

You can bypass the transactions and view the distributions directly from the Material Transaction Distributions. This gives the capability to search based on General Ledger (G/L) batch and account number, which are not available in the material transaction search.

WIP Value Summary

With the WIP Value Summary, you can review the value of the jobs and repetitive schedules that are completed, closed, or currently still in WIP. For each cost element, you can see the accounting code combination that it is held in G/L and the costs that have flowed into and out of the job. The outflow can be in costs relieved or variances. The net activity should be reflected in a balance in G/L. You can click the Distributions button to review all the distributions for the job. An example of the WIP Value Summary form is shown in Figure 18-9.

WIP Distributions   You can also review the WIP distributions directly by navigating to the WIP Transaction Distributions form. Search criteria include job, production line, assembly, distribution account, the item or Item category being transacted, the operation, department or resource performing the transaction, and the transaction identifier or type.

Processing Costs

It is the cost processor that picks up the uncosted material and resource transactions. It updates the item cost, if appropriate, and determines the value for the transaction. It is the central processing engine in the costing system. If the cost processor is not running, there are no updates made. It is a concurrent program that you can set up to run at intervals. There is a separate cost processor for periodic costing. The periodic costing processor uses acquisition costs, including additional charges such as freight, customs, and insurance, to value receipts and returns. The Periodic Cost processor is run manually, by submission.

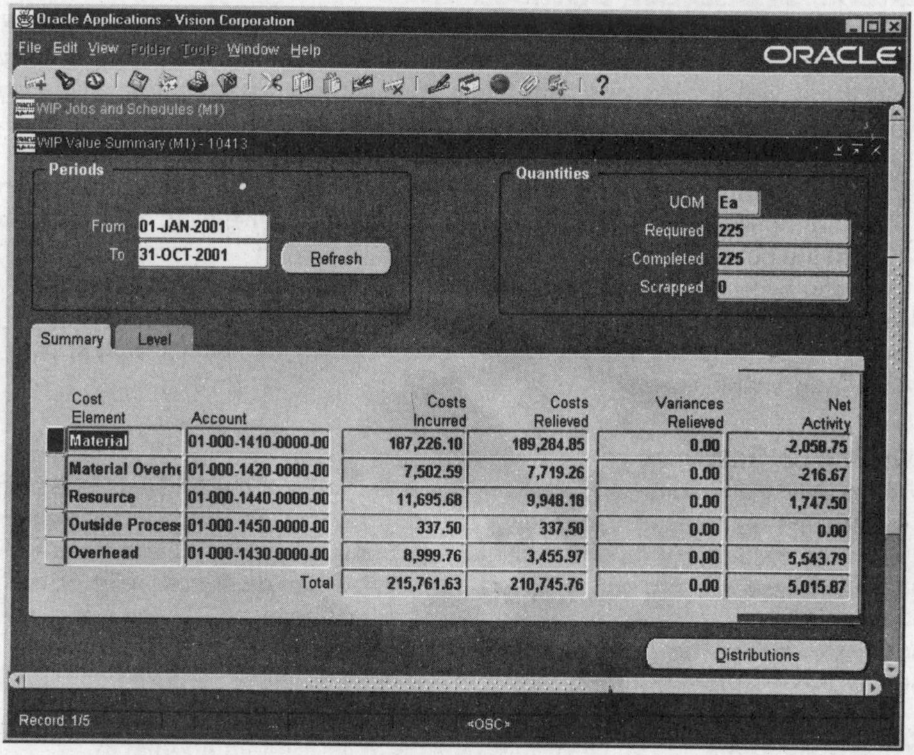

FIGURE 18-9. *Example of a WIP Value Summary form*

Costing Methods

The Oracle E-Business Suite is capable of supporting many costing methods and conventions. Costing methods include Standard and Average costing; cost layering methods of last in, first out (LIFO) and first in, first out (FIFO); and periodic methods of Periodic Average Cost and Periodic Incremental LIFO. The method you choose for your organization will depend on the legislative requirements of the country you are operating in, inflation in the economy, and the provision you wish to make for the replacement of goods sold.

Standard Costing

Standard costing values inventory and WIP at a standard value. All material transactions for an item are values at the standard cost. Any differences between the standard values flowing into manufacturing and the standard value of the material produced are recorded as variances in the period. Cost of sales in a period will be the standard cost of the goods sold plus any variances recorded in the period. You can model other costs in other cost types and update the frozen standard. Updating the frozen standard will cause a revaluation variance to be recorded when on-hand inventory is revalued.

Transactions processed from WIP can have an entry per cost element, or you can choose to combine the entries for cost elements that share the same account. For example, if the overhead and resource cost elements share the account manufacturing recoveries, you could choose to post both entries in one G/L transaction. The setting of the profile option would be CST: Account Summarization.

Setting Up for Standard Costing

Within the E-Business Suite you can create a new cost from the average purchase-order prices and average invoice prices for your buy items and roll them up into a pending cost type, using Bills, Routings, Resources, and Resource Rates. The pending cost can then be moved into a frozen standard cost.

Setting Up Manufacturing Resources   The costs of resource used in the conversion of material are set up under the Bill of Materials application. For each resource, you define the rate per unit for each cost type. For example, you might be currently charging at the rate of $30 an hour for Frozen Standard Cost and $40 an hour for a cost type of Contract Labor.

NOTE
If you are using standard costing, you need to set the profile options CST:Recognize Period Variance and CST:Require Scrap Account to Yes.

Rolling Up Standard Costs

When you roll up standard costs, you will define to a cost type for pending costs. To roll up the costs, navigate to the Assembly Cost Rollup concurrent request submission. You can run this process with or without reporting the output. You can also perform a cost rollup that will only be printed and will not affect the Item Costs in the database. You can roll up just a single level, or you can roll costs from the lowest level to the top. You can choose to rollup a single item, a range of items, or all items assigned to an item category. You can choose to roll up zero cost items only.

NOTE
Inactive items will be excluded from the rollup unless you roll up a specific inactive item.

Component items will be included if they are effective on the bill of material for the assembly. There can be many bills of material for an assembly: one primary and many BOM alternates. One of these BOM alternates is the one that is used for costing. You might have used and frozen a different BOM alternate when the costs were rolled up than your current manufacturing bill of material. The date against which their effectivity is measured is a parameter to the request. The rollup can include pending changes to those Bills of Material if you want. You can see the cost impact of pending changes in product structures. You can also include items, bills, and routings that are currently in engineering to check if target costs are being met. You can specify the BOM and routing alternates to use in this cost rollup.

If you choose to print a report with the cost rollup, you can choose to see the quantities of component parts level by level or as a total for the assembly. You can also choose to include or exclude the sub-element detail for a more consolidated report.

NOTE
You can include the operations associated with a component that is of the item type phantom. You need to set the BOM parameters. Use Phantom Routings and Inherit Phantom Operation Sequence. Costs for the phantom are reported at the level of its parent in the rollup structure.

Updating Standard Costs

When costs have been created against a pending cost type, you can review the pending changes and then apply those new costs to the frozen standard to revalue inventory on hand, in transit, and on the shop floor. When the costs are updated, an entry is also made in the cost history table to allow a full audit of the changes made to inventory balances.

Reviewing Pending Cost Adjustments   This report shows the effect on inventory, in-transit, and WIP of changing the costs from the current frozen standard to the cost type you supply as a parameter. To review pending cost adjustments, navigate to the Pending Cost Adjustments report. You can review changes for item costs, or you can include changes to resource and overhead rates.

Updating Costs   When updating the standard cost, you create a new entry for the frozen cost type and revalue on-hand, in-transit, and WIP inventories. The changes in value are posted to a revaluation account in G/L specified in a parameter to the report. Costs can be shared between facilities, so a change in the costs in a cost master organization will be reflected in the inventory values of all child organizations.

NOTE
The cost update will not run until Job Close, Period Close, or G/L Transfer processes are running. There will be conflict in having some of the transactions valued at the prior value at some at the new value.

To update standard costs, navigate to the Update Standard Cost concurrent submission. This report gives you the option to save the quantities and costs involved in the update and report on it later. There is a report set defined, with a report for On-Hand, In-Transit, and WIP. To run the report set, navigate to Report Standard Cost Adjustments.

Viewing Standard Costs History   You can view the updates from a cost update online by navigating to View Cost History form. All cost updates, whether from the Define Item Cost form or the Cost Update Concurrent program, are displayed in this form. If you are currently logged in to the costing master organization, you can view the cost information for the costing organization and all its children organizations. If you are logged in to a child organization, you can see information for only that organization. You can search based on a specific item and date combination, or you can search for a specific cost update run.

In the search results, you can see the item, date, and unit cost for each item cost and a description of the update. There are tabs that display the cost element break-down of the cost, the adjustment quantity for on hand, in-transit, and WIP, and the adjustment values.

Cost Flows in Standard Costing

The movement of material and flow of resources at an agreed engineering standard allow management to trap the differences between the expected flow of material and resources and the actual flow, and report the difference in the accounts. This is variance accounting. The variances identified under standard costing conventions in the E-Business Suite are as follows.

Purchase-Price Variance Purchase-price variance is the difference between the standard cost of the item and the value received. The received value will by default be the value on the purchase order. The transactions will be as shown here:

Inventory in Receiving	
Debit	**Credit**
@ Standard	
Goods Received Not Invoiced Accrual	
Debit	**Credit**
	@ Received Value
Purchase Price Variance	
Debit	**Credit**
Standard - Received Value	

Invoice-Price Variance Invoice-price variance is the difference between the received value and the invoiced value match in Oracle Payables. The transactions will be as follows:

Goods Received Not Invoiced Accrual	
Debit	**Credit**
@ Received Value	
Accounts Payable	
Debit	**Credit**
	@ Invoiced Value
Invoice Price Variance	
Debit	**Credit**
Invoiced - Received Value	

Cycle-Count Adjustments The standard cost of any quantity adjusted from or to on-hand balances during cycle count adjustments is charged or credited to cycle count adjustments.

Inventory	
Debit	**Credit**
Found Qty @ Standard	Lost Qty @ Standard
Cycle Count Adjustments	
Debit	**Credit**
Lost Qty @ Standard	Found Qty @ Standard

Material-Usage Variance   The standard cost of the differences in material quantities consumed versus quantities defined in the BOM for the manufacture of an assembly is charged or credited to material-usage variance. The transactions are as follows.

■ Material Issue

WIP Accounting Class Material Value	
Debit	**Credit**
Issue Qty @ Standard	
Material Usage Variance	
Debit	**Credit**
	Issue Qty @ Standard

■ Assembly Completion

WIP Accounting Class Material Value	
Debit	**Credit**
	Completed Qty @ Standard
Subinventory Finished Goods Material Account	
Debit	**Credit**
Completed QTY @ Standard	

■ Job Closure

WIP Accounting Class Material Value	
Debit	**Credit**
	Issued Material - Relieved Material @ Standard
Material Usage Variance	
Debit	**Credit**
Issued Material - Relieved Material @ Standard	

Move-Efficiency Variance   For overheads that are applied on move transactions, you can cause a variance by altering the operations in the routing from that used to calculate the standard cost. If you do this, a move-efficiency variance will occur. For example, if you had constructed the routing in the costed bill to include four operations, but through clever manufacturing cell design, the routing used in production has only three operations, a positive variance will be recorded on job completion. The transactions will be as follows:

■ Move Transaction

Overhead Recoveries Account	
Debit	**Credit**
	Overheads Charged @ Standard
WIP Accounting Class Overhead Value	
Debit	**Credit**
Overheads Charged @ Standard	

■ WIP Assemblies

WIP Accounting Class Overhead Value	
Debit	**Credit**
	Assembly Overhead Costs @ Standard
Subinventory Overhead Valuation Account	
Debit	**Credit**
Assembly Overhead Costs @ Standard	

■ Job Closure

WIP Accounting Class Overhead Value	
Debit	**Credit**
	Resources Consumed - Resources Relieved @ Standard
WIP Move Efficiencies	
Debit	**Credit**
Resources Consumed - Resources Relieved @ Standard	

Resource-Efficiency Variance   Resource-efficiency variances are created by more or less resources being charged to the job than are required on the routing used to arrive at the standard cost. For example, if the routing had required the printed circuit board to be glued into place, but the current design has press studs to secure them, then reduction in assembly time would be reflected as a positive resource-efficiency variance. You can generate an efficiency variance by charging more or less cost to the job, but you can also generate rate variance by charging resources with a different rate. There is a Standard Rate check box on the resource. If you check this box, resources will be charged to the job at standard rate. If you uncheck the box, you will be required to enter a rate for internal resources. Outside processing rates will be derived from the purchase order. Differences between the rates charged and standard rates will be charged to resource-rate variance.

NOTE
Rate and efficiency variances are reported in this account as the user can apply actual rates to the resource transactions on entry.

The transactions would be as follows:

Resource Recoveries	
Debit	**Credit**
	Actual Units @ standard (or actual) rate

■   Rate and Account defined in BOM Resources.

WIP Accounting Class Resource Value	
Debit	**Credit**
Actual Units @ Standard (or Actual) rate	

Revaluation Variance   The revaluation variance is caused when the standard cost of an item with quantities on hand or in transit is changed. For example, if the cost of Xenium III processors drops due to the introduction of the Xenium Starfire V, the value of inventory on hand will fall, causing a negative revaluation variance but a positive purchase price variance on new receipts. At the same time, autoplacement machinery needs circuit boards to be manually reseated after the first five placements. This has been reflected in a new cost rollup, causing a positive revaluation variance but negative resource efficiency variances. The revaluation account is defined in the Standard Cost Update Parameters. The in-transit valuation account is defined in the Interorg Parameters available from the Tools | Inventory Parameters form. The transactions are as follows:

Subinventory Valuation Accounts	
Debit	**Credit**
Increase in Value	Decrease in Value
In-Transit Valuation	
Debit	**Credit**
Increase in Value	Decrease in Value
Revaluation Variance	
Debit	**Credit**
Decrease in Value	Increase in Value

Average Costing

Average costing is a costing convention that updates the cost of an item with each receipt. It updates the cost to be the average of the quantity on hand and the previous average and the quantity received at the new price. Issues are made from inventory at the average price ruling at the time the material is issued. Receipts can be purchase-order receipts or WIP completions. For WIP completions, the receipt value is the material resource and overheads charged to the job at average cost.

NOTE
Average costing does not apply to repetitive scheduled items. If the cost conventions of the organization are average cost, you cannot define repetitive schedules in that organization.

Advantages of average-costing mechanisms are that any increase or decrease in price, quantity, or material and resources needed to manufacture an item are reflected against the item automatically. This essentially revalues quantities on hand and in transit with each receipt.

NOTE
Average costs cannot be shared among organizations. Each item has an average cost within each facility.

Under standard costing conventions, usage and price variances would be recorded as period costs, but not reflected against the items being manufactured. This has to be weighed against the control capability that standard costing gives.

Note that the following transaction processors should be run in online mode if you are using average costs:

- TP:INV:Transaction Processing Mode profile
- TP:WIP:Completion Transactions Form
- TP:WIP:Material Transactions Form
- TP:WIP:Move Transaction
- TP:WIP:Operation Backflush Setup
- TP:WIP:Shop Floor Material Processing

Enabling an Organization for Average Costing

To enable average costing in an organization, navigate to the Organization Parameters form in the Inventory Setup menu and set the Cost Method. You need to define cost type that resource rates can be defined against in this organization.

Cost Flows in Average Costing

The following is an analysis of the way costs flow through the organization when it is operating under average-costing convention. The same events are described, but inventory movements in and of themselves are revaluing inventory. There is capability to trap variances, but the flow of cost is not dictated by an agreed engineering and costing standard. Items may be costed higher than expected, and those costs are held in inventory until product ships and costs flow into costs of goods sold.

Labor Charges   You can perform labor time entries manually through the resource transactions, or you can backflush the resource transactions. For manual transactions, the rates can be defaulted from either the employee rates or from the resource rates associated to the cost type on the resource definition in BOM.

■ Resources Charged at Standard

WIP Accounting Class Resource Account	
Debit	**Credit**
Resource Charged @ Standard	
Resource Recovery Account	
Debit	**Credit**
	Resource Charged @ Standard

■ Resources Charged at Actual

You can choose to charge the job with the actual rates and units, or you can set Autocharge to manual, recognizing the rate variance immediately. In the latter case, the entries are as follows:

Resource WIP Accounting Class Resource Account	
Debit	**Credit**
Resource Charged @ Standard	
Labor Rate Variance	
Debit	**Credit**
Resource Charged @ Actual - Standard	Resource Charged @ Actual - Standard
Resource Recovery Account	
Debit	**Credit**
	Resource Charged @ Actual

Overhead Charges   For overheads that are based on resource units or resource value, the value charged to WIP will be based on the actual resource units and value used.

WIP Accounting Class Overhead Account	
Debit	**Credit**
Actual Overheads Charged @ Standard Charge Basis Rate	
Overhead Recoveries Account	
Debit	**Credit**
	Actual Overheads Charged @ Standard Charge Basis Rate

Component Issues   Components issued to the job will be valued at the average cost ruling at the time of the transaction. If a component item is issued to a job in several transactions, it is possible for them all to have different costs. The transactions would be as follows:

WIP Accounting Class Material Account	
Debit	**Credit**
Actual Units @ Current Average	
Subinventory Material Account	
Debit	**Credit**
	Actual Units @ Current Average

Material Overhead Charges   Material overhead is charged to the job according to the basis and overhead rate prevailing at the time. The rates may be changed at any time, but they will affect only future transactions and have no immediate effect on the item's costs. Material overheads are recovered on completion and applied to finished assemblies. They are not applied to WIP. The transactions would be as follows:

Inventory Organization Material Overhead Account	
Debit	**Credit**
Actual Units @ Current Basis and Basis Rate	
Material Overhead Recoveries	
Debit	**Credit**
	Actual Units @ Current Basis and Basis Rate

Scrap Charges   There is an entry in the WIP Parameters that defines if a scrap account is required. The value of the assemblies up to the operation at which they are scrapped is moved to the scrap account from the elemental costs. If the scrap account is not defined for the assemblies, the costs follow the assembly into inventory. Even if you don't require a scrap account, you can optionally enter one, which will relieve cost from the job at that point.

■   Scrap Account Required

Elemental Cost Accounts	
Debit	**Credit**
	Proportion of Costs to Current Operation
Scrap Account	
Debit	**Credit**
Cost to Current Operation	

■   Scrap Account not Required

The scrap value remains against the cost elements. No accounting is performed.

Assembly Completions   The values relieved from WIP on assembly completion depend on the value set in the Completion Cost Source on the WIP Parameters and defaulted down to the WIP Accounting Class. The Completion Cost Source is either user-defined or system-calculated. User-defined relieves costs according to the cost elements of a cost type that you need to specify. Balances remaining at the end of the job are moved to inventory or variance accounts in the Job Closure transaction.

If you choose a Completion Cost Source of System Calculated, it must be further refined to be based on actual or standard resources. For actual resources, a proportion of the costs of the job are moved to inventory based on the quantity moved as a proportion of the quantity in the job. If you choose standard resources, resource costs are relieved from the job based on the routing. The transactions will be as follows:

Inventory Organization Cost Element Valuation Accounts	
Debit	**Credit**
Resource Value from Routings	
WIP Accounting Class Cost Element Valuation Accounts	
Debit	**Credit**
	Resource Value from Routings

On completion the inventory is revalued. The formula for the revaluation is as follows:

New Average = (Qty on Hand × Previous Average + Completion Qty × Completion Cost) / (Qty on Hand + Completion Qty)

If you check the Final Completions flag, the final completion option can be set. If you choose a final completion option of Enabled, any balances remaining in the job will be spread over the quantity being completed if such balances are positive. If such balances are negative, you have consumed less material and resource than expected to produce the assemblies. The positive variances that this represents will not follow the items into inventory but will be reported in Profit and Loss. If you choose a final completion option of Disabled, the completions are costed according to the costing source of the WIP Accounting Class.

Returns from inventory to WIP are valued at the average completion value for assemblies on the job being returned to.

Job Closures and Variance Calculations   There are many ways to leave costs in the job when all pending completions have been done.

- If the completions from the job were not done as final completions.

- If there were more completions from the job than the scheduled quantity and you are relieving resources based on standard values.

- A transaction was posted after all completions were performed.

- The job was cancelled with value accrued.

Positive job balances follow the assemblies into inventory. Negative job balances are reported in the variance accounts defined in the WIP Accounting Class.

WIP Accounting Class Variance Accounts	
Debit	**Credit**
Negative job balances	Positive job balances
WIP Accounting Class Cost Element Accounts	
Debit	**Credit**
	Negative job balances
Completion Subinventory Cost Element Accounts	
Debit	**Credit**
Positive job balances	

Maintaining Average Costs

You can directly maintain the average cost of an item by navigating to the Update Average Costs form. You can enter a new average cost and have the system allocate the cost increase at the element level, or you can maintain the costs at the element level manually. You can also update item costs by a percentage. Costing also allows you to specify a change to the value of inventory on hand and have that drive a change in the average cost of those items. This might happen with an audit specifying a new value or material moving into an obsolescent stage in its lifecycle. The potential change to the value of the material is shown for each change. The average cost is also updated from many transactions:

- **Invoice Price Variance Application**   You can apply invoice price variance back to items by navigating to the Transfer Invoice Price Variance to Inventory concurrent submission. This is one piece of the value movement that is not captured in a material movement and will not be reflected in the item's average cost unless this process is run.

- **Purchase Order Receipts**   These are valued at PO-line shipment values.

- **Inter Organization Receipts**   These are valued at cost from the sending organization plus freight and transfer credit.

- **Returns to Vendor**   These are valued at original PO receipt value.

Cost Layering Methods

With Release 11.i of the E-Business Suite, Oracle introduced LIFO and FIFO costing methods. These methods rely on keeping costs not only at the item and warehouse level, but also at the cost layer. The stack of receipts may be consumed from the top (LIFO) or the bottom (FIFO). The cost layer is a quantity of inventory at the same received cost. An illustration of the cost layers moving into and out of inventory value is shown in Figure 18-10.

FIFO/LIFO costing conventions are well accepted within Generally Accepted Accounting Principles (GAAP). FIFO costing conventions will tend to value inventory higher and report profits higher in times of rising prices. Cost of sales will provide for the oldest purchase prices. It might not reflect the replacement cost of the inventory sold. LIFO costing conventions will tend to value inventory lower and report profits lower in times of rising prices. Cost of sales will provide for the most recent purchase prices. It might more closely reflect replacement cost of the inventory sold. A small data model of the structure of cost layers is shown in Figure 18-11.

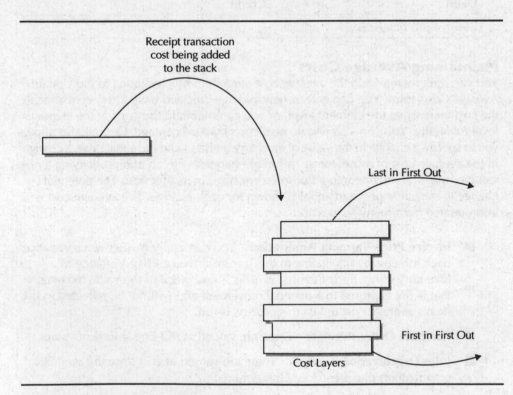

FIGURE 18-10. *Stack of cost layers*

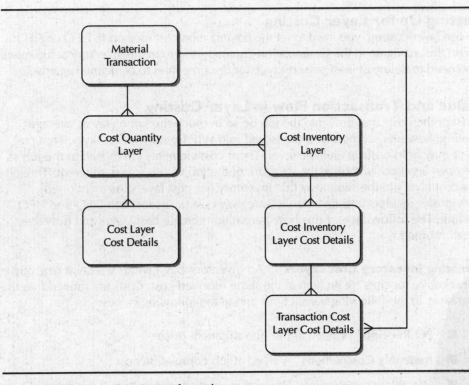

FIGURE 18-11. *Structure of cost layers*

Every purchase or work in process receipt transaction causes a cost layer to be created. Some transactions will not cause a cost layer to be created. For example, a Miscellaneous Receipt transaction would be an inventory layer at the same cost layer as the previous PO receipt. The costs of the transaction at an element level are held in the Cost Layer Cost Details. The elemental breakdown of the inventory layer within the cost layer are held in the Cost Inventory Layer Cost Details. A transaction that consumes part of a cost layer has the cost layer consumed in the transaction cost layer cost details.

You cannot share LIFO/FIFO costs with other organizations, and you cannot apply LIFO/FIFO costing conventions to a repetitive schedule. If the costing convention of a facility is a layer cost type, you cannot create repetitive schedules in that organization.

The system maintains cost layers within WIP. As material is issued to a job, it is issued to its own cost layer.

Setting Up for Layer Costing

To use layer costing, you need to set the organization cost method to LIFO or FIFO. To do this, navigate to the Organization Parameters form in the inventory Setup menu. You need to define at least one cost type for resource rates to be defined against.

Value and Transaction Flow in Layer Costing

Most of the costs that flow into the job do so in much the same way as average costing; however, components are issued into WIP from their cost layer. That cost layer may hold costs at element level. These cost elements are moved to the job as previous level costs, though the structure of the Job values is very different. The job has cost layers in the same way that inventory has cost layers. As mentioned previously, receipts into inventory create new cost layers for both LIFO and FIFO costing. The following explains how transactions create cost layers and how they are consumed.

Creating Inventory Cost Layers   An inventory cost layer is a receipt or group of consecutive receipts for an item at the same received cost. Costs are moved into the cost layer in the following transactions and at the following values:

- **PO Receipts**   Valued at PO-line shipment price

- **Assembly Completions**   Valued at job completion cost

- **Miscellaneous Receipts**   Valued at user-entered cost, or if not entered, at the latest received cost

- **Inter-Org Transfers**   Valued at the cost from the shipping organization, plus freight plus transfer credit

- **WIP Component Returns**   Valued at the last layer issued to the job, irrespective of LIFO or FIFO cost basis

- **Positive Inventory Adjustments**   Valued at the latest received cost

- **RMA Receipts**   Valued at latest received cost

Cost layers are consumed when the inventory quantity in them is issued, adjusted, sold, or returned to a vendor.

Creating WIP Cost Layers   A WIP cost layer is a component issue to the job. The material issued to the job is held as a stack of cost layers. Each cost layer keeps references back to the inventory layer from which it was issued. A component issue transaction can consume many inventory cost layers.

Consuming WIP Cost Layers   When an assembly is completed, the material cost is relieved from WIP. The Costs are taken from the top (LIFO) or bottom (FIFO) of the stack of Inventory Cost Layers for earliest (FIFO) or latest (LIFO) WIP cost layer. The component cost computation for assembly completions uses the same algorithm as for average costing.

View Transaction Cost Layers

You can view all the cost layers that make up an item's layered cost. Navigate to the View Transaction Layer Cost form in the View Transactions menu. You can search by transaction dates, item, and transaction source. The Results window shows two regions. The first is a list of items and quantities. The second is a set of cost layers. The cost layers block shows the quantity and cost in the cost layer and the breakdown by cost element.

Updating Layer Costs

You can directly update the cost of a layer. Navigate to the Update Layer Cost form. An example of a cost layer for item AS62444 is shown in Figure 18-12. It shows a downward revision of the cost from $153–$140 for layer 1036, which has 25 units.

You can update the cost of a particular layer. Navigate to the Layer Cost Update form. You must specify the date for the transaction and the account for the revaluation in the same way as other cost conventions. When you specify the item to be updated, you must also specify the layer that you are updating. Cost updates can be made by new cost, percentage change, or adjustment amount. The change in value is apportioned among the cost elements in proportion to their current values. The accounts used to hold those values is displayed in the Accounts tab and can be overridden.

Periodic Costing

The Oracle E-Business Suite also offers two periodic costing methods. These are methods for calculating a cost for the items from the transactions that have happened in a costing period. Costs are based on invoice prices or order prices for goods delivered but not yet invoiced in the period. Acquisition costs such as freight can be matched to the receipts. Costs are averaged for the entire period rather than on a transaction-by-transaction basis. Overheads are fully absorbed for the period because the cost pool to be applied is known. Therefore, the rate-per-basis unit can be determined and applied.

Costing requires that there is also a perpetual cost available to value transactions as they occur. You might want to use the periodic costs to set standards for your organization. In some countries, such as Italy, periodic costing is a legal requirement. For this reason, periodic costing is very focused on external reporting. Periodic costs can be shared between inventory organizations and costs groups that are part of the same legal entity.

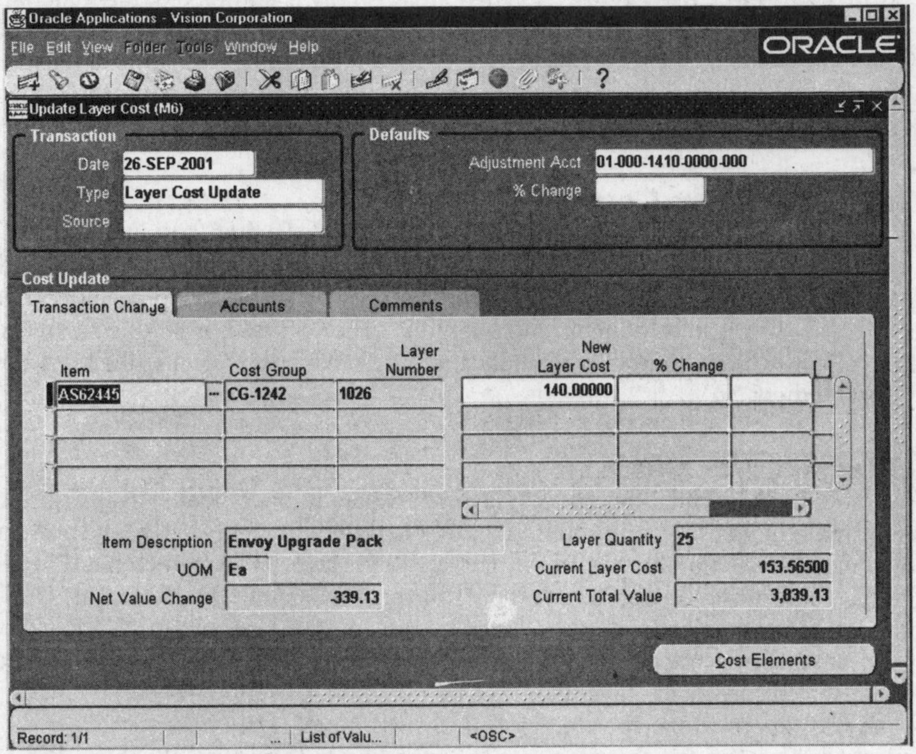

FIGURE 18-12. *Layer Cost update*

There are some restrictions for using periodic costs:

■ Cost types must be multi-org and not enabled for update.

■ The cost type for the periodic rates must be multi-org and updateable.

■ The cost group must have only one item master organization.

■ Organization cost groups can have only one legal entity.

Much of the functionality for periodic costing is centered around external reporting. This means that the legal and ownership organization groupings of cost group and legal entity play a much bigger role.

Important Concepts

There are some important concepts to introduce to let you understand how periodic costs are calculated. These are centered around whether the transaction has a value or whether the value is derived from elsewhere and where the organizational boundry is for deriving periodic costs.

Cost-Owned Transactions   These transactions have their own cost. Cost-owned transactions include the following:

- PO receipt
- WIP completion
- WIP labor/resource

Cost-Derived Transactions   These transactions do not have their own costs. The average cost for these transactions will be computed. Cost-derived transactions include the following:

- Material issues
- Returns to WIP
- Returns to vendor

Organization Cost Group   This is a group of organizations that share the same set of periodic costs. Transactions will be accumulated across all the member organizations to arrive at average costs.

Periodic Average Cost

Periodic average cost accumulates the value of inventory at the previous periodic average cost and adds it to the sum of all cost-owned transactions. It divides this value by the quantity in inventory at the start of the costing period plus the quantity received in the period. This is the average cost that all cost-derived transactions are valued at for the period.

Periodic Incremental LIFO

Periodic Incremental LIFO costing accumulates the value of all cost-owned transactions and divides it by the quantity received in the period. This is the average cost that all derived transactions are valued at for the period. If there is a quantity left in inventory at the end of the period, a cost layer is created for the period. The following period, the same process takes place. Only if the quantity issued on derived cost transactions exceeds the quantity of owned cost transactions received will prior periods cost layers be consumed. In this manner, the most recent costs are passed to costs of sale and the value of inventory is based on the oldest receipt costs.

Setup for Periodic Costing

There are a number of steps to set up an organization for periodic reporting. There is a separate setup menu for Periodic Costing, under the main Periodic Costing menu.

- **Set Up Organization Cost Groups** Set up an organization cost group and associate it with both a legal entity and an item master organization. To define cost group organizations navigate to the Setup menu underneath the Periodic Costing menu and open the Organization Cost Groups form.

- **Set Up Cost types and Periodic Rates Cost Type** This is done from the Cost Types definition form in the Costing Setup menu.

- **Associate Cost Types to Legal Entities** This is done from the Periodic Cost Setup menu.

- **Set the Accounting Options for the Cost Type Association** From here you can define whether the cost type should create accounting entries and the set of standard accounting rules it should follow. This is currently limited to U.S. Generally Accepted Accounting Principles (GAAP) and Brazilian Periodic Average Cost. This is done by clicking the Accounting Options button from the Cost Type to Legal Entity Associations form.

- **Associate Accounts with Item Categories within a Legal Entity Cost Group** For each costing item category, you can define a set of accounts with the organization cost group. Each organization cost group is defined within a legal entity.

Procedures for Periodic Costing

The following are the procedures for using periodic costs in an organization. The collection, the cost processor, and the Create Distributions run for a combination of legal entity, cost type, period, and cost group.

Collecting Costs To collect costs, navigate to Periodic Acquisition Cost concurrent submission from the Periodic Cost menu. The cost collection engine sums the invoiced value, freight and special charges, and nonrecoverable taxes. The purchase-order price is used where no invoices have been matched to the receipt at period end.

You can rerun the collection if invoices are matched at a later time. The received quantities are frozen as at period end.

Calculating Average Costs   To calculate the average cost for the period, submit the Periodic Cost Processor from the Periodic Cost menu. The process can calculate Periodic LIFO and Periodic Average Costs.

Creating Subledger Distributions   Entries are made into the manufacturing subledger if the accounting option Post to G/L is set to Yes. To create accounting entries according for the Organization and Cost Type, navigate to the Periodic Cost Distributions Processor in the Periodic Cost menu. You pass transactions valued at periodic cost by submitting the Transfer Periodic Cost Distributions to G/L concurrent request.

Reporting on Periodic Costs and Valuations   There are a number of reports that allow you to review the costs and valuation of inventory at periodic cost. These are listed here:

- **Periodic Acquisition Cost Report**   Shows the acquisition cost of each receipt quantity in the period.

- **Periodic Incremental LIFO Valuation Report**   Shows the LIFO valuation for each item reported in the inventory balance in G/L. It is a very useful report for backing up year-end accounts.

- **Periodic Accrual Reconciliation Report**   Shows all the receiving transactions that are in the goods received accrual.

- **Periodic Accrual Write-Off Report**   Shows all the receipt transactions for which accrual has been written off.

- **Periodic Inventory Valuation Report**   Shows the periodic average cost of each item in inventory.

- **Periodic WIP Value Report**   Shows the value of jobs in the organization cost group at the end of the period.

- **Periodic Material and Receiving Distributions Reports**   Show the periodic cost of the material and receiving transactions both in summary and detail by account, account and item, or item and account.

- **Periodic WIP Distributions Reports**   Show the periodic cost of WIP transactions, both in summary and detail.

Period Close

Period close establishes closing values for each subinventory, transfers the value of transactions to G/L, and prevents transactions being posted to G/L for a period for which a trial balance has been struck. Costing and General Ledger share the same period definitions. A batch reference is created for the transactions created in the Inventory and WIP systems when they are transferred to General Ledger. This enables drill back from General Ledger to the Manufacturing Subledgers.

When you close a period, transactions will no longer be able to be posted to that period. You should ensure that there are no pending transactions in any of the following interfaces:

- Inventory and WIP Transaction

- Cost Management Cost

You should also ensure that all shipped Order Management orders are processed through inventory.

To close a transfer transactions to G/L, navigate to the Accounting Close Cycle menu and submit the Transfer to G/L concurrent submission. To close the period, navigate to the Inventory Accounting Period Close form. An example of this form with the closing values for June 1998 is shown in Figure 18-13.

When you have completed all the transfers, it is good practice to reconcile the inventory values in G/L with the inventory valuation from the costing system. It would be very good practice to ensure that any manual adjustments that you need to make to inventory balances in G/L do not go through the same accounts as that posted to from the costing system. You can use the summary account capability in G/L to aggregate the account reserved for automatic posting and any accounts used for adjustments. Reports that can be used for reconciliation include

- Inventory Value

- Period Close Summary

- Material Account Distribution Detail

- Material Account Distribution Summary

If you are using average costing conventions within an organization, and therefore store all subledger balances in the same set of accounts, you can use the Inventory Subledger Report.

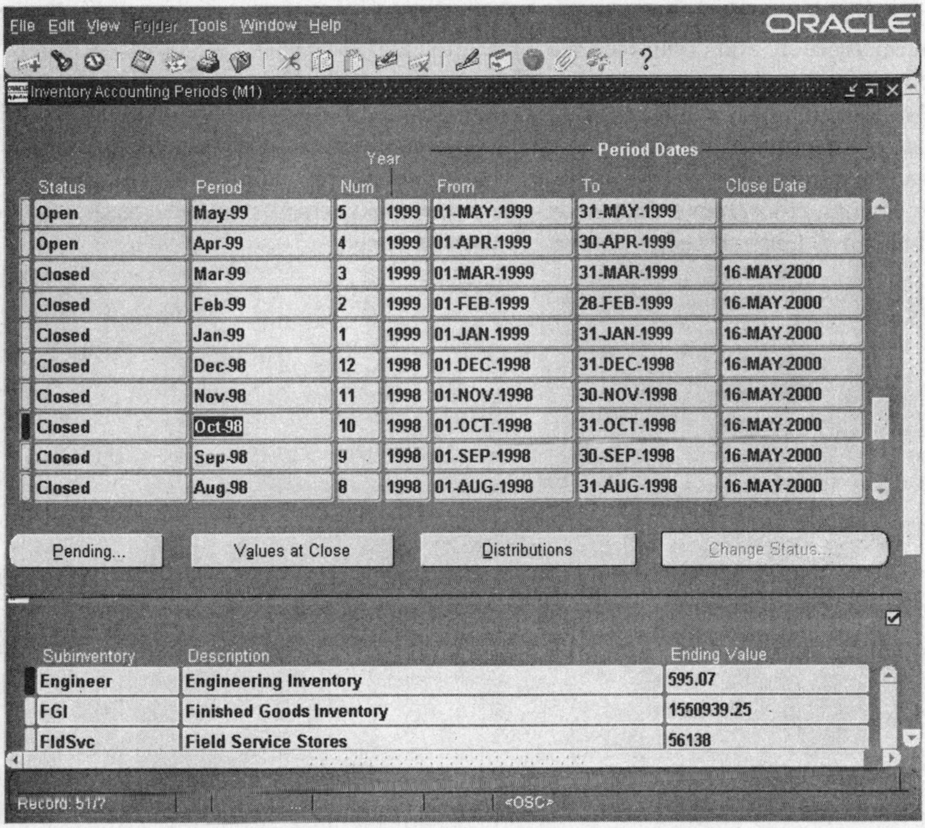

FIGURE 18-13. *Period Close with Subinventory values*

Summary

This chapter covered the organization structures for cost information and the structure of the item costs themselves. It reviewed the attributes in the item definition that influence costing and learned how to efficiently update large volumes of cost data.

This chapter showed you how accounts are assigned to inventory and WIP balances and where variances are charged. It examined the process of creating and editing costs and the many ways of viewing the item cost information. And it reviewed the ways that you can see transaction values flow through the organization.

This chapter examined the main costing methods of standard, average, layer, and periodic and what each cost type is best used for. Standard costing gives the best accountability and control for manufacturing and purchasing but does not reflect changes in purchase prices or manufacturing capability into inventory valuation. Average costing gives an arguably more accurate statement of inventory valuation but less accountability for any margin variation. Periodic costing is a fiscal view of inventory valuation that is mandated in some countries.

Finally, this chapter looked at how to close the period, post the transactions through to General Ledger, and reconcile the results.

CHAPTER
19

Quality Management

n this highly competitive world, quality is a very important component in the strategy of any enterprise. It is one of the three most important drivers of any business, called collectively as the QCD (Quality, Cost, Delivery) parameters. Oracle Quality provides sophisticated support for capturing data, analyzing data, and finally implementing corrective actions when quality problems arise.

This chapter is broadly organized into two topics: data collection and data analysis. All the data-collection features such as collection plans, collection elements, and specifications are covered in the first part. The data-collection part also talks about quality actions, which help you in putting short-term solutions in place. The latter part of the chapter talks about the various features that allow you to analyze the data that is collected.

Collection Elements

Collection plans and collection elements constitute the data-collection mechanism of Oracle Quality. Collection elements are the basic building blocks of collection plans (covered in the "Collection Plans" section later in this chapter), the data structures that you use to collect quality results. If you are familiar with tabulating data, you can imagine the collection plan to be the table and each column in the table to be a collection element.

Before you can collect data with Oracle Quality, you must first create a collection plan. You begin by creating collection elements, which define the characteristics of the product or process that you want to monitor, record, and analyze. You can create an unlimited number of your own collection elements (which are referred to as user-defined collection elements), or you can use any of the predefined collection elements.

To save you time and to automate data entry, Oracle Quality provides you with several predefined collection elements that are available on a list of values when you set up collection plans.

NOTE
If you are collecting quality data during transactions, and your collection plan uses predefined collection elements that also are on the parent form, their values are automatically entered for you.

Collection-Element Types

Collection elements are categorized by type for easy searching and reporting. You assign collection-element types to collection elements when you define them.

You can create your own collection-element types and add them to collection plans, or you can use any of Quality's predefined collection-element types. If you create your own collection-element types, you must define them before you define collection elements. There are three predefined collection-element types: attribute, variable, and reference information.

Attribute Collection-Element Type

Attributes are data that represent discrete characteristics, for example, characteristics of an object, or the possible outcomes of an experiment. The collection-element type attribute identifies collection elements with these characteristics. These collection elements often have a limited list of acceptable values.

Variable Collection-Element Type

The Collection-element type variable identifies collection elements that are used for numeric measurements. They often have a range of acceptable values or specification limits expressed as preferred values with an acceptable degree of tolerance.

Reference Information Collection-Element Type

The collection-element type reference information identifies collection elements that reference common objects defined in Oracle applications.

Defining Collection-Element Types

In addition to the three predefined types—attribute, variable, and reference information—you can create your own collection-element types in the Collection-Element Type QuickCodes window. You specify the name, meaning, description, and effective dates and enable the collection-element type. If you do not check this box, the collection-element type will not appear on the list of values when you define collection elements. You can disable, but you cannot delete, collection-element types. Disabled collection-element types are not available for future assignments. Existing collection elements that use the disabled type will still continue to work properly.

Defining Collection Elements

You can define an unlimited number of collection elements, which you can then add to collection plans to determine what quality results data will be collected and tracked. You can add, change, and delete collection elements as your requirements change.

You define new collection elements in the Collection Elements form. The collection element name can contain alphanumeric characters, spaces, underscores (_), and single quotation marks (').

NOTE
There are some reserved words that are used by Oracle Quality for column names in collection plans. For example, NAME, OCCURRENCE, ORGANIZATION_ID, and CREATED_BY are all reserved words and cannot be used as collection element names. A complete list of the reserved words can be found in the product documentation.

The Enabled check box activates the collection element. Only enabled collection elements can be added to collection plans and specifications. The collection-element type helps in searching and reporting. The prompt is displayed as the name of the collection element field while entering quality results. Prompts also become the column headings on reports and online inquiries. The default prompt is the name of the collection element, but you can overwrite it. Hints appear in the message line as the user enters quality results. Figure 19-1 shows the Collection Elements form.

The available data types are numeric, character, and date. You can select any data type; however, it's not updateable. The Mandatory check box indicates if a value must always be entered for this collection element when entering quality results. At the collection plan level, you can override this mandatory setting.

The reporting length specifies the display length for this collection element. The reporting length does not determine the amount of space used to store quality result values in the quality data repository. Values can be up to 150 characters in length.

If the data type is number, enter the decimal precision. The decimal precision here controls the decimal precision of the specification limit values that you can define and the results data. Units of measure can be entered for any collection elements regardless of data type. When you set a default value for the collection element, it is automatically entered when the user enters quality results. You can override this value. Collection-element default values can be copied to any collection plan that contains that collection element.

The SQL Validation Statement is used for validation when you enter quality data. You can base a collection element's data validation on any table in the database. To do this, you can define a SQL validation statement that is used for validation when you collect quality data.

NOTE
If you define both a SQL validation statement and a list of collection element values (covered in the "Collection-Element Values" section), only the list of values is used for validation; the SQL validation statement is ignored.

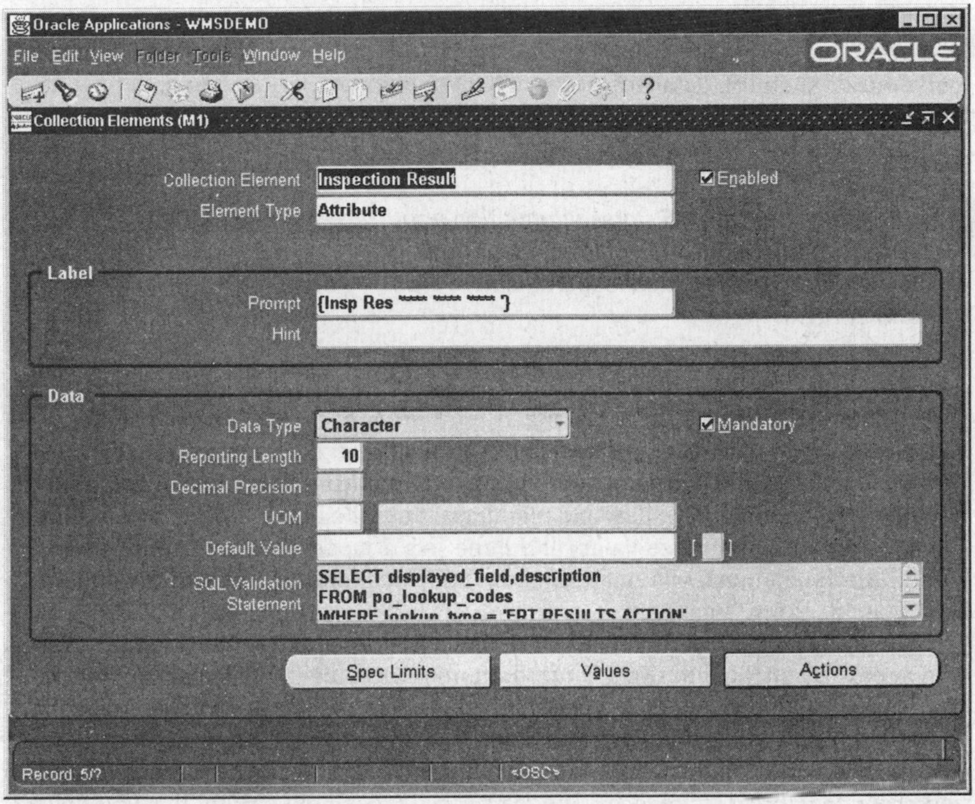

FIGURE 19-1. *The Collection Elements form allows you to define collection elements*

Collection-Element Values

If you want to ensure that the data capture process uses a limited set of values, you define a list of values for them when you create collection elements. When you use a collection element in a collection plan, however, the values are not copied into the plan, and you therefore must reassign some or all of them to the collection-plan element or create new values for it.

NOTE
You can delete collection-element values only if they have not been copied to a collection-plan element.

You define collection-element values in the Values window, which you can access by clicking the Values button in the Collection Elements window. The short code generally is an abbreviation of the value and is used to speed data entry. The short code must match the data type of the collection element. For example, if the data type is number, the short code must be numeric.

NOTE
The table QA_CHARS stores information about collection elements. QA_CHARS also stores information about the collection-element type and context.

Collection-Element Specification Limits

Specifications are useful in representing the product specifications against which the various measurements are compared during quality inspections. Specification limits establish the acceptable values and tolerances for collection elements and include a target value (the preferred value) and three sets of upper and lower range limits, which can be changed without restriction. Specifications are covered in detail in the "Specifications" section.

You define specification limits in the Specification Limits window, which you can access by clicking the Spec Limits button in the Collection Elements window. The Target Value represents the preferred value. The user-defined range limits can be used to represent a process control limit. Your user-defined limits can be inside, be outside, or overlap your specification range limits. The specification range limits can represent engineering tolerances. The reasonable range limit ensures that you collect values that make sense. The upper limits must exceed the lower limits in all cases.

NOTE
During data collection, you cannot collect data that is outside the reasonable range limits.

Quality Actions

Once a problem has been detected, corrective actions need to be taken. Often, you can take short-term corrective actions. For example, you might simply want to stop the production line from producing more defective products. Another simple example is to send an e-mail to all the appropriate parties if a test result on a critical component is entered as "Failed."

Oracle Quality can issue alerts and electronic notifications, launch workflows created in Oracle Workflow, as well as place jobs, repetitive schedules, items, suppliers, and purchase-order lines on hold. An action rule consists of two parts: a condition that needs to be tested and the corresponding action that needs to be invoked if the condition evaluates to true. Action rules are evaluated and executed during the quality data collection process. You can copy actions and action rules to other collection plan elements. Figure 19-2 shows the Quality Actions window.

Message Actions

Message actions either display a message or post it to the Quality Action Log. You can use message actions to prompt an operator to take immediate action. Message

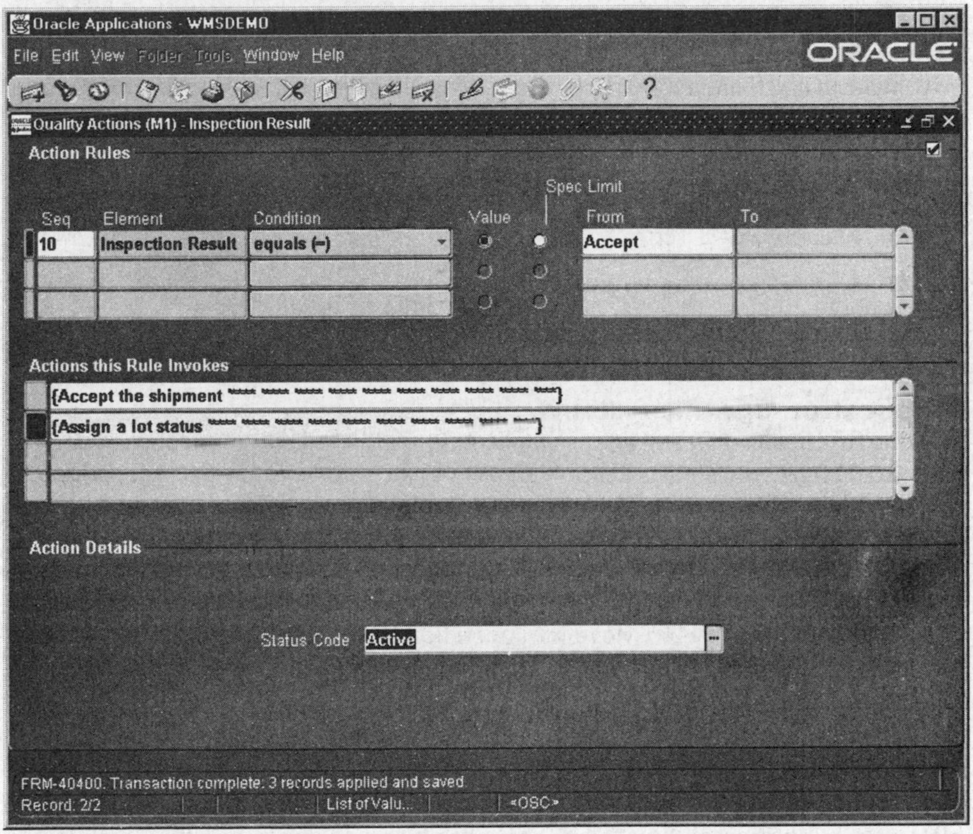

FIGURE 19-2. *The Quality Actions window allows you to define the various actions*

actions provide immediate feedback and help resolve problems at the source but require action details. There are three message action options:

- Display the message entered to the operator.

- Display the entered message and reject the input. Before you can continue with quality data collection, you must reenter an acceptable quality results value.

- Post the message entered to the Quality Action Log. For example, you can post an entry each time a critical part is found to be defective so that the source of the problem can be determined and eliminated. This creates a quality results audit trail.

Alert Actions

Alert actions can launch various processes, as well as send electronic mail notifications to users. Alert actions include the following:

- Execute an operating system script

- Execute a SQL script

- Launch a concurrent request

- Send an electronic mail notification

Application-Specific Actions

Actions are classified into two types: application-specific and non-application-specific. Application-specific actions act on database objects associated with that product. There also are dependencies between some application-specific actions and context elements. Non-application-specific actions do not have any restrictions.

In Oracle Work in Process, there is an application-specific action to assign shop-floor statuses. This action assigns the specified shop-floor status to the assemblies that you are moving into the To Move intraoperation step of the operation. Shop floor statuses were covered in Chapter 16. There are also application-specific actions for placing a job/schedule on hold.

Action Rules

Action rules define conditions that are evaluated before invoking actions during the data-collection process. You can define more than one action rule for a collection element or collection-plan element. You can also define one or more related actions per action rule.

Some actions require that you supply details, such as the text of a message or the number of a particular step. For example, when you associate the Assign a Shop Floor status to the Intraoperation Step action with an action rule, you must specify the shop-floor status that is to be assigned when the action is invoked during data collection. Other actions, such as the Place the Job on Hold action, do not require action details.

Action-Rule Sequencing

Since you can define more than one action rule for a collection element or collection-plan element, the sequence number establishes the order in which each action rule is evaluated. If the action rules are mutually exclusive, you must assign each a unique sequence number. If the action rules are not mutually exclusive, you can assign more than one action rule to a sequence. Figure 19-3 illustrates the rule evaluation and action invocation process.

As you can see from the figure, once a rule evaluates to true, all the rules with the same sequence are executed; rules with a different sequence number are not executed.

Collection-Element Actions

You define collection-element actions in the Quality Actions window, which you can invoke by clicking the Actions button in the Collection Elements window. In the Action Rules region, enter the Sequence number for the action rule. The sequence number can be from 0–99999.

Select the condition that must be met to invoke the action. Choose either the Value or Spec Limit option to specify the evaluation method. Value allows you to compare your result with a prespecified value, whereas Spec Limit allows you to check if your result is within a range.

If you choose Value, as quality data is collected, the action rule is evaluated using the results value and the value or values entered here. If you have defined values for the collection element, you must choose a value from this list. If you have not defined values for the collection element, you can enter any value. If you choose Spec Limit, as quality data is collected, the action rule is evaluated using the quality results value and the specification limit target value, the upper or lower user-defined range limits, or the upper or lower specification range limits.

If the selected condition requires a range of values, enter both the From and To values. If the selected condition requires only a single value, enter only the From value.

NOTE
Some conditions do not require values. Examples include Is Entered and Is Empty. These conditions result in Boolean values (true or false) themselves, without needing a comparison.

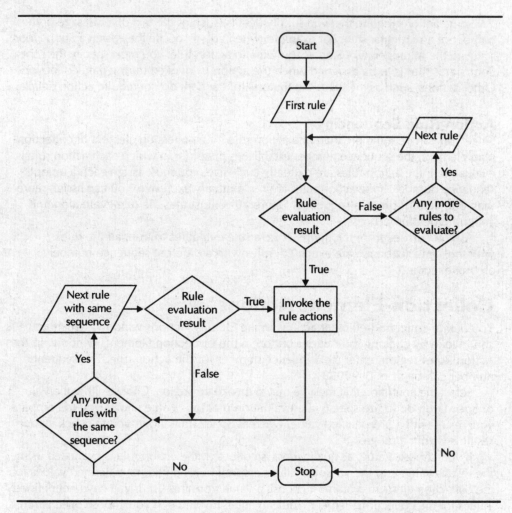

FIGURE 19-3. *The process of rule evaluation and action invocation*

For each rule you can associate one or more actions. Some dependencies exist between collection plan elements and actions. For example, you can define an Assign a Shop Floor status to the Intraoperation Step action only if you have first created the To Operation Sequence and To Intraoperation Step collection elements.

Collection-Element Alert Actions

Alert actions are special types of actions that are based on the Oracle Alert technology. Quality alert actions often require action details such as recipients (for electronic mail notifications), arguments, and filenames (for SQL and operating system scripts). Further, you can customize alert action details using output variables. Output variables represent quality results values and are dynamically defined as action rules are evaluated. All the alert actions are also defined in the same window as the collection element actions—the Quality Actions window.

E-mail Alert Actions

In the Actions This Rule Invokes region, select the Send an Electronic Mail Notification action. In the Action Details tab, choose the Action Details button to complete the action details in the Actions: Send Electronic Mail window. In the To field, enter the electronic mail IDs of the mail message recipients, separated by spaces or commas. You can enter many mail IDs—up to 240 characters. You can dynamically distribute mail messages by including output variables in the recipient fields. For example, you could define and use an output variable for an Inspector ID collection-plan element if Inspector IDs are equivalent to electronic mail IDs. Specify the Subject, Cc, and Bcc fields of the mail notification.

Define your message source by selecting either File or Text. If you specified file, enter the filename including the full path. If you specified text, enter the text in the text area. You can include output variables in the text, and this is covered in detail in the upcoming "Associating Output Variables with Actions" section.

Concurrent Request Alert Actions

In the Actions This Rule Invokes region, select the Launch a Concurrent Request action. In the Action Details region, click the Action Details button and complete the action details in the Actions: Concurrent Program window. Specify the concurrent program and enter the arguments, separated by spaces.

Operating System Script Alert Actions

The Execute an Operating System script action should be selected to define this action. In the Action Details region, click the Action Details button and complete the action's details in the Actions: Operating System Script window. The source of the operating system script can be either a File or Text.

If you selected File, you can enter the filename in two ways: as a relative path from an application top directory or as the absolute (complete) path. If you have placed your script in an application's top directory, select the application and enter the relative path of the file. If the file is not in any application top directory, enter the full path and filename of the operating system script source file. Enter the arguments to pass to the operating system script file, and separate them by spaces.

If you choose to enter the text for the operating system script, enter the script in the text area. You can include output variables in the text. You cannot select an application or enter arguments if you choose to enter a text script. You can include output variables in the text, and this is covered in detail in the "Associating Output Variables with Actions" section. If these output variables select character or date data, place single quotes around the output variable to correctly pass the argument.

SQL Script Alert Actions

In the Actions This Rule Invokes region, select the Execute a SQL Script action. In the Action Details region, click the Action Details button and complete the action details in the Actions: SQL Script window. Choose the source of the SQL system script by selecting either File or Text. The action details of the SQL script and the OS script are essentially the same and, therefore, are not explained here in detail. In SQL script however, you can use only the Insert and Update statements.

Launch a Workflow Action

The technology for executing these actions is Oracle Workflow. You create a workflow that performs all the tasks that you want as a part of implementing your corrective actions. Select the Launch a Workflow action from the list of values. In the Action Details window, select the corrective action workflow that you defined for this purpose.

You can dynamically pass quality results values to the workflow during data collection. You must create output variables for the collection plan elements for which you want to pass values and assign them a token. The token that you assign is the internal name for the workflow attribute that corresponds to the collection element. Associating output variables is covered in detail in the "Associating Output Variables with Actions" section.

CAUTION
For the output variables to work, the token name must be entered exactly the same as the workflow attribute's internal name.

Associating Output Variables with Actions

You can incorporate quality results values into the action details using the output variables feature for various types of actions. Output variable tokens are defined by entering an ampersand (&) followed by a token name that represents a results value. For example, you can define a token called &ITEM_NUMBER to represent the item number.

You define output variables from the Action Details windows of the various actions that allow output variables. Examples of these actions are Actions: Send Electronic Mail, Actions: SQL Script, Actions: Operating System Script, Assign a Value, or Launch a Workflow. In these windows, navigate to the Output Variables window by clicking the Variables button.

Enter the token name. The token name should not contain the ampersand in this window. The ampersand is required only when this variable is referenced in the action details. Associate a collection element with the token name. You can associate token names with any collection element, including common collection plan elements. For example, you can associate the item collection element with the &ITEM_NUMBER token name. Figure 19-4 shows all the entities and relationships that support the data collection functionality in Oracle Quality. Some of these entities are covered in the following sections.

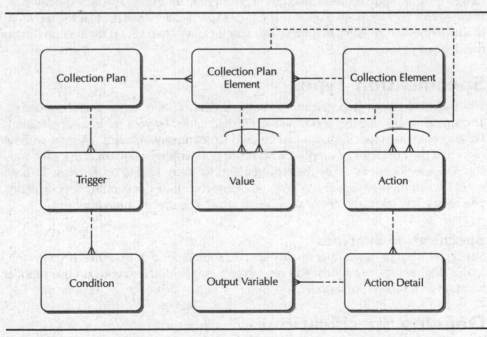

FIGURE 19-4. *Logical data model covering the data collection entities in Oracle Quality*

NOTE
The table QA_ACTIONS stores action definitions. Action logs are stored in the table QA_ACTION_ LOG. The actions associated with collection elements are tracked using the tables QA_CHAR_ ACTIONS, QA_CHAR_ACTION_OUTPUTS, and QA_CHAR_ACTION_TRIGGERS.

Specifications

Specifications define product requirements. In other words, they define what is expected from an item for it to be usable. You can define specifications for the key characteristics of the products that you produce or for the materials that you receive from suppliers. You can attach documents to specifications. These attached documents can be used to document processing instructions as well as inspection and disposition procedures.

Specifications are normally defined in terms of nominal (+/–) tolerances or ranges (low to high). A specification for a piston ring, for example, might specify that the diameter be 74mm +/– 0.05mm. The upper specification limit (USL) is the top limit of the defined range. Similarly, the lower specification limit (LSL) is the bottom limit of the defined range.

Specification Types

There are three types of specifications in Oracle Quality: item, supplier, and customer. The specification type that you can select is determined by your business application. For example, item specifications can be used to define requirements for items without regard to the customer or supplier who might purchase or sell them. Customer and supplier specifications define the requirements for items sold to or purchased from specific customers or vendors. When you define a customer or supplier specification, you also select the customer or supplier to which the specification applies.

Specification Subtypes

Specification subtypes further qualify specification types. For example, if you want to use different specifications with respect to supplier location, you can use supplier location as a subtype of supplier.

Defining Specifications

You define specifications in the Specifications form. Enter the specification name and effectivity date and choose a specification type. The available specification types are Item, Supplier and Customer. Each type of specification can be based on either an Item or Item category. If your specification is based on an Item, you must assign an item and, depending on the item, an item revision. If you intend to base your specification on an Item category, you must have specified a default category set using the profile option QA: Quality Category Set. You can then select one of the Item categories within this set from a list of values. Figure 19-5 shows the Specifications form.

Specification Elements

You create specification elements by adding collection elements to your specifications. Collection element specification limits are defaulted to these specification elements. For example, if you create a specification element by adding the Frequency collection element to a specification, the target value of 20.0000 and user-defined, specification, and reasonable range limits—19.7800–20.2200, 19.7600–20.2400, and 19.7400–20.2600, respectively—are defaulted to the specification element.

NOTE
The tables QA_SPECS and QA_SPEC_CHARS store information about specifications and specification elements.

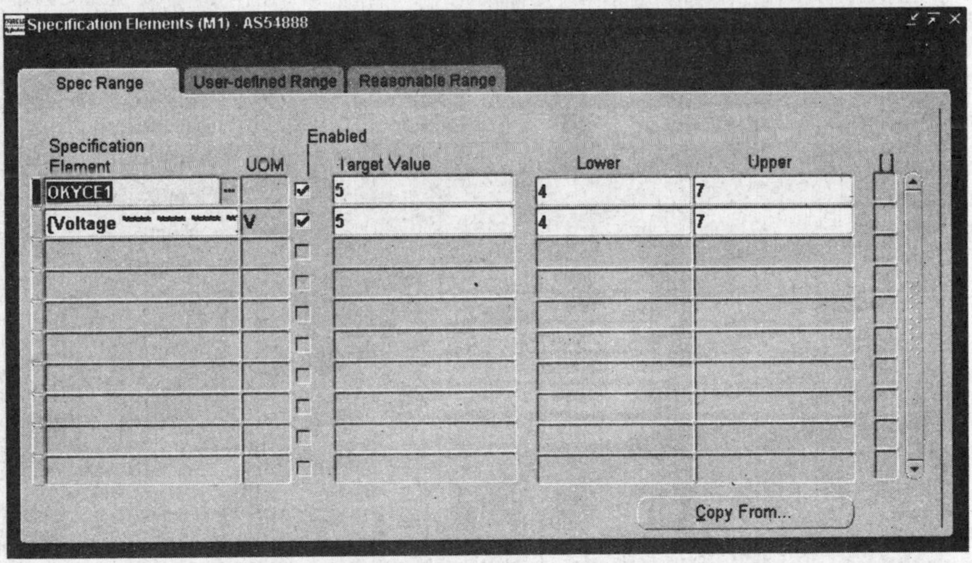

FIGURE 19-5. *The Specifications form allows you to define specifications and spec limits*

Collection Plans

Collection plans are composed of collection elements, their values and specifications, and any actions that you want to initiate in response to quality results. Collection-plan elements are the building blocks of collection plans. You can create collection-plan elements by adding individual collection elements to your collection plan. In addition to the collection elements that you explicitly add to a collection plan, there are a number of common collection-plan elements that are added to every collection plan. For example, item is a typical collection-plan element that can appear in all the collection plans in which you want to collect information about items. You create collection plans in the Collection Plans form, which is shown in Figure 19-6.

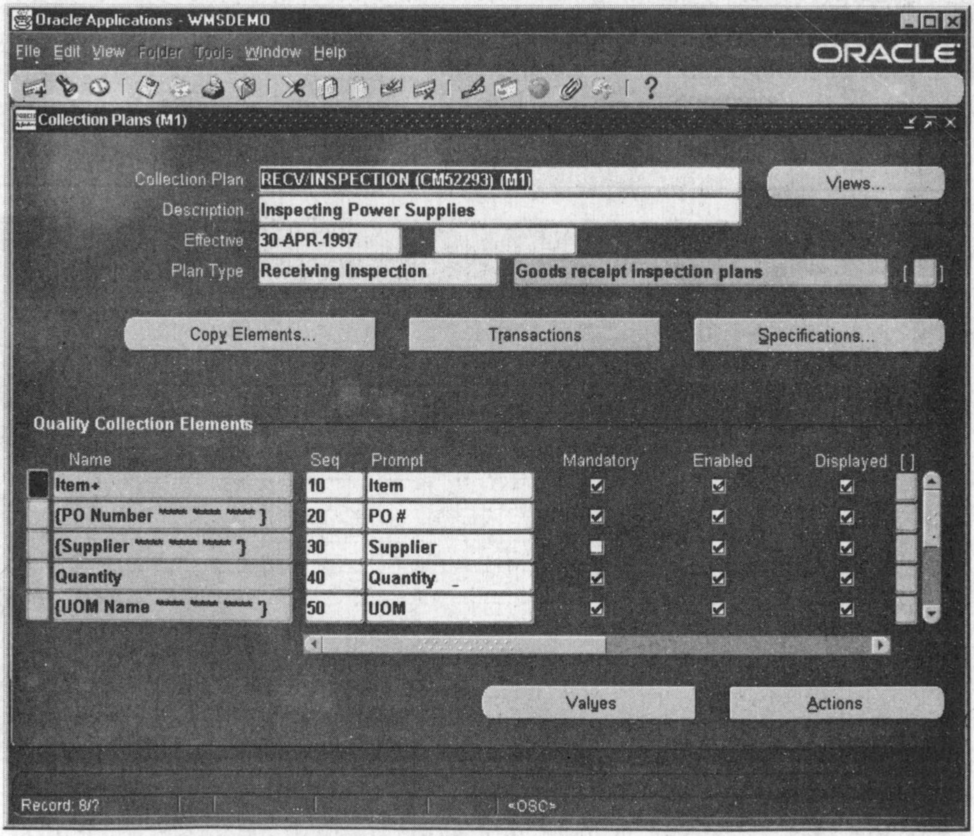

FIGURE 19-6. *The Collection Plans form allows you to define collection plans and associate collection-plan elements*

Specify the name, description, and effectivity dates. Once a collection plan expires, you cannot enter quality results using the plan, but you can query records that already use it.

The collection-plan type allows you to categorize your collection plans. You can define your own collection-plan types, or you can use any of these five predefined collection-plan types: WIP Inspection, Receiving Inspection, FGI Inspection, Field Returns, and Service Requests. Collection-plan types are only informational; they do not affect a collection plan's association with transactions.

NOTE
The table QA_PLANS stores information about collection plans.

Collection-Plan Elements

Collection elements are generic until you use them in collection plans. Whenever you use collection elements in collection plans, they are associated with the plans and thereafter are referred to as collection-plan elements. Collection-plan elements can have different actions, specifications, and values that make their use specific to that collection plan.

You can define the collection-plan elements by selecting them individually or by copying from another collection plan. You can also define the collection-plan element values and actions similarly. Some actions are independent of the collection-plan elements they are associated with. For example, you can define message actions, such as Display a Message to the Operator, or alert actions, such as Send an Electronic Mail Notification, for any collection-plan element. Some other actions, however, require the existence of a context element. For example, the action Place the Job on Hold can be selected only if Job is present.

NOTE
The table QA_PLAN_CHARS stores information about collection-plan elements.

User-Defined Formulas Using Assign a Value Actions

You can dynamically assign values to collection-plan elements as you enter quality results. Values are assigned when action rules associated with Assign a Value actions are evaluated and found to be true. When you assign a value to a collection-plan element, its current value is overwritten.

CAUTION
Formulas and SQL scripts might fail to process if the value represented by an output variable token is null.

In addition to the normal action details, you specify the mode in which a value is assigned and the appropriate details. Choose the appropriate check box to define the value using either a Formula or SQL script.

Use the formula option to define arithmetic expressions. Arithmetic expressions can include the following:

- Operators - +, –, *, /

- Specific values –3, A

- Functions

- Output variable tokens that represent quality results values

Use the SQL option when data must be read from database tables. You can include specific values and output variable tokens in your SQL text as well. If you have included output variable tokens in your Formula or SQL Text, click the Variables button to associate these output variable tokens with the action.

Associating Collection Plans with Transactions

Once you define a collection plan, you must associate it with the transaction and enable it, so that the collection plan is available on the transaction's list of values during quality collection. Integrating quality data collection with standard manufacturing transactions provides the following benefits:

- You can combine the data recording and data entering steps into one.

- You can enforce mandatory data collection if required.

- You can collect quality results automatically in the background without user intervention.

You associate collection plans with transactions in the Collection Transactions window, which you can invoke by clicking the Transactions button. In the Quality Collection Transactions region, select a collection transaction and indicate if quality data collection is mandatory when the transaction is entered using the Mandatory check box. The Mandatory check box also ensures that all the conditions specified in the collection triggers must be met. If you do not check the Mandatory box, you can skip quality result entry for this transaction.

NOTE
The complete list of transactions supported for quality data collection can be found in the documentation.

The Background check box enables background data collection that allows you to collect quality results without invoking the Enter Quality Results window. Inspection collection transactions and self-service transactions cannot be set to background. Finally, check the Enabled box to indicate that data collection for this quality collection plan is enabled.

Collection Triggers

Collection triggers consist of conditions, which if evaluate to true, trigger the results entry process. You define triggers in the Collection Triggers region. The trigger name specifies which context collection element is used to define the trigger. The condition entered determines when quality data collection is triggered. For example, for the WIP Move transaction you might choose to trigger data collection when assemblies are moved from the To Move intraoperation step of Operation Sequence 20 to the Queue intraoperation step of Operation Sequence 30. Based on the condition, enter a value or range of values for the specified trigger.

NOTE
The table QA_PLAN_TRANSACTIONS stores the association between collection plans and transactions. The collection triggers associated with a plan and a transaction are stored in the table QA_PLAN_COLLECTION_TRIGGERS. QA_TXN_COLLECTION_TRIGGERS contains all the collection elements that can be used as collection triggers for a specific collection plan associated with a transaction.

Collecting Data

When the data collection framework (consisting of collection elements, specifications, and collection plans) is in place, you can start collecting data. You can enter quality results into the quality data repository directly as you perform transactions or by using Collection Import. When you enter quality data using a collection plan that has been associated with a specification type, you are prompted to find and assign a specification before you can enter quality results.

Direct Data Collection

You can enter quality results directly in stand-alone mode. You can then update, view, report, and chart these results as required. When you enter results in stand-alone mode, the data entered is validated, using acceptable values and valid data types, and actions are executed per the collection plan used.

You use the Enter Quality Results window to enter quality results directly. When you enter quality results for collection-plan elements with specifications, the Spec Name, UOM, Target, Upper Limit, and Lower Limit fields are displayed at the bottom of the window. If you do not want the specifications to be displayed, set the QA: Blind Results Entry profile option to On.

Data Collection During Transactions

You can collect data during transactions, and you can specify that it be mandatory or optional. You must create a collection plan specific to the transaction, and in the plan, you can indicate whether or not quality results are to be collected automatically or in the background as you transact. If you indicate that quality results are not to be collected in the background, you use the Enter Quality Results window to enter them. As with direct data collection, the data that you enter is validated, and actions executed, per the collection plan. This was covered in detail in the "Associating Collection Plans with Transactions" section.

Collection Import

You can load quality results data from external systems into the quality data repository using the Collection Import Interface. This allows you to feed data directly from testing devices and measuring instruments. For example, if you use infrared systems for inspecting incoming goods, you can use the collection's import functionality to directly feed the data into Oracle Quality.

You use SQL or PL/SQL to load the Collection Import interface table. From the Launch Collection Import Manager window, open the Collection Import Manager. This process validates records in the Collection Import Interface, and then imports the data into the quality data repository. Results data that fail validation or processing are marked. You can use the Update Collection Import window to view, update, and resubmit this information.

NOTE
*The tables QA_RESULTS and QA_RESULTS_*
UPDATE_HISTORY store the data that is captured
during transactions. You can use the QA_RESULTS
INTERFACE to populate data programmatically.

Mobile Quality Applications

Oracle Mobile Quality Applications are part of the suite that enable companies to extend the benefits of their mobile supply chain applications. The following data entry pages are provided in mobile quality:

- Enter Quality Results
- View Specifications
- Transactional Data Collection—WIP Move, WIP Return, WIP Scrap/Reject, WIP Completions, WIP Workorderless Completions, WIP Material Transaction, and Flow Manufacturing Completions

Analysis Tools

Popular statistics texts say that there are three types of lies: lies, damned lies, and statistics. Statistics can be very misleading. Care should be taken every step of the way—data collection, data analysis, and verification of solution. Your analysis can be only as good as your data. Oracle quality supports the generation of Pareto charts, histograms, trend charts, and control charts. These charts can be very useful in different conditions to analyze your data. This section talks about these charts in detail.

Copying Settings

You can view the same subset of data in different ways using the Copy Settings function. Copy Settings copies the saved settings from a source chart to a destination chart. The settings that are copied include the collection plan and the record selection criteria, and, depending on the source chosen, might also include the primary collection element, specification limits, or both. You can change all the settings that are copied except the collection plan.

Copying settings is explained as a part of explaining the various analysis tools. A general point to remember is that there might be data losses when you copy data between the various tools. For example, if you create a Pareto chart by copying the settings from a trend chart, information about the specifications are lost, since Pareto chart doesn't require specifications. If you create a control chart from the Pareto chart thus created, which requires specifications, you should manually include the specifications information after copying the settings from the Pareto chart.

Pareto Charts

In 1897, the Italian economist Vilfredo Pareto showed that the distribution of income is uneven; 80 percent of the income was in fact earned by 20 percent of the population. Quality management guru Dr. J. M. Juran extended this theory to classify problems into the vital few and the trivial many. Pareto's Law, named after the Italian economist, states that 80 percent of the effects can be attributed to just 20 percent of the possible causes. The Pareto chart, which is based on Pareto's Law, allows you prioritize the list of possible causes and focus on the most important ones.

TIP
*Use Pareto charts in the problem-identification
phase of your problem-solving methodology.*

You can chart quality results for any collection plan element. For example, you can chart the top defects entered for a particular production line during a week. You can create Pareto charts from scratch, or you can create them by copying settings from another chart, descriptive statistic view, or custom report. You can save your chart settings so that you can re-create charts using the same settings. Only those results that are to be charted can be selected. When you are satisfied with your settings and record selection, you can view your chart. You can optionally export chart information for further analysis.

Chart Settings

Enter the chart name in the Pareto Chart window. This allows you to save your chart parameters. You can select any collection plan, even those that are no longer effective. The collection plan cannot be modified during subsequent chart generations. The chart title, if specified, is displayed at the top of the chart. Figure 19-7 shows the chart settings for the Pareto chart.

The X-axis of the chart represents the problem classification scheme. If you are generating the top defects, the list of defect codes should be chosen as the collection element for the X-axis. If you are analyzing the causes of a particular defect, the list of causes should be chosen as the collection element for the X-axis.

The Y-axis of the chart usually represents a quantity or count of occurrences. If a numeric collection element is selected, you can choose to plot the sum, count,

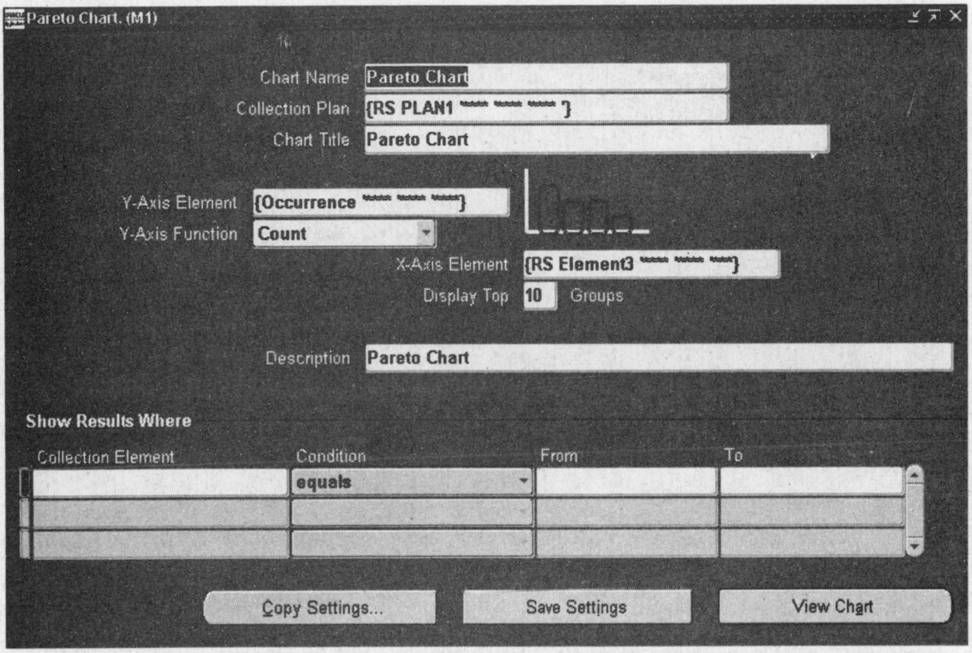

FIGURE 19-7. *Use the Pareto Chart form to define the settings for your Pareto chart*

minimum, maximum, or average of the values associated with that collection element. If a nonnumeric collection element (character or date) is selected, you can select only count.

Enter the maximum number of groups to display on the chart. For example, enter **5** to chart the top-five defect codes. The chart description is displayed at the top of the chart, under the chart title. Select the quality results to chart in the Show Results Where region of the Pareto Chart window. If you do not select which quality results to chart, all results associated with the collection plan are used.

Generating and Viewing the Pareto Chart
If you want to copy the settings from another chart, click the Copy Settings button in the Pareto Chart window. You can change all copied settings except the collection plan.

Click the View Chart button to view the Pareto chart (see Figure 19-8). Click the Save Settings button if you want to save the inquiry settings. To export the chart, choose Tools | Export Results.

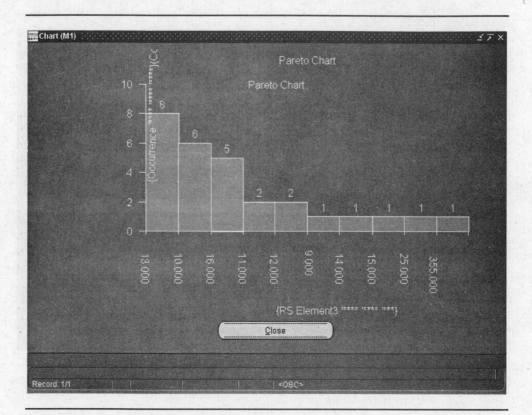

FIGURE 19-8. *Pareto Chart generated by Oracle Quality*

Histograms

Histograms provide a graphic summary of variations in a set of data. It is an objective way of looking at the population at a glance. The diagram is constructed by partitioning the range of data into several intervals of equal length, counting the number of points in each interval, and plotting the counts as bar lengths. Typically, the shape of the distribution should be bell shaped. Any significant deviation from this normal pattern has one or more assignable causes, which can shed light on the variability in the process.

You can graphically display, in histogram form, quality results for any collection-plan element with a numeric data type. You can select and graph a subset of the quality results values. You can create histograms from scratch or by copying settings from another chart, descriptive statistic view, or custom report. You can save your chart settings so that you can re-create charts using the same settings.

Chart Settings

Enter the chart name in the Histograms window. This allows you to save your chart parameters. You can select any collection plan, even those that are no longer effective. The collection plan cannot be modified during subsequent chart generations. The chart title and chart description, if specified, are displayed at the top of the chart.

Select any collection element on the collection plan with a numeric data type. The X-axis of the chart represents the computed intervals of the selected collection plan element. You can influence the interval by specifying the number of bars that you want in the histogram. If you do not specify the number of bars, it is calculated as the square root of the number of data points. The number of points represents the total number of data points to be included. If you do not enter a specific number of points, all the points are used. If you enter a specific number, the most recently collected results are used.

The Y-axis of the chart represents the count or sum of occurrences of the primary collection element on the X-axis. You can specify whether you want your histogram to be based on count or sum using the Group By field.

You can select only specifications that have specification elements in common with the selected collection plan element defined. You can find and select any specification, even specifications that do not have the selected collection element as a specification element. If this is the case, upper and lower specification limits and the target value are defaulted from the collection element.

Select the quality results to chart in the Show Results Where region of the Histograms window. If you do not select which quality results to chart, all results associated with the collection plan are used.

Generating and Viewing the Histogram

If you want to copy the settings from another chart, click the Copy Settings button in the Histograms window. You can change all copied settings except the collection plan.

Click the View Chart button to view the histogram. Figure 19-9 shows a histogram. Click the Save Settings button if you want to save the inquiry settings. To export the chart, choose Tools | Export Results.

Trend Charts

You can use trend charts to analysis data collected over a period. By observing trends, you can identify the pattern of problem occurrence over time. You can then analyze the causes that are associated with the unfavorable trends and develop solutions to overcome them.

Chart Settings

Enter the chart name in the Trend Chart window. Select the collection plan to chart. If you are creating a chart, you can select any collection plan, even those that are

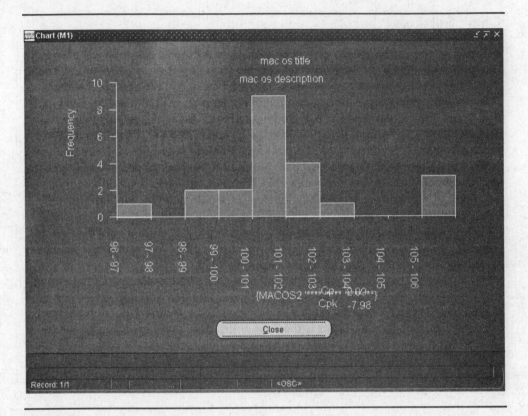

FIGURE 19-9. *Histogram generated by Oracle Quality*

no longer effective. If you are changing a chart, you cannot change the collection plan. The chart title and chart description will be displayed at the top of the chart.

The X-axis of the chart can be any collection plan element that usually represents time or groups of quality results collected consecutively over time. You can view results by any one of the following three options:

- ■ **Occurrence** Plots individual quality results consecutively over time, from the oldest occurrence to the most recent occurrence

- ■ **Collection Number** Plots a group of individual quality results or readings, grouped into a collection and identified by a collection number

- ■ **Entry Date** Plots a group of individual quality results or readings, grouped by the date in which they were entered

For the collection number and entry date options, you must select an appropriate grouping function such as average or sum.

The Y-axis of the chart represents the variable that is studied with respect to time. If the X-axis represents a grouping, you must select a grouping function for the Y-axis. For example, if the X-axis is Entry Date, you can select a function such as Average to display average values for the collection element for each day.

Select the quality results to chart in the Show Results Where region. If you do not select which quality results to chart, all results associated with the collection plan are used.

Generating and Viewing the Histogram

If you want to copy the settings from another chart, click the Copy Settings button in the Trend Chart window. You can change all copied settings except the collection plan.

Click the View Chart button to view the trend chart. Click the Save Settings button if you want to save the inquiry settings. To export the chart, choose Tools | Export Results.

Control Charts

Control charts help gauge the stability of a process. The main purpose of control charts is to detect the existence of assignable causes.

For some types of control charts, the data that is collected to construct a control chart needs to be grouped into subgroups. Selection of a subgroup is extremely important when defining these types of control charts. Improper subgroup selection can lead to misleading results and false corrective actions.

Prior to subgrouping, consider the variation that you want to eliminate. Construct your subgroups in such a way that the variation by permissible factors alone constitutes the variation within the subgroup. If these variations are unknown, a control chart cannot be used effectively.

Control Chart Types

Control charts are typically pairs of charts. The first chart plots a measure that represents the within-subgroup variation or individual data points, while the second chart plots a measure that represents the between-subgroup variation, such as range or standard deviation. Oracle Quality has three types of control charts: Xbar-R, X-mR, and Xbar-S.

Xbar-R Chart   An Xbar-R chart is a pair of line graph charts that plot subgroups of data collected over a continuous period. The Xbar chart plots the average value for each subgroup. The R chart, or range chart, plots the range of values within each subgroup.

X-mR Chart   The individual X chart simply plots individual data points. The moving range chart plots a specified range of the data points up to and including the current data point. For example, if a subgroup size of five is specified, then the tenth point on the Moving Range chart is plotted, using the range of 6–10 points. These charts are commonly used when the process results do not fall into subgroups, for instance, when the process is slow and data does not form clusters over time.

Xbar-S Chart   This pair of line charts is similar to the Xbar and R charts except that when the S chart is plotted, the standard deviation is used instead of the range. This pair of charts is commonly used instead of the Xbar and R chart when the subgroup size is large (more than 10) because it mitigates the effects of outliers.

Chart Settings

Enter the chart name in the Control Charts window. Select the collection plan to chart. The chart title and chart description are displayed at the top of the chart. Select the chart type—Xbar-R, X-mR, or Xbar-S. If the subgroup size is greater than 10, Xbar-S is recommended. Select the collection element that you want to analyze. It must have a numerical data type. Select the quality results to chart in the Show Results Where region. If you do not select which quality results to chart, all results associated with the collection plan are used.

Control limits can be defined based on collection results, saved limits, or manual entries. To define control limits based on collection results, click the Control Limits button in the Control Charts window. Enter the control limit name and description. You must enter a subgroup size that is between 2–25. If you change the subgroup size, you must recalculate control limits. The number of subgroups allows you to specify the number of subgroups to be used by Oracle Quality in the calculation of control limits. The Compute New button calculates the control limits. Figure 19-10 shows the Control Charts form and the Control Limits window.

If you want to base your control limits on saved limits instead of defining a new control limit, select the control limit name of the saved set of control limits. You can also select saved limits from other charts; however, the selection is limited by the chart type and the collection element.

Generating and Viewing the Control Chart

If you want to copy the settings from another chart, click the Copy Settings button in the Control Charts window. You can change all copied settings except the collection plan.

Click the View Chart button to view the histogram. Choose the Save Settings button if you want to save the inquiry settings. To export the chart, choose Tools | Export Results.

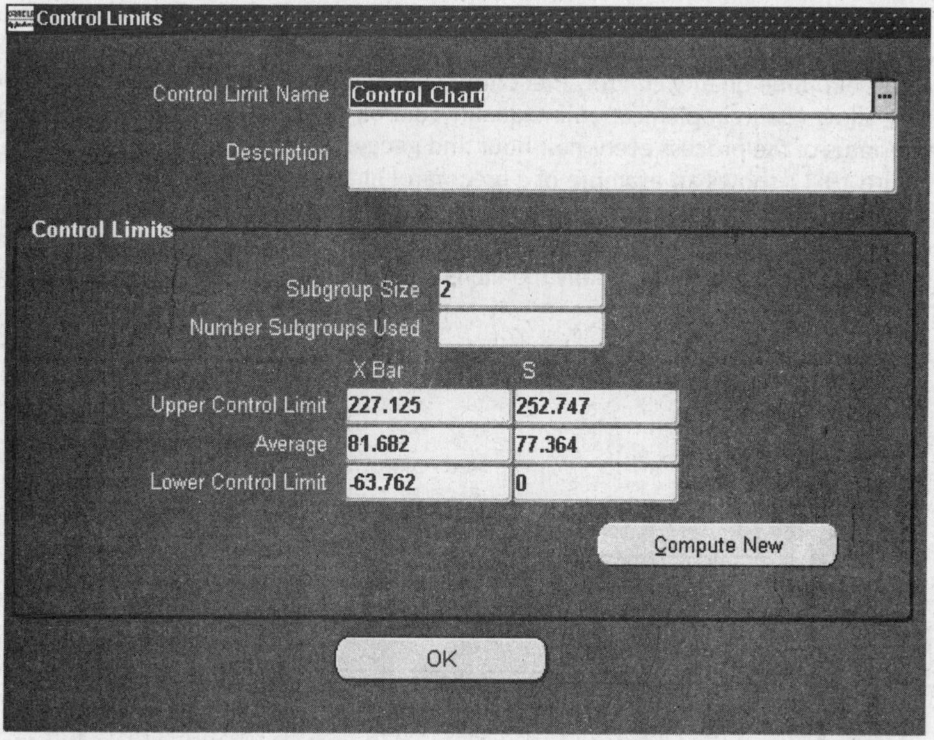

FIGURE 19-10. *Control Chart Settings and the Control Limits window*

How to Read Control Charts

Points outside the control limits clearly indicate process instability. Even when the points are inside the control limits, the process is not stable if you can detect one or more *runs*. Run is a state in which points occur continually on one side of the control line. The number of points in a run is called the length of the run. A seven-point run is considered abnormal.

Trend represents a state of instability. When the points have a continuous upward or downward sequence of points, they are said to be in a trend. *Periodicity* occurs when you see the upward and downward trends forming a repeating pattern.

If two out of three points fall outside the two sigma lines, then this condition is referred to as *approaching the control limits*.

Precontrol Charts

The tools in Statistical Process Control (SPC) significantly improve the ability to detect and prevent potential problems, but they do not function in real time. They are still a part of offline quality control. Precontrol charts are a variant of control charts, and they allow you to implement online quality control, by which the operator can check the status of the process every half-hour and gauge the stability of the process. Figure 19-11 shows an example of a precontrol chart.

After identifying the critical process parameters using the various tools including control charts, you can develop precontrol charts for these critical parameters to make sure that the process is continually monitored. Since it is an online quality control tool,

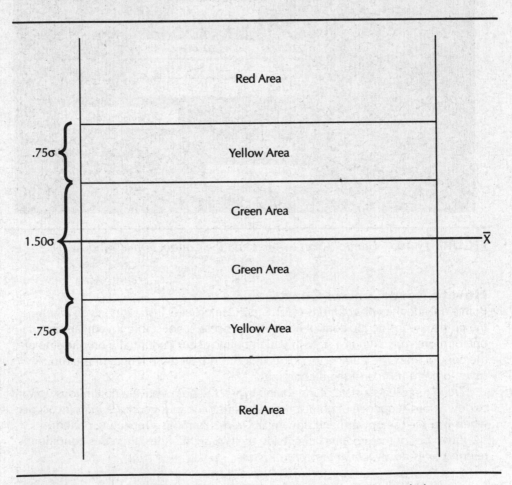

FIGURE 19-11. *Implement online quality control using precontrol charts*

this is plotted by the operator. Typically, a measurement is taken every half-hour or every batch of five to 10 parts. The simple rules are as follows:

- If you get a point in green, continue with the process.

- If you get a point in yellow, take another measurement. If the next measurement also falls in yellow, stop the process and inform the appropriate authority.

- If you get a point in red, stop the process and inform the appropriate authority.

Descriptive Statistics

Once you collect data, you can generate descriptive statistics on the collected data using the Descriptive Statistics form. The statistics generated are as follows:

- Sum

- Mean

- Minimum value, maximum value, range, standard deviation, and variance

- Total occurrences and null occurrences

- USL, LSL, Cp, and Cpk

Along with the appropriate charts, these descriptive statistics are very useful in studying quality problems.

Statistical Process Control (SPC)

SPC is the application of statistical tools and methods to evaluate important process parameters for continuous improvement. Quality assurance departments have inspectors who measure the quality of products after they are made. The tools of SPC allow you to detect potential problems ahead of time and implement corrective actions.

The most important aspect of SPC is the splitting of variability into two types: variability due to chance causes and variability due to assignable causes. Chance causes are present inherently in the process; they cannot be controlled, at least not without substantial investment. For example, you don't have a lot of control over the atmospheric temperature, unless you move the process into a controlled environment.

Assignable causes, on the other hand, represent deviations from the process specification or process design flaws. For example, using the wrong coolant is an assignable cause. If the coolant that is used is in fact the specified coolant, then this is a process design issue; you have to change the process specification. If this was an error on the part of the operator, this nonconformance needs to be addressed. Control charts are excellent tools for studying a process. They are covered earlier in the "Control Charts" section.

Process Capability Studies

Process capability studies are performed periodically by quality engineers to make sure that a particular production process is capable of producing a certain dimension, with an acceptable level of repeatability. The two indices Cp and Cpk are commonly used in the process capability studies to measure the health of the production process that is being investigated.

A sample size is established prior to the study. When the samples are ready for analysis, the process characteristic is measured for all the samples. The arithmetic average of this group of values is denoted by the mu character (μ), and the standard deviation of all the values from the calculated average is denoted by the sigma (σ) character. Standard deviation is a measure of variability in a process. Defined as the root mean square (RMS) deviation from average, it indicates how much a process can be expected to vary from the average.

The focus of a process capability study is to understand two aspects of the process: variability and centering. Variability is the inherent variation that occurs in the process around the average, and centering represents the ability of the process to adhere to its target value. The approach to improving process capability is to reduce variability first, and once variability is under control, concentrate on centering.

Cp

The index Cp is calculated using specification limits and the standard deviation of the process. This index indicates, in general, whether the process is capable of producing products to specifications. The specifications are denoted by LSL and USL for lower specification limit and upper specification limit, respectively. The formula for Cp is shown here:

$$Cp = \frac{USL - LSL}{6\sigma}$$

The recommended value for Cp is 1.67 or greater. Since it doesn't include the mean in its calculation, it is not a very reliable index and can be very misleading if used in isolation. Figure 19-12 explains this.

In the two scenarios shown in Figure 19-11, the Cp is exactly the same—a value of 1.75 that is greater than the recommended value of 1.67 and so would seem normal.

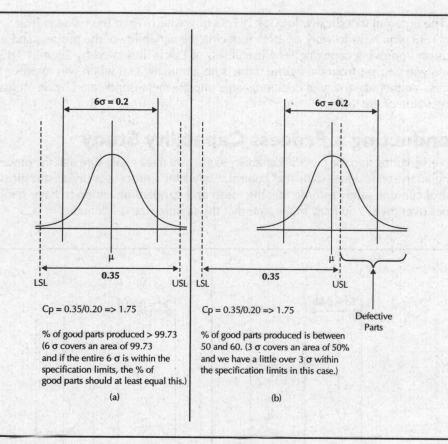

FIGURE 19-12.   *How reliable is Cp if used in isolation?*

Although, as you can understand from scenario (b), the process is operating way off its target value, and approximately 40 percent of its output will be defective.

This shortcoming of Cp notwithstanding, the index gives meaningful insights on the variability of the process.

Cpk

Cpk is calculated using specification limits, the standard deviation, and the mean. The index indicates whether the process is capable of producing within specification and is also an indicator of the ability of the process to adhere to the target specification. The formula for Cpk is shown here:

$$Cpk = Minimum\left[\frac{USL - \mu}{3\sigma} \quad \frac{\mu - LSL}{3\sigma}\right]$$

The recommended value for Cpk is 1.33 or greater. When the value is lesser than 1.33, you have to work on both reducing the variability of the process and also focus on improving centering. The usefulness of Cpk is illustrated by Figure 19-13.

As you can see from the figure, there is no ambiguity that when you improve the process—either variability or centering—the improvement is indicated by an increase in the value of the index.

Conducting a Process Capability Study

Before venturing into the process capability study, you must make sure that the process being analyzed is under statistical control. Only after a process is under statistical control can one safely assume that the mean and standard deviation to have stable values over time. You must make sure that the sample size is adequate.

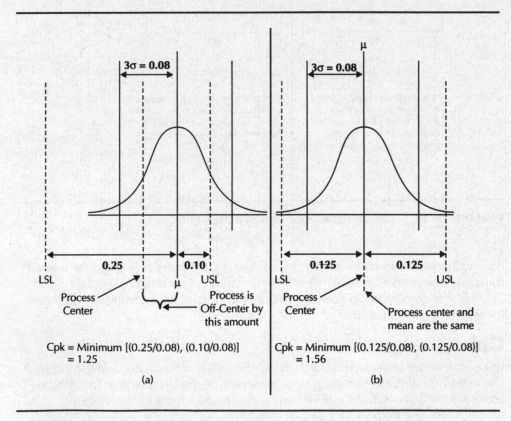

FIGURE 19-13. *Usefulness of Cpk in improving the process capability*

The data should be tested for normality before you can use the data in the study. Histograms are very useful for this purpose. After satisfying all these conditions, you can calculate Cp and Cpk. Both Cp and Cpk are calculated with the generation of descriptive statistic views and histograms (as shown in Figure 19-8).

Summary

Quality is everybody's business. Assuring quality depends on how controlled your processes are. Keeping your processes under control depends on the analysis methods and the accuracy of your data.

Oracle Quality provides a sophisticated data collection framework comprising collection elements, specifications, and collection plans. Collection elements identify the characteristic that you want to measure or some reference information. Specifications represent the target and permissible upper and lower limits.

Collection plans are a collection of collection elements. You can associate actions with collection elements and collection plan elements. Actions allow you to put short-term corrective actions in place. You can also implement long-term corrective actions using the workflow actions. You can implement and assign value actions at the collection-plan element level. You also associate transactions and the corresponding collection triggers at the collection plan level.

Oracle Quality supports the generation of four graphical tools: Pareto Chart, Histogram, Trend Chart, and Control Chart. These charts allow you to conduct your problem investigation meaningfully. The process capability indices Cp and Cpk are generated when you construct a histogram or when you generate descriptive statistics.

CHAPTER
20

Pricing

n Release 11i, Oracle rewrote its pricing functionality. Release 11i offers two methods for pricing goods that you sell to your customers: basic pricing functionality, included with the Order Management application, and advanced pricing, which you must license separately.

Basic pricing is essentially the same functionality as was provided prior to Release 11i—the ability to define multiple price lists and discounts.

Advanced pricing builds on the basic functionality, adding the ability to handle deals, promotions, and other sales incentives. Advanced pricing also serves the pricing needs of other applications, including the Order Capture or quoting systems in the CRM products, Oracle Contracts, and others. It attempts to address business-to-business pricing needs that you might find in the automotive industry or consumer packaged goods, as well as the business-to-consumer needs in Web stores and telecommunications.

Figure 20-1 provides an orientation to the fundamentals of advanced pricing.

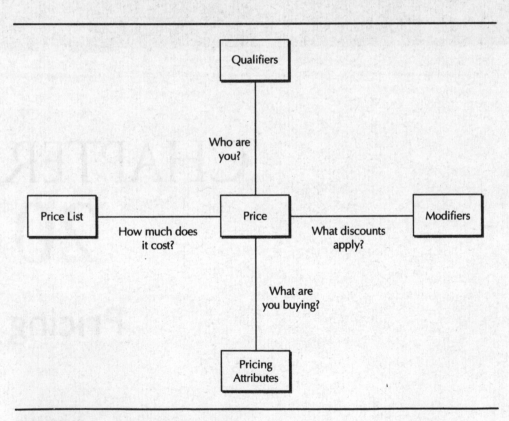

FIGURE 20-1. *Main pricing concepts*

Defining Price Lists

Price lists are the core of the pricing functionality. An order can be placed only if a price list line can be found for the ordered item. To define a price list, navigate to the Price List Setup form in the Pricing menu. The price list is expressed in a currency. The rounding precision of the currency is defaulted as the rounding precision of the price list. The payment term, freight term, and freight carrier defined at the header are possible default sources for defaulting rules.

NOTE
The pricing engine uses the rounding factor to round the final price only if the calling application requests that the price be rounded. The rounding factor will not prevent the user from entering a price that is a greater precision than that given by the rounding factor.

Price List Lines

You identify what is being priced through the product context, product attribute, and attribute value. The price list line can therefore be for an item, item category, or anything defined within the Pricing Attributes Descriptive Flexfield. You may define volume breaks for price lists by making the line type a price break line. The Price Break button then becomes enabled. Price breaks may be quantity-based or value-based.

NOTE
Price breaks may actually be based on any attribute in the volume context of the Pricing Descriptive Flexfield. Value and quantity are two of the most obvious examples of how this is used.

The application method is discretionary only for service items for which you must choose between pricing by unit or percent of the price of the item being serviced. You can choose a formula for your price list line and effective dates. Because many price list lines may be effective to price a line on an order but only one can apply, precedence can be set for the line. The price list line with the lowest precedence will be the one applied.

NOTE
The precedence assigned to the list line by the pricing engine is the lowest precedence on the list line itself or any of its qualifiers.

Pricing attributes can further define the item being priced. For example, Neptune defines premium, standard, and economy support services, but defines an item only for support services. When entering an order in Order Management, the order-entry operator will choose the service item and then be presented with a choice of the service level in a separate window.

NOTE
You can define a Pricing attribute as being either user entered or sourced. If the Pricing attribute is user enterable, when entering an order in Order Management, the order-entry operator will be presented with a descriptive flexfield to enter the value of the Pricing attribute; if sourced, the Sourcing API will populate the Pricing Attribute value.

Administering Price Lists

Oracle Pricing offers a number of tools to help ease price list administration for volatile catalogs, or if you manage a large number of price changes.

Creating New Price Lists from Old

You can create a new price list by copying an old price list. Navigate to the Copy Price Lists form in the Pricing menu. You can copy all or a category of items, and you can bring the discounting structure and effective dates over to the new price list.

Managing Price Increases or Reductions

You can adjust the price of a(n):

- Item or range of items

- Item category—for example, Neptune has decided to reduce the price of all Pentium II Desktops.

- Item status—for example, Neptune may decide to reduce the price of all products with a status Retiring.

- Creation date—for example, Neptune updates its price lists twice every year, so it has a June 1 and a December 31 price list.

NOTE
You cannot use wildcards in the Beginning or Ending items.

You can adjust the price by a percent or an amount. To adjust prices, navigate to the Adjust Price List form in the Price List menu.

Adding Items to Price Lists

You can bulk-load items onto price lists using the same criteria as adjusting price lists. You can choose to set the price equal to the cost from the standard cost type in a specified organization. If you build your prices on a cost-plus basis, you can create the price list and then uplift the price accordingly.

Setting Up Pricing for Government Services Administration (GSA)

The GSA is the buying arm of the U.S. government. A condition of selling to the GSA is that you can show you have systems that guarantee no one will be offered a lower price than the government. Oracle Pricing uses the Modifiers form with an application type of override price to implement the special pricing that is needed for GSA. The basic logic is that GSA customers are offered the lowest price. This means that non-GSA customer orders should be placed on hold if the price on the order is less than the agreed GSA price. For countries that do not have a need for such pricing, the feature is very useful to set minimum prices. Salespeople can negotiate freely, but orders placed that are below the minimum price will be placed on hold. To set up a GSA price list, navigate to the GSA Pricing Setup form in the Price List menu.

NOTE

The application type of New Price is used so that whenever a GSA customer receives a GSA price, a discount will be created for the amount of the reduction. This allows the cost of giving a lower GSA price to be captured.

Secondary Price Lists

If the item you are ordering cannot be found on the primary price list on the order, the pricing engine will search through the secondary price lists in order of precedence to see if a price can be found. Advanced pricing supports multiple secondary price lists; basic pricing supports only a single secondary price list.

Price Qualifiers—Setting Up Rules of Eligibility

Price lists, discounts, and surcharges can be qualified to determine the orders to which they apply. It is the "Who you are?" piece of the pricing equation. For example, Neptune qualifies a price list to use for distributors. You can also qualify a price list to be used only with other order characteristics, such as a particular order type. For example, Neptune applies a surcharge to the order type Rush Order.

Qualifier Groups

You may choose a qualifier group to restrict the use of a price list. You can set up new qualifiers in Qualifier Groups in Oracle Pricing. An example of a qualifier group might be retail distributors. Under one qualifier group, you can set up attributes that must all evaluate to true for the list or modifier to apply. These groups are identified by a grouping number. By putting attributes under different grouping numbers, you are saying that all the attributes within at least one group must evaluate to true.

NOTE
Grouping Number may also be NULL, which means this qualifier becomes a condition that applies to all other qualifier groups.

Figure 20-2 shows how the qualifier attributes are evaluated within grouping numbers to qualify an order for the retail distributor price list.

Modifiers

Modifiers cover discounts, surcharges, freight charges, and deals and promotions. The Modifiers form is capable of creating them all. While discounts enable you to adjust prices, deals and promotions allow you the full range of sales incentives: coupons, upgrades, discounts on other items, and improvements in payment or freight terms. The different sales incentives are implemented as different line types within the form. Modifier lists are under version control and have date effectively in the header. You state who is eligible for the modifier list or modifier list line by clicking the List Qualifiers or Line Qualifiers button. You can choose from existing qualifier groups, or you can create qualifiers directly.

NOTE
Copying a qualifier group will actually copy rather than reference the qualifier group, hence, any changes made to the original qualifier group will not be reflected in the qualifier group where it has been copied to a List or List Line.

To create a modifier, navigate to the Modifiers form in the Pricing menu. Figure 20-3 shows a sample discount in the Modifiers form. It shows Version 1 of a discount list called "Compact Disk Discount." It shows a line-level lump-sum discount of $2. Only customers with a customer status of "Silver" will qualify for this discount.

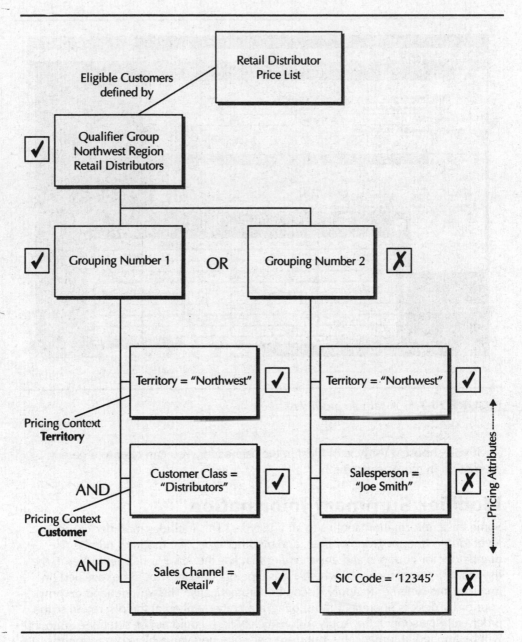

FIGURE 20-2. *Qualifying an order for the retail distributor price list*

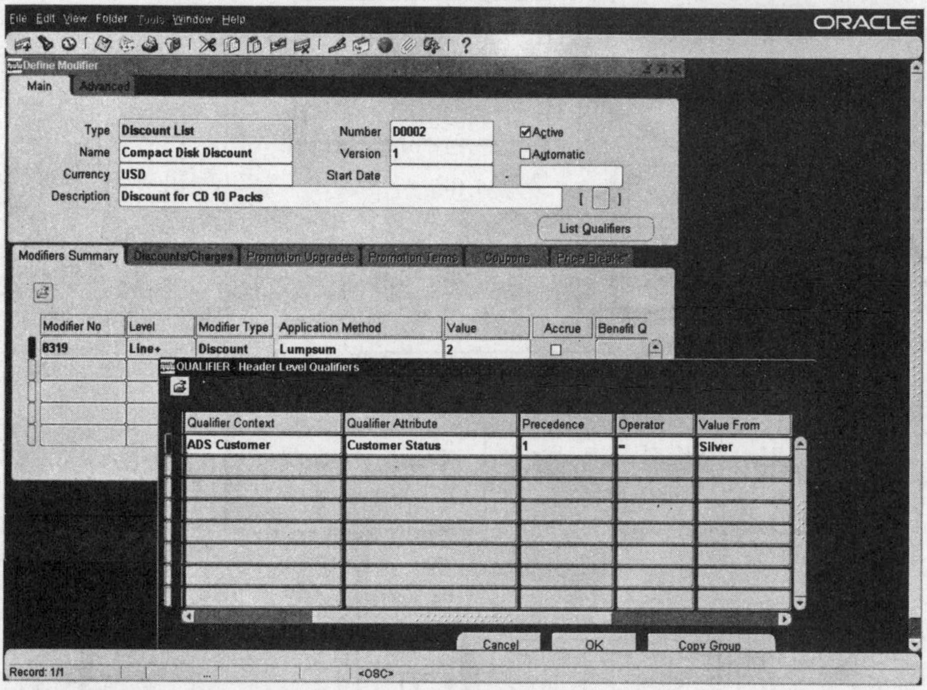

FIGURE 20-3. *A sample modifier screen*

If you choose a list type of Deal in the list header, you can refer to a parent promotion in the Advanced tab.

Modifier Summary Information

Some basic information applies to all line types. This includes modifier number, level (order, line, or group of line), and modifier type. The modifier number is mandatory for coupons and any modifier that has the Ask For flag set to Yes in the list header. You can choose whether this type of discount should be revealed on invoices and whether to apply discounts automatically. This will depend on how your order desk is operating. If discounts are being applied at the discretion of the order-entry personnel, the Apply Automatically flag should not be set. If the discount will be applied automatically, but the order-entry personnel have discretion to override the discount, the Allow Override flag should be checked.

Combining Discounts

When a number of discounts are eligible, you need to decide whether and how they will affect the overall price. You could choose to allow only one of the eligible discounts to be applied, or you could combine discounts. When discounts are combined, you might wish to apply all the discounts to the list price (called *additive discounts*) or apply discounts to the previously discounted value (*cascading discounts*).

Exclusive Discounts

If you choose to allow only one of the eligible discounts to be applied, you need to set up incompatibility groups. For example, in a retail environment, it is common to print on a coupon that the coupon cannot be combined with any other discount. Oracle Pricing enforces this through incompatibility groups. Modifiers can be defined as being incompatible within a given phase.

Pricing Phases   Oracle Pricing evaluates the lists and modifiers to be applied to the order at different phases. The incompatibility groups are defined within a pricing phase. Phases are needed because an order line might qualify for a discount based on many order lines. For example, a line might qualify for a volume discount based on the volume on all order lines of a product category. The order line will be priced when entered and then might be repriced in the All Lines phase. Incompatibility resolve codes are defined for the pricing phase. To set up a pricing phase, navigate to the Event Phases form in the Setup menu.

Incompatibility Groups   Oracle Pricing can resolve the modifier to apply within an Incompatibility group through its precedence or whether it returns the best price. The precedence of a given modifier is assigned on the line. It is defaulted from the Segment Number in the Pricing Descriptive Flexfield definition, explained in the technical overview. Incompatibility groups are set up in pricing lookups. Incompatibility groups can be assigned to modifier lines in the Modifier form and in the Modifier Incompatibility Setup form in the Modifiers menu. An overview of the how the exclusive discount is selected is laid out in Figure 20-4. Two modifiers would both be eligible, but they are within the same incompatibility group. The modifier with the lowest precedence is selected and applied to the order line.

Cascading and Additive Combinations

You can make combinations of discounts cascade or be additive. Additive discounts apply all the discounts to the list price. Cascading discounts apply a discount to an already discounted value. Oracle Pricing will treat as additive all discounts that are within the same pricing bucket. A pricing bucket is a grouping mechanism for

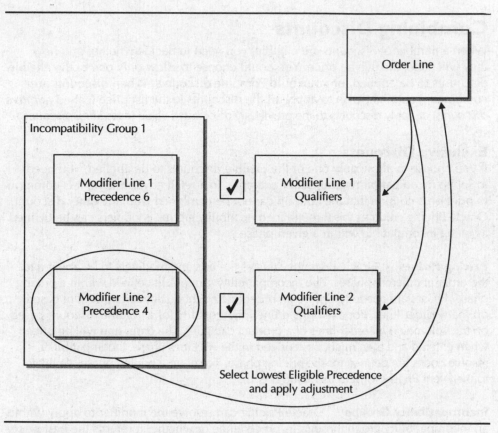

FIGURE 20-4. *Selecting exclusive discounts in an incompatibility group*

discount lines. Buckets are applied in Order. Bucket 1 is applied to the list price. Bucket 2 is applied to results of bucket 1 being applied. Putting all the discounts in the same bucket makes them additive. Putting discounts in different buckets makes them cascading. For example, if a set of writeable CDs has a list price of $10, and Neptune modifies the price by $1.50 for distributors and further discounts it by 10 percent from the list price for the San Francisco Bay Area, Bay Area distributors will be charged $7.50. Grill's is a discount warehouse that Neptune decides to grant an extra 10 percent from the *discounted* price. The calculation would look as follows.

List Price = $10.00
Bucket 1 percent discount = 10%
Bucket 1 amount discount = $1.50
Subtotal ------------------------= $7.50
Bucket 2 percent discount = 10%
Subtotal ------------------------= $6.75

NOTE
You can also place a modifier in an unnumbered bucket, known as a null bucket. Modifiers in this bucket are calculated off the list price and then applied to the last bucket's subtotal. Manual and Order Level modifiers are always in the null bucket.

Defining the Subject of the Modifier

The subject of the modifier can be refined through pricing attributes, price breaks, and exclusions. A brief explanation of each method for defining what is modified is outlined next.

Defining Pricing Attributes

You can define the Product or Product category that the modifier applies to in the Modifier Summary. You can define the subject of the modifier line to be more specific than the item using pricing attributes. To define pricing attributes, click the Pricing Attributes button. For example, Neptune provides service coverage for its enterprise servers, but it will charge the customer based on the age of the machine and the distance from the service center. Rather than record combinations of service, machine age, and distance as items, Neptune has decided to define service as the item and machine age and distance as pricing attributes.

Defining Price Breaks

You can create a single line discount with a volume or value qualifier. For example, spend more than $10 on item A, get a 10 percent discount. You can also create a price break by defining a Price Break header and Price Break lines in the modifier details, where you have multiple ranges. For example, spend more than $10 on item A, get a 10 percent discount; spend more than $50, get a 25 percent discount. All attributes, phases, buckets, etc., of the Price Break header apply to all Price Break lines.

A price break can be a point- or range-type break. With a point break, the entire volume is priced at the highest price break. With a range break, the volume within the range attracts the price within that range. The volume in the next price break range attracts the price in its range. A volume qualifier on a single line discount can be of type point or recurring. For example, if every fourth item is at 20 percent discount, the discount applies only to the fourth, eighth, and twelfth items.

Defining Exclusions

You can exclude pricing request lines from qualifying for the prices and discounts from a modifier by stating the excluded items, categories, and pricing attributes in the Exclusions window. You define exclusions by selecting the modifier and clicking the Exclusions button.

Discount and Charges

A discount creates a negative price adjustment. A surcharge creates a positive price adjustment. To create a discount line you must have a discount, freight charge, surcharge, deal, or promotion modifier list. If you have chosen a discount, only the Modifier Summary and Discount Surcharge tabs apply.

Charges

If this is a charge, you need to record the charge name. You can include or exclude charges from returns. If your list is of types surcharge or freight and special charges, the charge name will be required.

Discounts

You can state how the discount should be applied:

- Percentage

- Amount per unit

- New price for the line

- Lump sum (amount for the Line)

Pricing Formulas

Oracle Pricing allows you to price using a pricing formula. You can state the formula you are using for this discount. How to set up pricing formulas is covered later in this chapter.

Accrued Discounts

You can state that the discount is to be rebated rather than given as a deduction on the invoice. The system supports both monetary and nonmonetary accruals, such as shopper points or air miles.

NOTE
Non-monetary accruals *are defined as units of measure in the UOM Class defined by the Profile Option: QP Accrual UOM Class. For example, a flight may have a unit of measure of Seat and accrue a number of air miles.*

You need to record the quantity of the nonmonetary unit and its conversion into a monetary value. At press time, there was no automated functions for creating credit memos or payables vouchers to discharge such accrued liabilities. You can mark accruals as having been redeemed in the Accrual Redemption form in the Modifiers menu.

Differences Between Pricing with and without Advanced Pricing

There are many features that are only available if Advanced Pricing has been licensed. A few of them are as follows. If only Order Management has been licensed, the List Type Code LOV shows only Discount, Surcharge, or Freight List types when defining lists.

Advanced Pricing adds capability to utilize price breaks on price lists. The following break types are supported:

- Point break
- Range break

Advanced Pricing includes the Basic Pricing types and adds

- Coupon Issue
- Item Upgrade
- Other Item Discount
- Terms Substitution
- Promotional Goods

Defining Other Types of Discounts and Sales Incentives

The other types of discounts can be created through the line types shown in Table 20-1. The list type determines the line types that you can create within it.

Promotional Upgrades

In this tab, you indicate that the system should replace a specific item ordered with another item for the same price. The items that are available for upgrade are related through the Related Items form in inventory.

Terms Substitution

In this tab, you define the freight charges, shipping charges, and payment terms to be replaced with typically more favorable terms. For example, you might want to give preferential payment terms of 90 days on a promotional order that would normally attract a 45-day term via defaulting rules.

List Type	Discount	Surcharge	Freight	Promotion	Deal
Line Type					
Discount	✔			✔	✔
Surcharge	✔	✔		✔	✔
Freight Charge			✔		
Price Break	✔	✔		✔	✔
Item Upgrade				✔	✔
Other Item Discount				✔	✔
Terms Substitution				✔	✔
Coupon Issue				✔	✔
Promotional Goods				✔	✔

TABLE 20-1. *Modifier Line Types by List Type*

Other Item Discount

This gives a price adjustment or benefit to a specified item on an order when the customer orders one or more other items on the same order. For example, the customer might order a desktop PC from Neptune and be eligible for 50 percent off Internet service for 12 months.

> **NOTE**
> *The Benefit or Get Items on an Other Item Discount are optional. For example, if you set up Buy A and Get 10% on B, 25% on C, if either B or C are on the order, the discount will be given.*

Promotional Goods

In this tab, you define an item to be added to the order free of charge when the modifier line item is ordered. For example, Neptune is offering a free printer with the order of a new desktop PC.

Coupon Issue

Issues a coupon on one order for the customer to redeem for a price adjustment or benefit on a later order. The price on the originating order is not changed, but a new modifier is created for the coupon. It is the coupon modifier that will attract the discount when it is redeemed at a later date.

Formula-based Pricing

With Oracle Pricing, you can price based on a formula rather than a price list entry. For example, Neptune charges for extended warranty as a percentage of the list price for some customers and as a percentage of the order value for others. You can use formulas to create the price or to calculate a price adjustment. To create a formula, navigate to the Formulas Setup form in the Pricing menu. You can express a calculation based on a number of components. These components are used at steps within the calculation. Components can be

- **Numeric Constant**   For example, 20 percent of order value.

- **Function**   Oracle provides a PL/SQL hook to external pricing functions through a function, GET_CUSTOM_PRICE. For example, Neptune takes orders for extended warranty on printers. The price for printers is calculated through an external package and passed to Oracle Pricing through this function. GET_CUSTOM_PRICE must return a number to the calling application.

- **List Price**   For example, 20 percent of the list price on the order line. This might be used for a formula where the list price will be decreased if the customer is in education.

NOTE
Attach a formula that has a List Price component only to price list lines, not to modifier lines.

- **Price List Line**   For example, 20 percent of the North American standard list price, irrespective of the price list used on the order.

- **Pricing Attribute Value**   For example, Neptune offers service coverage on older equipment. It captures the age of the equipment as a pricing attribute.

- **Factor**   Neptune will increase the service charge by 30 percent if the equipment being covered is between two and four years old, and 50 percent if the equipment is between four and six years old.

Prior to advanced pricing, the support for formula-based pricing required you to create price list lines for all possible outcomes. For example, if a manufacturer of aluminum sheeting will charge for area of an ordered sheet in multiples of meters to a maximum of 200 square meters, it might choose to create the price list of Length and Width entries ahead of time. The pricing attributes of Length and Width would be created for every possible rectangle of aluminum sheeting that it sells. This has some performance benefits, and the capability still exists, but you define the price list line formula as a static formula and run the Update Formula Pricing concurrent request.

Agreements

There are two types of agreements: Standard and Pricing, determined by the Price List Type that you attach to the agreement. With Standard agreements, a price list can be attached to many agreements, and you can edit the price list through the Price List form. Pricing agreements Price Lists can only be edited through the Pricing agreements.

Pricing agreements are a way to store a more formal pricing arrangement with a customer. Although you can make price lists and discounts specific to a customer, the agreement makes it much easier to set up. Agreements are under revision control and have effectivity dates and signature dates. The salesperson and customer contact that were the signatories are also recorded. You can define the items on the agreement in terms of either your item number or your customer's item numbers. The lines themselves are under revision control. If you define a line as a price break, you can set up volume breaks, making this an ideal way to set up volume purchase agreements. Pricing can be taken from an existing agreement price list, or you can define it in the Pricing tab. The Payment tab enables you to set up a billing address and contact for this agreement.

Overview of the Pricing Flow

The Calling application prepares a pricing request. The pricing request includes what is being sold and how the purchaser qualifies for the price. The calling system will create the product hierarchy and pass this to the pricing engine in the pricing request. An example of a product hierarchy used for pricing is shown in Figure 20-5.

For example, a manufacturer of cake mixes might sell a stock-keeping unit (SKU) but price at the product group/brand/variant (cake mix, greens, lemon sponge, 2 dollars) level and discount at the product group/brand (greens, cake mix, 10 percent off) level.

Different customers might qualify for a discount. The qualification of a customer for a discount is through their position in a customer-pricing hierarchy. An example of a customer-pricing hierarchy is shown in Figure 20-6.

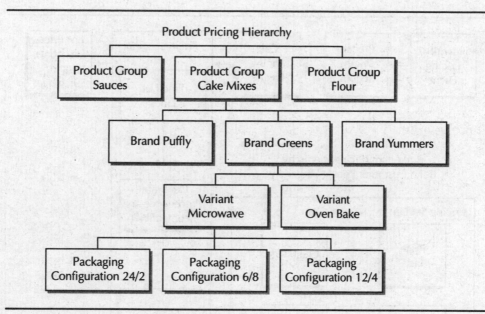

FIGURE 20-5.   *Product pricing hierarchy for a cake-mix company*

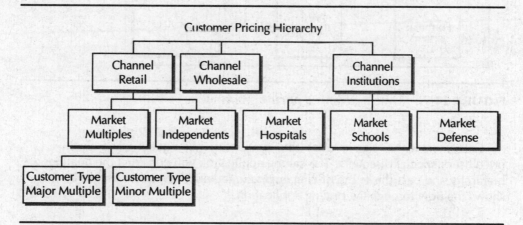

FIGURE 20-6.   *Customer pricing hierarchy for a cake-mix company*

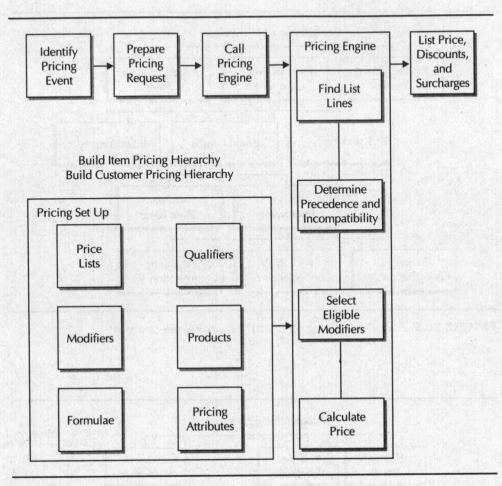

FIGURE 20-7. *Oracle advanced pricing process flow*

Customers within a given class (retail multiples) might qualify for a given price list or special discounts. The calling application will construct the qualifier hierarchy and pass this to the pricing engine in the pricing request. Figure 20-7 shows the flow through the pricing application.

Extending Oracle Pricing

Oracle Pricing provides seeded qualifiers and pricing attributes in associated contexts with defaulting rules. The following paragraphs explain how to extend the application for the inclusion of new qualifiers and pricing attributes. Pricing uses descriptive flexfields to define the qualifier and pricing contexts. Descriptive flexfields define attributes within a given context. Attributes are assigned a segment number. Pricing uses this segment number to resolve incompatible discounts. It is the segment number that is defaulted to the Precedence field in the Modifier form.

NOTE
To resolve incompatibility between discounts, you must assign segment values in pricing contexts that are unique across all contexts.

Setting Up Qualifiers

As explained earlier, qualifiers define eligibility for a given list or discount. Oracle provides seeded contexts that include customer, order, coupons, and other modifiers and volume.

Setting Up Qualifier Contexts

To set up a new context, navigate to the Define Descriptive Flexfield form. Query the Qualifier Contexts descriptive flexfield in the Pricing application. In the Contexts block, create a new row and give the context a new short name. You can optionally give the context a long name and description.

Setting Up Qualifier Attributes

In the Descriptive Flexfield form, query the Qualifier Contexts descriptive flexfield in the Pricing application. Choose the context that you want to add the attribute to. Click the Segments button. In the Segments column, give the new attribute a segment number that is unique across all qualifier contexts.

NOTE
Segment numbers 1–30 are reserved for applications development.

Create a name and prompt for the attribute. Select the column that you want to store the attribute in and the value set that defines the valid values for the attribute.

Setting Up New Pricing Attributes

As explained earlier, Pricing attributes define what is being sold. Oracle provides seeded pricing attribute contexts that include Item, Line Amount, and Pricing attributes. A pricing context is a way to model a product marketing hierarchy. Each attribute in the context represents a level in the hierarchy.

NOTE
When the pricing engine qualifies a list line for a given order line, it checks qualifiers and the product Pricing attributes. When it searches for the most specific price to apply, it looks for the lowest precedence. The precedence is defaulted from the segment number, so you need to ensure the segment number is unique across the product context and all qualifier contexts.

Setting Up Pricing Contexts

To set up a new context, navigate to the Define Descriptive Flexfield form. Query the Pricing Attributes descriptive flexfield in the Pricing application. In the Contexts block, create a new row and give the context a new short name. You can optionally give the context a long name and description.

Setting Up Pricing Attributes

In the Descriptive Flexfield form, query the Pricing Attributes descriptive flexfield in the Pricing application. Choose the context that you want to add the attribute to. Click the Segments button. In the Segments column, give the new attribute a segment number that is unique across all pricing contexts.

Create a name and prompt for the attribute. Select the column that you want to store the attribute in and the value set that defines the valid values for the attribute.

Defaulting Rules in Pricing

Pricing uses the same defaulting engine as Order Management to determine a value for a missing attribute on a pricing request. It does this for both Pricing attributes and Qualifier attributes. For a full explanation of how defaulting rules work, refer to Chapter 12.

Brief Technical Overview

The following paragraphs outline the technical specifications of the pricing system. Pricing is based on Oracles PL/SQL API standards. These implement PL/SQL procedures that you can call to interface your own systems into Oracle Pricing. Table 20-2 lists some of the packages and their purposes.

Package	Purpose
QP_CALCULATE_PRICE_PUB	Calculate a price
QP_GSA_ERROR_PUB	Raise a GSA error
QP_INT_LOADER_PUB	Process from interface tables
QP_LIMITS_PUB	Process discount limits
QP_MODIFIERS_PUB	Get a modifier
QP_MOD_LOADER_PUB	Load modifier lists
QP_MSG_PUB	Initialize the message table
QP_PREQ_PUB	Process pricing request
QP_PRICE_LIST_PUB	Get a price list
QP_PRL_LOADER_PUB	Load price lists
QP_QUALIFIER_RULES_PUB	Process qualifier rules
QP_REBATE_PAYMENT_PUB	Process accrued discounts
QP_SOURCING_API_PUB	Gets source attributes

TABLE 20-2. *Public Pricing APIs*

Specification of the Calculate Price API

The following listing shows the PL/SQL tables that are passed in and out of the Calculate Price API.

```
/*  PROCEDURE Calculate_Price
(p_request_line                 l_request_line_rec,
 p_request_line_details         l_request_line_details_tbl,
 p_related_request_lines        l_related_request_lines_tbl,
 x_request_line          OUT    l_request_line_rec,
 x_request_line_details  OUT    l_request_line_details_tbl,
 x_related_request_lines OUT    l_related_request_lines_tbl,
 x_return_status         OUT    VARCHAR2,
 x_return_status_txt     OUT    VARCHAR2);  */
```

Main Tables

The functionality for price lists and modifier lists is very similar, and they are implemented in the same tables, QP_LIST_HEADERS and QP_LIST_LINES. QP_LIST_HEADERS and QP_LIST_LINES are qualified through QP_QUALIFIERS. Details of products and other Pricing attributes are held in QP_PRICING_ATTRIBUTES.

Summary

This chapter explained the main pricing concepts of price lists, modifier lists, and pricing agreements. It showed how the basic pricing capability that comes with Order Management has been extended to include a range of pricing and discounting tools that serve business-to-business and business-to-consumer needs. These tools now include coupons, accrued discounts, upgrades, improved payment terms, and discounts on other items. You reviewed how these tools are built on a few key concepts of price lists, modifier lists, qualifiers, and pricing attributes. Pricing attributes define what you are buying, and price lists define how much you pay, which can be modified up or down with a modifier that you may be eligible for through a qualifier.

This chapter also reviewed how the pricing is administered by the commercial functions of the organization and the special functionality that exists for companies selling under GSAs. The chapter explained how the pricing functionality can be extended. It showed how to price and qualify discounts using other attributes in descriptive flexfields. Finally, it showed how the pricing engine is implemented in PL/SQL APIs that can be used by other applications.

PART
VI

Business
Intelligence

CHAPTER
21

Business Intelligence
for Manufacturing and
Supply Chain

racle introduced a set of business intelligence products with Release 11 of the E-Business Suite. These are applications that are targeted at senior and middle managers to monitor business process and help in setting organization strategy. These applications are based on a number of business intelligence technologies.

Business Intelligence Technologies

There are a number of job types supported through the business intelligence system. Each job type is supported through a different blend of the business intelligence technologies. The technologies include

- Personal Home Page and Portals
- Balanced Scorecard
- Activity-based Costing/Activity-based Management
- Performance Management Viewer
- Performance Management Framework
- Discoverer Worksheets and End-user Layer
- Business Views and View Generator
- Enterprise Data Warehouse

How the components fit together is laid out in Figure 21-1.

The needs of the executive are met with Performance Management Viewer (PMV) and Performance Management Framework (PMF). The PMF allows you to set targets for key business metrics. You can relate metrics into a business strategy that can be rendered as a strategy map or balanced scorecard. A strategy map is a set of metrics linked to show how movement in one metric influences another.

The needs of an analyst are met with Discoverer Workbooks for analysis, drilling into details, and finding patterns and exceptions. The summarized data is built using data warehouse technologies. Analysis is provided by an end-user layer (EUL) that allow users to move up and down levels of summarization and to related information. A business view generator creates views that include columns for key and descriptive flex.

Personal Home Page and Oracle Portal

At press time, most of the intelligence products for the E-Business Suite were delivered as predefined personal home pages. Personal Home Page (PHP) is the Extranet menu system. The PHP is how the self-service applications are exposed. It

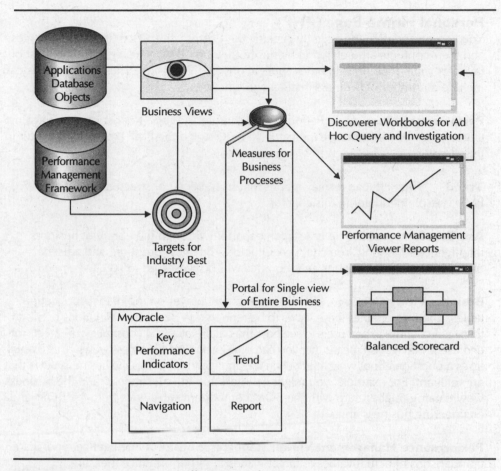

FIGURE 21-1.   *Business intelligence architecture*

has the capability to allow those outside the firewall secure access to a Web-based reporting application with rich graphical content.

Recently Oracle Portal has become part of the E-Business Suite technology stack. With this advent, there has been much greater concentration on how the information is delivered. Many smaller reports (*portlets*) are arranged on a portal page. Content for the portal page is both delivered by Oracle and syndicated by other providers. Portal has the capability to hold a user's password to many systems. Other systems can delegate the management of authentication to portal completely, obviating the need for many passwords. A portal page can be constructed from portlets from many sources that may all require authentication. *Single sign-on* (SSO) through Oracle Portal means that the user signs on only once but authenticates to many systems.

Personal Home Page (PHP)

You can personalize the page by clicking the Customize (pencil) icon. These pages and their contents are defined in menus in the normal way. You can define a list of favorites to include links to other applications and Web sites. These home pages can include a number of business intelligence functions.

Performance Measure   Performance Measure is a report of performance against target for a Key Performance Indicator (KPI). KPIs and the PMF are explained later in this chapter.

Trend   The PHP can display graphs that have been constructed from the PMV. PMV is explained later in this chapter.

Ask Oracle   Ask Oracle is a search capability through the library of business intelligence functions. You can "Ask Oracle" a business question, and a list of business intelligence reports and inquiries will be presented to you.

Business Views Catalog   Business views are a layer on top of the Application's tables. The EUL enables these views to be rendered in discoverer. Relations between these views allow expert users to see how the data relates and construct worksheets for end users. Navigation means that you can query on related business views. This inquiry takes a question about what might be in the application and lists the business views that are relevant. For example, you might be interested in "substitutes," and the business view catalog might return with the BOM component substitutes from the BOM and engineering business area.

Performance Management Viewer Reports   Business intelligence reports are comparisons of actual values to target values for a performance measure.

Portal

Oracle Portal is the new deployment of business intelligence. PMV and PMF are capable of producing portlets for both tabular and graphical data that can be used in Oracle Portal. SSO capability lets you access data from many data sources within one page. For example, you might choose to have My Stock Quotes from My Yahoo on the same page as a set of KPIs and a trend graph. The page design with Oracle Portal is much closer to what you might expect from a printed executive briefing than an enterprise applications page. You can navigate from the portal to Oracle or other applications without having to log on to those other applications.

Balanced Scorecard

The balanced scorecard, a strategic management concept developed by Robert Kaplan and David Norton, has shown successful results in many private-sector companies, as well as in some government organizations.

The Oracle Balanced Scorecard is an application to help organizations in their process of successfully implementing a business strategy. It organizes business metrics and the relationship between them into a strategy map. You can review the list of metrics as this map or as a scorecard. The scorecard lets you see metrics in the traditional four-quadrant scorecard with quadrants for financial perspective, customer perspective, internal processes, and learning and growth. For example, understanding customer needs might be a learning and growth metric. Having sufficient customer focus group meetings before committing to a design might be an internal process metric. Win/loss ratio might be a customer metric, and sales growth might be a financial metric.

Balanced scorecard lets you work backward from a financial perspective, through the processes and improvements needed to achieve them. It provides simulation capability to allow you to see the improvements that need to be made to achieve the business strategy and drill capability to allow you to navigate to the root cause of an out-of-tolerance metric.

At press time, the integration between balanced scorecard and the PMF was planned. The intelligence products within the E-Business Suite are not shipping preconfigured scorecards.

Activity-based Costing and Management

The E-Business Suite includes an activity-based costing module. This is beyond the activity-based costing that resides within the costing module. It includes the ability to model cost objects other than items, such as customers, services, product lines, and events. The system allocates costs based on activities and activity rates. It also includes a budgeting capability. The system is not a costing system in the same way that Oracle costing is. It is mostly a way to allocate nonfactory costs for finding the "true" costs of servicing an account or selling and supporting a product. Activity-based costing comes with a set of Discoverer Workbooks to analyze returns after the allocation of these costs.

Performance Management Framework (PMF)

The PMF is where you record the targets for the KPIs. The targets can be set at different levels. These targets may form part of the management-by-objective process in your company. The targets can have tolerances surrounding them. When an actual value exceeds one of the tolerances, a corrective action workflow is initiated. As delivered, the corrective action workflows simply notify the owner of the tolerance level for a target and level; you can tailor the workflows to be as complex as you want.

Oracle delivers more than 40 performance measures with the E-Business Suite. To define targets, navigate to the Targets form in the Business Intelligence System (BIS) responsibility. You are presented with a list of targets. Select a target and click the Go button. You are then presented with a list of levels for which the target can be set. Click Go, and record the target value for a given business plan.

Performance Management Viewer (PMV)

The PMV is a reporting tool, dedicated to reporting against targets in the PMF. It is driven by the Web Applications Dictionary. You define views to the dictionary, and you can rename the column names to user-oriented descriptions. You define report regions and report columns in this dictionary. The report column can be a target in PMF. When you define the function for PMV, you simply name the region to be displayed.

Discoverer Worksheets and End User Layer (EUL)

Discoverer is an end-user data-access tool. It provides a way for an "expert user" (not a developer) to create reports from the wealth of information in Oracle Applications. People can use these workbooks with no expertise in the tool or how the data is structured. For example, Oracle provides a number of prebuilt workbooks in the margin analysis and purchasing analysis areas. Discoverer has two editions: Admin and User.

Admin Edition

The Admin edition is where the EUL is created and users are granted access. Discoverer has a security mode for Oracle Applications. It can grant access to a database role or an applications responsibility. The switch in the Discoverer invocations is as follows:

```
<Drive>:\<Oracle Home>\DISCVR31\DIS31USR.EXE /APPS_USER
```

When an application user connects to the database, they can connect with the following:

```
<User Name>:<Responsibility>/<Password>
```

Bridges and Gateways   Discoverer comes with gateways to build the EUL from the database data dictionary or the designer repository. It includes bridges to other metadata repositories such as Oracle Warehouse Builder. This allows you to build start points for an EUL that can be tuned to be more understandable by end users.

Business Areas   The primary grouping of the Discoverer content is by business area. Business areas for the EUL delivered by Oracle Applications create a business area per application. The business area needs to be granted to a responsibility.

Folders   A folder corresponds to either a table or a view. Folders are composed of items. The items can be assigned to an item class. The item class defines the list of valid values for the item.

Hierarchies   The hierarchy definition allows you to define items that you can drill up and drill down on. This allows you to see summary data and drill-to details.

Joins   Joins allow you navigate through different folders in the EUL. You can declare joins in the EUL that are not necessarily foreign keys implemented in the database. Oracle Applications deliver joins in the EUL that correspond to the relationships in the published logical data models in the Business Objects manual.

User Edition

The User Edition is the part of Discoverer that the end users access. Users can open existing workbooks, or they can open folders and set conditions and calculations to create new workbooks. Workbooks can be scheduled to run at periods of low system load. Workbooks can be saved to the database or saved as a file.

Business Views and View Generator

The Discoverer EUL is based on a set of business views. The business views are a set of views that abstract the applications tables to a level that is understandable by end users. For example, the table MTL_SYSTEM_ITEMS might be renamed ITEMS. Foreign keys that might be difficult to resolve without knowledge of the application are resolved in the views. The views can also reflect applications configurations such as key and descriptive flexfield definitions. This will label the column with the title from the key or descriptive flexfield definition. Once your flexfields are configured, you can generate the business views by running the Generate Business Views concurrent request from a BIS super-user responsibility.

Business View Security

The whole business intelligence solution is aimed at cross-enterprise reporting. Those familiar with the multi-organization views will know that these views are restricted to a single operating unit. They are the organization in which the transaction is being performed. When you log into the applications, your transactions are within an operating unit. For example, if an employee places a purchase order, the terms used on-the PO are those negotiated within a specific operating unit.

Business views use security profiles. These were originally used within the HR applications. They implement organizational security by specifying a level in the organization hierarchy. HR can support many organization hierarchies. The hierarchy and top organization unit are specified in the security profile. A user logs in with a responsibility. This responsibility is associated with a security profile. The security profile grants access to a point in an organization hierarchy and all organization units under the node specified.

Enterprise Data Warehouse

The E-Business Suite also comes with an enterprise data warehouse (EDW). When a reporting solution needs to collect data from many data sources, the data warehouse can be very valuable. The business intelligence solutions are available on Release 11. The EDW can collect data from Releases 10.7, 11, and 11.i into a data warehouse.

The data warehouse also provides archiving capability. The main components of the data warehouse are facts, such as purchases, and dimensions, such as item. Each dimension can have many hierarchies. Each hierarchy can have many levels. For example, you might want to analyze purchase by item or commodity code. These dimensions ensure information is comparative between data collected in different applications. For example, if you are comparing revenue information from Order Management and Accounts Receivable up and down item hierarchies, these hierarchies are defined once.

Information is collected from the transaction system and loaded into the data warehouse on a net-change basis. Oracle Applications update a Last Update column whenever a row of data is changed. Data with a last-update date earlier than your last collection will not be collected. There are Performance Management targets and reports delivered over the data warehouse. The data warehouse is supplied with its own EUL for analytical and ad-hoc query access. The flow of information into the data warehouse is shown in Figure 21-2.

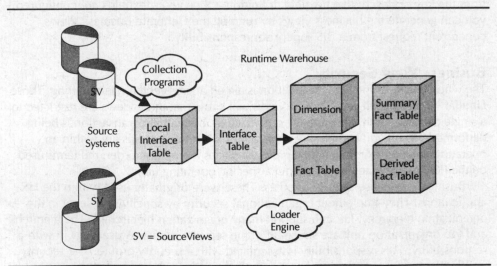

FIGURE 21-2.   *Flow of information into the data warehouse*

Business Intelligence Applications

The E-Business Suite comes with a number of prebuilt intelligence applications. These applications use the technologies listed previously to answer the business questions for senior and middle management.

Supply Chain Intelligence

Supply Chain Intelligence provides business intelligence for the Order Management and Distribution area. It includes a portal focused on the order management and cash collection activities. It also includes reports and workbooks based on both the transaction system and a datamart dedicated to supply-chain decisions.

Order to Cash Portal

A portal is a collection of portlets arranged on a page. There are many more portlets than are on the default Order to Cash portal. At press time, the Order to Cash portal included portlets for the following:

- **Order to Cash Performance** A list of KPIs covering the order-to-cash process, including revenue, growth, past-due shipments, book to fulfill days, and days sales outstanding (DSO).

- **Product Revenue Trend** Shows quarter-by-quarter revenue against quarters in the prior year with a projection of the current quarter revenue extrapolated from the current date.

- **QTD Revenue by Manager** Shows the quarter-to-date (QTD) revenue versus prior year, listed by sales manager.

- **Order to Cash Summary** Shows number and value of orders booked, fulfilled, and invoiced, and cash collected for the last week and current quarter against prior year.

- **QTD Revenue by Product** Shows the revenue for the current quarter against prior year with rate of growth.

- **Top Orders Summary** Shows a listing of the largest orders booked in the period.

- **Most Returned Items** Shows a list of the most returned items, with the value of those returns and the quantity of the item returned.

- **Backorder Summary** Shows the number of items and orders backordered and revenue not able to be shipped and invoiced, listed by operating unit.

- **Overdue Shipments Summary**   Shows the number of lines and orders with the revenue affected and the percentage of the QTD revenue that revenue represents.

- **Past Due Receivables**   Shows an aging analysis of overdue receivables, listed by credit manager.

- **Revenue Projection**   Shows the current QTD revenue versus QTD revenue from the prior year, as of the same day in the quarter. The percentage growth is extrapolated to give the projected full quarter revenue.

- **Current Year and Prior Year Revenue**   Shows quarter-by-quarter revenue by the highest levels in the product hierarchy.

Supply Chain Intelligence Reports

Supply Chain Intelligence includes reports over the continuum of the supply chain. These reports are executive-level reports against targets that form both the strategy of the company and the objectives that managers are incented on. An example of a Business Intelligence report is shown in Figure 21-3.

- **Sales Order Execution—Bookings**   The bookings reports include Bookings and Billings; Cancellations and Returns; and a Bookings, Billings, and Shipping analysis workbook.

- **Sales Order Execution—Backlog**   The Sales Order Execution Backlog Reports include Billing Backlog, Shipping Backlog, Delinquent Backlog, Unbilled Shipment Backlog, and a Backlog Analysis workbook.

- **Sales Order Execution—Shipping**   The Sales Order Execution Shipping reports include Order Shipment Volume, One Day Book to Ship, and One Day Pick to Ship. Analysis capability includes workbooks for On-Time Shipment Analysis and Order Fulfillment Analysis and one workbook that covers shipping volume and cycle time analysis.

- **Supply Chain Velocity—Order to Cash**   The Supply Chain Velocity reports decompose the order-to-ship cycle time into Book to Ship, Book to Fulfill, Book to Pick, and Pick to Ship elements.

- **Supply Chain Velocity—Procure to Pay**   The Supply Chain Velocity reports decompose the procure-to-pay cycle into Order to Pay, Order to Receive, and Receive to Pay. Analysis capability is provided in the Procurement Cycle Time Analysis workbook.

- **Supply Chain Inventories**   The Supply Chain Inventories reports are all data warehouse-based. You can select and view by levels in different hierarchies in the organization and item dimensions. The reports show how often inventory is turning over. This is measured as the ratio between the

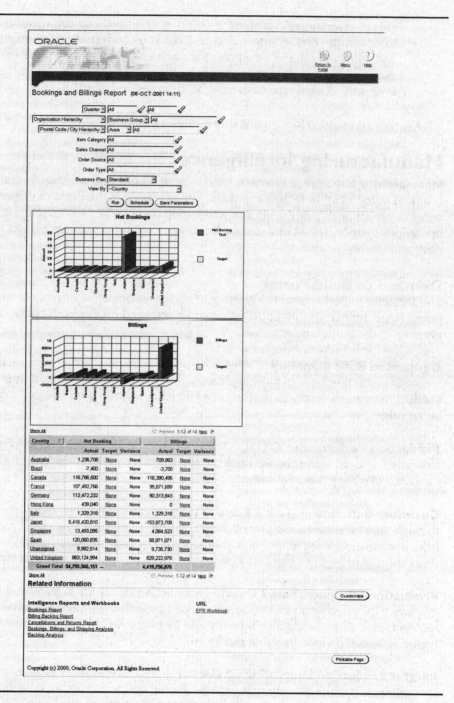

FIGURE 21-3. *Sample Business Intelligence report*

cost of inventory on hand to the cost of goods sold. You can measure the turnover for years, quarters, and periods. You can report on the quantity and value of on-hand inventory, the value of WIP inventories, the value of expired lots, the value of inventory by type, and the percentage of the total inventory in each type (receiving, WIP, stores, in-transit).

Analysis is provided in the Inventory Analysis workbook.

Manufacturing Intelligence

Manufacturing Intelligence is a portal and a set of reports and workbooks that is aimed at the plant or factory manager. The portal gives the plant manager a window on actionable problems and where they stand on key manufacturing and operations metrics. The Manufacturing Intelligence reports cover the mantra time, cost, and quality.

Demand to Build Portal

The Demand to Build portal is a number of portlet reports arranged onto a single page. There are many more portlets than those arranged on this portal page. At press time, the portlets were as follows:

Demand to Build Summary   This is a list of key manufacturing performance indicators with the status of those indicators. The indicators are on-time shipments, product margin, inventory turns, resource efficiency, resource utilization, and scrap value.

Production Performance QTD   The Production Performance QTD graph shows forecasted demand against booked orders, production schedule, and actual production measured in money, week by week.

Customer Satisfaction (Last 7 Days)   Customer satisfaction is measured through the percentage of shipments made on time and the percentage of order lines that customers are returning. On-time shipments are measured as the proportion of order lines planned to ship on a given day that did ship that day.

Production Efficiency (Last 7 Days)   Production efficiency is measured through efficiency (planned resource consumed divided by actual resource consumed), resource utilization (productive time divided by time available), and scrap value (value scrapped divided by value produced).

Largest Production Shortfall QTD (Units)   Production shortfall highlights production quantities that are in the master production schedule but have not been manufactured. It summarizes by product category the units of production scheduled and produced. It shows the value of sales orders that have been promised against the master production schedule but not been produced.

Largest Overproduction QTD (Units)   Largest overproduction highlights production for which there is no master production schedule. It attempts to show product that is subject to holding costs and obsolescence risk because no buyer exists. It shows the production scheduled and produced and the value of that production.

Product Margin   Product margin shows the target and actual margin percentages for the current and four prior quarters by product category.

Manufacturing Cost Variances   Manufacturing cost variances show the target and actual variances for the current and four prior quarters. The manufacturing cost variances are calculated as the total of all the manufacturing variances divided by the expected cost for the items and are aggregated by category.

Inventory Turns   The Inventory Turns portlet shows target and actuals for the current and prior four quarters. Inventory turns are calculated as the value of cost of goods sold in the period divided by the value of inventory at the end of the period.

WIP Days on Hand   The WIP Days on Hand shows target and actuals for the current and prior four quarters. It is the number of days' worth of production that has sat on the shop floor. It is measured as the value of WIP inventory divided by value of production multiplied by days of production.

Manufacturing Intelligence Reports

Manufacturing intelligence comes with a set of reports built over the data warehouse. These reports are broken down into areas of production management, product quality, variance analysis, critical resources, and performance to plan.

Production Management Reports   For all the production management reports, you can restrict and view by levels in selected hierarchies in the organization and item dimensions and compare with targets from a specified business plan over a given period.

- **Resources Utilization**   Compares aggregate available resources with resource applied in comparison to targeted utilization.

- **Material Efficiency**   Compares the cost of material issued to WIP with the planned cost of material issued for the quantity of assemblies produced. It is what might more traditionally be called *material usage variance*. If material is backflushed, material efficiency will be merged with inventory count adjustments, as actual usage will be identified only when components are counted.

■ **Resource Efficiency** Compares the cost of resources charged to the job with the planned cost of resources for the quantity of assemblies produced. If resources are autocharged, resource efficiencies are not normally generated, although you could have resource efficiency variances if you backflushed resources from an alternate routing.

■ **Production Efficiency** Compares the time consumed by time-based resources charging to the job with the aggregate time planned for time-based resources from the manufacturing routings.

■ **Late Production Completion** Compares the number of jobs completed on time with the total number of jobs completed. You can select a production line or report across production lines.

■ **Linearity Index** Compares the aggregate quantity output with the quantity planned for one, some, or all production lines.

Production Management Workbooks There are workbooks provided for drill and analysis into the areas of production effectiveness analysis, WIP analysis, resource analysis, and continuous improvement analysis.

Product Quality Manufacturing Intelligence provides quality information from the Oracle Quality product. Reports are available for nonconformity value, quantity, and analysis by defect code. As well as the organization and item dimensions, you can also select and view by the trading partner dimension.

■ **Quality Nonconformity Value** Compares the aggregate value of nonconformant material with the total value of material tested.

■ **Quality Nonconformity Quantity** Compares the aggregate quantity of nonconformant material with the total quantity tested.

■ **Quality Nonconformity by Defect Code** Compares the aggregate quantity of nonconformant material for each defect code.

Quality Management Workbooks There are workbooks provided for drill and analysis into the areas of defect analysis and test reports.

Cost Variance Reports The cost variance reports give you a view of how well you are controlling production activity to standards and the accuracy of those standards.

■ **Manufacturing and Purchase Price Variance**   Shows the total manufacturing variances and total purchasing variances (Purchase Price Variance and Invoice Price Variance) as both a raw value and a percentage of product cost.

■ **Actual Scrap**   Shows scrap value and percentage of assemblies scrapped against target. You can further refine your selection or set your view-by to production line.

A workbook for detailed cost variance analysis is also provided.

Purchasing Intelligence

Purchasing Intelligence is the intelligence product that serves the professional buying community. It includes a portal that covers the entire procure-to-pay cycle and a set of reports and workbooks.

Procure to Pay Portal

The Procure to Pay portal is composed of a set of portlets laid out to give you a view of the entire cycle on a single Web page; it spans the time from the moment a need is recognized to the disbursement of funds. It might be used by a vice president of procurement or as a tab on a Chief Executive Officer portal. The actual page is somewhat longer than the section shown in Figure 21-4. Again, there are more portlets defined than have been arranged on the Procure to Pay portal.

Performance Measures   The Performance Measures portlet on the Procure to Pay portal has KPIs for QTD, purchases (POs approved), and QTD spend (invoices received). Contract leakage identifies spend for commodities for which contracts exist but have not been used. The procure-to-pay cycle time is broken down into PO approval, order to payment, order to receive, and receipt to pay.

Monthly Travel and Entertainment Expenses   Monthly Travel and Entertainment is a graph broken out period by period for the current and prior years and with month-to-date for current month.

QTD Purchases by Supplier   QTD Purchases by Supplier shows the total value of POs approved in descending order of aggregate spend by supplier. Each supplier is shown with the percentage of total spend and the overall score. The overall score is an index constructed from the price, quality, delivery, and service scores for the supplier.

Monthly Purchases—Total Company   Monthly Purchases is a graph of POs approved period by period.

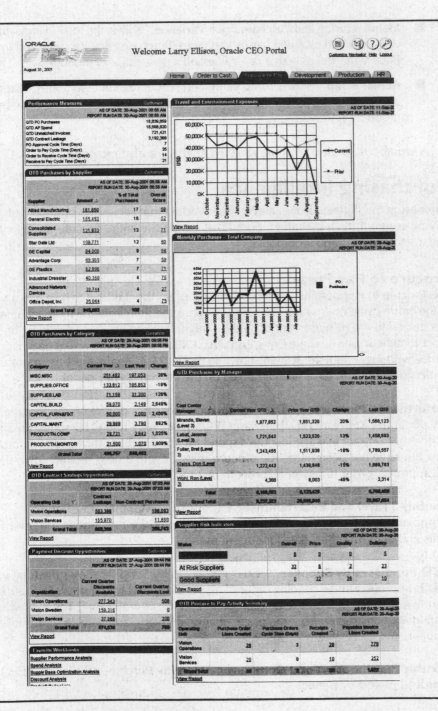

FIGURE 21-4. *Procure to Pay portal*

QTD Purchases by Category   The QTD Purchases by Category shows the aggregate value of POs approved by category. It displays current and prior year with growth or reduction percentage.

QTD Purchases by Manager   Purchases by Manager shows the POs approved by cost center manager. The purchases are rolled up the management chain. Top-level managers are shown against all the spend that they control, either directly in their cost centers or indirectly through the cost center budgets that they have delegated to their managers. For example, Jane Smith is the general manager of the Consumer Products and Accessories Division. Her direct managers are Bob Jones and Fred Clark. Bob runs the Palmtop product line. He has cost center managers that run service, research and development, and marketing. When the CEO of Neptune is reviewing spend by his managers, he will see the spend of Palmtop R&D included in the purchases for Jane Smith. You can drill up and down the management chain by clicking the names. You can see the current and prior year and QTD spend with a growth or reduction percentage. The previous quarter purchases are also shown.

QTD Contract Savings Opportunities   Contract Savings Opportunities shows the contract leakage and noncontract purchases in the quarter. Contract leakage, as explained earlier, is the value of POs that have been raised without the benefit of negotiated contracts that the company has in place for the commodity purchased. Noncontract purchases are an indicator for the purchasing department that the company is spending money on commodities for which no negotiated contract exists.

Supplier Risk Indicators   Supplier Risk Indicators shows the number of suppliers that are categorized as problem suppliers, at-risk suppliers, and good suppliers. You can see the numbers that fall into each of these categories based on service, delivery, quality, price, and overall.

Payment Discount Opportunities   Payment Discount Opportunities shows the terms discounts that have been lost in the quarter because of missing terms discount dates, as wells as the terms discounts available on accounts payable that are due within the quarter.

QTD Pay Activity Summary   This portlet shows the transaction throughput for each operating unit across PO lines created, receipts created, payables invoices created, and payments created, as well as PO cycle time.

Current Activity Transaction Backlog   The Current Activity Transaction Backlog shows activity that is behind schedule within the procure-to-pay cycle by operating unit. Supplier late activities are late acknowledgements, both number and days late, and overdue receipts. Internal measures are the number of open payments and the average number of days late within accounts payable.

Purchasing Intelligence Reports

In the Purchasing Intelligence Reports, you can restrict and view by levels in hierarchies in the organization, trading partner, and item dimensions.

PO Purchases   This report shows the value of POs approved. You can also restrict and view by the buyer and geography dimension, as well as the operating unit, item, time, and trading partner dimension.

Accounts Payable Spend   Accounts Payable Spend shows the value of invoices received. You can also restrict and view by the AP clerk.

Supplier Scorecard   The Supplier Scorecard shows the score for price, quality, delivery, survey, and total, with a target for each score.

Contract Leakage Report   The Contract Leakage Report tells managers if rogue buying is happening. It is a very powerful report that is worthy of a little explanation.

- **PO Purchases**   Shows the value of purchases

- **Contract Purchases**   Shows the value within those purchases that were made under a negotiated contract

- **Leakage**   Shows the value of purchases that could have been made under negotiated contract, but were not

- **Potential Savings**   Shows the value of the difference between the price paid for the commodities and the price available under the negotiated sources.

- **Actual and Target**   Shows the percentage leakage percentage of purchases against target

Purchasing Workbooks

The E-Business Suite provides workbooks for analysis in spend, contract, supplier performance, supply-base optimization, discount, productivity, and buyer.

Supplier Scorecard Calculations

The Supplier Scorecard and Risk Indicators incorporate a scorecard that shows the relative performance on axes of price, delivery, quality, and survey. The relative scores are displayed. An explanation of how those scores are calculated follows.

Weighted Price Score   The Weighted Price Score displays the price score multiplied by the corresponding weight factor entered in the parameter page for this worksheet. This score is determined by comparing the average price that a supplier gives for an item with the target price. The target price is the "best" price given for an item from any supplier during the same time period. The closer a supplier is to the target price, the higher the supplier's price score will be.

The price score is calculated in the following way:

```
Price Score =(Transaction Quantity Ordered * (Target Price/ Price))/
Total Quantity Ordered
```

NOTE
Target price has a detailed algorithm for determining the correct value. The method varies depending on the type of PO, whether there are price breaks, and several other conditions.

Weighted Quality Score   The Weighted Quality Score displays the quality score multiplied by the corresponding weight factor entered in the parameter page for this worksheet. This score is a reflection of the percentage of goods accepted after inspection for a given supplier. The quality score is calculated in the following way:

```
Quality Score = ((Quantity Received - Quantity Rejected)/Quantity Received)
    * 100
```

NOTE
The Quantity Received and Quantity Rejected columns come from the receiving transaction table in Oracle Purchasing.

Weighted Delivery Score   The Weighted Delivery Score displays the delivery score multiplied by the corresponding weight factor entered in the parameter page for this worksheet. This score is a reflection of the percentage of on-time deliveries for that supplier. The delivery score is calculated as follows:

```
Delivery Score = (Quantity Received - Quantity Received Early - Quantity
Received Late)/(Quantity Received + Quantity Past Due) * 100
```

Weighted Survey Score   The Weighted Survey Score displays the survey score multiplied by the corresponding weight factor entered in the parameter page for this worksheet. This score is a reflection of the average score received by that supplier during a given time period. Scores at the lowest time period are averaged together. For each level in the time dimension, scores continue to be averaged as they are rolled up to the level that you want to analyze. Each individual survey score is calculated as follows:

```
Survey Score = ((Score - Minimum Score)/(Maximum Score - Minimum Score))
* 100
```

Survey scores are entered through special survey forms available in the Oracle Applications source environment. The surveys themselves are created in the same environment, which is where the maximum and minimum scores are defined.

Aggregate (Overall) Score   The overall score displays the aggregate, or total, score for a supplier. Each component score, including price, quality, delivery, and service, is weighted using the corresponding weight factor entered in the parameter window. The weighted scores are then added together to determine the total supplier score.

Summary

This chapter reviewed the various technologies that Oracle employs to provide Business Intelligence within the E-Business Suite. It reviewed the portals that Oracle provides and showed how to customize the portals to your own needs. The chapter also reviewed the performance management framework, illustrated the setting of set targets and tolerances, and showed how the Performance Management viewer reports against these targets. Drilling and pivoting capabilities of Oracle Discoverer and how to move through the end-user layer were also covered. You also looked at the business views and learned how to run the business view generator, build the data warehouse, and adapt the warehouse definition with Oracle Warehouse Builder.

The Business Intelligence Applications were examined, first looking at supply chain intelligence, then manufacturing intelligence, and finally purchasing intelligence. The intelligence products have a portal, a set of reports, and a set of workbooks. In this chapter you reviewed the portal that gathers the business intelligence for a whole process and presents the information in a comprehensive page of information with drills to related reports and information. The reports have a common set of dimensions to view and restrict access to the information; each report and the workbooks that provide analysis capability for each area were discussed.

CHAPTER
22

Case Study: Neptune Corporation

he functional chapters have occasionally cited examples using Neptune Corporation. This case study will explain Neptune's operations. The case sections correspond to the various chapters in this book. Each case section also comes with a list of activities. Analyze the case section, and use the activities listed in each section as questions for your implementation effort. These activities are not meant to be a comprehensive list of implementation steps; you are encouraged to explore areas and options that are not explicitly mentioned in the list of activities.

Design and Manufacturing Engineering

To understand Neptune's design and manufacturing engineering functions, it is first necessary to understand its enterprise structure. The company's manufacturing philosophy also influences its design of items, bills, and routings, and its industry places a premium on rapid product-design cycles. Neptune uses the Oracle E-Business Suite to facilitate communication between its various business units, and thus maintain its competitive advantage in bringing new products to market.

Customer pressure also has led Neptune to adopt flow manufacturing practices, to respond to customer orders quickly while minimizing its investment in inventory.

Enterprise Structure

Neptune manufactures a full range of computers including servers, desktops, and laptops. Neptune offers an Internet service as an option in its products. A company named World Online (WOL) provides this service, and Neptune receives commission from WOL when a customer chooses this option.

Saturn is a 100 percent subsidiary of Neptune and manufactures network communication products such as switches, routers, and related products.

Neptune has two divisions: Neptune Products (NP), which designs, develops, manufactures, and distributes their products; and Neptune Professional Services (NPS), which performs onsite installation and maintenance of computers and networks and also operates parts and service centers around the world.

NP has manufacturing and distribution facilities all over the world. The manufacturing facilities are located in the following cities:

- Sacramento, California
- Pittsburgh, Pennsylvania
- Taiwan

The distribution facilities are in the following locations:

■ Orlando, Florida

■ Denver, Colorado

■ Madrid

■ Singapore

Each facility accounts for inventory in its local currency. The U.S. facilities (Sacramento, Pittsburgh, Orlando, and Denver) use the same chart of accounts. Taiwan uses the same chart of accounts as the U.S. locations. Singapore and Madrid each has its own chart of accounts.

To minimize shipping costs and times, the supply chain is designed primarily by geography; however, alternate sources are modeled, particularly for expensive or long lead-time items. The "Supply Chain Planning" section discusses this further.

Each manufacturing plant has a central store and many RIP (raw in process) stores that serve the various machining and assembly cells. Once the materials are received at the receiving dock, they are normally transferred to the central stores. In some cases, the material that is received is sent directly to the RIP stores. The warehouses are designed to support a serpentine picking model, using Locator Picking Order to define the pick path.

Enterprise Structure Activities

Consider the following activities, as they pertain to Neptune's enterprise structure and your own:

1. Define the set of books and business groups that are required by this client.

2. Define the legal entities under the appropriate set of books.

3. Define the operating units under the appropriate legal entities.

4. Set up the workday calendar(s) that Neptune will need.

5. Define the inventory organizations under the appropriate operating units.

6. Define appropriate subinventories and locators for each inventory organization.

Managing Items, Bills, and Routings

Neptune uses one item master organization for all its manufacturing and distribution facilities. As part of its implementation planning, it identified the item attribute control levels. To simplify item maintenance, the implementation team began with the assumption that attributes would be master-controlled whenever possible. The team reviewed each attribute with team members from the various functional areas to identify fields that required organization-level control; most planning attributes are controlled at the organization, for example, to enable more flexibility in the planning process.

When new items are added to the item master, each of the functional areas is notified to review and modify the item attributes that affect its function. For example, the procurement department is responsible for an item's purchasing and receiving attributes, cost accounting is responsible for costing, etc. To prevent unauthorized or inadvertent changes to item attributes, Neptune uses security on the different attribute groups.

To more easily understand the function of the different items in its operation, Neptune has identified a number of item types to classify its items: Finished Good, Subassembly, Subassembly/Spare, Purchased Item, and Phantom. It has developed a unique template for each item type to facilitate item entry.

Neptune uses item status primarily to identify phases in an item's lifecycle. The default status is New, which prohibits all activities. Other statuses include Prototype, which allows most activities except sale to customers; Active, which allows all activities; and Obsolete, which permits inventory stocking and inventory transactions, but prohibits other activities.

Item status can vary by organization. For example, an item might be in Prototype status in one manufacturing plant, but fully active in another, therefore, item status and the attributes it controls are maintained at the organization level. The one exception to status control is the BOM Allowed attribute. This is controlled at the master level and is set when the item is initially defined; it does not change during the product's lifecycle.

Because of the extensive use of categories for reporting and processing across the Oracle E-Business Suite, Neptune's implementation team carefully reviewed the categorization needs of the various functional departments within the company. The Engineering, Materials Management, and Planning departments agreed on a common categorization scheme that groups items by anticipated usage: raw material, subassembly, finished good, or mixed usage. The Procurement department determined that it would use categories to represent an item's commodity code. The Cost Accounting, Order Management, and Service organizations identified a need to group items by their primary product family.

Item relationships are used to identify items that have superceded other products and to maintain a relationship between a product and its repair kit(s). Neptune also uses customer-item cross-references to identify customer part numbers for some of its larger customers and item cross-references to specify the UPC code for some of its products.

High-volume products produced on flow lines have flat bills of material, in keeping with demand-flow best practices. Complex and specialized products, such as large servers, might have deeper bills of material, but Neptune strives to keep the bills as flat as possible. If a specialized product proves popular enough, it will be moved to a flow line. In this case, Neptune might temporarily identify some subassemblies as phantoms to quickly affect the "flattening" of the bill; for long-term production, such bills are ultimately revised to eliminate the phantom level.

Neptune maintains some component substitutes in its bills of material for items it has identified as frequently on allocation. This enables planning to automatically generate requisitions for the alternate components and also serves as documentation of acceptable substitutes for manufacturing.

Routings are relatively simple and are used primarily for standard cost development. Most components are set up to be backflushed at operation completion. Because labor is a small percentage of the products' cost, all labor resources are set up to be automatically charged. Operation method sheets for flow production are maintained as operation attachments, so they are visible in the flow and discrete workstations.

Neptune maintains alternate bills and routings for a few high-volume items. Optimized planning occasionally suggests an alternate routing (and associated bill) to alleviate short-term capacity problems. It also maintains product families for its popular products, such as the Asteroid laptop family. These product families are used in manufacturing engineering and reporting.

Item, Bill, and Routing Activities

The following activities will help you think about how Neptune and your own company can best use the Oracle E-Business Suite for item, bill of material, and routing maintenance:

1. Review the item attribute controls, and determine the appropriate control level for each attribute in order to meet Neptune's needs.

2. Review the status control attributes, define appropriate status codes, and specify their effect on each of the status control attributes.

3. Define the category sets, category codes, and default categories that this client requires.

4. Identify the item types that Neptune is likely to use.

5. Review seeded item templates and modify as necessary to meet the company's requirements.

6. Define cross-reference types to meet Neptune's needs.

7. Define appropriate resources, departments, and resource availability.

8. Define alternate designators for bills and routings.

9. Define the appropriate items, bills, and routings.

Design Engineering

Neptune designs and develops products in a research facility, which is located in the primary manufacturing location. The new product development process includes gathering of requirements, design, prototype development, and product proving. The manufacturing engineering teams take this information and establish their manufacturing processes to deliver the products that have been developed.

A typical design cycle begins with a prototype (engineering) bill of material to control access to the bill and prevent unnecessary confusion on the shop floor. A WIP job is created to build the prototype, with most components and labor charges entered manually.

The completed prototype is often issued to the service organization for field testing using an internal transfer. Field test data is collected using a quality collection plan, and the data is analyzed.

Engineering Change Orders (ECOs) are used to change products after they have been released to manufacturing. Change requests can be initiated based on a variety of factors: customer requests or complaints, production problems, or cost-reduction opportunities. Typically, an engineer studies the request or problem and proposes an ECO as a remedial action. ECO types at Neptune correspond to the source of the change (Customer Request, Production Improvement, Cost Improvement, etc.). The ECO is approved or rejected by an ECO committee made up of the department heads of Research and Develpoment, Quality, Manufacturing Engineering, Procurement, Marketing, Finance, and Service. The committee also decides on the effectivity of the change and the disposition of existing material.

Mass change ECOs are occasionally used. For example, if a component is found to have a high defect rate, it might be replaced in all the bills where it is used, or a customer might request a change to the configuration of all the machines that are supplied to them. Neptune will use a mass change to make the appropriate changes to all the configuration items that were created for that customer.

Design Engineering Activities

Use the following activities to analyze how you would apply the Engineering module of the Oracle E-Business Suite to Neptune, and to your own company:

1. Define appropriate responsibilities and profiles to control access to Engineering bills and routings.

2. Determine the numbering method for Neptune's Engineering Change Orders, and set up the numbering controls.

3. Define the ECO types and priorities needed by this client.

4. Review ECO approval workflow for proper routing of ECOs.

5. Transfer engineering items and bills to manufacturing.

6. Set up and implement mass change orders using category sets and categories.

Assemble-to-Order and Pick-to-Order Products

Popular product families, such as the Asteroid laptop family, are offered with a variety of options. For example, customers can order an Asteroid with his or her choice of processor, memory, hard drive, and CD-ROM/DVD. As a result, the Asteroid product is configured and assembled only in response to customer orders. An Assemble-to-Order (ATO) model bill defines the available options and is used in the configuration process.

Sometimes customers will order the Asteroid as part of a kit that might include a carrying case, spare battery, external floppy drive, or other options. These kits are identified as Pick-to-Order (PTO) models and include the ATO model for the computer itself as part of the model bill of material.

For some large corporate customers, Neptune will apply the customer's logo to the CPU as part of the final assembly process.

ATO/PTO Activities

Consider the following ATO/PTO activities as they pertain to Neptune's and your own business:

1. Define appropriate option classes for the Asteroid laptop.

2. Define the model bills and routing for the Asteroid line.

3. Determine which routing operations are option-dependent, and set the appropriate flags.

Manufacturing Engineering

Neptune has many production lines to manufacture its products. The Asteroid line is used for regular production runs of the Asteroid model laptops. A schematic layout of this line is shown in Figure 22-1.

The line design began with identification of all the discrete events in the process; identification and removal of all non-value-added events; and the grouping of events into logical, standard line operations. After this was done, Neptune created a forecast that represented the anticipated mix and volume for the intended line design and used this forecast to generate the Mixed Model Map. This process identified line operations with a takt time higher than the line takt time. For such operations, Neptune's engineers reviewed the events within each line operation. In some cases, they could move the events to other line operations; in other cases, they redesigned the process. They

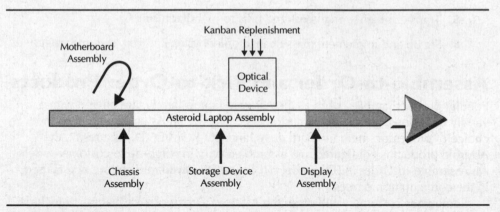

FIGURE 22-1. *Asteroid laptop line*

repeated the process until the line was reasonably balanced and designated the use of in-process kanbans where necessary.

As part of the process, manufacturing engineering identified alternative resource deployment scenarios for demand levels that are 60 and 80 percent of the designed capacity.

Line designs are reevaluated with each major new product release and are evaluated weekly using actual demand to determine if the alternate scenarios must be used or if the line should be redesigned.

Because the Asteroid model can be supplied in over a hundred configurations, Neptune starts assembling its laptops only after it receives a firm order. The speed of the line is adjusted to suit the demand requirements, so there is minimal inventory buildup between processes. Other assembly lines operate based on an anticipated build schedule, which in turn is constructed based on forecasts. The motherboard assembly is produced in batches using discrete jobs.

Manufacturing Engineering Activities
Use the following manufacturing engineering activities to analyze how you would apply the Oracle E-Business Suite to Neptune, and to your own company:

1. Define the Asteroid production line and other needed lines for flow production.

2. Define the standard events, processes, and line operations needed for the Asteroid line.

3. Design a preliminary flow routing for the Asteroid product family.

4. Using a forecast or other source of demand, generate the Mixed Model Map for the Asteroid line.

5. Review the results, and adjust the line design if necessary.

Supply Chain Planning

Neptune's planning process covers its entire supply chain. It begins with a forecast, generated by the Marketing department, with collaboration from some of its larger customers, and reviewed weekly before being published back to individual forecasts in each organization. Forecasts are consumed by sales orders, and the combination of unconsumed forecast and actual orders is used as input to its supply chain plan.

Demand Planning

Neptune uses the item and customer dimensions for forecasting aggregation. The Item dimension uses the following item categories:

- PDAs
- Laptops
- Desktops
- Servers
- Imbedded systems
- Professional services

The customer dimension groups customers into the following customer classes:

- Industrial
- Consumer
- Distributor
- Education
- Export

Demand planning is an activity carried out by a forecasting and demand planning group within Neptune's Marketing organization. There is a planner for each combination of customer class and product category.

The demand planning cycle is a monthly activity. Planners are notified every day of deviations between the forecast and the orders received. An example alert might be:

```
"Select Geography within Geography:Country by Value where Difference
between Sales and Customer Forecast is greater than the value 100".
```

Demand plans are reviewed on a weekly basis and pushed back into ERP on a monthly basis. Distributors have extranet access to review and adjust forecasts.

Demand Planning Activities

The following activities will help you think about how Neptune and your own company can best use the demand planning capabilities of the Oracle E-Business Suite:

1. Define the dimensions that Neptune will use for demand planning.

2. Assign the appropriate dimensions to the correct demand planners.

3. Determine forecast scenarios to be generated, and select the forecast method and parameters for each.

4. Determine the allocation method for spreading aggregate forecasts.

5. Review standard reports, and assign the desired reports to the demand planners.

6. Set up usernames for external distributors, and ensure that the appropriate security is enforced so that external users can view and update only their assigned portion of the demand plan.

7. Review the demand planning cycle for completeness.

Advanced Supply Chain Planning

Neptune includes both orders and forecasts in its production plans and uses a single, holistic, advanced supply chain plan that covers all manufacturing and distribution facilities. The company is subject to various constraints in its manufacturing facilities and uses the advanced planning system to model and factor its constraints into its plans.

The supply chain for Neptune, illustrated in Figure 22-2, is determined primarily by geography. The Pittsburgh manufacturing plant typically replenishes the distribution centers in Denver, Orlando, and Madrid, while the Taiwan plant replenishes the Singapore distribution center. The Sacramento plant is the sole plant for large servers, which are shipped directly to their customers. Sacramento also provides extra manufacturing capacity, if needed, to supply Singapore.

Customer orders are normally fulfilled from the closest distribution center, except in the case of large servers that are shipped directly from Sacramento. Alternate sources of supply are defined for some high-ticket items, such as high-end desktop systems.

Neptune uses ASCP but has approached the process gradually. Its planners began with a basic, unconstrained, multiple-organization plan that encompassed their manufacturing facilities and distribution centers. Over time, they added internal constraints and optimization. At each stage, they ran simulated plans that incorporated the new options, compared those plans to the current state, and designated the new plan as the "production" plan only when they were ready.

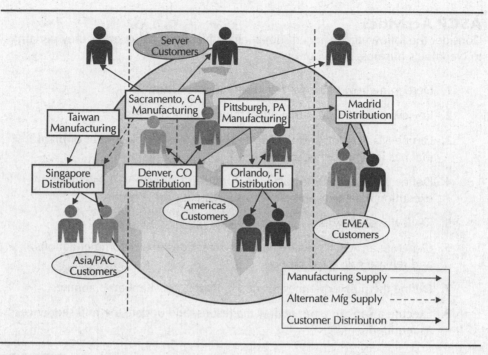

FIGURE 22-2. *Neptune's supply chain*

Planners and buyers are in the process of identifying supplier capacity from a few of their largest suppliers to further optimize their planning process.

Many of Neptune's items are kanban-controlled, and its planners use Kanban planning regularly, as part of their new product release process, to evaluate the kanban assumptions. At least once per quarter, they run the Kanban planner using actual demand to verify that the kanban sizes are suitable for the actual demand; they make adjustments if necessary.

All component items appear on the ASCP plan. The purchasing department uses this information in its pricing negotiations. Most items are single-sourced, but Neptune has identified a few alternate suppliers for critical items that are often allocated due to limited supply. For many single-sourced components, global sourcing rules are used to define the supplier and are assigned by item categories; exceptions are made by item/organization if necessary.

Although most items are procured using kanban signals, purchase orders for some long lead-time items are released from the ASCP plan.

On occasion, customer service will receive an unusually large order and contact planning to assess when it can be built. A planner will perform an online simulation of the new demand, to determine when it can be added to the production schedule, or what additional resources are needed.

ASCP Activities

Consider the following advanced supply chain planning activities, as they pertain to Neptune's business and your own:

1. Determine how to model Neptune's supply chain.

2. Review item attributes that affect the planning process.

3. Define Master Demand Schedules in each distribution center or plant that has independent demand.

4. Define the "production" plan (i.e., the plan Neptune will use for its execution activities) and alternates to be used for analysis.

5. Review workflows for appropriate routing of exceptions.

6. Generate an ASCP plan, review the exceptions and recommendations, and release suggested orders.

7. Define the pull sequences needed for Neptune's Kanban planning.

8. Execute a kanban plan, review the results, and update the pull sequences as required.

Supply Chain Execution

Neptune supplies its computers to corporate customers worldwide and also sells computers to individual customers. A common order desk serves the two divisions of Neptune. The same order desk serves Saturn. A few products such as monitors are drop-ship products. Neptune's warehouse personnel also perform light assembly and merge-in-transit in their distribution centers. Some of the products arrive directly at the customer from different supply points.

Order Management

Neptune has defined several order types to support different order-processing characteristics:

■ Standard

■ Priority

■ Export

■ Promotional

■ On Site configuration

■ Special configuration

Using Global Order Promising, the order service desk quotes each customer an available date as the order is entered. Because most of Neptune's products are assembled to order, order promising is based on the availability of key components and critical resources used in the final assembly process. Order promising attempts to satisfy customer orders from the closest distribution center, although alternate distribution centers are defined so that a customer service representative can select an alternate warehouse if the requested item is unavailable at the preferred location.

Distributors can order using their own item numbers, which are set up as customer item numbers at the customer level. Industrial customers can order using UPC numbers set up in item cross-references. Consumers can order using the Neptune number.

PDAs are available with a gift-wrap option. The PDAs are defined as a pick-to-order model with the gift wrap as a separate order line. There is no attempt to model the light-assembly operation as a job.

Order Management Activities

The following activities will help you think about how Neptune and your own company can best use the Oracle E-Business Suite for order management:

1. Determine the order types that Neptune needs.

2. Review the associated workflows, and modify as necessary.

3. Define the sourcing rules to be used for order promising, and perform the appropriate setup steps.

4. Review processing constraints and defaulting rules.

5. Enter and process a sales order for each of the following scenarios: standard products, ATO products, PTO products, and customer returns.

Supply Base and Procurement Management

Neptune buys most of its components from outside suppliers and has worked very hard to limit the number of suppliers in its supply chain. Direct materials are procured from established vendors. Neptune sends planning schedules to its largest suppliers so they can plan ahead; this advance visibility has facilitated the negotiation process and resulted in better terms for the company and less uncertainty for its suppliers. Much material is actually ordered based on kanban signals, which automatically generate releases against approved blanket purchase agreements. For some long lead-time and low-volume items, Neptune sends shipping schedules as required and occasionally creates individual purchase orders from its planning process.

Neptune also provides its largest suppliers access to purchasing information through the Internet Supplier Portal; this has proven to be a very effective communication tool. The selected suppliers can see notifications and details of new requests for quotations, orders, schedules, and releases. They can see Neptune's measurement of their performance in terms of on-time delivery and returns, and they can view order and payment history. A few suppliers even provide Neptune with capacity information, which Neptune is starting to use as a constraint in its planning process.

In the case of indirect materials, users create purchase requisitions. On approval, the required products are procured from pre-established vendors or new vendors, depending on the requirement. All employees have access to self-service procurement for normal supply orders.

Supply Base and Procurement Activities

Consider the following activities, as they pertain to supply base and procurement activities within Neptune's business and your own:

1. Set up suppliers, blanket agreements, and supplier-item relationships needed to automatically create releases based on kanban signals.

2. Research supply sources using RFQs and quotations.

3. Select and set up the appropriate items for supplier scheduling.

4. Review approval and account generation workflows.

5. Review the requisition pool and create purchase orders.

6. Review supplier performance, and update approved supplier lists accordingly.

Inbound Logistics

Neptune has three receiving dock locations, as illustrated in Figure 22-3. One is used for back-to-back orders that are received to the loading bay. For example, Neptune uses Sanyc monitors, which it delivers with its processor units. These are not put away in inventory; they are purchased to order and delivered to Neptune to assemble the load for delivery.

The layout of the main receiving bay splits the deliveries into quality-inspected and non-quality-inspected deliveries. QA is informed when inventory for inspection is delivered. To reduce non-value-added movement of material, it is inspected in the receiving bay.

More than 50 percent of Neptune's direct material suppliers have access to quality specifications on the Web and can record their test results. QA can review the results online; on receipt, they need only to verify batch numbers.

Neptune uses mobile devices for receipts from 80 percent of its suppliers. Purchase order number, item, supplier item, and shipment number all appear on the label.

Deliveries for indirect purchases are picked up by internal distribution twice a day. Deliveries into Inventory of verified material are continuous. The receiving pipeline must be clear of material at the end of each shift. Receiving and QA work

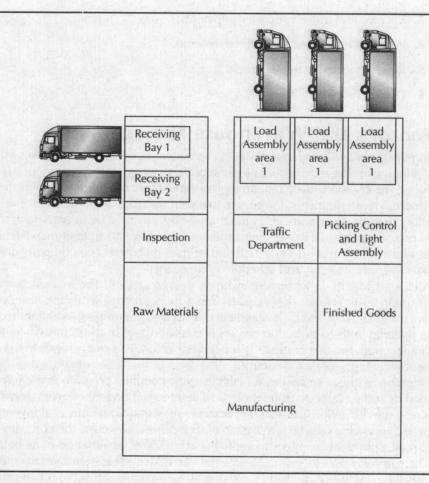

FIGURE 22-3. *Neptune's receiving dock and warehouse layout*

two shifts, from 6 AM to 2 PM and 1:30 to 9:30 PM. The receiving dock is closed to deliveries for one hour before the end of shift.

Inbound Logistics Activities

Use the following activities to analyze how you would use the Oracle E-Business Suite to manage inbound logistics at Neptune, and at your own company:

1. Review receiving controls at the organization, supplier, and item levels.

2. Define the location codes needed to represent Neptune's receiving dock.

3. Receive and inspect supplier shipments.

4. Process unexpected (unordered) receipts.

5. Return rejected material to vendors.

6. Deliver to material to stores.

Inventory and Warehouse Management

To simplify the planning of low-value, high-volume products, Neptune uses Min-Max Planning for these items and has its suppliers manage the inventory of a few products. The company uses kanban replenishment for both internal replenishments and external replenishments. In order to maintain the accuracy of their inventory, inventory personnel perform cycle counting weekly. Neptune performs ABC analysis based on various criteria; it uses annual planned usage dollars in their manufacturing plants and forecast usage dollars in their distribution centers. The company uses this analysis to group its items and schedule cycle counts.

ABC assignments vary from organization to organization. The manufacturing plants use five ABC classes—A, B, C, D, and X (uncounted)—while the distribution centers use only A, B, and C. Assignment criteria also vary by organization; most of the material in the distribution centers is classified as A in the plants where it is manufactured, but that material is subdivided into A, B, and C classes in the distribution centers for better control.

Neptune has been so successful with its cycle counting program that it has satisfied its auditors that an annual physical inventory is no longer necessary. This has saved the disruption and inherent inaccuracy of traditional physical inventory practices. Following conversion of each of its facilities, however, the company performed a physical inventory to verify the accuracy of its initial on-hand balances.

The company uses lot control and serial control for a few items and maintains the genealogy of the products they sell (the as-built configuration) so it can better serve its customers. For example, the customer-service organization proactively sends service bulletins to the appropriate customers if a defect is discovered with a particular lot.

Neptune uses LPNs to track each container in its warehouse and often consolidates multiple items in small cartons into larger cartons or pallets, also identified with an LPN. It uses cartonization rules to instruct pickers how to pack material for shipment.

Several material statuses are used within the warehouse, to identify locations or LPNs where the count is inaccurate, or the material, its containers, or locations appear to be damaged. These status codes effectively place such material on hold, by prohibiting selected transactions, until the problem is resolved and the hold removed.

Neptune uses third-party labeling software in conjunction with the labeling rules in Oracle Warehouse Management. It has defined different material label types for material that is lot or serial controlled and prints the appropriate label at material receipt. Most customers accept Neptune's standard shipping label, but a few have special requirements, which the labeling rules also accommodate.

Warehouse resources are identified by instance (individual people and serial-numbered equipment) to allow task dispatching.

Neptune's warehouses receive material from the manufacturing facility and other suppliers. Warehouse employees sometimes perform packing and light assembly operations before shipping material to the customers. From the receiving dock, operators choose containerized stock and are directed to the appropriate putaway location, based on predefined rules. For example, hazardous material (identified by item category) is stored in special subinventories; some items are stored based on their supplier.

Similarly, when a customer order is released for shipment, these releases are broken into warehouse tasks and scheduled against the appropriate resources. To minimize operator travel and repacking activities, typical picking rules respect the picking unit of measure of the different zones (subinventories) in their distribution centers. For example, a large corporate order might require a full pallet of a single product. Such a pick will be directed to the "Pallet" zone of the warehouse, and the task will be dispatched to an operator logged on to the required forklift.

Inventory and Warehouse Management Activities

The following activities will help you think about how Neptune and your own company can best use the Oracle E-Business Suite for inventory and warehouse management:

1. Identify appropriate items for min-max planning, and set the required item attributes.

2. Define ABC classes, perform an ABC analysis, and assign ABC classes to all items.

3. Set up an organization-wide cycle count for each manufacturing plant and distribution center.

4. Review physical inventory setup and procedures for initial inventory verification.

5. Define material status codes for Neptune.

6. Define container items.

7. Define the appropriate rules, strategies, and strategy assignments to meet Neptune's putaway, picking, labeling, and task dispatching requirements.

Manufacturing Execution

Neptune uses demand flow manufacturing techniques for its most popular products. Flow schedules are created each day for a two-day window, looking at orders within a five-day window. Performance to schedule is evaluated daily, and uncompleted schedules are rolled forward if necessary. Production is completed using the Work Order-less Completion transaction.

Prototypes and high-end servers are built on specific discrete jobs for better analysis of the cost. Prototypes often use engineering bills of material, and security limits the number of people who can create jobs for a prototype. If a manufacturing routing is available for a prototype, the supply type of all components is typically changed to "Push" so that material usage can be more closely monitored.

A few manufacturing processes are performed by suppliers outside of Neptune, for example, conformal coating on circuit boards that will be used in certain environments. For such processes, purchase requisitions are created when the discrete jobs are released. In most cases, blanket purchase agreements are in place for such services, and the blanket releases are automatically created at the same time.

For prototypes of some high-value items, labor costs are entered manually and are reviewed against the routing standard, which is adjusted if necessary before the product is released to full production. By definition, work order-less completions automatically charge labor at the standard rate and amount; most discrete jobs also auto charge labor because it is a small constituent of the product's total cost.

Non-standard discrete jobs are also used for repair or upgrade of returned material. Orders are created as products are returned, necessary components are issued as needed, and no bill of material is used. One exception is when Neptune promotes a specific upgrade of existing products. In that case, it will create an alternate BOM that is used to specify all the required upgrade components for a product; additional components can still be added or replaced as needed.

Manufacturing Execution Activities

Consider the following activities, as they pertain to the manufacturing processes at Neptune and your own company:

1. Review WIP Parameters.

2. Set up appropriate accounting classes and reason codes for WIP transactions.

3. Review and modify scheduling rules for flow scheduling.

4. Define any needed shop floor statuses.

5. Set up the appropriate items, resources, and blanket purchase agreements to meet Neptune's outside processing needs.

6. Create and process a standard discrete job to completion.

7. Record flow production using a work order-less completion.

Outbound Logistics

The arrival and departure of carriers are maintained using a dock appointment scheduling system. Consumer products are shipped from Neptune's distribution centers on a regular basis. Orders are normally prioritized by scheduled ship date, using a default Release Sequence rule; however, at the end of the quarter, a special rule is used that gives priority to orders with the highest revenue potential. Pick release is run nightly and automatically generates and details the move orders to stage the material. Material handlers transact the move orders (using RF scanners) as they move material to the designated staging lane. Ship confirm is performed as material is picked up, usually by UPS for consumer goods.

Most corporate orders and parts orders follow the same process.

Rush orders (most often for parts) are processed immediately. Pick release is run on line, the orders are typically shipped using next-day delivery, and special shipping charges are added when the shipping method and carrier are determined.

Some large orders, including many of the internal shipments to Neptune's distribution centers, are planned in advance. This has resulted in more favorable freight terms and significant cost savings for Neptune.

Outbound Logistics Activities

The following activities will help you think about how Neptune and your own company can best use the Oracle E-Business Suite for outbound logistics:

1. Define Release Sequence rules.

2. Define special freight charges.

3. Define carriers and ship methods.

4. Ship a simple order by running pick release, transacting the resulting move order, and confirming the shipment.

5. Define a trip to represent a shipment of material from Sacramento to Orlando, with a stop in Denver. Assign the appropriate delivery lines to the trip.

6. Record the progress of the trip by stop.

Support Functions

The following sections discuss the support functions of Cost Management, Quality, and Pricing. These functions often require the input and cooperation of many other departments within the enterprise, so they are described separately.

Cost Management

Neptune uses standard costing throughout its enterprise and identifies variances on a period basis. Every quarter, the company goes through a profit forecasting exercise, which includes review and revision of its standard costs.

The company undertook an activity-based costing exercise 18 months ago. This identified that Neptune's imbedded systems division, long considered an "also-ran" in the portfolio, was a major contributor. Support and development costs for imbedded systems were much smaller than for consumer or industrial products, thus its contribution to corporate profits was higher than anticipated.

Chip prices are very volatile, so costs for chips are forecast according to the R&D and obsolescence cycles of the major chip manufacturers. Purchasing standards are updated every month and reflected in inventory balances. Affected assemblies have their costs re-rolled and updated accordingly. Often, this can be done by product family, but occasionally Neptune's cost accountants perform a where-used inquiry to determine all affected assemblies.

For consumer products, packaging is a significant component of the costs. For easy identification of these costs, Neptune has defined a material cost subelement for packaging material, as well as a generic "material" subelement.

Resources are initially defined by manufacturing engineering, in order to define routings, but their costs are set and maintained by the cost accounting department. Neptune's resources include major work centers, machinery, labor, and outside processing. The paint shop and anodizing bath are defined as resources. Each auto-insertion and surface-mount machine is defined as a separate resource. Wiring, PCB assembly, and final assembly have resources defined for the number of trained personnel.

Although its prior ERP system provided only one plant-wide overhead rate, Neptune uses several overhead subelements to more discretely identify product cost and more equitably absorb indirect costs. Each overhead has its own absorption account for comparison against actual expenses for that cost. For example, the cost of employee benefits is defined as a separate overhead, assigned to labor resources on the basis of labor cost. Each absorption account is compared with the discrete expense account that captures the corresponding actual expenses, such as insurance and vacation pay.

Cost Management Activities

Use the following activities to analyze how you would apply the Cost Management module of the Oracle E-Business Suite to Neptune, and to your own company:

1. Define the cost types and subelements needed by Neptune.

2. Review standard costs and reset as necessary.

3. Perform cost rollup, review the results, and update standard costs.

4. Investigate variances from purchasing and manufacturing.

5. Verify engineering standards.

6. Review overhead absorption against actual expenses. Revise rates as needed.

Quality Management

For new purchased products, Neptune's product engineers typically develop item specifications. The Quality department will define collection plans, usually requiring incoming inspection. Data that are outside of the specifications trigger an e-mail to the item's buyer. Quality data for new products are analyzed weekly; when a particular supplier-item combination is deemed certified, the inspection requirement and the quality plan are removed.

Quality collection plans are also used for new manufactured products, most often required with a manufacturing completion transaction. The data are analyzed to determine process capability, and the results are shared with engineering if corrective action is needed.

When an item is moved to flow production, quality plans are no longer required, as Neptune feels that its manufacturing engineering process has incorporated quality events and visual operation method sheets in the flow routings.

Quality Management Activities

Consider the following activities as they pertain to Neptune's quality programs and those of your own company:

1. Define quality specifications for purchased and manufactured items for this client.

2. Define collection elements.

3. Define collection plans.

4. Generate the various charts and analyze the results.

5. Perform a process capability study on the process of your choice.

Pricing

Neptune has separate domestic price lists for distributors, business customers, consumers, and education customers. There are Export price lists for Canada, Mexico and Brazil, Western Europe, Eastern Europe, and Scandinavia. Price Lists in the Americas are expressed in U.S. dollars (USD). Price lists in Europe are expressed in euros.

There are discounts that are qualified to apply only to customer classes of "research institutions" and "elementary schools" when buying desktop computers. There is a surcharge for "dot.com" business customers. The Neptune brand is well-respected in the server segment, and the company provides extensive after-market support for its "dot.com" customers; therefore, it can command a premium price.

Neptune is heavily promoting its products in lifestyle magazines as it launches a range of entertainment appliances with Internet access, video on demand, TV tuner with playback, DVD, and video-editing units. Customers must ask for the promotion. Coupons have been placed in three magazines for $75 toward the purchase of a digital video recorder when a customer buys an entertainment appliance.

Pricing Activities

Use the following pricing activities to analyze how you would apply the Oracle E-Business Suite to Neptune, and to your own company:

1. Define the price lists that Neptune will need.

2. Set the prices for products and categories of products on price lists.

3. Define discounts and other sales incentives, such as coupons and promotions.

4. Qualify discounts for appropriate customers and products.

5. Rebate customers for retroactive discounts.

Business Intelligence

Neptune has implemented Oracle Portal as the desktop for all its employees. The VP of Operations has a Portal with tabs for Order to Cash and Demand to Build. Buyers use the Savings Opportunities Analysis workbook to focus their energies on consolidation opportunities. The VP of Procurement checks the Savings Opportunities Portlet on his Portal Page every day to see if there is any rogue (or "maverick") buying that should be using negotiated contracts.

Because Neptune still performs some Order Management on a legacy system from a recent acquisition, Neptune has implemented Oracle's Enterprise Data Warehouse. It uses Oracle Warehouse Builder to map data from the legacy systems.

Summary

Neptune is presented in this chapter as a hypothetical company making good use of the Oracle E-Business Suite to manage its manufacturing and supply chain activities. This chapter described how Neptune has modeled its enterprise structure, its design and manufacturing engineering activities, its supply chain planning practices, and its execution of the plan: order management, procurement, inbound logistics, warehouse management, manufacturing, and shipping. This chapter detailed the costing techniques the company uses to manage and evaluate product costs, quality management activities, and the pricing techniques it employs to maintain profitable margins in a very competitive business environment.

This chapter also outlined the business intelligence capabilities that Neptune employs to measure its performance, identify problems early, and work for continuous improvement. Hopefully the examples presented here and throughout the book will help you do the same in your business.

Index

Symbols and Numbers

\# of line operations, calculating for Manufacturing Engineering, 174

& (ampersand) used with output variable tokens, 731–732

* (asterisk) delimiter character, using with BOM parameters and profile options for ATO/PTO, 150

4/5 Weekly Pattern, reporting in, 97

5/4/4 Weekly Pattern, reporting in, 97

A

ABC analysis, maintaining inventory accuracy with, 512–514

Acceptable Early Days field of MRP/MPS Planning Attributes tab, 243

Accounting information, role in inventory organization, 39

Accounting Rule attribute for items, 69

Accounts receivable customers, providing credit checking for, 376–377

Accounts, receiving for inventory organization, 44

Action definitions, storage of, 732

Action rules for Quality product, 726–727

Actions, associating output variables with, 730–732

Actions button, functionality of, 392–394

Actions tab in ASCP Planner Workbench, 332–334

Activity-based costing module in E-Business Suite, 683, 783

Ad-hoc reports
generating for demand planning, 272

Address information, specifying with Order Organizer, 390–391

Addresses for delivery locations, specifying with Purchasing product, 454

Adjustment approval, specifying for cycle counts, 516

Admin edition of Discoverer tool and EUL creation, 784

ADS (Application Data Store), role in data collection, 325

Advanced Pricing, benefits of, 767

Advanced Pricing module in Order Management product, 374

Aggregate forecasts
creating, 215–216
reviewing for demand planning, 270

Aggregation tab in ASCP, 323

Alert actions, defining with Quality product, 726

Alerts, defining for demand planning, 272–273

Allocation percentages, specifying with Purchasing product, 432

Allocation rules, specifying for demand planning, 264–265

Alternate resources, associating for routings, 111

Alternate routings, switching from primary routings, 112–113

Alternates, setting up for BOMs, 81

Always condition, setting up for Order Management product, 368

Ampersand (&) used with output variable tokens, 731–732

Analysis tools, 739–749

AOL (Applications Object Library), role in Order Management product, 364

APIs (application programming interfaces)
BOM business object, 93–96
Calculate Price, 775
Cycle Count Entries, 564
ECO business object API, 139–142
Forecast Entries, 210

823

D

J

K

Q

T

X

Y

Z

INTERNATIONAL CONTACT INFORMATION

AUSTRALIA
McGraw-Hill Book Company Australia Pty. Ltd.
TEL +61-2-9417-9899
FAX +61-2-9417-5687
http://www.mcgraw-hill.com.au
books-it_sydney@mcgraw-hill.com

CANADA
McGraw-Hill Ryerson Ltd.
TEL +905-430-5000
FAX +905-430-5020
http://www.mcgrawhill.ca

**GREECE, MIDDLE EAST,
NORTHERN AFRICA**
McGraw-Hill Hellas
TEL +30-1-656-0990-3-4
FAX +30-1-654-5525

MEXICO (Also serving Latin America)
McGraw-Hill Interamericana Editores S.A. de C.V.
TEL +525-117-1583
FAX +525-117-1589
http://www.mcgraw-hill.com.mx
fernando_castellanos@mcgraw-hill.com

SINGAPORE (Serving Asia)
McGraw-Hill Book Company
TEL +65-863-1580
FAX +65-862-3354
http://www.mcgraw-hill.com.sg
mghasia@mcgraw-hill.com

SOUTH AFRICA
McGraw-Hill South Africa
TEL +27-11-622-7512
FAX +27-11-622-9045
robyn_swanepoel@mcgraw-hill.com

**UNITED KINGDOM & EUROPE
(Excluding Southern Europe)**
McGraw-Hill Education Europe
TEL +44-1-628-502500
FAX +44-1-628-770224
http://www.mcgraw-hill.co.uk
computing_neurope@mcgraw-hill.com

ALL OTHER INQUIRIES Contact:
Osborne/McGraw-Hill
TEL +1-510-549-6600
FAX +1-510-883-7600
http://www.osborne.com
omg_international@mcgraw-hill.com